The International Library of Critical Writings in Economics

Series Editor: Mark Blaug

Professor Emeritus, University of London
Professor Emeritus, University of Buckingham
Visiting Professor, University of Exeter

This series is an essential reference source for students, researchers and lecturers in economics. It presents by theme an authoritative selection of the most important articles across the entire spectrum of economics. Each volume has been prepared by a leading specialist who has written an authoritative introduction to the literature included.

A full list of published and future titles in this series is printed at the end of this volume.

The Economics of Ageing

The Economics of Ageing

Edited by

John Creedy

The Truby Williams Professor of Economics
University of Melbourne

THE INTERNATIONAL LIBRARY OF CRITICAL WRITINGS IN ECONOMICS

An Elgar Reference Collection

Published by
Edward Elgar Publishing Limited
Gower House
Croft Road
Aldershot
Hants GU11 3HR
England

Edward Elgar Publishing Company
Old Post Road
Brookfield
Vermont 05036
USA

British Library Cataloguing in Publication Data
Economics of Ageing. – (International
Library of Critical Writings in Economics;
Vol. 51)
I. Creedy, John II. Series
339.4

Library of Congress Cataloguing in Publication Data
The economics of ageing / edited by John Creedy.
p. cm. — (International library of critical writings in economics : 51) (An Elgar reference collection)
1. Ageing—Economic aspects—Statistics. 2. Aged—Economic conditions—Statistics. 3. Aged—Social conditions—Statistics. 4. Aged—Government policy—Statistics. 5. Social security–
–Statistics. I. Creedy, John, 1949– . II. Series. III. Series: An Elgar reference collection.
HQ1061.E26 1995
305.26′021—dc20

94–49066
CIP

ISBN 1 85278 827 5

Printed in Great Britain by Galliard (Printers) Ltd, Great Yarmouth

Contents

Acknowledgements

The editor and publishers wish to thank the following who have kindly given permission for the use of copyright material.

American Economic Association for articles: Barbara Boyle Torrey (1982), 'Guns vs. Canes: The Fiscal Implications of an Aging Population', *American Economic Review Papers and Proceedings*, **72** (2), May, 309–13; Ray C. Fair and Kathryn M. Dominguez (1991), 'Effects of the Changing U.S. Age Distribution on Macroeconomic Equations', *American Economic Review*, **81** (5), December, 1276–94.

Association for Social Economics for article: Robert Clark (1977), 'Increasing Income Transfers to the Elderly Implied by Zero Population Growth', *Review of Social Economy*, **XXXV** (1), April, 37–54.

Atlantic Economic Society for articles: William J. Serow (1976), 'Slow Population Growth and the Relative Size and Productivity of the Male Labor Force', *Atlantic Economic Journal*, **IV** (2), Spring, 61–8; Joseph J. Spengler (1978), 'Population Aging and Security of the Aged', *Atlantic Economic Journal*, **6**, March, 1–7.

Basil Blackwell Ltd for article: John Creedy and Richard Disney (1992), 'Financing State Pensions in Alternative Pay-As-You-Go Schemes', *Bulletin of Economic Research*, **44** (1), January, 39–53.

Brookings Institution for article: David M. Cutler, James M. Poterba, Louise M. Sheiner and Lawrence H. Summers (1990), 'An Aging Society: Opportunity or Challenge?', *Brookings Papers on Economic Activity*, **1**, 1–56 and 71–3.

Cambridge University Press for article: Jane Falkingham (1989), 'Dependency and Ageing in Britain: A Re-Examination of the Evidence', *Journal of Social Policy*, **18** (2), April, 211–33.

Canadian Journal of Economics and Political Science for article: Henry Aaron (1966), 'The Social Insurance Paradox', *Canadian Journal of Economics and Political Science*, **XXXII** (3), August, 371–4.

Chapman & Hall for article: Brian S. Ferguson (1986), 'Labour Force Substitution and the Effects of an Ageing Population', *Applied Economics*, **18** (8), August, 901–13.

Econometric Society for article: Harold Lydall (1955), 'The Life Cycle in Income, Saving, and Asset Ownership', *Econometrica*, **23** (2), April, 131–50.

Elsevier Science B.V. for articles: A.F. Shorrocks (1975), 'The Age-Wealth Relationship: A Cross-Section and Cohort Analysis', *Review of Economics and Statistics*, **LVII** (2), May, 155–63; F.A. Cowell (1975), 'Income Tax Incidence in an Ageing Population', *European Economic Review*, **6** (4), October, 343–67; Christopher A. Pissarides (1989), 'Unemployment Consequences of an Aging Population: An Application of Insider–Outsider Theory', *European Economic Review*, **33**, 355–66.

Elsevier Sequoia S.A. for article: P.A. Diamond (1977), 'A Framework for Social Security Analysis', *Journal of Public Economics*, **8** (3), December, 275–98.

Foundation Journal *Public Finance* for article: Robert K. von Weizsäcker (1990), 'Population Aging and Social Security: A Politico-Economic Model of State Pension Financing', *Public Finance*, **45** (3), 491–509.

International Economic Review for article: Paul A. Samuelson (1975), 'Optimum Social Security in a Life-Cycle Growth Model', *International Economic Review*, **16** (3), October, 539–44.

International Monetary Fund for articles: William A. Halter and Richard Hemming (1987), 'The Impact of Demographic Change on Social Security Financing', *International Monetary Fund Staff Papers*, **34** (3), September, 471–502; Paul R. Masson and Ralph W. Tryon (1990), 'Macroeconomic Effects of Projected Population Aging in Industrial Countries', *International Monetary Fund Staff Papers* **37** (3), September, 453–85.

MIT Press Journals for article: James L. Medoff and Katharine G. Abraham (1980), 'Experience, Performance, and Earnings', *Quarterly Journal of Economics*, **XCV** (4), December, 703–36.

Oxford University Press for articles: A.B. Atkinson (1971), 'The Distribution of Wealth and the Individual Life-Cycle', *Oxford Economic Papers*, **23** (2), July, 239–54; John Creedy (1974), 'Income Changes over the Life Cycle', *Oxford Economic Papers*, **26** (3), November, 405–23.

Population Investigation Committee for article: Alfred Sauvy (1948), 'Social and Economic Consequences of the Ageing of Western European Populations', *Population Studies*, **II** (1), June, 115–24.

Royal Bank of Scotland Plc for article: A.R. Prest (1970), 'Some Redistributional Aspects of the National Superannuation Fund', *The Three Banks Review*, No. 86, June, 3–22.

Southern Economic Journal for articles: Thad W. Mirer (1980), 'The Dissaving Behavior of the Retired Aged', *Southern Economic Journal*, **46** (4), April, 1197–25; John A. Turner (1984), 'Population Age Structure and the Size of Social Security', *Southern Economic Journal*, **50** (4), April, 1131–46.

University of Chicago Press for articles: Paul A. Samuelson (1958), 'An Exact Consumption-Loan Model of Interest with or without the Social Contrivance of Money', *Journal of Political Economy*, **LXVI** (6), December, 467–82; Yoram Ben-Porath (1967), 'The Production of Human Capital and the Life Cycle of Earnings', *Journal of Political Economy*, **75** (4, Part 1), August, 352–65; Martin Feldstein (1974), 'Social Security, Induced Retirement, and Aggregate Capital Accumulation', *Journal of Political Economy*, **82** (5), July/August, 905–26; Finis Welch (1979), 'Effects of Cohort Size on Earnings: The Baby Boom Babies' Financial Bust', *Journal of Political Economy*, **87** (5), pt 2, August, S65–S97; Edward P. Lazear (1979), 'Why Is There Mandatory Retirement?', *Journal of Political Economy*, **87** (6), December, 1261–84.

Western Economic Association International for article: Michael J. Boskin (1977), 'Social Security and Retirement Decisions', *Economic Inquiry*, **XV**, January, 1–25.

Every effort has been made to trace all the copyright holders but if any have been inadvertently overlooked the publishers will be pleased to make the necessary arrangement at the first opportunity.

In addition the publishers wish to thank the Library of the London School of Economics and Political Science and the Alfred Marshall Library, Cambridge University, for their assistance in obtaining these articles.

Introduction

This volume collects 32 journal papers concerned with a variety of economic aspects of individual and population ageing. They have been arranged under four main headings as follows: individual ageing and the life cycle; population ageing; ageing and social insurance, and macroeconomic effects. The present Introduction makes no attempt to summarize the articles or to survey the wider literature (much of which is contained in books rather than journal articles). Rather, it aims to set the context and discuss some of the major issues. In view of the central role of population dynamics, it seems useful to provide a discussion of the systematic demographic changes that have taken place over time, along with an examination of the basic analytics of population change. The implications for social expenditure are then discussed.

The fundamental role of individual ageing is something that everyone is necessarily aware of, and the division of the life cycle into a number of distinct stages has been recognized for many centuries. The best known statement of these stages is perhaps that of Jaques in Shakespeare's *As You Like It*. He described the 'seven ages of man', beginning with 'the infant, mewling and puking in the nurse's arms' and ending with 'the last scene of all, that ends this strange eventful history ... sans teeth, sans eyes, sans taste, sans everything'. While the ageing process has for long played a prominent role in some other disciplines, extensive investigations into the economics of ageing are relatively recent. Few published data contain decompositions according to age or life-cycle stages, so that there are still large gaps in knowledge of cross-sectional age comparisons, never mind knowledge about true cohort variations.

An important distinction must be drawn between individual and population ageing. The latter concerns the age distribution of the population and is influenced more by fertility patterns than by mortality or longevity characteristics of individuals. It might be thought that, in view of the importance of the population model associated with the famous work by Malthus, concern with population ageing would stem at least from the early classical economists. However, the major area of interest was rapid population growth, even though changes in death rates were recognized as important; concern for ageing is also relatively modern. The analytics of population growth and age structure were not explored at length until the early years of the present century. Furthermore, in view of the early age of death of the large majority of people, population growth was regarded by the classical economists as being synonymous with labour force growth, so that no independent role was attached to the age distribution.

Demographic Transitions

It is possible to distinguish several demographic stages or transitions through which most industrialized societies have been observed to pass. The time taken to move through the various stages has varied between countries, however, and there is evidence to suggest that more recently industrialized countries have passed through some later stages relatively more quickly.

The different stages are characterized mainly by their birth and death rates (expressed per 1000 of the population) and the associated age distribution of the population. They are shown in Table 1 under four main headings. The figures given in the table must be regarded simply as representative values rather than indicating precise orders of magnitude for a particular country.

The pre-modern stage is characterized in Table 1 by quite high fertility and high mortality. The expectation of life at birth is only about 25 years, so there are very few individuals in the 'over 60' age group. The high birth rate, while imposing very heavy burdens on families, is nevertheless associated with a growth rate of the total population of only about half of one per cent, so that reproduction is sometimes described as being very inefficient.

The middle two stages are shown as 'early transition' and 'later transition' periods, though they are sometimes amalgamated into a single demographic transition or movement towards the 'modern' period. The early transition period is characterized by a fall in mortality, particularly infant mortality, which is associated with a rise in the expectation of life to about 30 years. In the later transition period, improved health conditions reduce mortality and increase longevity further, while the birth rate continues to be high. This period is thus associated with a high 'youth dependency' ratio, with about 45 per cent of the population under the age of 15 years. Despite the much higher expectation of life at birth, the proportion of people over 60 years remains relatively low, while the population growth rate is increased to about 3 per cent. Indeed, it can be shown that the extent of population ageing is more sensitive to fertility than to mortality changes.

Table 1 Demographic Transitions

	Pre-modern	Early transition	Later transition	Modern
Births/1 000	45	45	45	20
Deaths/1 000	40	33	15	10
% $\leq$ 15	36	38	45	26
% $\geq$ 60	5	5	5	15
Expectation of life at birth	25	30	50	70
Population growth rate	.5	1	3	1

Despite increased longevity, the later transitional period is one in which the idea of retirement from employment does not really exist. Individuals continue to work, unless illness prevents labour market participation. For example, during this transitional period in Britain, the various Friendly Societies were able to cope with the requirements of such sickness insurance for their members and were also well placed to handle the potential moral hazard problems. Hence increased longevity did not lead to a breakdown of family support systems, despite the high 'youth' burden already faced.

As shown in Table 1, the modern period experiences a continued reduction in mortality and an increase in the expectation of life at birth to about 70 years. A significant feature is the reduction in the birth rate so that, despite the extra longevity, the population growth rate falls to about 1 per cent. The age composition of the population shifts dramatically, with a reduction in the proportion below 15 years and an increase in the proportion aged over 60 years. Given the difficulty of making life cycle savings, these later transitions place great strain on family support systems, despite the reduction in the youth burden. In Britain, the significance of these changes was not at first fully appreciated by the Friendly Societies, who were initially opposed to the introduction of government Old Age pensions; however, the demand for some kind of government pension became irresistible in the major industrialized countries at the turn of the century. The shift from family support to government support in the form of a tax and transfer system involves a complex range of factors, including the very high costs – particularly health costs – of supporting the aged relative to those of the young. Hence the overall burden of dependency increased despite the reduction in birth rates.

The modern period shown in Table 1 corresponds to the industrialized countries around 1960 and must be augmented by a yet 'more modern' period through which many countries are currently passing. The expectation of life at birth has increased further, and it has been found that support costs (again particularly health costs) rise dramatically for individuals over 75 years who form a growing proportion of the population. The birth rates have also fallen further, implying significant population ageing in the early years of the 21st century. This prospect is also associated with the ageing of members of the post-war baby boom. The implications of the more recent demographic transition are, however, more complicated than is often portrayed in popular debate.

The recent 'post-modern' period has also seen a substantial increase in the labour force participation rate of women (partly associated with the lower birth rate) along with a certain amount of variability in unemployment rates. Following a shift of the 'aged burden' to the tax and transfer system during the modern period, the commonly expressed fear is that future working populations will renege on the 'implicit social contract' between generations. Intergenerational equity issues are therefore now receiving some attention from economists. It is also of interest that, despite the much lower birth rate, more recent times have seen increased pressure from some quarters for a further shift of the 'youth burden' to the tax and transfer system. Others have expressed concern over such a shift, partly associated with what some commentators have referred to as a breakdown of the nuclear family. The potential costs associated with population ageing are considered further below, following a brief discussion of the analytics of population dynamics.

Population Projections

It is useful to appreciate some of the basic determinants of the population age structure and population growth. There are of course well-established models developed by demographers and used by, among others, actuaries. However, their notation and methods are less familiar to economists, and for this reason the present discussion presents a social accounting framework. The analysis makes use of matrix methods which are more widely known among economists.

Population flows can be represented by a social accounting framework as follows.

Table 2 Demographic Flows

t+1 \ t		Ages 1 2 3............N	Births	In migration	Total
Ages	1	0 0 0............ 0	b_1	v_1	p_1
	2	f_{21} 0 0............ 0	0	v_2	p_2
	3	0 f_{32} 0............ 0	0	v_3	p_3
		: :	:	:	:
	N	0 0 0............ 0	0	v_N	p_N
Deaths + out migration		d_1 d_2 d_3...........d_N			
Total		p_1 p_2 p_3...........p_N			

The square matrix of flows (from columns to rows) has N–1 non-zero elements which are placed on the diagonal immediately below the leading diagonal. No one is assumed to survive beyond the age of N. Define the coefficients, a_{ij}, showing the proportion of people in the jth age who survive in the country to the age i, as:

$$a_{ij} = f_{ij}/p_j \tag{1}$$

only the $a_{i+1,i}$, for $i=1,\ldots, N-1$ are non-zero. This framework applies to males and females separately, distinguished by subscripts m and f. The 'forward equations' corresponding to this framework are therefore:

$$p_{m,t+1} = A_m \, p_{m,t} + b_{m,t} + v_{m,t} \tag{2}$$

$$p_{f,t+1} = A_f \, p_{f,t} + b_{f,t} + v_{f,t}. \tag{3}$$

Given population age distributions in a base year and information about the relevant flows, equations (2) and (3) can be used to make projections. In general the matrices A_m and A_f, along with births and inward migration flows, may be allowed to vary over time. Changes in the As can arise from changes in either mortality or outward migration.

Further specification can be added to the model by considering births. Suppose that c_i represents the proportion of females of age i who give birth per year. Many elements, for young and old ages, of the vector, c, will of course be zero, and in general the c_is may vary over time. Suppose that a proportion, δ, of all births are male, and define the N-element vector τ as the column vector having unity as the first element and zeros elsewhere. Then births in any year can be represented by:

$$b_m = \delta \tau c' p_f \tag{4}$$

$$b_f = (1-\delta) \tau c' p_f \tag{5}$$

where c' is the transpose of the vector c (that is, the column vector written as a row). The b vectors contain only one non-zero element, of course. Equations (2) to (5) can thus be used to make population projections for assumed immigration levels.

Stable Populations

If all the coefficients, represented by the elements of the A matrices and the c and v vectors, remain constant over time, the population should eventually reach a stable level and age distribution. The age distribution of males and females will be such that total 'entrants' are exactly matched by total 'exits' from the country. In practice, such a stable population is unlikely ever to be experienced, given the time required for convergence from some initial non-stable distribution, so that the coefficients are bound to change before stability is reached. Yet it is sometimes useful to have an idea of the population structure towards which any given system may be thought to be approaching.

First, consider the female population. Combine (3) and (5) and set $p_{f,t+1} = p_{f,t} = p_f$. With constant migration $v_{f,t} = v_f$ per year, so that:

$$p_f = [A_f + (1-\delta)\ \tau c']p_f + v_f. \tag{6}$$

Notice that the matrix $\tau c'$ takes the simple form:

$$\tau c' = \begin{bmatrix} c_1 & \ldots\ldots & c_N \\ 0 & \ldots\ldots & 0 \\ \vdots & & \vdots \\ 0 & \ldots\ldots & 0 \end{bmatrix} \tag{7}$$

Rearranging (6) gives:

$$[I - A_f - (1-\delta)\tau c']p_f = v_f \tag{8}$$

where I is the unit matrix. It is convenient to denote the matrix in square brackets in (8) as M, so that:

$$Mp_f = v_f. \tag{9}$$

This matrix takes the form:

$$M = \begin{bmatrix} 1-(1-\delta)c_1 & -(1-\delta)c_2 & -(1-\delta)c_3 & \ldots \\ -a_{21} & 1 & 0 & \ldots \\ 0 & -a_{32} & 1 & 0\ldots \\ \ldots\ldots & \ldots\ldots & \ldots\ldots & \ldots\ldots \end{bmatrix} \tag{10}$$

The first few terms c_i (for $i=1,\ldots,N$) will, as noted above, be zeros. However, this matrix will in general be non-singular, so that the stable female distribution is given by:

$$p_f = M^{-1} v_f. \tag{11}$$

The model has the property that if there are no inward female migrants, so that $v_f=0$, then equation (9) represents a set of linear homogeneous equations. Given the non-singularity of M, this means that the model has only the trivial solution whereby the stable population is $p_f=0$.

If $v_f=0$, and denoting the matrix in square brackets in equation (6) as A_f^*, then:

$$\begin{aligned} p_{f,t+1} &= A_f^* \, p_{f,t} \\ &= (A_f^*)^t \, p_{f,1}. \end{aligned} \tag{12}$$

Therefore with constant birth and death rates and no migration, the total population will grow at a constant geometric rate (which may be positive or negative), while the relative age distribution will settle down to be constant whatever the form of $p_{f,1}$. The population growth will be either 'explosive' or will converge to zero, which again confirms the earlier result. The population grows steadily if the largest characteristic root of A_f^* is greater than unity, and declines steadily if the largest root is less than one. The process shown in equation (12) can converge to a stable value of p_f only if the matrix A_f^* has a largest characteristic root of exactly unity, which is extremely unlikely.

The stable male population is determined by substituting (4) into (2) and setting the coefficients constant, so that

$$p_m = A_m \, p_m + \delta\tau c' \, p_f + v_m. \tag{13}$$

Substituting for p_f from (11) and further rearranging gives:

$$p_m = [1-A_m]^{-1} \, [\delta\tau c' \, M^{-1} \, v_f + v_m]. \tag{14}$$

A stable non-trivial solution for p_m does not therefore require any male migrants.

Social Expenditure

It has been mentioned earlier that an increase in longevity in the industrialized countries led to a demand for the introduction of some kind of government age pension and health 'insurance' scheme. The difficulty of providing adequate personal savings for old age, combined with the strain placed both on family support and the existing sickness support schemes (which anyway covered only a small minority of workers), resulted in a situation in which the aged formed the vast majority of those found to be living below a designated poverty level. At around the same time, there was much wider recognition of a role for the government in other areas of social insurance, such as sickness and unemployment. It is no accident that this movement coincided with wider support for redistribution, involving also the use of progressive income taxation.

Social insurance schemes are typically financed on a pay-as-you-go (PAYG) basis – that is, from current taxation – with pensions forming by far the largest component of social expenditure. A variety of market failure arguments have been advanced to justify the use of such social insurance. In addition, the inter-generational transfers involved in PAYG pension schemes are often described in terms of an implicit social 'contract' between three generations: each generation stands to gain from such an arrangement so long as there is sufficient productivity and population growth. The increased ageing of the population (expected to be most prominent in the early years of the next century) has been widely anticipated as placing great strain on this metaphorical contract. It is possible that the post-war 'baby boom' generation will once again be squeezed.

Pensions and health are not, however, the only age-related forms of social expenditure. Indeed, given the many elements involved, the implications of population ageing for aggregate social expenditure are far from clear. Many projections can perhaps be criticized for not providing sufficient sensitivity analyses, given the wide range of assumptions and the many uncertainties involved. A basic projection framework, which formalizes the approach used by a number of investigators, may be described as follows.

The population is divided into, say, N age groups and the numbers in each group at time t are placed in a vector p_t, where $p_t = p_{m,t} + p_{f,t}$. The per capita social expenditures within each group are placed in a matrix with N rows and k columns, where there are k items of social expenditure (education, medical care, pensions and so on). If this matrix is denoted S, then the i, j th element s_{ij} measures the per capita cost of the j th type of social expenditure in the i th age group. Suppose that the j th type of social expenditure per capita is expected to grow in real terms at the annual rate ψ_j in each age group. Then define g_t as the k-element column vector whose j th element is equal to $(1 + \psi_j)^{t-1}$. Aggregate social expenditure at time t, C_t, is thus equal to:

$$C_t = g'_t \, S' \, p_t \tag{14}$$

where, as above, a dash indicates transposition. This could of course be complicated by allowing for expenditure per person in each category and age to differ for males and females, but such information is rarely available.

The relevant cost is not, however, the absolute value as in (14), but the ratio of this cost to GDP in each year. Projections of Gross Domestic Product depend on assumptions about five factors: initial productivity defined as GDP per employed person, productivity growth, employment rates, participation rates and the population of working age. Total employment is the product of the population, participation rates and the employment rate. Employment is calculated by multiplying the labour utilitization rate by the labour force. If U_t is the total unemployment rate in period t, the utilization rate is $1-U_t$. The aggregate unemployment rate is calculated by dividing the total number of unemployed persons in period t, V_t, by the total labour force in that period, L_t. The value of V_t is in turn calculated by multiplying the age distribution of unemployment rates by the age distribution of the labour force, where these differ according to both age and sex. Let the vectors U_m and U_f be the N-element age distributions of male and female participation rates. If the symbol â represents diagonalization, whereby the vector is written as the leading diagonal of a square matrix with other elements equal to zero, the total number of people unemployed in period t is

$$V_t = U'_{m,t}\, \hat{L}_{m,t}\, p_{m,t} + U'_{f,t}\, \hat{L}_{f,t}\, p_{f,t}. \tag{15}$$

The labour force in period t, L_t, is given by:

$$L_t = L'_{m,t}\, p_{m,t} + L'_{m,t}\, p_{f,t}. \tag{16}$$

Suppose productivity grows at the constant rate, θ. Then GDP in period t is calculated as the product of the utilization rate, $1 - U_t$ $(= 1 - V_t/L_t)$, the labour force, L_t, and productivity, whence:

$$GDP_t = \left\{\frac{GDP_1}{(1 - U_1)\, L_1}\right\} (1 + \theta)^{t-1} (1 - U_t)\, L_t. \tag{17}$$

If the population age distribution, along with the sex and age specific participation and unemployment rates, are constant, then the social expenditure to GDP ratio will remain constant if all items of expenditure grow at the same rate as productivity; that is, if $\theta = \psi_j$ for $j = 1,\ldots,k$.

This framework illustrates that there are many assumptions required to make projections, as well as many potential interdependencies which are not easy to model. For example, productivity may itself depend on social expenditures and the age distribution of workers. Furthermore, participation rates and population growth are interdependent. The changing age distribution is just one component of the ratio of aggregate social expenditure to GDP, and its effects may be swamped by changes in unemployment rates, for example.

Hypothetical Examples

The approach outlined above can be illustrated by considering a hypothetical example where, for simplicity, there are just five age groups. Suppose the constant survival rates for males and females, and fertility rates, are as shown in Table 3. With no migration and the additional assumption that half of all births are male, the application of the above population projection method gives a constant rate of population growth of 1 per cent, with age distributions as shown also in Table 3. Suppose there are just four categories of social expenditure, nominally defined as education, labour market related (including unemployment benefits), health and pensions. Hypothetical costs per capita are shown in Table 4. Suppose male participation rates are zero for ages 1 and 5, and 0.95 for the other ages, and female participation rates are 0.7, 0.7 and 0.4 for the middle three age groups. Furthermore, assume that unemployment rates are 0.05 for all age groups for males and females. If labour productivity is initially 180 units, and if both productivity and all social expenditures per capita grow at a constant rate of 0.018, then total social expenditure as a rate of GDP is found to be constant at 0.2185.

Consider the alternative survival and fertility rates shown in Table 5. These rates represent lower mortality and fertility and imply a steady rate of population growth which is negligible, as well as a stable relative age structure as shown in Table 5. It can be seen that the population in this alternative case is substantially older than in Table 3. With the same assumptions about productivity, unemployment and so on as in the first case, this new population structure implies a ratio of social expenditure to GDP of 0.2394. Hence population ageing in these examples implies increased total expenditures as a proportion of GDP. These orders of magnitude reflect those of the major industrialized countries.

Table 3 Hypothetical Population Structure 1

Age	Survival rates		Fertility	Age distribution		
	M	F	rates	M	F	Total
1	.99	.99	0	0.2484	0.2453	0.2468
2	.955	.955	.95	0.2434	0.2403	0.2418
3	.755	.775	.755	0.2300	0.2272	0.2286
4	.625	.655	.55	0.1719	0.1742	0.1731
5	0	0	0	0.1063	0.1130	0.1097

Table 4 Social Expenditure Per Capita

Age	Education	Labour	Health	Pensions
1	10	0	5	0
2	8	5	4	0
3	0	5	5	0
4	0	5	12	5
5	0	0	20	25

Table 5 Hypothetical Population Structure 2

Age	Survival rates		Fertility	Age distribution		
	M	F	rates	M	F	Total
1	.99	.99	0	0.2335	0.2215	0.2274
2	.955	.955	.9	0.2312	0.2193	0.2251
3	.8	.9	.75	0.2208	0.2094	0.2150
4	.78	.855	.47	0.1767	0.1885	0.1828
5	0	0	0	0.1378	0.1612	0.1498

The higher expenditure requires correspondingly higher tax revenues and, depending on the tax structure, increases in tax rates. This may perhaps generate pressure for some items of social expenditure to be reduced, for example by cutting state pensions and government health benefits.

It is, however, most unlikely that changes in the population structure would occur without any other changes, for example in participation rates. Furthermore, social expenditures are also influenced by productivity and other variables. If the participation rates of women in the middle three age groups are increased to 0.8, 0.8 and 0.5 respectively, the social expenditure ratio would become lower, at 0.2247. If, in addition, all unemployment rates were 0.04, the ratio would again be lower, at 0.2223. Higher productivity would of course reduce the ratio further, though a differential between the expenditure growth of each category and productivity means that the ratio falls steadily over time. What is clear is that population ageing is just one component of the aggregate social expenditure-to-GDP ratio, which is sensitive to a wide range of variables. Some of the variables (such as unemployment rates) may be independent of ageing, but there are several interdependencies about which very little is known.

Many industrialized countries may be regarded as entering a largely unfamiliar territory whose characteristics are very difficult to predict. The present collection of articles is intended to provide an initial reference source for those wishing to examine the varied and important issues relating to the economics of individual and, particularly, population ageing.

Part I
Individual Ageing and the Life Cycle

[1]

ECONOMETRICA

VOLUME 23 April, 1955 NUMBER 2

THE LIFE CYCLE IN INCOME, SAVING, AND ASSET OWNERSHIP

BY HAROLD LYDALL

1. INTRODUCTION

THE SUBJECT of econometrics, as I understand it, is an attempt to discover empirical laws of economic behaviour which can be expressed in mathematical terms. Clearly, a task of this nature requires the services of the economist to suggest reasonable hypotheses, the statistician to collect and analyse appropriate data, and the mathematician to supervise the formulation of the "laws." The work may also start from the other end, the mathematician suggesting convenient formulae, the statistician collecting the data, and the economist trying to interpret the results. But I suspect that the latter method is usually of dubious validity. In the social sciences, empirical study of society must usually take precedence over deductive reasoning; in econometrics, the mathematician must be the ally, not the master, of the economist.

In the past, the development of econometrics—and of economics itself—has been hampered by lack of suitable data to which to apply the mathematical and statistical tools at our disposal. As a consequence, there is sometimes a tendency amongst econometricians to devote more time to the improvement and sharpening of their tools—in readiness for the great occasion when they may be used—than in demonstrating by practical example what results can be obtained by the use of these same tools. Like surgeons without a cadaver they console themselves by burnishing their scalpels.

In order to increase our understanding of how the economic system functions and of how it can be made to work more efficiently, we need more facts as well as more theories—we need more and better corpses as well as more and better scalpels. And if the corpses are not produced in sufficient quantity for our purposes in the normal course of events, then we must go out and find more of them and of the right kind. In the following paper I shall describe the results of such an exercise in "body-snatching."

The development of modern Keynesian economics has led to an increasing emphasis on the importance of "income effects" and a diminution of the importance attributed to "price effects." This leads immediately to a study of the relations between fluctuations in aggregate income, consumption, and investment, and hence to the whole mass of macroeconomic models which have sprouted in the past twenty years. But once the doors are opened in this direction it becomes clear that macro-models are not good enough. The aggregate volume of consumption or investment is the consequence of thousands or millions of individual decisions, each of which may have been taken to some degree independently. Clearly, the effect on consumption of an increase in total personal income will be of one kind if the extra income goes mainly to entrepreneurs, for example, and of another if it goes mainly to old age pensioners; or again the effect of an increase in wages will be different from that of an increase in dividends. So it becomes necessary to go beyond the macro-phenomena and examine the micro-organisms, the households and individuals who make up society.

Statistically, the study of the economic behaviour of households is possible only by means of sample surveys. Information of the quantity and quality required cannot be obtained by compulsory censuses, and the only possible method is to approach a sample of households and win their cooperation. If this can be achieved, we immediately tap a vital new source of knowledge, which has the inestimable advantage that the information it yields can be collected in the form that we desire. The sample survey begins to occupy a similar place in social science to that occupied by the laboratory experiment in the natural sciences. It is not, of course, of quite the same quality, nor can it ever take the place of strictly experimental conditions; but it is a valuable alternative, whose potentialities have scarcely begun to be explored.

In 1952 the Institute of Statistics at Oxford began a series of national surveys of personal incomes and savings. The surveys were made among samples of 2,000–3,000 families or single persons living in private households in Great Britain. The major results obtained from the first survey have been published in articles appearing in the *Bulletin* of the Institute between November, 1952 and April, 1954. In this paper I propose to examine some of the data, drawn principally from the results of the 1953 survey, which throw light on the question of the life cycle in personal economic behaviour.

2. THE ECONOMIC LIFE CYCLE

The cycle of changes in economic behaviour of human life is, when one thinks of it, a very obvious fact. It is not surprising, therefore, that various authors have made mention of it. I suppose Shakespeare was one of the first to produce what an econometrician would call a "model" when, in *As You Like It*, he put into Jaques's mouth the great speech on the Seven Ages of Man. But it was not until the development of large-scale sample surveys in the United States that suitable data became available for a factual study of the question. The great 1935–36 Consumer Purchases Study provided the first set of data; and the annual Surveys of Consumer Finances have, since 1946, provided regular post-war data from which a study of the economic life cycle can be made. A paper written by Dr. Janet Fisher draws on these sources for its material.[1]

As people pass from youth to middle-age, and thence to old age and senility, their economic behaviour passes through various phases. The pattern of these changes is sufficiently stable in any one country and period to warrant our dignifying it with the title of an "economic life cycle." Broadly, the course of

[1] "Income, Spending and Saving Patterns of Consumer Units in Different Age Groups," *Studies in Income and Wealth*, Vol. 15, National Bureau of Economic Research, New York, 1952.

events is as follows: Emerging from adolescence, the young adult goes out to work. His first earnings are usually lower than those he will gain later. As he grows in skill and experience he earns more; but at some stage he reaches a peak from which his income begins to fall. This may be due to a decline in his skill or in his strength, or to the onset of periods of illness or unemployment. Whatever the reason, the phenomenon exists and deserves to be studied. In the end there is an abrupt change with retirement, when income generally falls very far below its previous level.

Western man is not only an earner and a consumer but also a saver. The essence of capitalist progress is accumulation, and the path of individual advance appears to be along the same channel. Moreover, the lengthening of the span of life has made men conscious of the importance of putting aside part of current income for use in their old age. The doctrine of thrift has gained control of wider and wider sections of the population, and the total volume of savings produced has become a vital factor in the stability of the economy.

The volume of personal saving also follows a life cycle pattern. While income rises from youth to middle-age and then declines, saving follows an irregular path, probably reaching its summit rather later on in life. The volume of capital owned at any time is partly an integration of the rate of saving over the past years of life and partly a result of windfall gains, of which the most important are caused by the inheritance of wealth. As we shall see, the average net worth per single adult or married couple in the population starts from a very low level in youth, rises rapidly between 25 and 54 years, and stabilises approximately at the level attained in the 50's. There are, however, discordant movements at about this time. Those who retire from work almost certainly begin to use up their capital to some degree, while those who continue to work beyond the normal retiring age add further to their capital holdings.

We shall see in detail below how these different movements appear in the figures at our disposal, and what causes can be identified from the other data available about the individuals and families making up the sample. But before we advance to the actual figures it is necessary to say a little about the methods employed in collecting them.

3. METHODS EMPLOYED IN THE SURVEY

Most of the data referred to in this paper are derived from the 1953 Survey; but in a few cases, where the information has not been so conveniently tabulated from that survey, tables will be taken from the 1952 Survey. The essential principles of both surveys were the same: the only differences were that the effective sample in 1953 was about 2,100 interviews compared with 2,600 in 1952 and that the questionnaire employed in the 1953 Survey covered rather more detail than that employed in the earlier year. Notably, the 1953 Survey provides information on the total net worth of each person or family interviewed, whereas the 1952 Survey obtained information on only some parts of the personal balance sheet.

The 1952 Survey of Personal Incomes and Savings was the first survey of its kind in Britain or, so far as I know, anywhere outside the United States. It was initiated and organised by the Oxford Institute of Statistics after a preparatory phase of study, during which a pilot survey of 400 interviews was made among households in the City of Oxford. Valuable advice was given by the Survey Research Center of the University of Michigan, who are responsible for conducting the American Surveys of Consumer Finances on behalf of the Federal Reserve Board. Technical advice and co-operation were also given by the British Social Survey, which is an organisation established by the government for undertaking sample surveys in Britain, mainly for official purposes.

The principal aim of the survey was to discover, by means of direct interviews, which sections of the population were adding to their savings and which were drawing on them, and in what form these savings were being made in each case. It was hoped that the survey would provide an additional source for estimates of the personal saving component of the national income, but the survey has not proved itself yet as a reliable method of estimating aggregates. Even if we recognise this difficulty, however, we can still claim that the Survey sheds some light on the component parts of personal saving and on their relative importance; and it gives the first real picture of the behaviour of different income groups and other sub-sections of the population that has ever been obtained in Great Britain.

The elementary unit whose characteristics and behaviour are studied in this survey is called an "income unit," which is defined as follows. Each single person of 18 years or over and each married couple is a separate income unit, children of under 18 being attached to the income unit of their parents or guardians. Thus the income unit may be a family consisting of husband, wife and several young children, or it may be simply a married couple without children, or a single person, aged 18 years or over, with or without dependent children. This definition is not, unfortunately, identical with the definition of a "spending unit" used by the American Surveys of Consumer Finances. In those surveys, all members of a family are grouped together if they pool the greater part of their incomes. Whether such pooling is deemed to take place is determined by a question which is asked in the early part of the interview. We thought it preferable to make our elementary unit one which could be defined by objective characteristics of age and marital status; but in the few cases in which an individual was found to have an income of less than £50 and was living with relations, he or she was "amalgamated," at a later stage, into his relations' income unit.

One convenient result of defining an income unit in the way described is that it corresponds fairly closely with the income unit employed by the British revenue authorities for the assessment of income tax. It is, therefore, possible to compare the distribution of income obtained in the survey with that part of the distribution which is covered by tax assessments.

The sample, in both years, was drawn in the following manner. Like all national samples in large countries, it was necessarily of multi-stage design. In the first stage 69 towns and rural districts were drawn from the more than 1,500 local authority areas in Great Britain. These areas were stratified by several characteristics so as to produce 69 separate strata and one town or district was drawn from each stratum for inclusion in the sample. The probability of selection of each town within each stratum was proportionate to its population and, to compensate for this, the sampling rate employed in the second stage of sampling—within each town—was inversely proportional to the population of that town. The sample within each town was drawn from the lists of property kept by the local authorities for purposes of local taxation. The traditional source of local finance in Britain is local rates, which are levied on all property within the boundaries of the district. Each piece of property is valued officially at a figure which is intended to correspond to its rental value. In fact, the valuations are out-of-date and have been much distorted by the effects of rent control and other influences. The rateable values of private houses are, however, generally associated quite closely with their rental values; and they are also associated, but to a much smaller degree, with the incomes of their inhabitants. Consequently, rateable value can be used with advantage as a means of stratifying property when a sample of private houses is to be drawn. In this survey the sample was divided into two strata at the second stage of sampling: houses with a rateable value of under £30 and houses with a rateable value of £30 and over. Moreover, the latter stratum was sampled at a rate five times as great as the former (eight times as great in 1953), partly to take account of the greater variability of economic behaviour in the upper stratum and partly in order to strengthen the representation in the sample of people with larger incomes.

The list of houses having thus been drawn up, interviewers were sent out to try to interview all the income units discovered in every house.[2] A questionnaire form was to be returned for each income unit. Of course, there was a considerable number of income units who could not be interviewed because they were always out or away from home, too ill or unfit to be interviewed, or because they refused to give information on this subject. In the 1952 Survey the proportion of non-respondents—for all these reasons—was 25 per cent (when the strata are re-weighted into correct proportion), but in the 1953 Survey the response was less satisfactory and the percentage of non-respondents rose to 34.

The data from the 1952 Survey have been submitted to a large variety of tests, including comparisons with outside estimates, and in general they stand up to these, showing no serious signs of bias. However, there is almost certainly one deficiency in the sample, namely, that it contains too few *rentiers* who, as one might expect, are not very willing subjects for an enquiry of this sort. This deficiency does not appreciably distort the income distribution, by size of income, but shows itself in the composition of aggregate income and in the estimates of aggregate liquid asset holdings.

The fall in response in the 1953 Survey is unfortunate, and the 1953 sample is undoubtedly less representative than the sample obtained in the previous year. Nevertheless, the broad lines of the conclusions that emerge from both surveys are similar and, since the 1953 Survey contains information on a wider

[2] With the exception that where a house contained more than three households only the income units in three of the households, selected at random, were to be included.

range of subjects than the earlier one, I have chosen to use its results for illustrating most of the discussion in this article. The 1952 results are, however, used in special cases where they are thought to be more reliable.

4. SOME DEMOGRAPHIC CHARACTERISTICS OF THE POPULATION

It might be argued that people vary in the speed at which they develop, some reaching a particular phase in their "life cycle" at an earlier age than others. Some people may, indeed, never pass through a particular phase of development, such as marriage or parenthood. On these grounds one might draw the conclusion that single people should be treated separately from the married, and families with children separately from childless couples. However, since this would add further complications to the analysis, I have, in this paper, ignored such differences within age groups and I have taken age as the sole index of the stage reached in the personal life cycle.

People enter our field of vision, in this survey, when they reach their eighteenth birthday. At that age they become separate entities—income units—whose behaviour can be studied. Both males and females are treated equally in this respect so long as they are unmarried. As soon as a woman marries, however, she becomes merged in her husband's income unit and loses, from our point of view, her independent identity. From that point on, so long as the marriage lasts, she is classified by the characteristics of her husband with respect to age, sex, occupation and similar attributes or, alternatively, by the aggregate characteristics of her whole income unit with respect to income, asset holdings and similar variables. Later on in life she generally emerges again as the "head" of an income unit, because she frequently outlives her husband. Sometimes, also, the marriage is terminated by divorce or separation.

The distribution of income units according to the age of head, as it appeared in the 1953 Survey, is given in Table I. The distribution corresponds fairly closely with what might be expected from Census data, although the Census figures are not strictly comparable. But there is some evidence to suggest that the sample contains rather too few younger members of the population (in the age group 18–24) and too many in the oldest age group. The distortion on this account, however, is not likely to affect seriously our conclusions about the variability of behaviour at different ages.

TABLE I

DISTRIBUTION OF INCOME UNITS BY AGE OF HEAD, 1953 SURVEY

Age of head	Per cent
18–24	11
25–34	18
35–44	20
45–54	18
55–64	13
65 and over	20
	100

TABLE II

DISTRIBUTION OF VARIOUS CHARACTERISTICS OF INCOME UNITS WITHIN AGE GROUPS, 1953 SURVEY
(percentage distributions)

Characteristics of income unit	Age of head of income unit						All ages
	18–24	25–34	35–44	45–54	55–64	65 and over	
Sex of head							
Male	55	84	88	84	67	56	74
Female	45	16	12	16	33	44	26
	100	100	100	100	100	100	100
Number of persons in income unit							
One	87	25	12	17	39	59	36
Two	6	18	13	36	48	38	27
Three	5	26	24	23	8	2	16
Four	1	19	28	16	3	*	13
Five	*	8	13	5	1	*	5
Six or more	1	4	10	3	1	—	3
	100	100	100	100	100	100	100
Occupation of head							
Self-employed	*	4	7	6	3	3	4
Managers and technical	2	8	12	11	7	2	7
Clerical and sales	34	22	12	13	10	1	14
Skilled manual	40	50	47	40	27	5	35
Unskilled manual	19	13	19	22	25	8	17
Retired and unoccupied	5	3	3	8	28	81	23
	100	100	100	100	100	100	100
Position in household							
Head of household	9	70	89	91	89	86	77
Younger relative of head	89	28	9	7	5	1	19
Older relative of head	—	—	*	1	5	13	3
Boarder	2	2	1	1	*	*	1
Employee	*	*	*	*	1	*	*
	100	100	100	100	100	100	100

* Less than one-half of one per cent.
Note: Details do not always add to totals because of rounding.

In order that we may have a picture in our minds of the sort of people who are to be found in each of the six age groups (in terms of which our analysis will proceed) I have brought together in Table II some distributions of attributes within each age group. It will be noted that nearly half the income units of which the age of the head is less than 25 are single women but that after that age, for the next three age groups, the proportion of single women is less than one-sixth. Later again they re-emerge, and, in the final age group, resume the importance they held in the first. The same kind of development can be traced in the second section of the table, where distributions of income units by size are given. Nearly 90 per cent of income units of which the head is aged 18–24 are unmarried, 6 per cent are married without children, 5 per cent have one child, and 2 per cent more than one. In later age groups a few of the multi-person income units are headed by widowed or divorced people; but in general it is safe to assume that the two-person income units are childless married couples and that the larger income units are married couples with children of less than 18 years of age. It will be observed that over a third of all income units are single people and about a quarter are childless couples. Hence not much more than a third of the total are "families" in the accepted sense of the word.

In the next section of the table are given the occupational distributions of the age groups. It will be seen that the proportion who are retired or unoccupied begins to grow in the 45–54 group and becomes considerable in the next group. Among those aged 65 and over, less than one-fifth are still occupied. The proportion of self-employed persons (*i.e.*, those owning their own business, farm or professional practice) rises to a peak in the middle age groups and then falls away; and the same tendency can be discerned with managers and other professional and technical employees (called "managers and technical"). However, as a proportion of the occupied population in each age group these two classes do not decline to the same extent. The proportion of clerical and sales workers falls sharply from one-third in the first age group to less than a quarter in the next and so to about one-eighth of the remaining groups aged less than 65. This is due primarily to the disappearance of female clerical and sales employees who marry and so cease to be employed, or to be heads of income units.

In the final section we see something of the household living arrangements of each type of income unit. Nine out of ten of those aged 18–24 are living with their relations, usually their parents, and over a quarter of those aged 25–34 are still in the same position. After that, separate households are the rule and only 10 per cent or less of each age group live with their relations. Among those aged 65 and over only one in eight is living as a subsidiary to his younger relatives, but there are others in this group who are themselves heads of households and share their accommodation with younger members of their family.

5. THE VARIATION OF INCOME WITH AGE

As people grow older their income tends to increase, up to a certain point, and then to decline. Numerous different influences are at work to produce this result, some of which we shall attempt to analyse below. But first, we shall consider the actual changes in income that take place in the population as a whole.

Table III shows distributions of income units in each age group according to their gross income (before tax). The large proportion of income units below £200 in the first age group is due mainly to the existence of many single women in this group, receiving fairly low wages. In the next age group the distribution assumes a more typical appearance, with a mode in the range £400–599. In the third group the upward tail of the distribution grows longer and there are more

TABLE III

DISTRIBUTION OF INCOME WITHIN AGE GROUPS, 1953 SURVEY

Gross income (before tax)	Age of head of income unit						All ages
	18–24	25–34	35–44	45–54	55–64	65 and over	
	Percentages of income units in each age group						
Under £200	31	6	3	6	27	66	23
£200–399	53	30	26	28	36	23	30
£400–599	14	43	40	39	22	7	29
£600–799	2	16	17	16	8	1	11
£800–999	—	3	7	7	2	1	4
£1,000–1,499	—	1	5	2	3	1	2
£1,500 and over	—	1	2	2	2	1	1
Total	100	100	100	100	100	100	100
	Mean amount per income unit in each age group						
Gross income £	269	482	574	560	409	240	434
Direct taxes £	24	34	50	68	46	25	42
Net income £	245	448	524	492	363	215	392
Number of persons	1.24	2.80	3.52	2.67	2.09	1.44	2.36
Net income per person £	197	160	149	184	174	149	166

large incomes. After this the tail appears to shorten a little and the proportion of low incomes begins to grow again until, in the last two age groups, there re-emerge large numbers of people with incomes of less than £200.

In the lower part of the table we show the average gross income in each age group, as found in the sample. These averages are subject to fairly large sampling errors (their standard errors are of the order of 5 per cent) and hence the point at which income reaches its maximum cannot be exactly determined. But there can be no doubt that these figures describe the broad pattern correctly, as is confirmed by other surveys both in Britain and in the United States.

The table also shows the average amount of direct taxes paid in each age group and the net income available for consumption or saving. Generally, this follows a similar course to gross income. If we divide average net income by the average number of persons per income unit in each age group, we arrive at a figure showing the average amount of disposable income per person in each group. This figure fluctuates much less violently than aggregate income per income unit, since the number of persons per income unit follows a path similar to that of gross income. On the average, in other words, fluctuations over the life cycle in the number of dependents are broadly offset by fluctuations in the size of income available for their support. This is, however, only broadly true; and it is worth noting that there is an appreciable fall in average net income per person among the families in the age groups from 25 to 44, as well as among elderly people in the final age group.

TABLE IV

COMPONENTS OF PERSONAL INCOME, ANALYSED BY AGE OF HEAD OF INCOME UNIT, 1953 SURVEY

Source of income	Age of head of income unit						All ages
	18–24	25–34	35–44	45–54	55–64	65 and over	
	Mean income per annum in £s						
Employment	260	429	468	448	293	100	339
Business, professional and farming profits	1	24	62	51	48	18	36
Rent, interest and dividends	1	9	14	35	25	34	21
Government transfers	5	14	27	22	37	87	35
Private transfers	2	6	3	4	6	1	3
Total	269	482	574	560	409	240	434
	As per cent of total income						
Employment	97	89	82	80	72	42	78
Business, professional and farming profits	*	5	11	9	12	8	8
Rent, interest and dividends	*	2	2	6	6	14	5
Government transfers	2	3	5	4	9	36	8
Private transfers	1	1	*	1	1	*	1
Total	100	100	100	100	100	100	100

* Less than one-half of one per cent.

We pass now to consider the composition of total income in each age group. From Table IV it will be seen that income from employment (which includes wages, salaries and pensions arising from employment) rises to a peak in the third age group, as does total income, and then declines. Entrepreneurial income also reaches its maximum in the same group, but remains at a comparatively high level for the next twenty years. Investment income, on the other hand, grows more slowly in the early years and reaches a plateau in the 45–54 age group, from which it does not fall appreciably. Government transfers (which consist principally of family allowances, health benefits and retirement pensions) represent not more than 5 per cent of total income in the first four age groups but become of increasing importance both absolutely and relatively in the last two groups. Private transfers are regular income receipts by way of gift from relatives or friends not living in the same household as the recipient. They are mostly paid to women, either by separated husbands or by children living away from home.

The conclusions to be drawn from this table seem to be: (1) that the earning power of the income unit reaches a maximum and then declines; and (2) that the share of income derived from active employment, including entrepreneurial income, steadily falls from one age group to the next, being replaced by two other sources of income in particular—investment income and government transfers. In other words, as a person's direct earning capacity declines with advancing age the fall in his income is partially broken, and his income is to

TABLE V

GROSS INCOME IN RELATION TO AGE AND OCCUPATION, 1953 SURVEY
(mean gross income per income unit in each cell)

Age of head	Occupation of head			All occupations
	Salaried and self-employed	Manual workers	Retired and unoccupied	
	£	£	£	£
18–24	219	309	153	269
25–34	541	463	243	482
35–44	772	494	278	574
45–54	788	464	439	560
55–64	752	377	222	409
65 and over	970	382	163	240
All ages	642	437	195	434

some extent sustained, either by the proceeds of private investment or by government assistance. The latter element has clearly been of increasing importance in Britain in the past fifteen years and may well continue to grow, while the proportionate importance of investment income may fall. It should be noted, however, that the survey's estimates of income from investment are biased downwards.

What are the causes of this apparent decline in earning power from somewhere in middle age? To those of us who are on salary scales that increase with age it may seem an odd result. In Table V estimates of average total income (before tax) are given for three occupational groups. The salaried and self-employed group includes all those who work on their own account or employ others, and managers, professional, technical, clerical and sales employees. In these occupations, especially among the employees, one might expect average earnings to increase right up to retiring age. The figures appear to confirm the existence of such a tendency, although there is some fall in the 55–64 age group. It must be remembered, however, that the self-employed are not subject to precisely the same influences as salaried employees. Evidence from various surveys, both in Britain and the United States, suggests that the earnings of self-employed professional people, such as doctors and dentists, reach a maximum in the 40's or early 50's and then decline.[3]

The most striking thing about Table V is the marked peak in the average income of manual-worker income units in the 35–44 age group. This pattern of income may, of course, be due to various causes. It may be the result of changes in the composition of the income unit, e.g., through marriage or death, or to changes in the number of members of the income unit who go out to work, as

[3] See A. Bradford Hill, "The Doctor's Day and Pay," *Journal of the Royal Statistical Society*, Vol. CXIV, Pt. I, 1951, p. 1; William Weinfeld, "Income of Dentists, 1929–48," *Survey of Current Business*, January, 1950; and "Income of Physicians, 1929–49," *Survey of Current Business*, July, 1951.

TABLE VI

ANNUAL EARNINGS OF MALE MANUAL WORKERS WORKING FULL-TIME, ANALYSED BY AGE GROUP, 1953 SURVEY

(mean annual earnings in each age group)

Age of worker	Skilled	Unskilled	All manual
	£	£	£
18–24	335	335	335
25–34	444	383	432
35–44	470	381	447
45–54	454	345	421
55–64	409	317	370
65 and over	478	323	388
All ages	441	352	414

well as to changes in the physical or mental capacity of the individual worker himself. In order to focus attention on this last aspect, we present in Table VI a special tabulation of the estimated annual earnings of male manual workers, working in full-time employment, who were absent from work on account of sickness or unemployment for not more than 4 weeks in the year. In these figures we find the same tendency for average earnings to reach a peak: among skilled workers it appears in the 35–44 age group, and among unskilled workers even earlier. This pattern of earnings may be due to changes in the average hours of work at different ages, to changes in piece-work earnings, or, in the case of skilled workers, to changes in the rate of pay for skill. It is interesting to note that skilled workers who continue to work after the age of 65, the normal retiring age, earn more than the average amounts received by the two preceding age groups. This suggests that it is the better workmen, whose abilities have suffered least from the effects of age, who are kept on after 65.

6. VARIATIONS IN ASSET HOLDINGS WITH AGE

We have seen that there is a clearly marked cycle in the movement of average income with age. Can we find any similar pattern in the holding of assets? In the 1953 Survey information was collected on the value of the following types of assets held by each income unit: cars, real estate, unincorporated businesses or farms, liquid assets of all types except actual cash, stocks, shares and other securities, and debts owed to the income unit. These were offset by the following liabilities: mortgage debt, hire-purchase debt, overdrafts at banks, and money owed on personal loans. The net amount of these assets and liabilities constitutes the net worth of the income unit. The coverage of the assets side is not complete, since it excludes cash in hand, household goods, furniture, clothes, jewellery and other "chattels," life assurance policies and the expected benefits under pension schemes. On the liabilities side no account was taken of short-term debts to retailers or others for services rendered. Moreover, the valuation of such assets as cars, real estate, stocks and shares and businesses was left to the judgement of the owner, who was asked to give the best estimate he could make of their value at current market prices. In spite of these qualifications, I believe that the figures obtained from this inquiry are indicative of the relative net worth of the different age groups of the population.

The distribution of income units according to their net worth is given in Table VII, and Table VIII contains the estimated mean values of the principal components of net worth, analysed by age group. It will be seen that, whereas income reaches its maximum somewhere in the third or fourth age group, net worth continues to increase up to the penultimate group. Nor does its average level decline appreciably even after that. From the frequency distributions it will be noted that in the first age group half the income units have no net worth or a negative amount, and very few of them have any substantial sum of capital. In the next group the proportion of income units who are in debt rises quite sharply,

TABLE VII

DISTRIBUTION OF NET WORTH WITHIN AGE GROUPS, 1953 SURVEY
(percentages of income units in each age group)

Net worth of income unit	Age of head of income unit						All ages
	18–24	25–34	35–44	45–54	55–64	65 and over	
Negative	9	21	17	11	8	5	12
Nil	42	15	14	19	20	32	22
£1–49	32	20	16	14	17	11	17
£50–199	12	21	16	10	15	7	14
£200–999	4	15	19	17	14	16	15
£1,000 and over	1	7	16	24	23	25	17
Not ascertained	—	1	2	5	3	4	3
	100	100	100	100	100	100	100

TABLE VIII

ASSETS, LIABILITIES AND NET WORTH, ANALYSED BY AGE GROUP, 1953 SURVEY
(mean per income unit in each age group)

Age of head of income unit	Assets				Liabilities	Net worth
	Liquid assets	Own home	Other	Total		
	£	£	£	£	£	£
18–24	30	10	10	50	−10	40
25–34	90	170	170	430	−110	320
35–44	140	450	340	930	−170	760
45–54	290	510	500	1,300	−140	1,160
55–64	310	600	380	1,290	−90	1,200
65 and over	280	450	470	1,200	−20	1,180
All ages	190	380	330	900	−100	800

TABLE IX

RELATION BETWEEN NET WORTH AND INCOME, BY AGE GROUPS, 1953 SURVEY

Age of head of income unit	Gross Income		Net Worth		Net worth as per cent of gross income
	Mean	As per cent of population mean	Mean	As per cent of population mean	
	£		£		
18–24	269	62	40	5	15
25–34	482	111	320	40	66
35–44	574	132	760	95	132
45–54	560	129	1,160	145	207
55–64	409	94	1,200	150	294
65 and over	240	55	1,180	148	492
All ages	434	100	800	100	184

but there is also an increase in the proportion with substantial amounts of assets. After this, the proportion of net debtors declines steadily and the positive tail of the distribution grows. It is only in the last group that there is a counter-movement, one-third of income units in this group reporting the ownership of no assets.

The figures in Table VIII give some indication of the growth of each type of asset with age and of the movement of liabilities. One interesting feature is the importance of home ownership as a component of total net worth: even when allowance is made for mortgage debts, this type of asset accounts for over £300 out of the £800 of total net worth. The bulk of the liabilities are, in fact, mortgage debts, and the net worth of owner-occupied houses is therefore increasing more sharply in the middle age groups than is indicated by the second column of figures in the table.

It is clear from the data given so far that income and net worth follow different paths as age increases. The relations between these two variables, as averages for each age group, are exhibited in Table IX. The final column in this table shows clearly how the relative importance of income and capital changes as age increases. The economic position of those in the first age group depends almost entirely on current income (except in so far as they benefit from their parents' ownership of capital) but the relative importance of asset holdings grows rapidly and without interruption as age advances.

While it is obvious that income and net worth are not independent of one another, it is of some interest to find that the relation between them varies from one age group to another. The relation between net worth and the two variables, age and income, is shown in Table X. From these data it is clear that at each level of income net worth is an increasing function of age.

7. VARIATIONS IN SAVING PROPENSITIES WITH AGE

One of the principal objects of this analysis is to give support to the view that there are significant differences between age groups in the propensity to

TABLE X

NET WORTH IN RELATION TO AGE AND INCOME, 1953 SURVEY

(mean net worth per income unit in each cell)

Gross income	Age of head of income unit				All ages
	18–24	25–44	45–64	65 and over	
	£	£	£	£	£
Under £200	30	50	540	480	380
£200–399	30	200	350	1,050	340
£400–599	70	260	540	2,870	480
£600–999	100	670	2,060	3,480	1,300
£1,000–1,499	—	2,020	5,680	11,950	3,800
£1,500 and over	—	12,430	19,370	22,240	16,740
Total	40	550	1,170	1,180	800

save. We have shown that income varies with age, and that net worth follows a somewhat different path. It is widely accepted that both these variables are likely to be of importance in determining the volume of saving. Lawrence Klein, in several papers, has examined models in which income and liquid asset holdings are used as principal independent variables; and his results, as well as other work in Oxford, has convincingly proved the importance of retaining both variables in the system. (Whether one uses liquid asset holdings or net worth as the indicator of the capital side is probably not important, since they are closely correlated with one another.) In some of his equations Klein has introduced age as an independent variable,[4] but his regression coefficients for this variable proved to be insignificant. I think that this result was caused by putting age in the equation as a linear variable. If it is to be a helpful explanatory variable, its influence must clearly be allowed to pass through a maximum at some point.

In Table XI, we present figures drawn from the 1952 Survey showing the average amounts saved or dissaved per income unit in each age group, and the breakdown of saving into some of its component parts. The reason for using 1952 figures instead of 1953 figures at this stage is that the full analysis of this part of the problem has not yet been made for the latter year. Saving is an awkward variable to try to explain, since it is subject to extremely wide variations in any given period of time. Even in a period as long as a year there are many people whose saving or dissaving is wildly erratic in comparison with their normal behaviour. For example, if a person has saved up for five years to buy a car or to take a specially expensive holiday, his saving in the year in which he makes the outlay for this purpose will be heavily negative, although if we considered the whole period of five or six years there would be no such heavy dissaving. Hence, we must not be surprised to find that mean figures of saving in different age or income groups are subject to relatively large random influences

[4] See, for example, his paper "Estimating Patterns of Savings Behavior from Sample Survey Data," ECONOMETRICA, Vol. 19, No. 4, October, 1951.

TABLE XI

TOTAL SAVING AND ITS COMPONENTS, ANALYSED BY AGE GROUPS, 1952 SURVEY
(mean amount per income unit in each age group)

Age of head of income unit	Contractual saving (1952)				Other saving 1952	Total saving	
	Life assurance premiums	Superannuation contributions	Mortgage capital repayments	Total		1952	1953
	£	£	£	£	£	£	£
18–24	3	1	—	4	−4	*	+3
25–34	11	4	5	20	−15	+5	+4
35–44	17	5	6	28	−28	*	+15
45–54	16	4	7	27	*	+27	+6
55–64	12	5	3	20	−13	+7	+8
65 and over	4	*	*	5	−24	−19	−13
All ages	11	3	4	18	−14	+ 4	+ 4

* Less than 10s. per income unit.

which throw them out of alignment. The problem of reducing random variance is more acute in this case than perhaps with any other variable which has been systematically studied.

One group of components of total saving is, however, relatively stable, namely, the various forms of contractual saving. From Table XI, it will be seen that contractual saving is of comparatively small importance in the first age group. Most of the total consists of life assurance premiums. In the next group average contractual saving becomes much larger: life assurance premiums are up, superannuation contributions have become significant, and there is now a new source of saving in the form of regular repayment of capital borrowed on mortgage for home purchase. Contractual saving reaches a peak in the middle age groups and falls away in the older groups. After the age of 65, superannuation contributions and mortgage repayments are of negligible importance, but there is still an appreciable volume of life assurance premiums being paid.

In Table XII, the figures of total contractual saving are expressed as a percentage of net income (after tax) in each age group. From them it will be seen that contractual saving is nearly 5 per cent of net income on the average, but, if we exclude the two extreme age groups, the average for those aged 25–64 is over 5 per cent.

"Other saving" represents a mixed bag of transactions, including changes in liquid asset holdings, changes in investment in property and securities, loans given and received, and so on. Purchases of durable goods, other than houses, are not treated as saving, and people who receive cash windfalls during the year are not credited with saving them if they merely keep them intact. On the contrary, people who spend windfalls or sell durable goods are regarded as having dissaved to that extent. In the period to which these figures refer, the year 1951–52, "other" saving appears to have been on balance quite heavily

TABLE XII

SAVING AND DURABLE CONSUMPTION, ANALYSED BY AGE GROUPS, 1952 SURVEY

Age of head of income unit	Durable consumption	Contractual saving	Total saving	Durable consumption plus:	
				Contractual saving	Total saving
	Mean amount per income unit in £s				
18–24	13	4	*	17	+13
25–34	26	20	+5	46	+31
35–44	29	28	*	57	+29
45–54	21	27	+27	48	+48
55–64	14	20	+7	34	+21
65 and over	4	5	−19	9	−15
All ages	18	18	+4	36	+22
	Percentages of net income in each group				
18–24	5.5	1.7	*	7.2	+5.5
25–34	6.2	4.6	+1.3	10.8	+7.5
35–44	6.3	6.0	*	12.3	+6.3
45–54	4.3	5.8	+5.7	10.1	+10.0
55–64	3 9	5.5	+1.9	9.4	+5.8
65 and over	2.3	1.8	−9.4	4.1	−7.1
All ages	4.9	4.9	+1.0	9.8	+5.9

* Less than half of last digit shown.

negative, so that total saving was only £4 per income unit for the whole population.[5]

Total saving, as has been said, is subject to serious random fluctuations, and the pattern of its variation with age is not easy to determine. Broadly, however, the results shown in the table follow the course that one would expect, and the results of the 1953 Survey, which are given here for comparison, are of the same general type. In the first age group, saving is very low; it rises a little in the next group, however, and becomes substantial in the middle age groups; it falls again in the 55–64 group and becomes strongly negative in the final group. At what point in the middle age groups saving is at its maximum is difficult to determine, but it seems probable that the 1952 figures give a better indication of the tendencies in these groups than the 1953 figures.

One of the items of expense which is heavy and discontinuous in its incidence is the purchase of durable goods. Such purchases are treated in this study as consumption expenditure, even though many durable items are capable of being re-sold. There is, however, an appreciable negative correlation between saving and durable consumption, and it seems reasonable to regard such con-

[5] An attempted reconciliation between these figures and the national income estimates of saving will be found in my article "Personal Saving and Consumption Expenditure," *Bulletin of the Oxford Institute of Statistics*, Vol. 15, Nos. 10 and 11, Oct.–Nov., 1953.

sumption expenditure as being an important influence on saving behaviour. In Table XII figures are given from the 1952 Survey, of average expenditure on durable goods in the six age groups. The figures cover all major durable goods costing £25 or more, but exclude clothing and soft furnishings. It will be seen that expenditure on durable goods, unlike saving, is comparatively large in the youngest age group and takes over 5 per cent of the net income of this group. Durable consumption continues to increase rapidly in the next age group (in which many people are getting married and setting up home) and it reaches its maximum in the 35–44 group. After that it falls away quite quickly.

If we compare saving and durable consumption over the life cycle, it is evident that durable consumption is more important in the earlier years and saving in the later years, up to the age of retirement. Durable consumption takes over 6 per cent of net income in the years from 25 to 44, when, according to the 1952 Survey, saving is barely positive. In the next twenty years, however, durable consumption is only about 4 per cent of net income while saving rises to about the same level. It is not implausible to conclude that saving and durable consumption are fairly close substitutes for one another in the household sector.

Finally, we present in Tables XIII and XIV the results of an analysis of average saving and durable consumption for various combinations of age and income. While these figures cannot be interpreted directly as savings functions for the different age groups, they give some indication of the form that the functions are likely to assume. From Table XIII, it seems that the income-elasticity of saving increases as age increases up to retiring age. The change between the first and second age groups is not very marked, but in the third group, extending from 45 to 64, there are signs of a definite increase in the elasticity. Janet Fisher has suggested that older people are unable to adjust their expenditures to changes in their income with the same facility as young people. This may well be true, but a further explanation of the greater income-elasticity of saving in the older age groups, before retirement, is the increasing importance of entrepreneurial income in these groups. Such income is subject to

TABLE XIII

TOTAL SAVING IN RELATION TO AGE AND INCOME, 1952 SURVEY

(mean saving per income unit in each cell)

Net income (after tax)	Age of head of income unit				All ages
	18–24	25–44	45–64	65 and over	
	£	£	£	£	£
Under £200	−1	−10	−31	−17	−16
£200–399	−2	+1	+4	−31	−1
£400–599	+8	−1	−2	*	−1
£600–999	+25	+18	+34	−74	+20
£1,000 and over	—	+43	+410	+132	+308
Total	+*	+4	+19	−19	+4

*Less than 10s. per income unit.

TABLE XIV

TOTAL SAVING PLUS DURABLE CONSUMPTION IN RELATION TO AGE AND INCOME, 1952 SURVEY

(mean amount per income unit in each cell)

Net income (after tax)	Age of head of income unit				All ages
	18-24	25-44	45-64	65 and over	
	£	£	£	£	£
Under £200	+3	−6	−25	−16	−12
£200–399	+14	+12	+11	−29	+8
£400–599	+48	+30	+19	+8	+27
£600–999	+99	+71	+64	−27	+67
£1,000 and over	—	+242	+503	+172	+432
Total	+13	+30	+35	−16	+22

sharper fluctuations from year to year than other types of income and these fluctuations are very largely offset by adjustments in saving.

When both saving and durable consumption are taken into account, as in Table XIV, there appears to be less difference between the behaviour of the three pre-retirement age groups. Indeed, there seems to be a tendency for total outlay on both items to decline at each equivalent level of income. The figures given for the £1,000-and-over income group are not strictly comparable, because of variations in the income composition of this group in different age classes.

8. CONCLUSION

The figures derived from the savings survey undertaken by the Oxford Institute of Statistics indicate a definite life cycle pattern in income receipts. Average income reaches a maximum in middle age and then declines with increasing speed.

Capital holdings and net worth, on the other hand, grow more slowly in the earlier years but continue to grow after income has started to decline. They become stabilised in later life and do not show a marked tendency to decline. However, different people have different experiences in this respect, and there is a considerable increase in the number of people in the older age groups who possess no capital.

Personal saving follows a less regular pattern than either of the former variables. Its general trend is to increase in middle age, especially in the latter part of this period, and to decline sharply in old age. While saving is generally at a low level in the first half of working life, durable consumption expenditure is rather high; and there is some reason to believe that these two influences interact on one another. In other words, young people devote their surpluses to building up their stock of durable goods, while older people who are still at work devote theirs to saving.

Perhaps we may hazard an impressionistic picture of the typical life cycle. Young men and women, before marriage, do not normally earn very large incomes. They spend what they earn very freely, with little thought for the future. Immediately before and after marriage, however, they begin to set aside what surplus they can for building up a home. In the next twenty years or so they are usually preoccupied with supporting their children, and their savings are not, on balance, very great. After middle age, the number of dependents declines more rapidly than income, expenditure on durables also falls away, and people begin to put aside larger sums for their old age. After retirement they usually draw down their capital in order to supplement their shrunken incomes.

In the light of the figures presented in this paper, I believe that any attempt to construct satisfactory savings functions from cross-section data must take into account the factor of age.

Oxford University Institute of Statistics

[2]

THE PRODUCTION OF HUMAN CAPITAL AND THE LIFE CYCLE OF EARNINGS

YORAM BEN-PORATH*
University of Chicago

The application of capital theory to decisions on individual improvement, and in particular improvement of earning capacity, has provided a framework for the understanding of many aspects of observed behavior regarding education, health, occupational choice, mobility, etc., as rational investment of present resources for the purpose of enjoying future returns. The formulation by Friedman and Kuznets (1945) and the significant development of the theory by Becker (1962, 1964) and Mincer (1958, 1962) provided a novel view of the life cycle of earnings by linking it to the time profile of investment in human capital: People make most of their investments in themselves when they are young, and to a large extent by foregoing current earnings. Observed earnings are therefore relatively low at early years, and they rise as investment declines and as returns on past investments are realized. The main reason why investment is undertaken mostly by the young is that they have a longer period over which they can receive returns on their investment. The purpose of this paper is to combine that part of the argument concerning the demand for human capital with a more explicit treatment of the supply, or cost conditions, facing the individual.

It is hard to think of forms of human capital that the individual can acquire as final goods—he has to participate in the creation of his human capital. His own abilities, innate or acquired, the quality of co-operating inputs, the constraints and opportunities offered by the institutional setup—all determine the "technology," or the production function.[1] Together with the relevant factor prices, the properties of the production function determine the optimal way in which any quantity of human capital is to be produced and determine the cost of production. I shall show how the production function (through supply or cost conditions) enters into the determination of the optimal path of investment, analyze some of the implications for the individual's allocation of time, and demonstrate how the life cycle of earnings can be affected by various properties of the production function.

The basic model generates some of the qualitative characteristics of the observed life cycle of earnings—typically, an initial period of no earnings followed by a period in which earnings rise at a declining rate and, eventually, decline.

* This paper is based on part of my Ph.D. dissertation submitted to the Department of Economics, Harvard University, February, 1967. I benefited from discussing earlier drafts with my adviser, Professor Simon Kuznets, and with Professor Rodney A. Dobell, Gur Ofer, and Christopher A. Sims; I received many useful comments from Professors Gary S. Becker, Zvi Griliches, Theodore W. Schultz, Lester G. Telser, and other friends. Financial support was provided by a Ford Dissertation Fellowship and a grant from the Ford Foundation to the University of Chicago for Research on Investment in Human Capital.

[1] Such a production has been recently introduced also by Becker (1966).

Actual, or observed, earnings turn out to be always lower, to change faster, and to peak at a later age than the attainable maximum, the earning capacity of the individual. The reverse is true of the relation between observed earnings and earnings net of all investment costs: the former are always higher, change slower, and peak at an earlier date than the latter. The model thus specifies the nature of the bias that may exist when earnings are used, as they often have been, to infer changes in productive capacity with age.

I. THE MODEL

In addition to the assumptions incorporated in the production function, to be discussed later, I assume:

1. Individual utility is not a function of activities involving time as an input.
2. There is a fixed amount of time to be allocated every period to activities that produce earnings and additions to the stock of human capital.
3. The stock of human capital, K, of which every individual has some initial endowment, is homogeneous and subject to an exogenously given rate of deterioration, δ.
4. The stock of human capital is not an argument in the individual's utility function.
5. Unlimited borrowing and lending take place at a constant rate of interest, r.

The first two assumptions express the fact that leisure is ignored in this analysis. In conjunction with the other assumptions they allow the partition of the individual's decision-making into two stages:

a) The individual allocates the given periods of time between earning and producing human capital and finds the corresponding outlays on investment that maximize the discounted value of any time t of disposable earnings (defined below) from t to T, where T is assumed with certainty to be the end of life.

b) Given the optimal time path of disposable earnings, the individual decides on the timing of the consumption. This is the point of departure of the life-cycle theories of consumption, which take the stream of earnings as given and explain consumption as dependent upon it.

The stock of human capital is defined as a concept analogous to "machines" in the case of tangible capital. There is a market in which the services of human capital are traded, and a rental, a_0, is determined for the services of a unit of human capital, K, per unit of time. The sum of the services offered in the market by various individuals is an input into the production of other goods and services. It may well have a diminishing marginal productivity, which will cause a downward-sloping aggregate demand curve for the services of human capital. Each individual is assumed, however, to possess only a small fraction of the total homogeneous stock of human capital in the economy and is regarded as a perfect competitor facing a given rental a_0, which is independent of the volume of services that he offers in the market. Earning capacity at time t, Y_t, is therefore the maximum services of human capital the individual can offer in the market valued by the rental a_0.

$$Y_t = a_0 K_t . \quad (1)$$

Let E_t be disposable earnings in period t—the portion of current earnings disposable for purposes of consumption or the purchase of non-human assets. It may be smaller than earning capacity if the individual engages in production of human capital; other uses for time are excluded by assumption. The difference

$(Y_t - E_t)$ is the cost of investment I_t; it depends on the production function and on input prices.

Let (2) be the production function of human capital:

$$Q_t = \beta_0 (s_t K_t)^{\beta_1} D_t^{\beta_2}, \quad (2)$$

where $\beta_1, \beta_2 > 0$ and $\beta_1 + \beta_2 < 1$; Q is the flow of human capital produced. D is the quantity of purchased inputs, the price of which is denoted by P_d; s_t is the fraction of the available stock of human capital allocated to the production of human capital, so that $s_t K_t$ is the quantity of human capital allocated for the purpose. If activities are not "mixed," that is, if there is no joint production of earnings and of human capital, then s_t is also the proportion of time devoted to the production of human capital. The fraction s_t is constrained by the condition

$$0 \leq s_t \leq 1. \quad (3)$$

(The properties of the production function including the assumption of decreasing returns to scale are discussed in a subsequent section.) The rate of change of the capital stock is given by (4):

$$\dot{K}_t = Q_t - \delta K_t \quad (4)$$

(a dot above any variable indicates a derivative with respect to time), where δ is the rate by which the stock of human capital deteriorates. Equations (1) and (4) imply that a unit of capital can be used from the moment that it is produced.

Investment costs have two components:

$$I_t = a_0 s_t K_t + P_d D_t, \quad (5)$$

that is, (a) opportunity costs, or "foregone earnings" (the value of the productive services withdrawn from the market), and (b) the direct costs of purchased goods and services. Minimizing I_t with respect to s_t and D_t, subject to (2) and ignoring (3), we get (6) as a condition for a minimum of (5):

$$\frac{a_0 s_t K_t}{P_d D_t} = \frac{\beta_1}{\beta_2}. \quad (6)$$

From (2) and (6) substituted into (5) we get investment costs as function of output:

$$I_t = \frac{\beta_1 + \beta_2}{\beta_1} a_0 \left(\frac{\beta_1 P_d}{\beta_2 a_0}\right)^{\beta_2/(\beta_1+\beta_2)} \times \left(\frac{Q_t}{\beta_0}\right)^{1/(\beta_1+\beta_2)} \quad (7)$$

The objective of the individual at any time t is to maximize the present value of his disposable earnings:

$$W_t = \int_t^T e^{-r\nu} [a_0 K(\nu) - I(\nu)] d\nu. \quad (8)$$

The objective expressed by (8) is treated as applicable to an individual from birth; up to a given age actual decisions are made by his parents, and if they were to take into account the full future life of their child, (8) still expresses the relevant maximand under the assumptions of the model. If the parents do not take into account the full economic life of their child, or in the extreme case where only the period of attachment to the present household is considered, less investment would be undertaken, and the age of entry into the labor force would be lower.

The problem posed here is suitable for treatment by the techniques of optimal control. Three phases are suggested by the constraints on s, the fraction of human capital, or time, allocated to the production of human capital: (i) The available stock of human capital K_t, even when fully allocated to produce human capital, is not large enough to provide the flow of services demanded given the relevant prices. The upper bound on s is thus an effective constraint. (ii) The available stock is large enough to supply the services demanded and more, so that $0 < s < 1$ and the services of human capital are truly a variable factor. (iii) The stock of capital is too big so that the optimal policy requires more disinvestment than is feasible through deterioration, that is, to produce negative quantities of human capital. Here s_t is constrained by its lower bound.[2]

The first phase is by definition a period in which no human capital is allocated to the market so that no earnings are realized. Using conventional tools, we shall first analyze the later phases in which $s < 1$ and then shall return to discuss the first.

Differentiating (7) with respect to Q we get (9), the marginal cost of producing human capital; it is a rising function of the quantity produced starting from the origin and is independent of the size of the existing stock of capital of the individual.

$$MC_t = \frac{a_0}{\beta_0\beta_1}\left(\frac{\beta_1 P_d}{\beta_2 a_0}\right)^{\beta_2/(\beta_1+\beta_2)} \times \left(\frac{Q_t}{\beta_0}\right)^{[1/(\beta_1+\beta_2)]-1}. \qquad (9)$$

The value at time t of acquiring an additional unit of human capital is the discounted value to that time of the additions to earnings that the undepreciated part of this unit will bring about. This is the "demand price" of human capital, given by (10). This price is

$$P_t = a_0\int_t^T e^{-(r+\delta)v}dv = \frac{a_0}{r+\delta}[1-e^{-(r+\delta)(T-t)}], \qquad (10)$$

independent of the number of units added or the existing stock. It is a declining function of time because of the presence of the finite horizon.[3] The optimal production of human capital is determined by equating the marginal cost to the price. Equating (9) and (10) we can solve for Q as shown in equation (11).

$$Q_t = \beta_0\left(\frac{\beta_0\beta_1}{r+\delta}\right)^{(\beta_1+\beta_2)/(1-\beta_1-\beta_2)}\left(\frac{\beta_2 a_0}{\beta_1 P_d}\right)^{\beta_2/(1-\beta_1-\beta_2)}[1-e^{-(r+\delta)(T-t)}]^{(\beta_1+\beta_2)/(1-\beta_1-\beta_2)}$$
$$= N[1-e^{-(r+\delta)(T-t)}]^{(\beta_1+\beta_2)/(1-\beta_1-\beta_2)} \geq 0. \qquad (11)$$

[2] In terms of the techniques developed by Pontryagin *et al.*, the maximization of (8) subject to (2), (3), and (4) involves the maximization of the Hamiltonian

$$H: e^{-rt}[(1-s)a_0K - P_dD] + q(Q-\delta K), \qquad (1')$$

where q is the discounted shadow price of investment in human capital

$$\dot{q} = -\frac{\partial H}{\partial K} = -e^{-rt}(1-s)a_0 - q\left(\beta_1\frac{Q}{K} - \delta\right).$$

In terms of current prices $\psi = qe^{rt}$

$$\dot{\psi} = -(1-s)a_0 - \psi\left[\beta_1\frac{Q}{K} - (\delta+r)\right]; \qquad (2')$$

Transversality condition:

$$\psi(T)K(T) = 0. \qquad (3')$$

First-order conditions for the maximization of (1′):

$$\frac{\partial H}{\partial s} = -a_0Ke^{-rt} + \psi e^{-rt}\frac{Q}{s}\beta_1 \geq 0. \qquad (4')$$

$$\frac{\partial H}{\partial D} = -P_de^{-rt} + \psi e^{-rt}\frac{Q}{D}\beta_2 = 0. \qquad (5')$$

A systematic analysis of a variant of this problem, using the techniques of optimal control, is pursued in an unpublished note by Eytan Sheshinski.

[3] In terms of the framework of n. 2 we are operating in the phase where (4′) holds exactly as equality. Substituting (4′), (5′), and (2) into (2′), and given (3′), we get a differential equation to which (10) is a solution.

The production of human capital, Q, the gross additions to the stock, are always positive except when $t = T$. At the date of compulsory retirement, T, the human capital loses its value, $P(T) = 0$ (see eq. [10]). No production is undertaken at period T, and the stock of human capital is reduced by sK (see eq. [3]). The point $t = T$ lies in the third phase. The reason why only this point lies in this phase is that for any earlier age, $t < T$, the demand price of human capital is positive, and the fact that the marginal cost curve starts from the origin insures that some positive quantity will always be produced. This would be true of any production function homogeneous of a degree less than 1 in these inputs.

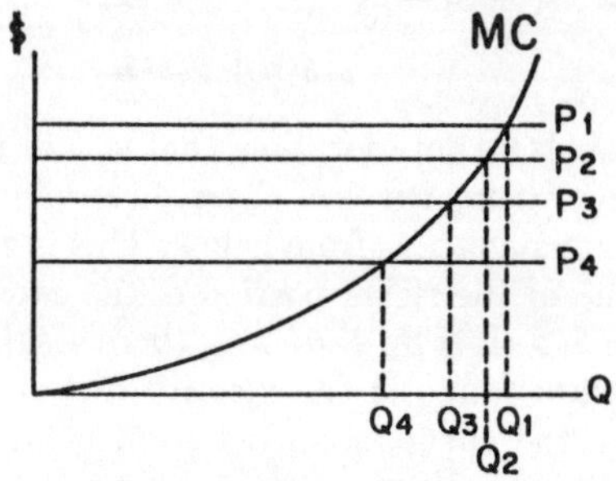

FIG. 1

The market prices that enter into the determination of the optimal production of human capital Q are: r, the rate of interest; a_0, the rental on human capital; and P_d, the price of purchased inputs. Differentiating (11) with respect to these shows that Q varies inversely with the rate of interest and with the price of purchase inputs and directly with the rental on human capital. It is, however, only the *ratio* between the last two that is important. The elasticity of Q with respect to the relative price a_0/P_a is $\beta_2/(1 - \beta_1 - \beta_2)$. When $\beta_2 = 0$, that is, when purchased inputs do not enter into the production of human capital, changes in a_0, the price of the services of human capital, do not affect the quantity produced. The obvious reason is that in this case, when the services of human capital are the only input, a rise in a_0 raises marginal cost by exactly the same amount that it raises the value of a unit of human capital. Needless to say, all this discussion refers to alternative stationary price levels when the current prices are expected to prevail throughout the individual's lifetime. Q_t is larger the larger the parameters of the production function β_0, β_1, β_2; the greater the length of economic life T; and the lower the rate of deterioration, which has exactly the same effect as the rate of interest.

As t rises, the flow of Q produced declines, as indicated by (12), the derivative of Q with respect to t:

$$\dot{Q} = \frac{\beta_1 + \beta_2}{1 - \beta_1 - \beta_2} N[1 - e^{-(r+\delta)(T-t)}]^{[(\beta_1-\beta_2)/(1-\beta_1-\beta_2)]-1} \times e^{(r+\delta)(T-t)}[-(r+\delta)] \leq 0 \,. \tag{12}$$

What we have here is a marginal cost curve as a function of Q starting from the origin and remaining stationary through time, and a perfectly elastic demand curve which slides down with time, thus creating a pattern of positive but declining optimal quantities of Q to be produced (Fig. 1). If the horizon were infinite, the demand curve would not slide down, and there would be at this phase one stationary rate of production of human capital (given by N in eq. [11]). Note that we are saying something about the *gross* additions to stock of human capital but not about the *net* additions, which depend also on the rate of depreciation and the size of the existing stock. If the initial stock is very high, net additions may be negative from an early age. If we think of the normal case as one where the capital stock does rise over a period, eventually as gross additions become very small and the stock becomes large this must be reversed, and toward the end of life, T, the stock will decline, if there is any deterioration.

What are the implications of this pattern of investment for the life cycle of earnings? Disposable earnings were defined as the difference between earning capacity and investment outlays; their rate of change over time is given by (13).

$$\dot{E}_t = a_0\dot{K}_t - \dot{I}_t . \qquad (13)$$

Let us define "observed earnings" $\hat{E}$ to be actual earnings realized in the labor market (14).

$$\hat{E}_t = a_0 K_t - \frac{\beta_1}{\beta_1 + \beta_2} I_t . \qquad (14)$$

They are larger than disposable earnings by the direct costs $P_d D$ and smaller than earning capacity by foregone earnings. Their rate of change over time is given by (15).

$$\dot{\hat{E}} = a_0\dot{K}_t - \frac{\beta_1}{\beta_1+\beta_2}\dot{I}_t = a_0 Q_t - \frac{\beta_1}{\beta_1+\beta_2}(MC_t)\dot{Q}_t - a_0\delta K_t . \qquad (15)$$

$\dot{I}$ is always negative (except when $t = T$), so that the change in observed earnings is always algebraically larger than the change in earning capacity and smaller than the change in disposable earnings

$$\left(\frac{\beta_1}{\beta_1+\beta_2} < 1\right).$$

Thus, the curve of observed earnings exaggerates the rate of increase of earning capacity when the latter increases and understates its decline when it declines. In particular, when we observe an individual at the peak of his earnings he is already past the peak of his productive capacity. The existence of a downturn in observed earnings is here only a consequence of depreciation (recall that interactions with "leisure" are excluded by assumption). If depreciation is zero, there is always, except at T, an increase in the three types of earnings, and at each point in time their rank by rate of change will be the reverse of their rank by level.

From the second derivative of observed earnings with respect to time (16), we learn more about the shape of the life cycle of earnings:

$$\ddot{\hat{E}} = Q_t\left\{a_0 - \frac{(r+\delta)MC_t}{1-e^{-(r+\delta)(T-t)}}\frac{\beta_1}{\beta_1+\beta_2} \times\left[1 - \frac{1}{1-\beta_1-\beta_2}e^{-(r+\delta)(T+t)}\right]\right\} - a_0\delta Q_t + a_0\delta^2 K_t . \qquad (16)$$

If there is no deterioration, that is, $\delta = 0$, the ever rising curve of observed earnings is always concave from below. This is also true of the rising portion of the curve when $\delta > 0$. If $\beta_1 + \beta_2 > \frac{1}{2}$, there will be a certain range in the vicinity of $t = T$ where the curve is convex from below.[4] All these qualitative results hold for any production function homogeneous of a degree smaller than 1 in sK and in D.

[4] Q is negative, and the term in braces is positive: from the equality between (11) and (12)

$$a_0 = \frac{r+\delta}{1-e^{-(r+\delta)(T-t)}} MC .$$

The right-hand side of this equality is here multiplied by a term always smaller than +1 and deducted from the left side so that the difference is positive and the first term is negative. If $\delta = 0$ and there is no deterioration, the other two terms vanish, and the curve of observed earnings is always concave from below. This is also true of the curve of disposable earnings with 1 substituted for $\beta_1/(\beta_1+\beta_2)$. When $\delta > 0$, concavity is assured for the range where $\dot{K} = Q - \delta K > 0$ If $\beta_1 + \beta_2 > \frac{1}{2}$, the first term tends to zero as $t \to T$; in the vicinity of $t = T$, $\dot{K} < 0$, so in this case the earnings curve will have there a shape that is convex from below.

The preceding discussion relates to the phase where the optimal s, the fraction of human capital or time allocated to the production of human capital, is smaller than 1. As indicated before, the maximization of (8) may, however, require that there will be a phase of complete specialization in the production of human capital in which $s = 1$ and the size of the stock is an effective constraint.

Movement along the marginal cost curve (7) by increasing Q implies an increase in the required sK. Once $s = 1$ is reached, larger rates of production can be achieved only by combining more purchased inputs with a fixed flow of services of human capital, thereby increasing costs at a higher rate than is implied by (7). The marginal cost curve described by (7) is a long-run envelope from which steeper marginal cost curves rise up, corresponding to alternative levels of the available stock of human capital. When people are young the value of a unit of human capital is only negligibly affected by the finite horizon T, so demand for human capital is relatively high. On the other hand, the available stock is still small; therefore the marginal cost curve rises up from the long-run curve, (7), at relatively small output, so that at a young age production is likely to occur at outputs where $s = 1$.

Note that the demand price given by (10) is now only the lower limit of the true shadow price of human capital. An increase in the stock of human capital implies a reduction in future costs of production of human capital. The precise value of this depends on the future quantities of Q that will be produced between t and t^*, the date of transfer from the first to the second phase. While in phase (ii), where $0 < s < 1$, we were able to determine the optimal Q_t by the intersection of demand and supply schedules independent of the future levels of Q, here only a complete, dynamic program in which the effects of present actions on future condition are explicitly taken into account will generate an optimal path of investment.

Phase (i) is identified by the absence of earnings. Another distinguishing characteristic of this phase is that the relaxation of the constraint K_t which lowers the marginal cost curve may induce a pattern of increasing investment with age, both through the allocation of the services of a growing stock of human capital for the purpose and through higher direct expenditure on D, justified by the higher marginal productivity of D that the increased K brings about. A phase of increasing direct costs in the early period when no earnings are realized is certainly not inconsistent with the real world.[5]

The age t^* when the individual enters the second phase and leaves the first is of great importance, because this is the date at which positive earnings begin to be realized. From the preceding discussion it should be clear that $K(t^*)$ is a declining function of t^*.[6] K_0 is the initial endowment of human capital, which, following the definition of K, is proportional to the maximum earnings the individual can realize when he "starts." All other parameters given, the larger this initial endowment, the earlier will be the date t^* at which specialization stops, noting that K_0 is an initial endowment only in terms of the capacity to earn, while we hold constant the capacity

[5] An explicit solution of our problem for the case in which $\beta_2 = 0$ is simple but not interesting. The interesting aspects of the problem derive from the possibility of using purchased inputs.

[6] This can be verified by substituting $s = 1$ into (4′), letting it hold as an equality, and substituting into it also the value of Q and ψ using (2), (5′), and the solution of (2′) referred to in n. 3.

to increase human capital thus defined, which is reflected in the β's of the production function.

II. THE PRODUCTION FUNCTION ROLE AND IMPLICATIONS

The technology which the individual faces when he makes decisions about investing in himself is a complicated system of technical and institutional relationships covering a wide spectrum of activities including formal education, acquisition of skills on the job, child care, nutrition, health, etc. By writing down a simple production function of the sort used here we are attempting, not to reproduce this system, but only to provide a framework within which some of the possible characteristics of the technology can be considered and their implications studied.

A. PURCHASED INPUTS, TIME, AND THE SERVICES OF HUMAN CAPITAL

Both the theory and the measurement of investment in human capital (see Schultz, 1963) emphasize the importance of foregone earnings alongside direct cost. A composite surrogate for direct cost here is D, the index of purchased inputs which stands for anything from tuition to vitamin pills. The presence of opportunities for some substitution between purchased and own inputs has a "smoothing" effect on behavior and helps the individual overcome the constraints of his limited time and sometimes modify the effects of its increasing cost.

The nature of and the role played by own inputs require some further discussion. In the production function so far considered, own inputs are represented by the product sK. K is the total stock of human capital; s is described as a fraction that can take any value between 0 and 1. We shall first regard s as a measure of the allocation of time to the production of human capital, although this interpretation is not necessary.[7]

At any time t the stock of capital K_t is given. If we were to assume that any activity the individual engages in produces either human capital or earnings but not both, then the allocation of time between these two types of activities is also the allocation of the services of the existing stock of human capital. The larger the stock of human capital, the larger the earnings per unit of time that the individual could get in the market and therefore the higher the foregone earnings from diverting a unit of time away from the market (see Becker, 1965). Whether this should or should not affect the relative attractiveness of non-market activities hinges on whether the change that made an hour in the market more rewarding also made more productive an hour outside the market, in our case an hour of producing human capital.

The question is whether the real production relation involved is stable in terms of time or in terms of some other variable. The way we *defined* human capital was to make the production of earnings stable in terms of its services, rather than in terms of time as such. By making (sK) the relevant input in the production function of human capital we are also *asserting* that this other process is stable in terms of the services of human capital rather than in terms of time as such. The main implication of this formulation in terms of the alloca-

[7] Note that time enters in two completely different ways—t, which moves the individual along his life cycle and which is being treated as continuous, and s_t, which is a measure of the allocation of time at any point in t. If we were to treat t as an index of discrete periods, and if s were understood as referring to the allocation of each such period, this dual meaning probably would have posed no problem.

tion of time is that, when K is higher, the higher costs of an hour diverted away from the market (because of the higher foregone earnings) are exactly matched by the greater productivity of time in the production of human capital, so that the marginal cost curve of producing the latter is independent of the stock of human capital in the range where the constraint on s is not effective.

By arguing that in the production of human capital the services of human capital rather than time as such are relevant we gain some analytical simplicity, because beyond the period of complete specialization in the production of human capital the benefits associated with acquiring a unit of human capital, the addition to future disposable earnings, do not depend on the future allocation between the market and the production of human capital. This is the reason why the dynamic programing problem that was referred to in relation to phase (i) degenerated into a much simpler decision problem in phase (ii). Analytical convenience is, however, no substitute for relevance. In a general production function both time as such and human capital would appear as inputs, and if we consider again the Cobb-Douglas case, s and K may appear with different coefficients. Thus, consider (17):

$$Q = \beta_0 s^{\gamma_1} K^{\gamma_2} D^{\beta_2} = \beta_0 s^{\gamma_1 - \gamma_2} (sK)^{\gamma_2} D^{\beta_2}; \quad 0 < \gamma_1, \gamma_2, \beta_2 < 1. \tag{17}$$

The corresponding marginal cost curve is (18):

$$MC_t = \frac{\alpha_0}{\beta_0 \gamma_1} \left(\frac{\gamma_1}{\beta_2} \frac{P_d}{\alpha_0} \right)^{\beta_2/(\gamma_1+\beta_2)} \times \left(\frac{Q_t}{\beta_0} \right)^{[1/(\gamma_1+\beta_2)]-1} K_t^{(\gamma_1-\gamma_2)/(\gamma_1+\beta_2)}. \tag{18}$$

If $\gamma_1 = \gamma_2$, we get an expression identical to (2), with γ_1 replacing β_1. If $\gamma_1 > \gamma_2$, the marginal cost curve is shifting upward as K increases. This can be viewed as a case where time plays an independent part in the production of human capital or, more directly, as a case where the larger productivity of time in the market indicated by an increase in K is not completely matched by a larger productivity in the production of human capital, so that the cost of the latter in terms of the former rises. The case where $\gamma_1 = \gamma_2$ implies, for example, that the more highly educated person is also better equipped for learning, so that his higher opportunity cost is matched by the greater amount of skills that he can acquire per hour. If this is not so, then the situation that we are describing now is relevant. A limiting case would be one in which human capital does not at all affect the ability to produce more human capital, $\gamma_2 = 0$.

In the basic model considered before, the decline over time in investment beyond the period of complete specialization is brought about by the downward drift, due to the approaching horizon T of the demand function, along a stationary, upward-sloping marginal cost curve. In the situation now described, as K increases the cost curve shifts upward. In young age, when $T - t$ is large, the quantitative effect of changes in t on the demand price is small, and the shifts in the cost function may be more important for changes in investment than in the downward drift of the demand curve. The role of purchased inputs here is also clear—the larger the β_2, the smaller the effect of K on the marginal cost.

The other case, in which $\gamma_2 > \gamma_1$, also cannot be ruled out. Here capital accumulation reduces the cost of producing human capital, and it is possible even in phase (ii) to have a stretch of time over which investment rises rather than declines (the downward shift in the costs being more important than the declines in demand). The corresponding life cycle may then have an early convex portion. Eventually the declining marginal productivity of K (due to $\gamma_2 < 1$) and the growing effect of the approaching horizon T will turn the rise in investment into a decline, and the life cycle will have the familiar S-shape.

B. THE ROLE OF RISING COSTS

With a homogeneous stock of human capital, the services of which are sold at a fixed price in a competitive market, both the determination of a finite desired stock and the speed in which the available stock is adjusted to the desired level depend on the cost of acquiring human capital. If human capital could be acquired at a fixed (or declining) cost without limitation, that is, if the supply schedule were perfectly elastic or declining, the desired stock would be either zero or infinite, and the optimal adjustment would be instantaneous. In the case of the demand for tangible capital, costs of adjustment are sometimes introduced to explain investment as a function of the interest rate. In the case of the aggregate economy, it is the rising cost of investment goods in terms of consumption goods that provides the negative slope of the aggregate demand function of investment (the marginal efficiency of investment curve) and a finite rate of investment.

The nature of human capital, the fact that it has to be produced by the individual, makes for some similarity in the considerations involved and provides a natural basis for dealing with the question of what makes the rate of investment and the attained stock of human capital finite. One form in which constraint on the rate of investment could come about is from individual capacity limitations solely. Thus, consider the case in which (2) $\beta_1 + \beta_2 = 1$, $\beta_1 > 0$, and $\beta_2 \geq 0$. In every period the available stock of human capital K_t is given. Costs would be constant up to that level of output which implies $s = 1$, that is,

$$Q = \beta_0 K \left(\frac{a_0}{P_d}\frac{\beta_2}{\beta_1}\right)^{\beta_2}.$$

For larger outputs marginal costs would rise (if $\beta_2 > 0$) or become infinite (if $\beta_2 = 0$). In either case, given the nature of the demand for human capital, the optimum rate of investment would always imply a value of 1 or 0 for $s > n$, the allocation of all the services of the available stock of human capital either to the production of human capital or to the labor market, but not to both. Because of the declining demand over time for human capital, a period of complete specialization in the production of human capital (phase [i]), if it comes, must precede the period of complete specialization in market work (phase [iii]). The resulting life cycle of (observed) earnings would therefore have a portion of zero earnings and then a jump to some positive level, which would be stationary in the absence of depreciation and declining in its presence.

Neither this implied life cycle of earnings nor the behavior to which it is related is supported by what we know of the real world. The basic model allows for an initial period of complete specialization in the production of human capital and, correspondingly, a period of zero observed earnings. But if we assume that the sum of the production elasticities of the variable inputs is smaller than 1 ($\beta_1 + \beta_2$ in eq. [2] and $\gamma_1 + \beta_2$ in eq. [17], the more general formulation), marginal cost rises continuously even before the capacity constraint is reached. This is the source of the existence of a phase (ii), a period in which $0 < s < 1$, when the individual engages simultaneously, or alternately, in work in the market and in the production of his human capital. (A more complicated functional form could have allowed increasing returns to scale at small outputs and eventually decreasing returns. This may be more plausible and still would provide the eventual check on the rate of investment.)

In this framework, where there is not "automatic" growth in earnings, increase in earning can come only from the allocation of more services of human capital to the market. This can be either because of a reduction in what is allocated to investment (s_t) or because of an increase in the total stock available (K). In order for some positive earnings to be observed there must be some work in the market; in order for earnings to decline there must be some investment that either increases from period to period the total available stock or, by itself declining, raises the fraction allocated to the market. The closer the sum of the production elasticities of the variable factors to 1, that is, the closer we get to constant returns to scale in terms of the variable factors, the more concave is the life cycle of earnings; the case of constant marginal cost in which the life cycle of earnings is a one-step function is the limiting case.

Throughout the preceding discussions s_t has been interpreted as a parameter of the allocation of time. If there are, however, activities in which earnings and human capital can be jointly produced, then s_t loses this meaning. We have many examples of learning on the job in which the time spent on the job cannot be allocated in any meaningful sense between pure work and pure learning; jointness is too prevalent to be excluded. We can still think of the individual as being faced with a production frontier indicating the possible combination of flows of earnings and of human capital that he can produce. Movements along this frontier, however, would not necessarily represent shifts between pure activities but, rather, represent movement between activities, each offering a different mix of earnings and additions to productive capacity. Shifts along this frontier are represented by the control s_t, and they may involve a change in occupations, of jobs within the occupation, or of function with the job. The less numerous and close together are these alternative combinations, the smaller is the justification for the continuous differentiable frontier implied by our formulation. Discontinuities and kinks in this production frontier are translated into kinks and jumps in the life cycle of earnings. In either case, it is clear that s_t becomes an empty concept once it has lost its link with the observable phenomenon of the allocation of time.

III. THE MODEL AND AGGREGATE EARNING PROFILES

The preceding section clarifies the role played in this framework by increasing costs in the explanation of a gradually rising portion in the *individual* life cycle of earnings. The purpose of the present section is to show that even within this framework an explanation of cohort life cycles of earnings, or of the cross-section profile of earnings, can be provided without the assumption of rising costs. Thus, assume for simplicity that $\beta_2 = \delta = 0$ and $\beta_1 = 1$. By the argument presented in the preceding section, the individual life cycle will be a stepwise function.

The marginal (and average) cost of

producing human capital is (a_0/β_0), β_0 differing among people. The higher is β_0, the later comes the date t^* when the downward-drifting demand price crosses it from above—which is the date when people jump from observed earnings of zero to their earning capacity. By equating a_0/β_0 with P (10) we get (19):

$$t^* = T + \frac{1}{r} \ln \left(1 - \frac{r}{\beta_0}\right). \quad (19)$$

The time path of the stock of human capital is given by

$$K_t = K_0 e^{\beta_0 t} \quad \text{for} \quad 0 \leq t \leq t^* ;$$
$$K_t = K_0 e^{\beta_0 t^*} \quad \text{for} \quad t^* \leq t \leq T . \quad (20)$$

Observed earnings are zero for $0 < t < t^*$ and are equal to earning capacity afterward.

$$E_t = a_0 K_0 e^{\beta_0 t^*}$$
$$= a_0 K_0 e^{\beta_0 [T + (1/r) \ln[1 - (r/\beta_0)]]} . \quad (21)$$

Using (21) we can see that, given $a_0 K_0$, earnings on the time of "emergence," t^*, and beyond it, are an increasing convex function of t^*. If in a given cohort K_0 and β_0 are not negatively correlated, we can expect to observe a rising curve as we follow the earnings history of the cohort through time (or as we examine the cross-section profile of earnings of a completely static population, with stationary distributions by β_0 and K_0, in a static economy). The exact form of the curve depends on the distribution of the cohort by β_0; reasonable distributions by β_0 can generate a curve with the familiar S-shape.

SUMMARY AND SOME OPEN QUESTIONS

To the theory of investment in man we have added here a production function of human capital and explored some of the implications of its properties for the optimal path of accumulation of human capital and the life cycle of earnings. The concepts and parameters introduced raise again some familiar problems and are used to focus attention on some others. In lieu of a summary we shall now refer to a few of these.

1. The particular definition of human capital K used is a measure of a quantity of a source of productive services. It is the stock that produces labor services in "standard units" and is thus the analogue of "machines" in the case of tangible capital. This should be sharply distinguished from W_t (defined in [8]), which is the *value* of the individual as a productive factor. It is affected by a broader view of the individual's productivity, by his durability, and by the rate of interest, and it can be misleading as a quantity measure of an input in any given point in time. Being a part of the individual's net worth (and the price that he could get for himself in a competitive slave market), it is probably better described as "human wealth."

2. The speed of adjustment, the rate at which the individual increases the stock of human capital, determines the ultimate size of this stock. The considerations affecting the speed of adjustment and the path of investment with age merit an explicit analysis. The mechanism provided here relies on the introduction of dependence between the marginal cost of producing human capital and the rate of production (a justification for this can come from the "learning curve" considerations). Beyond a certain point the saving in costs from postponing investment to the next period compensates for the loss of the returns that would have come from getting the unit of capital a period earlier.

Rising costs result here from a certain specification of the technology. The properties of the production function and the parameters introduced draw attention to certain distinctions that have to be made when the conglomerate of abilities and external conditions is considered and the implications of its properties are explored.

3. In discussing the "initial endowment" of individuals a different role is played by the initial endowment in terms of the ability to earn in the market (K_0) and the abilities to produce additions to earning capacity. These consist of the ability to make efficient use of inputs purchasable in the market, D (expressed by β_0 and β_2), and of one's own time (β_0, β_1, or γ_1 in [17]). A related issue is to what extent the individual, as he increases his human capital, K, also raises his efficiency in the production of K (in eq. [17] this is expressed by the distinction between γ_1 and γ_2). This question is related to the homogeneity of human capital.

4. The possibility of producing human capital in addition to earnings means that the "real output" of the individual consists of earnings plus the value of human capital produced, when the latter is evaluated by its shadow price. This will be a measure of by how much total inactivity at a given period would affect W.

5. Not much has been said of δ, the rate of deterioration. Consideration ought to be given to cases where δ is negative rather than positive as assumed here and also to the dependence of deterioration on the allocation of human capital to different activities.

6. The horizon T is treated here as exogenous. Opening the analysis to include leisure will, of course, make retirement endogenous, but even if T is the date of death there can be types of investments that will affect that date.

7. The three market prices—the rate of interest r, the rental on human capital a_0, and the price of purchased inputs P_d—affect behavior in the expected way. These are the parameters of the models that public policy can most directly attack. The framework presented here may prove convenient for mapping possible effects of public policy and their interaction with ability factors.

8. Various problems of measurement are implied but not directly discussed. One of these is the relation between the integral of investment costs, (7), over stretches of time and the integral of $\dot{K}$, or of Q. The problem of measurement in this model hinges on the measurability of s_t, which is a question about the prevalence of activities in which human capital and earnings are jointly produced. When s_t is an observable phenomenon of the allocation of time, the model becomes operational, but, without it, much is lost.

9. We have abstracted here from uncertainty and from capital rationing two important considerations in investment in human capital which should be incorporated in a complete analysis.

10. A natural extension of the two-way choice analyzed here between activities producing current earnings and investment in human capital would be to deal with the three-way choice involving also the allocation of time for activities of a consumptive nature, following the approach of Becker (1965).

The reader probably does not have to be told how simplifying many of the assumptions are and how many additional aspects of investment in human capital and of the determination of the life cycle of earnings are relevant. The main purpose of this paper was to raise some more questions rather than provide definite answers.

REFERENCES

Becker, G. S. "Investment in Human Capital: A Theoretic Analysis," *J.P.E.*, LXX, No. 5, Part 2 (October, 1962), 9–49.

———. *Human Capital*. New York: Columbia Univ. Press (for the National Bureau of Economic Research), 1964.

———. "A Theory of the Allocation of Time," *Econ. J.*, Vol. LXXV (September, 1965).

———. "Human Capital and the Personal Distribution of Income: An Analytical Approach." New York: National Bureau of Economic Research, October, 1966 (mimeographed).

Friedman, M., and Kuznets, S. *Income from Independent Professions*. New York: National Bureau of Economic Research, 1945.

Mincer, J. "Investment in Human Capital and Personal Income Distribution," *J.P.E.*, LXVI, No. 4 (August, 1958), 281–302.

———. "On-the-Job Training: Costs, Returns, and Some Implications," *ibid.*, LXX, No. 5, Part 2 (October, 1962), 50–79.

Schultz, T. W. *The Economic Value of Education*. New York: Columbia Univ. Press, 1963.

[3]

INCOME CHANGES OVER THE LIFE CYCLE

By JOHN CREEDY[1]

'And so, from hour to hour we ripe and ripe, and then from hour to hour we rot and rot, and thereby hangs a tale.' (*As You Like It*)

I. Introduction and basic framework

THE relative neglect of dynamic aspects of the income distribution in recent work is surprising in view of the tremendous interest in very closely related problems such as dynamic models of demand (often in the context of life-cycle planning) and the changing distribution of wealth. While it is continually emphasized that current household behaviour depends crucially on expectations of future income and responsibilities, and that welfare and taxation policy should be concerned with lifetime equity rather than the income distribution at any particular time, it remains true that most models dealing with these problems do not consider the dynamics of income change through life in sufficient detail.[2]

Any model of demand which takes the household, or nuclear family, as the unit of analysis must of course face the difficulty that income changes are often associated with changing household composition and the labour force participation of its members (births, retired parents entering, young earners leaving, etc.). Closely associated with these problems is that of the concept of income itself, since the different kinds of 'income' are all generated in fundamentally different ways and their relative importance changes over the life cycle.[3] The following discussion will therefore abstract from these problems by concentrating on changes in the earnings from employment of individuals in particular occupations. It will be shown, however, that this is not a severe constraint in the applicability of the model.

In the previous analytical literature which has been concerned with the genesis of the income distribution, and in particular with its functional form, there has been a dichotomy between the so-called stochastic models which regard income as the outcome of a succession of 'random shocks', and the 'human capital' models where income is increased by the acquisition

[1] I would like to thank Professors Alan Brown and Peter Hart for help and encouragement in the preparation of this paper.

[2] For example, both Friedman and Modigliani use distributed lags in terms of past aggregate income as a proxy for 'anticipated' income, without carrying out the aggregation process. Modigliani and Ando's explanation for the smaller cross-section slope of the consumption function involved the untested assumption that rich people are likely to have just received an increase in income (and vice versa for poor) which was unanticipated, so that adjustment was not complete.

[3] As well as the value of services produced in the home. Also from considerations of 'social justice' people usually have different attitudes towards inequalities according to their genesis.

of skills and education over life. On one side the 'justification' for stochastic models has been neatly expressed by Champernowne (1953, p. 318):

> The forces determining the distribution of incomes . . . are so varied and complex, and interact and fluctuate so continuously, that any theoretical model must either be unrealistically simplified or hopelessly complicated.

While Mincer (1970) argued that

> . . . the stochastic models say nothing about age . . . profiles of earnings. They do little more than predict a growth of variance with age. Distinction between aggregates, and components, . . . are outside the reach of these models.

Both of these arguments are of course very persuasive when considered from their own points of view; since the stochastic models were concerned specifically with obtaining the limiting (functional) form of the distribution on the most general assumptions, while the human capital models were more interested in the age profiles of mean income for various professions and levels of education.

The approach adopted in this paper, however, is a combination of both of these—whereby for any individual the proportionate change in his income from one year to the next is regarded as being the same as that of the geometric mean income of his age group, apart from an additive (stochastic) term which governs the extent of movements within the distribution. This framework can therefore be written:

$$\frac{1}{y_{it}}\frac{\mathrm{d}y_{it}}{\mathrm{d}t} = \frac{1}{m_t}\frac{\mathrm{d}m_t}{\mathrm{d}t} + u_{it} = f(t) + u_{it}, \tag{1}$$

where y_{it} is individual i's income at 'age' t (t is measured in years from entry into the occupation, or labour force), m_t is the geometric mean income in 'age' group t, and u_{it} is a stochastic component. Thus, everyone's income is assumed to change by the same proportion, except for the term u_{it}, whose expected value must by definition be zero. The framework represented by equation (1), and which as yet has no empirical content, has obvious affinities with that of Friedman and Kuznets (1945) so that $f(t)$ and u_{it} may (loosely) be referred to as 'permanent' and 'transitory' components respectively of the *change* in income. They should not, however, be confused with their use by Friedman (1957, 1963), where the term 'permanent' as applied to *levels* of income has a completely different meaning.[1]

The use of a deterministic formulation for $f(t)$ combined with a stochastic term (u_{it}) is also supported by Friedman and Kuznets (1945),[2] who—

[1] In that context it is, of course, the amount which can be consumed (in perpetuity) from a stock of wealth equal to the anticipated value of lifetime income; and the horizon is the 'average period' of an infinite stream whose capital value is equal to lifetime income. See Hicks (1939) and Friedman (1963).

[2] Friedman and Kuznets (1945, ch. 7) considered changes in 'relative income status' which took place within the aggregate distribution—and therefore combined the changes associated with age with those caused by u_{it} above.

although they would have liked to isolate all the causal influences—concluded that

It is probably not possible to do so for the transitory factors; these are likely to be largely 'chance' influences that have no counterpart in objectively determinable attributes of the individual, [but on the other hand] . . . there is more likelihood of naming the factors considered permanent.

A further important reason for isolating the effect of age is that it (or stage in life cycle) is thought to be a significant determinant of consumer behaviour. In constructing models which will be of use to the demand analyst it is useful to determine the extent to which income change is associated with ageing and to express this in a model which will be tractable when included in others as a component.

II. Changes in relative income status

The characteristics of u_{it} determine, then, the changes in relative income status[1] which take place from one year to the next in age group t. This section will examine the implications of various assumptions about u_{it} for such mobility within the distribution—so that to abstract from changes in geometric mean income it is convenient to consider proportionate changes in the ratio of income to geometric mean income. Thus equation (1) can be rewritten:[2]

$$\frac{m_t}{y_{it}}\frac{\mathrm{d}}{\mathrm{d}t}\frac{y_{it}}{m_t} = u_{it}, \tag{2}$$

and defining

$$x_{it} = \log y_{it}, \quad \mu_t = \log m_t, \quad \text{and} \quad z_{it} = \log(y_{it}/m_t) = x_{it}-\mu_t,$$

(2) simply states that

$$\mathrm{d}z_{it}/\mathrm{d}t = u_{it}. \tag{3}$$

(a) *Gibrat's 'law of proportionate effect'*

Perhaps the best-known model of the genesis of income distribution is Gibrat's so-called 'law of proportionate effect' (1931), which assumes that the u_{it} are distributed independently of previous changes and with constant variance σ^2, say. If (3) is converted to discrete time, and if the variance of x_{it} is denoted σ_t^2, then[3]

$$\sigma_t^2 = \sigma_{t-1}^2+\sigma^2,$$

whence by continual substitution

$$\sigma_t^2 = \sigma_0^2+\sigma^2 t, \tag{4}$$

where σ_0^2 is the variance of log-income in the year of entry into the occupa-

[1] Again Friedman and Kuznets argued (1945, p. 350), '. . . individuals do not have the same relative income status year after year . . . these differences must be ascribed largely to accidental occurrences that impinge on the individual in one year but not in another'.

[2] Since from (1) $u_{it} = \frac{\mathrm{d}}{\mathrm{d}t}(\log y_{it}-\log m_t) = \frac{\mathrm{d}}{\mathrm{d}t}\log(y_{it}/m_t)$.

[3] As $z_t^2 = z_{t-1}^2+u_t^2+2z_{t-1}u_t$ and since u_t is assumed to be independent of previous values the last term is zero.

tion. Gibrat originally applied this 'law' to all earners (rather than to particular age groups as here) so that the implication of a linearly increasing σ_t^2 seems to be highly implausible. For this reason Kalecki (1946) suggested that there may be a tendency for those in the higher deciles to obtain proportionately smaller increases than below the median. Although in this context (with entry into and retirement from the labour force)[1] there is no problem with equation (4) it may be useful to examine the consequence of such 'regression towards the mean' when applied to changes within an age group.[2]

(b) Galtonian 'regression towards the mean'

Within the present framework this phenomenon can be represented by subtracting a term $\beta \log(y_{it-1}/m_{t-1})$ from the right-hand side of equation (1). Thus when income is above the geometric mean the change in income is less than the average (since $\beta > 0$, and $\log(y_{it-1}/m_{t-1}) > 0$). Thus

$$\begin{aligned} z_{it} &= z_{it-1} - \beta \log(y_{it-1}/m_{t-1}) + u_{it} \\ &= (1-\beta) z_{it-1} + u_{it}. \end{aligned} \tag{5}$$

Here, letting $\phi = 1-\beta$, continual substitution yields

$$z_{it} = \phi^t z_{i0} + \sum_{j=1}^{t} \phi^{t-j} u_{ij}$$

whence, using the sum of a geometric progression to evaluate the second term,

$$\sigma_t^2 = \frac{\sigma^2}{1-\phi^2} + \left(\sigma_0^2 + \frac{\sigma^2}{1-\phi^2}\right)\phi^{2t} \tag{6}$$

which for large t ($\phi < 1$) tends to the constant value $\sigma^2/(1-\phi^2)$. This kind of 'regression' therefore tends to stabilize the degree of inequality within a particular cohort, while allowing mobility within the distribution. As demonstrated by Hart (1973) a high positive value of β indicates 'egalitarian' movements, and must be considered along with σ_t^2 in assessing inequality. Indeed, it is quite possible for an increase in σ_t^2 to be regarded as an 'improvement'[3] if the changes in the rankings of individuals are such that income measured over a longer period is more equally distributed.[4]

Although there are no data (at least in Britain) for the same group of income earners over life, a large amount of evidence from cross-section data (see later) indicates that σ_t^2 does increase with t, rather than approach a

[1] This has been considered in much more detail in Creedy (1973b).

[2] This concept of 'regression' was, of course, originally suggested by Darwin's cousin Francis Galton (1889) in connection with the inheritance of genetic characteristics. It has been applied to stochastic models of firm size by Hart and Prais (1956), and to income distributions by Hart (1973). Galton was referring to the geometric mean.

[3] From an egalitarian point of view.

[4] Since ϕ in equation (5) is a simple regression coefficient it can be expressed in terms of the correlation, r, between z_t and z_{t-1}. As $\phi = \text{Cov}(z_t\, z_{t-1})/\sigma_{t-1}^2$ and $r = \text{Cov}(z_t\, z_{t-1})/\sigma_t\, \sigma_{t-1}$ then $\phi = r\sigma_t/\sigma_{t-1}$ and $\sigma_t^2 > \sigma_{t-1}^2$ if $\phi^2 > r^2$.

stable value. This suggests that either the 'parameters' of the model change over age (for example, a higher value of σ^2 or a lower tendency to regress towards the mean in older age groups) or there is a further component of income changes which has so far been omitted. The latter case will be considered first.

(c) *Serial correlation in the u_{it}*

It may be thought that individuals in certain occupations are able to move through the income distribution (of their contemporaries) in a fairly systematic way; or indeed that significant improvements may depend crucially on previous success. This may apply, for example, in a profession where 'merit' awards are commonly paid, or where prospects for increasing income depend on a reputation which is established on the basis of previous work. Where successive proportionate changes in income are correlated this means that the relative stability of an individual's position in the distribution is increased—since income now depends on that of the past few years rather than simply the previous year. This can be seen by assuming a first-order autoregressive form for the u_{it}, such that

$$u_{it} = \rho u_{it-1} + \epsilon_{it}, \tag{7}$$

where ρ is assumed to be the same for all individuals,[1] and ϵ_{it} is now distributed independently of previous values with (constant) variance σ_ϵ^2, say. Combining this with equation (5) and eliminating the u's from each gives the reduced form[2]

$$z_{it} = (\rho+\phi)z_{it-1} - \rho\phi z_{it-2} + \epsilon_{it}. \tag{8}$$

The implications for the age-profile of σ_t^2 are rather more cumbersome to derive, but from (6) above,

$$\sigma_t^2 = \phi^{2t}\sigma_0^2 + E\Big(\sum_j \phi^{t-j}u_j\Big)\Big(\sum_j \phi^{t-j}u_j\Big). \tag{9}$$

With no serial correlation the cross-product terms in (9) cancel, though they must now be included to give

$$\sigma_t^2 = \phi^{2t}\sigma_0^2 + E\sum_j \phi^{2(t-j)}u_j^2 + E\sum_{i\neq j}\sum \phi^{(t-i)(t-j)}u_i u_j,$$

and using the fact[3] that

$$E(u_t^2) = \sigma_\epsilon^2 \sum_{i=1}^{t} \rho^{2i} \quad \text{and} \quad E(u_t u_{t-s}) = \rho^s E(u_t^2)$$

this can be written as

$$\sigma_t^2 = \phi^{2t}\sigma_0^2 + \sigma_\epsilon^2 \sum\sum \phi^{2(t-j)}\rho^{2i} + 2\sigma_\epsilon^2 \sum_{j=1}^{t-1}\ \sum_{i=j+1}^{t}\ \sum_{r=0}^{i} \phi^{(t-i)(t-j)}\rho^{2r+i-j} \tag{10}$$

[1] It is sometimes argued that large inequalities are needed to preserve incentives (and are therefore discussed in terms of σ_t^2) whereas it is probably more appropriate to relate incentives to the ability to *change* one's income or ranking in the distribution, or to prevent it from falling successively (so that ρ is more relevant here).

[2] If (7) is combined with the discrete form of equation (3) then income in any year is simply a weighted average of income in the previous two years.

[3] See for example Johnston (1972, p. 245).

which is clearly inconvenient. The case of no 'regression' combined with serial correlation can be found by setting $\phi = 1$, though even in this case it will not be possible to discriminate between the more complex kind of income changes and the simple Gibrat model, given only a series of σ_t^2's (the relation between the latter and t is only non-linear for low values of t and rapidly becomes linear).[1]

The characteristics of mobility within the income distribution can, therefore, only be analysed in detail if information is available for a constant sample of individuals over at least three consecutive years (or at least where the two time intervals are equal). Unfortunately this kind of data is extremely rare for British income earners (though it could be obtained from the tax authorities), mainly because of the desire to maintain anonymity in surveys. Some interesting results for income in two consecutive years have recently been published in the Department of Employment Gazette (1973), where manual and non-manual workers were treated separately by age groups. The regression coefficients obtained from fitting equation (5) to the various groups were presented (table 15, p. 348), though it is well known that the estimates obtained from an autoregressive form will not be consistent if the disturbances are serially correlated. In this case it can be shown[2] that an ordinary least-squares estimate of ϕ in (5) will be biased by an amount given by $\rho(1+\phi^2)/(1-\rho\phi)$. Furthermore, an estimate of the serial correlation coefficient from the residuals of such a regression will also be biased.[3] The only alternative is therefore to start from an examination of equation (8) above, and to proceed from this to the less complex cases, where it seems justified. If (8) is rewritten as

$$z_{it} = az_{it-1} - bz_{it-2} + \epsilon_{it} \tag{11}$$

and if the parameters ρ and ϕ are considered as the roots of a quadratic equation, then the coefficients a and b of (11) actually give the two relationships between those roots. Thus the two roots of the quadratic

$$x^2 - ax + b = 0$$

can easily be calculated, though exact identification is not possible because of the fact that (11) does not include an exogenous variable. Nevertheless ϕ can be chosen as that root nearest to unity, since this would be expected from *a priori* consideration.

[1] Using a variant of the method of estimation described below, equation (10) was used to obtain estimates of σ_0^2, ρ, and σ_ϵ^2 (ϕ was set to 1). Convergence was slow, however, and the goodness of fit not significantly better than that obtained from equation (4) fitted to the same data.

[2] See, for example, Malinvaud (1970, p. 556). Multiply (8) by z_{t-1}, sum and divide by Σz_{t-1}^2. Denote $\hat{\phi} = \Sigma z_t z_{t-1}/\Sigma z_{t-1}^2$, then $p\text{-lim}\,\hat{\phi} = (\rho+\phi) - \rho\phi(p\text{-lim}\,\hat{\phi})$ and

$$p\text{-lim}\,\hat{\phi} = (\phi+\rho)/(1+\rho\phi).$$

[3] Since $p\text{-lim}\,\hat{\rho} = \rho\phi(\rho+\phi)/(1+\rho\phi)$.

A survey has recently been carried out by the Royal Institute of Chemistry in order to obtain information about the past earnings of a random sample of its members who were aged 47 years in October 1973. Respondents were asked to give their annual earnings from 1971 onwards,[1] with all the usual precautions having been made to ensure anonymity. The R.I.C. is in fact the only professional body to have conducted such an inquiry, and has a long history of very useful remuneration surveys.[2] When equation (11) was fitted to these data the following results were obtained:

$$z_t = \underset{(0{\cdot}0010)}{1{\cdot}0358}z_{t-1} - \underset{(0{\cdot}0009)}{0{\cdot}0594}z_{t-2}, \qquad R^2 = 0{\cdot}947$$

(where t is January 1973 so that income is from January 1972 until January 1973, and as usual time is in units of one year).

This implies values of 0·975 and 0·061 for ϕ and ρ respectively, which indicate very little regression and serial correlation. Indeed a simple regression (equation (5)) gave a value for ϕ of 0·977 ($\pm$0·0148).

The results given in the Gazette (1973) do seem to indicate slightly more 'regression' (especially as the coefficients shown may be biased towards unity), with β falling in the older age groups. It is important to note, however, that they are based on age groups (rather than a single age as above) and a combination of occupations—so that the increased regression could well represent 'between occupations' regression towards the over-all mean, while that 'within occupations' may be just as small as in chemistry. Much more information would, of course, be desirable here, especially for other age groups.[3]

Empirical specification must now be given to the 'permanent' component of income changes.

III. Systematic changes associated with age

The most popular explanation of the large variety of profiles of mean income over age is that of the 'human capital' approach, where education and on-the-job training are regarded as investment in a future stream of income. Thus the proportionate change in the geometric mean income from one year to the next can be regarded as the product of the proportion of income invested during the period, d_t, and the average rate of return to

[1] I would like to thank the R.I.C. for the use of these data, and in particular the helpful co-operation of Barry Henman (Professional Activities Officer).

[2] For an analysis of these surveys see Creedy (1974).

[3] Respondents were also asked to anticipate their income at 1 Jan. 1974 (most questionnaires were returned in November 1973). A corresponding regression of this income on the previous two years gave values of 1·139 ($\pm$·0009) and 0·147 ($\pm$·0009) for a and b respectively; whereby ϕ = 0·991 and p = 0·148. The changes in these coefficients have interesting implications for the effect of incomes policies.

investment in human capital, r_t. Thus

$$f(t) = \frac{1}{m_t}\frac{dm_t}{dt} = r_t d_t. \tag{12}$$

Using the definition of $\mu_t = \log m_t$ and converting to discrete time equation (12) can be rewritten:

$$\mu_t = \mu_{t-1} + r_t d_t = \mu_0 + \sum_{j=1} r_j d_j, \tag{13}$$

where μ_0 is the mean of log-income in the year of entry into the occupation.

Empirical content can be added to the model by the assumption (made by Becker (1964), Mincer (1970), and Mincer and Chiswick (1972)) that the rate of return remains constant over age at r, while the proportion of income invested falls steadily with age according to

$$d_t = d_0 - gt. \tag{14}$$

Substituting into (13),

$$\mu_t = \mu_0 + rd_0 t - rg \sum_{j=1} j$$
$$= \mu_0 + r(d_0 - \tfrac{1}{2}g)t - \tfrac{1}{2}rgt^2, \tag{15}$$

using the sum of the first n integers as $\sum_{j=1}^{t} j = \frac{1}{2}n(n+1)$. Thus equation (15) implies that mean log-income is a quadratic function of age with coefficients μ_0, $\alpha = r(d_0 - \frac{1}{2}g)$, and $\gamma = \frac{1}{2}rg$—and thereby reaches a maximum at age $\alpha/2\gamma = (d_0/g - \frac{1}{2})$. This has the convenient interpretation that the larger the initial investment d_0, and the slower the rate at which this falls over life, the greater is the age at which income is a maximum (the slower is the rate at which $f(t)$ falls to zero).[1]

Although equation (15) gives the profile of mean log-income (log-geometric mean) over age, and (4), (6), and (10) describe the changing variance of log-income with age under various assumptions about individual movements within the distribution,[2] the question of the functional form of that distribution has so far been tacitly ignored. Since this is subsidiary to the main topic of the paper it will, of course, be necessary to make assumptions which are to some extent 'question-begging'.

IV. The changing distribution of income with age

In order to derive more testable predictions it is assumed that income in each age group is log-normally distributed, so that log-income x_{it} is

[1] In fact (12) can be written $d \log m_t/dt = rg(d_0/g - t)$ so that, neglecting the term $-\frac{1}{2}$, the proportionate change in the geometric mean is a constant proportion rg of the time from t to that at which geometric mean income is a maximum.

[2] It may be thought that the 'second order' nature of the process with serial correlation would affect the profile of μ_t, since a second initial condition is required. However, it is shown in Creedy (1973 a) that if $\mu_1 = \mu_0 + r(d_0 - g)$, then there is no problem.

normally distributed with parameters μ_t and σ_t^2. Thus y_t is $\Lambda(y_t \mid \mu_t, \sigma_t^2)$ and

$$d\Lambda(y_t) = \frac{1}{\sigma_t y_t \sqrt{(2\pi)}} \exp\left\{-\frac{1}{2\sigma_t^2}(\log y_t - \mu_t)^2\right\} dy_t, \quad y_t > 0. \tag{16}$$

For (16) to hold for all t it is necessary to assume that the distribution in the year of entry is log-normal and that the distribution of percentage changes is normal, since the product of Λ variates is itself Λ.[1] Discussion of the genesis of the initial distribution would, of course, require a separate paper; so from the present point of view this must be taken as 'given' (though the log-normal does satisfy the criteria suggested by Aitchison and Brown (1954)). The available evidence also suggests that the second assumption is not unreasonable.[2]

Thus if (15) is combined with Gibrat's simple assumption of independent proportionate changes the conditional distribution of income, given t, can be written as

$$F(y \mid t) \quad \text{is} \quad \Lambda(y \mid \mu_0 + \alpha t - \gamma t^2, \sigma_0^2 + \sigma^2 t). \tag{17}$$

The log-normal distribution also has the convenient implication that the median income is equal to the geometric mean (the log of which is the mean of log-income), and that the moments can easily be obtained from the moment-generating function of the normal distribution.[3] In particular the mean and variance of income in each age group t are given by

$$E(y_t) = \exp(\mu_t + \tfrac{1}{2}\sigma_t^2) \tag{18}$$

and

$$V(y_t) = E(y_t)^2 \exp(\sigma_t^2 - 1). \tag{19}$$

Equation (19) immediately resolves the apparent conflict between Lydall's remark (1968, p. 124) that

> . . . there is some doubt whether this . . . increase in variance with age . . . is true; and if it were true it does not seem to be very important, except for a relatively small group of highly educated people

and the results of previous researches on this topic (for example, Fisher (1952) and Morgan (1962)). While the latter either transformed to logs or explicitly plotted Lorenz curves, Lydall actually measured $V(y_t)$ which, on expanding (19), is given by

$$V(y_t) = \exp\{(\sigma_0^2 + 2\mu_0) + (2\alpha + \sigma^2)t - 2\gamma t^2\}\{\exp(\sigma_0^2 + \sigma^2 t) - 1\} \tag{20}$$

and is obviously concave with respect to t. The fact that increasing σ_t^2 and decreasing $V(y_t)$ are not inconsistent is easily explained by the 'relative'

[1] Much stronger assumptions are needed here than in the usual stochastic models of genesis—where the limiting form is independent of the initial distribution and appeal is made to the central limit theorems. A very useful discussion of these problems is contained in Hart (1973).

[2] The 1973 Gazette provides some support here, as well as the distributions of percentage changes obtained from the Royal Institute of Chemistry Survey.

[3] See Aitchison and Brown (1957), ch. 2.

nature of the former, which does not depend on levels of income and is therefore independent of the profile of μ_t.

Furthermore, comparison of equation (18) with (15) indicates that arithmetic mean income reaches a maximum $\sigma^2/2\gamma$ years after median income attains a maximum. The tendency for higher deciles to reach a peak later than the lower deciles was noted long ago by Woytinsky (1943), and this also carries over to 'between occupations' comparisons of median income (as demonstrated by, e.g., Blaug (1970, p. 27)). This should, however, be interpreted with some caution, since to a large extent it may simply be a 'statistical' phenomenon. Individual earners are shifting between the deciles, so that the variance of the age at which income is a maximum would be expected to be quite large—although the relationship between age and income would be upward sloping and convex.[1]

According to the assumptions made above, the joint distribution of income in any two years, t and s, say, is bivariate log-normal. Thus the conditional distribution of y_s, given y_t $(s > t)$, can easily be obtained as[2]

$$f(y_s \mid y_t) \quad \text{is} \quad \Lambda\left(y_s \mid \mu_s + r\frac{\sigma_s}{\sigma_t}(\log y_t - \mu_t),\ (1-r^2)\sigma_s^2\right), \tag{21}$$

where r is the correlation between log-income in the two years.[3] The value of this will of course depend crucially on the assumptions made about changes in relative income status, though in the case of Gibrat's law and Galtonian regression it is particularly simple. For the former the term $r\sigma_s/\sigma_t$ is always unity, and for the latter case it is ϕ^{s-t}. Thus for periods t and $t+\delta$ the conditional distribution is given by[4]

$$\Lambda(y_{t+\delta} \mid \mu_{t+\delta} + \phi^\delta(x_t - \mu_t),\ (\sigma_{t+\delta}^2 - \sigma_t^2)\phi^{2\delta}). \tag{22}$$

This enables a matrix of 'age-specific' transition probabilities for movement from one income class to another between any two years to be constructed simply by integrating (22) over the appropriate income range. The case of serially correlated changes is, of course, more complicated, though the transition matrix for income over any two years provides no information about this anyway since (as argued above) income for at least three years is required.

It has been mentioned that the large majority of available data concerning income over the life cycle is in the form of a series of cross-section distributions for a number of age groups—and that this kind of data contains very little information about movements of individuals within

[1] A more rigorous demonstration of this proposition can be found in the appendix to Creedy (1973a).

[2] See, for example, Mood and Graybill (1963), ch. 9.

[3] The correlation between income, as opposed to log-income, is derived in Creedy (1973b).

[4] For Gibrat's case it is simply $\Lambda(y_{t+\delta} \mid x_t + (\mu_{t+\delta} - \mu_t),\ \sigma^2\delta)$ and the conditional variance is homoscedastic and independent of age.

the distribution (thereby making it almost impossible to discriminate between the assumptions considered in Section II above). For this reason the following section of the paper will concentrate on the model represented by equation (17), the estimation and testing of this model and its use in larger models of economic behaviour.

V. Estimation and results

(a) Use of cross-section data

The need to use cross-section data here raises the perennial problem of interpretation, since the conditions under which a cross-section can be identified with a lifetime income stream are never likely to be met in practice. The most obvious factor is that of a trend in real/money income, as Woytinsky (1943) argued,

> There is no evidence that most of the aged persons now living are worse off than they were several decades ago.

In the case of a constant proportionate increase of p, say, this simply changes the profile of μ_t to $\mu_t = \mu_0+(\alpha+p)t-\gamma t^2$; whereby median income increases for $p/2\gamma$ years longer than otherwise.

When dealing with data relating to particular occupations, much greater problems are created by mobility, since income change is often a process of successive promotion through various stages. The data necessarily relate to those remaining in the occupation so that it may be difficult to interpret the results in terms of riskiness or incentives provided. For example the term σ^2 in the Gibrat model governs the extent to which people move within the distribution and may be thought to provide a measure of the 'riskiness' of the occupation—although excessive risks may induce (or force) people to move to a more 'stable' occupation. Thus the resulting data, covering those left, may indicate a misleadingly low value of σ^2.

Nevertheless, from the (behaviouristic) point of view of the demand analyst the actual rate of return or lifetime income is not really relevant, since the central concept is 'expected' future income over life, which as Modigliani (1960) has stated, '. . . has never been measured; and indeed may forever defy meaningful measurement'. The approach taken here will therefore be to assume that expectations are based largely on the earnings distribution of older employees. Marshall also argued in this context (1890, p. 475),

> . . . the majority assume without a further thought that the condition of each trade in their own time sufficiently indicates what it will be in the future.

A study of occupational choice or future demand for education may, for example, be based on cross-section data although it would be inadequate to measure rates of return for a cost–benefit analysis.

(*b*) *The method of estimation*

The available data are usually in the form of k independent samples at ages t_j ($j = 1,\ldots, k$) with n_j observations in each. If the incomes are first transformed to logs and the unweighted means and variances of log-income, m_j and s_j^2 respectively, are calculated[1] then of course a straightforward method of estimation would be to simply carry out an ordinary least-squares regression on the two equations

$$m_j = \mu_0 + \alpha t_j - \gamma t_j^2 \tag{23}$$

and

$$s_j^2 = \sigma_0^2 + \sigma^2 t_j. \tag{24}$$

In estimating each equation separately, however, a large amount of information would be neglected, so that a more efficient method is required which uses all the information in the sample. If initial estimates of σ_0^2 and σ^2 are obtained from O.L.S. in equation (24) the corresponding 'expected' values of σ_j^2, $\hat{\sigma}_j^2$ say, can be calculated and used to form a set of weights $w_j = n_j/\hat{\sigma}_j^2$ ($j = 1,\ldots, k$). Using these weights (proportional to the number of observations, and inversely proportional to the variance) the weighted regression of equation (23) can be carried out. Again, using these estimates the 'expected' values of μ_j, $\hat{\mu}_j$ say, can be calculated for each age group.

Then, using the same set of weights w_j, a weighted regression of (24) can be carried out—except that instead of using s_j^2 as the dependent variable the mean sum of squares $(1/n_j) \sum (x - \hat{\mu}_j)^2 = s_j^2 - 2\hat{\mu}_j m_j + \hat{\mu}_j^2$ is used. This provides a second set of estimates of σ_0^2 and σ^2, which can be compared with the initial set. This comparison completes, therefore, the second stage of the first iteration of the estimation procedure. If there is any change in the coefficients from one iteration to the next a new set of weights w_j is calculated (from the latest 'expected values' of σ_j^2) and the whole process repeated. In the cases reported below the iterative process was stopped when the percentage change in the coefficients was less than 10^{-3}, convergence usually being fairly rapid.[2]

(*c*) *Results for various occupations*

The method of estimation described above has been applied to a considerable variety of data covering many occupations and levels of skill (both from Britain and the U.S.). A selection of these results is given in Table I.

[1] In some published results only the deciles (or often only the quartiles and the median) are available. Nevertheless estimates of m and s^2 can easily be obtained using the 'method of quantiles' (see Aitchison and Brown (1957), p. 40).

[2] It can be shown that this method of estimation is equivalent to the application of Fisher's 'Method of Scoring' to the (non-linear) system of equations obtained for maximum likelihood. The full derivation is given in Creedy (1973a). The log-likelihood is proportional to

$$\sum_{j=1}^{k} \left\{ n_j \log \sigma_j^2 + \sum_{i=1}^{n_j} (x_{ij} - \mu_j)^2/\sigma_j^2 \right\}.$$

It can also be shown that convergence of the technique is quadratic. The method was first devised by Alan Brown.

TABLE I

Parameter estimates: selected occupations and education levels

Group	μ_0	α	γ ($\times 10^2$)	σ_0^2	σ^2 ($\times 10^2$)
(from Cmnd. 1064, June 1960, U.K. Annual Incomes)					
Surveyors	1·75	0·077	0·12	0·099	1·34
	(0·035)	(0·0043)	(0·005)	(0·01)	(0·08)
Solicitors	1·81	0·079	0·11	0·225	0·63
	(0·063)	(0·0059)	(0·005)	(0·022)	(0·10)
Gen. Medical	2·57	0·048	0·10	0·145	0·33
Practitioners	(0·01)	(0·001)	(0·002)	(0·003)	(0·01)
Gen. Dental	3·0	0·032	0·10	0·199	0·70
Practitioners	(0·033)	(0·004)	(0·005)	(0·012)	(0·065)
Consultants	2·99	0·056	0·10	0·068	0·34
	(0·014)	(0·002)	(0·003)	(0·003)	(0·02)
University	1·76	0·072	0·10	0·084	0·14
Teachers	(0·017)	(0·002)	(0·002)	(0·003)	(0·015)
Engineers	2·14	0·038	0·05	0·034	0·70
	(0·008)	(0·0013)	(0·002)	(0·001)	(0·016)
(from D.E.S. Survey, U.K. 1966–7 ss. 3)					
a/b Women	2·25	0·029	0·05	0·05	0·95
	(0·029)	(0·004)	(0·005)	(0·006)	(0·064)
c Women	2·07	0·022	0·04	0·048	0·35
	(0·012)	(0·0018)	(0·005)	(0·0025)	(0·018)
a/b Men	2·45	0·06	0·10	0·059	0·59
	(0·01)	(0·002)	(0·002)	(0·003)	(0·02)
c Men	2·32	0·047	0·10	0·06	0·30
	(0·014)	(0·0018)	(0·002)	(0·003)	(0·019)
Unqualified	2·19	0·051	0·10	0·075	0·36
Males	(0·01)	(0·0016)	(0·002)	(0·0027)	(0·02)
(from Wharton School Survey (1950, table 8, p. 86), income $100's per annum)					
Unskilled	3·19	0·015	0·04	0·153	0·78
	(0·039)	(0·0034)	(0·003)	(0·0132)	(0·06)
Semi-skilled	3·39	0·015	0·03	0·116	0·30
	(0·027)	(0·0026)	(0·0025)	(0·007)	(0·036)
Skilled	3·46	0·022	0·04	0·069	0·30
	(0·024)	(0·0023)	(0·002)	(0·005)	(0·025)
Salaried Prof.	3·4	0·039	0·05	0·11	0·44
and Official	(0·033)	(0·003)	(0·002)	(0·009)	(0·04)
Self Employed	3·69	0·012	0·04	0·304	0·90
	(0·088)	(0·0066)	(0·0025)	(0·035)	(0·13)

These results demonstrate the wide applicability of the model, and provide some interesting comparisons between occupations. It is perhaps not surprising that (for the U.S. data) the self employed show both more initial inequality and much more variability within the distribution, and that the best-qualified women (U.K., D.E.S. survey) have the least stability of relative income status. Of the various medical professions included the dentists seem to show much less stability than the consultants and general practitioners; so that although the latter have less initial inequality than dentists it is likely that lifetime incomes are much more unequally distributed.

From the large variety of professions for which data is available, that for which the extent of inter-decile movements is by far the lowest is in fact university teaching!

Although the parameters are virtually all highly significant it may nevertheless be thought desirable to test the 'goodness of fit' of the model further. Using the estimates of the five parameters the 'expected' frequency in each cell (age/income group) can be obtained by integrating a normal distribution over the relevant range of log-income. If e_{ij} denotes the (estimated) probability that an individual selected at random from the jth age group will fall in the ith income class, and if the actual frequency in that class is f_{ij}, then a value of χ^2 can be calculated as

$$\chi^2 = \sum_j \sum_i (f_{ij} - n_j e_{ij})^2 / n_j e_{ij} \tag{25}$$

where one degree of freedom is lost for each parameter estimated. As the sample size increases the calculated value of χ^2 increases without any commensurate increase in degrees of freedom, so that it is desirable to compare the model with an alternative hypothesis in order to carry out a classic F test (obtained as a ratio of the two χ^2s, each divided by their respective degrees of freedom). The alternative considered here was simply that income is log-normally distributed in each age group, where the e_{ij} were obtained using the ordinary maximum likelihood estimates of μ_j and σ_j^2 for each j. Some results are given in Table II, where the fit of the complete model is seen to be not significantly worse than that provided by the straightforward assumption of log-normality.

It is therefore argued that the above provides a useful framework with which to analyse many dynamic problems in economics, and especially where consumer expectations are thought to play an important role. It also indicates those aspects of income change which are important from the point of view of social policy, and provides a convenient descriptive summary of those characteristics.

VI. Some further applications

It has already been noted that we may prefer not to regard differences in income which can be attributed to the fact that people are in different stages of the life cycle as 'genuine inequalities' so that when considering the aggregate distribution (over all ages) it is important to be able to separate the component of 'inequalities' which is determined by the age distribution alone.[1] This has obvious implications for taxation policy (although virtually all the optimal tax literature ignores dynamic aspects of the distribution) and for the measurement of the impact of tax changes on the distribution.

TABLE II

F-statistics. Selected occupations

Occupation	*Degrees of freedom* *Numerator*	*Denominator*	*F*
a/b Women	49	34	0·86
c Males	86	70	1·05
c Women	56	41	0·94
Unqualified males	92	76	1·31
a/b Males	107	94	1·15
Graduates	139	123	1·12
Gen. Med. Pract.	180	165	2·52
Consultants	140	130	0·93
Solicitors (E and W)	94	77	0·85
Accountants	117	100	0·96
Univ. Teachers	112	96	1·10

N.B. First 5 from D.E.S. 1967. Remainder from U.K. Cmnd. 1064, 1960.

In positive (behavioural) problems the most obvious application is of course in life-cycle models of consumption; indeed any case where expectations of future income are important.[2] Of course, any model of the genesis of the wealth distribution must include models of savings behaviour and income over life as components. Since these subjects are much too large to be dealt with here, this section will show how the basic 'unit of analysis' can be extended to include the household rather than the individual, and how the model can be used in a simple treatment of occupational choice.

(a) The inclusion of household size

A common procedure adopted by the demand analyst is to convert household expenditure and income into 'per equivalent adult' terms, where the equivalent household 'size' is obtained as a weighted average of the number of people of each (age/sex) type in the household. If the equivalent household size, h_t, is also assumed to be log-normally distributed in each age group (taking the age of the 'head' of the household) as $\Lambda(h_t \mid m_t, s_t^2)$

[1] For a further treatment of this problem see again Creedy (1973b).

[2] None of the present 'expectations models' explicitly deals with the problem of aggregation over the cross-section. As Hicks (1939, p. 178) pointed out, where different people have (possibly inconsistent) expectations, '. . . an aggregate of their incomes has little meaning. It has no more to its credit than its obedience to the laws of arithmetic.'

and the correlation between log-household income and size is r_t, then the distribution of income per equivalent adult can be obtained as

$$f(h_t/y_t) \text{ is } \Lambda\left(\frac{h_t}{y_t}\,\middle|\, \mu_t - m_t,\ \sigma_t^2 + s_t^2 - 2r_t s_t \sigma_t\right) \tag{26}$$

by a straightforward application of theorem (2.4) in Aitchison and Brown (1957, p. 12). Thus the changing distribution of incomes per equivalent 'household member' is completely specified once the profiles of m_t, s_t^2,..., etc. are known, and equation (26) represents the confluence of the two cycles of household income and size (and their interdependence) which is familiar from Rowntree's original diagrams (1899). The extension of the model to cover household income therefore presents no fundamental difficulties for its application.[1]

(*b*) *Occupational choice*

The subject of occupational choice has, of course, a long and fairly consistent history in economic literature. Adam Smith's arguments that the relative attractiveness of occupations is determined by net advantages rather than simply pecuniary returns and that occupational choice is distorted by

> ... that natural confidence which every man has ... not only in his own activities, but in his own good fortune (1790)

are often repeated. Combined with Smith's last point is Marshall's argument that

> ... if an occupation offers a few extremely high prizes, its attractiveness is increased out of all proportion to their aggregate value (1890, p. 461).

Notwithstanding these distortions[2] in the 'distribution of labour between industries' the problem is often discussed in the context of the relative 'actuarial attractiveness' of different occupations. This has recently been considered by Weiss (1972), who specifically limited his analysis to the aspect of decision making under risk which results from incomplete knowledge about future income prospects. The individual is assumed to maximize the expected value of utility from anticipated future income—where the ultimate choice naturally depends on the attitude towards risk as reflected in the degree of 'risk aversion' shown by his utility function. Concerning the formation of expectations Weiss uses a similar approach to the above, and states (1972, p. 1207)

> ... the individual assumes that his income at each future age will fall within the currently observed distribution of the corresponding age group.

[1] Although, e.g. in demand analysis, there are difficulties in extending the utility function to cover the household, such as those of decision making within the household, learning by doing, and changing tastes as household size changes.

[2] Pigou (1952, p. 493) also noted the interesting distorting factor, 'Fathers who invest in their sons' activities unremuneratively are not expelled by bankruptcy from the profession of fatherhood.'

The objective function to be maximized is therefore written (Weiss, p. 1208)

$$E_T = E\left\{\int_0^T e^{-rt}U(y_t)\,dt\right\}$$
$$= \int e^{-rt}E\{U(y_t)\}\,dt, \quad (27)$$

where T is the career length (fixed), r the subjective discount rate, and U the utility function. Using the well-worn function with constant relative risk aversion $1-a$ (equal to $yU''(y)/U'(y)$) given by

$$U(y_t) = \frac{1}{a}\,y_t^a, \quad (28)$$

then from the convenient properties of the log-normal distribution,

$$E\{U(y_t)\} = \frac{1}{a}\exp(a\mu_t + \tfrac{1}{2}a^2\sigma_t^2). \quad (29)$$

The substitution of (29) into (27) presents obvious difficulties, and it is certainly not clear that its evaluation would give an explicit solution which is a convenient function of the subjective discount rate. This led Weiss to consider

> ... the special case where the parameters of the earning distributions are independent of age, and life is infinite (p. 1209).

In this way Weiss obtains a simple solution for the 'rate of return' from investment in education, defined as

> ... the subjective discount rate at which the individual would be indifferent between acquiring that level of education and having no education at all.

This does, however, seem a rather artificial way of avoiding the usual problems associated with the calculation of rates of return—though consider the model summarized by equation (17), whence

$$E_T = \frac{1}{a}\int \exp\{A+(B-r)t - Ct^2\}\,dt, \quad (30)$$

where $A = a\mu_0 + \tfrac{1}{2}a^2\sigma_0^2$, $B = a\alpha + \tfrac{1}{2}a^2\sigma^2$, $C = a\gamma$.

By completing the square inside the exponent and rearranging terms, (30) can be simplified to give

$$E_T = \frac{1}{a}\,kN(M, V^2), \quad (31)$$

where $k = (\pi/C)^{\frac{1}{2}}\exp\{A+(B-r)^2/4C\}$ and $N(M, V^2)$ denotes the normal distribution function with parameters M and V^2 given by

$$M = (B-r)/2C \quad \text{and} \quad V^2 = 1/2C. \quad (32)$$

Now when appropriate values for the parameters are substituted into (32), for any reasonable value of T the normal integral on the right of (31) becomes unity. This considerably simplifies the problem, since log E

is now only a quadratic function of r. Thus the 'rate of return' from entering an occupation yielding a stream of expected utility of income over life of $(1/a)\exp(a\mu_t+\frac{1}{2}a\sigma_t^2)$ for $t = 0,\ldots, T$ over another occupation yielding a stream of $(1/a)\exp(a\mu_t'+\frac{1}{2}a\sigma_t'^2)$ is that discount rate r for which $k = k'$. This can be seen to yield a quadratic in r, which can easily be solved.

For the very simple case where the two occupations differ only in respect of their 'riskiness'—as defined above in terms of σ^2—then r is given as the solution to

$$(B^2-B'^2)/4C-(B-B')r/2C = 0$$

so that

$$r = (B+B')/2$$

and

$$r = a\alpha+\tfrac{1}{2}a^2(\sigma^2+\sigma'^2). \quad (33)$$

This, then, provides a clear demonstration of the tractability of a simple and widely applicable model of the changing distribution of income over the life cycle when included in larger models of economic behaviour.

Department of Economics, University of Reading

REFERENCES

Aitchison, J., and Brown, J. A. C. (1954), *Metroeconomica*, 'On criteria for description of income distribution'.

—— —— (1957), *The Lognormal Distribution*, C.U.P.

Becker, G. S. (1964), *Human Capital*, Princeton University Press.

Blaug, M. (1970), *Economics of Education*, Allen Lane.

Champernowne, D. G. (1953), *Economic Journal*, 'A model of income distribution'.

Creedy, J. (1973a), 'The dynamics of income change', University of Reading discussion papers in Economics, Series A, No. 53.

—— (1973b), 'Aggregation and the income distribution', University of Reading discussion papers in Economics, Series A, No. 55.

—— (1974), 'Earnings in Chemistry', *Chemistry in Britain*, Vol. 10, No. 2.

Fisher, J. (1952), *N.B.E.R. Vol. 15, Studies in Income and Wealth*, 'Income, spending and savings patterns of consumer units in different age groups'.

Friedman, M. (1957), *A Theory of the Consumption Function*, N.B.E.R.

—— (1963), 'Windfalls, the horizon and related concepts in the permanent income hypothesis', from Christ *et al.*, *Measurement in Economics*.

—— and Kuznets, S. (1945), *Income from Independent Professional Practice*.

Galton, F. (1889), *Natural Inheritance*, London, Macmillan.

Gibrat, R. (1931), *Les Inégalités économiques*, Paris, Sirey.

Hart, P. E. (1973), 'The comparative statics and dynamics of income distribution', University of Reading discussion papers in Economics, Series A, No. 49.

—— and Prais, S. J. (1956), 'The analysis of business concentration: a statistical approach', *J.R. Statist. Soc. A*, 119.

Hicks, J. R. (1939), *Value and Capital*, O.U.P.

Johnston, J. (1972), *Econometric Methods* (2nd edn.), McGraw Hill.

Kalecki, M. (1946), *Econometrica*, 'On the Gibrat distribution'.

Lydall, H. (1968), *The Structure of Earnings*, O.U.P.

Malinvaud, E. (1970), *Statistical Methods of Econometrics* (2nd edn.), North Holland.

Marshall, A. (1890), *Principles of Economics*, Macmillan.

MINCER, J. (1970), *J. Econ. Litt.*, 'The distribution of labour incomes. A survey'.
—— and CHISWICK, B. (1972), *J.P.E.*, 'Time series changes in personal income inequality in the U.S.'
MODIGLIANI, F. (1960), In, *Study of Consumer Expenditure*, vol. II, edited by Friend & Jones.
MOOD, A. M., and GRAYBILL, F. A. (1963), *Introduction to the Theory of Statistics*, McGraw Hill.
MORGAN, J. N. (1962), *R.E. Stats.*, 'Anatomy of income distribution'.
PIGOU, A. C. (1952), *The Economics of Welfare* (5th edn.), Macmillan.
ROWNTREE, B. S. (1899), *Poverty: A Study in Town Life*.
WEISS, Y. (1972), 'The risk element in occupational and educational choice'. *Journal of Political Economy*.
WOYTINSKY, W. S. (1943), *Earnings and Social Security in the U.S.*

[4]

EXPERIENCE, PERFORMANCE, AND EARNINGS*

JAMES L. MEDOFF AND KATHARINE G. ABRAHAM

This study provides direct evidence concerning the relationship between experience and performance among managerial and professional employees doing similar work in two major U. S. corporations. The facts presented indicate that while, within grade levels, there is a strong positive association between experience and relative earnings, there is either no association or a negative association between experience and relative rated performance. If we are correct that the performance ratings given to managerial and professional employees in any grade level adequately reflect those employees' relative productivity in the year of assessment, the results imply that the human capital on-the-job training model cannot explain a substantial part of the observed return to labor market experience.

There is abundant evidence that earnings grow with labor market experience over most of a normal worklife. Since the advent of human capital theory,[1] the vast majority of labor economists have accepted, or at least not openly challenged, this theory's contention that the upward sloping segment of the experience-earnings profile reflects on-the-job training, which causes the relevant underlying experience-productivity profile to slope upwards. However, there are other potential explanations of the relationship between experience and earnings in which productivity growth plays a very minor role. For instance, Mincer [1974, p. 80] recognizes the possibility that the positive association between experience and earnings might only "reflect the prevalence of institutional arrangements such as seniority provisions in employment practices." He then makes the observation that sets the stage for this study: "Such practices, however, do not contradict the productivity-augmenting hypothesis, unless it can be shown that growth of earnings under seniority provisions is largely independent of productivity growth."[2]

Thus, the human capital interpretation of the experience-earnings profile is distinguished from other interpretations by the pre-

* We are most grateful to C. Brown, G. Chamberlain, J. Dunlop, R. Freeman, Z. Griliches, H. Leonard, H. G. Lewis, J. Mincer, A. Rees, S. Rosen, M. Wagner, and participants in seminars at Berkeley, the University of Chicago, Columbia, Harvard, the National Bureau of Economic Research, the University of Pennsylvania, and Princeton for their helpful criticisms and suggestions. We are also indebted to J. Fay and M. Van Denburgh for their invaluable assistance in carrying out the research to be discussed. The study was supported by the National Bureau's program for research on labor economics. Any opinions expressed are not necessarily shared by the individuals who have aided us or by the National Bureau.

1. This event can be marked by the publication of Becker [1964].
2. Mincer has seniority provisions under collective bargaining agreements in mind when he makes this statement, but his logic applies equally well to other institutional settings.

The Quarterly Journal of Economics, December 1980 0033-5533/80/0095-0703$03.40

diction that earnings growth reflects productivity growth.[3] Despite the dominance of human capital theory over labor economics during the past fifteen years, there exists no evidence that corresponding pieces of the experience-earnings and experience-productivity profiles have slopes of the same sign. There is a simple explanation of why this important proposition has not been addressed empirically: it is very difficult to measure an individual worker's productivity in an advanced industrial society. However, if the hypothesis is to be tested, this measurement problem must be addressed.

This study has as its basis the assumption that job performance ratings done by immediate supervisors are valid indicators of the relative current productivity of white male managerial and professional employees engaged in comparable work (i.e., that an employee rated ahead of X percent of his peers is more productive than X percent). Under this assumption, which will be supported at length below, it is possible to compare the relative earnings and relative productivity of employees in similar jobs who have different amounts of experience. The evidence to be presented, drawn from the personnel records of two major U. S. corporations, has as its most important implication that, while greater experience moves white male managerial and professional employees toward the upper tail of the earnings distribution for their grade levels, it does not move them toward the upper tail of the relevant performance distribution. Thus, the primary finding to be discussed appears to be at odds with what would be expected, given the human capital interpretation of the experience-earnings profile.

Section I describes the two company personnel files used in the research and discusses how they were transformed for statistical analysis. Section II demonstrates that, while there is a positive association within grade levels between relative earnings and experience, there is not a positive association between relative performance and experience. Potential criticisms of the way in which we have come to our main conclusion, that a substantial fraction of experience-earnings differentials cannot be explained by experience-productivity differentials, are considered in Section III. Factors that might possibly explain the finding are briefly considered in Section IV.

3. In the human capital model, productivity growth does not necessarily produce earnings growth; if a worker's productivity were enhanced by firm-specific on-the-job training financed solely by the firm, the earnings profile would be flat. However, if growth in earnings is observed, according to the model, either general or specific training (financed partially by the worker) and thus growth in productivity must have occurred.

I. The Company Personnel Files

Company personnel departments are a rich and little-explored source of economic microdata. Most major U. S. corporations collect and computerize extensive information on the demographic characteristics, earnings, and job performance of their employees. Hence, they represent a primary potential supplier of evidence concerning the relationship between experience-earnings and experience-productivity profiles.

The Company A and Company B Personnel Data Files

Two large corporations in the U. S. manufacturing sector, hereafter called Company A and Company B, have provided computerized personnel records for virtually all the members of their exempt workforces.[4] The Company A file contains information computerized (and, thus, roughly current) through March 15, 1977; it has only a limited amount of historical data and only persons active during at least one pay period since mid-1975 are included on the file. The Company B records contain information entered through July 1, 1977, including a complete log of all personnel actions since 1971 for persons active on or after September 1, 1976, and an abbreviated personnel action log for persons active on or after January 1, 1974.

All samples drawn from the Company A data set were limited to employees in jobs categorized as managerial or professional under the Equal Employment Opportunity Commission's job classification scheme. The samples extracted from the B file include only employees in those grade levels into which the Company classifies its managerial and professional jobs. To be included in an analysis, an employee in a selected position or grade level had to be white, male, "active," full time, regular, and domestically based as of the appropriate date(s).

Both the A file and the B file contain data on each employee's education, birth date, service date, and current physical work location. Both files also record each individual's most recent performance rating and current salary. In addition, the Company B file contains usable information on each individual's performance evaluation history and salary history.

Time with the company was calculated for each individual by reference to his service date. The schooling information in each file

4. Both companies deleted information on the name, address, and social security number of each worker to insure employee anonymity. Neither company provided the personnel records for a very small number of their top executives, as the records contained sufficiently detailed information that these individuals might have been identifiable even without name, address, or social security number.

was used to categorize individuals by highest level of educational attainment: less than high school, high school diploma, bachelor's degree, master's or law degree,[5] or doctorate. A pre-company experience variable was computed to equal age minus schooling minus company service minus five. For this purpose, it was assumed that those with less than a high school education had spent 10 years in school, high school graduates 13 years, college graduates 16 years, master's degree holders and lawyers 18 years, and Ph.D.'s 21 years. Dummy variables were created for the Company A and Company B physical work locations which place each site in one of four regions: Northeast, North Central, South, or West.

Performance Ratings at Company A and Company B

One piece of information that distinguishes a typical company personnel file from other sources of economic microdata is the assessment of how well each individual performs his or her job. At both Company A and Company B, supervisors review each managerial and professional employee's performance roughly once a year. Company A's "Employee Assessment" form instructs the reviewer to:

> List the six most important job duties or Areas of Accountability in decreasing order of importance. Next establish standards of performance or Expected Results for each area. Be sure to set your standards and/or objectives so that successful accomplishment falls into the 2 (Good) column. These standards should be discussed with the employee at the *beginning* of the assessment period. At the end of the assessment period, indicate the extent to which the results were obtained. . . .

The reviewer is then instructed to rate the subordinate's overall performance in his or her current job as: outstanding, good, acceptable, not acceptable, or too new to rate. In addition, the reviewer is asked to provide a separate assessment of each employee's potential for advancement, rating each employee as follows: promotable with no apparent limitations, promotable beyond next level, promotable one higher level, not promotable, or too new to rate. After a feedback session, the completed rating form is signed by both the rater and the ratee, and then given to the rater's superior for comments and a signature.

Company B's "Supervisor's Guide for Performance Review and Development Planning," in use from 1970 through the end of 1976, offered the following suggestions to the reviewer:

> The performance review of employees demands care and attention and should be carried on without distractions or interruptions. Before you begin a performance

5. The Company A education coding system does not include a separate law degree category. There are nine lawyers included with those holding master's degrees in the basic Company B regression sample.

review, refresh your knowledge of the content of the employee's position description. If only a generalized description is available, take time to think through the specific components of the job. It is very important that you analyze how the employee is performing in *each* of his areas of major responsibility. The more concrete your thoughts are, the more helpful your suggestions will be. The review should cover a sufficiently long span so that a pattern of performance can be observed. Except for extremely unusual cases, a period of 4 to 6 months experience with the employee should be sufficient to enable you to make objective judgments about him and thus complete a performance review.

Considering the employee's performance over an extended period will aid greatly in minimizing the influence of recent incidents and will help you to be objective and fair minded. Each factor being reviewed should be considered separately and be based on fact rather than opinion.

Reviews should be based on the employee's performance in his present position and only for the period since his last review. Since previous ratings should not be allowed to influence the current reviews, many managers prefer to make their evaluations without having the past records at hand.

The supervisor began the review by listing up to four of his subordinate's strengths ("He is particularly good at:"), and indicating whether "each is (essential, important, supplementary) to his job." The supervisor then indicated up to four areas where there was room for improvement ("He could use help in:") and the relative importance of each to the subordinate's job. Finally, the reviewer was told:

Now that you have completed your analysis of his strengths and opportunities for improvement, check the box opposite the paragraph that most nearly describes your evaluation of his overall performance:

- ☐ EXCELLENT: Consistently exceeds expected performance in accomplishing objectives and position requirements.
- ☐ SUPERIOR: Exceeds expectations and demonstrates high level performance in accomplishing objectives and position requirements.
- ☐ GOOD: Accomplishes objectives and position requirements as originally anticipated and in a manner resulting in expected performance.
- ☐ SATISFACTORY: Acceptable performance of position requirements with indication of ability for improvement.
- ☐ MINIMUM ACCEPTABLE: Probationary performance level for employees in same position for more than twelve months, requiring consultation with the employee and a specified plan for improvement within a designated period of time.
- ☐ UNACCEPTABLE: Unsatisfactory. Does not perform at an acceptable level of accomplishment.

The rating chosen then became the basis of the rater's recommendation for a salary action (which was reviewed by the appropriate group of the rater's superiors). No ratings in the bottom two categories were observed.

At the beginning of 1977, the Company B performance/salary review process was altered. One relevant change was in the number and description of the overall performance rating categories. Under the new program there are only four rating categories. Even though only the first four rating categories were ever used under the old program, the different descriptions under the old and new plans led to different rating distributions in the two regimes. For this reason, the performance ratings done before January 1, 1977, are not comparable to those done after that date.

As both companies' evaluation procedures indicate, a performance rating should be based on how well an individual, in the year of evaluation, is carrying out the responsibilities of his or her job. Thus, a performance rating should reflect an employee's current level of performance relative to the level of performance deemed normal for someone in his or her position. It follows that the ratings of two employees are comparable only if the workers are in similar jobs.

For compensation purposes, companies assess the relative importance and difficulty of their myriad positions and group them in light of these assessments into grade levels. For both companies under analysis, this grading is based on a position description filled out (and kept current) by the supervisor of the job (with the concurrence of higher level supervisors, when necessary). The "Exempt Position Description" form in Company B (which is quite typical) obtains information about the following: the basic purpose of the job, the duties and responsibilities of the position, and the job holder's relationship to others within or outside the organization. In addition, the form elicits:

> Functional Scope Data: A listing of the functional statistics commonly used in the industry and/or profession to indicate scope and size of responsibility, e.g.: a) Sales Volume, b) Total Employment, c) Operating Budget, d) Department Payroll, e) Total Assets, f) Number Supervised—direct and indirect, g) Cost of Rentals, h) Purchasing Volume, i) Other.

and

> Position specifications: The normal knowledge or training required; the normal minimum experience and the required personal characteristics such as level of maturity, tactfulness, judgment, creativity, etc. All of the foregoing should be regarded as being necessary for an average employee in order to attain a satisfactory level of proficiency in the job.

The jobs held by sample members from Company A fall into nineteen grade levels; those held by sample members from B fall into twelve. In light of the way in which jobs are classified into grade levels, it is assumed that positions within a grade level are of equal importance and difficulty.[6] Thus, within a grade level it seems most rea-

6. Interviews with a number of Company B supervisors lent strong support to this assumption.

TABLE I

CHARACTERISTICS OF WHITE MALE MANAGERIAL AND PROFESSIONAL SAMPLES USED IN REGRESSION ANALYSIS

	Mean (standard deviation)	
	Company A (N = 4,788)	Company B (N = 2,841)
Highest level of educational attainment:		
Less than high school diploma (yes = 1)	0.050	0.026
High school diploma (yes = 1)	0.449	0.466
Bachelor's degree (yes = 1)	0.444	0.401
Master's or law degree (yes = 1)	0.049	0.082
Doctorate (yes = 1)	0.007	0.025
Age (years)	43.1	44.1
	(10.5)	(9.9)
Pre-company experience (years)	6.8	9.5
	(6.7)	(7.7)
Company service (years)	16.8	14.9
	(10.4)	(9.6)
Annual salary (dollars)[a]	17,884	20,008
	(3,240)	(4,916)
Performance rating:		
(1) Not acceptable/satisfactory (yes = 1)[b]	0.002	0.012
(2) Acceptable/good (yes = 1)[b]	0.053	0.366
(3) Good/superior (yes = 1)[b]	0.743	0.584
(4) Outstanding/excellent (yes = 1)[b]	0.202	0.038

a. These figures are based on current dollar salaries as of March 15, 1977, for Company A and as of July 1, 1976, for Company B.

b. Performance rating 1 is worst, and performance rating 4 is best. The Company A performance category description precedes the slash and the Company B description follows the slash.

sonable to assume that a higher performance rating implies higher productivity.

A Comparison of the Two Companies' Workforces

Examination of Table I reveals great similarity in the demographic characteristics of the basic Company A and Company B regression samples.[7] In both companies, nearly 50 percent of the sample

7. The basic regression samples consist of all white males who were "active" full-time regular domestically based managerial and professional employees as of March 15, 1977, at Company A and as of July 1, 1976, at Company B for whom valid information on education, birth date, service date, physical work location, most recent performance rating, current salary, and current grade level was available. The requirements that education, birth date, service date, and physical work location be available resulted in the exclusion of 22 Company A employees and 791 Company B employees. At the time we obtained the Company B data, the firm was in the process of adding educational codes to its computerized personnel system. Almost all of the Company B exclusions resulted from not yet complete (and apparently randomly missing) educational information.

did not graduate from college. The Company B sample contains a somewhat higher proportion of people with advanced degrees; this is consistent with the organization's involvement in research and development activities. On average, Company A's employees have somewhat less pre-company experience than Company B's employees (6.8 years versus 9.5 years), but somewhat longer company service (16.8 years versus 14.9 years). The average annual salary at Company B exceeds the average annual salary at Company A by nearly $2,900.[8] There is a larger concentration of people in the top performance categories at Company A than at Company B; this is most likely attributable to the differences in the sets of rating instructions given the supervisors at the two companies.

II. Relative Earnings and Relative Performance

This section offers evidence for three propositions:

1. Managerial and professional employees with more than average pre-company experience and company service have higher than average salaries;

2. About 40 percent of the earnings differentials associated with pre-company experience and with company service occur within grade levels;

3. These within-grade-level earnings differentials cannot be explained by within-grade-level differentials in job performance. The third proposition, which is the study's major finding, is demonstrated both by a test in which performance rating dummies are entered into a within-grade-level human capital earnings function and by estimating and contrasting multinomial logit earnings and performance category equations.

Earnings Function Results

The regression results presented in Table II allow us to compare the earnings of groups of managerial and professional employees stratified by both educational attainment and labor market experience. These findings are based on a standard semi-log earnings function:

$$\ln(y) = \mathbf{x}\beta + \epsilon,$$

8. This figure was produced by inflating the Company B mean salary to March 1977 dollars using the Consumer Price Index to make it comparable to the Company A mean salary, then taking the difference between the two mean salaries.

where y equals annual salary rate, x is a vector whose elements capture highest level of educational attainment, pre-company experience, company service, and region, β is a vector of parameters to be estimated, and ϵ is an equation error. As stated above, the pre-company experience variable was constructed to equal age minus years assumed spent in school by those with different degrees minus company service minus five. Thus, in the presence of dummy variables capturing highest degree received and a company service variable, differences in pre-company experience will be indistinguishable from differences in age.

Equations (1) and (4) indicate that, with pre-company experience and company service held constant, individuals with advanced degrees receive substantially higher salaries than individuals with less education. The proportional reward to education within the two companies studied appears quite similar, except that, holding experience constant, college graduates are relatively better off at Company B; the percentage earnings differential between those with a high school diploma but not a bachelor's degree and college graduates with comparable labor market experience is only 13 percent at Company A as compared with 22 percent at Company B.

In both companies, controlling for educational attainment and company service, there is a positive association between salary and pre-company experience, and, controlling for schooling and pre-company experience, a positive association between salary and company service, which weakens with length of service but does not vanish within the set of feasible differences in years of service.

Regressions (2) and (5) include grade-level dummies, and hence provide information on within-grade-level earnings differentials. These within-grade-level salary differentials are central to this study, since performance ratings are conditional on the importance and difficulty of an employee's position, and thus, on his grade level. This implies that the performance ratings can at most explain the fraction of a total earnings differential that occurs within grade levels.

As can be seen by comparing regressions (1) and (4) with regressions (2) and (5), relatively little of the return to educational attainment takes the form of higher within-grade-level earnings. Controlling for pre-company experience and company tenure, systematic within-grade-level earnings differences account for an average of only 12 percent in Company A and 10 percent in Company B of the total earnings differential between those with a bachelor's degree and less educated workers and for an average of only 22 percent and 13 percent

TABLE II

EARNINGS FUNCTION ESTIMATES

	Company A Dependent variable = ln (annual salary as of March 15, 1977)[a] (N = 4,788)			Company B Dependent variable = ln (annual salary as of July 1, 1976)[a] (N = 2,481)		
	(1)	(2)	(3)	(4)	(5)	(6)
Less than high school diploma (yes = 1)	−0.247 (.010)	−0.075 (.007)	−0.077 (.007)	−0.263 (.024)	−0.014 (.012)	−0.016 (.012)
High school diploma (yes = 1)	−.131 (.005)	−.013 (.003)	−.015 (.003)	−.221 (.008)	−.022 (.005)	−.024 (.005)
Master's or law degree (yes = 1)	.104 (.010)	.022 (.006)	.020 (.006)	.099 (.014)	.011 (.007)	.015 (.007)
Doctorate (yes = 1)	.214 (.025)	.051 (.016)	.054 (.016)	.256 (.024)	.051 (.012)	.052 (.012)
Years of pre-company experience/10	.043 (.008)	.023 (.005)	.027 (.005)	.070 (.014)	.026 (.007)	.028 (.007)

Continued overleaf

TABLE II (continued)

(Years of pre-company	−.003	−.003	−.004	−.001	−.002	−.002
experience)^2/100	(.003)	(.002)	(.002)	(.005)	(.002)	(.002)
Years of company	.202	.087	.088	.192	.056	.056
service/10	(.008)	(.006)	(.006)	(.013)	(.007)	(.007)
(Years of company	−.031	−.013	−.013	−.028	−.005	−.005
service)^2/100	(.002)	(.001)	(.001)	(.004)	(.002)	(.002)
Performance rating 1	—	—	−.053	—	—	−.036
(worst; yes = 1)			(.027)			(.016)
Performance rating 2	—	—	−.039	—	—	−.018
(yes = 1)			(.006)			(.004)
Performance rating 4	—	—	.025	—	—	.026
(best; yes = 1)			(.003)			(.009)
Constant	yes	yes	yes	yes	yes	yes
Region dummies (3)	yes	yes	yes	yes	yes	yes
Grade level dummies (18; 11)	no	yes	yes	no	yes	yes
R^2	.356	.741	.747	.335	.849	.851
SEE	.144	.091	.090	.190	.091	.090

a. The mean (standard deviation) of the dependent variable is 9.776 (0.179) at Company A and 9.876 (0.233) at Company B.
Note. Standard errors are in parentheses below coefficient estimates.

of the total earnings differential between advanced degree holders and those with only a bachelor's degree.[9] Thus, college graduates earn more than less educated workers almost entirely because they are assigned to jobs in grade levels with higher mean earnings; the same is somewhat less true of advanced degree holders as compared with those with only a bachelor's degree.

In contrast, a large fraction of the return to pre-company experience and to company service reflects higher within-grade-level earnings. At the appropriate sample mean for pre-company experience, 48 percent (in A) and 34 percent (in B) of the salary differential associated with an additional year of this construct occurs within grade levels. At the appropriate mean for company service, 44 percent (in A) and 38 percent (in B) of the return to an additional year of tenure occurs within grade levels. Thus, a substantial fraction of the observed relationship between experience and earnings cannot be explained by between-grade-level differences in mean salaries.

Why do workers with more education, more pre-company experience, and more company service have higher within-grade-level earnings? One possible explanation would be that such workers have acquired valuable skills during their years in school and in the labor force, and as a result their productivity exceeds that of less educated and less experienced workers in the same grade level. If this explanation were valid, it would be expected that the introduction of performance rating dummies into the ln(earnings) equations which have grade-level controls would move the estimated coefficients of the schooling, pre-company experience, and company tenure variables toward zero. However, comparison of equations (2) and (5) with equations (3) and (6) reveals that, although higher rated performance is associated with significantly and substantially higher earnings, introduction of the rating dummies has virtually no effect on the relevant education and experience coefficients. *Thus, performance does not appear to be a mediating factor in the within-grade-level positive relationship between either education or labor force experience and earnings.* In other words, within groups of similar jobs, despite the positive correlation between "human capital" and earnings, there does not appear to be a positive correlation between "human capital" and performance.

9. These figures are weighted averages. The weights for the first set are the proportions of those with less than a high school education and of high school graduates in the less educated worker group; the weights for the second set are the proportions of master's or law degree holders and of doctorates in the advanced degree group.

Multinomial Logit Results

The multinomial logit models estimated for Table III offer another way of looking at the earnings-performance nexus.[10] In constructing the models, employees rated either "not acceptable" or "acceptable" (in A) or "satisfactory" or "good" (in B) were categorized as below-average performers for their grade level.[11] Employees rated "good" (in A) or "superior" (in B) were categorized as average performers for their grade level. Employees rated "outstanding" (in A) or "excellent" (in B) were categorized as above-average performers for their grade level. Next, employees were categorized as having either a below-average salary, an average salary, or an above-average salary for their grade level. Salary categories were assigned on the basis of each individual's percentile ranking in the relevant within-grade-level salary distribution in such a way as to make the salary and the performance categories comparable. Suppose, for example, that X_1 percent of the individuals in grade level k were in the lowest performance category, X_2 percent were in the middle performance category, and X_3 percent were in the top performance category. An individual in the bottom X_1 percent of the grade level k salary distribution would be assigned to the lowest salary category, an individual in the next X_2 percent of the grade level k salary distribution to the middle salary category, and an individual in the top X_3 percent of the grade level k salary distribution to the top salary category. Assuming that performance ratings accurately reflect relative productivity, if more productive workers were always paid more than less productive workers, the assignment of individuals to salary categories would be identical with the assignment of individuals to performance categories.[12]

A maximum likelihood multinomial logit procedure was used to estimate the effects of education, pre-company experience, and

10. Nerlove and Press [1973] discuss the multinomial logit model.

11. The small number of employees with the lowest observed performance rating, "not acceptable" in Company A and "satisfactory" in Company B, made it seem advisable to combine the bottom two categories at each company to create a "below-average" category.

12. The samples used for constructing the performance and salary categories consisted of all "active" full-time regular domestically based white male managerial and professional employees in each grade level for whom both a valid salary and a valid performance rating were available. There were fewer people in the multinomial logit samples due to the more stringent data availability requirements that had to be satisfied. Thus, unless relative rated performance in the larger sample is perfectly related to relative salary, our procedure need not (and does not) result in the number of logit sample members in each salary category equaling the number of logit sample members in the corresponding performance category.

TABLE IIIA

MULTINOMIAL LOGIT SALARY CATEGORY AND PERFORMANCE CATEGORY EQUATION ESTIMATES

	Company A ($N = 4{,}784$)				Company B ($N = 2{,}822$)			
	Salary category (1)[a]		Performance category (2)[a]		Salary category (3)[a]		Performance category (4)[a]	
	Category 2[b]	Category 3[b]	Category 2[b]	Category 3[b]	Category 2[b]	Category 3[b]	Category 2[b]	Category 3[b]
Less than high school diploma (yes = 1)	−2.538 (0.287)	−3.036 (0.342)	0.214 (0.308)	0.503 (0.367)	−0.330 (0.288)	−0.054 (0.553)	−0.026 (0.271)	1.774 (0.585)
High school diploma (yes = 1)	−0.583 (0.186)	−0.571 (0.203)	0.231 (0.166)	0.470 (0.184)	−0.279 (0.113)	−0.848 (0.283)	0.217 (0.108)	0.491 (0.287)
Master's or law degree (yes = 1)	—	—	—	—	0.265 (0.167)	0.413 (0.390)	−0.665 (0.159)	−0.656 (0.383)
Doctorate (yes = 1)	—	—	—	—	1.414 (0.341)	0.282 (1.076)	−0.682 (0.287)	−0.332 (0.524)
Master's degree, law degree or doctorate (yes = 1)[c]	1.156 (0.474)	1.645 (0.489)	0.105 (0.348)	0.238 (0.362)	—	—	—	—

Continued overleaf

TABLE IIIA (continued)

Years of pre-company experience/10	0.439 (0.268)	0.834 (0.296)	−0.806 (0.267)	−1.318 (0.292)	0.546 (0.165)	0.441 (0.393)	−0.512 (0.162)	−0.991 (0.405)
(Years of pre-company experience)^2/100	−0.072 (0.094)	−0.081 (0.106)	0.198 (0.099)	0.273 (0.110)	−0.073 (0.055)	0.078 (0.120)	0.040 (0.054)	0.147 (0.134)
Years of company service/10	1.122 (0.280)	2.890 (0.322)	0.429 (0.261)	−0.122 (0.290)	1.131 (0.164)	0.928 (0.402)	0.095 (0.153)	−0.582 (0.408)
(Years of company service)^2/100	−0.133 (0.070)	−0.408 (0.078)	−0.127 (0.063)	−0.060 (0.070)	−0.132 (0.046)	0.035 (0.100)	−0.068 (0.042)	0.014 (0.117)
Constant	yes	yes	yes	yes	yes	yes	yes	yes
Region dummies (3; 2)[d]	yes	yes	yes	yes	yes	yes	yes	yes
Grade level dummies (15; 8)[e]	yes	yes	yes	yes	yes	yes	yes	yes
χ^2	711.30		351.70		413.37		216.96	
d.f.	50		50		36		36	

a. All equations were estimated using a maximum likelihood multinomial logit procedure.

b. Category 1 represents the lowest level, category 2 the middle level, and category 3 the highest level of salary or performance. The coefficient estimates reported are equal to $\beta_2 - \beta_1$ (under category 2) and $\beta_3 - \beta_1$ (under category 3).

c. Since none of the thirty-five Company A doctorates were in the lowest salary category, individuals at Company A with doctorates were included with the master's or law degree group.

d. In the Company B sample, individuals in the West region were included with the North Central region group.

e. Individuals in grade levels where not all of the salary and performance categories were represented were excluded from the sample.

Note. Standard errors are in parentheses below the coefficient estimates.

company service on the probability of an individual's being in each of the salary categories and in each of the performance categories. The multinomial logit model specifies the probability that an individual is in category i to be of the form, $e^{\mathbf{x}\beta_i}/\Sigma_{j=1}^{3} e^{\mathbf{x}\beta_j}$, $i = 1, 2, 3$, where $\mathbf{x}$ is a vector of individual characteristics containing education dummies, pre-company experience and company service variables, region dummies, and grade level dummies, and the β_1, β_2, and β_3 are vectors of parameters. The coefficients presented in Table IIIA are estimates of the elements in vectors equal to $\beta_i - \beta_1$, $i = 2, 3$.

If the higher within-grade-level earnings of those with more education, more pre-company experience, and more company service were a reflection solely of the higher relative productivity of such workers, one would expect the estimated coefficients in salary category equations (1) and (3) to equal the estimated coefficients in performance category equations (2) and (4). In fact, the estimated coefficients in the salary category equations are markedly different from the estimated coefficients in the performance category equations. At both Company A and Company B, those with less than a college education appear to have a much lower probability of being in one of the top two salary categories than do those whose highest degree is a bachelor's degree, but an equal or higher probability of being in one of the top two performance categories. Those with advanced degrees, on the other hand, appear to have a substantially higher probability of being in one of the highest two earnings categories than do those whose final degree was a bachelor's degree, without having a substantially higher probability at A and actually having a substantially lower probability at B of being in one of the top two performance categories.

At both Company A and Company B, pre-company experience appears to decrease an individual's chances of being in the bottom salary category, while increasing his chances of being in the bottom performance category. At both companies, additional company service has a significant and strongly positive effect on the probability that an employee will be in one of the top two salary categories; at Company A the incremental effect of an additional year of service falls as the amount of accrued seniority gets larger but does not vanish within the feasible set of values for the variable. While the initial years of service at Company A have a small but significant positive effect on the probability of an individual being in the middle performance category rather than in either the top or the bottom performance category, this effect vanishes in under seventeen years (i.e., within two years beyond the mean amount of company service). At Company

TABLE IIIB

MULTINOMIAL LOGIT SALARY CATEGORY AND PERFORMANCE CATEGORY EQUATION ESTIMATES

	Company A (N = 4,784)			Company B (N = 2,822)		
	Bottom category	Middle category	Top category	Bottom category	Middle category	Top category
Salary categories						
Probability of average sample member being in category (sample means in brackets)	0.030 [0.052]	0.758 [0.748]	0.212 [0.200]	0.330 [0.380]	0.644 [0.582]	0.025 [0.038]
Percentage change in probability attributable to:						
(1) an additional year of pre-company experience	−4.117 (1.536)	0.098 (0.212)	1.027 (0.751)	−2.771 (0.517)	1.319 (0.268)	1.997 (1.898)
(2) an additional year of company service	−8.331 (0.903)	0.184 (0.130)	2.241 (0.465)	−5.028 (0.388)	2.373 (0.208)	3.480 (2.785)
Performance categories						
Probability of average sample member being in category (sample means in brackets)	0.048 [0.055]	0.783 [0.743]	0.169 [0.202]	0.368 [0.381]	0.606 [0.582]	0.026 [0.037]
Percentage change in probability attributable to:						
(1) an additional year of pre-company experience	5.784 (1.427)	−0.270 (0.165)	−1.147 (0.691)	2.827 (0.477)	−1.648 (0.291)	−2.682 (1.846)
(2) an additional year of company service	0.537 (0.760)	0.001 (0.097)	−0.704 (0.414)	0.787 (0.335)	−0.410 (0.205)	−2.103 (1.343)

a. The probability figures reported here were derived using the fitted values of the multinomial logit coefficients reported in Table IIIA. The sample mean values of the education dummies, region dummies, and grade dummies and the mean amount of both pre-company experience and company service were assumed. The standard errors are "back-of-an-envelope" approximations calculated with the probability of an average sample member being in each category treated as known rather than estimated.

Note. Standard errors are in parentheses below the percentage change estimates.

B, length of tenure has no significant effect on a person's performance category.

The point estimates (and approximate standard errors) presented in Table IIIB were calculated using the estimated coefficients from the multinomial logit models (and the variance-covariance matrix of the parameter estimates). In both Company A and Company B, the point estimates of the multinomial logit coefficients imply that for the mean sample member an additional year of either pre-company experience or company service would do the following: (1) substantially reduce the probability of being in the below-average salary category, increase the probability of being in the average salary category, and increase by a larger percentage the probability of being in the above-average salary category; and (2) increase the probability of being in the below-average performance category, reduce or leave unaffected the probability of being in the average performance category, and reduce by a larger percentage the probability of being in the above-average performance category. Thus, the multinomial logit coefficient estimates strongly suggest that while pre-company experience and company service tend to move individuals with average measured characteristics toward the top of the relevant within-grade-level salary distribution, they tend to move them toward the bottom of the relevant within-grade-level performance distribution. It seems clear that at least among the samples of employees at Company A and Company B under analysis, higher relative productivity cannot be offered as a satisfactory explanation of the higher relative within-grade-level salaries associated with additional labor force experience.[13]

III. Potential Criticisms

Our finding that a substantial fraction of the experience-earnings differential among managerial and professional employees in major U. S. corporations cannot be explained by an experience-performance differential is inconsistent with the explanation of the experience-earnings profile associated with human capital theory. Thus, it is likely that this paradigm's adherents will argue that the test which we have conducted was ill-conceived. In this section we attempt to anticipate and address potential criticisms of our approach. We have grouped these criticisms according to whether they question our econometric

13. It is perhaps worth commenting that, although the data used in this study only permit us to conclude that at Companies A and B the within-grade-level portion of the experience-earnings differential cannot be explained by an experience-performance differential, there is no direct evidence on the extent to which the cross-grade-level portion of the experience-earnings differential at Companies A and B reflects higher productivity of more experienced workers.

methods or our key assumption that within similar jobs, rated performance is monotonically related to productivity.[14]

Econometric Issues

As stated above, the key piece of information used in our analysis is the performance rating given to each employee. Since this assessment seems to be conditional on an employee's job assignment and, hence, his grade level, our analysis has focused on whether the within-grade-level portion of the experience-earnings differential (a substantial part of the total experience-earnings differential) could be explained by a within-grade-level experience-performance differential.

A critic might correctly point out that by looking within grade levels at a given firm, we most likely induce a negative partial correlation between experience and unobserved ability. Even if in the whole relevant sample, experience and ability have a zero correlation, within a given grade level, more experienced employees most likely are less able than less experienced employees, since otherwise they probably would have been promoted to jobs in higher grade levels. A critic might also point out that performance ratings are almost surely error-ridden proxies for relative within-grade-level productivity.

With regard to our earnings function results, it can be shown formally that neither the existence of a negative within-grade-level correlation between experience and ability nor random error in the performance ratings we have used to capture relative productivity can explain the failure of the estimated within-grade-level return to labor market experience to move toward zero when performance rating controls are introduced.[15]

14. Another potential criticism might be that our work is flawed because we look at cross-sectional data rather than at changes over time in the relative earnings and relative performance of members of a cohort. This argument is dealt with in Medoff and Abraham [forthcoming]; longitudinal data from another large company yield the result that, for white male managers or professionals remaining in a grade level, relative earnings rise and relative performance falls with the passage of time.

15. For a sample of people in a grade level, let earnings be a function solely of productivity:

$$\ln Y = \alpha_1 C + \epsilon_1, \quad \alpha_1 > 0, \tag{1}$$

and productivity be a function of both experience and ability:

$$C = \alpha_2 X + \alpha_3 A + \epsilon_2, \ \alpha_2, \alpha_3 > 0, \ \text{cov}(X,A) < 0. \tag{2}$$

Suppose that we have a variable which captures productivity with error for those in the given grade level:

$$P = C + \epsilon_3. \tag{3}$$

Assume that these three equations accurately describe the relevant relationships and that ϵ_1, ϵ_2, and ϵ_3 are uncorrelated with each other, with X, and with A. Under these conditions, if ln Y is first regressed on X alone and then regressed on both X and P, the expected value of the experience coefficient falls toward zero when P is added. This model is laid out more fully in Medoff and Abraham [forthcoming].

The conclusions that can be drawn from our multinomial logit results also appear to be unaffected. It is true that if there is a negative within-grade-level correlation between experience and ability, the estimated effect of experience on performance will be biased downward. It should not be forgotten, however, that the estimated effect of experience on earnings will *also* be biased downward. The goal of our multinomial logit analyses is *not* to derive consistent estimates of the effect of experience on either performance or salary. Rather, they are intended to yield an answer to the question: Can the 40 or so percent of the total earnings advantage enjoyed by more experienced managers and professionals at the firms we have studied that occurs within grade levels be explained by the fact that the more experienced employees within these grade levels are better performers? Our answer of "no" does not depend on the consistency of either our estimate of the impact of experience on performance or our estimate of the impact of experience on earnings. All that the response depends on is that the *difference* between these two estimated experience effects be a consistent estimate of the difference between the two "true" experience effects. We know of no reason why it should not be.

It also seems unlikely that classical measurement error in our performance variable should in any way affect the main conclusions derivable from our multinomial logit models. In a linear model, error in the dependent variable of the type under discussion will weaken the equation's overall explanatory power but will not lead to inconsistent estimated coefficients. In the relevant multinomial logit models, the performance ratings form the basis for the dependent variables. We do not see how errors that arise out of random error in the performance ratings would lead to inconsistency in the estimated multinomial logit coefficients. Consistency is all that matters for our purpose.

Use of Performance Ratings

The validity of our analysis depends on the assumption that within a grade level, for the samples studied, performance ratings are valid indicators of relative productivity. There is an extensive literature on white-collar performance evaluations.[16] Since critical articles are more likely to find their way into personnel journals than those that applaud current practices, performance evaluation programs have been subject to a fair amount of criticism.

16. For good general discussions and further references, see Barrett [1966], Bass and Barrett [1972], Landy and Trumbo [1976], and McCormick and Tiffin [1974].

Much of this criticism focuses on the possibility that supervisors may be overly lenient in rating their subordinates. While inflated ratings are a matter of concern for personnel administrators, there is no evidence to suggest that such inflation distorts the relative rankings of employees by true performance. Even if the ratings of all employees are biased upwards, the best employees should be rated above average, and the worst employees below average. This is all that matters for the present study.

A second criticism of performance ratings asserts that since different supervisors may have divergent beliefs about what constitutes good performance, ratings done by different supervisors should not be compared. While it does seem unlikely that any two supervisors would be completely consistent in their ratings, the results of laboratory studies suggest that a high degree of interrater reliability can be expected.[17] In any event, so long as subordinates with particular observed characteristics are not systematically paired with superiors who rate more or less generously, our findings cannot be called into question on account of variation in supervisors' rating standards.

A third potential weakness of performance ratings is that employees' personal characteristics (race, sex, age, time with company) might influence supervisors' performance assessments. Whether race or sex affects ratings is irrelevant in the context of the present study, since we have restricted our analysis to samples of white males. Evidence that supervisors systematically underrate the relative performance of older or more senior workers would be very relevant. However, in our review of the pertinent literature, we have found no such evidence.

One cannot conclude a priori that any systematic bias in performance ratings associated with age or tenure should be in the direction of understating rather than overstating older or more senior workers' relative productivity. While one might argue that the typical supervisor would tend to give a higher than deserved rating to an employee in a given grade level with less than average experience because of, say, lack of familiarity with his or her weaknesses or because of lower performance expectations, it seems equally plausible to argue that the typical supervisor would favor an employee with greater than average experience because of, say, friendship developed over a period of years or because of lower expectations for someone

17. Relevant research includes Borman [1975] and Whitlock [1963]. Lawler [1967, p. 371] refers to Whitlock's work and asserts that "other studies have shown that raters tend to agree upon the weight to be assigned to . . . different behavior specimens; thus, inter-rater reliability is possible." Unfortunately, he does not specify what other studies he has in mind.

who is more likely to be a "stayer" as opposed to a "mover" in the corporate hierarchy. (If the idea that a supervisor would implicitly assume there to be a negative partial correlation between experience and what one can expect from an employee seems implausible, the reader should reassess its plausibility remembering that the relevant partial correlation is with grade level held constant.) In fact, the limited empirical evidence that is available on the issue of age- and seniority-related bias in performance ratings suggests that more experienced employees tend to be rated somewhat *higher* than is warranted by their true relative performance.[18] Thus, it appears that, so long as older or more senior workers are not systematically below superiors who underrate subordinates with these characteristics (which we find most doubtful), unequal treatment in ratings is not an acceptable explanation for more experienced workers in a grade level receiving ratings that are no higher and perhaps somewhat lower than those received by otherwise comparable less experienced workers.

Another related possibility is that perhaps even within grade levels at a company, more experienced workers might tend to be assigned more difficult tasks than less experienced workers (perhaps because more is expected of those with more experience). If this were the case, employees with greater than average experience could have greater productivity than their less experienced peers and still receive no higher or even lower performance ratings. However, since jobs are grouped into grade levels on the basis of the importance and difficulty of the tasks the job holder must perform, any difference in the potential value of the tasks performed by employees in the same grade level should be small. Further, the only evidence we have seen that bears on this point suggests that older workers in a group of employees holding similar jobs tend to be assigned *less* difficult rather than *more* difficult tasks. In an article discussed at greater length in Section IV of this study, Dalton and Thompson [1971] report that among engineers at six companies there was a negative relationship between supervisors' assessment of the complexity of the tasks a subordinate was typically asked to perform and the subordinate's age. (Their finding is illustrated graphically in Figure I in Section IV.)

18. Two studies of blue collar workers, one by Rothe [1949] and one by Rundquist and Bittner [1948], contain some evidence that the ratings of long service laundry workers and of container inspectors tend to be inflated. A study by Ferguson [1949] of ratings given to assistant life insurance sales managers and another study by Stockford and Bissell [1949] of ratings given to first line supervisors at a manufacturing plant suggest that superiors tend to be more lenient in rating those whom they have known for a longer period of time.

An analysis of promotion probabilities and percentage salary increases in Company B can provide two tests of our contention that performance ratings mirror relative true performance. These tests are based on the seemingly reasonable assumptions that, holding educational attainment, experience, and grade level constant, differentials in promotion probabilities reflect differentials in productivity and that, holding the same variables plus ln(salary) constant, differentials in percentage salary increases also reflect productivity differentials.[19] Under these assumptions, a strong positive association between rated performance and probability of promotion or a strong positive association between rated performance and percentage salary increase among employees in the same grade level who have the same amount of schooling and experience can be taken as evidence of a strong association between relative performance rating and relative productivity.

Table IV presents estimates of the effects of educational attainment, experience, and rated performance on promotion probabilities and percentage total salary changes.[20] A maximum likelihood logit procedure was used to estimate the promotion equations; ordinary least squares was used to estimate the percentage salary change equations.

The partial effect of rated performance in 1976 on the probability that a Company B employee received a promotion between July 1, 1976, and July 1, 1977, is estimated in equation (1). The results imply that individuals with either of the bottom two performance ratings were substantially and significantly less likely to have been promoted than otherwise comparable individuals with either of the top two ratings. The equation (2) results support the same conclusion with regard to the effect of rated performance as of July 1, 1974, on the probability of having received a promotion between July 1, 1975, and July 1, 1977.

19. Holding productivity constant, ln(salary) should be negatively related to percentage salary increase if firms tend to increase the relative earnings of those who are paid less and decrease the relative earnings of those who are paid more than they are currently contributing. The assumptions made in the text also permit education, experience, and grade level to have independent effects on probability of promotion and percentage salary increase, although a priori it is not clear in which direction these effects should go.

20. Estimates for Company A are not presented in Table IV because the Company A file does not contain the necessary historical performance rating data. The Company B samples consist of all white males who were "active" full-time regular domestically based managerial and professional employees throughout the relevant periods, for whom education, experience, and physical work location are known, for whom a valid initial performance rating and grade level are available, and, when relevant, for whom the requisite salary data exist.

TABLE IV

ESTIMATES OF THE RELATIONSHIP OF SCHOOLING, EXPERIENCE, AND PERFORMANCE RATING TO THE PROBABILITY OF BEING PROMOTED AND TO PERCENTAGE SALARY INCREASES AT COMPANY B

	Dependent variable = 1 if promoted between July 1, 1976 and July 1, 1977, 0 otherwise (N = 2,728) (1)[b]	Dependent variable = 1 if promoted between July 1, 1975 and July 1, 1977, 0 otherwise (N = 2,491) (2)[b]	Percent salary change July 1, 1976 to July 1, 1977[a] (N = 2,763) (3)[b]	(Percent salary change July 1, 1975 to July 1, 1977)/2[a] (N = 2,491) (4)[b]
Mean (standard deviation) of dependent variable	0.064	0.209	9.712	9.580
	(0.245)	(0.407)	(4.098)	(3.168)
Less than high school diploma (yes = 1)	0.089	−0.072	0.125	0.304
	(0.656)	(0.420)	(0.496)	(0.411)
High school diploma (yes = 1)	−0.390	−0.282	−0.057	−0.317
	(0.229)	(0.143)	(0.194)	(0.158)
Master's or law degree (yes = 1)	0.250	0.045	−0.486	−0.335
	(0.276)	(0.178)	(0.289)	(0.218)
Doctorate (yes = 1)	−0.002	0.169	−0.348	0.321
	(0.488)	(0.314)	(0.504)	(0.395)
Years of pre-company experience/10	−0.711	−0.741	−0.706	−0.743
	(0.318)	(0.220)	(0.287)	(0.249)
(Years of pre-company experience)^2/100	0.083	0.094	0.035	0.051
	(0.112)	(0.083)	(0.096)	(0.090)

Continued overleaf

TABLE IV (continued)

Years of company service/10[c]	−1.277	−0.818	−1.517	−0.743
	(0.303)	(0.211)	(0.283)	(0.240)
(Years of company service)^2/100[c]	0.227	0.096	0.256	0.058
	(0.085)	(0.062)	(0.076)	(0.067)
Ln(annual salary)[c]	—	—	−8.296	−9.255
			(0.799)	(0.613)
Performance rating 1 (worst; yes = 1)[c]	—	−1.517	−2.879	−2.155
		(0.743)	(0.684)	(0.488)
Performance rating 2 (yes = 1)[c]	—	−0.631	−1.735	−1.134
		(0.125)	(0.158)	(0.132)
Performance rating 1 or performance rating 2 (worst; yes = 1)[c,d]	−0.992	—	—	—
	(0.205)			
Performance rating 4 (best; yes = 1)[c]	−0.139	0.285	0.991	0.949
	(0.377)	(0.208)	(0.382)	(0.270)
Constant	yes	yes	yes	yes
Region dummies (3)	yes	yes	yes	yes
Grade level dummies (8; 11; 11; 11)[c,e]	yes	yes	yes	yes
χ^2	139.07	225.92	—	—
d.f.	21	25	—	—
R^2	—	—	0.147	0.178
SEE	—	—	3.802	2.888

a. Percent salary change was calculated as the natural logarithm of the annual salary in the ending year minus the natural logarithm of the annual salary in the starting year times 100.
b. Equations (1) and (2) were estimated using a maximum likelihood logit procedure, equations (3) and (4) using ordinary least squares.
c. Years of company service, salary rating, and grade level are as of July 1, 1976, if used in equations (1) and (3) and as of July 1, 1974, if used in equations (2) and (4).
d. Since none of those with the lowest performance rating in 1976 received a promotion between July 1, 1976, and July 1, 1977, the two bottom performance categories were combined in estimating equation (1).
e. Individuals in grade levels where either everyone or no one received a promotion were excluded from the logit samples.
Note. Standard errors are in parentheses below the coefficient estimates.

Promotion-related salary increases are a relatively small part of total salary increases at Company B. Between July 1, 1976, and July 1, 1977, only 9 percent of the total dollar amount of salary increases granted were associated with promotions, while 83 percent were labeled "merit" increases. Regression (3) demonstrates a substantial and significant positive partial correlation between 1976 relative performance rating and 1976–1977 percentage total salary increase. This result suggests that, while a part of so-called "merit" increases is relatively automatic, part does in fact reflect merit. The fourth regression shows that individuals with a given amount of schooling and experience who received higher performance ratings in 1974 received substantially and significantly higher average percentage salary increases between July 1, 1975, and July 1, 1977, than did their lower rated grade-level peers.

Critics of the use of performance ratings in the analysis presented in Section II might make one further argument: since a major use of ratings is to condition decision-making concerning promotions, rated performance is likely to reflect not only a manager's or professional's productivity in his current job but also his supervisor's assessment of his potential for advancement within the company. Holding education constant, more experienced (older) managers and professionals are typically less likely to be promoted out of any given grade level than less experienced (younger) managers and professionals and, hence, apt to be perceived as having limited potential for future advancement.[21] Thus, to the extent that performance ratings are affected by supervisors' assessments of individuals' future potential, more experienced workers might typically receive lower performance ratings than warranted simply on the basis of their current productivity.

The institutional basis for this argument is weak insofar as at both Company A and Company B, the instructions to supervisors preparing ratings clearly ask for an assessment of how well each employee is fulfilling the requirements of his or her current job, not for a forecast of the employee's productivity profile over his or her work life. At Company A supervisors are asked to make entries on a per-

21. Estimation of promotion equations similar to those in Table IV but without performance rating controls yielded education and experience coefficients virtually identical to those reported in Table IV. The coefficients from the equations without rating controls imply that, for a Company B employee with the relevant sample mean characteristics, an additional year of either pre-company experience or company service was associated with a 6 percent lower chance of receiving a promotion between July 1, 1976, and July 1, 1977, and with a 5 percent lower chance of receiving a promotion between July 1, 1975, and July 1, 1977.

formance review worksheet *"during the year* for the purpose of *providing supporting information for the annual employee assessment"* [our italics]; the intent is clearly that each employee's annual performance rating should reflect his or her performance during the appraisal year. At Company B, as seen above, the "Supervisor's Guide for Performance Review and Development Planning" states that "[r]eviews should be based on the employee's performance in his present position and *only for the period* [typically one year] *since his last review"* [our italics].[22]

Finally, it should be noted that at Company A, as at many U. S. corporations, each employee's promotability is formally assessed separately from his performance. A Company A supervisor who believed that a particular employee would do well in a higher level job would not have to convey that information to higher management indirectly by giving the employee a higher than deserved performance rating but could convey his belief directly by awarding the employee an appropriate promotability rating. Statistical results discussed in Medoff and Abraham [forthcoming] based on data from another U. S. manufacturing corporation indicate that the performance ratings and the promotability measure used at that company really do capture different things; while the performance ratings do very much better in explaining current salary, the promotability measure strongly dominates in predicting advancement to a higher grade level.[23]

In light of what we have been able to learn from our review of the relevant personnel literature, from the case studies we have done, and from various analyses with company personnel data, we feel very comfortable in assuming that performance ratings are good indicators of employees' relative productivity in the year of evaluation. Hence, we believe that this diverse evidence strongly supports the interpretation we have given to our results.

22. A small number of Company B supervisors were asked to "list the five most important factors (in order of importance) that you consider when you give a performance rating to a subordinate." Of the thirteen supervisors responding to this question, only one indicated that he considered an employee's potential when awarding a performance rating. For this supervisor, potential was the last factor listed, coming behind "achievement against action plan," "creative element brought to assignments," "need for supervision to complete assignments," and "attitude." All of the thirteen supervisors' responses were consistent with a belief that the actual practices followed by Company B raters closely matched the instructions they were given.

23. The Company A performance measure contributes more to explaining current salary than does the Company A promotability measure. However, we were not able to test whether at Company A the promotability measure dominated the performance measure in predicting promotions because the Company A file did not contain the historical performance rating and promotability rating information such a test would have required.

IV. Toward a Richer Explanation of the Experience-Earnings Relationship

The finding that at least a substantial fraction of the experience-earnings differential cannot be explained by an experience-performance differential among samples of white male managerial and professional employees at Companies A and B does not appear to be an aberration. We observed the same phenomenon in two comparable studies, Medoff [1977] and Medoff and Abraham [forthcoming], of a major airline and of another manufacturing firm. Dalton and Thompson [1971] also obtained similar results in an analysis (supported by the Harvard Business School) of the relative performance and earnings of 2,500 managerial and professional employees of different ages in six technology-based companies. Figure I is based on the information presented by Dalton and Thompson. The average percentile performance ranking of employees in each age group depicted in this figure is determined by supervisors' assessments of the "contribution made to the company during the past year" by their subordinates. Dalton and Thompson's findings imply that although engineers older than thirty five received relatively low performance ratings, they received relatively high earnings. In addition, the Dalton and Thompson results indicate a negative relationship between relative performance and age among first and second level managers after their late thirties.[24] While information on the managers' compensation was not presented, it would be most exceptional if there were a corresponding negative association between relative earnings and age among those past their late thirties. In comparing the relative salaries and performance of older and younger engineers, Dalton and Thompson [p. 59] write:

> While performance rankings begin to fall after the mid-thirties salaries continue to climb until the early forties before leveling off. This increasing discrepancy between a person's performance rankings and his "salary ranking" is one of the factors that makes project leaders reluctant to have older engineers assigned to their projects.

The divergence between experience-earnings and experience-performance differentials among managerial and professional employees in major U. S. firms raises a number of questions: (1) Why might the relative performance of a managerial or professional employee stay constant or decrease over much of his or her worklife? (2) What factors condition the salary determination process such that

24. For a summary of other studies concerning the relationship between experience or age and performance that strongly support the main assertion of this study, see Medoff and Abraham [April 1980].

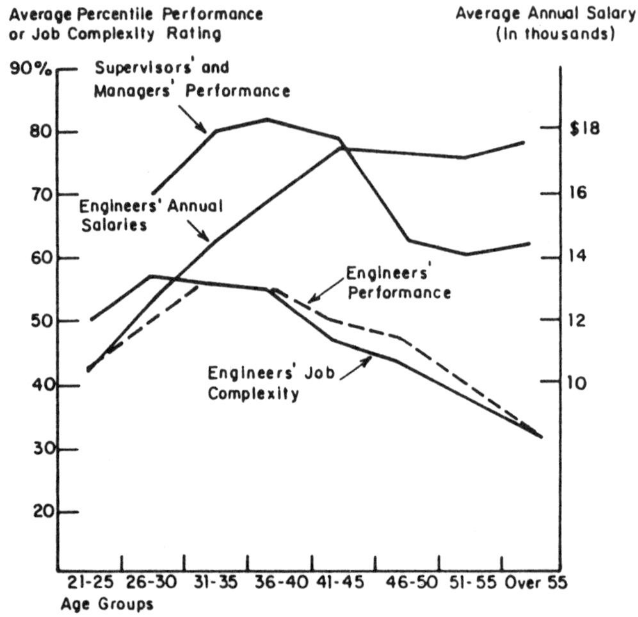

FIGURE I
Age, Performance, and Salary of Engineers; Age and Performance of Supervisors and Managers; Age and Job Complexity of Engineers
(Adapted from Dalton and Thompson [1971])

within grade levels the experience-earnings differential cannot be explained by an experience-performance differential? (3) While the observed divergence between these two differentials appears to be inconsistent with a strictly human capital interpretation of the experience-earnings profile, can the finding be reconciled with competitive theory?

Why Might Relative Performance Not Increase with Experience?

Human capital theory argues that with the passage of time workers accumulate productivity-augmenting skills. While on-the-job learning is undoubtedly of some importance, especially when a person is just beginning a job, other factors change over time in a direction that implies a decrease in workers' capacity for their assignments. Most importantly, during periods of rapid technological change, skills workers acquired during the formal education process may soon become obsolete. Skill obsolescence creates the largest problems for those in technical fields; for instance, revisions in college engineering curricula since the 1950s have given increasing emphasis to basic science and mathematics, which appears to have greatly reduced the "half-life" of an engineering education.[25] Similarly, the recent emphasis on quantitative techniques has most likely caused the business training of many older managers to become substantially obsolete.

A second factor that can be expected to affect performance is the stimulation (or lack of it) offered by an assignment. While learning most likely occurs with doing (at least for a short period of time), boredom is apt to set in eventually. Thus, the passage of time can come to have a negative effect on productivity, mediated by what might be called "on-the-job sensory deprivation."[26]

Motivation is a final potential determinant of within-grade-level performance that is also, most likely, a function of time. Within a grade level, workers with greater than average experience are relatively behind their cohort in terms of movement up the corporate hierarchy. Hence, within a grade level, workers with more experience are likely to have a stronger feeling that they are not on their company's fast track or on any track at all and thus become discouraged. This can lead to a reduction in effort expended on the job, especially since companies appear to avoid discharges (at least among those who are not new hires), demotions, and substantial cuts in relative salaries, fear of which might give employees an incentive to avoid slackening off. Dalton and Thompson [1971, p. 63] observed that the effort of the engineers they studied seemed to decline with age and offered the following explanation of the phenomenon:

> An older engineer often views the future with pessimism. He expects little positive reward, even if he does put forth greater effort.

Further, it has been claimed that older employees value promotions less highly than do younger employees.[27] This suggests that age can be expected to reduce the effort employees expend in trying to advance.

25. See Kaufman [1974].

26. For a discussion of the extensive literature on the importance of boredom in industrial settings, see Maier [1973]. While most of the relevant studies have focused primarily on production jobs, there is no reason why boredom should not have an effect on those who remain in a given nonproduction assignment. Indeed, Kaufman [June 1974, p. 379] argues that, "Although the emphasis on such techniques as job enrichment in recent years has focused mainly on nonprofessional employees, it is the professionals in the organization who are likely to be most affected by the intrinsic motivation of their work."

27. The issue of what rewards are most valued by different groups of employees has received a great deal of attention from industrial psychologists. The study by Hall and Mansfield [1975] lends support to the argument that older workers care less about promotions than younger workers. Their paper also contains references to earlier studies that reached similar conclusions.

Thus, even if obsolescence and encroaching boredom were not a problem for older workers in a job, motivational considerations could explain why, within grade levels, relative performance might not increase with experience. Next, we must address the more difficult question of why within-grade-level earnings do increase with experience.

Why Might Relative Earnings Increase with Experience Even If Relative Productivity Does Not?

At this point in time, neither we nor, to the best of our knowledge, anyone else can provide direct evidence in support of a new interpretation of the experience-earnings relationship; our findings demonstrate only that productivity-augmenting on-the-job training should play a substantially smaller role in any new explanation than it does under human capital theory. Moreover, since we feel that, to be of value, any new interpretation must have an empirical basis, all we wish to do at present is to suggest several alternatives whose validity must be assessed through the collection and analysis of additional information on the origins and functioning of firms' compensation policies.

First, for any of a variety of reasons, employees and employers may enter into implicit contracts that provide for relative earnings growth unrelated to changes in relative productivity over the course of a worker's tenure with the firm.[28] One reason for both firms and workers to prefer such a pay scheme is that deferring part of workers' compensation may deter quitting or behavior that would lead to discharge, increasing the expected present value of each employee's net contribution to the firm and (assuming competition) increasing the expected present value of each employee's lifetime compensation.[29] Moreover, the regular receipt of raises may improve workers' morale, which may in turn increase their productivity and present value of lifetime compensation. Alternatively, steep wage profiles might serve as a self-selection device. For example, workers with high innate quit propensities might be less likely to come to work for a firm that underpaid people at the start of their work lives and made up the difference later on.[30] A different rationale for implicit contracts providing that at least some workers be paid less than they produce

28. For discussion of another type of implicit contract, see Baily [1974] and Azariadis [1975].
29. One implicit contract model that offers a cheating deterrence story is developed in Lazear [1979].
30. See Salop and Salop [1976] for a formal development of this argument.

when young and more than they produce when old might rest on workers being risk-averse and owners of firms being risk-neutral. Not knowing at the beginning of their work lives whether their productivity would grow rapidly or slowly, workers might want a pay scheme that guaranteed annual pay increases of a certain amount independent of whether they turned out to be high-productivity or low-productivity employees. Still another possibility is that workers might prefer deferred compensation if the rate of return on assets the firm can earn exceeds the rate of return on assets accessible to the employee.

While all of the preceding seem at least on the surface to be plausible hypotheses, so far as we know none has any empirical basis. Furthermore, under implicit wage agreements of the sort discussed above, the firm could increase current profits by violating its pledge to pay long-service employees more than their productive value. Thus, some enforcement mechanism must be introduced. One potential *deus ex machina* is the firm's reputation (among present employees, future employees, and the society at large), which is a determinant of its long-run profitability. Whether or not such a mechanism exists is an open question.[31]

A second issue that merits consideration as a factor in the divergence between the earnings and performance of senior employees involves the relationship between a superior and subordinate. It is likely that the disutility from firing or reducing the relative salary of a long-time subordinate employee conditions a supervisor's decisions. This is just an extension of the point that factors other than profits are likely to enter the utility function of a manager.

A third issue which deserves mention is that workers have beliefs concerning "just" relative compensation. These beliefs could stem from certain societal values (e.g., "elders should be respected") and could be quite strong. Thus, a compensation policy which pays each employee his or her value of marginal product at each point in time may not be the policy that would be chosen by the marginal or average employee in the firm.

Each of these points is a member of a larger set that share the realization that individuals are quite likely to prefer a compensation policy which does not relate relative wages only to relative productivity. If any of the points is valid, long-run profit maximization need not imply that when an employee's relative earnings are increasing, the worker's relative performance could not be constant or decreasing. Thus, it is not true that the divergence of experience-earnings and

31. For an empirical analysis of this issue, see Medoff and Abraham [April 1980].

experience-performance profiles must be inconsistent with the tenets of competitive theory. However, whether it is or is not remains to be demonstrated.

V. CONCLUSION

This study has provided direct evidence concerning the relationship between experience and performance among managerial and professional employees doing similar work at two major U. S. corporations. The facts presented indicate that while, within grade levels, there is a strong positive association between experience and relative earnings, there is either no association or a negative association between experience and relative performance. Since the fraction of the experience-earnings relationship that occurs within grade levels is substantial, at a minimum a substantial portion of this relationship cannot be explained by the human capital model of productivity-augmenting on-the-job training.

An explanation of why in U. S. corporations more experienced workers doing a given job receive higher salaries than their less experienced, but no less productive, peers remains to be documented. At present, there are a number of theories that have been offered as consistent with our findings, but each of them suffers the same deficiency as the human capital theory about the experience-earnings profile: absence of an empirical basis. Nevertheless, we are confident that through future explorations within firms guided by those who administer and those who are affected by corporate compensation policies, the requisite evidence can be obtained. This will represent an important step toward an empirically based interpretation of experience-earnings differentials in particular and earnings differentials in general.

HARVARD UNIVERSITY
MASSACHUSETTS INSTITUTE OF TECHNOLOGY

REFERENCES

Azariadis, Costas, "Implicit Contracts and Underemployment Equilibria," *Journal of Political Economy,* LXXXIII, No. 6 (Dec. 1975), 1183–1202.

Baily, Martin, "Wages and Employment Under Uncertain Demand," *Review of Economic Studies,* XLI, No. 125 (Jan. 1974), 37–50.

Barrett, Richard S., *Performance Rating* (Chicago: Science Research Associates, Inc., 1966).

Bass, Bernard M., and Gerald V. Barrett, *Man, Work and Organizations: An Introduction to Industrial and Organizational Psychology* (Boston: Allyn and Bacon, Inc., 1972).

Becker, Gary S., *Human Capital: A Theoretical and Empirical Analysis with Special Reference to Education* (New York: National Bureau of Economic Research, 1964).

Borman, Walter C., "Effect of Instructions to Avoid Halo Error on Reliability and Validity of Performance Evaluation Ratings," *Journal of Applied Psychology*, LX, No. 5 (Oct. 1975), 556–60.

Dalton, Gene W., and Paul H. Thompson, "Accelerating Obsolescence of Older Engineers," *Harvard Business Review*, XLIX, No. 5 (Sept.–Oct. 1971), 57–67.

Ferguson, Leonard W., "The Value of Acquaintance Ratings in Criterion Research," *Personnel Psychology*, II, No. 1 (Spring 1949), 93–102.

Hall, Douglas T., and Roger Mansfield, "Relationships of Age and Seniority with Career Variables of Engineers and Scientists," *Journal of Applied Psychology*, LX, No. 2 (April 1975), 201–10.

Kaufman, H. G., *Obsolescence and Professional Career Development* (New York: Amacon, 1974).

——, "Relationship of Early Work Challenge to Job Performance, Professional Contributions, and Competence of Engineers," *Journal of Applied Psychology*, LIX, No. 3 (June 1974), 377–79.

Landy, Frank J., and Don A. Trumbo, *Psychology of Work Behavior* (Homewood, IL: The Dorsey Press, 1976).

Lawler, Edward E., "The Multitrait-Multirater Approach to Measuring Managerial Job Performance," *Journal of Applied Psychology*, LI, No. 5 (Oct. 1967), 369–81.

Lazear, Edward P., "Why Is There Mandatory Retirement?" *Journal of Political Economy*, LXXXVII, No. 6 (Dec. 1979), 1261–84.

Maier, Norman R. F., *Psychology in Industrial Organizations* (Boston: Houghton Mifflin Company, 1973).

McCormick, Ernest J., and Joseph Tiffin, *Industrial Psychology* (Englewood Cliffs, NJ: Prentice-Hall, Inc., 1974).

Medoff, James L., "The Earnings Function: A Glimpse Inside the Black Box," mimeographed, Dec. 1977.

——, and Katharine G. Abraham, "Are Those Paid More Really More Productive?: The Case of Experience," *Journal of Human Resources*, forthcoming.

——, and ——, "Involuntary Terminations under Explicit, Implicit, and No Employment Contracts," mimeographed, April 1980.

Mincer, Jacob, *Schooling, Experience, and Earnings* (New York: National Bureau of Economic Research, 1974).

Nerlove, Marc, and S. James Press, *Univariate and Multivariate Log-Linear and Logistic Models* (Santa Monica, CA: The Rand Corporation, 1973).

Rothe, H. F., "The Relation of Merit Ratings to Length of Service," *Personnel Psychology*, II, No. 2 (Summer 1949), 237–42.

Rundquist, E. A., and R. H. Bittner, "Using Ratings to Validate Personnel Instruments: A Study in Method," *Personnel Psychology*, I, No. 2 (Summer 1948), 163–84.

Salop, Joanne, and Steven Salop, "Self-Selection and Turnover in the Labor Market," this *Journal*, XC, No. 4 (Nov. 1976), 619–27.

Stockford, Lee, and H. W. Bissell, "Factors Involved in Establishing a Merit-Rating Scale," *Personnel*, XXVI, No. 2 (Sept. 1949), 94–116.

Whitlock, Gerald H., "Application of the Psychophysical Law to Performance Evaluation," *Journal of Applied Psychology*, XXXXVII, No. 1 (Feb. 1963), 15–23.

[5]

Why Is There Mandatory Retirement?

Edward P. Lazear

University of Chicago and National Bureau of Economic Research

This paper offers an explanation of the use of mandatory-retirement clauses in labor contracts. It argues that the date of mandatory retirement is chosen to correspond to the date of voluntary retirement, but the nature of the optimal wage profile results in a discrepancy between spot wage and spot VMP (value of the worker's marginal product). This is because it is preferable to pay workers less than VMP when young and more than VMP when old. By doing so, the "agency" problem is solved, so the contract with mandatory retirement is Pareto efficient. A theory of agency is presented and empirical evidence which supports the hypothesis is provided.

Mandatory retirement has recently become an important issue. Congress has enacted legislation that extends coverage under the Age Discrimination in Employment Act to workers up to age 70 rather than to age 65 as it previously stood. This essentially outlaws the use of mandatory retirement at age 65, a common practice. Furthermore, Congress is considering the extension of the Age Discrimination Act such that exemption would be eliminated entirely. The current legislation already does this for federal workers. In order to understand whether or not legislation outlawing mandatory retirement would benefit society, it is first essential to ask why this institution exists. The primary task of this paper is to offer an analysis of that institution, with testable implications, and then to discuss policy proposals that are consistent with and implied by this analysis. As an outgrowth, a

The author wishes to thank Charles Brown, Dennis Carlton, Linda Edwards, Victor Fuchs, Nathaniel Gregory, Victoria Lazear, Jacob Mincer, Sam Peltzman, Melvin Reder, Sherwin Rosen, and Lester Telser for useful suggestions. Victoria Lazear provided substantial assistance in solving the problem discussed in Section IA of the text.

[*Journal of Political Economy*, 1979, vol. 87, no. 6]

theory of agency is presented which provides insight on how to compensate an agent in a manner that creates a harmony of interest between the principal and the agent.

There are many defenses and explanations of mandatory retirement. Most rely on the notion that a worker's productivity declines significantly after some age, say 65, and that mandatory retirement is the employer's way to deal with this reduced productivity. Yet, there is a significant diversity of talent in the labor force. No one claims that only the most talented individuals are the ones who can find jobs. Instead, economists believe that differences in wage rates reflect differences in productivity. The same is true of older workers. If older workers are less productive than younger workers, employers in a competitive labor market would be forced to pay older workers a lower wage rate than they pay younger workers. There is no necessity to lay off the older workers simply because their productivity is not as high as the younger workers'. In fact, very young workers earn less than middle-aged workers as a reflection of their lower productivity. Yet, we do not find researchers arguing that the minimum age for employment should be 45. The correct question then is, Why does employment rather than wage adjust?

Some have argued that morale would be adversely affected by lowering the wages of older workers. But it is not obvious that terminating workers rather than lowering their wages will improve the morale of the remaining work force. A 60-year-old worker who is faced with approaching termination is not necessarily going to have a better attitude than one who knows his wage rate will be lowered 5 years from now. Another view often expressed is that one cannot judge the decrease in productivity so that it would be impossible to adjust wages accordingly. But laying off a worker adjusts his wage rate to zero. This is a poorer approximation of his true productivity decline than any smooth wage adjustment. Furthermore, employers face the problem of gauging productivity for all workers. There is nothing unique about 65-year-olds in this regard. Thus, a productivity decline is not a sufficient explanation for the existence of mandatory retirement. One must ask why the productivity decline is dealt with by terminating the worker rather than by reducing his wages.[1]

Another "explanation" is that a uniform retirement policy avoids the disadvantage of discrimination between employees. Two questions arise. First, there is nothing that requires that a uniform retirement policy be one that has a provision for mandatory retirement. One could easily set up a flexible retirement scheme, where payment varies with length of service, that is invariant across individuals but

[1] See Gordon (1960), Kreps (1961), National Industrial Conference Board (1964), and U.S. Department of Health, Education, and Welfare (1976) for some commonly offered explanations of mandatory retirement.

does not require mandatory retirement at any given age. The second problem is that employers discriminate between employees at every level: some are promoted, others are terminated, others experience wage gains while others do not, and the existence of differences between workers is dealt with in many ways. Why should employers or employees favor a system that reduces the ability of the employer to compensate workers differentially?

Another "explanation" is that mandatory retirement creates promotion possibilities for younger workers. This explanation ignores at least two factors: First, young workers know that they will become old workers at some date in the future. They care about the present value of some lifetime wage path rather than the present value of any segment of it. Although they would prefer to be promoted when young, they also would, if their retirement is truly mandatory, prefer to continue working when old. Second, promotion may be interpreted as an increase in one's wage rate (and perhaps a change in the accompanying job title) that occurs as one's productivity rises over the life cycle. The firm will, in competition, pay the worker his marginal product, no matter how old he is. Thus, there would be no incentive for a firm to mandatorily retire a worker whose marginal product was equal to or greater than his wage rate to "promote" a younger worker.

Needless to say, none of the so-called explanations satisfactorily describes why it is optimal to terminate a worker at a certain age rather than reduce his wages accordingly and in a continuous fashion. In fact, explanations of mandatory retirement suffer from the same drawback as explanations of layoffs. Economists have been puzzled by layoffs as an alternative to spot VMP payments as well. I suggest that the two phenomena are linked.

The purpose of this paper is to give a theoretical explanation for the existence of mandatory retirement that is consistent with economic theory and then to test this theory empirically. Before proceeding, it is important to make clear what is meant by "mandatory retirement." The phenomenon that we wish to explain has the following characteristics: First, there is a definite date when a contract (either explicit or implicit) ends. Second, at that date there will be some workers who will wish to remain with the firm at their previous wage rates, but whom the firm will not choose to employ at that wage.[2]

[2] Given this definition, the institution of term contracts with up-or-out employment arrangements (i.e., arrangements where the worker is either promoted or forced to leave the firm) is a form of mandatory-retirement contract. The model to be presented in this paper could be applied to the analysis of that problem as well. In a recent theoretical paper by S. Freeman (1977), retirement and promotion decisions are linked. His model will not, per se, yield mandatory retirement, however. The reason is that in his framework there is no reason to distinguish between lump sums at critical time points and smooth payment streams with the same present value. The former will not yield mandatory retirement as it is commonly used.

Thus, mandatory retirement has the characteristic that at some time T, the worker earned some wage $\overline{W}$. But at $T + \epsilon$, the firm is no longer willing to employ the worker at wage $\overline{W}$, nor is the firm's wage-offer function continuous at that point (i.e., it takes a discrete jump downward for some workers). This story, by definition, implies that at T the firm is paying some workers more than the value of their marginal products. This is a necessary condition for the firm to desire to terminate the worker, and this is the bottom line to virtually all explanations of mandatory retirement. The argument here will be that, for reasons discussed below, it will be optimal for firms and workers to have a payment scheme such that the worker receives less than his marginal product when young and more than his marginal product when old. This implies that there be some date at which the firm is no longer willing to pay the worker his current wage. He is, therefore, mandatorily retired.

In some recent work, Feldstein (1976) has employed the notion that a worker's commitment to the firm tends to be permanent. He presents evidence which reveals that a large proportion of total job separations consist of layoffs, and, further, that layoffs are, in large part, temporary. That is, the worker is reemployed by the same firm which has laid him off in the first place. The lifetime commitment to the firm is the starting point from which we attempt to explain the existence of mandatory retirement. A sketch of that explanation follows.

Workers care about the present value of their wage stream over the lifetime (i.e., their wealth), whereas firms care about the present value of the worker's marginal product over his lifetime. Other things equal, a worker would be indifferent between a wage path which paid him a constant dollar amount over his lifetime and another one which had the same present value but paid him less when he was young and more when he was old. Other things equal, the firm would be indifferent between paying the two streams. But other things are not equal. It will be shown that a wage profile which pays workers less when they are young and more when they are old will allow the worker and firm to behave in such a way as to raise the present value of marginal product over the lifetime. For example, by deferring payment a firm may induce a worker to perform at a higher level of effort. Both firm and worker may prefer this high wage/high effort combination to a lower wage/lower effort path that results from a payment scheme that creates incentives to shirk. Thus, it may pay the firm and worker to set up a scheme such that the worker is paid less than his marginal product when he is young and more than his marginal product when he is old to compensate.

The efficiency condition for retirement is that the value of the worker's marginal product is just equal to his reservation wage. This will determine the optimal date of retirement. But if workers are paid less than their marginal products when they are young and more when old, their wage rate at T (the optimal retirement date) will exceed VMP and, therefore, the reservation wage. Although this is the efficient and equilibrium date of retirement (the date such that the present value of the lifetime marginal product equals the present value of the lifetime wage payment), the worker will not voluntarily retire at this date because wage exceeds reservation wage. Wage exceeds reservation wage at this point because that payment scheme produces a superior lifetime profile which workers prefer ex ante. Therefore, mandatory retirement is required to induce them to leave the firm at the optimal date. Thus, the existence of mandatory retirement is optimal from the worker's point of view. The worker is actually better off as the result of a contract which specifies a mandatory termination date. This allows the worker's present value of marginal product to be higher than it would be in the absence of such a contract, and these "rents" will spill over to the worker.

I. The Model

Consider an individual who has a value of marginal product over his lifetime, $V^*(t)$, and a wage rate $W^*(t)$ as illustrated in figure 1. This worker is receiving an amount less than his VMP for $t < t^*$ and an amount greater than his marginal product for $t > t^*$. Let T be the point such that

$$V^*(T) = \tilde{W}(T), \tag{1}$$

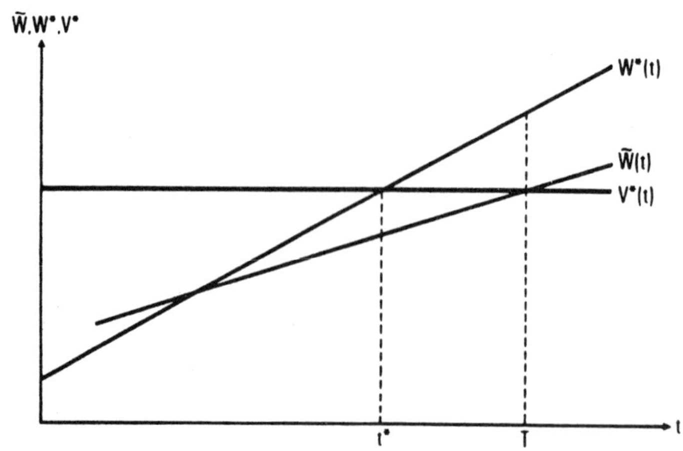

FIG. 1

where $\tilde{W}(t)$ is the individual's reservation wage at t. Any $W^*(t)$ path that satisfies the condition that

$$\int_0^T W^*(t)e^{-rt}dt = \int_0^T V^*(t)e^{-rt}dt \quad (2)$$

will be an equilibrium path.[3] That is, other things equal, a worker is indifferent between a path which pays him his spot VMP at each point in time and one which pays him a wage less than VMP initially and more than VMP later. As long as each path yields the same present value, workers have no preference. The argument in this paper, however, is that other things are not equal. A path which pays less than VMP when young and more than VMP when old may yield the worker a higher lifetime wealth. The reason is that a steeper path reduces the worker's incentive to cheat, shirk, and engage in malfeasant behavior. That is, it affects the amount of output per hour worked by altering the worker's incentive structure. This generates a preference for a path that has a wage greater than VMP at the date when VMP equals the reservation wage. Since this is the point when retirement should occur, and since workers would not voluntarily leave at this point (since $W^*[T] > \tilde{W}[T]$), "mandatory" retirement is a necessary consequence. But what is important here is that retirement is "mandatory" only in an ex post sense. It is negotiated in advance and is part of an optimal contractual arrangement which insures that firm-worker separation occurs at the appropriate time.[4]

A. *Incentives-induced Mandatory Retirement*

A steeper-than-VMP wage path is generated when we consider the notion of optimal effort, honesty, and malfeasance on the job.[5] These

[3] This assumes that the worker can borrow and lend at rate r. To the extent that this does not hold, a utility-maximizing framework must replace the wealth-maximizing one. The fundamental analysis and its conclusions, although somewhat more complex, remain essentially the same.

[4] That is, the worker is "mandatorily retired" at T. This is not the same as saying that the worker leaves the firm at T. He is retired from his old contract, but not necessarily from his old firm. For example, at age 65 many professors are mandatorily retired from their former contracts and renegotiate a new contract frequently called "emeritus." The wage rate changes, as do the working conditions. In this case, the worker stays with the former firm. In most cases, however, "mandatory retirement" will be coupled with firm-worker separation as well. The reason is that at T when renegotiation occurs, it is no longer necessarily the case that the worker-firm match and corresponding working conditions (hours, flexibility, effort, etc.) that were optimal between 0 and T will also be optimal between T and retirement (or death). For example, older workers may want shorter and more flexible hours with limited responsibility (or they may want zero hours of work, i.e., retirement). This is not necessarily the type of work conditions/wage trade-off that they would choose between 0 and T. If not, T will be characterized by a reshuffling of workers among firms. What is crucial is the termination of the former contract.

[5] Papers which have dealt with this issue are Becker and Stigler (1974) and Stiglitz (1975).

are treated symmetrically because performing at a level of effort lower than expected is merely a special type of worker "cheating."

Let a worker's marginal product at time t be given by $V^*(t)$; his reservation wage is $\tilde{W}(t)$, and the optimal wage path is $W^*(t)$ (as defined above). Worker "cheating" is assumed to be detectable immediately and the worker is dismissed when he cheats.[6] A worker will cheat when the present value of cheating exceeds the cost of cheating. The major cost of cheating is the loss of the current job which carries with it earnings greater than the individual's reservation wage. This immediately suggests that if wage paths are steeper than VMP paths (and reservation wage paths as the result), this will discourage cheating by workers since it raises the costs of termination. Stated otherwise, a firm which withholds payment until the end of an individual's work life is less likely to experience worker cheating than one that pays workers more at the beginning and less at the end of the worker's career. But if the former path discourages cheating, it results in a higher expected lifetime value of the marginal product. Thus, workers produce more and are paid more if their wage paths are steeper than VMP. But this implies that $W^*(T) > \tilde{W}(T)$. Given that, the worker would not choose to retire at T. Since his VMP is equal to his reservation wage at T, however, it is optimal for him to leave the firm. Therefore, both worker and firm will, at $t = 0$, agree on a "mandatory" retirement date of T. I reiterate that it is only mandatory in the sense that, once at T, the worker would prefer to continue working at $W^*(T)$ if it were available. It is not available because his VMP is less than $W^*(T)$, his reservation wage equals his VMP at that point, and he has been paid exactly the full present value of his lifetime VMP at point T. Time T is the date of ex post mandatory, but ex ante voluntary, retirement.

In order to determine the exact shape of the $W^*(t)$ path, it is necessary to formalize the model: To make the model completely general, we start out with the possibility not only of worker cheating, but of firm cheating as well. Firm "cheating" takes the form of promising a worker a stream $W^*(t)$ from 0 to T, but dismissing the honest worker at some $t < T$ and depriving him of the promised wage stream. The firm's cheating may be intentional or may be "unintentional," if, for example, the firm goes bankrupt before T.[7] Initially, let us assume that firm cheating is unintentional or exogenous and that the distribution of dates t at which the firm "cheats" on the worker is known

[6] This is a result rather than an assumption. It is true because any worker who finds it optimal to cheat at $t = t_0$ will cheat with certainty at $t > t_0$. Therefore, the firm gains by replacing him with a worker whose probability of cheating is less than one at that point.

[7] "Unintentional" is in quotes because the value of bankruptcy depends upon how much the firm owes workers and so is at least in part endogenous.

and given by $\bar{g}(t)$. Exogeneity of $\bar{g}(t)$ will be dropped below, but it is useful to adopt the assumption for comparison's sake.

Let the ith worker be assigned a $\theta_i \sim f(\theta_i)$, where θ is defined as the benefit that the worker derives from cheating. It may reflect the utility increase he derives when he works at a low effort level rather than the high effort level promised, or it may reflect something as tangible as revenue from the sale of stolen merchandise. For simplicity, assume that θ_i is constant over the worker's lifetime. If the worker "cheats," assume that he is caught with certainty and that as a result he is terminated. (The problem is complicated somewhat if there is a time lag for detection. As it turns out, that will necessitate pensions as part of the optimal wage path. For now this is ignored.)[8] The expected rent to a worker at time t is

$$R(t) = e^{rt} \int_t^T \Big\{ W^*(\tau) - \tilde{W}(\tau) - \bar{g}(\tau)e^{r\tau} \int_\tau^T [W^*(\delta) - \tilde{W}(\delta)]e^{-r\delta}d\delta \Big\} e^{-r\tau}d\tau. \quad (3)$$

This rather complicated expression is the value in period t dollars of nominal rents to the worker $[W^*(t) - \tilde{W}(t)]$ minus the probability that the firm will cheat on the worker in the form of early termination $(\bar{g}[\tau])$ times the cost to the worker of that cheating $(e^{r\tau} \int_\tau^T [W^*(\delta) - \tilde{W}(\delta)]e^{-r\delta}d\delta)$. The worker cheats at time t if $\theta_i > R(t)$. From this, $\bar{f}(t)$, the probability of worker cheating at time t, is derived:

$$\bar{f}(t) = \begin{cases} F[R(0)] & \text{for } t = 0, \\ f[R(t)][R'(t)] & \text{for } R' < 0 \text{ and } t > 0, \\ 0 & \text{for } R' > 0 \text{ and } t > 0, \end{cases} \quad (4)$$

where $F \equiv 1 - \int_{-\infty}^{R} f(\theta)d\theta$. That is, at $t = 0$, some individuals, $F[R(0)]$, will have $\theta > R(0)$ and will choose to cheat. If $R'(t) > 0$, then those who did not cheat at $t = 0$ are even less likely to do so now or $\bar{f}(t) = 0$. If $R'(t) < 0$, some individuals who did not cheat at zero, namely, $f[R(t)]$ $[R'(t)]$, will now find it profitable to cheat, so $\bar{f}(t) = f[R(t)]$ $[R'(t)]$.

The problem then for the firm is to choose T and $W^*(t)$ so as to maximize the payment to the worker subject to the constraints that lifetime earnings equal lifetime expected VMP and that T is efficient. This can be written:

[8] It is a trivial extension of the model to allow the worker a probability of detection less than one. In the terminology below, $R(t)$ is merely replaced by $R(t) \cdot P$, where P is the probability of detection.

maximize over T, $W^*(t)$

$$\text{wealth} = \int_0^T \left\{ W^*(t) + \bar{f}(t)\left[\theta - e^{rt}\int_t^T W^*(\tau)e^{-r\tau}d\tau\right] - \bar{g}(t)e^{rt}\int_t^T W^*(\tau)e^{-r\tau}d\tau \right\} e^{-rt}dt \tag{5}$$

subject to

$$\begin{aligned} \text{wealth} &= \text{expected VMP} \\ &= \int_0^T \left[V^*(t) - \bar{f}(t)e^{rt}\int_t^T V^*(\tau)e^{-r\tau}d\tau - \bar{f}(t)c(t) - \bar{g}(t)e^{rt}\int_t^T V^*(\tau)e^{-r\tau}d\tau \right] e^{-rt}dt - \xi, \end{aligned} \tag{6}$$

where ξ are hiring costs and the boundary condition is

$$V^*(T) - \bar{f}(T)c(T) = \tilde{W}(T). \tag{7}$$

Equation (5) says wealth is equal to the wage rate ($W^*[t]$) plus the probability of worker cheating, $\bar{f}(t)$, times the gain from worker cheating to the worker (θ) minus the cost to the worker ($e^{rt}\int_t^T W^*[\tau]e^{-r\tau}d\tau$), minus the probability of firm cheating, [$\bar{g}(t)$], times the cost to the worker ($e^{rt}\int_t^T W^*[\tau]e^{-r\tau}d\tau$). Expected VMP consists of nominal VMP, [$V^*(t)$], minus the costs imposed by worker cheating equal to the sum of the loss of his output between t and T ($e^{rt}\int_t^T V^*[\tau]e^{-r\tau}d\tau$), and exogenous costs imposed on the firm, $c(t)$,[9] times the probability that the worker cheats, [$\bar{f}(t)$], minus the probability that the firm cheats, [$\bar{g}(t)$], times the effect on marginal product ($e^{rt}\int_t^T V^*[\tau]e^{-r\tau}d\tau$), minus hiring costs, ξ. Equation (7) says that net VMP at T must equal the reservation wage $\tilde{W}(t)$ for efficiency. The complete solution to the problem is complicated and relegated to an appendix.[10] We merely sketch the solution here.

If $\bar{g}(t)$ is exogenous, that is, the probability of the firm cheating on the worker is independent of $W^*(t)$, the solution boils down to choosing $W^*(t)$ so as to set $\bar{f}(t) = 0$, that is, completely eliminating worker cheating. Payment should be weighted sufficiently toward the end of the career so that at every point t it does not pay for the worker to cheat. The exact form of the solution depends upon the distribution of θ_i. In the simplest case, where all workers have $\theta_i = \bar{\theta}$, the solution is indeterminate, but it has the characteristic that at $W^*(T)$, $W^*(T) - \tilde{W}(T) \geq \bar{\theta}$, and that $V^*(T) = \tilde{W}(T)$.[11] The intuition behind this solution

[9] The $c(t)$ may be zero or positive. One example is the loss suffered when the worker takes customers with him upon his departure.

[10] Available from author upon request.

[11] The Becker-Stigler (1974) solution is a special case of this general form.

is clear: If the worker cheats, he imposes cost $c(t)$ on the firm, but receives $\bar{\theta}$. Therefore, the cheating lifetime net VMP and wealth is

$$\int_0^T V^*(t)e^{-rt}dt + [\bar{\theta} - c(t^*)]e^{-rt^*}$$

if the worker cheats at t^*. If he never cheats, his lifetime VMP and wealth is simply $\int_0^T V^*(t)e^{-rt}dt$. As long as $c(t) > \bar{\theta}$, the cost imposed on the firm by worker cheating exceeds the value of cheating to the worker (stolen machines sell at a price less than the replacement cost to the firm) and the zero-cheating path will be preferred. The zero-cheating equilibrium is produced by paths having $R(t) > \theta$ for all t.

Figure 2 illustrates some possible $W^*(t)$ paths. One path is *ABP*. Here the worker receives a constant amount less than his VMP over his lifetime, but receives a large lump sum at T to set present values of payment and marginal products equal. There is no worker cheating because $R(t)$ is always greater than $\bar{\theta}$; it never pays to cheat. Another possibility is the more conventional *LQ* curve. Again, there is no worker cheating, and at T the worker receives more than his marginal product. Again, of course, present values of lifetime earnings and marginal products are equal. Another possibility is *LKHQ*. This is the Becker-Stigler (1974) solution where the worker posts a "bond" equal to *LM*, is paid interest on it (*KM*), and gets back the principal at T (*HQ* = *LM*). A fourth possibility is *LHNX*. Here the worker is paid less than his VMP initially, more at T, and receives a pension equal to *NX*. As long as the present value of remaining rent exceeds $\bar{\theta}$ and the present

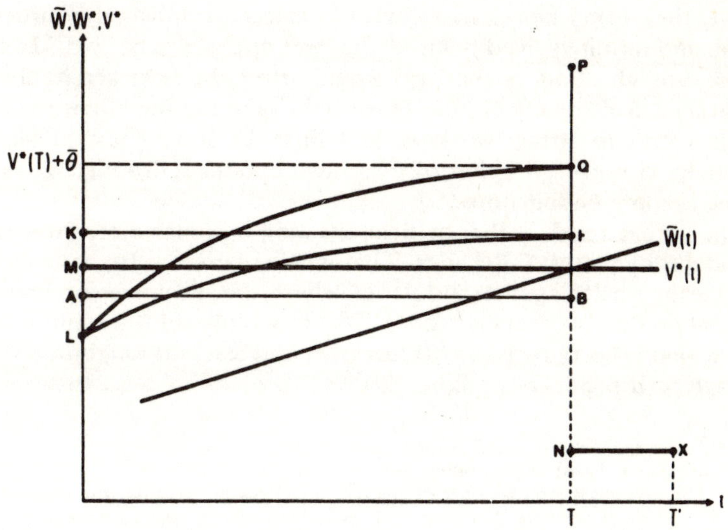

FIG. 2

value of earnings equals present value of payments, this will be an optimal path. This path is probably the most typical.

The important point that comes out of the above analysis is that in all these cases, $W^*(T) > \tilde{W}(T)$. That is, if the worker could continue to earn $W^*(T)$, he would not choose to retire. If he were paid $V^*(T)$, on the other hand, he would choose to retire. Mandatory retirement is warranted because it is optimal for the worker to retire at T, but paying him a wage that would induce him to do so voluntarily would result in more than the optimal amount of cheating. Thus, a path that is optimal from a cheating point of view coupled with mandatory retirement is superior for both worker and firm.

Without going into the details of the analysis, suffice it to say that when $\bar{g}(t)$, the probability of firm cheating, is endogenous and influenced by the amount owed to the worker, the indeterminacy disappears (as it does for certain distributions of θ_t). The complete analysis is contained in an appendix.[12] The sense of the main result is this: As the amount owed to the worker above his marginal product increases, the gains to the firm from cheating on the worker increase. Therefore, minimizing the sum of cheating costs (which is essentially what [5] does) will trade off reduced worker cheating against increased firm cheating as $W^*(t)$ becomes more end weighted. This eliminates the indeterminacy and tends to reduce the end weighting of the payment stream. Mandatory retirement will still be required, however, since $W^*(T) > \tilde{W}(T)$.

As an aside, it is interesting to ask whether or not $\bar{g}(t)$ is endogenous. That is, does the firm have a greater incentive to cheat when it owes the worker more? In a world of perfect (or unbiased)[13] information and infinitely lived firms, the answer appears to be "No." In that case, any cheating by the firm would affect the next generation of workers' assessments of $\bar{g}(t)$. This would raise the wage that the firm has to pay to attract workers, and this cost should just offset the benefit. However, if either of these assumptions is dropped, $\bar{g}(t)$ may well become endogenous.[14]

A second result is that as firm cheating becomes more profitable and $\bar{g}(t)$ increases, T declines. That is, mandatory retirement should occur at earlier ages in industries where the incentive for firms to cheat on their workers is higher. This is because the left-hand side of equation (7) is reduced as $\bar{f}(t)$ increases and less end weighting of the wage path produces a higher $\bar{f}(t)$.

[12] Again, available from the author upon request.

[13] See Fama (1978) on this point.

[14] This suggests that a firm with an unanticipated decrease in its horizon will be more likely to cheat on workers. Thus, one may expect to find that the incidence of pension default and early termination is higher in declining industries.

One final and important implication results from the analysis: Other things constant (including education, ability, etc.), workers who have steeper profiles are more likely to have entered a long-term contract designed to prevent cheating. A necessary consequence of this contract is mandatory retirement. Therefore, individuals whose lifetime wage growth rate is higher than anticipated are more likely to have mandatory retirement. This somewhat counterintuitive implication that the high-performing, honest workers, with high wage growth rates, are more likely to have mandatory retirement is tested in the empirical section. The prediction is unequivocally supported by that evidence.

Note that pensions are a possibility, but not a necessity up to this point. Path *LHNX* in figure 2, for example, is one possible path. Two added considerations make pensions part of the optimal determinate wage path. The first, and most obvious, is a progressive income tax structure which makes a lump-sum payment at T less desirable than a smooth pension flow from T to T'. The second is relaxation of the assumption that cheating is observed immediately. If there were a lag time required for detection, then it would be optimal to withhold some payment until after T, or until the results were in, as it were. Pensions would act as such a holdback. This argument is somewhat less compelling than the first, however, because it requires that firms be allowed to terminate pension payments after they have already begun to make them. As an empirical phenomenon, the significance of midstream termination is doubtful.[15]

B. Stochastic Variation

Another consideration is important. There is a potential inefficiency in this model which is tied to the question of early retirement. One observes that individuals sometimes leave the firm before T, the date of mandatory retirement. Does this suggest a mistake or inefficiency implicit in the lifetime contract? The answer is no. Consider figure 3.

Suppose that we introduce a stochastic component to the analysis such that at time t^*, the worker receives an unexpected offer of $\tilde{W}_{t^*}$ from another firm. Under these circumstances, the worker would not leave the original firm, because $W^*(t^*) > \tilde{W}_{t^*}$. However, if $\tilde{W}_{t^*}$ mea-

[15] An alternative justification for a wage profile which rises more steeply than VMP is risk aversion coupled with uncertainty about VMP. If some workers will have low VMPs in the future relative to others, but neither workers nor firms can identify these workers initially, workers will prefer to buy "insurance" from the firm. This notion, which is described in detail in an earlier version of this paper, is related to the insurance ideas of Baily (1974), Azariadis (1975), Grossman (1977), and the self-selection analyses of Rothschild and Stiglitz (1976) and Salop and Salop (1976). The empirical evidence, however, is at odds with this view and so I only mention it in passing.

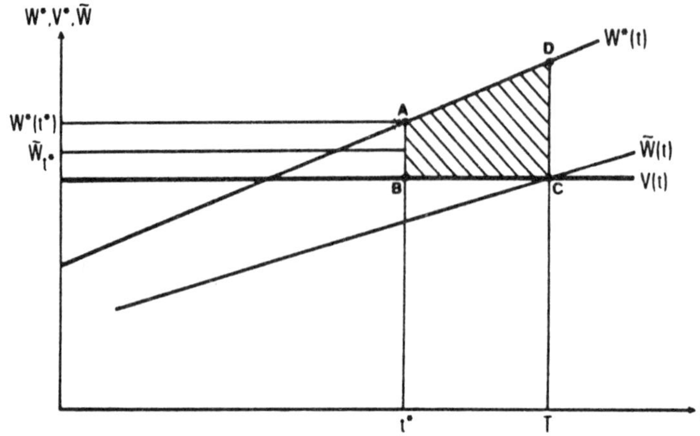

FIG. 3

sures his VMP in the alternative firm, it is inefficient for him to remain with the original firm since $\tilde{W}_{t^*} > V(t^*)$. That is, his social value is greater at the alternative firm, yet he remains with the original firm only because his wage rate is higher there. This is clearly inefficient, and it is unnecessary. An appropriate severance payment will eliminate the inefficiency which seems at first glance to be a necessary consequence of long-term contracts. At t^*, the original firm still "owes" the worker area *ABCD* as payment (with interest) for service rendered between 0 and t_0. If the firm were to make a lump-sum payment to the worker at t^* equal to area *ABCD* in t^* dollars, the firm would have paid out over the worker's lifetime an amount exactly equal to the present value of his marginal product. This is the equilibrium condition for the firm's payment through T, so the firm suffers no loss by allowing the worker to quit at t^* with severance pay. The worker, however, is better off. As the result of taking the job at the alternative firm and receiving severance pay, he will receive the present value of $W(t)$ from 0 to T plus the present value of the difference $\tilde{W}(t^*) - V(t)$ from t^* to T. That is,

$$\text{the present value of earnings} = \int_0^{t^*} W^*(\tau)e^{-r\tau}d\tau + \int_{t^*}^{T} [W^*(\tau) - V^*(\tau)]e^{-r\tau} + \int_{t^*}^{T} \tilde{W}(t^*)e^{-r\tau}d\tau$$

$$= \int_0^{T} W^*(\tau)e^{-r\tau}d\tau - \int_{t^*}^{T} V^*(\tau)e^{-r\tau}d\tau + \int_{t^*}^{T} \tilde{W}(t^*)e^{-r\tau}d\tau$$

$$= \int_0^{T} W^*(\tau)e^{-r\tau}d\tau + \int_{t^*}^{T} [\tilde{W}(t^*) - V^*(\tau)]e^{-r\tau}d\tau,$$

which exceeds his earnings at the original firm $\left[= \int_0^T W^*(\tau)e^{-r\tau}d\tau\right]$ by the difference between $\tilde{W}(t^*)$ and V^* for the appropriate period. Thus, the worker and firm behave efficiently as long as severance pay is permitted.

One form that the severence-pay arrangement may take is increased pension benefits. Thus, we expect that workers who retire early would receive a larger expected pension than those who work through T. This is a characteristic of many pension plans (as will be discussed below).

The qualification raised in the last few paragraphs is an important one because it reconciles the phenomenon of early retirement with the lifetime payment scheme suggested earlier. It is also important because it means that unexpected changes either in the alternative use of time (as another employment offer or a change in the value of leisure, say, due to poor health) or in the value of the marginal product at the original firm (say, due to business-cycle conditions) do not result in an inefficiency. This long-term contract carries no immobility costs as long as severance pay (or pension adjustment) is permitted.

C. *The Choice of* T

The past few pages have argued that mandatory retirement is the necessary consequence of an optimal wage scheme which makes both workers and firms better off. There, the existence of some T or date of mandatory retirement was determined optimal. But one important issue remains: The formal model presented in Section A yields a solution for T given the parameters. However, one observes that the actual distribution of T is not as smooth as one might expect from that model. That is, the reservation wage functions are likely to be smooth, and this would imply a smooth distribution of T. The real world seems to be characterized by a set of T's that take particular values. One source (Banker's Trust 1975), which sampled firms which employed a total of 8.4 million workers (about 10 percent of the civilian labor force) in 1970–75, reports that of firms which stated an age of mandatory retirement, over 87 percent had that age equal to 65. This suggests that there is some exogenous factor which pulls T to age 65. An obvious candidate for prime mover is the social security provision which becomes available at age 65. Consider the reservation wage function in figures 1 and 2. If at 65 an individual becomes eligible for a social security subsidy to leisure, the reservation wage $\tilde{W}(t)$ is likely to take a discrete jump upward at 65. This means that voluntary retirement takes a discrete jump at age 65 as well, which implies that the choice of T such that age equals 65 is most likely. An implication of this argument is that before social security, the distribution of mandatory-retirement ages among firms with mandatory retirement would have been more dispersed. Unfortunately, no data are available on this point.

Social security is one possible determinant of T. There may be others as well. Social security payments do not affect all individuals in the same way. High-wage workers, for example, may find the social security subsidy to leisure relatively less attractive than do low-wage workers. As a result, ages of mandatory retirement might vary by the characteristics of the workers. An obvious determinant of retirement date is education. If education increases the value of work by more than the value of leisure, one would expect more educated workers to retire later (Bowen and Finegan [1969] find this positive relationship). If, as this paper claims, mandatory retirement is the outgrowth of an optimal long-term contract, we might then expect that conditional upon having mandatory retirement, education and the age of mandatory retirement will be positively correlated. This is explored in the empirical analysis below. In addition, anything that affects $\tilde{f}(t)$ and $\tilde{g}(t)$ will affect the choice of T. If either probability of cheating is higher, T will be lower. Thus, the age of mandatory retirement will be negatively related to the probability of early termination.

II. Some Implications of the Model

In the previous section, a model was presented which has implications for the incidence of mandatory retirement by job and demographic characteristics. In this section I will explore these implications in greater detail and outline the empirical tests which will be discussed in the next section.

The first and most important implication of the model is that mandatory retirement is more likely to be found where job tenure is long. That is, we portray mandatory retirement as the consequence of an optimal long-term contract between a worker and firm. If contracts are short term, say week by week or even year by year, profiles where wages are below VMP early in life and above VMP late in life are infeasible. Mandatory retirement is only useful in a long-term context.

Another implication, already discussed, is that unanticipated wage growth and the existence of mandatory retirement should be positively correlated. This, too, can be tested easily. By looking at an individual's work history and corresponding wage growth one can see how it relates to mandatory retirement. The argument on wage growth relates to the part that is unobservable at $t = 0$. Some differences are anticipated. We know, for example, from the outset that more educated workers learn more rapidly than the less educated. We therefore want to compare two individuals with the same observable characteristics.[16] The one with the most rapid wage growth, given these characteristics, is then the one with the higher probability of mandatory retirement under the incentives view. We therefore expect the probability of mandatory retirement to be positively related to the difference between actual wage growth and predicted (at time $t = 0$) wage growth.

Wage growth and job tenure are not exogenous variables. They are themselves the result of a choice process that is based on lifetime optimization. This suggests that mandatory retirement will be correlated with those variables that underlie wage growth and job tenure determination. That is, a reduced form, as well as structural approach, may prove interesting. For example, to the extent that whites have longer job tenure than nonwhites, whites should have a higher incidence of mandatory retirement. Similarly, if males enjoy longer job tenure than females, they will experience more mandatory retirement. Similarly, union workers, who have longer job tenure than nonunion workers (see Medoff 1976), should be more likely to experience mandatory retirement. It should be noted that these implications are the opposite of those derived from a queue or discrimination theory. If mandatory retirement were a way to reduce the labor force and make room for the younger, more desirable workers, one would expect that blacks, females, and the poorly educated would be the most affected. (They are the workers who suffer most from layoffs—the phenomenon that queue theory was formulated to explain.) The hypothesis in this paper, where mandatory retirement is viewed as the result of optimal lifetime contracting, suggests that it is the more favored rather than least favored workers who face mandatory retirement.[17]

Pensions are one way to compensate the worker at T. It was argued above that if there is a progressive tax structure which taxes lump-sum payments at a higher rate than it does pensions, or if cheating is detected with a lag, pensions will be part of the optimal path. Thus, pensions should be positively correlated with mandatory retirement since they both are manifestations of the same contractual arrangement. Also important is that it is necessary to have some type of severance pay in order to avoid the inefficiencies of a long-term contract. As argued above, paying higher pensions to those who retire

[16] What is observable to the economist may be much more limited than that which is observable to the employer. It is the latter that is relevant. We are, unfortunately, restricted to the former.

[17] It has been suggested that this view explicitly characterizes the Japanese labor market. Mandatory retirement takes place at age 55 after a long-term contract with the firm has been completed. Often, renegotiation takes place and the worker remains with the firm after 55 (see, e.g., Hashimoto [1977]).

before T is one such arrangement. Burkhauser (1976) finds that workers who leave the firm before the normal retirement date receive a pension, the actuarial value of which is a monotonic increasing function of the years to normal retirement. This is strong support for the long-term contract view.

This model reinforces the implication of many firm-specific labor models that older workers, if laid off, will have a difficult time finding another job at the same wage. If wage exceeds VMP for older workers, a new firm will be unwilling to pick this worker up at his previous wage.

An additional implication comes from considering types of compensation. Since the steep wage path which necessitates mandatory retirement is seen as the result of an agency problem, piece-rate workers are unlikely to experience mandatory retirement. Mandatory retirement was the necessary consequence of a payment scheme which induced workers to perform optimally. A piece-rate compensation scheme is a substitute. Under this type of payment scheme, workers always have an incentive to reveal their true ability or effort.[18]

The explanation of mandatory retirement provided in this paper also suggests a particular life-cycle pattern of preference for mandatory retirement. In this scheme workers at $t = 0$ prefer the payment arrangement that implies mandatory retirement. Firms prefer this arrangement as well. At time T, however, given that the worker and firm have followed the mandatory-retirement plan, firms favor mandatory retirement for the old worker, but the worker may oppose it vehemently, even though he favored it when he was young. That is, his lifetime wealth is higher with the mandatory-retirement scheme than without it, but given the wage path, his wealth would be even higher if he could continue to work at $W^*(T)$ beyond T. Thus, firms will oppose laws that restrict the use of mandatory-retirement contracts (explicit or implicit). Labor, in general, will also oppose these laws. Old workers, however, will push for legislation that makes mandatory retirement illegal since they can increase their wealth levels by doing so, given that they enjoyed wage paths $W^*(t)$ from $t = 0$ to $t = T$. This closely parallels the demographic breakdown of support of revisions to the Age Discrimination in Employment Act. Both business and organized labor opposed raising the age of exemption to 70. Major support, however, came from lobbying groups which represent the interests of the elderly.[19]

[18] Unfortunately, data on piece-rate vs. time-rate compensation are very difficult to obtain. They are unavailable in the data set used below in this study.

[19] It should be pointed out, however, that there are many other models of mandatory retirement which generate the same structure of preferences. On the other hand, Ehrenberg (1978) finds that firefighters and policemen who have mandatory-retirement provisions also obtain higher wages. This is consistent with this model.

III. An Empirical Model

In this section, the implications discussed above will be given specific functional form and will be tested empirically. Let *MR* be a dummy which equals one if the individual in question has a mandatory retirement provision on his current job, and zero otherwise.[20] Let *E* be the number of years that the worker has been employed with his current firm. Let *AWG* be the average level of wage growth over the individual's lifetime. Then the theory above predicts that

$$\text{prob}\ (MR = 1) = \frac{1}{1 + \exp\{-[\alpha_0 + \alpha_1 E + \alpha_2(AWG - \hat{AWG})]\}}, \quad (9)$$

where $\hat{AWG}$ is the predicted level of wage growth from a wage growth regression. Further, there will be equations for the determination of *E* and *AWG* as well:

$$E = \beta_0 + \beta_1\ \text{Male} + \beta_2\ \text{White} + \beta_3\ \text{Ed} + \beta_4\ \text{Urban} + \beta_5\ \text{Married} + \beta_6\ AFJ, \quad (10)$$

where Male, White, Urban, and Married are zero-one dummies, and Ed is the years of schooling completed; *AFJ* is the age of first job. (This corrects for vintage and inflation effects.)

$$AWG = \gamma_0 + \gamma_1\text{Male} + \gamma_2\ \text{White} + \gamma_3\ \text{Ed} + \gamma_4\ \text{Urban} + \gamma_5\ \text{Married} + \gamma_6\ AFJ. \quad (11)$$

Alternatively, one can specify the following reduced-form equation:

$$\text{prob}\ (MR = 1) = 1/\{1 + \exp[-(\eta_0 + \eta_1\text{Male} + \eta_2\text{White} + \eta_3\text{Ed} + \eta_4\text{Urban} + \eta_5\text{Married} + \eta_6 AFJ)]\}. \quad (12)$$

The signs of the coefficients in (14) should be the same as the product of the sign on the corresponding variable in (12). This is because α_1 is positive and because $AWG - \hat{AWG}$ should not vary with any of these variables if (13) is specified correctly.

The same set of equations can be estimated with *MR* replaced by *PP*, where *PP* is a dummy equal to one if there is a pension plan. Thus,

$$\text{prob}\ (PP = 1) = \frac{1}{1 + \exp\{-[\delta_0 + \delta_1\text{Ed} + \delta_2(AWG - \hat{AWG})]\}}. \quad (13)$$

[20] This variable actually understates the true incidence of mandatory retirement. Some retirement is mandatory as a result of pension schemes which essentially prevent anyone from continuing to work past 65. For example, mandatory retirement is likely to be unnecessary in a firm that offers no pension to individuals who leave the firm after age 65, and a full salary pension to those who leave at 65. This points out that the mandatory-retirement response is itself a function of price. Some attempt to deal with response bias is made below.

If δ_1 and δ_2 have the same signs as α_1 and α_2, we might expect a positive simple correlation between *PP* and *MR*.

The data used in this analysis came from the Longitudinal Retirement History Survey, 1969–71. This is a panel study of about 11,000 individuals who were 58–63 years old in 1969. A follow-up survey was done in 1971, and the data used in this analysis are derived from that wave. Only those working in 1971 were used so that data on wages could be obtained.

All were asked whether or not their firm had a mandatory-retirement provision which applied to them. An affirmative answer to this question was coded as $MR = 1$. The wage rate, W, is the hourly (actual or derived) wage rate on the current job. The measure of job tenure used, E, is the difference between the question date and the date at which the individual reports to have started his current job. Average wage growth, *AWG*, is constructed as follows: Individuals were asked what their wage rates were on their first full-time jobs. (The starting wage on their current job was not reported.) They also reported the age at which they took this job. Thus, define

$$AWG \equiv \frac{W_t - W_{t_0}}{t - t_0}, \qquad (14)$$

where t_0 is the age of first job and t is the individual's current age. All other variables were defined above.

IV. Results

First and most important, it should be noted that both job tenure and wage growth affect mandatory retirement positively. This is seen in equation (9) in table 1. Individuals who have longer job tenure and more rapid unanticipated wage growth are the ones who are most likely to face mandatory retirement. This finding, although consistent with the theory of this paper, is hard to reconcile in terms of queue or discrimination theories of mandatory retirement. Note that the effect of $AWG - \widehat{AWG}$ is positive and substantial. This is consistent with the incentives or agency view of mandatory retirement. Second, note that the reduced-form coefficients in equation (12) go in the direction predicted by this theory but seem inconsistent with theories of discrimination. Note in particular that males and highly educated workers are the ones most likely to have mandatory retirement.[21]

It is interesting that the pension-plan equation (13) and the mandatory-retirement equation (9) are very similar and that the reduced-form versions are not very different. The theory related to

[21] The reversal in signs on the urban variable may reflect the fact that information is easier to obtain in small towns and there is, therefore, less need for payment schemes which require mandatory retirement.

TABLE 1

LOGIT AND OLS RESULTS

	Eq. (9): *MR*			Eq. (10): *E*	Eq. (11): *AWG*	Eq. (12): *MR*			Eq. (13): *PP*			*PP*		
	Logit	$\frac{\partial \bar{MR}}{\partial X_i} \cdot \frac{X_i}{\bar{MR}}$	$\frac{\partial \bar{MR}}{\partial X_i}$	OLS	OLS	Logit	$\frac{\partial \bar{MR}}{\partial X_i} \cdot \frac{X_i}{\bar{MR}}$	$\frac{\partial \bar{MR}}{\partial X_i}$	Logit	$\frac{\partial \bar{PP}}{\partial X_i} \cdot \frac{X_i}{\bar{PP}}$	$\frac{\partial PP}{\partial X_i}$	Logit	$\frac{\partial PP}{\partial X_i} \cdot \frac{X_i}{\bar{PP}}$	$\frac{\partial PP}{\partial X_i}$
E	.02727 (.00249)	.31	.006	...	...	...	...	...	.02958 (.00249)	.28	.007	...	...	...
AWG–AŴG	2.8992 (.502)	*	.661	...	...	...	...	...	5.8557 (.5791)	*	1.46	...	...	...
Male	...	...	...	2.25 (.87)	.0640 (.0135)	.2268 (.1398)	†	.051	...	...	...	.3451 (.1345)	†	.086
White	...	...	...	1.00 (.77)	.0118 (.0119)	.0757 (.1299)	†	.017	...	...	...	.2650 (.1231)	†	.066
Ed	...	...	...	.153 (.062)	.0084 (.0009)	.0963 (.0100)	.655	.021	...	...	...	.0945 (.0097)	.51	.023
Urban	...	...	...	−.289 (.423)	.0183 (.0065)	.2254 (.0672)	†	.051	...	...	...	.3492 (.0652)	†	.087
Married	...	...	...	1.015 (.769)	−.0201 (.0118)	−.0244 (.1230)	†	−.007	...	...	...	.0221 (.1185)	†	.006
AFJ	...	...	...	−.174 (.030)	.0014 (.0004)	.0011 (.0049)	.014	.0002	...	...	...	−.0129 (.0048)	−.14	−.003
DMR	...	...	...	...	...	...	...	...	...	...	...	...	...	...
Constant	−1.1067 (.057)	...	...	16.1 (1.2)	−.0833 (.0194)	−1.9852 (.2105)	...	...	−.5582 (.0545)	...	...	−1.4727 (.200)	...	...
SEE	...	...	...	13.27	.205	...	...	...	...	...	...	...	...	...
N	4,123	...	...	4,123	4,123	4,123	...	...	4,123	...	...	4,123	...	...
−2 log λ	186.7	...	...	...	...	119.9	...	...	324.9	...	...	180.7	...	...
R^2	...	...	...	.025	.029	...	...	...	...	...	...	...	...	...

NOTE.—Standard errors are in parentheses.
*$AWG - \hat{AWG} = 0$ by construction; $\overline{AWG} = .088$.
†Dummy variables; $\bar{MR} = .352$, $\bar{PP} = .485$.

lifetime labor force contracts predicts that this would be the case (note that the mean value of *MR* is .35 and the mean value of *PP* is .49). The exogenous variables seem to have virtually the same effect on the existence of mandatory retirement as they do on the existence of pension plans. Furthermore, the correlation between mandatory retirement and pension plans in a simple sense is extremely high. In this sample, 62 percent of those with a pension plan have mandatory retirement. Further, 86 percent of those who have mandatory retirement also have a pension plan. This finding is important. It is strong support for the coupling of mandatory retirement and pensions. The theory above suggests that they should be linked directly as each is the outcome of the same optimal contract. That is, in a world where the tax rate is higher on a lump-sum payment than on a smooth flow of income with the same present value, or in a world where cheating is detected with a lag, all wage paths that have mandatory retirement will also have pensions.

As mentioned above, there may be reporting bias associated with the *MR* variables. New workers, for example, may be less aware of the rules of the firm and less likely to report the existence of mandatory retirement. To treat this, individuals with tenure levels in the twentieth percentile were separated from the rest of the sample, and the estimation contained in table 1 was repeated for each group separately. (The low-tenure group had $0 \leq E \leq 4.3$; the high-tenure group had $4.3 \leq E \leq 59.0$.) The results, only summarized here for the sake of brevity, reveal the same basic story as table 1. Deletion of the low-tenure individuals leaves the results for the top 80 percent essentially unchanged. In addition, the results for the low-tenure group were similar to those for the high-tenure group. The only notable difference is that for this group, married workers were less likely to face mandatory retirement than unmarried ones.

Some empirical evidence can be obtained on variations in T, the age of mandatory retirement, across individuals. Earlier it was suggested that more highly educated individuals would have optimal dates of retirement later in their lifetimes. If the skills which they acquired in school were relatively more useful in the labor market, then they would have an incentive to continue working longer than less educated workers. It follows, then, that if mandatory retirement is a manifestation of an optimal long-term contract, more educated workers should have older ages of mandatory retirement.

In table 2, a regression is presented in which the age of mandatory retirement is regressed on demographic variables, education, and job tenure. The sample contains only those who face mandatory retirement. The first point is that education has an important (in size and precision of estimate) effect on the age of mandatory retirement. It

TABLE 2

Regression and Logit Results

	MR Age OLS
Male	−.093
	(.256)
White	−.387
	(.246)
Ed	.118
	(.017)
Urban	−.133
	(.120)
Married	.198
	(.225)
AFJ	−.005
	(.009)
E	−.032
	(.004)
Constant	66.4
	(.4)
R^2	.066
N	1,429
SEE	2.25

Note.—Standard errors are in parentheses.

appears as though more educated workers make contracts which end at a later point in their life cycles. This is consistent with the notion that they choose to retire later voluntarily as well.

Second, note that job tenure has a negative effect on the age of mandatory retirement. In the context of this sample of old workers, all of whom are about the same age, job tenure is a proxy for the date at which the employment contract was made. Holding age about constant, those workers with fewer years of job tenure also have more recently made a "contract" with the employer than those with longer tenure. The results suggest that more recent contracts specify a later age of mandatory retirement. Individuals who have made more recent contracts may have done so either because the value of their leisure did not rise as rapidly as they expected ($\tilde{W}[t]$ is flatter than had been anticipated) or because they ended up being more productive in the labor force than expected ($V^*[t]$ is higher than anticipated). In either case, it is optimal for them to be "bought out" of their previous contract (through severance pay or early pensions) and to negotiate a new one. The new one will have a later date of mandatory retirement because, as equation (6) shows, the higher is $V^*(t)$ or the flatter is $\tilde{W}(t)$, the later will be the date of mandatory retirement.

Third, the coefficient on White is negative. Other things constant, whites have earlier ages of mandatory retirement than blacks. Although the explanation of this phenomenon is not obvious, let us conjecture. Even holding education and urbanization constant, whites have substantially higher income than blacks. This is especially true of nonwage income. Thus, if the education effect captures most of the wage variation, the white variable may well proxy higher property income. Since the income effect on leisure is positive, holding education constant yields an increase in the demand for leisure via income effects, so whites are richer individuals with the same wage rate. As such, whites prefer to work less and therefore set up contracts with earlier retirement dates.

V. Summary and Conclusions

This paper provides an explanation of the institution of mandatory retirement that is derived from optimizing behavior on the part of both workers and firms. The theory, simply stated, is that it pays both parties to agree to a long-term wage stream which pays workers less than their VMPs when young and more than the VMPs when old. By using this payment schedule, the worker's lifetime VMP is higher than it would be in the absence of that scheme because this provides valuable incentives to the worker which would otherwise be lost to moral hazard. A necessary consequence of this payment schedule is mandatory retirement, that is, a date at which the contract is terminated and the worker is no longer entitled to receive a wage greater than his VMP. Its mandatory nature is illusory, however. The date of mandatory retirement is the social and private optimum date of retirement.

This theory has some perhaps counterintuitive implications. It suggests that the long-tenured and most able workers will face mandatory retirement rather than the least tenured. It predicts that the highly educated, white, male workers are the ones most likely to be mandatorily retired. These predictions are borne out in the empirical section.

The most important implication of this theory is that workers and firms all benefit from the existence of mandatory retirement. Although older workers may be unhappy about this provision when the retirement day draws near, their lifetime wealth levels are increased as the result of being able to enter into these kinds of contracts. What they lose by being mandatorily retired is more than offset by what they have gained during working years as the result. As mandatory retirement is made illegal before age 70 and the social security payment age is not raised accordingly, there will be an efficiency loss as voluntary and mandatory retirement ages diverge. If the ability to enter into mandatory-retirement contracts is eliminated through legislation, this analysis argues that current older workers will enjoy a small once-and-for-all gain at the expense of a much larger and continuing efficiency loss that affects all workers and firms adversely.

References

Azariadis, Costas. "Implicit Contracts and Underemployment Equilibria." *J.P.E.* 83, no. 6 (December 1975): 1183–1202.

Baily, Martin N. "Wages and Employment under Uncertain Demand." *Rev. Econ. Studies* 41 (January 1974): 37–50.

Banker's Trust Company. *1975 Study of Corporate Pension Plans.* New York: Banker's Trust, 1975.

Becker, G., and Stigler, G. "Law Enforcement, Malfeasance, and Compensation of Enforcers." *J. Legal Studies* 3, no. 1 (1974): 1–18.

Bowen, W. G., and Finegan, T. A. *The Economics of Labor Force Participation.* Princeton, N.J.: Princeton Univ. Press, 1969.

Burkhauser, R. "Early Pension Decision and Its Effect on Exit from the Labor Market." Ph.D. dissertation, Univ. Chicago, 1976.

Ehrenberg, Ronald. "Retirement System Characteristics and Compensating Wage Differentials in the Public Sector." Unpublished paper, Cornell Univ., 1978.

Fama, Eugene. "Agency Problems and the Theory of the Firm." Mimeographed. Univ. Chicago, 1978.

Feldstein, Martin. "Temporary Layoffs in the Theory of Unemployment." *J.P.E.* 84, no. 5 (October 1976): 937–57.

Freeman, S. "Wage Trends as Performance Displays Productive Potential: A Model of Application to Academic Early Retirement." *Bell J. Econ.* 8, no. 2 (Autumn 1977): 419–43.

Gordon, M. S. "Older Workers and Retirement Policies." *Monthly Labor Rev.* 83, no. 6 (June 1960): 577–85.

Grossman, H. "Risk Shifting, Layoffs, and Seniority." Working Paper no. 76-7, Brown Univ., 1977.

Hashimoto, M. "Variable Wages, On-the-Job Training, and Lifetime Employment in Japan." Unpublished paper, Univ. Washington, September 1977.

Kreps, J. "A Case Study of Variables in Retirement Policy." *Monthly Labor Rev.* 84, no. 6 (June 1961): 587–91.

Medoff, J. "Layoffs and Alternatives under Trade Unions in United States Manufacturing." Discussion Paper no. 525, Harvard Inst. Econ. Res., 1976.

National Industrial Conference Board, Inc. *Corporate Retirement Policies and Practices.* Studies in Personnel Policy, no. 190. New York: NICB, 1964.

Rothschild, Michael, and Stiglitz, Joseph. "Equilibrium in Competitive Insurance Markets: An Essay on the Economics of Imperfect Information." *Q.J.E.* 90, no. 4 (November 1976): 629–49.

Salop, Joanne, and Salop, Steven. "Self-Selection and Turnover in the Labor Market." *Q.J.E.* 90, no. 4 (November 1976): 619–27.

Stiglitz, J. "Incentives, Risk, and Information: Notes toward a Theory of Hierarchy." *Bell J. Econ.* 6, no. 2 (Autumn 1975): 552–79.

U.S. Department of Health, Education, and Welfare. *Reaching Retirement Age.* Social Security Administration Research Report no. 47. Washington: Government Printing Office, 1976.

[6]

THE DISTRIBUTION OF WEALTH AND THE INDIVIDUAL LIFE-CYCLE[1]

By A. B. ATKINSON

THE distribution of wealth in Britain has been the subject of considerable discussion in recent years, and many people have drawn attention to the extreme inequality which it exhibits. On the basis of the distribution derived by the Inland Revenue from the Estate Duty returns, it can be estimated that the top 1 per cent of the adult population own about a third of the total personal wealth and the top 10 per cent as much as three-quarters. In interpreting this evidence it must be borne in mind, however, that it relates to the distribution of *current wealth* among all people alive at a particular date, and that this includes the wealth that people have accumulated for life-cycle purposes (particularly saving for retirement). It may therefore exhibit inequality simply because people are at different stages of the life-cycle: the top 10 per cent may own more than their share because they are older and have saved more for old age. If this were the case, we should be less concerned about inequality, and there are strong grounds for arguing that our primary concern should be with the distribution of *inherited wealth* rather than the current distribution. We should assess inequality in terms of the value of wealth that a person receives over the course of his life in the form of bequests, gifts, and other capital receipts, and not in terms of his wealth-holding at some arbitrary date. This lifetime view of equity is clearly more appropriate if our concern is with unequal 'life chances', and has the merit of treating an individual's lifetime as a whole rather than considering each year in isolation.

If this viewpoint is accepted, we have to consider the importance of life-cycle factors and the inferences that can be drawn from the observed current distribution regarding inequality in inherited wealth, and it is with this problem that the present paper is concerned. In considering the importance of life-cycle factors, the natural reference standard is the case of a *perfectly egalitarian* society where everyone has the same inherited wealth (and is identical in all other relevant respects). In such a society there is still likely to be inequality in the current distribution of wealth as a result of differences in wealth-holding according to age—a point that was made very clearly in an editorial in *The Times* (28 September 1968):

> Quite obviously in the most egalitarian of societies one would not expect the new-born babe and the man on the point of retirement to have identical savings, or even the fifty-year-old and the sixty-year-old, and there must therefore be a concentration of wealth in a minority of hands in any society one can conceive of.

[1] I am grateful to J. E. Meade, J. R. S. Revell, and A. Shorrocks for their comments on an earlier draft of this paper.

The editorial goes on to argue that

> This effect is more marked than most people would suppose. If one calculates the probable pattern of savings in a hypothetical society with total equality of male incomes and a total prohibition on inheritance, and if one assumes that the savings will belong to men as the main earners, then in that most egalitarian society over 80 per cent of the total private wealth would be in the hands of men over fifty who would comprise less than 15 per cent of the population. Where inheritance is not allowed, only the old can be rich.

It is not obvious, however, that the quantitative importance attached by *The Times* to life-cycle differences is correct, and the first section of the paper examines in more detail the likely degree of inequality in a hypothetical egalitarian society of this type. The second section of the paper adopts a rather different approach and discusses the evidence that can be derived by breaking down the Estate Duty statistics by age groups. By examining the distribution of wealth among people of the same age, we can hope to eliminate the major life-cycle differences and this provides an alternative way of assessing their importance.

I. Life-cycle differences in a hypothetical egalitarian society

Suppose everyone were identical in every respect apart from age (having the same market opportunities and the same tastes) and inheritance and gifts were prohibited. How much inequality would there still be in the current distribution of wealth as a result of differences in age? This part of the paper attempts to answer this question in the context of a number of explicit (although inevitably rather stylized) models of individual savings behaviour.

Let us consider first a model where all individuals live for a fixed period (T years). They spend the first N years of their lives working for a wage $w(t)$, and during this period they save for their retirement. They can borrow or lend freely at a constant interest rate r. They are assumed to know for certain that they will live for T years and to plan for their consumption to grow at a constant exponential rate g. (This would be the optimal consumption policy for a person maximizing an additively separable, iso-elastic utility function.) They leave no bequests and make no gifts. Everyone faces the same r and $w(t)$ and chooses the same g. Simplifying still further and setting $r = 0$, $g = 0$, and $w(t)$ constant all t gives the Modigliani–Brumberg model [4]. If in this case we set $T = 50$, $N = 40$ (assuming that life begins at 25) and assume a constant population, the pattern of wealth-holding has the particularly straightforward form shown in Fig. 1. From this it can readily be calculated that the wealthiest 10 per cent of the population (those aged 62–6) account for 19 per cent of the total wealth, which is considerably less than the figures estimated for Britain.

Even within the context of the models discussed here, the Modigliani–Brumberg case is a very special one and it is interesting to examine the effect of allowing positive interest rates (as well as for the growth over time of consumption, earnings, and population). The upper part of Table I shows the results obtained from the model described earlier for different values of r and g (on the assumption that both population and real earnings

FIG. 1

grow at the rate of 2 per cent). In general the shares are broadly similar to those suggested by the very simple model: the share of the top 10 per cent ranges from 17 per cent to 27 per cent of total wealth. The degree of concentration tends to rise with the rate of interest, but a *real* (after tax) rate of 6 per cent would be quite high. Concentration also tends to increase as we take lower rates of growth of consumption; it seems reasonable, however, to suppose that consumption would grow at least as fast as earnings. It might be expected that a faster rate of population growth would lead to more concentration, since there would be proportionately fewer old (and therefore rich) people. The results given in the lower part of Table I, however, suggest that variations in the rate of growth of population do not have a particularly marked effect. They also show that a higher rate of growth of earnings increases concentration but that again the effect is fairly small.

The demographic assumptions made so far are *simpliste* to an extreme, and it might be thought that more realistic assumptions would give rather different results. To see whether this is so, further calculations on the basis of the actual survival rates observed in England and Wales are shown in Table II.[1] Since it is no longer reasonable to assume that individuals expect to live for a fixed period, it is assumed instead that they plan for their

[1] *Annual Abstract of Statistics*, 1967, Life Tables for England and Wales. The rates used are those for the male population and relate to 1964–6.

TABLE I

Inequality in a hypothetical egalitarian society

Rate of growth of population 2%, rate of growth of real earnings 2%

Rate of growth of consumption		Real rate of interest r 3%	4½%	6%
2%	Share of top 1%	2·4	2·8	3·1
	,, top 5%	11·7	13·1	14·6
	,, top 10%	22·5	24·7	27·4
3%	Share of top 1%	1·9	2·1	2·2
	,, top 5%	9·4	10·1	10·8
	,, top 10%	18·4	19·6	20·9
4%	Share of top 1%	1·7	1·8	2·0
	,, top 5%	8·6	9·1	9·7
	,, top 10%	17·1	18·0	19·0

Rate of growth of consumption 3%, real rate of interest 4½%

Rate of growth of population		Rate of growth of real earnings 1%	2%	3%
0%	Share of top 1%	1·7	1·8	2·2
	,, top 5%	8·5	9·1	10·6
	,, top 10%	16·9	17·8	20·6
2%	Share of top 1%	1·9	2·1	2·5
	,, top 5%	9·5	10·1	12·1
	,, top 10%	18·7	19·6	23·2
4%	Share of top 1%	2·2	2·4	3·0
	,, top 5%	10·8	11·4	14·1
	,, top 10%	21·1	22·0	26·4

In all cases $T = 55$, $N = 45$.

consumption to grow at a constant rate subject to the condition that their expected wealth at death must be zero (the conditions under which this behaviour can be derived from utility maximization are described in the Appendix, which also discusses the treatment of cases where people die in debt). These calculations also allow for a more realistic lifetime earnings profile reflecting the tendency for earnings to rise and then fall with age.[1] Comparing the results with those from Table I, it is clear that there is no

[1] *Ministry of Social Security Annual Report*, 1967. It is assumed that an individual now aged u expects to earn at age t the current average earnings of people now aged t increased by the general growth of earnings (i.e. by a factor of $e^{g(t-u)}$).

major difference: the share of the top 10 per cent is on average higher but only by a few per cent.

TABLE II

Inequality with realistic survival rates and earnings profile

Rate of growth of consumption		Real rate of interest r		
		3%	4½%	6%
2%	Share of top 1%	2·6	3·0	3·5
	,, top 5%	12·4	14·2	16·4
	,, top 10%	24·0	27·1	30·9
3%	Share of top 1%	2·0	2·2	2·3
	,, top 5%	10·0	10·7	11·6
	,, top 10%	19·8	21·2	22·7
4%	Share of top 1%	1·9	1·9	2·0
	,, top 5%	9·2	9·7	10·1
	,, top 10%	18·4	19·2	20·0

(Rate of population growth = 2%, earnings growth = 2%.)

The effect of introducing equal inheritance

The hypothetical egalitarian society considered so far ruled out inheritance and gifts altogether; however, a more general case of a perfectly egalitarian society is one where wealth *is* transmitted from generation to generation, but in such a way that everyone receives the same amount. If, as seems likely, this inheritance is not received until middle age or later, this would tend to increase the degree of 'apparent' concentration, since it would increase still further the wealth of the old relative to that of the young. It is interesting, therefore, to examine the effect of equal inheritance on the degree of inequality in the current distribution.

Let us consider first the effect on the simple Modigliani–Brumberg model (with constant population). At the age of 50 everyone inherits I from their fathers; they hold this intact until they die, when it passes to the next generation (since the population is assumed not to be growing, the estate does not have to be divided). The effect of this on the share of the top 10 per cent (those aged 62–6) can be calculated quite simply: it becomes

$$\frac{38w+5I}{200w+25I} = 0{\cdot}19+0{\cdot}01\left[\frac{I}{8w+I}\right].$$

In other words, their share goes up by less than 1 per cent however large is I. This results from the fact that the share of the top 10 per cent in inherited wealth is only very slightly larger than their share in total wealth. The degree of concentration of inherited wealth is clearly largest when it is held for the shortest possible period. However, if each generation passes on its wealth at the same age, this period equals the difference between the ages of the father and the son and is not likely to be less than 20 years. In that case (where the son inherits at the age of 55) the share of the top 10 per cent could rise at most by 6 per cent—so that it was 25 per cent in all.[1]

The results derived from this simple model suggest that the introduction of equal inheritance does not lead to a large increase in the degree of apparent inequality. This model takes no account, however, of the fact that even if inheritance is equal, everyone does not necessarily inherit at the same date. Those whose fathers die young will inherit early and those whose fathers are octogenarians (and hang on to their estate) may not inherit until they are well into their sixties. For this reason, it may be interesting to examine the effect of equal inheritance in the context of the model based on actual survival rates (assuming that the fathers were subject to the same mortality pattern). Table III shows the results obtained from

TABLE III

Equal inheritance in a hypothetical egalitarian society

Present value of inheritance at age 25 expressed as multiple of annual earnings	*Share in total wealth of top* 1%	5%	10%
$I = 0$	2·4	11·5	22·4
1	2·6	12·8	24·9
5	3·1	15·2	29·6
25	3·1	15·4	30·0
50	3·1	15·4	30·0

(Real rate of interest 3%, rate of growth of population 2%, earnings 3%, consumption 3%.)

this model with different amounts of inherited wealth. In each case the value of the inheritance discounted to age 25 is expressed as a multiple of earnings at that age (if we take earnings at 25 as £1,500, then with an interest rate of 3 per cent $I = 5$ is approximately equivalent to £20,000 inherited at the age of 55).[2] As I increases, the distribution approaches that of inherited wealth taken by itself (which depends on the mortality of the fathers) and there is little change as I rises above 25. The results show

[1] The effect of inheritance on the distribution of wealth depends on the point at which it is transferred. It is largest when inherited wealth is held during that part of the person's lifetime when his 'accumulated' wealth is at its peak—as is the case with the example given here.

[2] The index of inter-generational equity used here is the ratio of inherited wealth to the present value of earnings. If inherited wealth accumulates at a rate r and this is equal to the rate of growth of earnings (as in the example given in Table III), then inter-generational equality (in this sense) is preserved.

that the introduction of equal inheritance increases the degree of inequality, but even where the inheritance is substantial the share of the top 10 per cent is only some 30 per cent.

Women and the distribution of wealth

So far no explicit account has been taken of the role played by women in the distribution of wealth. At one extreme, we could assume that women own no property at all. It is clear, however, that this is not the case: in 1967, 38 per cent of the personal wealth in Britain recorded in the Inland Revenue estimates was owned by women. At the same time, it is not obvious that in their effect on wealth-holding they can be regarded in the same way as men. Revell has commented as follows [5]:

> In any distribution of wealth owned by individuals women have a rather peculiar role. They have some savings before they marry, but most of the wealth which accrues to a married couple (except perhaps direct gifts and bequests to the wife) will go into the husband's name and appear in his estate when he dies. . . . Once the husband dies, however, what is left of her husband's estate after the payment of estate duty partly or wholly falls to the widow.

If the pattern described by Revell is broadly correct, it may not be seriously inaccurate to regard married women as having no wealth while their husbands are alive but inheriting their estates when they die. Since married women account for about a third of the adult population, we ought to allow for approximately 1 propertyless person per 2 propertied adults, so that what was referred to earlier as the share of the top x per cent becomes the share of the top $2x/3$ per cent.

Conclusions—The Times *view*

In *The Times* editorial quoted earlier, it was claimed that in a perfectly egalitarian society with no inheritance there would be substantial apparent concentration of wealth: 80 per cent of the total wealth would be in the hands of men over 50 who would comprise less than 15 per cent of the population. The results reached here, however, are rather different. Even stacking the cards in one direction by taking a high interest rate (6 per cent in real terms), a low rate of growth of consumption over the individual's lifetime (2 per cent in real terms), and assuming that married women are propertyless, the share of the top 15 per cent is 53 per cent—or considerably less than 80 per cent. For other values of the parameters it is typically around 40 per cent. There are two main reasons for the discrepancy between our results and the view of *The Times*. Firstly, *The Times* assumed that no women held wealth, an assumption which we have seen not to be justified. Secondly, it expressed the number of men over 50 as a percentage of the total *population* rather than as a percentage of total *adults*, which is the base generally used in the estimates of inequality in Britain. The importance of this can be seen from the following figures for the United Kingdom in June 1969:[1]

Men over 50 as % of total population	13%
Men over 50 as % of population over 25	22%

II. Evidence from the estate duty statistics

In the introduction to the paper it was argued that our primary concern should be with the distribution of inherited wealth—or the total that a person receives over his life in the form of bequests, gifts, or other capital receipts. The information required to measure directly the concentration of inherited wealth is not available, but it is possible to make estimates from the Estate Duty statistics of the distribution of wealth within age (and sex) groups. By standardizing for age in this way, we should be able to eliminate the major life-cycle differences, and hence throw some light on the distribution of inherited wealth and the importance of life-cycle factors in giving rise to 'apparent' inequality in the current distribution.[2]

Inequality by age groups

The approach used to estimate the distribution of wealth within each age group is basically the same as that adopted in estimating the over-all distribution. The method, which dates back to the work of Mallet and others at the beginning of the century, has been described in detail by a number of writers.[3] Essentially it is assumed that those dying in a particular year are a representative sample of the living, so that we can blow up the Estate Duty figures by a 'mortality multiplier' to give an estimate of the total wealth of the living. The mortality multiplier is in general the inverse of the mortality rate for a particular age group (adjusted for differences by social class): so that if the mortality rate for a particular group is 0·05 we assume that their total wealth is 20 times that recorded in the Estate Duty statistics. When considering individual age groups, the application of the method is particularly straightforward, since the only differences in the multipliers are those reflecting the adjustment for social class.[4]

The deficiencies of this method of estimating the distribution of wealth have been well documented. The most important are:

(i) The Estate Duty statistics cover only those estates for which probate

[1] Most of the studies of wealth-holding in Britain have defined the adult population as those over the age of 25.

[2] A similar study for the years 1911–14 and 1923–5 was made by Wedgwood [9], Chapter VII.

[3] Cf. Langley [2].

[4] For estates under £3,000 the mortality multipliers were those for the general population (Source: *Annual Abstract of Statistics*); for estates over £3,000, the mortality rate was adjusted using the figures given by Revell [6], Table 5.4 (the same adjustment is made for males and females).

is granted, so that there is only limited coverage of estates below the exemption limit (£5,000 from 1963–4 to 1968–9).[1]

(ii) The small numbers in certain cells mean that the results are subject to large sampling errors—particularly in the case of the youngest age groups: in 1967–8 only one person died between the ages of 25 and 34 with an estate of over £200,000.

(iii) Certain kinds of property disappear at death and therefore do not appear in the Estate Duty statistics. The most important of these are pensions and annuities. Other kinds of property are also excluded from the statistics: for example, property settled on the spouse and passing on his/her death, and property held under discretionary trusts (for the period considered here).

There is also the problem of wealth avoiding Estate Duty through gifts *inter vivos*, but this is more a question of interpretation than a deficiency of the figures as such.

The importance of the incomplete coverage of the Estate Duty figures can be seen from the fact that in 1967 the returns accounted for only 44 per cent of all deaths in that year. We have, therefore, to decide what allowance should be made for the wealth of those not covered. In its estimate of total personal wealth the Inland Revenue just ignores this group, and since this is the simplest approach it is adopted initially here (the effect of alternative assumptions is discussed below). The importance of the second problem (the small numbers in certain cells) can be reduced by averaging over a number of years, and the five-year period 1963–7 is taken as a basis for the estimates. This also serves to reduce the error introduced by the fact that the Estate Duty statistics do not relate precisely to deaths occurring in one year,[2] and by short-term fluctuations in the prices of assets such as shares and real property. The third of the problems listed above (wealth not appearing in the Estate Duty statistics) is discussed below.

Using the method and the assumptions described above, we obtain the estimates of the inequality in the distribution of wealth by age (and sex) groups for 1963–7 shown in Table IV. These estimates suggest that wealth within age groups is still very unequally distributed. In no case do the top 10 per cent of a group own less than 60 per cent of the group's total wealth; and the share of the top 1 per cent ranges from 26 per cent to 55 per cent. It is interesting to note that the degree of inequality is very similar for all groups except that of women aged 25–54, where the share of the top

[1] The deficiency has become more important since the Small Payments Act 1965, which raised the limit below which probate was not necessary.

[2] For this reason the general practice is followed of treating the Estate Duty returns for the year ending in March as relating to deaths in the preceding calendar year.

10 per cent is over 80 per cent (this presumably reflects the tendency of married women to have little property in their own name).

To put these figures in perspective, we may compare them with the degree of inequality in the over-all distribution. Applying the same method of estimation, we arrive at the figures for the whole adult population (male and female combined) shown at the bottom of Table IV, and we can see that

TABLE IV

Inequality by age and sex group—Great Britain, 1963–7

	Male			Female		
	Proportion of wealth in that class owned by top					
Age	1%	5%	10%	1%	5%	10%
25–34	31·2	50·5	64·1	54·8	80·6	92·7
35–44	27·5	49·3	63·1	43·9	74·6	88·5
45–54	28·3	52·7	66·8	38·2	66·4	81·2
55–64	26·8	51·2	66·0	29·0	56·9	71·5
65–74	27·5	52·8	68·1	26·8	54·1	69·3
75–84	28·9	57·1	72·4	26·4	53·6	68·8
85–	30·4	60·1	74·7	27·5	56·8	72·2
Whole population over age 25 (male and female combined)	31·5	58·3	72·7	31·5	58·3	72·7

the inequality within age and sex classes is not substantially less than that for the population as a whole.[1] In four out of fourteen groups the share of the top 10 per cent is actually greater than the share of the top 10 per cent in the wealth of the entire adult population. In the most egalitarian age group, the share of the top 10 per cent is 63·1 per cent—which is not a great deal less than the figure of 72·7 per cent for the entire population. These results suggest therefore that if we standardize for age and sex, the degree of inequality is not substantially reduced.

It is also interesting to examine the age distribution of total wealth-holding. If the life-cycle phenomenon were important, we should expect to find that those aged over (say) 55 would own nearly all of the total personal wealth—as *The Times* said: 'Where inheritance is not allowed only the old can be rich.' Table V shows, however, that the over-55s owned only slightly over half of the total personal wealth of the adult population in 1963–7,

[1] The over-all distribution of wealth differs from that given in the Inland Revenue Annual Reports, since different multipliers are used (the Inland Revenue multipliers are not published) and the estates of those aged under 25 and where age is not stated are not included here.

and those over 65 only slightly over a quarter. Moreover, if we look at the top wealth-holders, they are far from exclusively old: of those with wealth over £200,000 only a half were over 55 and only a quarter over 65.

TABLE V

Wealth and age, Great Britain, 1963–7

	Distribution of total wealth by age groups			*Proportion of total adults with wealth over £200,000*		
Age	*Male*	*Female*	*All*	*Male*	*Female*	*All*
25–34	9·4	2·4	11·8	13·1	2·5	15·6
35–44	11·6	4·3	15·9	13·0	2·2	15·2
45–54	12·9	7·3	20·2	15·4	3·8	19·2
55–64	14·5	10·3	24·8	16·4	8·5	24·9
65–74	8·2	8·4	16·6	8·4	5·4	13·8
75–84	3·7	5·1	8·8	4·8	4·1	8·9
85–	0·7	1·2	1·9	1·4	1·0	2·4
Total	61·0	39·0	100·0	72·5	27·5	100·0

Interpretation of the results

The figures presented above show that there is considerable inequality even among people of the same age, and this in turn suggests that there must be significant inequality in the distribution of inherited wealth. However, before we can draw any such conclusion, we must consider the role of two factors which may influence the interpretation of the results: the pattern of transmission of wealth between generations, and the importance of wealth not included in the Estate Duty estimates.

It is possible that some of the inequality within age groups can be explained by the way in which wealth is transmitted between generations. If it is passed on at death, inequality may simply reflect differences in the dates of death of the preceding generation. Those whose fathers died young would initially make up the top 1 per cent and would own a large share of the wealth of their age group. As they got older, they would find their share falling as successively more and more of their contemporaries inherited. The evidence presented in the earlier sections does not, however, suggest any clear tendency for inequality to decline with age—at least in the case of men. It is of course possible that the tendency for inequality to fall on this account is offset by certain families (those with good tax advisers) choosing to pass on their wealth well before death. However, this argument depends on the two factors cancelling more or less exactly, and it seems unlikely that this could explain a major part of the observed inequality. Wedgwood [9] argued that inequality in the age group 55–64 might provide a reasonable guide to the degree of inequality of inherited wealth on the grounds that they would in general have already inherited, but not yet made substantial gifts *inter vivos*. Unfortunately, our knowledge of the processes by which wealth is transmitted is so limited that it is hard to assess the validity of this argument. It is interesting to note, however, that the inequality among this group is not significantly lower than that for other age groups.

The estimates given above followed the method used by the Inland Revenue and as such excluded certain types of wealth 'missing' from the Estate Duty statistics: 'small' wealth-holdings, the value of pension rights and annuities, and property settled on the spouse or held in discretionary trusts. This procedure was justified on the grounds that we were *comparing* inequality within sub-groups with that in the population as a whole; and it does allow us to say that life-cycle differences are not an important explanation of the inequality shown by the estimates of the Inland Revenue. If, however, we are going to draw conclusions about the *absolute* degree of inequality within age groups, we clearly have to make allowance for the 'missing' wealth.

There are good grounds for expecting that the effect of such adjustments would be to reduce the degree of inequality. This is obviously true of those estates excluded because probate was not required, although the amount involved is likely to be small.[1] More important in quantitative terms is the value of rights to state pensions (and other National Insurance benefits). Their value is likely to be broadly the same for all those of the same age,[2] and their inclusion will definitely reduce inequality. In addition, there is the value of occupational pension rights and annuities. The estimates of Revell for 1961 suggested that the value of life and occupational pension funds (including an allowance for the actuarial value of non-funded rights) 'missing' from the Estate Duty figures was of the order of £10,000 million —or 13 per cent of total personal wealth. Unlike the state pensions, these are not distributed equally between people of the same age, and the same is true of property held in discretionary trusts or settled on a surviving spouse (it seems quite possible that this wealth would be at least as unequally distributed as that included in the Estate Duty statistics).

To give some indication of the importance of allowing for 'missing'

[1] It seems very unlikely that the average wealth of those not appearing in the Estate Duty statistics would exceed £1,000. For a person not to appear means either that no property was left or that the assets were of a kind where small amounts could be transferred without probate (principally National Savings and deposits in building and friendly societies). Lydall and Tipping [3] estimated that in 1954 those excluded from the Estate Duty Statistics had average wealth of under £300.

[2] Their value would tend to be higher for the wealthier, on account of their higher survival rates and of the differential pension under the graduated scheme (although this would have been extremely small for the period considered).

wealth, alternative estimates have been made of the degree of concentration based on the following assumptions:

(i) An average allowance is made of £750 per man and £250 per woman excluded from the Estate Duty statistics. These are essentially arbitrary figures, but give some idea of the sensitivity of the results.

(ii) It is assumed that the value of occupational pension rights and settled property is equal to 15 per cent of the wealth included in the Estate Duty statistics for each age group, and is distributed in the same way.

(iii) An allowance is made for the actuarial value of rights to National Insurance retirement pensions. The detailed assumptions underlying this estimate are described in the notes to Table VI, but the most important are the choice of interest rate and the fact that benefits are valued in terms of prospective benefits rather than contributions paid. The value of the rights would be higher if a lower interest rate were used, but it does not seem reasonable to suppose that it should be much lower than the figure of 5 per cent (in money terms) used in Table VI. Since the present value of benefits exceeds that of contributions at an interest rate of 5 per cent (see [1]), valuation in terms of contributions paid would tend to reduce the importance of pension rights.

Table VI shows the results obtained in the case of male wealth-holders in different age groups. As is to be expected, the effect of allowing for 'missing' wealth is most marked among those aged 45–74, since these have the most valuable pension rights. For these age groups, the share of the top 1 per cent is reduced by around 8 per cent, and the share of the top 10 per cent by some 15–20 per cent. However, even with these allowances, the degree of inequality within age groups is still very striking: the share of the top 1 per cent is in no case less than 18 per cent nor that of the top 5 per cent less than 36 per cent of the total wealth. If we compare the degree of inequality within age groups with that in the over-all distribution, the differences are smaller than in the 'unadjusted' case. In the most egalitarian age group, the share of the top 1 per cent is only 3 per cent lower than the corresponding figure for the distribution as a whole. These results do nothing, therefore, to alter the conclusion that life-cycle differences are not an important factor in explaining the observed inequality.

III. Concluding comments

It is clear from the analysis of the last section that life-cycle factors cannot explain the upper tail of the current distribution of wealth in Britain, and there are good reasons for believing that there is a high degree

TABLE VI

Inequality adjusted for 'missing' wealth—Great Britain, 1963–7

	Adjusted for 'missing' wealth			*Unadjusted*		
Male wealth-holders aged	*Proportion of total wealth owned by top* 1%	5%	10%	1%	5%	10%
25–34	25·1	40·9	52·3	31·2	50·5	64·1
35–44	20·9	37·7	48·9	27·5	49·3	63·1
45–54	20·2	38·4	49·4	28·3	52·7	66·8
55–64	18·8	36·4	48·0	26·8	51·2	66·0
65–74	18·7	36·4	48·2	27·5	52·8	68·1
75–84	22·8	45·4	58·4	28·9	57·1	72·4
85–	26·3	52·4	65·4	30·4	60·1	74·7
Distribution as a whole (male+female)	21·7	41·0	52·3	31·5	58·3	72·7

Notes on method of valuing rights to National Insurance pensions

(i) The present discounted value of the rights is calculated using an interest rate of 5 per cent (in money terms).

(ii) The pension is based on the average rate in force over the period 1963–7 (basic pension only, with no allowance being made for the graduated pension or other additions). It is assumed that both pensions and contributions rise at a steady rate of 5 per cent (in money terms), which has been approximately the long-run trend in the past.

(iii) The pension rights of a person aged 25–64 are valued in terms of expected benefits (calculated on the basis of the person's current life expectancy). A person is assumed to have earned a proportion of the benefit equal to the proportion paid to date of the present value of contributions over his life (assuming that contributions are paid from the age of 20 to the age of 64). The life expectancies used are those for the general population, and were taken from the Registrar-General's Decennial Supplement, *Life Tables for England and Wales*, 1961.

of concentration in the distribution of wealth inherited by people over their lives. It might be asked, however, whether we can reasonably regard inherited wealth as explaining the share of the top 1 per cent or 5 per cent, but life-cycle factors as explaining the rest of the distribution. If we were to take out the top 5 per cent, the distribution (allowing for 'missing' wealth) among the remainder would be as follows:

First 1%	3·9%
First 5%	18·3%
First 10%	30·6%

These figures are not too different from some of the more unequal distributions generated in the hypothetical egalitarian society considered in Section I. However, it should be emphasized that life-cycle factors cannot be expected to explain even this amount of inequality in the Inland Revenue distribution, since this excludes a large component of wealth acquired for life-cycle reasons.[1]

In the last part of Section II, I have presented an alternative estimate of the over-all distribution of wealth allowing for wealth 'missing' from the Inland Revenue figures. This estimate departs from earlier work in allowing for the value of rights to state pensions; and it is interesting to see that even with this allowance the degree of concentration remains very substantial: the top 1 per cent own more than 20 per cent of total wealth and the top 10 per cent more than half. The distribution of wealth is still much more unequal than the distribution of before-tax income. There are, however, two points that should be borne in mind with regard to this estimate. Firstly, the assumptions made (particularly the choice of interest rate, and the valuation of rights in terms of benefits) mean that it is likely to over-state the importance of pension rights and hence to *under-state* the degree of inequality. The 'true' degree of inequality probably lies, therefore, between these figures and those derived from the Inland Revenue estimates. Secondly, there are a number of important questions not discussed in this paper regarding the meaning of 'ownership'. Pension rights can be said to represent claims on future consumption; however, they are not assets over which the individual has current command (he cannot even borrow on the strength of them as with life insurance policies), and they are not relevant to assessing the distribution of *control* over wealth.

University of Essex

[1] The Inland Revenue distribution does show substantial variation in average wealth between age groups, but it increases steadily with age rather than exhibiting the inverse U-shape predicted by the life-cycle savings theories discussed in Section I.

APPENDIX

Suppose that the consumer plans his lifetime consumption to maximize

$$\int_0^T U(c_t)e^{-\alpha t}f(t)\,dt$$

where $f(t)$ is the probability of his being alive at time t and $U'(c) = c^{-\epsilon}$. Suppose further that his budget constraint is of the form

$$\int_0^T (w_t - c_t)e^{-rt}f(t)\,dt = 0,$$

i.e. the present discounted value of expected consumption must equal the present discounted value of his expected wage income.

The solution to this maximization problem is obtained by introducing a Lagrange multiplier λ and maximizing

$$\int_0^T [U(c_t)e^{-\alpha t} + \lambda(w_t - c_t)e^{-rt}]f(t)\,dt$$

which gives as a necessary condition

$$U'(c_t) = \lambda e^{-(r-\alpha)t} \quad \text{or} \quad c = c_0 e^{(r-\alpha)t/\epsilon}$$

so that the optimal policy involves consumption growing at a steady rate as assumed in the text. The rate of growth depends on the rate of interest, but also on α and ϵ and any combination of r and $g = (r-\alpha)/\epsilon$ is possible.

With the budget constraint assumed above, there is nothing to prevent a person planning to have negative net worth in a period when there is a non-zero probability of his dying, and we must consider under what institutional circumstances this is possible. The assumption made here is that borrowing is always secured by life insurance—as discussed by Yaari [10]. This raises the question of how negative net worth should be treated in estimating the degree of inequality. In the calculations given in Tables II and III, it is assumed that those with negative net worth would be treated as though they owned nothing, on the grounds that debts would not appear in estate-duty based estimates (in this respect assets and liabilities are treated asymmetrically—it being assumed that assets are included even though held in the form of annuities or pensions).

For further discussion of this model, see Tobin [8] and Yaari [10].

REFERENCES

1. ATKINSON, A. B., 'National superannuation: redistribution and value for money', *Bulletin of the Oxford Institute of Economics and Statistics* (Aug. 1970).
2. LANGLEY, K. M., 'The distribution of capital in private hands in 1936–1938 and 1946–1947', *Bulletin of the Oxford University Institute of Statistics* (Dec. 1950).
3. LYDALL, H. F., and TIPPING, D. G., 'The distribution of personal wealth in Britain', *Bulletin of the Oxford University Institute of Statistics* (February 1961).
4. MODIGLIANI, F., and BRUMBERG, R., 'Utility analysis and the consumption function: an interpretation of cross section data', in K. K. Kurihara (editor), *Post Keynesian Economics* (Rutgers University Press, 1954).
5. REVELL, J. R. S., 'Changes in the social distribution of property in Britain during the twentieth century', *Actes du Troisième Congrès International d'Histoire Économique*, volume i, Munich, 1965.
6. —— *The Wealth of the Nation* (C.U.P., 1967).
7. STROTZ, R. H., 'Myopia and inconsistency in dynamic utility maximisation', *Review of Economic Studies* (1955–6).
8. TOBIN, J., 'Life cycle saving and balanced growth', in *Ten Economic Studies in the Tradition of Irving Fisher* (Wiley, 1967).
9. WEDGWOOD, J., *The Economics of Inheritance* (1929).
10. YAARI, M. E., 'Uncertain lifetime, life insurance and the theory of the consumer', *Review of Economic Studies* (Apr. 1965).

[7]

THE AGE-WEALTH RELATIONSHIP: A CROSS-SECTION AND COHORT ANALYSIS

A. F. Shorrocks*

I. Introduction

THE age profile of individual asset holdings is frequently supposed to follow a hump pattern, increasing during the working lifetime and declining in later years. The theoretical explanation of such a relationship is firmly established, since it is a characteristic feature of life-cycle saving models. However, the empirical evidence has never been critically examined. A number of studies based on sample survey information have been regarded as confirming this hump pattern, but on closer examination the evidence is far from conclusive. Moreover the survey results conflict fundamentally with alternative estimates of the age-wealth relationship derived from estate tax data.

This paper begins in section II by examining this basic conflict. In the following section the relevance of cross-section studies is questioned, and a cohort is identified whose lifetime wealth characteristics can be studied. The sequence of observed wealth distributions for this cohort is obtained by selecting successive ten years age groups from the Estate duty statistics at intervals of a decade. Section IV is devoted to an analysis of the variation in the composition of any cohort as it ages. These composition changes arise from the fact that wealthier individuals have a lower mortality rate and therefore tend to become a larger proportion of the surviving cohort independently of accumulation behaviour. In these circumstances the characteristics of the representative individual will not necessarily correspond to the representative behaviour of the group. It is, however, possible to correct for this change in composition so that the empirical estimates can be compared with the predictions of economic theory.

Received for publication September 20, 1972. Revision accepted for publication May 20, 1974.

* This is based on chapter 4 of the author's Ph.D. thesis "Aspects of the Distribution of Personal Wealth," London University, 1973. Acknowledgements are due to Professors W. M. Gorman and F. H. Hahn who supervised the work, and to Professors J. D. Sargan and A. B. Atkinson who contributed useful comments on earlier drafts.

II. Empirical Estimates of the Age-Wealth Relationship

The asset holdings of individuals are estimated from two main sources of data: sample surveys of household behaviour and taxes on wealth, of which the most important is estate duty. Sample surveys have been conducted in a number of countries at different points of time, primarily for the purpose of investigating savings behaviour. The inclusion of questions concerning wealth ownership and demographic details such as age and family composition, have enabled some observations to be made on the variation of wealth with age.[1]

No attempt at a comprehensive review of this literature is made here. However, the general conclusion has been that the surveys confirm the existence of the hump pattern. For example, Straw concludes from the 1953 Oxford Savings Survey that

> In general, the ownership and value of the assets included in net worth seem to follow fairly standard patterns. They tend to increase with income and age, but to decline in the highest age group, as capital accumulated during the working years of life is run down.

Modigliani and Ando claim that the behaviour of net worth over the lifetime ". . . as revealed by the Oxford surveys seems to bear a fair relation to the pattern implied by the life cycle model." And Janet Fisher, reporting on a similar survey in the United States, concludes from her data that the mean value of liquid assets, taken as a proxy for wealth, ". . . continues to rise throughout middle age and declines only during old age."[2]

The main available alternative to surveys

[1] See Fisher (1952), Lydall (1955), Straw (1956), Modigliani and Ando (1957).

[2] Straw (1956), p. 26; Modigliani and Ando (1957), p. 110; Fisher (1952), p. 84.

are Estate duty statistics. For England and Wales the published data[3] include a number of years in which details of estate size are cross classified by age and sex. Assuming that those who die comprise a random sample from that age group, the numbers in any age-wealth class in the existing population can be computed simply by multiplying the numbers recorded in the corresponding age-estate class by the reciprocal of the mortality rate for that age. If mortality experience is not expected to be independent of wealth, the mortality rate can be adjusted to take this into account.[4]

The data used in this study are published in the Inland Revenue Reports for the years 1912, 1921, 1931, 1939, 1951, 1961 and 1971.[5] Minor adjustments have been made by reallocating the small number of estates recorded under the "age not stated" category and by estimating the male/female ratio in 1912 and 1921 when separate classifications were not published. The number of individuals recorded in any estate class can then be expressed as a proportion of the total deaths in that age group, obtained from the mortality statistics.[6] If mortality were independent of wealth, the proportion in any age-estate cell would be an unbiased estimate of the proportion in the same age-wealth category in the population as a whole. However, the evidence suggests that wealth and mortality are negatively correlated and in these circumstances the estate proportion will underestimate the population values. An adjustment has therefore been made using the mortality ratios m_w/m computed by Revell from the mortality experience of assured lives.[7] This correction assumes that, for those individuals whose wealth exceeds the minimum taxable estate size, the mortality rate m_w is independent of wealth and is less than the age-specific mortality rate m for the corresponding age group in the population as a whole.

The set of distribution curves for the various age groups contained in the 1961 Inland Revenue Report, constructed in the manner outlined above, is given in figure 1. The most

FIGURE 1. — DISTRIBUTION CURVES FOR SEPARATE AGE GROUPS

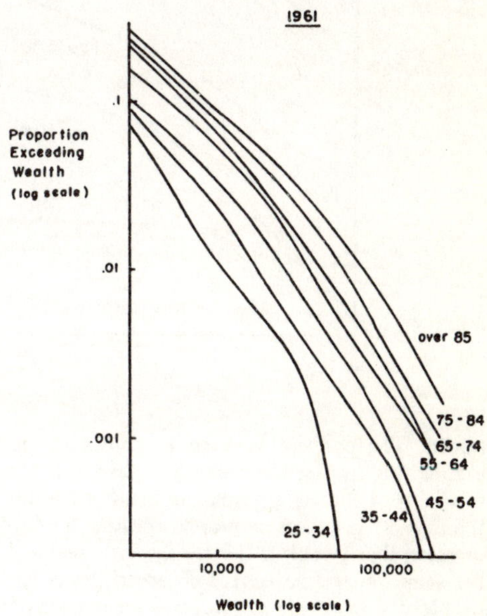

significant feature is that the distribution curves shift to the right with each successive age group, suggesting that wealth increases throughout the lifespan. Moreover, the shifts appear to be roughly of the same order of magnitude, indicating, because of the logarithmic scale, that the proportional wealth increase between age groups is similar.

As another indication of the age-wealth relationship, various percentiles have been calculated.[8] The computed values represent the

[3] *Report of the Commissioners of the Inland Revenue.* Various years. H.M.S.O., London.

[4] For a more detailed discussion of the Estate duty method and its deficiencies see Revell (1967), especially chapter 4, pp. 103–113.

[5] This paper concentrates on the wealth ownership of males in England and Wales during the past 60 years. Published data for 1971 covers only Great Britain and separate figures for England and Wales were kindly provided by the Inland Revenue.

[6] The data source for the number of deaths was the Registrar General's *Statistical Review of England and Wales.* H.M.S.O., London.

[7] Revell (1967), pp. 121–129. The actual mortality ratios used were

	15–24	25–34	35–44	45–54	55–64	65–74	75–84	over 85
m_w/m	.987	.729	.683	.697	.668	.718	.774	.845

and these have been assumed to remain constant for the period under consideration, 1911–1971.

[8] Throughout this study the wealth characteristics of different age groups are distinguished by the minimum

minimum wealth of the top 1%, 5%, and 10% in each age group. Plotting the age profiles for each of those percentile values figure 2 is ob-

FIGURE 2. — WEALTH PERCENTILES BY AGE 1961

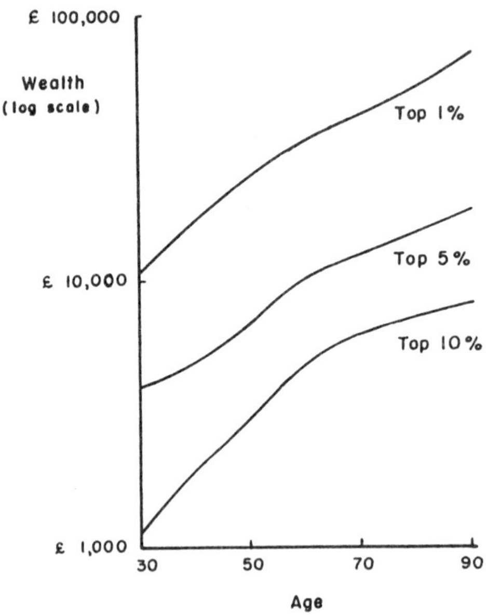

tained. The convention used to construct the graphs was to plot the percentile values at the midpoint of the age groups and at 90 years for the over 85 group. The graphs confirm the impression that wealth is increasing with age, and the same general pattern is observed if the age profiles for any other of the years are examined. These results correspond to Atkinson's observation that[9]

> The Inland Revenue distribution does show substantial variation in average wealth between age groups, but it increases steadily with age rather than exhibiting the inverse U-shape predicted by the life cycle savings theories. . . .

It thus appears that the evidence derived from the two sources of data is inconsistent in one major respect. The sample surveys suggest that wealth increases with age up to about age 60 and then declines, whilst the Estate duty estimates indicate that wealth is a monotonic function of age, with wealth growing at a constant rate throughout the latter period of the lifespan. This apparent conflict may be partly due to the deficiencies of both methods of estimation. In sample surveys only certain categories of assets are included in the questionnaire, and stock and shareholdings are valued by the individuals themselves. More important is the serious under-estimate of both the numbers and wealth of the more affluent households.[10] Estimates from Estate duty data relate to individuals rather than families and include only the wealthier members of the population. In addition, some assets may escape valuation due to legal exemption or tax evasion.[11] However, the most likely explanation is that the two data sources are representative of different sets of people — Estate duty evidence indicating the behaviour of the wealthier individuals and survey information that of the less affluent.

III. Wealth Ownership for a Cohort Over Time

In the examination of single period cross-section information it should be remembered that it is not admissible as evidence of accumulation behaviour over time. The existence of the hump savings characteristic is a statement about the asset behaviour of an individual or cohort over its lifespan. Any pattern discovered in wealth holdings of different age groups in any particular year does not necessarily imply a similar relationship for the ownership of wealth over a lifetime and cannot therefore be

wealth of the top 1%, 5% and 10% of wealth holders. The advantage of using percentiles, as opposed to more conventional statistics, is that they avoid making arbitrary assumptions about asset ownership at either end of the wealth spectrum. In estimating percentile values the observed distribution was not assumed to follow any specific frequency function. Instead a simple interpolation rule was applied between the known points of the distribution curve. In a few cases the estimated percentiles are less than the minimum taxable estate size and have consequently been derived by extrapolation. These may be less reliable than those obtained by interpolation and are indicated as they occur in the results.

[9] Atkinson (1971), p. 253 footnote.

[10] See Hill et al. (1955), Ferber (1966).

[11] One category of assets which escapes valuation are that vanishing at death, a category including human capital and pension and annuity rights. No attempt is made here to impute the value of these assets. The effect of avoidance is difficult to assess, particularly since the history of estate tax law has been one of progressive elimination of the legitimate loopholes.

used in support of such a hypothesis. In fact it is easy to produce a counterexample demonstrating that a hump in the cross-section profile can be derived when individual behaviour over the lifespan does not exhibit the hump savings characteristic.

Denote by $A(v, u)$ the asset holdings of the representative individual born in year v and aged u. For the specific example chosen here it will be assumed that individuals own no wealth up to the age of 25, after which point wealth is a linear function of age. The age-wealth profile after 25 years is a straight line and does not exhibit the hump savings feature. It will also be assumed that due to growth, either real or nominal, this profile is shifting upwards over time. In its simplest form this generation factor takes the form of a constant growth rate k so that

$$A(v,u) = \begin{cases} 0 & 0 \leqq u \leqq 25 \\ \alpha(u-25)e^{kv} & u \geqq 25 \end{cases}$$

Now consider the cross-section profile in year t. If $D(t, u)$ is the wealth of the representative individual aged u in year t, then

$$D(t,u) = A(t-u,u)$$
$$= \begin{cases} 0 & 0 \leqslant u \leqslant 25 \\ \alpha(u-25)e^{k(t-u)} & u \geqslant 25 \end{cases}$$

and when $u \geqq 25$

$$\frac{\partial D(t,u)}{\partial u} = \alpha e^{k(t-u)}\{1 - k(u-25)\}$$
$$\gtreqless 0 \text{ as } u \lesseqgtr 25 + 1/k.$$

A generation growth rate k equal to 2.5% would mean that the cross-section profile increases with age to a maximum at age 65 (independent of α) and then declines. It is easy to see from figure 3 how such a cross-section pattern might be misinterpreted as evidence for

FIGURE 3. — COHORT AND CROSS-SECTION PROFILES VIEWED AT TIME t

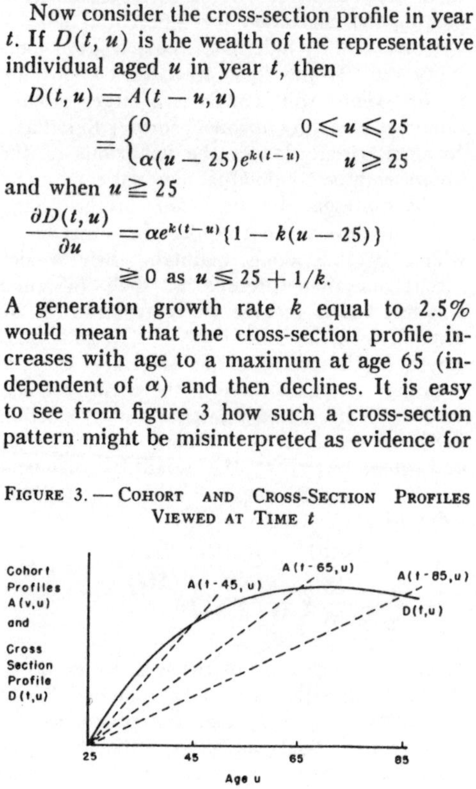

hump savings. When the assumption of linearity for the profiles $A(v, u)$ is discarded, and the multiplicative generation factor is restricted only to be monotonically increasing, then a cross-section hump feature is necessary but not sufficient to ensure a hump pattern in lifetime asset behaviour. If cross-section evidence shows that mean wealth decreases above a certain age, it is impossible to determine whether this indicates a corresponding pattern for the life cycle or whether it is the result of considering different generations at different points of their lives.

Perhaps the reason this point has been overlooked so frequently is that no satisfactory substitute for cross-section studies has been known. An alternative is, however, available. Despite the paucity of data on wealth ownership the British Estate duty statistics have a long history of publication and can be used to construct a sequence of distribution curves for the wealth of a particular cohort over its lifetime.

The construction of such a series is possible when Estate duty data for selected years are combined. The basis for this is the trivial observation that the 35–44 age group sample contained in the 1921 Inland Revenue Report comes from approximately the same cohort population as the 45–54 age group in 1931 and the 65–74 sample of 1951. Since the age groups span ten years the ideal situation would be to consider the Inland Revenue Reports at intervals of a decade. These data are not available for a long series of Estate duty statistics cross classified by age and estate size, but the series selected in this analysis is the best approximation, with gaps only in 1911 and 1941. The data for 1912 and 1939 are used to fill in these missing years by estimating the appropriate age group as a weighted arithmetic mean of the corresponding overlapping classes.

Table 1 shows how the percentile values for the cohort aged roughly 25–34 in 1910 can be traced over its lifetime. The estimates given are for the nominal percentiles of the surviving members of the cohort and the same estimates valued at 1960 prices.[12] These lifetime profiles are plotted in figure 4. The results show that

[12] Adjustments were made on the basis of the consumer price index.

TABLE 1. — CONSTRUCTION OF THE LIFETIME WEALTH CHARACTERISTICS OF A COHORT

Year of Report	1912	1921	1931	1939	1951	1961	1971
Age Group Considered	26–35	35–44	45–54	53–62	65–74	75–84	over 85
Minimum Wealth (nominal £) of the top							
1%	2,055	9,114	16,411	23,603	39,564	55,386	80,326
5%	*141*	1,490	3,567	5,172	10,331	15,828	26,982
10%	*23*	546	1,593	2,307	5,006	7,636	14,117
Minimum Wealth (1960 prices) of the top							
1%	7,267	12,573	35,676	51,978	58,726	55,386	53,979
5%	*499*	2,055	7,754	11,390	15,335	15,828	18,132
10%	*81*	753	3,463	5,080	7,431	7,636	9,487

Estimates in italics were derived by extrapolation.

FIGURE 4. — LIFETIME PERCENTILE VALUES FOR THE SURVIVING MEMBERS OF A COHORT

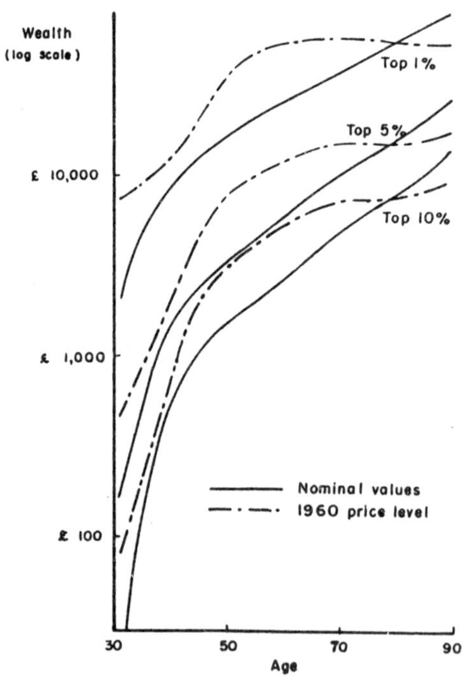

for the surviving members of this cohort nomimal wealth increases monotonically with age. In fact, since the curves are approximately linear above the age of 45, accumulation appears to be increasing exponentially. Correcting for price changes leads the profiles to flatten out around the age of 70, but there is no significant decline in wealth during retirement.

IV. The Composition Adjustment

It is tempting to deduce from the above results that wealth increases monotonically with age and that the hump characteristic is not observed. However, one important point has so far been neglected. It has been assumed, in making the correction for differential mortality, that wealthy individuals have a lower mortality rate. If this is so then the composition of any cohort will change as a larger proportion of the wealthy members survive to old age. In these circumstances the behaviour of the "representative" individual may not correspond to the representative behaviour of the group.

As an illustration consider the situation in which all individuals maintain their wealth throughout their lifetime at their inherited amount, which for the ith individual will be denoted by A_o^i. Thus $A^i(u) = A_o^i$. Call those whose assets exceed some arbitrary level w 'wealthy.' At age u those in the wealthy group number $N_w(u)$ and constitute a proportion $p(u)$ of the total population size $N(u)$. A proportion $S_w(u)$ of the wealthier members survive to age u compared with a population value of $S(u)$. Then

$$p(u) = \frac{N_w(u)}{N(u)} = \frac{N_w(O)}{N(O)} \frac{S_W(u)}{S(u)}$$
$$= p(O) \frac{S_w(u)}{S(u)}.$$

If the mortality ratio of the wealthy group to the total population is then less than one, $S_w(u)$ is greater than $S(u)$ and the proportion of wealthy individuals increases, although on an individual level no accumulation or decumulation has occurred. As the proportion of wealthy individuals grows, so will the average wealth of the group. The conclusion is somewhat paradoxical. In the absence of any accumulation, the "representative" individual is becoming more affluent.

The wealth characteristics of the existing population are naturally of interest to those concerned with policy matters. They may not, however, have much value as empirical evidence to set against theoretical predictions of accumulation behaviour. This is because the observed characteristics are those of *surviving* individuals, whilst economic theories are invariably described in terms of individuals for whom mortality, if explicitly recognised at all, is independent of wealth. Unless the changing composition is taken into account, the comparison between theory and empirical evidence will not be valid. For example, an increase in mean wealth may be used inappropriately as evidence of accumulation. This is essentially an aggregation problem which can be solved in either of two ways: the correlation between wealth and mortality can be incorporated into the theoretical models; or the empirical estimates can be corrected for this composition change so that they correspond to the experience of an "ideal" cohort for which mortality has been random. This latter approach is almost certainly the more convenient and is the one adopted here.

Where the mortality rate and wealth are negatively correlated, the wealth of the surviving population will overestimate the wealth of the hypothetical ideal cohort for which no such correlation exists. The composition adjustment effectively adds back to the cohort those who died, a group of individuals who would have been disproportionately poor had they lived. The correction involves dividing the proportion of individuals in the surviving population whose wealth exceeds a certain level by the survival ratio S_w/S for the appropriate age group and year. Compensating for this composition change is therefore similar to the adjustment for differential mortality, but works in the opposite direction.

For the younger age groups the survival ratio is close to one and the composition adjustment has little effect. However, the survival rate falls rapidly as the cohort ages and the magnitude of the adjustment becomes correspondingly large. For example, if only 5% of individuals aged 30 survive to the age of 90, and the mortality ratio m_w/m is constant at 0.8 throughout this period, then 24% of the wealthier members will still be alive and the survival ratio will be 4.8. The proportion of top wealth holders in the surviving population will exceed that of the corresponding theoretical ideal, from which mortality has been random, by a factor of almost five.

Efforts have been made here to standardise the cohorts at their composition when the groups were aged 25–34. Using a time series for the mortality rate by age group back to 1850,[18] the population survival probabilities for each of the years and age groups have been computed. The mortality ratios used previously for the differential mortality adjustment enable the corresponding survival probabilities for the wealthier individuals to be calculated and consequently the survival ratio S_w/S. The results are shown in the following table 2. These were the values used to standardise for composition with no modification made for the years out of sequence, 1912 and 1939.

TABLE 2. — SURVIVAL RATIOS BY AGE GROUP AND YEAR

End of Year	Age Groups						
	25–34	35–44	45–54	55–64	65–74	75–84	over 85
1910	1.000	1.022	1.069	1.170	1.384	1.855	3.034
1920	1.000	1.020	1.056	1.144	1.348	1.818	2.930
1930	1.000	1.017	1.050	1.122	1.303	1.756	2.942
1940	1.000	1.013	1.043	1.113	1.266	1.676	2.703
1950	1.000	1.010	1.033	1.101	1.254	1.603	2.558
1960	1.000	1.006	1.026	1.086	1.239	1.584	2.397
1970	1.000	1.005	1.021	1.075	1.217	1.555	2.374

[18] Registrar General, *Statistical Review of England and Wales*, Part 1. H.M.S.O., London 1974, table 4, p. 7.

The estimated percentile values, corrected for both differential mortality and changing composition, are given in table 3. As expected the composition adjustment is felt drastically in the older age groups. The table shows that for the cross section in any particular year, wealth initially increases with age but falls again before the last age group is reached. The cross-section maximum tends to occur later in the top one percentile estimates (generally 65–74) than for the 10% values (usually 55–64) with the maximum 5% value intermediate. Plotting the 10%, 5% and 1% percentiles by age for 1961 with a log scale for wealth, the impression given in figure 5 is that the hump

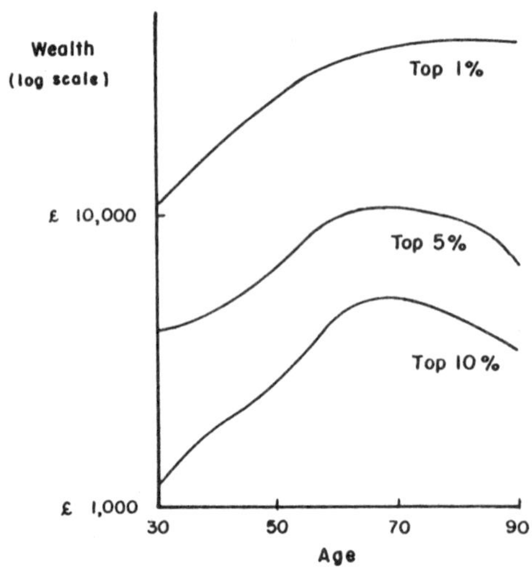

FIGURE 5. — WEALTH PERCENTILES BY AGE 1961 CORRECTED FOR COMPOSITION CHANGES

pattern is more pronounced for the less wealthy. The significance of the composition adjustment can be seen by comparing these profiles with those of figure 2.

For the cohort aged 25–34 in 1910 the age profiles for the top percentile values corrected for composition changes are given in figure 6. Nominal wealth still increases with age for the top 1% and 5%, but the minimum wealth of the top 10% reaches a maximum about the age of 80. When the estimates are valued at 1960 prices, the percentile values all increase with age up to approximately 65–70 years and then decline. Again the impression given is that the hump is more pronounced for the lower wealth holders. These results indicate that, allowing for changes in the composition of the surviving cohort, the real purchasing power of wealth owned by individuals exhibits the hump pattern, with maximum wealth attained approximately at the normal age of retirement. The characteristics of just one cohort is naturally not conclusive, but the same general features are observed in the age-wealth profile of other cohorts extracted from this series of estate statistics.

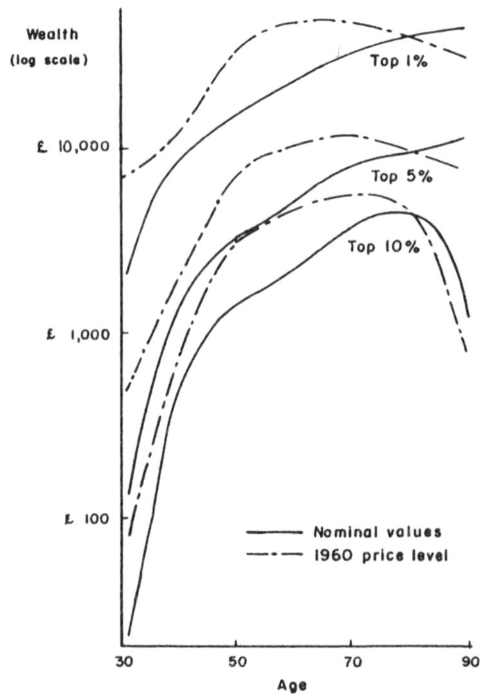

FIGURE 6. — LIFETIME PERCENTILE VALUES FOR THE COHORT STANDARDISED FOR COMPOSITION

V. Conclusions

It is clear from this study that wealth ownership varies considerably with age. In addition, the evidence contained in the previous section suggests that the lifetime ownership of assets does follow the hump pattern. However, this feature is not apparent unless the changing

TABLE 3. — MINIMUM WEALTH OF THE TOP 1%, 5%, 10% OF WEALTH HOLDERS BY AGE GROUP AND YEAR (£)
(Males. England and Wales. Adjusted for Differential Mortality and Composition Changes)

Age Groups	1912 1%	1912 5%	1912 10%	1921 1%	1921 5%	1921 10%	1931 1%	1931 5%	1931 10%
25–34	1,705	*74*	*16*	2,946	342	*42*	3,106	414	*58*
35–44	5,066	720	*77*	8,936	1,459	521	9,267	1,633	653
45–54	11,042	1,488	562	14,148	2,812	1,112	15,678	3,390	1,491
55–64	17,171	2,377	854	23,026	4,144	1,625	25,115	5,527	2,379
65–74	19,974	2,569	809	25,386	4,126	1,434	31,227	5,904	2,241
75–84	18,649	2,037	515	19,151	2,697	788	29,269	4,209	1,306
over 85	17,203	983	*42*	17,415	1,638	*82*	25,344	2,548	246

	1939 1%	1939 5%	1939 10%	1951 1%	1951 5%	1951 10%	1961 1%	1961 5%	1961 10%	1971 1%	1971 5%	1971 10%
25–34	4,964	702	136	7,411	*667*	*87*	10,803	4,028	*1,199*	22,454	*5,523*	*441*
35–44	8,739	1,995	788	13,378	4,375	2,284	17,263	4,853	*1,928*	33,232	12,609	*2,317*
45–54	16,679	2,774	1,167	20,981	6,300	3,281	25,189	6,769	*2,735*	37,205	13,108	*2,048*
55–64	23,244	5,097	2,239	27,850	7,852	4,010	34,306	9,914	4,566	52,659	15,249	*4,714*
65–74	28,963	5,570	2,253	33,423	8,278	3,839	37,615	10,656	5,269	49,843	15,233	*3,666*
75–84	29,236	4,838	1,691	32,941	7,192	2,973	40,915	9,740	4,571	48,296	14,574	*3,143*
85+	25,721	3,504	437	31,167	5,265	1,563	38,799	7,077	3,423	46,496	11,871	*1,201*

The estimates in italics were less than the minimum taxable estate and consequently obtained by extrapolation.

structure of the surviving population is recognised and suitable corrections made. The change in composition is particularly significant for the older age groups and will be relevant in the estimation of other age relationships, such as the income-age and consumption-age profiles.

The shortcomings of the estate duty method must obviously add qualifications to these results. Any interpretation of the trends should take into account that the data relate to the non-human wealth of individual males, and corresponding implications for households or families will not necessarily hold if changes in the structure of ownership within this group are taking place. Problems associated with the non-assessment of certain types of assets have already been outlined, and these may distort the comparison between age groups and years.

The greatest potential source of error, however, is in the differential mortality estimates. These influence both the estimation of the wealth ownership of the existing population and the calculation of the survival ratio used to make the quantitatively important corrections for changes in composition. These survival ratios are particularly sensitive to changes in the mortality ratio, and are unlikely therefore to be accurate until the relationship between mortality and wealth has been reliably established.

REFERENCES

Atkinson, A. B., "The Distribution of Wealth and the Individual Life-Cycle." *Oxford Economic Papers*, 23 (July 1971), 239–254.

Ferber, R., *The Reliability of Consumer Reports of Financial Assets. Studies in Consumer Savings No. 6.* (Urbana: University of Illinois, 1966).

Fisher, J., "Income, Spending and Saving Patterns of Consumer Units in Different Age Groups" in *Studies in Income and Wealth*, XV (New York: National Bureau of Economic Research, 1952).

Hill, T. P., L. R. Klein, and K. H. Straw, "The Savings Survey 1953: Response Rates and Reliability of Data." *Bulletin of the Oxford Institute of Statistics*, 17 (Feb. 1955), 89–126.

Lydall, H. F., "The Life Cycle in Income, Saving and Asset Ownership." *Econometrica*, 23 (Apr. 1955), 131–150.

Modigliani, F., and A. K. Ando, "Tests of the Life Cycle Hypothesis of Saving." *Bulletin of the Oxford Institute of Statistics*, 19 (May 1957), 99–124.

Revell, J. R. S., *The Wealth of the Nation* (Cambridge: Cambridge University Press, 1967).

Straw, K. H., "Consumer's Net Worth: The 1953 Savings Survey." *Bulletin of the Oxford Institute of Statistics*, 18 (Feb. 1956), 1–60.

[8]

The Dissaving Behavior of the Retired Aged*

I. Introduction

What do retired people do with the wealth that they have accumulated during their lifetimes? Simple life-cycle theory suggests that they will decumulate their wealth (i.e., dissave) in order to finance consumption, because that is why they saved in the first place. Some studies of the wealth-age relation confirm this pattern [4; 10], and the life-cycle theory has had considerable success in explaining aggregate saving behavior. However, precautionary, bequest, and status motives call for holding on to wealth rather than dissaving it, and examinations of the wealth-age relation among the aged by Smith [11] and Mirer[5] even suggest a tendency to save rather than dissave.[1]

This paper examines the saving (or dissaving) behavior of the retired aged using data from the 1963 and 1964 Federal Reserve surveys of wealth [9; 8]. These data have been used before to examine age-specific saving patterns [8; 3], but in those studies the specification of saving behavior was the same for all age classes. Here, models are formulated specifically for the aged: attention is focused on the saving/wealth ratio as the favored dependent variable, and factors such as life expectancy and bequest intentions are included. The analysis is restricted to the retired, rather than all the aged, because it is employment status rather than number of years lived that distinguish the aged economically.

The economic environment has changed markedly for the aged during the fifteen years since the data were collected. New government programs, including Medicare and Supplementary Security Income, and the inflation indexing of Social Security benefits have decreased the uncertainty that retired persons face. These make life-cycle dissaving more practicable, and thus the behavior analyzed here cannot be assumed to have remained unchanged.

The wealth examined here is fungible wealth, which does not include the capitalized value of future pension and Social Security income. To some extent, these plans have institutionalized the process of life-cycle saving, and to ignore them may be to rob the theory of its application. However, the proper valuation of these non-marketable assets is debatable and difficult in practice. The findings presented here must be understood as relating to only part of the total wealth-income-saving nexus that makes up the financial status of the aged.

In this paper, the next section discusses the data. The third section analyzes the distribution of saving rates and then presents a regression analysis of the determinants of saving and dissaving.

*The author thanks Robert A. Moffitt and Joseph W. Hunt for comments on earlier versions of this paper (presented at meetings of the Eastern Economic Association and the American Economic Association) and Erling Thoresen of the Federal Reserve for help in obtaining the data tapes.

1. The simple life-cycle theory has been under a state of siege lately [1; 14], but most investigators have been concerned with questions other than the behavior of the aged.

Table I. Extant Wealth (As a Percentage of Wealth at Age 65)

Age	Rate of Dissaving (percent per annum) 1	3	5	7	9
65	100	100	100	100	100
70	95	86	77	70	62
75	90	74	60	48	39
80	86	63	46	34	24
85	82	54	36	23	15
90	78	47	28	16	9

II. The Data

The 1963 and 1964 Federal Reserve wealth surveys, formally known as the Survey of Financial Characteristics of Consumers and the Survey of Changes in Family Finances, are widely regarded as the best available survey data on the distribution of wealth in the United States. The two surveys were a re-interview panel and provided information on a total of 2,164 consumer units (families or individuals) of which 347 had a head who was 65 years or older. More than half of these were fully retired (i.e., reported working zero months in 1963) and they are the relevant group for this study. Consumer units which underwent major demographic change in the two years were excluded from further study, in order to focus on realized dissaving plans.

The wealth examined here is a net worth concept aggregating detailed survey questions on family and personal ownership of investments, homes, automobiles, and outstanding debt at the end of 1962. The main assets not counted by the survey were certain life insurance items. Among fully retired families and persons aged 65 and over, median wealth was about $10,000; the lower and upper quartiles were about $2,000 and $28,000. (Note that these are 1962 dollars.)

In this study "saving" is simply the change in wealth from the end of 1962 to the end of 1963. Two features of the 1964 re-interview help reduce error in the saving response. First, respondents were shown the information they had provided the previous year about their assets and debts at the end of 1962. Second, for some assets the questionnaire asked directly about changes in holdings during the year.

The (proportional) saving rate is measured as the ratio of saving to wealth at the end of 1962, and hence it is the rate of change of wealth holdings. For zero and negative values of wealth, this ratio is not well defined. Also, for small positive values of wealth, the saving/wealth ratio is subject to considerable variability due to measurement error. Accordingly, in the work reported below only observations with wealth of $1,000 or greater are included. During 1963 the rate of inflation in the Consumer Price Index was 1.2 percent, and in the preceeding five years it averaged slightly less than that. Therefore, the nominal rate is adjusted by subtracting 1.2 percent in order to estimate the real rate of saving. When the saving rate is negative, it can be called the "dissaving rate" (with a change of sign).

Other variables used in the regression analysis are discussed below.

Table II. The Distribution of Saving Rates

Percentile	.10	.20	.30	.40	.50	.60	.70	.80	.90
Saving Rate	-10.8	-5.8	-3.0	-1.2	-1.2	-.3	1.0	3.1	7.1

III. Analysis and Results

The Distribution of Saving Rates

How much dissaving would one expect to see if the aged were planning to use their wealth simply to finance their own consumption? How little dissaving would reject the hypothesis that this is what families are doing? In the absence of specific knowledge about persons' utility functions, it is possible to conjecture some tentative answers to these questions, assuming retirement at age 65. Suppose that the optimal plan called for decreasing wealth by a fixed proportion each year, so that the dissaving rate is constant. (This would imply a decreasing consumption-age profile, which is theoretically appropriate). Table I shows the proportion of initial wealth (at age 65) that would remain on hand at various ages, for alternative values of the dissaving rate. Each column gives six points along the wealth-age profile.

To assess the alternatives, note that the expectation of life at age 65 was 12.7 years for men and 15.9 years for women [12], so that the expected age of death for an individual was about 80. With a constant dissaving rate of 3 percent, over half of the initial wealth would still remain at the expected age of death: this is not a very aggressive plan for wealth decumulation. As a tentative criterion, if the dissaving rate is less than 3 percent (i.e., if the saving rate is algebraically greater than -3 percent) then the dissaving implication of simple life-cycle theory should be rejected. This is meant to be a conservative test criterion, making it difficult to reject the simple life-cycle hypothesis.

Turning to the data, the frequency distribution of saving rates in the represented population of the retired aged was analyzed, and the saving rates at the decile points along the distribution are given in Table II. The median rate of saving (after adjustment for inflation) is -1.2 percent, and the lower and upper quartiles (not shown in the table) are -4.1 and 1.6 percent respectively. More than a third of the represented population show an increase in wealth (i.e., positive real saving), while less than a third show rates of dissaving greater than 3 percent. Thus, most of these retired units do not dissave their wealth so fast as would be expected on the basis of the life-cycle hypothesis.

Following an idea of Feldstein's [2] that the life-cycle hypothesis may be appropriate for most of the population but not for the very wealthy, the distribution of saving rates was analyzed also for a population restricted to those with wealth of less than $100,000. The resulting distribution was essentially the same as that for the whole population, and the same conclusion follows.

Determinants of the Saving Rate

The broadest form of the life-cycle theory of saving is simply an assumption of rational planning in an intertemporal context. Thus, in addition to providing for consumption during retirement, wealth may be held as a precaution for emergency needs and to provide bequests. Indeed, in their seminal paper on life-cycle behavior, Modigliani and Brumberg [6] noted all these motives but abstracted away from the latter two.

Beyond this, there also may be a desire to hold wealth for power or similar reasons that have not been treated customarily by economists. In addition, practical considerations such as the illiquidity of an owned home may inhibit dissaving behavior. On the other hand, wealth will be decreased if emergencies occur or if gifts are given to potential heirs—two uses of wealth that are related to motives for holding wealth rather than dissaving it. Thus, not all observed dissaving should be attributed to life-cycle consumption smoothing.

In most regression analyses of saving behavior, the dependent variable is the level of saving or the saving/income ratio. Here, attention is focussed on the saving/wealth ratio—called the "saving rate". Like the saving/income ratio, it is preferred to the saving level because it reduces the problem of heteroscedasticity. Further, for the aged it is natural to think of dissaving as being an allocation of wealth (not income), and hence the saving/wealth ratio is a behavioral variable—it is an indicator of wealthholding decisions.

The general statement of the regression model used here is:

$$\text{Saving Rate} = f(\text{Wealth, Income, Life Expectancy, Bequest Intentions, Insecurity, Other Factors}).$$

The income concept taken from the data is total income for 1963, excluding capital gains (which were not measured accurately in the survey). In some of the regressions, total income is broken into "pension" and "other" components to see if there are different propensities to save out of different types of income.

To account for life-cycle consumption smoothing, a good measure of life expectancy is needed. In addition to knowing each person's age and sex, it would be desirable to know specific aspects of his health and family history. Unfortunately, these latter variables are not measured in the survey. The life expectancy variable constructed here is designed to provide an index of the number of years of equivalent consumption over which wealth is allocated. (Of course, it may not be rational to plan to exhaust one's wealth by the expected date of death, since there is a good chance of living beyond). For single persons, it is taken as the age- and sex- specific expectation of life based on the 1963 life tables of the U.S. Public Health Service[12]. For married couples, the expected life of each spouse is calculated first, and the expected life of the couple is taken as the shorter of the two plus two-thirds of the excess of the longer over the shorter.[2]

Bequest intentions might be measured both subjectively and objectively. The 1963 survey asked about persons' reasons for saving, and if either of the first two reasons indicated a desire to leave a bequest, a dummy variable so indicates. One anticipates that those who desire to leave a bequest would dissave less than those who do not. Also, the survey asked whether people had received inheritances themselves. If they responded that inherited assets constituted a substantital portion of their current assets, a dummy variable so indicates. The hypothesis is that inheritors will be more inclined to leave a bequest than others. It would be desirable to have some objective measures that might lead to bequest intentions, such as the number of children and their economic status, but these are not available.

2. This approach is similar to that of Weisbrod and Hansen [13]. Note that it was considered above that the dissaving rate might be constant and therefore independent of life expectancy. More likely from a life-cycle view, however, is the hypothesis that the saving rate is positively related to life expectancy (i.e. negatively related to age); this would obtain if an equal absolute amount were dissaved each year.

No measure of insecurity or desire to hold wealth for precautionary reasons is directly available. A dummy variable indicating if the unit is a single person rather than married couple is included—partly because these types of units may have different perceptions of need and security, but also to allow for more general differences in behavior.

Finally, a variable measuring the proportion of home equity in total wealth is used to test the hypothesis that holding an illiquid asset will inhibit one's ability to dissave, at least in the short-run. Homeownership is quite prevalent among the aged in general, with about 60 percent of aged units being in this category [9, 33]. Overall, about 22 percent of the wealth of the aged is in the form of home equity, although the proportion is substantially higher in the sample examined here.

The saving functions are estimated for two samples of data —the complete sample of 160 observations[3] on fully retired families and persons with wealth greater than $1,000, and a restricted sample (N = 120) which excludes those with wealth greater than $100,000. Since the complete sample contains some very wealthy families, this restriction enables us to get better estimates for the range of wealth that includes most of the represented population. Also, as noted above, the life-cycle hypothesis may be appropriate for most of the population but not for the very wealthy.

The saving rate regression results[4] are presented in Table III. For the complete sample (equation (1)) wealth and income have significant effects when entered quadratically, but not linearly. Some strict versions of the life-cycle theory include a homogeneity postulate that would imply no relation between the dissaving rate and wealth. Here, the saving rate is significantly related to the level of wealth: it decreases with wealth up to the level of $3 million, and increases thereafter. The impact of income on saving is positive up to about $100 thousand, and negative beyond there. None of the other variables representing controls and auxiliary hypotheses are at all significant. When they are deleted, the wealth and income effects are not much affected.

For the sample that is restricted to observations with wealth less than $100,000, the results are different in several respects (equation (2)). When wealth and income are entered quadratically, neither is significant. In the linear form, the saving rate is found to increase rather than decrease with the level of wealth, and the estimate is significant at the .10 level: the greater the wealth, the less is the tendency to use it up.[5] The impact of income is positive and significant.

Among the auxiliary variables, only the home/wealth ratio is at all significant (using a one-tailed test at the .10 level). The impact is sizeable: a family with half its wealth in a home saves at a rate 1.5 percentage points more (or dissaves less) than it would if none of its wealth were in the form of an owned home. This supports the hypothesis that the illiquidity of a home inhibits dissaving. Surprisingly, the other variables were insignificant and of mixed signs. The expected length of life had a small negative effect on saving, contrary to life-cycle

3. Two observations were deleted as outliers: one had a home/wealth ratio of 1.5, which was 50 percent greater than the next highest value; the second had a saving rate of -86 percent (this woman seems to have lost her home), which was about nine standard deviations below the mean. The observations were not deleted in examining the distribution of saving rates above.

4. The regressions did not take into account the sampling weights. Porter [7] argues that if the regression is correctly specified, then the weighting pattern does not affect the validity of the least squares results. There are, of course, some arguments for taking the weights into account, especially in cases when the regression model coefficients are not homogeneous for the whole population or when the disturbance term depends on the sample weight. However, the correct procedure for taking these weights into account is not the standard weighted regression approach.

5. This finding is opposite to that in Mirer [5, 438].

Table III. Saving Regressions

	(1)	(2)	(3)
Dependent Variable	Saving Rate	Saving Rate	Saving Level
Constant	-2.05 (.80)	-5.74 (1.84)	- .715 (.79)
Wealth	- .00696 (2.15)	.0690 (1.72)	.0245 (2.11)
Wealth Squared	.00000113 (2.24)	--	--
Income	.277 (3.33)	.530 (2.44)	.162 (2.58)
Income Squared	- .00148 (3.47)	--	--
Expected Life	- .0616 (.36)	- .0368 (.19)	- .0155 (.27)
Bequest Motive	1.51 (.62)	.740 (.21)	2.75 (2.71)
Inheritance	-1.37 (.80)	-2.03 (.92)	- .616 (.96)
Single	.528 (.41)	1.18 (.78)	.452 (1.03)
Home/Wealth	1.65 (.97)	3.03 (1.52)	- .0323 (.06)
R^2	.09	.14	.25
N	160	120	120

Note: Parentheses contain absolute t-values. Saving, Wealth, and Income are in $ thousands; Saving Rate is in percentage points.

anticipations. The intention to leave a bequest had a small positive effect, but was quite insignificant. This may reflect the weakness of the bequest motive or of the measure itself. Those who had received an important inheritance dissaved more than others; the effect is sizeable, but not significant. Finally, single persons seemed to save slightly more than married couples.

The restricted sample provides a better fit than the complete sample, and estimation over the complete sample seems seriously to have distorted the impact of wealth. Hence, the estimation using the sample restricted to those with wealth less than $100,000 is considered the preferred form. Of course, these results cannot be extrapolated to the very wealthy.

To assess the importance of wealth and income in determining saving rates, Table IV shows the predicted saving rates for different values of these variables. Derived from equation (2), these predictions are based on the mean values of the other independent variables.[6] As noted above, the interquartile range for wealth among fully retired families (not just the

6. The approximate means (unweighted) are: 11.3 for Expected Life, .04 for Bequest Motive, .11 for Inheritance, .56 for Single, and .51 for Home/Wealth.

Table IV. Predicted Saving Rates

	Income				
Wealth	$0	$1,000	$1,700	$3,400	$10,000
$0	-4.15	-3.62	-3.25	-2.35	+1.15
$2,000	-4.01	-3.48	-3.11	-2.21	+1.28
$10,000	-3.46	-2.93	-2.56	-1.66	+1.84
$30,000	-2.08	-1.55	-1.18	- .28	+3.21
$50,000	- .70	- .17	+ .20	+1.10	+4.59

estimation sample) runs from about $2,000 to $28,000; this range yields a difference in savings rates of about 1.80 percentage points. The interquartile range for income runs from about $1,000 to $3,400; this range yields a difference in saving rates of 1.27 percentage points, suggesting that wealth may be considered more important than income as a determinant of saving rates. The table shows that families with below-average wealth and income may dissave sufficiently to be in accord with the predictions of life-cycle theory, while those with above-average resources may not. Of course, predicted saving rates also vary with the other independent variables: they would be noticeably lower for families who did not own their home and for those who had received a sizeable inheritance.

A regression explaining saving levels rather than saving rates is also estimated for the restricted sample, and it is presented as equation (3). The positive and significant impact of wealth on the saving level contradicts the simple life-cycle hypothesis: one would expect that dissaving would be greater if wealth were greater.[7] The marginal propensity to save out of income is estimated to be about 16 percent and is significant. Among the other variables, the home/wealth ratio loses its significance and changes its sign. Interestingly, the bequest motive shows up strongly positive and significant; persons naming a bequest as a reason for their saving saved $2,751 more per annum (or dissaved less) than those who did not.

Saving level regressions for the aged were also estimated with the Federal Reserve data by Projector [8] and by Friend and Lieberman [3] as part of studies of savings by all age groups. A major difference is that they included all the aged—the employed and the very wealthy, as well as the sample used here—in their samples. Both found that saving decreased as wealth increased, in contrast to the positive effect found here. The marginal propensities to save out of income were quite similar.

Regressions corresponding to the three presented here are also estimated with total income broken into "pension" and "other" components. In no case is there a significant difference between the two income coefficients.

IV. Conclusion

The evidence examined in this paper indicates that most of the retired aged do not dissave their wealth so fast as would be expected on the basis of simple life-cycle saving theory.

7. This finding is perhaps a more striking contradiction of the life-cycle theory than the test of dissaving rates examined above. However, when equation (3) is estimated for the complete sample, the coefficient on wealth is positive but not significant.

Among the retired, those who have the greatest rates of dissaving are those with modest levels of wealth and income. Some evidence suggests that owning a home or desiring to leave a bequest may inhibit dissaving, but the findings are mixed. These results are based on an analysis of fungible wealth, and do not include the wealth value of pensions and Social Secutity.

These results seem to be in accord with recent studies [1; 14] that dispute the basic claim of life-cycle theory: that saving for later retirement accounts for the bulk of total saving. However, evidence on the behavior of the retired aged does not necessarily tell us anything about the motives for saving by younger persons. The aged may very seriously misperceive their life expectancy or find it hard to break the habit of saving. Also, the finding of modest (or non-existent) dissaving behavior does not necessarily support the hypothesis of a strong motive to leave a bequest, because precautionary and status motives would lead to the same observable behavior. The evidence here shows only a small proportion of the sample expressing a desire to leave a bequest, and the impact of this intention on actual behavior is of mixed significance (though of the right sign).

The wealthholding behavior of the aged is relevant in determining the structure and benefit levels of income maintenance programs, including Social Security, that are aimed at the aged. If increases in benefits are partially saved (as they seem to be), then the consumption-effectiveness of these programs may be reduced and we may find recipients with larger wealthholdings at the time of death. Also, in means-tested programs there arises the question of how wealth ought to be treated. Should it be ignored (as in Social Security) or should it be subject to an implicit tax or manatory spend-down? The answer to this question depends, in part, on the behavior of the aged. If they behave as pure life-cyclists, then a mandatory spend-down rate would not be much of an imposition. If they hold their wealth for precautionary or status motives, it would be.

Thad W. Mirer
State University of New York at Albany

References

1. Darby, Michael R. *The Effects of Social Security on Income and the Capital Stock*. Washington: American Enterprise Institute, 1979.

2. Feldstein, Martin, "Social Security, Induced Retirement and Aggregate Capital Accumulation." *Journal of Political Economy*, September/October 1974, 905–26.

3. Friend, Irwin and Charles Lieberman, "Short-Run Asset Effects on Household Saving and Consumption: The Cross-Section Evidence." *American Economic Review*, September 1975, 624–33.

4. Lydall, Harold, "The Life-Cycle in Income, Saving, and Asset Ownership." *Econometrica*, April 1955, 131–50.

5. Mirer, Thad W., "The Wealth-Age Relation Among the Aged." *American Economic Review*, June 1979, 435–43.

6. Modigliani, Franco and Richard Brumberg. "Utility Analysis and the Consumption Function: An Interpretation of Cross-Section Data," in *Post-Keynesian Economics*, edited by K. Kurihara. New Brunswick: Rutgers University Press, 1954.

7. Porter, Richard D., "On the Use of Survey Sample Weights in the Linear Model." *Annals of Economic and Social Measurement*, 2, 1973, 141–58.

8. Projector, Dorothy S. *Survey of Changes in Family Finances*. Washington: Federal Reserve, 1968.

9. ——— and Gertrude S. Weiss. *Survey of Financial Characteristics of Consumers*. Washington: Federal Reserve, 1966.

10. Shorrocks, A. F., "The Wealth-Age Relationship: A Cross-Section and Cohort Analysis." *Review of Economics and Statistics*, May 1975, 155–63.

11. Smith, James D. "White Wealth and Black People: the Distribution of Wealth in Washington, D.C. in 1967," in *The Personal Distribution of Income and Wealth*, edited by J.D. Smith. New York: National Bureau of Economic Research, 1975.

12. U.S. Public Health Service. *Vital Statistics of the United States*, 1963, Vol. II.

13. Weisbrod, Burton A., and W. Lee Hansen, "An Income-Net Worth Approach to Measuring Economic Welfare." *American Economic Review*, December 1968, 1315–29.

14. White, Betsy Buttrill, "Empirical Tests of the Life Cycle Hypothesis." *American Economic Review*, September 1978, 547–60.

Part II
Population Ageing

[9]

Social and Economic Consequences of the Ageing of Western European Populations

By Alfred Sauvy

Of all the phenomena which have been affecting Western civilization in the last 50 years, the ageing of the population is the one least open to dispute, the easiest to measure and also the most stable.

It is least open to dispute because a person's age is an inexorable and inescapable fact which cannot be concealed: easiest to measure, because statistics based on the ages of the population are among the most reliable, at any rate in the countries with which we are concerned: the most stable, because the age structure is subject only to gradual changes, save in cases of exceptional disaster. It takes 20 days to start a business, 20 weeks to build a house, 20 months to build a factory or a dam, but 20 years to make a human being. A progressive unlevelling occurred because of the considerable progress of techniques and the almost total powerlessness of biology upon senility. Though the infant in its cradle finds its expectation of life increased, and the woman of 40 can seem younger than her grandmother did at the same age, thanks to sport, hygiene and cosmetics, on the other hand, sclerosis of the crystalline always begins at 25, and the change of life has not been postponed by science, which has been equally powerless as regards mortality at the older ages.[1]

Accordingly, the basic phenomenon of the ageing of the population must be the foundation of any explanation of Western European evolution as well as of any estimates of the future.

Facts

Several indices may be used for measuring the ageing of the population, the most usual being the ratio of old people to the total population.

In Western Europe, the proportion of persons aged 60 years or over has increased from about 80 per 1000 in 1850 to 140 per 1000 at the present time.

Persons aged 60 years and over per 1000 total population

	About 1850	About 1900	End of 1947
Switzerland	79	93	142
France	101	124	160
England	72	75	152
Belgium	89	95	156
The Netherlands	77	92	116
Germany	70	78	138
Denmark	82	99	131
Sweden	78	119	153
Norway	88	109	137

[1] This statement is made without prejudice to the possible progress of science in the future.

This ageing process will become more marked and will even accelerate at least for the next 20 years, even if the birth-rate should rise appreciably.

By about 1970 it is probable that there will be a new high level at the ratio of 220 persons, aged 60 years and over, per 1000 of the total population.

The curve may flatten out at that point. But if fertility rates should continue to fall, even higher percentages of old persons would have to be expected after an interval of a further generation.

Such advances in medicine, as the discovery of a cure for cancer, might cause a substantial increase in the proportion of old persons.

At the same time, within the adult population aged 20–60, there occurs and will continue to occur a kind of balancing action around the age of 40: the proportion of young people will decrease while the 40–60 years age-group will increase.

This movement is peculiar to Western Europe and some other countries with a similar civilization. In Central and Southern Europe the process has developed to a much smaller extent. As far as countries in the Far and Middle East are concerned, they continue having very young populations, and so does the Soviet Union.

Ageing happens, as it were, from both ends, that is to say by a decrease in natality (fewer young people) and by the lengthening of human life (more old people).[1] We should note that both these immediate causes are characteristics of a civilization which has gradually developed.

There are two types of consequences of this fundamental phenomenon:

(*a*) Direct consequences, almost 'mechanical', i.e. those directly resulting from structural changes. It is assumed here, that man does not change, and that a person of a given age, when faced by a given situation, will react in the same way as in the past.

(*b*) Changes in man himself which, though more difficult to observe and still more difficult to foresee, are no less important.

'Mechanical' consequences

Economically, a change in the age structure may influence consumption and production.

An aged person will not consume exactly the same products as a child. But the changes which may result from such substitution are slow enough to give the economy time to adjust itself.

A reduction in the demand for equipment affects savings and the state of productive machinery. The proportion of old machinery increases like that of old people.

The ageing of tools ultimately leads to unfavourable repercussions on the standard of living, a phenomenon clearly noticeable in France even before the war.

Is ageing a factor in unemployment? Upon the whole, in spite of the complexity of such a question, it may be answered in the affirmative. Persons over 50 have great difficulty in being re-employed once they have lost their jobs. Young people can easily find manual work, but appointments involving greater responsibility are

[1] The decline in infant mortality retards the process of ageing, but this is not the case with the fall in adult mortality.

a different matter. Owing to demographic stagnation, no sizeable new businesses are started, so that enterprising young men must enter an inflexible, slow-moving machine, without any hope of promotion to posts of higher responsibility until relatively late in life. In an expanding army with a heavy percentage of losses, a lieutenant may become a colonel or a general fairly soon; when the contrary applies, he is pained to find that there are more lieutenants than generals in an army.

Another phenomenon is actually occurring now. As we said above, young men easily find manual work. The number of such jobs is actually larger than the number of applicants, who naturally select the easiest jobs; that is why coal mines and 'primary industries', for instance, have great difficulty in finding labour. The coal shortage, in its turn, causes activity in other branches to contract. Great Britain experienced a new type of unemployment in March 1947; the same is happening in France where, every year, a number of factories have to close in January and work on a 'short time' basis throughout the year.

An increase in the number of old persons entails an additional burden on the adult population, to the full extent to which old age implies inactivity. Indeed, whatever the legal sources of income of an old person (direct support by his children, retired pay or old age pension, annuities, income from capital, etc.), such income is a charge upon the production of adult persons.

In particular, the wealth in the hands of the old is gradually increasing. In France, calculations have shown that the income of persons aged over 60 represents 20% of the national income.

Thus, the adult producer is confronted by a novel situation: his social, fiscal and family burdens are growing seriously. More precisely, the burdens are heavier than those borne by preceding generations. In these circumstances, three reactions are open to him. He may (i) have fewer children, (ii) reduce his standard of living, or (iii) refuse to shoulder the added burden.

In fact, all three reactions are visible:

(*a*) The fall in the birth-rate is partly attributable to this decrease of resources.

(*b*) Some fiscal or social burdens are accepted.

(*c*) But the third reaction is not the least interesting: the adult population *refuses* to bear the excessive burden. This refusal does not appear to be deliberate or even conscious, but is a manifestation of social biology. When the rate of interest does not come down far enough, pressure bears on the weak point, i.e. on currency. Accordingly, we see France, which entered the ageing process well before other countries, resorting to successive devaluations, which result in reducing the incomes or, more exactly, certain kinds of income of old persons.

Thus there appears a connexion, new in history, between demographic ageing and currency depreciation.

There are other ways in which the middle-aged generation can refuse to accept the burden of old age: housing offers a curious example.

After reaching a certain stage, ageing is always accompanied by demographic stagnation. The need for new housing then becomes less acute, a fact which makes it possible, without causing any serious untoward consequences, to fix rents much below the free market rate. If the demand for housing were heavy, such a measure—the effects of which are to halt or to slow down building operations—could not be maintained for long. On the contrary, it would last only so long as the advantage to established tenants exceeds the disadvantages to newcomers as well as to landlords. This is already the case in France, a country further advanced than others in the ageing process: present rents represent about 3% of the tenant's income and 20% of the rent required to make building profitable.

This is a new aspect of the 'silent struggle' between the adult generation and old age, since landlords are usually fairly old.

The electorate

Ageing of the electorate should also be mentioned as one of the 'mechanical' consequences. The approximate age-composition of the electorate in France, at various periods, is shown below:

Age-composition of the French electorate (%)

	1850	1901	1947	1970
Less than 40 years of age	49·3	47·1	39·8	35·5
From 40 to 60	35·7	34·7	37·0	36·5
Over 60	15·0	18·2	23·2	28·0
	100·0	100·0	100·0	100·0

Thus, people under 40 who, a century ago, represented half the electorate, are to-day a minority. The time is fast approaching when half the electorate will be over 50 years of age.

At first sight this change should make for conservatism; public opinion polls have shown that younger generations vote more for the 'Left' than old generations. But other and more complex factors, also connected with ageing, very strongly counteract this tendency.

In the first place, the demographic evolution of a country frequently runs on lines parallel to its social evolution. In France the political graph is very closely related to the birth-rate graph: the most progressive regions have the smallest number of children.

Moreover, the young embrace extreme left-wing doctrines as a form of escapism and as an expression of their refusal to accept an increasingly heavy burden.

The longing for security

In countries suffering from ageing, the spirit of enterprise, and hence the willingness to accept risks without which capitalism cannot function, gradually atrophies and is replaced by a new feeling: the desire for security.

This is not simply due to the 'mechanical' change resulting from the increase in the proportion of aged persons; both the young and the old modify their conduct.

An increasing number of elderly people are childless or live so far away from their children that family solidarity ceases to play a great part. At the same time, rising prices have greatly curtailed their savings. These rising prices primarily result from the war. But, as we have seen, they are accentuated by excessive ageing. In this respect, the landlord, as we have observed, is hardly better off than the stockholder.

Thus the 'problem of the aged' came into existence and was the reason for most social security schemes. Wages are now divided into two parts, economic wages and social wages, or, to put it in other words, working wages and non-working wages.

The problem of the aged brought with it, as its unavoidable corollary, the problem of children. These, like the young shoots of a tree with excessive growth, are in danger of choking. That is why family allowances or similar measures were destined to appear in countries suffering from ageing, as compensatory or balancing measures, or else as measures showing a dynamic reaction to the threat of accelerated decline.

But since the desire for security can hardly be reconciled with the spirit of enterprise, a hybrid situation results, viz. a transition situation between classic capitalism and an unknown system, often spoken of by economists or sociologists, but not delineated as yet, because the incentive urging a person to create and produce, which takes the place of the profit motive existing under capitalism, has not yet been found.

This is a curious situation, for while the previous rules of the game are honoured less and less, they still exist because nothing has yet been found to take their place.

The same kind of development has, from time to time, been found in the past. Old, decadent dynasties and obsolete institutions persisted because they possessed this great advantage over others, that they were already in existence.

At the present time, particularly in France, a reaction against social security is taking shape. Social contributions have become extremely heavy (about 35%) and producers are offering a resistance against which the Government is so impotent that at times it actually helps the resistance to become vocal.

Technical progress

This reaction, on the part of the adult population, to the fresh burdens, raises the problem all over again.

Happier solutions than the three mentioned above may be conceived. It may be asked if, perhaps through the help of technical progress, and without having fewer children or making any self-sacrifice, the adult producer could not bear the increasing burden.

Let us assume that, as a rule, work ceases completely at 60 years of age. On this assumption the number of persons working to every (non-working) aged person is 3·8 in England, 3·3 in France, 3·7 in Belgium, 3·9 in Sweden. Even this weak support is to become weaker still, and in 1970 the ratio will be 2·6 in England and in France, 2·5 in Belgium, 2·4 in Sweden. This shows that the situation in the various countries is comparable. Thus, let us take an average of 3·5 for the present and 2·5 for a generation later. Let us assume the pension or average income of an old man to be equal to 60% of an adult's income. This is a conventional figure used as an example.

In these circumstances, the average adult to-day who produces 6 units, keeps 5 for himself or his children, and has to put 1 aside for his old age. But a generation hence, if he still produces only 6, he will have to give away 1·4 and keep only 4·6. On the other hand, if his output goes up to 6·4, he will be able to ensure the same income to the aged without worsening his own position. Now, an increase of from 6 to 6·4 in 25 years' time is very small and very much below the rhythm recorded up till now. It would consequently be enough to devote a small proportion of technical progress to the maintenance of aged persons to enable them to keep their present standing.

But a great difficulty arises at this point. If technical progress takes place, surely the standing of each old person will have to be raised in consequence. Should some 'super-penicillin' be discovered, it can surely not be withheld from anybody! If housing, food, and clothing improve and if new needs are felt, by what right could old people be denied these improvements, to which their generation obviously contributed?

An uncompromising moralist might argue that, had they had more children, the number of producers would be larger; but if the optimum level of population has not been reached in France, it may have been exceeded in other countries like Belgium and England. An unlimited increase of the population would meet with other difficulties, in turn causing impoverishment.

In any case, whatever may be the juridical or moral arguments, efforts will be made to bring technical progress within reach of all and also to maintain the ratio between wages and income, or old-age pensions, which we have conventionally determined at 60%, at a constant level. In these conditions, however great the technical progress, the deduction from the adult's production will have to be increased.

This is an economic and social problem which deserves attention, particularly because the increase of the nation's general expenditure is tending in the same direction.

It is observed, admittedly, that taxes and deductions are coming to be regarded as normal. Englishmen and Frenchmen are bearing fiscal burdens which would have been inconceivable 30 years ago. But the greater the proportion of the national income to be redistributed, the more difficult it becomes for the capitalist system to function. At that point collectivism becomes more attractive. It is easy enough to give a producer a profit lower than his production justifies when he does not know its value—at all events easier than depriving him of that part of his profit which he already regards as his own property.

It is probable that the reluctance of the capitalist system to grant social compensation for old age has contributed to the development of collectivist doctrines. No relief is given in this direction by the nationalization of important industries, because that does not change any of the facts and because the producer in the nationalized industries cannot, in the present state of the national accounts, be sacrificed to the non-producer. He has the evidence of the wages in non-nationalized industries and demands a similar wage, even if the industry is working at a loss.

Prolongation of active life

Thus, technical progress solves the economic problems without touching the social scheme. Another method for reducing the producer's burden has appeared: it consists in shifting the dividing line between working life and retirement. The age we assumed for this break, in the previous example, was 60.

By this means, the number of producers is increased, while the number of retired people is decreased. The gain is considerable. By raising the critical age from 60 to 65 years, all other things being equal, retirement benefits are increased by more than 50%.

Lord Beveridge has shown that a social security scheme can be applied only by lengthening the active part of life as far as possible.

Such a process is unattractive, because it runs counter to general progress and thus appears retrogressive. Progress, indeed, makes for an increasingly better life in return for less and less work. Sustained by progress, or rather by their confidence in progress, both young and old favour a lower age for retirement.

This gives us serious food for thought. Like film stars and boxing champions, society does not realize it is ageing and even goes so far as to fly in the face of facts. Out of 100 Western Europeans, there are not 10, not even 5, who are aware of the ageing of the population among which they are living.

Human capital not having been 'amortized' by the production of younger generations, impoverishment follows the initial well-being.

Yet prolongation of working life may be less retrogressive and less inhuman than appears at first sight.

(1) While medical science has so far been powerless to cope with senility, nevertheless, a 60-year-old worker is less tired and less worn out than in former times, because working conditions have greatly improved.

(2) It is bad for health to switch suddenly from an active to an inactive life. The first year of retirement is marked by a heavy mortality rate. The farmer, being his own master, provides a good example by working all his life, but gradually reducing his work, and by keeping his work in proportion to his abilities.

A woman running her household, often in difficult circumstances, does not give up working on account of age. All that may happen is that her work is kept within the limits of her physical capacity.

A very large number of easy jobs (as, for instance, that of a watchman) can be retained until a very advanced age. Such jobs may be reserved for aged persons.

This process might even enable workers engaged in hard and difficult work to give it up when they are about 50 years old, which would mean an advance on present practice.

Thus the prolongation of working life, viz. the utilization of fairly old persons, is one of the problems which have hardly received any attention hitherto but which should be among the first to be studied.[1]

[1] The *Institut National d'Études Démographiques*, being responsible for elucidating the French Government's demographic and social policy, has conducted an investigation into the possibilities opened up by a longer working life and into the psychological—rather than technical—difficulties which this extension encounters. Cf. J. Davic, *Vieillissement de la Population et prolongation de la vie active*. Paris, 1948.

Emigration or immigration?

The insufficiency of young blood has some curious consequences: it may, at the same time, cause both an immigration movement and an emigration movement.

The shortage of young miners and workers in the heavy occupations causes gaps harmful to the whole of the economy. Workmen or clerks can hardly be asked to give up their existing jobs in order to take harder ones. And since the professional structure is modified but very slowly by the introduction of new blood, immigration appears to be the only means of filling the gaps quickly enough.

Such immigration can only come from a country with surplus labour and a lower standard of living. The Slav countries, which answered both these requirements before the war, have closed their frontiers and even recalled their nationals from abroad. Germany raises a very special problem, which we shall not consider here. Spain and Rumania are isolated. The only country left in Europe is Italy, which receives urgent offers from various countries and which admits, without any false shame, that men being her only wealth, she has to derive some profit from them.

A region which is a little, but not much more remote, North Africa and Algeria particularly, i.e. an area of high demographic pressure, is already sending men to France; this has obvious hygienic and social disadvantages. Will Europe some day look further afield and draw upon the Middle East or Asia?

That moment has not yet come. In spite of the acute shortage of young workers, the memory of the great depression is still too vivid in industrial countries for them to embark on such an adventure, which, at best, would raise particularly difficult social and political problems.

In any case, nobody can affirm that the present period of full employment—and even over-full employment—will continue. Accordingly the immigration schemes prepared in Britain, Sweden and elsewhere met with strong opposition from the trade unions. Even in France, where the threat of unemployment springs from the shortage of miners and of primary producers, an extremely cautious policy is stopping at the frontier Italian workers anxious to leave their overcrowded country. Last year, 30,000 of them secretly crossed the Alps on foot and, more than once, men, and even women and children, were found dead in the snow on their way to France.

Will Europeans be reduced to introducing large numbers of young people from a more primitive civilization in order to be safe in their old age? So far, this picture requires an effort of imagination. This contingency is outside the scope of conjecture, unless extremely unlikely events take place.

Together with the question of immigration of young foreign workers, ageing raises the question of emigration. This particularly concerns Great Britain. In France, just after the liberation, large numbers of young men from upper middle-class families eagerly contemplated leaving their country for a foreign land. But this was a rather vague dream, easily given up in view of the difficulties of the undertaking. In Britain the movement seems more serious because it concerns wage-earners who find in the Dominions a welcoming country and a population speaking their own language.

Britain's economic difficulties are to a large part due to ageing: internally, there are the burdens of the New National Insurance Scheme and of the public debt; internationally, foodstuffs have to be bought abroad for the non-active population. The attraction of new countries is all the stronger, because at home the producer is heavily burdened.

Let us imagine that the emigration movement, at the present moment hindered by lack of shipping, takes shape and that the first settlers invite others to come. What will happen?

As emigration will take young people, it will weaken the British economy still further by reducing an already inadequate support. The more the burdens increase, the more will young people be tempted to leave, so that the movement may become continuous until a very difficult situation arises.

But the interest of the British Empire, considered as a whole, lies in a fairly large migration, since the productivity of an Australian or a Canadian worker is higher than that of an Englishman. But then the Dominions, as a compensation, ought to grant an income to the mother-country which deprives herself of her sons. Possibly, some day, a social security scheme covering the whole of the Empire may be conceived, providing for the remittance of part of the subscriptions to the mother-country. However, no such compensations are contemplated for the time being, and so the problem remains or rather has not yet fully arisen.

In any case, a migration from the British Isles towards oversea countries is of an entirely different nature from the migrations by which these territories were populated in the last century.

British official circles do not regard the emigration of young people to Canada, Australia and South Africa with disfavour, because they hope that thereby the bonds of Empire will be knit more closely. To make good the resulting losses and to fill the gaps in some basic industries they may propose to look to immigration.

If large scale emigration from England towards her Dominions occurred at the same time as an immigration of Mediterranean or Asiatic workers towards England, we should be witnessing a social phenomenon unique in history. Its accomplishment implies, at any rate, a long period of full employment. Nobody can give a reliable forecast on this point and we sincerely hope the reader will forgive our incautious speculations regarding an uncertain future.

Conclusion

Ageing, being a lengthy process which began a century ago, is only now beginning to show its first effects. Its slowness, its inertia and its bare perceptibility make it particularly formidable. Unless there are sensational discoveries, human science is bound to aggravate it still further by its successful fight against premature death.

The danger of an eclipse of Western civilization owing to lack of replacement of its human stock cannot be questioned. Perhaps we ought to regard this organic disease, this lack of vitality of the cells, as a symptom of senility in the body politic itself and thus compare social biology with animal biology. That would be proceeding too rapidly; there is nothing to prove that an effort of conscience and of thought would be impossible in a modern society.

'The level of a civilization', said Paul Valéry, 'may be judged by the number of contradictions it accumulates.' We might add: 'by the number of contradictions it can tolerate.' At the very moment when living conditions are changing more quickly than ever before, the proportion of aged men has never been so high.

Since the beginning of the century, changes have been taking place in rapid succession, but half the men capable of action were born in the last century.

The frequently observed distortion in the rhythm of progress in various fields shows itself with full force in this field.

Of the various possibilities opened up by this longer span of life, we prefer to choose that of ensuring sufficient progress in knowledge to enable man to retain some influence over his own destiny.

[10]

Slow Population Growth and the Relative Size and Productivity of the Male Labor Force

WILLIAM J. SEROW*

I. Introduction

The current interest in the feasibility and desirability of a stationary population has led to several recent studies of the demographic conditions needed to produce a stationary population and of the long-run implications of alternate paths to the stationary state [8, pp. 379-97; 21]. The study of the economic and demographic implications of population stationarity has had a fairly extensive history in the literature [19, pp. 3-7], and there has been considerable revival of interest of late [5, pp. 495-54; 7, pp. 223-31].

Absolute stationarity of population will eventually result from the attainment of replacement level fertility and a zero level of net immigration. The purpose of this paper is to expand the scope of previous study by focusing on the size and composition of the American male labor force that will result from the attainment of the replacement level of fertility, and compare this labor force to that resulting from a moderately higher level of fertility. Females are excluded because of problems of productivity measurement. Only individuals in the primary working years (20 to 64) are included in the analysis.

In order to limit the scope of the discussion, only two alternative situations are analyzed, the Series D and Series E projections of the U.S. Bureau of the Census. There are two specific effects which will be analyzed: first, the effects of changes in the age composition of the labor force and subsequent effects of these changes on labor productivity; and, second, the effects of a diminution of population growth on the capital-labor ratio and subsequent effects of these changes on labor productivity.

*Tayloe Murphy Institute, University of Virginia. Presented at the third annual conference of the Atlantic Economic Society held in Washington, D.C., September 11-13, 1975.

There are a variety of reasons for considering the labor force in this context. First, as a factor of production, the volume of total output may be considered to be dependent upon the size of the labor force. Because in a situation of declining population growth rates, eventually leading to condition of both stationarity and stability of population, changes in the labor force will be determined by labor force participation rates rather than demographic change. Consequently, a major determinant of the level of output will also be the productivity of the labor force.

One might follow the line of reasoning of Leibenstein [16, pp. 175-98] who argues that aggregate labor productivity is enhanced by growth of the labor force, since new entrants are presumably better equipped (in terms, say, of education) for productivity. Thus, the higher the excess of entrants over departures (within reasonable limits), the more rapidly will labor productivity grow. However, Jones and Gingrich [12, pp. 226-48] found that in the context of developing counties such a process would be made more difficult due to the costs associated with providing educational services to relatively large numbers of persons about to enter the labor force. In the context of the United States, one might argue that the decline in the rate of replacement (as Leibenstein puts it) would permit increases in the volume of human capital embodied in the new entrants to the labor force. Presumably, these better endowed persons would add to aggregate productivity.

II. Demographic Implications of Fertility Reduction

The effect of a lessening of population growth upon the age composition of a population is well known to demographers. The age composition of a population at any point in time is, of course, a direct reflection of that population's history of fertility and mortality [2, pp. 61-116]. The absolute size of a population depends upon these factors, as well as on the size of the population on which these factors operated. The Series E projection assumes that each woman will bear an average of 2.11 children over her lifetime. Mortality is assumed to decline somewhat; the annual volume of net immigration is fixed at 400,000. The Series D projection is identical except that completed family size is pegged at 2.45 children. Because of what Keyfitz [15, pp. 71-80] calls the momentum of population growth, estimates for the United States suggest that it will take approximately 70 years for a stationary population to be attained once replacement is reached.

The Series E population would be considerably different in size and composition from that which would result from continuous growth of population under the Series D assumptions. By the year 2020, the population with replacement fertility (Series E) would have median age of 35.7 years, compared with 32.4 years for the Series D population. By way of contrast, the median age in the United States in 1970 was 27.9 years. Population size (about 205 million in 1970) would grow by nearly 50 percent to 307 million in 2020 in the Series E projection and by about 75 percent under the Series D projection.

In brief, an increase of about one third child per woman would add by 2020 about a fourth of the present U.S. population to the level consistent with the ultimate stationary population.

There will be a considerable shift in the ratio of persons of working age (20 to 64 years of age in this study) to the rest of the population (dependents). This is true under both the Series D and Series E assumptions, but is so to a somewhat greater extent in the Series E case. The number of dependents per 100 persons of working age (dependency ratio) was 90.6 in 1970. In the Series D projection, this would gradually fall to 78.6 in the year 2020. Under the Series E assumptions, the dependency ratio would be only 71.0.

III. Implications for Labor Productivity

A. General Considerations

With technical progress, one would anticipate increases in productivity of labor over time due to factors such as increasing training and education of the labor force and the possibility of increases in the capital-labor ratio.

One way of considering this is from a cohort approach. For each cohort (that is, a group of persons born within the same time interval), productivity at any age will be greater than that of an earlier cohort at the same age, and less than that of a later cohort at the same age. At any point in time, the aggregate level of productivity of the labor force will be determined by the relative levels of productivity of each cohort and by the relative size of that cohort in relationship to the entire labor force. Thus, productivity in this simplified schema is determined by the relative heights of the productivity curve of each cohort (which represents how education, training, more capital, and so on affect inter-cohort levels of productivity), as well as the shape of the curve itself (that is, how productivity is related to age or intra-cohort levels of productivity). Intra-cohort levels of productivity are assumed to be constant in a relative sense. The argument of this relatively simple approach, therefore, is that productivity differences between the Series D and Series E populations are a result of differences in the age composition and the capital endowments.

B. Demographic Considerations

Differences in the age composition of the male labor force aged 20-64 are given in Table 1. These are simply the result of multiplying adjusted 1970 labor force participation rates by the age composition. Labor force participation for men has been declining at all ages in recent years. The 1970 rates are adjusted simply by assuming a linear decline of 5 percent on all rates, spread over 50 years. After 1990 (when differential fertility becomes relevant to the labor force), the Series D labor force is clearly younger, although not to a considerable extent. The question now is whether or not the slightly older labor force of a population approaching stationarity would differ significantly from the labor force of a slowly increasing population in terms of per capita productivity.

TABLE 1

AGE DISTRIBUTION OF THE MALE LABOR FORCE[a] AGED 20-64 OF THE SERIES D AND SERIES E PROJECTIONS, 1970-2020[b]

	1970	1980	1990	2000	2010	2020
Series D						
20-24	15.4	16.0	12.0	13.7	12.7	12.3
25-34	24.9	31.1	31.1	25.1	27.9	26.4
35-44	22.7	21.1	27.5	27.1	22.1	26.1
45-54	21.9	17.7	17.4	22.3	22.1	19.2
55-64	15.7	41.1	12.0	11.8	15.2	16.0
Number of Persons (millions)	47.7	56.6	64.0	73.3	83.5	89.1
Percent of the Labor Force Under 45 Years Old	63.0	68.1	70.6	65.9	62.7	64.8
Mean Age	40.0	38.7	38.9	39.7	40.2	40.3
Series E						
20-24	15.4	16.0	12.0	12.6	11.7	11.1
25-34	24.9	31.1	31.1	25.0	26.3	25.1
35-44	22.7	21.1	27.5	27.7	22.8	25.6
45-54	21.9	17.7	17.4	22.7	23.3	20.6
55-64	15.1	14.1	12.0	12.0	15.9	17.6
Number of Persons (millions)	47.7	56.6	64.0	71.9	79.2	81.2
Percent of the Labor Force Under 45 Years Old	63.0	68.2	70.6	65.3	60.8	61.8
Mean Age	40.0	38.7	38.9	40.0	40.8	41.1

[a] Employed civilian only.
[b] All values in percent except mean age and size of labor force.

Brennan, Taft, and Schupack note that a relationship between productivity and age on an aggregate statistical level is not directly observable. However, in deriving demand equations for labor by age, they suggest the existence of such a relationship [1, p. 207]:

> "Older workers show a smaller increase in employment with respect to expansions of product demand and industry output. They also show relatively low wage elasticity of demand . . ."

These data suggest that, in general, the employment of workers aged 25-44 is most strongly affected by increases in industry output, followed by workers aged 15-24, and finally, by workers 45 years of age and older. To what extent these differences are due to observed or expected productivity differences and to what extent they are due to nonmarket forces is impossible to say. In discussing productivity as a function of age, Corson and McConnel note [4, p. 61] " . . . the evidence points to a gradual but continuous decline in productivity after the forties." Additionally, the most important factor may be, as Colberg and Windham [3, p. 40] suggest, the difference in the present relevance of the education of older and younger workers, as well as the amount of education (or human capital) as a function of age.

In order to estimate productivity as a function of age, U.S. Bureau of the Census data [20] giving earnings by age as a function of educational attainment were employed. In general, the higher the level of educational attainment, the higher the maximum level of annual earnings and the later in life would this maximum be reached.

Using these data, the weighted mean of earnings for several age groups was computed. The weights were 1970 levels of educational attainment for these age groups. Because the weights were used for the entire projections period, it is implicitly assumed that the relative level of intercohort differences in educational attainment would hold constant.

This measure of earnings was transformed into an index of productivity as follows. The highest cohort (in terms of weighted average annual earnings) was assigned a value of 1.0; the value for other cohorts was set as a percentage of this. The index values derived in this fashion were as follows: 20-24, .417; 25-34, .760; 35-44, .978; 45-54, 1.0; and 55-64, .824. It should also be noted that the rather strong assumption is made here that productivity is directly related to earnings, or that workers are paid the value of their marginal product.

The index values shown in Table 2 are the sums of the product of the labor force age distribution (found in Table 1) and the appropriate index of productivity. The 1970 values are set equal to 1.0; since the population base is the same for both the Series D and Series E, they are both equal to 1.0 initially. The resulting values for subsequent years under both productivity indices and both demographic situations are computed relative to their initial (1970) value. With a few exceptions, the index for both series shows marginal increases in aggregate labor productivity over the course of time. These are a function only of the changing age composition of the labor force; in other words, to this point we have made no effort to allow for productivity to be affected by technological change or changes in the capital-labor ratio. The index shows a higher level of productivity for the Series E projection than for the Series D projection. This, of course, is due to the relative differences in assumed productivity of younger (20-24) and older (45 and over) workers.

An implicit assumption contained in Table 2 is that the occupational distribution of the male labor force is unchanging during the 1970-2020 period. Such an assumption is clearly untenable, but not necessarily of compelling importance since we are concerned with the level of productivity of the alternative labor force projections vis à vis *each other* rather than vis à vis the initial level. Consequently, if occupation changes of the same type occur regardless of the future path of fertility, the ratio of productivity of one series to the other will be approximately the same as shown in Table 2, though the absolute values of the indices will be different (higher, if

TABLE 2

INDICES OF AGGREGATE LABOR PRODUCTIVITY, SERIES D AND SERIES E PROJECTIONS, SELECTED YEARS, 1970-2020

	1970	1980	1990	2000	2010	2020
Series D	1.0000	.9915	1.0080	1.0038	1.0015	1.0040
Series E	1.0000	.9915	1.0080	1.0072	1.0045	1.0063

the projections made by Johnston [11, pp. 159-87] are close to reality).

C. Economic Considerations

Thus far this study only begins to show how the labor force might be affected by variation in fertility over time. In order to demonstrate some of the probable effects, the Series D and Series E projections were employed in an economic-demographic model, which, although somewhat rudimentary in form, is capable of providing comparative estimates of economic indicators under alternative demographic situations. Although the output of this model should not be considered as a sophisticated econometric forecast, the fact that the model uses demographic change as a crucial input makes it quite useful for present purposes. With some minor revisions, this model is that developed by the General Electric Company's Center for Advanced Studies (TEMPO) [9]. The specifications of the model follow.

Given the projected population, P_t, at time t, and the age composition of this population, $P_{i,t}$, the employed labor force, L_t, at time t is defined as follows:

$$L_t = \sum_{i=20}^{64}(p_i P_{i,t}) \qquad (1)$$

where P_i are age and sex specific rates of labor force participation and employment. The values are initially taken to be equal to rates for 1970; following recent experience, labor force participation is assumed to decline linearly for a total of 5 percent over the projection period. Rates of unemployment are held constant.

The number of equivalent adult consumers, $P_{e,t}$, at time t is:

$$P_{e,t} = \sum_{i=0}^{n} E_i(P_{i,t}) \qquad (2)$$

where E_i is a weight chosen to reflect changing consumption patterns at various ages. E is equal to unity for persons aged 20 and over; correspondingly less for persons of younger age.

Total consumption, C_t, at time t is defined as:

$$C_t = C_1 Y_t + C_2 Y_t \qquad (3)$$

where C_1 is the propensity for public expenditure and is constant; and C_2 is a parameter reflecting the propensity to consume by the private sector. It is a function of both $P_{e,t}$ and the level of income per equivalent adult consumer. It is the weighted mean value of the average propensity to consume of the various age groups.

Investment, I_t, is simply the difference between total income (Y_t) and consumption:

$$I_t = Y_t - C_t\,. \qquad (4)$$

Capital stock, K_t, is:

$$K_t = K_{t-1} + I_t \qquad (5)$$

where K_{t-1} is the depreciated value of capital in the previous period.

Finally, total income, Y_t, is determined by the simple Cobb-Douglas expression:

$$Y_t = (A)(K_{t-1})^u (L_{t-1})^v\,; \qquad (6)$$

where A is a factor reflecting the level of technology and is equal to:

$$A = (Z)(1 + Q)^t\,; \qquad (7)$$

where Z is the initial level of technology and Q is the average annual rate of technical progress (3 percent). The fractional change in output resulting from a change in inputs of capital and labor is represented by u and v, respectively.

There are two aspects of this model which warrant further discussion: the production function (6); and the consumption, and hence, savings function (3). The Cobb-Douglas production function has a large number of useful properties which are well known to economists. One of these is that returns to scale are given by the sum of the exponents u and v. It can be demonstrated that as u and $v \gtreqqless 1$ returns will be increasing, constant, or decreasing to scale. For these projections, u is set .25, $\nu = .75$ (hence, constant returns to scale). It can also be shown that the marginal rate of substitution (the ratio of the marginal products of capital and labor) is functionally determined by the ratio of labor to capital and not to the rate of technological change. Finally, and perhaps most importantly, if the quantity of one input is held constant and that of the other is increased, increases in the latter will yield successively smaller increments to total output.

For example, if the supply of capital rises relative to that of labor (say as a result of an increase in the share of income saved), each dollar of investment adds less to potential output and growth rate of total output tends to diminish. The level of per capita output (Y/L) can be determined to be a function of the level of technology and the capital output ratio [6, pp. 426-28]:

$$\frac{Y}{L} = A^{1/1-u}(K/Y)^{u/1-u} \qquad (8)$$

In the long run, under conditions of this model, capital and labor must grow at the same rate. Hence, under the conditions of stationarity of population, absence of growth of the labor force implies that per capita output will be a function only of the rate of technical progress.[1]

The savings function in the model is simply that share of income not consumed by the public or private sector. The share of product consumed by the government is fixed at a level of 25 percent. No portion of this is assumed to be invested in such a way as to augment productivity through physical capital formation. Private consumption is related to the number of equivalent adult consumers. If two populations were of equal size, but differed in age composition, the one with fewer children would have a larger number of equivalent adult consumers. Hence, the share of income saved would be lower in this case. But, because per capita income would also be higher in the latter case (because the ratio of the labor force to total population is higher), the level of per capita savings would be higher in the latter case and possibly the level of aggregate savings as well (depending upon the size of aggregate income and population as well).[2]

As a result of the foregoing, it may be inferred that under the conditions set forth by the model employed, the relatively greater savings of the Series E projection will result in a relative increase in the capital-labor ratio for this series. However, it has also been suggested that, *ceteris paribus*, this will decrease the marginal productivity of capital relative to that of labor since the output-labor ratio would rise more rapidly than the output-capital ratio[3] and that the marginal rate of substitution of capital for labor will fall with the labor-capital ratio.

Data given in Table 3 give index values for the value of the output-labor, output-capital, and capital-labor ratios under the alternative demographic assumptions. These stem from application of the model shown above to the alternative projections.

The differences between the series are slight, especially for the first 20 years of the projection period when the full impact of fertility decline has not yet occurred (in terms of labor force participation). The ratio of GNP (1970 dollars) to the employed labor force would be slightly greater than three times the initial level by 2020 in either case. Part of this would be due to increased capital inputs per head (roughly about 80 percent more than the initial level), part due to technical progress (which we have assumed to be neutral), and a relatively small part due to the changed age distribution of the labor force.

The Series E situation is slightly higher than the Series D in terms of both output per unit of

---

[1] This point is taken up by Hieser [10, pp. 241-62].

[2] An excellent discussion of the very complex relationship between population growth and savings is found in Kelley [13, pp. 20-29].

[3] It can be demonstrated that the marginal product of each factor is equal to the appropriate factor share (u or ν) multiplied by the output-capital or output-labor ratio, respectively.

labor input and the capital output ratio. Given these, it is not surprising that the level of output per unit of capital is lower in the Series E case. Since the marginal products are the output-input ratio times a constant (u or v), we can conclude that the marginal product of labor would be a-bout three times the initial level in both series, but a slight advantage to the Series E case. On the other hand, the marginal product of capital would be 70-80 percent higher in 2020 than was the case in the initial period, with capital being relatively more productive in the Series D case. These results would appear to confirm assumptions made in previous writings by Phelps [17, pp. 71-84] and Spengler [18, pp. 91-133].

A few other aspects which might affect labor productivity are worthy of brief comment. The increase in savings per capita resulting from a higher level of income may be employed in the employment of adding to human capital, rather than physical capital as is assumed in the model here. This would have effects on overall productivity, of course, depending upon the relative magnitudes of the marginal products.

A second aspect, whose implications are far beyond the scope of this paper, deals with the problems of advancement in the labor hierarchy suggested by Spengler [18, pp. 91-133] and Keyfitz [14, pp. 335-52]. Conceivably, delays in deserved (actually or imaginarily) promotion could adversely affect individual's performance.

TABLE 3

RELATIVE VALUES FOR OUTPUT-LABOR, OUTPUT-CAPITAL, AND CAPITAL-LABOR RATIO FOR ALTERNATIVE DEMO-GRAPHIC SITUATIONS, 1970-2020 (1970 = 100.0)

	Series D	Series E		Series D	Series E
Output-Labor			**Output-Capitol**		
1970	100.0	100.0	2000	159.3	152.5
1975	104.5	108.7	2005	161.3	162.3
1980	119.0	118.0	2010	172.2	162.3
1985	134.4	138.0	2015	180.5	173.8
1990	150.4	154.4	2020	177.4	169.5
1995	167.3	174.2			
2000	188.9	191.2	**Capital-Labor**		
2005	208.5	217.0	1970	100.0	100.0
2010	235.9	246.8	1975	101.4	102.3
2015	287.2	288.1	1980	97.3	99.1
2020	314.0	321.9	1985	100.6	102.8
Output-Capital			1990	105.6	108.3
1970	100.0	100.0	1995	113.2	114.7
1975	103.1	106.3	2000	118.6	125.4
1980	122.3	119.1	2005	129.2	133.7
1985	133.6	134.3	2010	137.0	152.1
1990	142.4	142.6	2015	159.1	165.8
1995	147.8	151.9	2020	177.0	183.9

Finally, we have acted as though all potential sources of productivity increase will be utilized for this purpose. In reality, some portion of this may be taken in increased leisure (e.g., a decrease in the work week) which would lower aggregate productivity.

REFERENCES

[1] M. Brennan, P. Taft, and M. Schupack, *The Economics of Age,* New York, 1967.

[2] Ansley J. Coale, *The Growth and Structure of Human Populations: A Mathematical Investigation,* Princeton, 1972.

[3] M. R. Colberg and P. W. Windham, "Age Income Profiles and Individious Comparison," *Mississippi Valley Journal of Economics and Business,* 5, Winter 1970.

[4] J. J. Corson and J. W. McConnell, *Economic Needs of Older People,* New York, 1956.

[5] Herman E. Daly, "The Case for Zero Growth," *American Journal of Agricultural Economics,* 54, December 1972.

[6] T. F. Dernburg and D. M. McDougall, *Macroeconomics,* 3rd ed., New York, 1968.

[7] D. Eilenstine and J. P. Cunningham, "Projected Consumption Needs for a Stationary Population," *Population Studies,* 26, July 1972.

[8] Tomas Frejka, "Reflections on the Demographic Conditions Needed to Establish a U.S. Stationary Population Growth," *Population Studies,* 22, November 1968.

[9] General Electric Company (TEMPO), *Description of the Economic-Demographic Model,* Santa Barbara, 1968.

[10] R. O. Hieser, "The Economic Consequences of Zero Population Growth," *Economic Record,* 49, June 1973.

[11] Denis F. Johnston, "Illustrative Projections of the Labor Force of the United States to 2040," *Economic Aspects of Population Change,* E. R. Morss and R. H. Reed, eds., Washington, 1972.

[12] G. Jones and P. Gingrich, "The Effects of Differing Trends in Fertility and of Educational Advance on the Growth, Quality, and Turnover of the Labor Force," *Demography,* 5, 1968.

[13] Allen C. Kelley, "Demographic Changes and American Economic Development: Past, Present, and Future," *Economic Aspects of Population Change,* E. R. Morss and R. H. Reed, eds., Washington, 1972.

[14] Nathan Keyfitz, "Individual Mobility in a Stationary Population," *Population Studies,* 27, July 1973.

[15] ———, "On the Momentum of Population Growth," *Demography,* 8, February 1971.

[16] Harvey Leibenstein, "The Impact of Population Growth on Economic Welfare-Non Traditional Elements," *Rapid Population Growth-Consequences and Policy Implications,* Baltimore, 1971.

[17] Edmund S. Phelps, "Some Macro Economics of Population Levelling," *Economic Aspects of Population Change,* E. R. Morss and R. H. Reed, eds., Washington, 1972.

[18] Joseph J. Spengler, "Declining Population Growth: Economic Effects," *Economic Aspects of Population Change,* E. R. Morss and R. H. Reed, eds., Washington, 1972.

[19] ———, *Declining Population Growth Revisted,* Chapel Hill, 1971.

[20] U.S. Bureau of the Census, "Annual Mean Income, Lifetime Income, and Educational Attainment of Men in the United States, for Selected Years, 1956 to 1972," *Current Population Reports,* Series P-60, no. 92, March 1974.

[21] ———, "Illustrative Population Projections for the United States, The Demographic Effects of Alternate Paths to Zero Growth," *Current Population Reports,* Series P-25, no. 480, April 1972.

[11]

DAVID M. CUTLER
Massachusetts Institute of Technology
JAMES M. POTERBA
Massachusetts Institute of Technology
LOUISE M. SHEINER
Harvard University
LAWRENCE H. SUMMERS
Harvard University

An Aging Society: Opportunity or Challenge?

AN AMERICAN woman reaching childbearing age in 1960 would expect 3.6 children; an identical woman in 1990 would expect only 1.9 children. That dramatic demographic change makes it almost inevitable that the American population will age rapidly over the next 50 years. By 2025, the share of the American population that is 65 or older will exceed the share of Florida's population that is of retirement age today. The ratio of retirees to workers will have risen by nearly two-thirds. Even more dramatic demographic changes are occurring abroad. The share of the Japanese population that is 65 or over will rise from 11 percent to 19 percent over the next two decades. If current fertility levels in West Germany are maintained until 2050, the population will not only age but shrink more than one-third.

These demographic changes have aroused considerable anxiety in the United States. Economic concerns have focused on the burden that a

We are grateful to George Akerlof, Robert Barro, Greg Duffee, Rachel Friedberg, Ken Judd, Larry Katz, Laurence Kotlikoff, Julio Rotemberg, Robert Solow, and members of the Brookings Panel for helpful comments and to the National Science Foundation and Alfred P. Sloan Foundation for research support. A data appendix for this project is on file at the Inter-university Consortium for Political and Social Research in Ann Arbor, MI.

growing elderly population will place on the economy in general and the federal treasury in particular, as well as on a possible loss of dynamism as population growth slows. Those concerns have led to a potentially radical change in American fiscal policy. To ensure that social security taxes will be sufficient to fund benefits over the next 75 years, and to help the nation save in anticipation of increased demographic burdens, the social security legislation enacted in 1983 calls for social security taxes to exceed benefits over the next 30 years. This surplus will be accumulated in a trust fund, which will peak at 29 percent of GNP in 2020 and then be drawn down as the population ages.

This paper steps back from the current political debate over the social security trust fund and examines the more general question of how serious a macroeconomic problem aging is and how policy should respond to it. We focus primarily on issues relating to saving and capital accumulation. We do not consider the broader question of whether the current U.S. national saving rate is too high or too low, but focus on the effect of demographic changes on the optimal level of national saving. In addition, we consider the effects of demographic change on productivity growth and the optimal timing of tax collections.

Our general conclusion is that demographic changes will improve American standards of living in the near future, but lower them slightly over the very long term. Other things being equal, the optimal policy response to recent and anticipated demographic changes is almost certainly a reduction rather than an increase in the national saving rate. Slowing population growth will reduce the investment that must be devoted to equipping new workers and housing new families, while making it easier for the United States to attract foreign capital. Although there are many reasons for arguing that the United States currently saves too little, anticipated demographic change is not one of them.

Our analysis proceeds in five steps. First, we assess the coming dependency burden. While it is true that the share of the population aged 65 or over will increase sharply, it is also true that the share of children in the population will gradually decline, and that the fraction of the labor force that is near peak productivity will increase. Using information on projected fertility, mortality, and labor force participation rates as well as data on health care costs and the spending of different age groups, we assess past and future dependency trends. We find that demographic changes unaccompanied by changes in capital intensity would reduce per capita incomes by between 7 percent and 12 percent over the next 60 years, but would actually increase incomes over the next 20 years. In only one of the next six decades will demographic changes affect living standards as much as the "peace dividend" is likely to affect them in this decade. The decline in living standards caused by the increased dependence would be fully reversed by a 0.15 percent a year increase in productivity growth.

Second, we consider the consequences of the slower labor force growth that presages the increase in the retired share of the population. Between 2010 and 2060, the labor force is expected to decline slightly, compared with an average increase of 1.5 percent annually between 1950 and 1990. The projected decline in the labor force growth rate will permit a 3–4 percent reduction in the share of net investment in total income without reducing capital intensity. Since reduced labor force growth will occur *before* dependency burdens increase, projected demographic changes raise the short-term consumption path even if the steady-state consumption level declines. We show that in a standard growth model with plausible parameter values, optimal consumption typically rises in response to a demographic shock like that experienced in the United States over the past three decades.

Third, we consider the implications of integrated world capital markets for our analysis. The degree and speed of population aging in other major industrialized countries, particularly West Germany and Japan, is more dramatic than that in the United States. The increase in dependency abroad will coincide with a deceleration in labor force growth rates. Along an optimal path, therefore, the rest of the world will export capital to the United States—thus increasing U.S. consumption and reducing saving in the short run.

Fourth, we go beyond the standard growth theoretic approach and ask whether the coming demographic changes are likely to affect the rate of technical change. With slow labor force growth, labor is scarce; this scarcity may induce more rapid technical change. Such a development would sharpen our conclusion that diminished fertility represents an opportunity rather than a problem. Using international cross-section time series data for 1960–85, we find some evidence that nations with slower labor force growth do experience more rapid productivity growth. The estimates suggest that the reduction in labor force growth projected for the next 40 years may raise productivity growth enough to offset fully the consequences of increased dependence. This finding, however, is uncertain. A more definitive finding is the absence of any empirical support for the pessimistic view that aging societies suffer reduced productivity growth.

Fifth, we consider the implications of our findings for fiscal policy. Because demographic changes over the next decades are not likely to be associated with reduced private saving, they constitute no argument for reducing the budget deficit. There remains the question of efficiency in tax collection. Maintaining current service levels for the elderly will require an increase in government spending from about 32 percent to 37 percent of GNP. Since the deadweight loss from taxation rises with the square of the tax rate, financing these expenditures on a pay-as-you-go basis will involve higher deadweight losses than maintaining a constant tax rate. We find, however, that these effects are likely to be small, amounting to at most several tenths of a percent of annual GNP.

We conclude by discussing the implications of our results for social security, for intergenerational redistribution more generally, and for population and immigration policy. Our findings suggest that population aging does not constitute a strong argument for accumulating a large social security trust fund, although if national saving is deemed to be inadequate for other reasons, the trust fund may be a convenient way to increase it.

The Burden of Increased Dependency

The economic consequences of population aging depend on the nature of the underlying demographic change as well as the relationship between the resource needs of individuals at different ages and their capacity for self-support. This section presents our estimates of the economic burden of increased dependency, noting the uncertainties associated with each step in the calculation.

Changing Demographic Structure

Figure 1 plots the Social Security Administration's projections of the elderly dependency ratio, the number of people aged 65 and over as a fraction of the population aged 20–64, and the total dependency ratio,

Figure 1. Actual and Projected Dependency Ratios, United States, 1960–2065[a]

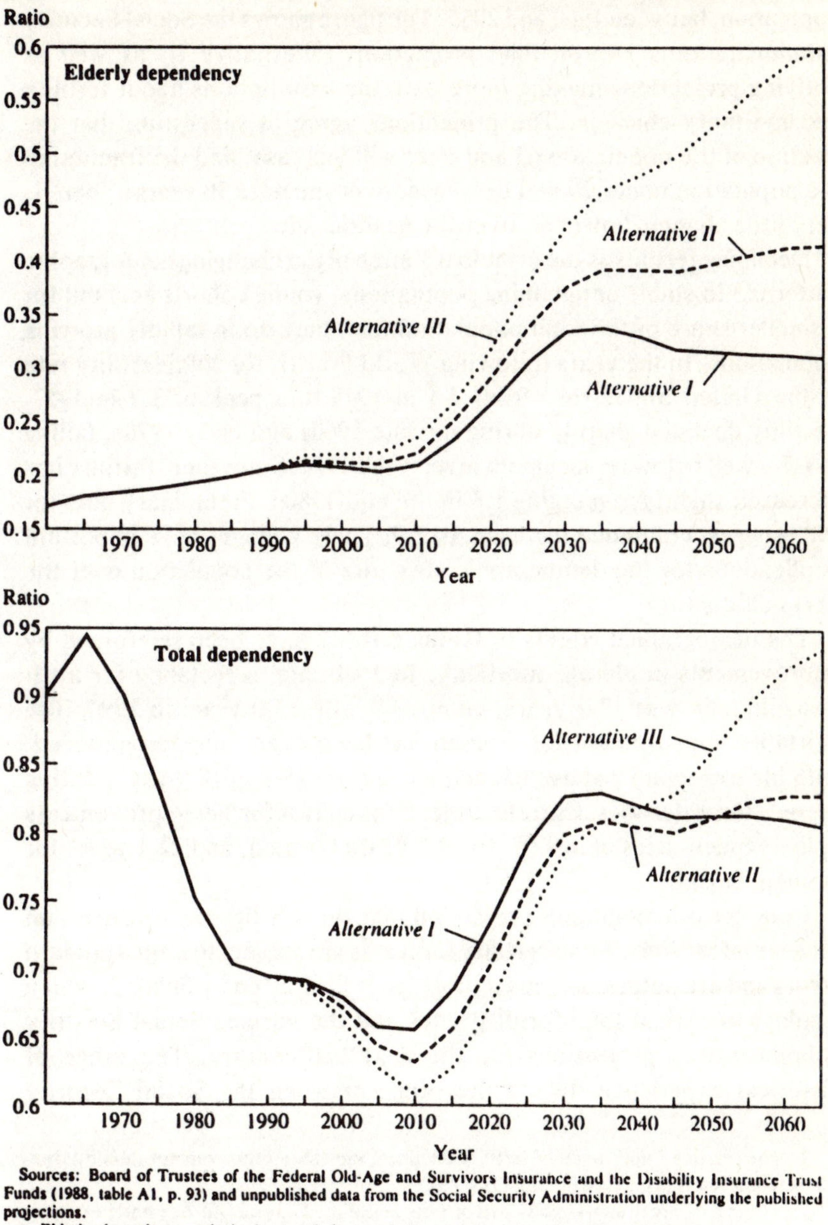

Sources: Board of Trustees of the Federal Old-Age and Survivors Insurance and the Disability Insurance Trust Funds (1988, table A1, p. 93) and unpublished data from the Social Security Administration underlying the published projections.

a. Elderly dependency ratio is the population aged 65 and over divided by the population aged 20–64. Total dependency ratio is population aged 65 and over plus the population under 20 divided by the population aged 20–64.

the number of children plus elderly as a fraction of the working-age population, between 1960 and 2065. The figure shows the Social Security Administration's intermediate projections (alternative II) as well as outlying projections making more extreme assumptions about fertility and mortality changes. The projections agree in suggesting that the fraction of the population 65 and over will increase, and the fraction of the population under 20 will decrease, over the next 50 years. There is very little change, however, over the next decade.

Declining fertility is the principal source of the changing demographic patterns.[1] In stable or declining populations, young cohorts account for a smaller share of the total population than they do in rapidly growing populations. In the years following World War II, the total fertility rate in the United States rose from 2.4 in 1945 to a peak of 3.7 in 1957. Fertility declined sharply during the late 1960s and early 1970s, falling to 1.7—well below replacement levels—by 1976. Since then, fertility has increased slightly, averaging 1.8 in the mid-1980s. Preliminary data for 1989 suggest continued increase, to 2.0. These changes have important implications for the demographic structure of the population over the next half-century.

The demographic effects of falling fertility have been reinforced by improvements in old-age mortality. In 1960, life expectancy for a 65-year-old man was 12.9 years, compared with 15.0 years in 1990. The mortality improvement for women has been even more pronounced, with life expectancy at age 65 increasing from 15.9 to 18.9 years during the past three decades. Current projections call for further improvements in life expectancies at age 65, to 18.0 years for men, and 22.1 years for women, in 2060.[2]

Long-term demographic projections like those in figure 1 are uncertain for several reasons. First, fertility forecasts are subject to large standard errors and are notoriously inaccurate, as is illustrated by figure 2, which displays historical total fertility rates and the various Social Security Administration projections for the next half-century. The range of historical experience dwarfs the range between the Social Security

1. The relative importance of fertility declines, mortality improvement, and international migration is discussed in OECD (1988).

2. These data are drawn from Board of Trustees of the Federal Old-Age and Survivors Insurance and the Federal Disability Insurance Trust Funds (1990, table 11). More detailed information on mortality improvements can be found in Poterba and Summers (1987).

Figure 2. Actual and Alternative Projected Total Fertility Rates, 1920–2080

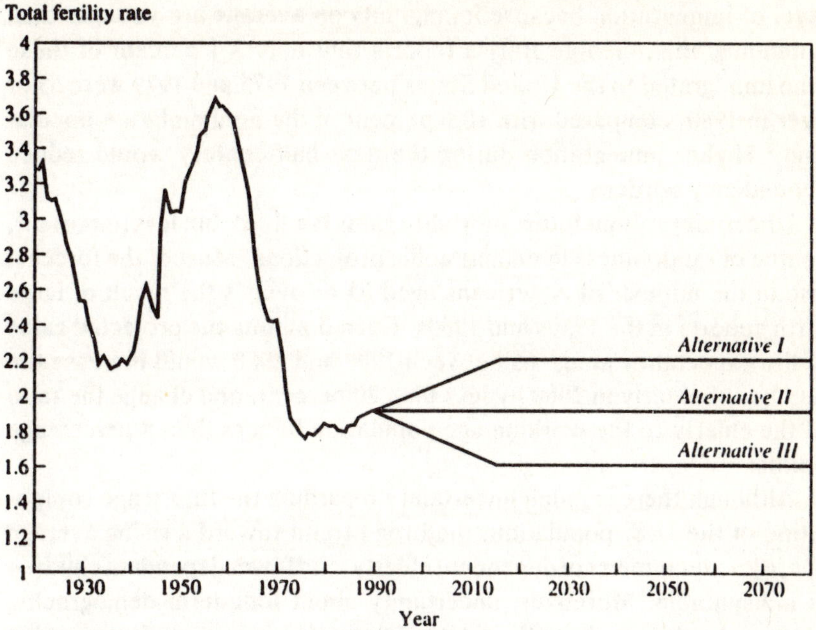

Source: Projected data are from Board of Trustees of the Federal Old-Age and Survivors Insurance and Disability Insurance Trust Funds (1988, table 11, p. 37). Historical data are from *Social Security Area Population Projections: 1989* (1989, pp. 3–4).

Administration's optimistic and pessimistic projections. Even the factor of two difference between the predicted share of the population 65 or over in 2050 in the optimistic and pessimistic projections shown in figure 1 probably understates the true degree of demographic uncertainty.[3] Postwar fertility projections in the United States anticipated neither the beginning, nor the end, of the baby boom.

A second important source of demographic uncertainty is the future course of immigration. The Social Security Administration's intermediate forecasts assume net immigration of 600,000 people a year until 2065—roughly the annual level of net legal and illegal immigration in the late 1980s. Assuming a constant immigrant flow for the next 75 years ignores potential changes in either immigration policy or the level of

3. The pessimistic case assumes an ultimate fertility rate of 1.6, high for example in contrast to West Germany's current rate of 1.3. On the other hand, figure 2 may be deceptive, in that uncertainty regarding the average fertility rate over a 75-year period may be much less than the uncertainty regarding fertility rates at any point in time.

illegal migration. The age structure of the population is sensitive to the level of immigration because immigrants on average are younger than nonimmigrants. George Borjas reports that only 3.1 percent of those who immigrated to the United States between 1975 and 1979 were 65 or over in 1980, compared with 10.6 percent of the nonimmigrant population.[4] Higher immigration during the next half-century would reduce dependency burdens.

Uncertainty about future mortality gains is a third, but less important, source of randomness in demographic projections. Most of the forecast rise in the number of Americans aged 65 or over is the result of large birth cohorts in the 1950s and 1960s. Even doubling the projected gains in life expectancy at age 65 between 1990 and 2060 would increase the number of elderly in 2060 by less than 20 percent, and change the ratio of the elderly to the working-age population by less than 8 percentage points.

Although there is much uncertainty regarding the future age composition of the U.S. population, the broad trend toward a rising average age, a greater number of dependent elderly, and fewer dependent children is indisputable. Moreover, uncertainty about long-term demographic change should not cloud the relatively certain *short-term* demographic outlook. Labor force growth in the next two decades, for example, is largely forecastable given the fertility experience of the past two decades. Along many dimensions, the near-term effects of demographic change operate in different directions from the long-term changes. To illustrate this we now explore alternative ways to calibrate the shifting burden of demographic change.

The Support Ratio

Demographic shifts affect the economy's consumption opportunities because they change the relative sizes of the self-supporting and dependent populations. We summarize these changes in the ***support ratio***, denoted α, which we define as the effective labor force, LF, divided by the effective number of consumers, CON:

$$\alpha = LF/CON. \tag{1}$$

The share of the population aged 65 and over is one, but not the only, determinant of this ratio. The support ratio is also influenced by the

4. Borjas (1990, pp. 41, 46).

relative consumption needs of people of different ages, as well as by changes in the retirement age, labor force participation rates, and the earning power of those who are working. Because there are several approaches to measuring and projecting each of these factors, we present several different measures of the support ratio.

The first issue in measuring the support ratio concerns the relative consumption needs of people at different ages. One assumption, which we label *CON*1, defines effective consumption as if all people have identical resource needs:

$$CON1 = \sum_{i=1}^{99} N_i, \quad (2)$$

where N_i is the number of people of age i. This measure of needs is implicit in the commonly cited total dependency ratio shown in figure 1.

An alternative approach involves differentiating the resource needs of people at different ages. We develop this approach in a second measure of effective consumption needs, *CON*2, which has three parts: private nonmedical expenses, public education expenses, and medical care. For private nonmedical outlays, we follow Edward Lazear and Robert Michael in assuming that all people 20 and older have identical needs, while those under 20 (18 in their work) have needs equal to one-half those of adults.[5] For public education expenses, we assume per capita outlays of $2,553 (1989 dollars) per person under 20, $309 per person aged 20–64, and $84 per person aged 65 and over. These estimates are explained in more detail below. For medical care, we assume that needs are proportional to total spending by age: $1,262 per person per year for those under 64 and $5,360 for those 65 and over.[6] Adding together

5. Lazear and Michael (1980, p. 102) estimate that a child raises equivalent scale consumption for a husband-wife family by 22.2 percent, or by 44.4 percent as much as the average consumption of either parent. There is some evidence that nonmedical consumption needs of the elderly may be lower than those for younger people. For example, the U.S. Department of Agriculture poverty line assumes that food expenditures by the elderly are 90 percent of those for prime-aged individuals. The ongoing trend toward more elderly living in single households, however, suggests that the relative expenditure needs of the elderly may rise in the future.

6. These relative medical costs are based on the current age structure of the elderly population. As the average age of those 65 or over rises, the relative cost of medical care for the elderly will increase. In 1987 total annual per capita health expenditures for people aged 65–69 were $3,728, compared with $9,178 for those aged 85 and over. Holding age-specific expenditure patterns constant at their 1987 level, average spending per person aged 65 and over would be approximately 10 percent higher with the age composition expected in 2060 rather than that in 1990. See Waldo and others (1989).

these three components, we construct a needs-weighted consumption measure, *CON*2, as 0.72 times the number of people under 20, plus the number aged 20–64, plus 1.27 times the number 65 and over.[7]

The relative needs of elderly and nonelderly consumers can be affected by demographic factors such as mortality improvements. Edward Schneider and Jack Guralnik observe that only 3 percent of men and 6 percent of women 65 and over reside in nursing homes, while 15 percent of men and 25 percent of women 85 and over are in such homes. The high cost of nursing home care ($23,600 per resident per year in 1985) makes it an important contributor to the total cost of caring for the aged population.[8]

The appropriate weighting of young and old dependents may depend on more than their consumption demands. Many of the transfers to children take place within the family, while those to elderly dependents are largely mediated by the government. A Scandinavian proverb, brought to our attention by George Akerlof, suggests that "one mother can care for ten children, but ten children cannot care for one mother." Individuals may derive more pleasure from caring for children than from caring for elderly dependents, making the burdens of an increasingly elderly population more onerous than the burdens of caring for a young population.[9]

We also consider two different measures of the effective labor force. The first, *LF*1, assumes that all people aged 20–64 are in the labor force, while individuals 19 and under or 65 and over are not:

$$LF1 = \sum_{i=20}^{64} N_i. \qquad (3)$$

Our second measure, *LF*2, recognizes that both human capital and labor force participation rates vary by age. We use data on the average 1989 earnings (w) of people of each age (measured in five-year intervals),

7. The needs-weighted consumption measure, *CON*2, is defined as

$$CON2 = \sum_{i=1}^{99} S_i N_i,$$

where S_i is the respective weight for an individual at age i.

8. Schneider and Guralnik (1990).

9. Provided the "warm glow" of caregiving does not affect the marginal utility of consuming goods, it should not affect our needs weighting of different-aged households. It will affect the total utility of households.

along with Social Security Administration forecasts of age-specific labor force participation rates, *PR*, to estimate *LF2*:[10]

$$LF2 = \sum_{i=15}^{80} w_i PR_i N_i. \quad (4)$$

This recognizes that the earning capacity of a society with a high fraction of people in middle age is higher than that of a society with many new entrants to the labor force.[11]

Support Ratio Projections, 1990–2060

Because the level of the support ratio is less informative than its changes from year to year, we focus on $\hat{\alpha}_t$, the percentage change in the support ratio between 1990 and year *t*:

$$\hat{\alpha}_t = (LF_t/CON_t)/(LF_{1990}/CON_{1990}) - 1. \quad (5)$$

We report support ratios corresponding to each combination of effective labor force and effective consumption measures.

Table 1 shows the historical and projected changes in *LF* and *CON* and demonstrates that regardless of measurement method, growth in both the labor force and consumption requirements declines during the next half-century. For example, the earnings-weighted labor force grew at a 1.7 percent annual rate during the 1980s, but will *shrink* in four of the five decades between 2010 and 2060. In the nearer term, labor force growth also slows. By the first decade of the next century, labor force growth is only one-fourth its rate during the 1970s. Total needs-weighted consumption, which grew at a 1.1 percent annual rate during the 1980s, rises by less than one tenth of 1 percent a year between 2040 and 2060.

Table 2 and figure 3 show the percentage change in the four alternative measures of the support ratio. Four conclusions stand out. First, because both our measures of the labor force grow more slowly than population

10. These data are from the Bureau of Labor Statistics, *Usual Weekly Earnings of Full-Time Wage and Salary Workers* and *Usual Weekly Earnings of Employed & Part-Time Wage and Salary Workers*. We adjust part-time workers to full-time equivalent employees.

11. This labor force concept includes only market activity, neglecting the value of labor devoted to household production. It may therefore overstate the historical changes in the effective labor force that were partly due to rising *market* labor force participation by women.

Table 1. Actual and Projected Average Annual Growth in Labor Force and Consumption, United States, 1950–2060
Percent

	Labor force		*Consumption*	
Period	*Population 20–64 (LF1)*	*Earnings-weighted population (LF2)*	*Unweighted (CON1)*	*Needs-weighted (CON2)*
1950–1960	0.74	1.18	1.77	1.66
1960–1970	1.25	1.19	1.23	1.28
1970–1980	1.73	2.05	0.91	1.13
1980–1990	1.29	1.69	0.95	1.08
1990–2000	0.83	1.07	0.70	0.75
2000–2010	0.80	0.48	0.57	0.65
2010–2020	0.06	−0.03	0.48	0.60
2020–2030	−0.26	−0.10	0.29	0.42
2030–2040	0.11	0.07	0.14	0.17
2040–2050	0.00	−0.03	0.04	0.05
2050–2060	−0.06	−0.02	0.03	0.05

Source: Board of Trustees of the Federal Old-Age and Survivors Insurance and Disability Insurance Trust Funds (1988). Projected data for 1990–2060 use alternative IIb. Data show geometric average annual changes in labor force and consumption needs under IIb.

during the next 70 years, there is a long-run decline in the support ratio. The size of the decline is more sensitive to our assumptions about consumption than to our measure of the effective labor force.[12] When consumption needs are assumed to be equal for people of all ages, the support ratio for *LF*1 (*LF*2) declines by 7.4 percent (7.8 percent) between 1990 and 2060. When we adjust consumption using our needs-weighted measure, the decline in the support ratio is more pronounced: 11.5 percent and 11.8 percent for *LF*1 and *LF*2, respectively.

It is difficult to know whether these estimates represent a large or a small burden spread over 70 years. They correspond to between a 0.10 percent and 0.15 percent reduction in the annual productivity growth rate, which is small relative to the uncertainty in secular productivity growth. They represent three to four times as large a cost as the peace dividend that the United States is likely to enjoy over the next decade.

12. For the period 1950–90, the support ratios *are* sensitive to our choice of labor force concept, primarily because of significant changes in labor force participation rates, most notably among women.

Table 2. Changes in Support Ratio Relative to 1990, United States, 1950–2060
Percent

Year	Unweighted population aged 20–64/ unweighted consumption (LF1/CON1)	Earnings-weighted population/ unweighted consumption (LF2/CON1)	Unweighted population aged 20–64/ needs-weighted consumption (LF1/CON2)	Earnings-weighted population/ needs-weighted consumption (LF2/CON2)
1950	−1.4	−11.5	1.4	−9.0
1960	−10.9	−16.5	−7.4	−13.2
1970	−10.8	−16.9	−7.7	−14.0
1980	−3.3	−7.0	−2.0	−5.8
1990	0.0	0.0	0.0	0.0
2000	1.3	3.7	0.8	3.2
2010	3.8	2.8	2.3	1.4
2020	−0.5	−2.3	−3.1	−4.8
2030	−5.9	−6.0	−9.5	−9.6
2040	−6.2	−6.6	−10.0	−10.5
2050	−6.5	−7.3	−10.4	−11.2
2060	−7.4	−7.8	−11.5	−11.8

Source: Same as table 1. The earnings-weighted labor force measure uses contemporaneous and projected labor force participation rates and the 1987 age-earnings profiles for men and women to form effective labor forces.

In yet another metric, a three- to four-year increase in the average age at retirement, or a 19 percentage point increase in female labor force participation, would be needed to offset the increase in dependency.

Second, in the next two decades there is a *decline* in economic dependency (a rise in the support ratio) because the declining number of dependent children more than offsets the rising number of dependent elderly. Between 1990 and 2010, when the baby boom generation is part of the labor force and relatively small birth cohorts are retiring, the labor force grows more rapidly than the dependent population. This leads to an improvement in the support ratio by 2010.[13]

Figure 4 provides further detail on the differential burdens of young and aged dependents. It plots the contributions of both children and the elderly to the support ratio defined using *LF*2 and *CON*2. In this case

13. Measures that define effective consumption with less weight on children show smaller gains in the support ratio during the next two decades. If the consumption weight based on needs is set equal to zero for children, the support ratio actually declines by between 1 percent and 2 percent during 1990–2010.

Figure 3. Actual and Projected Changes in Support Ratio (Relative to 1990), Four Alternative Measures, United States, 1960–2065

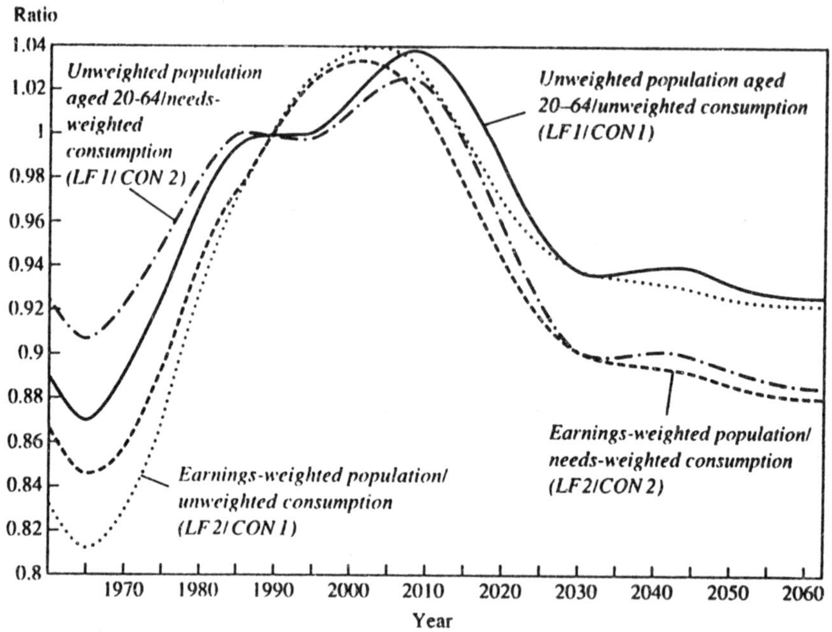

Source: Table 2.

$\alpha = P/(C + P + E)$, where P is the number of prime-aged adults, C the number of effective children, and E the number of effective elderly. Then the percentage change in the support ratio can be written in terms of the percentage change in its components:

$$(6) \quad \hat{\alpha} = (\hat{P} - \hat{C})\,[C/(C + P + E)] + (\hat{P} - \hat{E})\,[E/(C + P + E)].$$

The first term is due to differential growth rates of the prime-aged and dependent children populations, the second to the differential growth between the prime-aged and elderly groups. Figure 4 plots these two terms, showing that virtually all the improvement in the support ratio in the near term is from a shrinking share of children in the population. Most of the long-run decline is a result of rising numbers of elderly during 2010–2035.

Third, the changes in the support ratio between 1990 and 2060 are usually no larger than, and in some cases significantly smaller than,

Figure 4. Contributions of Young and Elderly Dependents to Percentage Changes in the Support Ratio (Relative to 1990), 1955–2065

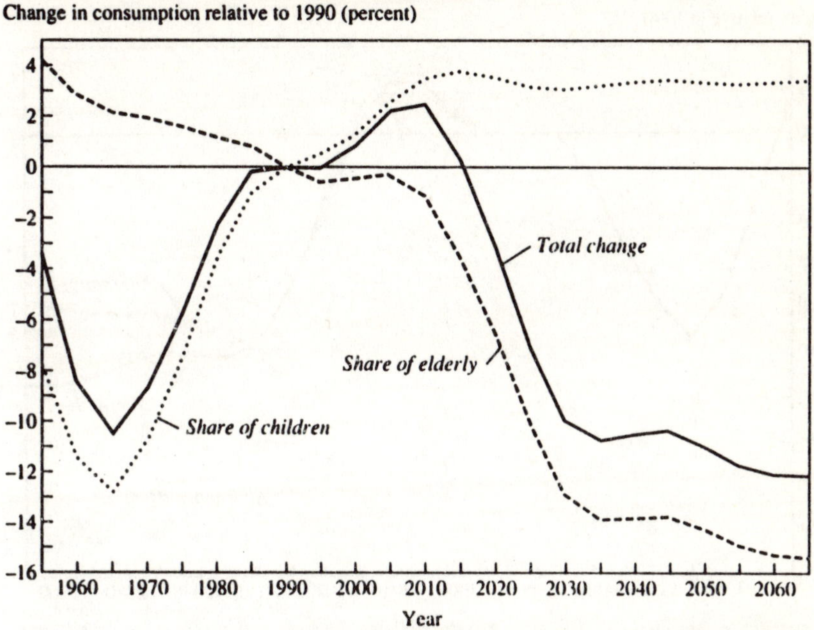

Source: Authors' calculations using equation 6. The earnings-weighted labor force measure (*LF2*) and the needs-weighted consumption measure (*CON2*) are used. See text for details.

those between 1960 and 1990. With our preferred measures, *LF*2 and *CON*2, the support ratio was 14.0 percent lower in 1970 than 1990. By 2060, it is projected once again to be below the 1990 level, this time by 11.8 percent. Our support ratio peaks around 2010. One reason why the slow growth of real wages in the U.S. economy since 1973 has been less burdensome than it might have otherwise been is that the labor force participation rate has risen. The figures show clearly that the gains in sustainable consumption from demographic developments are now nearly exhausted.

Finally, while the decline in the support ratio by the middle of the next century is large, there is still substantial uncertainty about the ultimate burden. Figure 5 presents support ratios using *LF*2 and *CON*2 under the three Social Security Administration demographic forecasts. There are substantial differences in the scenarios, particularly between the more pessimistic alternative III and alternative II, which is our

Figure 5. Percentage Change in Support Ratio (Relative to 1990), Alternative Demographic Assumptions, 1950–2065

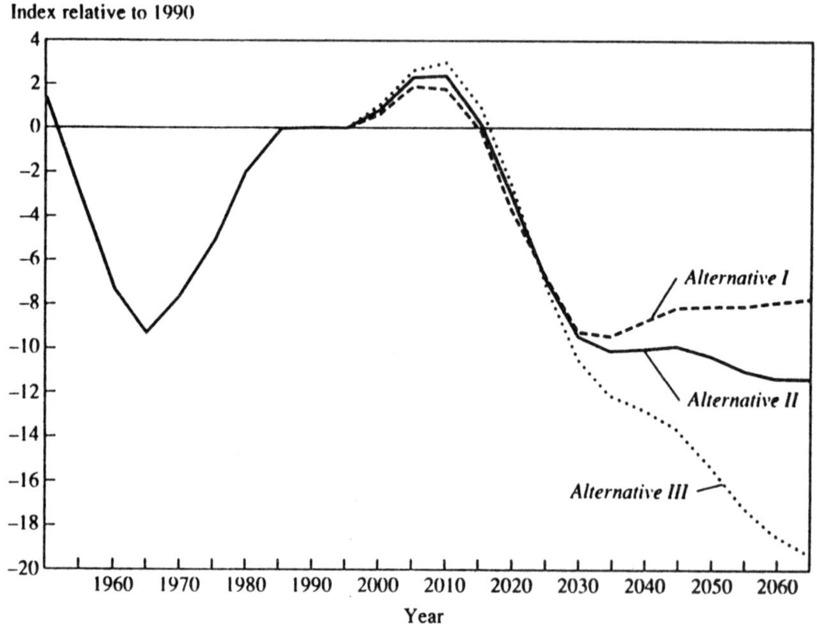

Source: Authors' calculations using Board of Trustees of the Federal Old-Age and Survivors Insurance and Disability Insurance Trust Funds (1988) and the needs-weighted consumption (*CON2*) and earnings-weighted labor force (*LF2*) measures.

standard case. The decline in the support ratio is almost twice as large in the pessimistic scenario as in our benchmark. Even in the optimistic alternative I, the support ratio still declines by almost 8 percent between 1990 and 2060.

Capital Accumulation and Shifting Dependency Burdens

This section explores how the demographic shifts described above affect the economy's sustainable level of consumption, and how society should plan for these changes. We find that sustainable consumption increases for the next several decades and that an economy with otherwise optimal national saving would reduce its saving in response to the coming demographic changes.

Steady-State Consumption Opportunities

Demographic change has two effects on consumption opportunities. First, an increase in dependency lowers output per person, thus reducing consumption per capita. Second, slower labor force growth reduces investment requirements, thus reducing the need for saving and increasing consumption per capita.

To examine the importance of these two changes for consumption opportunities, we assume that output per worker, $f(k)$, where k is the capital-labor ratio, is divided between consumption and investment. Maintaining constant capital intensity requires investment of nk, where n is the labor force growth rate.[14] For expositional ease, we have assumed away depreciation and technical change.[15] When the labor force and the population are not the same, consumption per capita is only a fraction of output net of investment per worker. This fraction is the ratio of the number of workers to the size of the population, precisely the support ratio (α) defined above. The resulting equation for per capita consumption is:

$$c = \alpha[f(k) - nk]. \tag{7}$$

This expression can be rewritten to find the change in steady-state consumption for changes in α and n:

$$\Delta c/c = \Delta\alpha/\alpha - [\alpha(k/c)\,\Delta n + \Delta\alpha\,(k/c)\,\Delta n], \tag{8}$$

with c, k, and α evaluated at the initial steady state.[16] Equation 8 illustrates the two steady-state effects of demographic change. A decline in the labor force-population ratio (α) reduces the level of per capita consumption that is feasible given the economy's capital stock. At the same time, a decline in the growth rate of the labor force (n) permits more consumption for a given capital-output ratio. Society receives a "consumption dividend" when it is able to invest less and still maintain

14. A substantial part of the U.S. capital stock is residential capital. The natural steady-state condition for housing requires investment at the rate of population growth, not the rate of labor force growth. In steady state, these two growth rates will coincide.

15. We incorporate both in our numerical simulations below.

16. We have arbitrarily assigned the second-order term to the second effect in our decomposition. We have also assumed that the capital-labor ratio, and thus the capital-consumption ratio, do not change with demographic change. The model we present below justifies this assumption.

Table 3. Shifting Steady-State Per Capita Consumption from Demographic Shocks, 1960–2065[a]
Percent

	Unweighted consumption (CON1)			*Needs-weighted consumption (CON2)*		
Year	*Effect of dependency*	*Effect of labor force growth*	*Total change in per capita consumption*	*Effect of dependency*	*Effect of labor force growth*	*Total change in per capita consumption*
			Population 20–64 as effective labor force (LF1)			
1960	−10.9	0.4	−10.6	−7.4	0.4	−7.1
1970	−10.8	−1.8	−12.6	−7.7	−1.8	−9.5
1980	−3.3	−2.4	−5.7	−2.0	−2.4	−4.5
1990	0.0	0.0	0.0	0.0	0.0	0.0
2000	1.3	0.0	1.3	0.8	0.0	0.8
2010	3.8	1.0	4.8	2.3	1.0	3.4
2020	−0.5	3.0	2.5	−3.1	2.9	−0.2
2030	−5.9	2.5	−3.4	−9.5	2.4	−7.1
2040	−6.2	1.8	−4.3	−10.0	1.8	−8.3
2050	−6.5	2.5	−4.0	−10.4	2.4	−8.0
2060	−7.4	2.1	−5.3	−11.5	2.0	−9.4
2065	−7.4	2.2	−5.2	−11.5	2.1	−9.4
			Earnings-weighted labor force (LF2)			
1960	−16.5	1.1	−15.4	−13.2	1.2	−12.1
1970	−16.9	−0.4	−17.3	−14.0	−0.4	−14.4
1980	−7.0	−1.9	−9.0	−5.8	−2.0	−7.8
1990	0.0	0.0	0.0	0.0	0.0	0.0
2000	3.7	2.2	5.9	3.2	2.2	5.4
2010	2.8	3.5	6.3	1.4	3.5	4.9
2020	−2.3	4.4	2.1	−4.8	4.2	−0.6
2030	−6.0	3.7	−2.3	−9.6	3.6	−6.0
2040	−6.6	3.6	−3.0	−10.5	3.5	−7.0
2050	−7.3	3.9	−3.5	−11.2	3.7	−7.5
2060	−7.8	3.6	−4.1	−11.8	3.5	−8.3
2065	−7.8	3.7	−4.2	−12.0	3.5	−8.4

Source: Authors' calculations.
a. The table shows the steady-state change in consumption relative to the 1990 base if demographic change were to reach a steady state at the level of the indicated year.

a given level of per capita output. This "Solow effect" offsets the long-run dependency effect on per capita consumption.

Table 3 reports the size of these two effects. For each year, we show the steady-state consumption change associated with changes in α (first column), n (second column), and the combined effect (third column). The consumption changes due to the dependency increase are the same as the changes in the support ratio shown in table 2; the other columns show the extent to which changing investment needs offset this effect.

Two results emerge from table 3. First, the consumption benefits from reduced investment requirements are substantial. During the next two decades, the benefits of slower labor force growth will be about a 1 percent to 3.5 percent increase in per capita consumption, using the 1990 base. Since the labor force was growing more rapidly in the 1970s and 1980s than in 1990, the effect of reduced investment requirements is even larger relative to earlier years. By the middle of the next century, the benefits of slower labor force growth will be between 2.1 percent and 3.7 percent of per capita consumption. This is between one-quarter and one-half of the adverse dependency effects of the changing population mix.

Second, while the investment effect offsets a substantial part of the long-term dependency increase, it magnifies the short-run effect of rising support ratios. Reduced dependency and slowing labor force growth both increase consumption possibilities so that by 2010, society will be between 3.4 percent and 6.3 percent richer, depending on the combination of labor force and needs measures. Only after 2020 does the increase in dependency outweigh the decline in investment needs and reduce consumption below its 1990 level.

The steady-state consumption decline between 1990 and 2060 is estimated at between 4.2 percent (with effective consumers set equal to total population and the earnings-weighted labor force) and 9.4 percent (with effective consumers computed using our needs-weighted measure and the unweighted labor force). As with the support ratios, this finding is more sensitive to our definition of consumption needs than to our definition of the effective labor force. For almost all cases, however, society is richer in the new steady state than in 1970 or 1980.

Demographic Change and Optimal Capital Accumulation

The results presented so far suggest that in the short run, demographic changes will raise the level of consumption that can be sustained while maintaining the level of capital intensity. In the long run, they will reduce the sustainable level of consumption. The question then becomes how society should adjust its saving policy to these developments. To study this question, we use the standard Ramsey optimal growth model.

We assume that a social planner seeks to maximize

$$V = \int_0^{\infty} e^{-\rho t} P_t \, U(c_t) \, dt, \tag{9}$$

where P_t denotes the number of individuals alive in period t, c_t is per capita consumption in period t, and ρ is the social time preference rate. We denote the current period as time zero. This social welfare function weights the utility, denoted as U, of a representative individual in each generation by the generation's size.[17] Using our earlier notation, $P_t = N_t/\alpha_t$, where N_t is the labor force in period t and α_t is the support ratio.

Our analysis abstracts from the overlapping generations structure of the actual population. Calvo and Obstfeld formally justify this procedure by demonstrating that if age-specific transfer programs like social security are available, and if individual utility functions are additively separable, then "the Cass-Koopmans-Ramsey framework can be used to evaluate paths of *aggregate* consumption even in models where different generations co-exist. . . . the planning problem facing the government can be decomposed into two subproblems, a standard problem of optimal aggregate capital accumulation and a problem of distributing consumption optimally on each date among the generations alive then."[18] The social planner maximizes equation 9 subject to a capital accumulation constraint analogous to equation 7:[19]

$$\dot{k}_t = f(k_t) - c_t/\alpha_t - n_t k_t. \tag{10}$$

If $\alpha_t = 1$, equation 10 reduces to the standard resource constraint in neoclassical growth models. The consumption profile that solves this problem satisfies:

$$\dot{c}_t/c_t = \sigma \, [f'(k_t) - \rho], \tag{11}$$

where $\sigma = [-U'(c_t)/c_t] \, [U''(c_t)]$, the elasticity of substitution in consumption.

17. Some might argue for using an alternative objective function that does not weight the average utility of different generations by the number of people in the generation. This will lead the social planner to raise average consumption in small cohorts relative to that in larger cohorts, because the aggregate resource cost of raising the average consumption of people in small cohorts is less than that for large cohorts. We see no compelling ethical argument for weighting people in different sized cohorts differently.

18. Calvo and Obstfeld (1988, p. 163).

19. The optimal plan must also satisfy transversality conditions noted for example by Blanchard and Fischer (1989).

Figure 6. Steady-State Consumption Response to an Increase in Dependency (Decline in α)

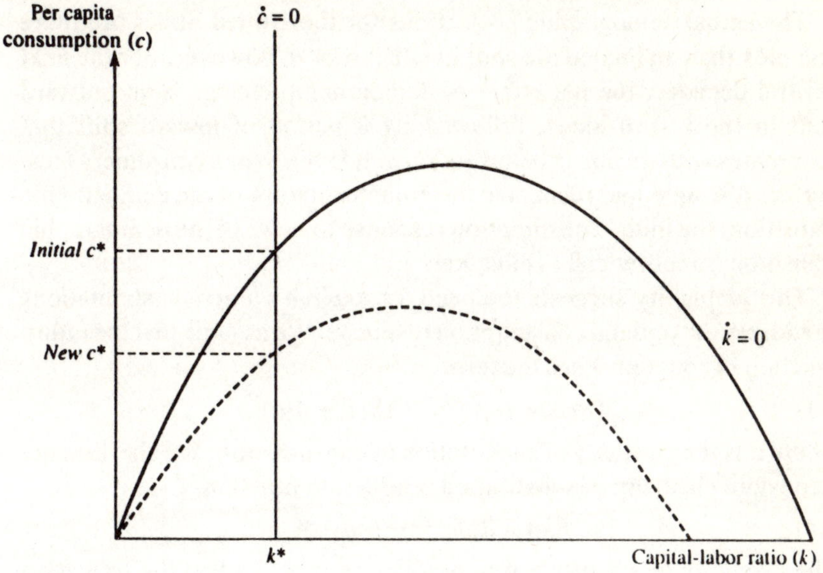

In steady state with no technical progress, per capita consumption and the capital-labor ratio must be constant. From the Euler equation 11, we find that constant consumption requires

$$k^* = f'^{-1}(\rho). \tag{12}$$

This locus, a vertical line in (*c*, *k*) space, is drawn in figure 6. Constancy of the capital-labor ratio given in equation 7 yields the second locus depicted in figure 6 as the solid line $\dot{k} = 0$.

Permanent reductions in α, the support ratio, scale back the feasible level of per capita consumption for each *k*, shifting the $\dot{k} = 0$ locus as shown by the dashed line in figure 6. The steady-state capital-labor ratio is unaffected by this change, so the only effect of this shock is an immediate and permanent decline in consumption per capita. Reductions in *n*, the labor force growth rate, would have the opposite effect, shifting the $\dot{k} = 0$ frontier *out*. The steady-state consumption effect of a demographic shift such as a fertility decline, which reduces both α and *n*, depends on which of these effects may be larger. Reductions in *n* would unambiguously reduce the optimal steady-state saving rate while increases in α would have no effect on steady-state savings.[20]

The actual demographic projections for the United States are more complex than an immediate shift in either α or n, however. For the next several decades, the net effect of demographic change is an outward shift in the $\dot{k} = 0$ locus, followed by a period of inward shift that terminates with the locus below its current level. When consumers have perfect foresight and recognize the complex nature of the demographic transition, the initial consumption response to news of the demographic transition is theoretically ambiguous.

This ambiguity suggests the need for explicit numerical simulations to address the optimal consumption response. We assume that the utility function in equation 9 has the form

$$U(c_t) = (c_t^{1-1/\sigma} - 1)/(1 - 1/\sigma), \qquad (13)$$

where σ is the elasticity of substitution in consumption. We also assume a constant elasticity of substitution production function:

$$f(k_t) = [ak_t^{1/1-\beta} + b]^{1-\beta}. \qquad (14)$$

The elasticity of substitution in production is β. To find the transition path between one steady state and another, we discretize differential equations 10 and 11 and employ a grid-search algorithm to find the initial consumption level that will lead the economy to the new steady state.[21]

Our simulations also allow for labor-augmenting technical change (g) and depreciation (δ), which are introduced into equations 10 and 11 in the standard way.[22] Although consumption grows over time when there is technical progress, the consumption numbers we report are *relative* to the consumption that would have been possible without demographic change. We assume that technical change is equal to 1.4 percent a year, the Social Security Administration's steady-state projection.[23] The depreciation rate is set equal to 4.1 percent, the U.S. average during 1952–

20. This is easily seen from the Harrod-Domar condition $k/f(k) = s/n$, where s is the saving rate out of national income, and the observation that neither changes in α nor changes in n affect optimal steady-state capital intensity in the Ramsey model.

21. Because the Social Security Administration forecasts population in every fifth year, we interpolate annual observations using a smooth interpolator. The results are not sensitive to the frequency of the data.

22. Following Blanchard and Fischer (1989), we express capital per "effective worker," where effective workers grow at $n + g$. Consumption is expressed per "effective person." In equation 11, the discount factor becomes $(\rho + \delta + g/\sigma)$.

23. Our results are insensitive to the choice of g.

87.[24] Finally, we use data for this period on payments to labor and capital to estimate capital's share in gross output—33.2 percent. Over this same period, the capital-output ratio averaged 2.3.[25] These two numbers imply a steady-state marginal product of capital of 14.4 percent. From equation 11, this implies an effective discount rate ($\rho + g/\sigma$) of 10.3 percent: that is, the steady-state marginal product of capital less depreciation.

We present results using two values of σ, a benchmark case of unit elasticity ($\sigma = 1$) and an alternative elasticity of substitution of one-tenth ($\sigma = 0.1$). We also choose two values for the elasticity of substitution in production, a benchmark of unit elasticity ($\beta = 1$) and an alternative elasticity of one-half ($\beta = 0.5$). When the elasticity of substitution in consumption is low, consumption today is not a good substitute for consumption tomorrow, and we expect more consumption smoothing. When the elasticity of substitution in production is low, saving does not get a high return since the extra capital does not substitute well for the smaller labor force, and we expect less consumption smoothing.

Demographic change has occurred gradually over the past 25 years, as the baby boom has given way to the baby bust. It is not obvious how best to model these changes as a single shock. Initially, we assume the economy is in steady state with values of α and n corresponding to those prevailing in 1990, and ask how consumption and saving should evolve henceforth. Because some of the consequences of demographic change were already known by 1990, we go on to examine how consumption and saving should have responded in 1970 and 1980 if news of demographic change had suddenly arrived.

For all our simulations, we use the trajectories of α and n implied by the Social Security Administration's alternative IIb forecasts, and further assume that the predicted values for 2065 persist as the economy's final steady state.[26] The resulting consumption changes are thus the

24. Our depreciation rate is estimated as capital consumption allowances divided by the aggregate capital stock. We define aggregate capital stock as national assets minus consumer durables minus one half of the value of land. Consumer durables are excluded since they are not included in output. One half of land is included in capital to allow for natural resource values to change.

25. Capital's share in output is total output less wages and salaries, two-thirds of proprietors' income (the estimated labor compensation), and indirect business taxes, divided by output less indirect business taxes.

26. Alternative IIb projections embody the alternative II forecasts regarding demographic change, as well as an intermediate set of economic forecasts.

Table 4. Optimal Consumption Response to Demographic Shocks, United States, 1990–2060[a]

Item	Static expectations	Perfect foresight with alternative elasticities[b] $\beta = 1$, $\sigma = 1$	$\beta = 1$, $\sigma = 0.1$	$\beta = 0.5$, $\sigma = 1$	$\beta = 0.5$, $\sigma = 0.1$
Case 1. Labor force population 20–64 and unweighted consumption					
Initial steady state	100.0	100.0	100.0	100.0	100.0
Initial adjustment	100.0	100.6	101.1	100.4	101.0
Time path					
2000	101.3	101.4	101.3	101.4	101.3
2010	104.8	103.3	101.7	103.8	102.1
2020	102.5	102.3	101.4	102.5	101.7
2030	96.6	98.3	100.3	97.7	99.8
2040	95.7	96.2	99.0	95.9	98.1
2050	96.0	95.9	98.1	95.9	97.1
2060	94.7	95.1	97.3	95.0	96.2
New steady state	94.8	94.8	94.8	94.8	94.8
Case 2. Earnings-weighted labor force and needs-weighted consumption					
Initial steady state	100.0	100.0	100.0	100.0	100.0
Initial adjustment	100.0	102.3	102.8	101.9	102.8
Time path					
2000	105.4	104.1	103.0	104.5	103.3
2010	104.9	104.1	102.8	104.5	103.0
2020	99.4	100.4	101.5	100.2	101.1
2030	94.0	95.7	99.6	95.0	98.3
2040	93.0	93.5	97.8	93.2	96.0
2050	92.5	92.7	96.3	92.6	94.5
2060	91.7	92.0	95.1	91.8	93.4
New steady state	91.6	91.6	91.6	91.6	91.6

Source: Authors' calculations.

a. Each column is the simulated path of consumption in response to a demographic shock like that which the United States will experience between 1990 and 2060. The static expectations column is the change in consumption if agents in each period assume that the current level of α and n will persist forever. The perfect foresight columns assume current knowledge of the entire path of demographic change. The initial steady state is the 1990 value of α and n.

b. β is the substitution elasticity in production; σ is the substitution elasticity in consumption.

optimal response to the demographic transition that the United States will undergo over the next seven decades, assuming these changes were unforeseen as of 1990.

The results of these simulations are shown in table 4. The level of per capita consumption in the 1990 steady state is normalized to 100. The first column, the static expectations response, is the change in consumption if consumers have no foresight about demographic change but rather assume at each date that current conditions will persist forever. It thus corresponds to the consumption path in table 3. The other four columns assume that consumers in 1990 have perfect foresight regarding future demographic changes.

For all the parameter values, consumption rises initially in response to the demographic transition, by up to 2.8 percent relative to the steady state implied by 1990 demography. This result is insensitive to the parameter choices we present.[27] Consumption remains above its 1990 level until 2020 or later. Thus, demographic shifts during the next half-century optimally *raise* present consumption. The initial effect is more pronounced when consumption is less substitutable over time (σ is small) and less pronounced when production is less substitutable over time (β is small).

Figure 7 shows the movements of consumption and capital for the simulations using unit elasticities of substitution in production and consumption. The corresponding saving rate is shown in figure 8. Consumption initially rises by 2.3 percent. This is followed by a period when capital per effective worker declines, during which consumption continues to increase. The shifting opportunity locus due to the decline in labor force growth ultimately causes an increase in saving and thus in capital intensity, even at the higher level of consumption. After the period of capital deepening, consumption begins to decline. Finally, when the increase in dependency overtakes the favorable effects of the slowing labor force growth, both consumption and capital decline to the new steady state, and saving remains low.

As figure 8 demonstrates, the saving rate falls almost 2 percentage points during the 1990 initial adjustment. It then increases for a few years, though it never attains its initial steady-state value. This increase is due to the increase in the support ratio, which allows both consumption per person and the saving rate to increase. Finally, the saving rate begins to fall toward its new long-run level, equal to the amount of saving necessary to equip the more slowly growing labor force.

We also ran the simulations using the Social Security Administration's alternative I and alternative III, with no substantive changes in results.

27. In addition to the parameter values reported, we have experimented with elasticities in substitution and production up to 10. For none of these cases is there an initial increase in savings.

Figure 7. Optimal Consumption and Capital-Labor Trajectory Following Demographic Shock, 1990–2060

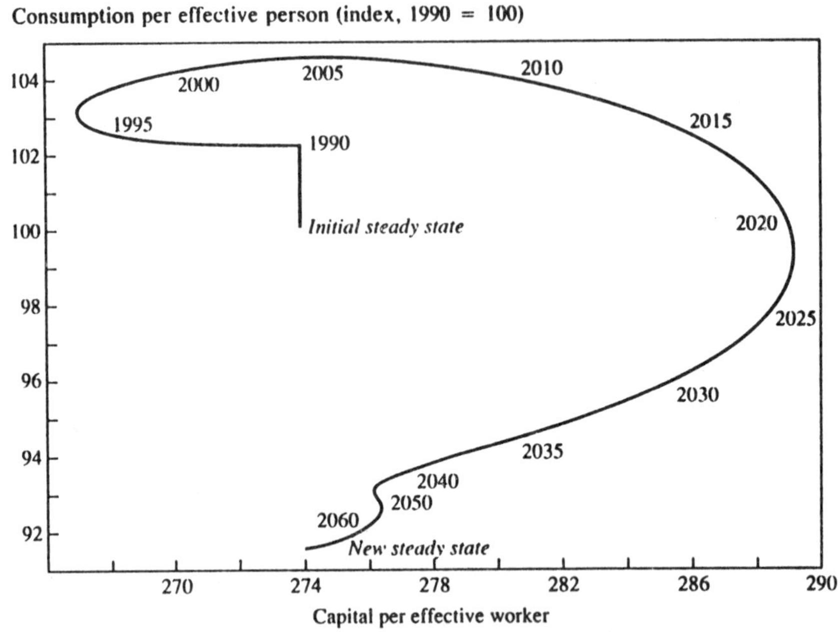

Source: Authors' calculations. Elasticities used are $\beta = 1$, $\sigma = 1$. Labor force measure is earnings-weighted (*LF2*); consumption measure is needs-weighted (*CON2*). Consumption at the initial steady state is normalized to 100. The resulting index yields capital per effective worker equal to 274 in the initial steady state.

Consumption rises less with the alternative I assumptions than with our benchmark alternative II assumptions, because the number of dependent children does not decrease as quickly, and more with the alternative III assumptions, where there is an even larger short-run benefit. In all three cases the response to the demographic news is a decrease in saving. We have also experimented with changing capital's share or the assumed initial level of capital intensity in order to vary the discount rate.[28] Even with a pure discount rate as low as zero, our conclusion that consumption rises following a demographic shock remains valid.

Finally, we explored how consumption would change if we began the simulations in 1970 or 1980. As table 2 demonstrated, consumption

28. Because the discount factor must equal the marginal product of capital in steady state, and the marginal product of capital is the ratio of capital's share in output to the capital-output ratio, changes in the discount factor have to be accompanied by changes in either capital's share or the capital-output ratio.

Figure 8. Optimal Saving Rates in Response to Demographic Shock, 1990–2070

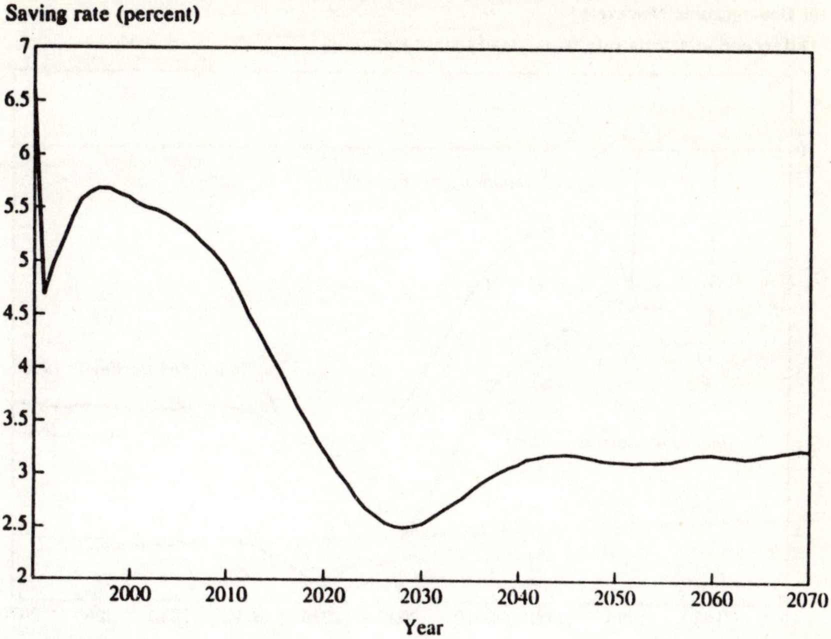

Source: Authors' calculations. Elasticities used are $\beta = 1$, $\sigma = 1$. The consumption measure is needs-weighted (*CON2*); the labor force measure is earnings-weighted (*LF2*).

possibilities are higher in 1990 than in any of the three previous decades. Figure 9 shows the deviation of the saving rate from its initial steady-state level after the demographic news. In all of the simulations, saving falls immediately following the demographic news, and is always falling by 2000. Even in the cases where saving begins to increase in the 1990s—when we begin the simulation in 1980 or 1990—the saving rate is lower throughout the 1990s than the original steady state, and it begins a period of prolonged decline by 2000.

While these figures help to develop perspective on the recent decline in U.S. saving and investment rates, the actual decline in U.S. national saving from an average of 7.1 percent in the 1970s to about 2 percent in the late 1980s is considerably more than our demographic analysis can justify.

The analysis in this section reaches a clear conclusion. For an economy choosing its consumption path in accord with a standard optimal growth model, the right response to the upcoming U.S. demographic change

Figure 9. Optimal Saving Responses to Demographic Change: Sensitivity to Date of Demographic Discovery[a]

Difference in saving rate from steady state (percent)

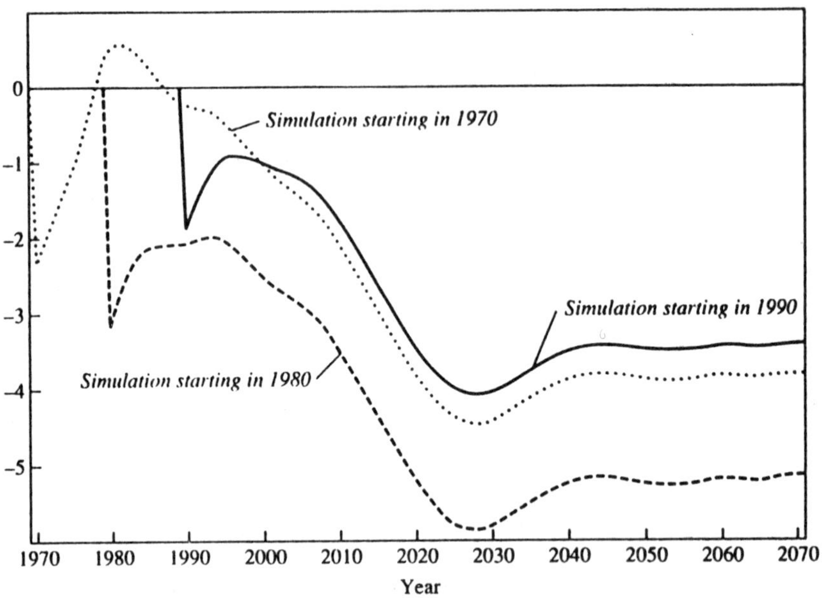

Source: Authors' calculations using Board of Trustees of the Federal Old-Age and Survivors Insurance and Disability Insurance Trust Funds (1988).

a. This figure presents the percentage point difference in saving rates from the initial steady state following a demographic shock. The three lines represent saving paths when the simulations are run starting in 1970, 1980, and 1990. These saving paths come from simulations using needs-weighted consumption (*CON*2) and the earnings-weighted labor force (*LF*2), and unit elasticities of substitution in both production and consumption ($\beta = 1$, $\sigma = 1$).

would be an increase in consumption and a reduction in national saving. For all plausible combinations of parameter values, the effects of reduced labor force growth and reductions in the number of children exceed the effects of increases in long-run dependency.

Open-Economy Aspects of the Demographic Shift

Our analysis thus far has focused on the demographic change in the United States. When capital markets are integrated, however, the demographic shift in the United States must be measured not only in absolute terms but *relative* to the coincident shifts in our major trading partners. This section compares the degree of population aging in

different nations and extends our earlier simulation model to consider the United States in relation to the other countries in the Organization for Economic Cooperation and Development (OECD). Our earlier finding that, other things being equal, demographic changes justify a reduction in optimal saving is reinforced when we allow for international capital flows, because demographic change is less pronounced in the United States than elsewhere in the OECD.

Relative Rates of Population Aging

To compare rates of population aging, we use projections by the OECD.[29] These projections differ in two important ways from the Social Security Administration projections for the United States. First, the OECD treats the 15–19 age group as workers rather than dependents. Second, and more important, the OECD assumes that fertility rates in all countries will converge to the replacement level of 2.1 by 2050. Because U.S. fertility rates are currently well above those in most of the OECD, this understates the likely contrast between the future U.S. and foreign demographic experiences.

Figure 10 shows the historical and projected elderly dependency ratio for the United States, Japan, and the European Community.[30] The elderly dependency ratio increases substantially in all countries, with the most rapid increase in Japan. By 2050, even with a 19 percentage point increase in the elderly dependency ratio from 1950, the U.S. ratio will be roughly 5 percentage points lower than those of the other countries.

Figure 11 shows the path of support ratios corresponding to the *LF*1 and *CON*1 assumptions. The broad outlines for all three regions are similar. All have higher support ratios in 1990 than in 1960, and all will have much lower support ratios by the middle of the next century than they do today. The ultimate level of U.S. dependency will be lower than that abroad.

Two differences in these indexes are notable, however. First, the United States will be better off for the next two decades than it is now, while the other countries experience declines in the support ratio

29. OECD (1988).

30. The multicountry index is a GDP-weighted average of the indexes for the individual countries.

Figure 10. Actual and Projected Elderly Dependency Ratios, United States, Japan, and European Community, 1950–2050

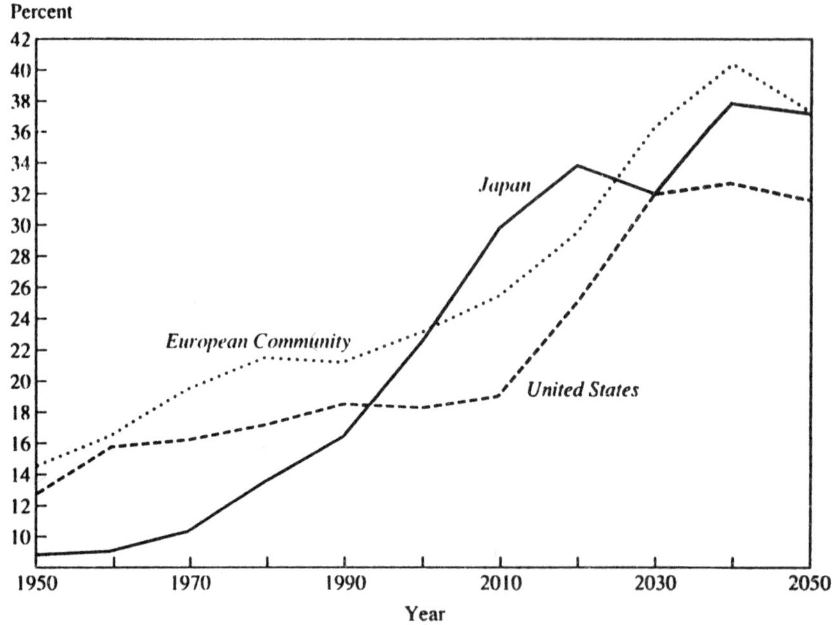

Source: OECD (1988). Working-age population includes all those aged 15–64.

beginning in 1990. Second, the U.S. and EC dependency ratios are driven principally by fertility changes, while the Japanese changes are driven to a much larger extent by reductions in mortality.[31] The decline in the support ratio in the 1950s in the United States and in the 1960s in the EC is due to increased numbers of children; the rise in the support ratio throughout the postwar period in Japan, in contrast, is caused by reduced mortality at middle and older ages. Because the labor force grows faster when fertility is higher, the reduction in labor force growth over the next several decades, and thus the consumption dividend from reduced investment requirements, will be larger in the United States and the European Community than in Japan.

To evaluate the size of the demographic transition abroad, table 5 reports the optimal consumption and saving responses to projected

31. OECD (1988) presents evidence on the importance of fertility and mortality declines for the different countries.

Figure 11. Actual and Projected Support Ratios, United States, Japan, and European Community, 1950–2050

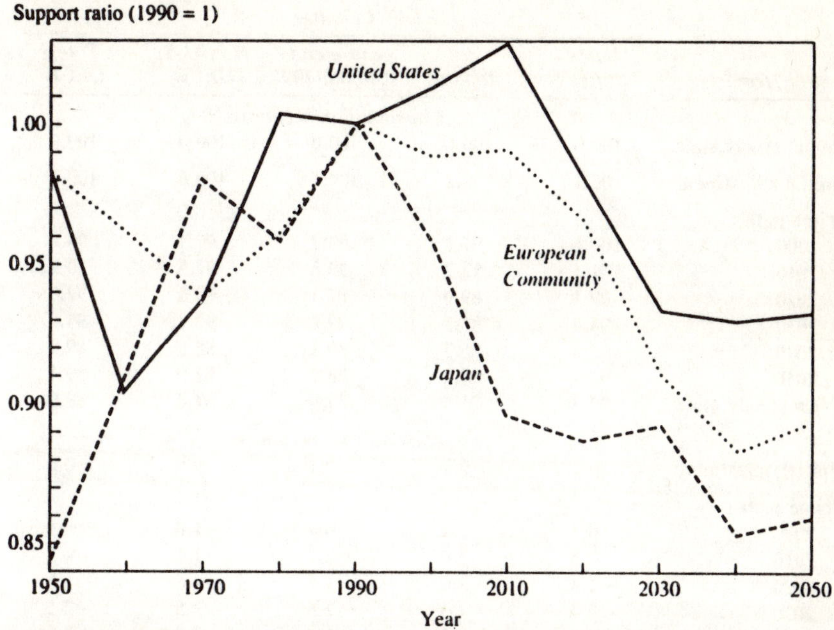

Source: OECD (1988) The consumption measure is total population (*CON1*). The labor force measure is the population 15–64 (*LF1*).

demographic changes in the United States, Japan, the European Community, the non-U.S. OECD, and the total OECD.[32] These consumption paths are simulated using the model of the previous section. For the United States, consumption rises only slightly initially, continues increasing until 2010, and then declines to the new steady state. This consumption increase is accompanied by an increased saving rate, however, since the relative increase in the working-age population increases output per person by more than consumption per person.

For Japan, the coming demographic changes reduce optimal con-

32. The table uses the case of unit elasticities of substitution and production. We assume that depreciation rates and rates of labor-augmenting technical progress are equal in all countries and are the same as the Social Security Administration forecasts for the United States. The assumption of equal productivity growth is obviously wrong but probably does not have a large impact on estimates of the change in saving due to changes in demographic structure.

Table 5. Autarky Response of Consumption and Saving to Demographic Shocks, United States and Various Nations, 1990–2050[a]

	Country				
Item	*United States*	*Japan*	*European Community*	*Non-U.S. OECD*	*Total OECD*
			Consumption response		
Initial steady state	100.0	100.0	100.0	100.0	100.0
Initial adjustment	100.1	99.2	100.1	100.0	100.1
Time path					
2000	100.6	97.2	99.7	99.3	99.8
2010	101.5	92.2	98.8	97.8	99.2
2020	99.1	89.0	97.1	95.5	97.0
2030	94.4	88.5	92.8	92.1	93.0
2040	92.0	86.3	89.1	88.8	89.9
2050	92.1	84.8	88.2	87.9	89.1
New steady state	92.3	84.4	87.9	87.8	89.0
			Saving rate response		
Initial adjustment	−0.1	0.7	−0.1	0.0	0.0
Time path					
2000	0.1	−1.4	−0.9	−1.0	−0.6
2010	0.5	−3.0	−0.7	−1.1	−0.5
2020	−1.4	−2.6	−1.5	−1.8	−1.6
2030	−2.4	−1.3	−2.8	−2.5	−2.5
2040	−1.5	−3.1	−2.9	−2.9	−2.3
2050	−1.4	−1.5	−0.8	−1.2	−1.3
New steady state	−1.5	−1.3	−0.7	−1.1	−1.3

Source: OECD (1988) and authors' calculations.

a. The values in the table are the optimal consumption and saving paths for each country without international capital flows. We use needs-weighted consumption (*CON2*) and the unweighted labor force (*LF1*). Consumption is relative to the initial steady state, which is normalized to 100. Saving paths are defined as the percentage point difference between the saving rate along the path and the initial steady state. The elasticities of substitution in production and consumption both equal unity.

sumption initially by just under 1 percent, and consumption continues to decline throughout the next 60 years, even as the saving rate declines. For the European Community, there is also a slight increase in consumption, but by 2000 consumption is lower, and continues to decline throughout the next half-century. This pattern of declining consumption after a small increase in initial consumption carries over to the non-U.S. OECD and total OECD simulations.

The initial decrease in the saving rate in the United States and the increase in the non-U.S. OECD imply that in an open economy, capital would initially flow from the non-U.S. OECD to the United States. After the initial change in saving, however, capital flows are more difficult to predict. In addition to the change in saving rates in the autarky case, the countries also have different changes in labor force growth rates, and thus in investment requirements. Because the desired capital inflow depends on the difference between saving and investment requirements, looking at saving rates or consumption alone does not indicate whether each country would borrow or lend. To address this issue, we turn next to simulations that allow for capital mobility.

A Two-Country Simulation Model

Our open-economy simulations aggregate the European Community, Japan, and the other countries of the OECD to form a non-U.S. OECD index. Figures 12 and 13 show the support ratio and labor force growth rates for the United States and this aggregate. The support ratios are consistent with those in figure 11. The United States has a 5 percentage point higher support ratio in 2050 than the non-U.S. OECD, and unlike the rest of the OECD has a rising support ratio over the next two decades. By 2050 the labor force in both areas is projected to stabilize, not grow. Between now and then they fluctuate, but with U.S. labor force growth always higher.

To assess the optimal response of U.S. saving in an open-economy context, we extend the model of the previous section to allow for capital mobility. We distinguish asset ownership from asset location by denoting period t asset ownership per person in country 1 by $a_{1,t}$. Asset accumulation is given by

(15) $$\dot{a}_{1,t} = w_t + a_{1,t}(r_t - n_{1,t}) - (c_{1,t}/\alpha_{1,t}),$$

where the wage, w_t, and the interest rate, r_t, are equalized across countries. The labor force growth rate, the support ratio, and the level of per capita consumption can differ across countries and therefore have both time and country subscripts.

The common capital-labor ratio is a weighted average of asset holdings in the two nations:

(16) $$k_t = \theta_{1,t}\, a_{1,t} + (1 - \theta_{1,t})\, a_{2,t},$$

where $\theta_{1,t}$ is country 1's share of world population. From equation 16 we derive the capital accumulation constraint for the two-country model:

(17) $$\dot{k}_t = \dot{\theta}_{1,t}(a_{1,t} - a_{2,t}) + \theta_{1,t}\dot{a}_{1,t} + (1 - \theta_{1,t})\dot{a}_{2,t}.$$

Figure 12. Actual and Projected Support Ratios, United States and Non-U.S. OECD, 1960–2050

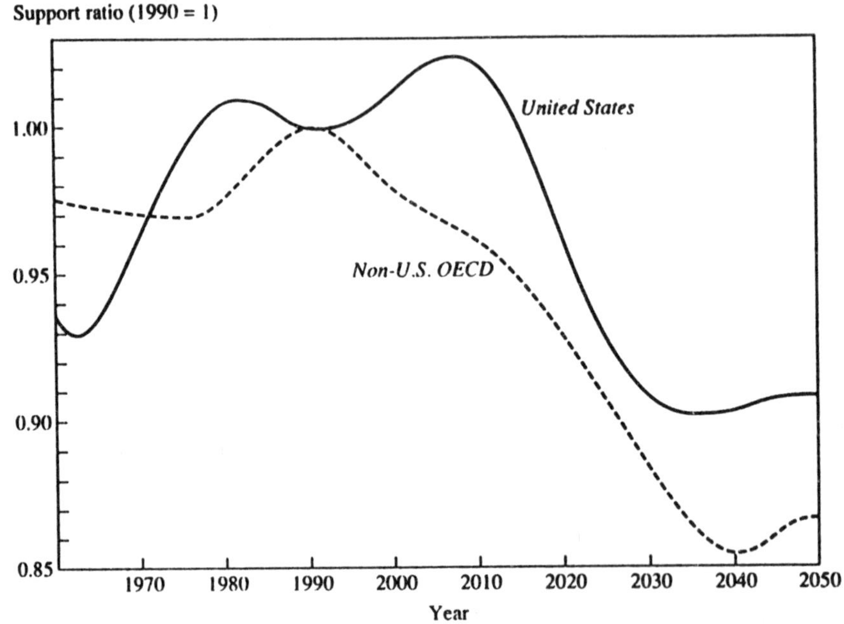

Source: Authors' calculations based on data in OECD (1988). Non-U.S. OECD includes all OECD countries except the United States, weighted by GDP. The consumption measure is needs-weighted (*CON2*), with the same weights as for the United States. The labor force is the population 15–64 (*LF1*).

This constraint replaces equation 10 in the one-country model. The optimal consumption profile (equation 11) and the steady-state saving-investment relation (equation 12) are identical to those in the one-country case.

We calibrate the two-country model assuming that both countries have Cobb-Douglas production functions and logarithmic utility functions. We assume that one nation is the United States and the other is the non-U.S. OECD, and set the relative labor force in the United States at four-tenths of the two-country total, roughly the value of the productivity-weighted U.S. labor force share for 1990. In addition, we begin the simulations assuming no net foreign investment position.[33] We also assume equal rates of technological progress and equal discount rates in the two countries.

33. This corresponds to the average U.S. net foreign asset position during the 1980s, but understates foreign holdings of U.S. assets at the beginning of the 1990s.

Figure 13. Actual and Projected Growth Rate of Labor Force, United States and Non-U.S. OECD, 1960–2050

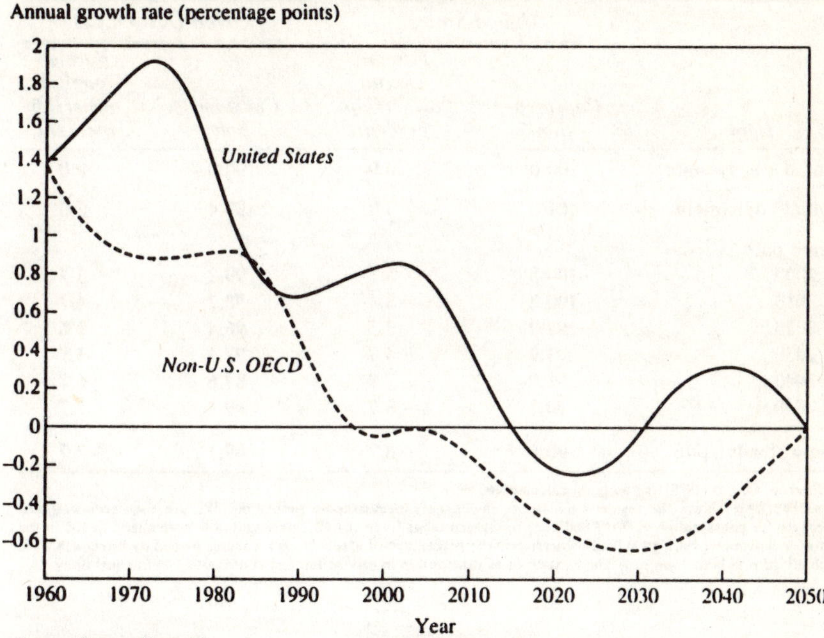

Source: Same as figure 12.

Table 6 presents the two-country simulation results. We normalize consumption to be 100 initially in both countries. While the shape of the consumption response is similar in the open- and closed-economy cases, the size of the responses is different. For the United States, the closed-economy analysis suggests a 0.1 percent consumption increase relative to the 1990 steady state. With capital flows between the relatively slowly aging United States and the more rapidly aging rest of the OECD, however, the U.S. consumption increase is 1 percent of the 1990 benchmark. Consumption in the United States increases more in the open-economy case because high saving elsewhere in the world reduces the rate of return to capital, inducing a positive shock to the value of human wealth.[34]

34. Although we assume that utility is logarithmic, the interest elasticity of saving is positive. When interest rates increase, holding wealth constant, saving is unaffected. However, with interest rates higher, the present discounted value of labor income decreases, and hence consumption falls. Wages in the United States also increase in the short run.

Table 6. Effect of Demographic Shock on Consumption and Foreign Capital Ownership, United States and Non-U.S. OECD, 1990–2050[a]

	United States		*Non-U.S. OECD*	
Item	*Consumption*	*Foreign capital ownership (percent)*	*Consumption*	*Foreign capital ownership (percent)*
Initial steady state	100.0	0.0	100.0	0.0
Initial adjustment	101.0	0.0	99.4	0.0
Time path				
2000	100.8	−5.5	99.2	3.7
2010	100.2	−6.4	98.7	4.7
2020	97.9	−3.5	96.4	2.6
2030	93.9	−4.7	92.4	3.7
2040	91.0	−7.9	89.6	6.7
2050	90.5	−8.7	89.1	7.7
New steady state	90.5	−8.7	89.1	7.7

Source: OECD (1988) and authors' calculations.

a. The table shows the results from the open-economy demographic simulation. We use the needs-weighted measure for consumption (*CON2*) and the unweighted labor force (*LF1*). Consumption is normalized to 100 in the initial steady state. Foreign capital ownership is the percentage of assets in each country owned by foreigners. It is initially zero in both countries. The elasticities of substitution in production and consumption both equal unity.

To finance the additional consumption indicated in the simulations, the United States runs a current account deficit. Figure 14 shows the path of net national saving and net investment, and, as residual, the current account. For about 15 years, the United States runs current account deficits, so that more than 6 percent of U.S. assets are owned by foreigners in 2010. High saving for the subsequent 15 years results in current account surpluses and reduces foreign capital ownership to 3.5 percent. Past 2020, however, with the rapid increase in the number of elderly, the United States again runs current account deficits, so that in the steady state almost 9 percent of U.S. assets are owned by foreigners.

For the non-U.S. OECD, consumption declines 0.6 percent when trade with the United States is permitted. The availability of investment projects in the United States means that higher saving in the short run will not depress rates of return by as much as in the closed-economy case.

The open- and closed-economy cases yield different consumption levels in both the short run and the steady state. In the open-economy

Figure 14. Net Saving and Investment Rates, United States, from Two-Country Simulations, 1990–2050

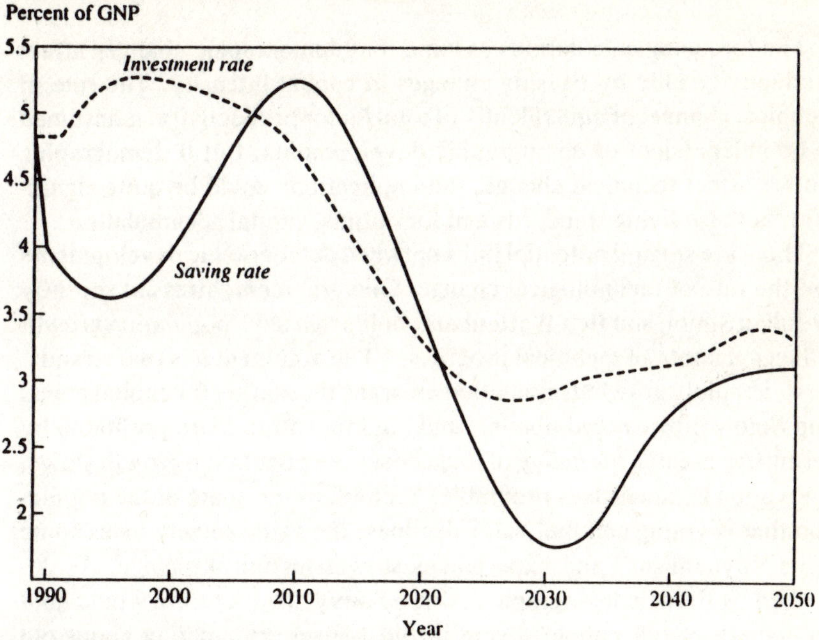

Source: Authors' calculations and OECD (1988).

case, U.S. consumption is higher in the early stage of the transition because of the availability of foreign capital. The resulting decrease in asset accumulation translates into a 1.8 percentage point reduction in steady-state consumption from the closed-economy simulation. For the non-U.S. OECD, the effect is reversed: greater capital accumulation along the transition path leads to steady-state consumption 1.3 percentage points higher than in the autarky steady state.

These results suggest two conclusions. First, the pattern of demographic change in other developed nations can have a large effect on the optimal consumption response to demographic change in the United States. The importance of these effects depends critically on the degree of capital market integration. Second, because the United States is aging more slowly than other OECD nations, the optimal consumption response in the open economy entails higher initial consumption than in the autarky case and thus a current account deficit.

Demographic Change and Productivity Growth

The foregoing calculations assume that demographic changes affect productivity only by causing changes in capital intensity. The rate of technical change, or equivalently of total factor productivity, is assumed to be independent of demographic developments. But if demographic factors affect technical change, the implications could be quite significant, both for living standards and for optimal capital accumulation.

There are several potential links between demographic developments and the rate of technological change. One argument, stressed recently by Julian Simon and Ben Wattenberg, holds that slow population growth reduces the rate of technical progress.[35] The argument has two strands. First, a rapidly growing population enlarges the market for capital goods (the Solow effect noted above), making innovation more profitable by permitting greater spreading of fixed costs. As population growth slows, innovation becomes less profitable. Second, as the share of the population that is young and innovates declines, the aging society loses some of its "dynamism" and experiences slower technical change. As described by French demographer Alfred Sauvy, such a future would hold "a society of old people, living in old houses, ruminating about old ideas."[36]

A more optimistic argument, advanced by H. J. Habakkuk, is that incentives to innovate are strongest when labor is scarce.[37] Habakkuk argued that industrialization proceeded faster in America than in England because attractive agricultural opportunities raised the price of labor in the United States relative to that in England, where labor was abundant and less expensive. Paul Romer has formalized this argument and used it to explain the apparent tendency for abnormally rapid U.S. productivity growth in periods of relatively slow labor force growth.[38]

The relative importance of these mechanisms can only be assessed empirically. Unfortunately, there are no ideal experiments for considering the effects of demographic change on productivity growth. Below we draw on the differing demographic experiences of relatively high-

35. Simon (1981) and Wattenberg (1987).
36. Wattenberg (1987, p. 65).
37. Habakkuk (1962).
38. Romer (1990).

income countries to assess the likelihood that an aging population will lead to economic stagnation.

Evidence on Productivity and Demographic Composition

Our empirical work uses the 1960–85 international comparison data of Robert Summers and Alan Heston.[39] Unfortunately, data on total factor productivity are not available for a wide sample of countries. Instead, we study the relation between labor force growth and labor productivity growth.[40]

We selected countries with 1960 labor productivity at least 30 percent of U.S. productivity (we use income per worker as our productivity measure) and excluded the OPEC countries, thus generating a sample of 29 countries. Selecting on initial income avoids the bias of including only countries that have experienced large productivity growth, as Bradford DeLong highlights.[41] We omit countries with very low initial productivity because the role of labor force growth may be very different in pre-industrial societies. Japan is omitted because its productivity was only 25 percent of U.S. productivity in 1960.

Figure 15 plots annual productivity growth and annual labor force growth during 1960–85. The data show a strong negative correlation. Slower-growing countries, including most European nations, exhibit above-average productivity growth, while more rapidly growing countries such as Canada and Australia have lower productivity growth.

To control for additional factors affecting growth, we estimate cross-section regressions of the form:

$$\ln(y_{1,i}/y_{0,i})/T = \alpha_0 + \alpha_1 \ln(LF_{1,i}/LF_{0,i})/T + \alpha_2 \ln(y_{0,i}) + \alpha_3 (I/Y)_i + \epsilon_i, \quad (18)$$

where $y_{1,i}$ and $y_{0,i}$ are, respectively, final and initial output per labor force member; $LF_{1,i}$ and $LF_{0,i}$ are the final and initial labor force; $(I/Y)_i$ is the average investment rate during the sample period; i denotes the country; and T is the length of the sample period. The investment rate is included to control for changes in capital that affect labor productivity but not

39. Summers and Heston (1990).

40. We present limited evidence below suggesting that the difference between labor productivity and total factor productivity does not have a large effect on our results.

41. DeLong (1988).

Figure 15. Productivity Growth and Labor Force Growth, Selected Countries, 1960–85[a]

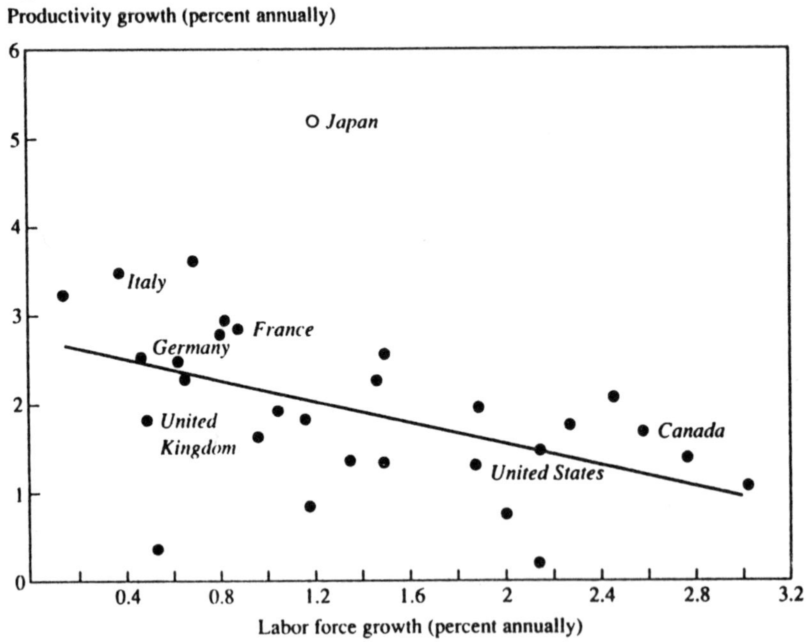

Source: Authors' calculations based on data in Summers and Heston (1990). The G-7 countries are labeled on the figure.

a. Japan is included in the figure but not in the regression line.

total factor productivity. Initial income is included to capture the possibility that lagging countries grow more rapidly as they converge toward leading ones. Productivity growth and labor force growth are expressed at annual rates.

The upper panel of table 7 reports ordinary least squares estimates of equation 18. The coefficients in the bivariate regressions, analogous to figure 15, imply that a 1 percentage point decrease in the annual labor force growth rate raises productivity growth by 0.62 percentage point a year. Controlling for the initial level of productivity and investment rates has little effect on the labor force growth coefficient, with the estimates still negative (−0.64) and large. The data also suggest that more rapid investment leads to faster productivity growth, although there is no evidence of productivity convergence for this sample.

We estimated equation 18 with other samples of countries, with similar results. If we include the six OPEC countries with 1960 produc-

Table 7. Demographic Change and Productivity Growth, 1960–85, Various Periods[a]

Period	No controls: Labor force growth	No controls: $\bar{R}^2$	With controls: Labor force growth	With controls: Logarithm of initial productivity	With controls: Investment rate	With controls: $\bar{R}^2$
Ordinary least squares estimates						
1960–85	−0.617	0.281	−0.637	−0.346	0.063	0.421
	(0.179)		(0.161)	(0.434)	(0.022)	
1960–73	−1.061	0.389	−1.044	−0.730	0.064	0.460
	(0.245)		(0.232)	(0.647)	(0.028)	
1973–85	−0.258	0.025	−0.295	0.154	0.075	0.175
	(0.198)		(0.195)	(0.546)	(0.031)	
Fixed effects	−0.903	0.085	−0.446	−6.290	0.032	0.600
	(0.477)		(0.355)	(1.177)	(0.057)	
Instrumental variables estimates						
1960–85	−0.711	. . .	−0.742	−0.337	0.064	. . .
	(0.216)		(0.189)	(0.438)	(0.022)	
1960–73	−0.977	. . .	−0.956	−0.763	0.064	. . .
	(0.297)		(0.272)	(0.651)	(0.028)	
1973–85	−0.436	. . .	−0.610	−0.150	0.085	. . .
	(0.272)		(0.296)	(0.610)	(0.033)	
Fixed effects	−0.840	. . .	0.332	−7.273	−0.017	. . .
	(1.151)		(1.440)	(2.174)	(0.107)	

Source: Authors' calculations based on data in Summers and Heston (1990).
a. The dependent variable is the annual productivity growth rate. The labor force growth rate and investment rate are both annual rates. The sample consists of the 29 non-OPEC countries with 1960 income per worker above 30 percent of the U.S. level. The upper panel reports ordinary least squares estimates. The lower panel instruments for the growth rate of the labor force with the growth rate of the population. Standard errors are in parentheses; $\bar{R}^2$s are adjusted for degrees of freedom.

tivity above 30 percent of the U.S. level, the coefficient in the multivariate regression rises to −0.517 (0.144). If we limit the sample to countries with 1960 productivity at least 50 percent of that in the United States, the coefficient becomes −0.263 (0.192). If we consider the current OECD countries, the coefficient is −0.372 (0.161). Finally, if we include all 114 countries in the Summers and Heston data with at least 20 years of data, the coefficient becomes −0.507 (0.159).

Dividing the period 1960–85 into two shorter intervals, 1960–73 and 1973–85, shown in the second and third rows of the upper panel, allows us to examine the importance of the productivity slowdown in the mid-1970s. The results from these regressions are consistent with those from the full sample, although the evidence is stronger in the 1960–73 period. In the earlier period, the coefficient (−1.044) is much larger and still statistically significantly different from zero. In the post-1973 period, the coefficient falls to −0.295 and is no longer statistically significant.

The fourth row of the table presents the results of treating the two sample periods as a panel and estimating a fixed-effects regression. This specification controls for other factors that can explain persistent differences in growth rates across countries but that are not included in our set of explanatory variables. The results are qualitatively similar to those without the fixed effects. The coefficient in the multivariate regression (−0.446) is within the range of the estimates for the two sample periods, although the coefficient is not statistically significantly different from zero when we control for initial income and the investment rate.

The lower panel of the table reports instrumental variables estimates of the same equations, using the population growth rate as an instrument for labor force growth. If rapid productivity growth leads to less rapid increases in labor force participation, the ordinary least squares estimates will be biased, but the instrumental variables regressions will not. The instrumental variables estimates strongly confirm the ordinary least squares estimates. In the 1960–85 regression, the coefficient on labor force growth becomes more negative in the instrumental variables regression (−0.742) and is still statistically significant. The coefficients on the other variables, in contrast, change little.

As the second and third rows of the bottom panel suggest, this is principally due to a more pronounced negative relation between labor force growth and productivity growth during 1973–85. This is consistent with Richard Freeman's claim that the decline in productivity growth in post-1973 Europe discouraged labor force participation, leading to a positive bias in the coefficient on labor force growth rates.[42]

The final row presents the results for the instrumental variables regression with the fixed-effects specification. While the coefficient in the bivariate regression is similar to the ordinary least squares estimate, the coefficient in the multivariate regression is positive. In both cases, the coefficients on labor force growth are not statistically different from zero.

Because reductions in the labor force growth rate tend to increase capital intensity, one would expect them to be associated with increases in labor productivity growth even if they had no impact on technical change.[43] We doubt that the equations in table 7 are primarily picking up

42. Freeman (1988).

43. Mankiw, Romer, and Weil (1990) explore this possibility with particular attention to the role of human capital accumulation.

this effect for two reasons. First, its theoretical magnitude is much smaller than the effects implied by the cross-country equations. Over a 25-year period, a 1 percentage point reduction in labor force growth holding the saving rate constant would raise labor productivity by at most 0.17 percentage point assuming a Cobb-Douglas production function with a 67 percent labor share.[44] Second, for a small sample of OECD countries with available data (18 countries) we estimated productivity growth equations using both labor productivity and total factor productivity and found only negligible differences in the results.[45]

These regressions imply substantively large effects of demographic change on future growth. Because the annual labor force growth rate is predicted to fall by about 1 percentage point between 1990 and 2050, with most of the change occurring between 1990 and 2010, our estimates imply an increase of about 0.6 percentage point in annual productivity growth. Such effects are large enough to offset the decline in living standards that we presented above. Even a 0.2 percentage point increase in annual productivity growth between 1990 and 2040 would offset the roughly 10 percent decrease in per capita consumption as a result of rising dependency burdens over that period. Thus, even if the effects are much smaller than those from our regressions, they are likely to have a large impact on future living standards.

The regressions thus far present little evidence for the more pessimistic view of demographic change. It may be, however, that part of the effect of demographic change occurs through the investment rate. If slower labor force growth reduces the rate of innovation because of decreased demand for capital goods, that will show up as a positive effect of investment rates on productivity growth, rather than as an effect of labor force growth.

To consider this hypothesis, we reestimated the equations in table 7 without controlling for the rate of investment. The results change little from those reported. For the full time period, for example, the coefficient

44. The predicted effect is this large only if the base year for our observations (1960) is the first year of the new labor force growth rates. If the countries were already in steady state with different labor force growth rates, there would be no predicted effect on productivity from this explanation.

45. Without controls for initial productivity and investment rates, the coefficient on the growth rate of the labor force is −0.788 (0.207) in the equation for labor productivity and −0.696 (0.257) in the equation for total factor productivity. In the multivariate regression, the coefficients are −0.305 (0.216) and −0.259 (0.324) in the two equations.

on labor force growth falls only slightly, from −0.637 (0.161) to −0.617 (0.182). In no case does the coefficient on labor force growth fall substantially, and in many cases it becomes more important.

It is also possible that our measure of demographic change is not the best measure for examining the productivity consequences of changes in the population structure. The argument that older work forces are less innovative than their younger counterparts suggests that a variable like the average age of the work force is a more direct measure of demographic conditions. Our measure of labor force growth rates is only partly correlated with this type of demographic variable.

We explored this possibility by adding the average age of the labor force to the equations in table 7.[46] In the basic specification in the first row of the table, when the average age variable is included, the coefficient on the labor force growth rate declines to −0.483 (0.225), and that on the average labor force age is 0.135 (0.138). Neither the coefficient on initial productivity nor that on the investment rate changes substantially. Similar conclusions emerge for the other specifications.[47]

To the extent that the labor scarcity hypothesis is correct, it reinforces our conclusion that the maturing of the labor force expands society's opportunities. Faster productivity growth has a theoretically ambiguous effect on the level of current consumption, however. It tends to increase consumption today because of the income effect of increased output, but this effect can be offset by a substitution effect from the increased investment return as the effective supply of labor grows more quickly.

To evaluate these effects for current consumption decisions, we calculated the optimal consumption path when productivity growth changes over time. We assumed that each percentage point decrease in labor force growth increases productivity growth by 0.5 percentage point, a number in the range of those in table 7. Figure 16 shows the resulting consumption path, as well as the consumption path without the

46. To account for changes in the average age of the labor force over the time period of our productivity growth measurements, we defined the average labor force age over any period as the mean of the average age at the endpoints of the period.

47. We intend to explore these issues further in subsequent work. Preliminary results suggest that the evidence for beneficial effects of slow labor force growth is much weaker for the 1870–1960 period than for the post-1960 period. This may be a consequence of the simultaneity caused by much larger immigration flows in the early period. At this point, it seems fair to conclude that there is no international evidence for the dynamism hypothesis that more rapid population growth or a younger population raises productivity, and some evidence for the contrary labor scarcity hypothesis.

Figure 16. Consumption Response with Induced Productivity, United States, 1990–2065

Per capita consumption (index, 1990 = 100)

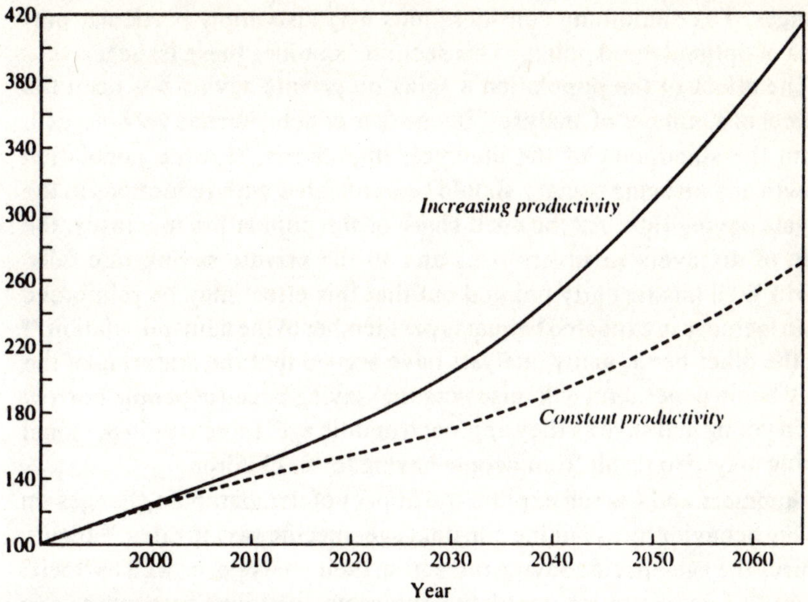

Source: Authors' calculations. For increasing productivity, it is assumed that productivity grows 0.5 percent for each 1 percent decline in annual labor force growth. The consumption measure is needs-weighted (*CON2*), and the labor force is earnings-weighted (*LF2*). The simulations assume unit elasticities of substitution in production and consumption.

productivity effects, following a demographic shock like those examined in the previous sections.[48] The effect of increased productivity growth is to increase current consumption even more, by an additional 0.2 percent. Further, because most of the productivity benefits occur in the next several decades, when the labor force grows slowly, consumption remains above its initial level throughout the transition path to the new steady state.

Demographic Change and Fiscal Policy

The preceding section suggests that, other things being equal, the optimal response to recent and projected demographic changes is a

48. We use the support ratio defined with the earnings-weighted labor force and needs-weighted consumption measure. We also assume unit elasticities of substitution in production and consumption.

decline in the national saving rate. The implications for fiscal policy depend upon how the private saving rate responds to demographic changes. Tax-smoothing considerations may also imply particular patterns of optimal fiscal policy. This section examines these issues.

The effect of the population's aging on private saving has been the subject of a number of analyses, but no firm conclusion has yet emerged. From the standpoint of the life-cycle hypothesis, slowing population growth and an aging society should be associated with reductions in the private saving rate. As the aged share of the population increases, the ratio of dissavers to savers rises and so the private saving rate falls. David Weil has recently pointed out that this effect may be reinforced by an increase in expected bequests per member of the adult population.[49] On the other hand, many analysts have argued that the maturing of the baby boom generation will raise personal saving because people borrow when young and save as they approach middle age. Increases in personal saving may also result from people having fewer children.

Summers and Carroll explore the impact of demographic changes on saving behavior by assuming constant age-specific saving rates.[50] Figure 17 uses the age-specific saving rates from their analysis, as well as Social Security Administration population forecasts, to project personal saving rates over the next 30 years. The results suggest that the maturing of the population will be associated with a small increase in saving rates during the next three decades. Calculations by Alan Auerbach and Laurence Kotlikoff reach similar conclusions.[51]

A near-term increase in private saving provides a further reason why an economy with an initially optimal saving rate should loosen fiscal policy in response to changing demographic conditions.

There is, however, a different argument for a tight fiscal policy. Projected demographic changes imply significant fluctuations in the level of government spending over the next century, since transfers to the

49. Weil (1989).

50. Summers and Carroll (1987).

51. Auerbach and Kotlikoff (1989). Both sets of calculations are flawed in ignoring pension saving, which may change as the age structure of the population changes. They also take no account of changes in the number of children or in the number of people supporting aged parents, although these factors may affect age-specific saving rates. David Weil (1990) uses aggregate data on OECD countries to study saving, recognizing these effects. His results suggest that private saving in the United States may rise about 1 percent in the next decade as a result of demographic factors.

Figure 17. Projected Private Saving Rate, United States, 1990–2065[a]

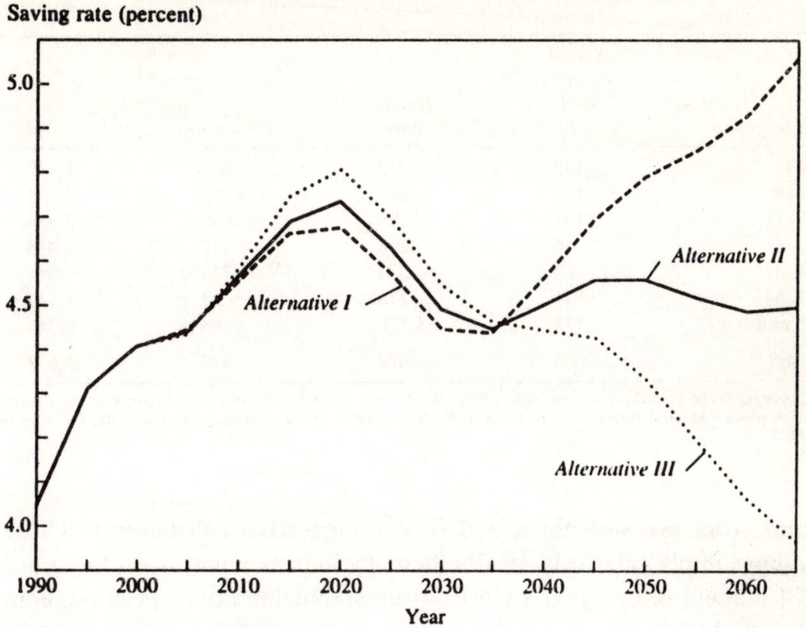

Source: Summers and Carroll (1987); Board of Trustees of the Federal Old-Age and Survivors Insurance and Disability Insurance Trust Funds (1988).

a. The calculations assume that the saving rate is held constant by age.

elderly are much larger than those to any other group. Efficiency considerations argue for higher current taxes to fund foreseeable increases in government outlays. Because the deadweight loss of taxation increases with the square of the tax rate, financing the anticipated rise in government outlays on a pay-as-you-go basis, with lower tax rates during the next few decades and higher ones in the middle of the next century, entails a larger deadweight burden than a constant tax rate policy.[52] This argument parallels the traditional justification for using debt to finance wars and other transitory shocks to government spending.

To evaluate the empirical significance of tax-smoothing considerations, we begin by describing the age-specific pattern of government outlays. We then present a simple framework for evaluating the efficiency

52. Barro (1979) describes the "tax-smoothing" view of optimal government financial policy.

Table 8. Per Capita Government Spending, by Age, United States, 1989
1989 dollars

Age group	*Social security and disability*	*Health care*	*Education*	*Total*
0–4	132	872	674	1,678
5–14	132	690	3,353	4,175
15–19	132	298	2,930	3,360
20–24	16	298	1,112	1,426
25–44	83	298	233	614
45–64	811	218	84	1,113
65 and over	6,138	3,526	84	9,748
Total	925	824	873	2,622

Sources: Social Security Administration (1987); Waldo and others (1989); Board of Trustees of the Federal Supplementary Medical Insurance Trust Fund (1988). For details regarding construction of the data, see notes to table 9.

gains from tax smoothing and report suggestive calculations. These findings imply relatively small efficiency improvements—on the order of 1 percent of one year's GNP—from stabilizing tax rates throughout the next half-century.

Age-Specific Patterns of Government Spending

Governments spend different amounts on individuals of different ages. Outlays on education, for example, benefit primarily children, while the elderly are the principal beneficiaries of most government spending on health care and social security. Even without changes in the structure of government programs, demographic shifts can therefore affect the level of government spending.

Table 8 presents age-specific government expenditure patterns for the United States, focusing on the three largest social expenditures: social security, health care, and education. The first column shows spending on Old-Age and Survivors and Disability Insurance. Virtually all such expenditures are directed to individuals aged 65 or over, with average outlays in 1986 of \$6,138 per person. The second column shows analogous age-specific spending patterns for health care, with average expenditures per person aged 65 and over (\$3,526) more than four times larger than outlays for any other age group. The third column reports

Table 9. Projected Government Expenditures, United States, 1990–2060
Percent of GNP

Year	*Social security and disability*	*Health care*	*Education*	*Other*	*Total*
1990	4.7	4.1	4.7	18.0	31.8
2000	4.5	5.3	4.9	18.0	32.9
2010	4.6	5.9	4.9	18.0	33.4
2020	5.6	6.5	4.8	18.0	35.0
2030	6.5	7.4	4.9	18.0	36.7
2040	6.5	7.8	4.9	18.0	37.1
2050	6.5	7.8	4.9	18.0	37.1
2060	6.5	7.8	4.9	18.0	37.0

Sources: Social security and disability spending are predicted from projected population growth rates. For the 1989 distribution of spending, we projected the year-end 1986 distribution from the Social Security Administration (1987) to 1989, using the GNP deflator. Spending at below retirement ages is the sum of OASDI payments to the disabled, payments to early retirees, and payments to surviving children and spouses. Spending on all persons below 20 years of age was treated as applying uniformly to the members of this group.

For health care spending, we combined four types of spending. We obtained 1987 estimates of Medicare and Medicaid per capita spending on the elderly for hospital care, physicians' services, nursing home care, and other personal health care from Waldo and others (1989). For the nonelderly population, we calculated government spending on each of these categories as the difference between the Division of National Cost Estimates, Office of Actuary, Health Care Financing Administration (1987) estimate of 1987 total government spending for that category and the implied spending on the elderly. This estimate includes both Medicaid spending for the nonelderly and medical care spending for government employees. We distributed this spending by age on the basis of Medicaid spending, as presented in Public Health Service (1989). All of the estimates were converted to 1989 dollars using category-specific projections of 1987–1990 inflation in Division of National Cost Estimates, Office of Actuary, Health Care Financing Administration (1987).

We forecast spending using estimates of inflation rates for the four categories of spending and projections of the age distribution of the population. Hospital care estimates are from the Board of Trustees of the Federal Supplementary Medical Insurance Trust Fund (1988). They imply a steady-state inflation rate above general inflation but below the growth rate of output. Inflation rates for the other three categories were projected to 2000 using the Division of National Cost Estimates, Office of Actuary, Health Care Financing Administration (1987) estimates, and were assumed to grow at the rate of hospital price inflation after that.

Finally, for age-specific spending on education, we obtained 1986 age-specific enrollment rates in school as well as the aggregate amounts spent on primary and secondary education, and higher education. We assumed that all persons under 17 who were enrolled in school were in primary and secondary schools, and all persons 18 and over who were enrolled were in higher education. Spending per person was then the weighted average of the population in each age group and the share of each age group in the two types of education. Our projections assume that education spending would grow at the rate of GNP growth, so that changes in the share of GNP devoted to education change only with changing numbers of young people.

the age profile of education spending. Per capita expenditures on schools for the younger cohorts are substantial, reaching $3,353 a year for children between the ages of 5 and 14. For the three programs combined, spending on the elderly is more than double that of any other group.

Demographic shifts can significantly alter government outlays. Table 9 reports projections of total government outlays as a share of GNP under the assumption that age-specific expenditure patterns remain at 1989 levels for the next 60 years. Primary government spending is assumed to equal a constant fraction of GNP. In these projections, government spending rises from 31.8 percent of GNP in 1990 to 37.0 percent of GNP in 2060, with nearly all the increase due to changes in medical expenditures and transfer programs to the elderly. Our tax-smoothing calculation assesses the efficiency gains from smoothing the time path of revenues needed to collect this variable expenditure stream.

The Efficiency Gains from Tax Smoothing

We evaluate the efficiency gain from tax smoothing by assuming that the deadweight burden of raising τ percent of national output in taxes is given by

(19) $$DWL_t = \epsilon\tau_t^2 Y_t/2.$$

The parameter ϵ depends on the elasticities of aggregate supply and demand and Y_t is national income.[53] The marginal deadweight loss per dollar of revenue raised is $\epsilon\tau_t$. We calibrate ϵ by setting the marginal deadweight loss from raising one dollar equal to 30 cents, the upper-bound estimate in Charles Ballard, John Shoven, and John Whalley's general equilibrium analysis of the U.S. tax system.[54] Their calculation employs 1973 data, when federal and state-local taxation in the United States was 31 percent of GNP, and therefore implies $\epsilon \cong 1.0$.

We assume that a government planner seeks to minimize the present discounted value of the deadweight losses from taxation over a T period horizon:

(20) $$V = \sum_{t=1}^{T} \left[\prod_{i=1}^{t} (1 + r_i)^{-1} \right] \epsilon\tau_t^2 Y_t/2,$$

where r_i denotes the one-period nominal interest rate in period i. This minimization is subject to an intertemporal budget constraint linking taxes and spending as a share of GNP (τ_t and h_t, respectively) with government debt as a share of GNP (d_t). For each period, this constraint is:

(21) $$d_t = d_{t-1}[(1 + r_t)/(1 + \gamma_t)] + h_t - \tau_t,$$

53. If governments set taxes to minimize deadweight loss, the marginal deadweight burden per revenue dollar should be equal across tax instruments. The aggregate tax-to-GNP ratio is then a simple proxy for the level of tax burdens. This convenient assumption neglects the voluminous public finance literature suggesting that marginal deadweight losses vary across tax instruments.

54. Ballard, Shoven, and Whalley (1985).

where r_t is the interest rate and γ_t is the rate of output growth.

Summing this forward yields a budget constraint of the form:

$$\sum_{t=1}^{T} \tau_t \delta_t = \sum_{t=1}^{T} h_t \delta_t + d_0 - d_T \delta_T, \tag{22}$$

where $\delta_t = \prod_{s=1}^{t} (1 + \gamma_s)/(1 + r_s)$. Minimizing equation 20 subject to equation 22 yields first-order conditions of the form

$$\epsilon \tau_t = \lambda, \tag{23}$$

so the optimal policy calls for equal tax rates in each period.

In the case where $r_t = \gamma_t$, the benefits of tax smoothing take a particularly simple form. The budget constraint is

$$\sum_{t=1}^{T} \tau_t = \sum_{t=1}^{T} h_t + d_0 - d_T. \tag{24}$$

If, further, $d_T = d_0$, then with a pay-as-you-go policy, taxes just cover government spending: $\tau_t = h_t$. Under the constant period-by-period debt-to-GNP policy, the deadweight loss is

$$DWL_1 = (Y_0 \epsilon/2) \Sigma h_t^2. \tag{25}$$

The constant tax rate satisfying the government budget constraint is just the average value of government spending, so that

$$DWL_2 = Y_0 \epsilon/2 \cdot T(\Sigma h_t/T)^2. \tag{26}$$

Thus, the relative deadweight loss from the optimal tax-smoothing policy is:

$$DWL_2/DWL_1 = (\Sigma h_t/T)^2/(\Sigma h_t^2/T). \tag{27}$$

For the expenditure path in table 9, the deadweight loss reduction in equation 27 is 0.3 percent.

The incremental deadweight loss from time-varying tax rates depends on the precise time path of taxes, hence on the government's choice of debt policy. We consider two such policies. The first assumes a constant debt-to-GNP ratio in every year, and the second assumes a constant primary surplus (equal to its value in 1989 of 0.5 percent of GNP) in each year.

Table 10 presents our estimates of the efficiency gains from tax smoothing. The upper panel presents results assuming a constant debt-

Table 10. Efficiency Gains from Smoothing Taxes, United States, 1990–2050[a]
Percent

Tax rate	Year 1990	Year 2010	Year 2030	Year 2050	Average deadweight loss as percent of average GNP
Constant debt-GNP ratio[b]					
Variable rate	32.6	33.5	36.8	37.1	6.23
Constant rate	35.3	35.3	35.3	35.3	6.22
Constant primary surplus[c]					
Variable rate	32.3	33.9	37.2	37.6	6.52
Constant rate	35.7	35.7	35.7	35.7	6.51

Source: Authors' calculations based on sources described in table 9.
a. For each spending category, total government expenditures are projected to 2060, as described in table 9. The two cases are described in more detail in the text.
b. Constant debt-GNP ratio is fixed at 1989 level of 50.2 percent.
c. Constant primary surplus assumes that a federal and state-local surplus equals its 1989 share of GNP throughout 1990–2000.

to-GNP ratio, fixed at its 1989 level of 50.2 percent. In this case the pay-as-you-go tax rate rises from 32.6 percent of GNP in 1990 to 37.1 percent by 2050. The average deadweight loss from this policy, shown in the last column, is 6.23 percent of the average value of GNP. The constant tax rate that achieves the same debt-to-GNP ratio of 50.2 percent in 2050 is 35.3 percent. Under this plan, taxes would rise by 3 percent of GNP—roughly $150 billion—in 1990. Despite this large change in the debt trajectory, however, the change in excess burden is small. The average value of deadweight loss is 6.22 percent of average GNP when tax rates are smoothed. The improvement in deadweight loss averages 0.017 percent of GNP annually, or less than $1 billion a year in 1990 dollars. The change in the *present value* of deadweight losses between 1990 and 2060 equals 1.1 percent of 1990 GNP, or approximately $55 billion.

The lower panel in table 10 shows parallel calculations assuming the combined federal and state-local primary surplus equals its 1989 share of GNP value throughout the 1990 to 2050 period. The results indicate that the average excess-burden-to-GNP ratio under this scenario is 6.52 percent, compared with 6.51 percent if the tax rate is smoothed. The difference between these two efficiency costs is similar to that in our first case, 0.017 percent of GNP. Plausible variations in our assumptions about the debt-to-GNP trajectory therefore do not appear to have large effects on the efficiency gains from tax smoothing. The general conclusion of these calculations is that there is only a weak tax-efficiency case for prepaying the costs of the future dependency burden.

Conclusions

Demographic changes currently in progress do not appear likely to worsen economic performance in the United States, at least during the next several decades. While increased dependency will reduce living standards by 5–10 percent in the long run, demographic changes will be beneficial over the next 20 years. In the short run, demographic change will have two important effects. First, slowing population growth will permit a smaller share of national output to be devoted to investment in plant, equipment, and housing. Second, the share of the population that is working will rise, largely as a result of the falling relative population of children. These positive effects of demographic change may be reinforced by increased foreign capital inflows and accelerating technical change as firms respond to an increasing scarcity of labor.

Recent and prospective demographic changes do not appear to warrant increasing the national saving rate. These changes increase wealth in the short run, reduce the rate of return to saving, and attract foreign capital. Holding all else equal, their net effect would be a *reduction* in the optimal national saving rate. Nor do tax-smoothing factors represent an important argument for trying to prepay the government's prospective liability to support a dependent population. There is little efficiency loss in following a pay-as-you-go policy with variable tax rates.

Our conclusion departs from analyses, such as that of Henry Aaron, Barry Bosworth, and Gary Burtless, that recommend accumulation of a large social security trust fund to bolster U.S. national saving.[55] These positions are not necessarily inconsistent, however. A first line of reconciliation would hold that apart from demographic considerations, American national saving is much too low right now and that the social security trust fund provides a politically convenient way of reducing the

55. Aaron, Bosworth, and Burtless (1989).

federal government's absorption of private saving.[56] The decline in the private saving rate from an average of 7.1 percent during the 1970s to about 3 percent during 1986–89 is greater than what our analysis suggests can be justified by demographic factors. There are even some reasons for advocating an increase in the U.S. national saving rate to levels above those observed historically, particularly in light of the emerging need for capital in Eastern Europe and the signs that saving is declining outside of the United States.

A second potential reconciliation of these views involves questions of optimal intergenerational redistribution. Some argue for using the social security trust fund to raise the national saving rate in order to avoid unfairly burdening our children. The primary thrust of this argument—that we need to prepare for the anticipated burden of increased dependency—is exactly what our support ratio calculations reject. This is because the dependency burden is remote, and because slower labor force growth means more rapidly diminishing returns to additional saving. Admittedly, our approach focuses on the economy's year-by-year consumption level, rather than the welfare of individual cohorts. It is therefore poorly suited to addressing arguments that certain cohorts will be greatly disadvantaged without additional capital accumulation. However, we do not find compelling the claim that our children will be unfairly burdened unless we increase capital accumulation today.

Two arguments militate against the intergenerational equity case for trust fund accumulation. First, if the aforementioned fears of inequity were correct, the appropriate response should be an adjustment in the level of prospective intergenerational transfers, not a change in capital accumulation policy. Just as concerns about the income distribution at a particular time are better addressed through transfer policies than through changes in the mix of products produced, transfers are the right way to respond to concerns about intergenerational equity.[57]

Second, other considerations operate to make the baby boom generation less well off than its successors. The baby boomers systematically lose because of their large cohort size. During their working years, wage growth is slow because of low capital-labor ratios. During their retirement years, the number of potential purchasers of capital will fall, thereby

56. See, for example, Hatsopoulos, Krugman, and Summers (1988).
57. This is the central point made by Calvo and Obstfeld (1988).

reducing the rate of return on saving.[58] Moreover, given productivity growth, the next generation will be considerably more affluent than the current one. If slower population growth or foreign capital inflows accelerate this tendency, the case for intergenerational redistribution is reduced. Even with our estimates of the path of optimal consumption, along which a declining support ratio reduces consumption, the lifetime utility of a person who lives for eighty years *rises* for those born from 1990 until 2020. Only after 2020 does the lifetime utility of new cohorts fall below that of those who lived before the demographic change.

Our aggregate analysis cannot resolve policy debates about raising the birth rate or increasing immigration, since these debates often focus on microeconomic effects and distributional consequences. Moreover, there is a fundamental political difficulty of deciding "who is us." How should the welfare of immigrants be treated in deciding whether or not to accept more of them? How should the utility of an otherwise unborn child be treated? Policy recommendations are impossible without a clear philosophical resolution of these questions.

Our analysis does, however, cast some doubt on the view that in narrow economic terms, higher fertility is helpful in reducing the burden of dependency in old age. Dependency at the beginning of the life cycle is between 50 percent and 100 percent as costly as dependency at the end of the life cycle. It also comes 60 years earlier. Furthermore, the weak available evidence suggests that slower population growth is more likely to raise than to reduce productivity growth.

For the set of issues captured by our analysis, there is a stronger case for increased immigration as a way of reducing dependency. Most immigrants arrive as young adults and so begin working without being dependents first. To the extent that they immediately start paying taxes for the support of the elderly, they may increase economic welfare of the preexisting population, even if they are ultimately eligible for transfer payments in old age.

We have only scratched the surface in assessing the macroeconomic implications of demographic change. Among the main priorities for future research, we would include the following. First, any effects of

58. Mankiw and Weil (1989) predict that real house prices will fall by almost 50 percent over the next 20 years because of demographic changes. While their results may overstate the coming decline, even small reductions in house prices would transfer large amounts of wealth to people who are very young today.

demography on the rate of technical change are likely to dwarf its other consequences. It would be valuable to refine our estimates by considering data spanning longer periods and by experimenting with alternative control variables. Second, how demographic changes affect private saving remains uncertain. Investigating the international experience on this question seems worthwhile, particularly if long-term data can be located. Third, our calculations have assumed that the nonmedical care needs of the elderly are equal to those for the nonelderly. Whether this assumption is correct, and whether it will remain correct as the aged population ages, needs to be investigated. Fourth, it would be useful to analyze more systematically the impact of demographic changes on the welfare of different cohorts. This would require a life-cycle analysis of the questions we address with an infinite horizon setting.[59]

It would also be useful to explore the microeconomic implications of changing demography. For example, our aggregation of capital may well be inappropriate if demographic change alters the relative demands for housing and nonhousing capital. Similarly, demographic changes may have important implications for the labor market position of aged workers and for the relative demands for workers in different occupations.

Further research on these and other related topics is likely to refine the conclusions about demographic change reached here. We doubt that it will alter our primary conclusion that demographic change provides opportunities as well as challenges.

59. Auerbach and Kotlikoff (1987) and Auerbach and others (1989) use a life-cycle model to consider demographic issues, but they assume counterfactually that consumers actually vary their saving rates as the model would predict and do not use the model for normative analysis.

D. M. Cutler, J. M. Poterba, L. M. Sheiner, and L. H. Summers 71

References

Aaron, Henry J., Barry P. Bosworth, and Gary Burtless. 1989. *Can America Afford to Grow Old? Paying for Social Security*. Washington: Brookings.

Auerbach, Alan J., and Laurence J. Kotlikoff. 1989. "Demographics, Fiscal Policy, and U.S. Saving in the 1980s and Beyond." Working Paper 3150. Cambridge, Mass.: National Bureau of Economic Research (October).

———. 1987. *Dynamic Fiscal Policy*. New York: Cambridge University Press.

Auerbach, Alan J., and others. 1989. "The Economic Dynamics of an Aging Population: The Case of Four OECD Countries. *OECD Economic Studies* 12: 97–130.

Baily, Martin N. 1981. "Productivity and the Services of Capital and Labor." *BPEA, 1:1981*, 1–50.

Baily, Martin Neil, and Charles L. Schultze. 1990. "The Productivity of Capital in a Period of Slower Growth." *BPEA: Microeconomics, 1990*, 369–406.

Ballard, Charles L., John B. Shoven, and John Whalley. 1985. "General Equilibrium Computations of the Marginal Welfare Costs of Taxes in the United States." *American Economic Review* 75: 128–38.

Bishop, John. 1989. "Is the Test Score Decline Responsible for the Productivity Growth Decline?" *American Economic Review* 79: 178–97.

Blanchard, Olivier J., and Stanley Fischer. 1989. *Lectures on Macroeconomics*. Cambridge, Mass.: MIT Press.

Barro, Robert J. 1979. "On the Determination of the Public Debt." *Journal of Political Economy* 87: 940–71.

Board of Trustees of the Federal Old-Age and Survivors Insurance and Disability Insurance Trust Funds. 1988. *1988 Annual Report*. Washington: Social Security Administration.

———. 1990. *1990 Annual Report*. Washington: Social Security Administration.

Board of Trustees of the Federal Supplementary Medical Insurance Trust Fund. 1988. *1988 Annual Report*. Washington: Social Security Administration.

Borjas, George J. 1990. *Friends or Strangers: The Impact of Immigration on the U.S. Economy*. New York: Basic Books.

Calvo, Guillermo A., and Maurice Obstfeld. 1988. "Optimal Time-Consistent Fiscal Policy with Finite Lifetimes: Analysis and Extensions." In *Economic Effects of the Government Budget*, edited by Elhanan Helpman, Assaf Razin, and Efraim Sadka. Cambridge, Mass.: MIT Press.

DeLong, J. Bradford. 1988. "Productivity Growth, Convergence, and Welfare: Comment." *American Economic Review* 78: 1138–54.

Denison, Edward F. 1985. *Trends in American Economic Growth, 1929–82*. Washington: Brookings.

Division of National Cost Estimates, Office of the Actuary, Health Care Financing Administration. 1987. "National Health Expenditures, 1986–2000." *Health Care Financing Review* 8(Summer): 1–36.

Freeman, Richard B. 1988. "Labour Market Institutions and Economic Performance." *Economic Policy* 6: 63–80.

Habakkuk, H. J. 1962. *American and British Technology in the Nineteenth Century*. Cambridge, England: Cambridge University Press.

Hatsopoulos, George N., Paul R. Krugman, and Lawrence H. Summers. 1988. "U.S. Competitiveness: Beyond the Trade Deficit." *Science*, July 15: 299–307.

Jorgenson, Dale, Frank M. Gollop, and Barbara M. Fraumeni. 1987. *Productivity and U.S. Economic Growth*. Cambridge, Mass.: Harvard University Press.

Lazear, Edward P., and Robert T. Michael. 1980. "Family Size and the Distribution of Real Per Capita Income." *American Economic Review* 70: 91–107.

Mankiw, N. Gregory, and David Weil. 1989. "The Baby Boom, the Baby Bust, and the Housing Market." *Regional Science and Urban Economics*, 235–58.

Mankiw, N. Gregory, David Romer, and David Weil. 1990. "A Contribution to the Empirics of Economic Growth" (February).

Organization for Economic Cooperation and Development. 1988. *Aging Populations: The Social Policy Implications*. Paris: OECD.

Poterba, James M., and Lawrence H. Summers. 1987. "Public Policy Implications of Declining Old-Age Mortality." In *Work, Health, and Income among the Elderly*, edited by Gary Burtless. Washington: Brookings.

Public Health Service. 1989. *Health United States 1988*. Hyattsville, Md.: Department of Health and Human Services (March).

Rivlin, Alice M., and Joshua M. Wiener. 1988. *Caring for the Disabled Elderly: Who Will Pay?* Washington: Brookings.

Romer, Paul M. 1990. "Capital, Labor, and Productivity." *BPEA: Microeconomics 1990*, 337–67.

Schneider, Edward L., and Jack Guralnik. 1990. "The Aging of America: Impact on Health Care Costs." *Journal of the American Medical Association* 263 (May 2): 2335–40.

Simon, Julian L. 1981. *The Ultimate Resource*. Princeton: Princeton University Press.

Social Security Administration. 1987. *Social Security Bulletin, Annual Statistical Supplement*. Washington (December).

———. 1989. *Social Security Area Population Projections: 1989*. Actuarial Study 105. SSA Pub. No. 11-11552. Washington (June).

Summers, Lawrence H., and Chris Carroll. 1987. "Why Is U.S. Saving So Low?" *BPEA, 2:1987*, 607–35.

Summers, Robert, and Alan Heston. 1990. "The Penn World Table (Mark 5):

An Expanded Set of International Comparisons." *Quarterly Journal of Economics* (forthcoming).

Tobin, James. 1988. "The Future of Social Security: One Economist's Assessment." In *Social Security: Beyond the Rhetoric of Crisis*, edited by Theodore R. Marmor and Jerry L. Mashaw. Princeton: Princeton University Press.

Waldo, Daniel R., and others. 1989. "Health Expenditures by Age Group, 1977 and 1987." *Health Care Financing Review* 10 (Summer): 111–20.

Wattenberg, Ben J. 1987. *The Birth Dearth*. New York: Pharos Books.

Weil, David. 1989. "Age and Saving in Micro and Macro Data." Harvard University.

———. 1990. "Prospects for Saving in the OECD over the Next 35 Years." Harvard University.

[12]

Effects of Cohort Size on Earnings: The Baby Boom Babies' Financial Bust

Finis Welch

University of California, Los Angeles

The arrival of the post–World War II baby boom cohorts in the job market raises many questions of effects associated with a rapidly declining average age of the labor force. This paper first summarizes 1967–75 wage behavior, showing that relative wages between schooling groups have not changed for prime-aged workers, but there is some evidence, for new job-market entrants, that wages of more educated workers have fallen relative to wages of less educated workers. However, changes among schooling groups are small in comparison to those between new entrants and peak earners within schooling group. The evidence is very direct: as work-experience distributions shifted toward increased proportions of young workers, their relative wages fell. After examining a career-phase model in which workers at different phases are imperfect substitutes, estimates of empirical relationships between cohort size and wages are presented. The main result is that income-depressant effects of (own) cohort size decline over the career but do not vanish altogether. Initial effects include reductions in wage rates and in hours and weeks worked, while persistent effects extend only to wages.

If everyone left school and started work on his twentieth birthday, the group of entrants into the U.S. labor market in 1977 would have been 44 percent larger than that in 1962. In fact the 1977 group would be this century's largest, and 15 years later—that is, in 1992—the entering group would be only slightly larger than in 1962. According

This project is supported by grants from the Rockefeller and National Science Foundations. I am indebted to Lee Lillard and James P. Smith for many valuable discussions during this work, to Marta Johnson for computational assistance, and to Richard Freeman for comments on an earlier draft. Views expressed are my own and I am responsible for any errors.

[*Journal of Political Economy*, vol. 87, no. 5, pt. 2]

to the assumption of entry at age 20, the number of new entrants has increased each of the last 20–25 years following the 1930s depression-related trough in number of births. But the number of births peaked in 1957 and has continued downward so that the number of new labor-market entrants will fall for at least the next 18 years (for which data on number of births are now available) with no clear indication of an ensuing rise.[1] Instead of labor markets adjusting to increasingly large numbers of entrants, adjustment will be to a declining pool.

It is, of course, true that not everyone begins work at the same age, and the higher the level of school attainment the later the age of job-market entry, so that cohort peaks for college graduates may not have passed. But in the last decade we witnessed a historically unique event—the market's responses to large entering cohorts.

Not only have labor markets been pressed by entry of those just out of school, but the work force has also been increased by the growing participation of married women and the influx of veterans of Vietnam. In the 8 years from March 1967 to March 1975, the (18–64-year-old) civilian labor force grew 21 percent. More important, new entrants during this period had more schooling than earlier cohorts. For example, even though the labor force grew by one-fifth, numbers of participants with 5–8 years of schooling fell 32 percent, as did numbers with 1–3 years of high school. In contrast, during these 8 years the number of high school graduates increased 35 percent, and both for those with 1–3 years of college and for college graduates the number of persons in the civilian labor force jumped an astonishing 64 percent.[2]

The unprecedented change in the age composition of the work force has undoubtedly affected earnings patterns, and this paper attempts to measure these effects. The main conclusion is that pressure of a work force whose average age is rapidly declining reduces wages of new entrants. This supports Richard Easterlin's and Michael Wachter's views of imperfect substitution among workers of different age or work experience.[3] While there is evidence that large cohorts

[1] The peak-sized baby boom cohorts may pull birth totals upward as they reach peak fertility ages, but the early evidence for these cohorts is of very low birthrates. They are so low, in fact, that numbers of births could conceivably continue the downward trend; see Butz and Ward (1979).

[2] These data refer to table A of "Educational Attainment of Workers" (U.S. Department of Labor 1975).

[3] Easterlin's cohort-effect fertility models are well known and in them imperfect substitution plays a central role. More recently, Wachter and Wachter and Easterlin have pursued ideas of imperfect substitution for implications of intermediate cycles both in labor force participation and economic stability. See, for example, Wachter (1977), Easterlin (1978), and Easterlin, Wachter, and Wachter (1978). Michael Wachter (1977) in particular pointed to recent changes in earnings of younger relative to older

receive reduced wages throughout their careers, most of the loss seems to be concentrated in the early years. Evidently the baby boom cohorts are taxed, but their future seems brighter than their experience to date.

The empirical analysis concentrates on earnings within school-completion level. The partition by schooling is used for two reasons. First, I think new entrants and experienced workers are more sharply distinguished at higher levels of education, and if they are, wage effects of expanded cohorts will be larger for them. Second, there is some evidence that during the early 1970s earnings of young college graduates fell relative to earnings of high school graduates. It obviously matters for assessments of the future of education as an investment and as an avenue of socioeconomic mobility whether this change signals a longer-run depression in markets for the products of higher education or is only an aberration as markets digest large entering cohorts.

The next section describes data sources and summarizes changes occurring between 1967 and 1975. Following that, a fairly simple model of career phases is examined for implications of effects of cohort size on earnings. Finally regression results are presented with estimates of these effects.

The Data Base and the Empirical Setting

The data refer to white males described in the 1968–76 March *Current Population Surveys* (*CPS*). Each of these nine surveys includes from 130,000 to 152,000 people. Of these, from 25 to 27,000 are included in the analytical population. They are civilian, white male, age 14 to 65, not now in school (as major activity last week), who either worked 50–52 weeks in the previous year or report the reason for working fewer weeks as something other than being in school or retired. Those self-employed or working without pay are also excluded.

The data are organized on the basis of years of school completed (8–11 years, 12 years, 1–3 years of college, or 4 or more years of college) and estimated years of work experience. Table A1 (see Appendix) reports number of observations by schooling class for each survey year.

One feature of the *CPS* public-use surveys that is especially noteworthy for earnings or wage comparisons is that nontrivial pro-

males and interpreted the decline as a result of the increased proportion of the population that is "young." While he did not analyze the relationship between wages and factor ratios, his presumption of this relationship served as the justification for examination of relationships between age-specific labor-force participation rates and the age distribution of the population. My approach takes participation as given and concentrates on wage determination.

portions of observations consist of respondents who apparently worked during the year in question, yet who did not report their earnings. In the *CPS* missing observations are filled with an imputation. Unfortunately the imputation procedure used in the first eight surveys differs from that of the ninth so that summary statistics for the 1976 survey (i.e., for 1975 earnings) are not comparable to other years.[4] To further confound analyses, individual records for the first eight surveys contain no flag to identify cases when earnings are imputed. Family records do however identify imputation of total family earnings, which presumably means that earnings for at least one family member are imputed. In contrast, the 1976 survey contains flags for individual imputations but none for families.

I exclude all individuals in the first eight surveys who are in families for which family earnings are imputed. For the final survey, a flag is constructed for families in which any member has imputed earnings, and all persons in these families are excluded. Table A2 (see Appendix) reports proportions by schooling level and survey year of otherwise valid observations excluded on this basis. These proportions range from 7 to 22 percent. They are generally higher for groups with more schooling and are trended, showing higher exclusion rates in more recent years. Unfortunately, exclusions are more frequent for the 1976 survey, suggesting that the constructed family-imputation flag may not correspond perfectly to those for earlier surveys.

Summary statistics reported in this section contain no correction for earnings not reported. There are, however, corrections included in the subsequent regressions to suggest that those not reporting are atypical and, on average, have higher wages than those reporting earnings.

Another feature of the *CPS* surveys is that work experience is not reported. While age, year of birth, and years of schooling are given, we do not know dates when the individuals observed entered the work force. This is troublesome because the purpose here is to examine effects of changing age or experience distributions on earnings patterns. Of course, missing information on dates of job-market entry and accumulated work experience is common to most "census-styled" data, and researchers concerned with income-experience relationships have resorted to various schemes for inferring experience. Here, too, experience is imputed. In fact the assumption of continuous participation following school completion and initial entry is explicit, so the imputation problem is that of estimating ages of job-market entry. This imputation is described in detail by Welch and Gould (1976). Briefly, the procedure estimates a year-of-job-market-

[4] I am grateful to Richard Freeman for pointing this out to me.

entry distribution for each birth–school completion cohort. Account is taken of the fact that more recent birth cohorts finished school at earlier ages. A person observed in one of the *CPS* surveys who worked in the preceding year is assumed to be representative of his cohort subject to the extra information that he began work last year or sometime earlier. Instead of treating an individual as being in a single year on the job, the full work experience is carried so that the number of people in their first year is the sum across individual observations of first-year probabilities. Accordingly, when examining statistics like wages by single experience years, averages are computed using individual probability weights. An example of these year-on-the-job probabilities is given for high school graduates in table A3 (see Appendix). Throughout the summary discussion and subsequent regressions, the data refer to national averages within schooling group for single years of job-market experience. For earnings comparisons, individuals who did not work last year and those who reported an average weekly wage of less than $10 are excluded, yet these people are included in cohort size calculations are those who failed to report earnings. Since earnings data refer to the year prior to the March survey, the dates used refer to earnings rather than survey year. That is, the reference period includes 1967–75.

To summarize changes over this period, I first examine earnings ratios between high school graduates and those with different amounts of schooling. Next, I turn to evidence, within schooling levels, of the general decline in average age of the work force and then compare earnings of recent job-market entrants to earnings of more experienced workers.

Table 1 reports average weekly earnings ratios, 1967–75, for two work-experience intervals, recent entrants (1–5 years) and peak earners (23–27 years). Each ratio is the (geometric) average weekly wage for the indicated schooling group relative to the wage of high school graduates. Table 2 gives corresponding ratios for annual earnings. Although these calculations are based on what by traditional standards are large numbers of observations, the adjacent-year comparisons suggest an uncomfortably high degree of variation relative to overall trend. Regardless of whether this variation refers to ordinary sampling error or to year-to-year variance in labor markets, it should be kept in mind in making trend comparisons.

Relative to high school graduates, new entrants with 8–11 years of schooling pretty much came full cycle over the period. Both weekly and annual earnings declined to 1971 and rose to 1967 levels by 1975. For peak earners, very little happened between 1967 and 1974. Relative earnings fell in 1975 which was by far the worst year of the survey vis-à-vis aggregate unemployment.

TABLE 1

WEEKLY WAGES OF THOSE WITH 8–11 YEARS OF GRADE SCHOOL, 1–3 YEARS OF COLLEGE AND COLLEGE GRADUATES, RELATIVE TO WAGES OF HIGH SCHOOL GRADUATES, 1967–75
(Ratios of Geometric Means)

YEARS OF SCHOOL COMPLETED	YEAR								
	1967	1968	1969	1970	1971	1972	1973	1974	1975
A. New entrants (less than 5 years of work experience):									
Grade school:									
8–11 years	.75	.71	.69	.69	.65	.71	.71	.74	.76
College:									
1–3 years	1.09	1.16	1.10	1.10	1.05	1.09	1.07	1.13	1.13
4 or more years	1.49	1.50	1.53	1.54	1.55	1.50	1.48	1.46	1.45
B. Peak earners (23–27 years of work experience):									
Grade school:									
8–11 years	.86	.86	.86	.86	.89	.88	.86	.87	.86
College:									
1–3 years	1.19	1.18	1.19	1.19	1.18	1.17	1.18	1.18	1.12
4 or more years	1.54	1.49	1.51	1.50	1.51	1.52	1.49	1.54	1.47

TABLE 2

ANNUAL EARNINGS OF THOSE WITH 8–11 YEARS OF GRADE SCHOOL, 1–3 YEARS OF COLLEGE AND COLLEGE GRADUATES, RELATIVE TO EARNINGS OF HIGH SCHOOL GRADUATES, 1967–75
(Ratios of Geometric Means)

YEARS OF SCHOOL COMPLETED	YEAR								
	1967	1968	1969	1970	1971	1972	1973	1974	1975
A. New entrants (less than 5 years of work experience):									
Grade school:									
8–11 years	.66	.62	.59	.61	.57	.63	.63	.63	.64
College:									
1–3 years	1.12	1.20	1.13	1.16	1.14	1.12	1.14	1.18	1.26
4 or more years	1.55	1.57	1.66	1.72	1.72	1.66	1.57	1.59	1.68
B. Peak earners (23–27 years of work experience):									
Grade school:									
8–11 years	.84	.83	.83	.83	.87	.85	.83	.85	.83
College:									
1–3 years	1.18	1.15	1.21	1.18	1.19	1.17	1.18	1.20	1.17
4 or more years	1.56	1.50	1.57	1.52	1.56	1.55	1.53	1.59	1.56

For those who attended but did not complete college, weekly wages of new entrants followed a similar pattern of relative decay until 1971 and returned at least to initial levels by 1974–75. For peak earners, weekly wages fell in 1975 relative to those of high school graduates but remained roughly constant until then. Annual earnings show no pattern. Only the 1975 jump for new entrants seems important.

Finally, for college graduates, the new-entrant weekly wage pattern is one of rising relative wages until 1971 and falling relative wages thereafter. Relative wages in 1975 are lower than in 1967. This, in a nutshell, is what has been called "the new depression in higher education." But even for new entrants, the annual earnings pattern contrasts with weekly wages. The rising profile to 1971 is consistent, but the subsequent decay is less pronounced. By 1974, relative annual earnings exceeded 1967–68 levels and the 1975 recession seems to have dramatically expanded weeks worked for college relative to high school graduates. For peak earners, there is little systematic change over the period in earnings of college relative to high school graduates.

Noting the decline in earnings of new-entrant college relative to high school graduates between 1969 and 1973 or 1974, Richard Freeman expressed concern that this trend signaled a longer-run depression in the earning power of higher education (see Freeman 1975, 1976, 1977). He conjectured that it occurred despite and not because of the deteriorating general level of economic activity during this period because the preponderance of the evidence suggests countercyclic motion in relative income of college graduates. Had Freeman awaited the 1975 data, or had his analysis extended backward to 1967 (the first annual survey available), his conclusion might have been less pessimistic.

Nonetheless, it is clear that comparisons like those of tables 1 and 2 are confounded by cyclic instability. It is true that college graduates appear to be generally less vulnerable to recessions than are those with less schooling. Most of the literature on this subject explains this phenomenon by reference to one of two closely related observations.

One is that capital goods are less substitutable for college-trained manpower than for high school graduates (see Rosen 1968; Griliches 1969; Welch 1970; Berndt and Christensen 1974). Since in the short run capital is largely fixed, reduced recessionary product demand is accompanied by disproportionate reliance on capital substitutes for reduced output. The other idea is that more educated workers carry larger firm-specific investments in them and, like other forms of capital, their employment is protected during recessions (see Oi 1962; Becker 1964; Rosen 1968). While both of these views have similar predictions for experienced workers, the firm-specific view sharply distinguishes new entrants from experienced workers. If experienced workers carry sunk investments, new entrants imply extra (training) costs, and the analogy to capital is precise: experienced workers are to fixed capital as new entrants are to investments in capital. In investments models it is the fixity of capital that destabilizes demand for investment, and for firm-specific skills it is the fixity of experienced workers that destabilizes demand for new entrants.

In a recent paper James Smith and I (Smith and Welch 1978) examined earnings of new-entrant high school and college graduates using data from the March 1968–75 *CPS*'s. Our finding is that, within industries, business cycles are neutral between high school and college graduates. Any aggregate nonneutrality for them seems to be an artifact of differences in the industrial composition of employment. But, college/high school graduate differences in employment patterns are large and there is much room for compositional effects. For example, 43 percent of all new-entrant college graduates work in service industries (largely health, education, and professional services), while only 11 percent of high school graduates work in these industries. In contrast, 39 percent of high school graduates and only 24 percent of college graduates work in manufacturing. High school graduates work in industries that are disproportionately vulnerable to business cycles and, for "normal recessions," they are more affected than college graduates.

In fact, 1971 appears to have been a normal recession, and as tables 1 and 2 show, relative earnings of college graduates were unusually high that year. But 1973 and 1974 were atypical. In both years industrial employment patterns were mixed with some industries lying above long-run trend and others below trend and in the aggregate employment was relatively depressed in industries disproportionately employing college graduates (Smith and Welch 1978, table 4). Even so, Smith and I could attribute little of the 1969–74 trend in relative earnings of college graduates to business cycles. Either our approach was faulty or the explanation of this change lies elsewhere.

I consider the bulge of entering cohorts a likely alternative. Table 3 shows, for each schooling group, the percentage of all workers in their first 5 years on the job. If experience distributions within schooling group are regular, the fraction of new entrants in the total signals the rate of growth of the total. Higher entry rates for college imply that average levels of schooling are rising. In this vein, convergence between 1967 and 1975 in differences among schooling groups suggests that the rate of growth in average schooling levels is itself falling. This points to what is well known, that rates of progression into college fell after 1969. Although cohorts entering since then

TABLE 3

PERCENTAGE OF WORK FORCE WITH LESS THAN 5 YEARS OF WORK EXPERIENCE BY YEARS OF SCHOOL COMPLETED, 1967–75

YEARS OF SCHOOL COMPLETED	YEAR								
	1967	1968	1969	1970	1971	1972	1973	1974	1975
Grade school:									
8–11 years	8.1	8.5	10.0	12.0	12.3	13.7	15.0	15.1	16.0
12 years	14.4	15.3	15.2	16.5	18.0	19.1	20.7	20.8	20.9
College:									
1–3 years	19.2	19.1	18.7	22.0	23.9	25.3	26.7	25.3	23.5
4 or more years	17.8	19.4	18.9	19.7	21.1	21.1	22.6	22.6	23.5

have more-than-national-average levels of schooling, so that their arrival increases the average, they are not as highly schooled as their recent predecessors. In any case, the changes in entering cohort shares are large for all levels of schooling, and unless new entrants and experienced workers are perfect substitutes, the entry bulge must have depressed new-entrant wages. Table 4 addresses this point. It compares weekly earnings of those with less than 5 years of experience to those with 23–27 years. In every schooling group new-entrant wages fell, and 1967–75 changes swamp anything shown in table 1 or 2. For example, relative to peak earners, weekly wages of new-entrant college graduates dropped 14 percent. Either for new entrants or peak earners, college/high school graduate wage ratios changed by less than 3 percent. Clearly, the most dramatic changes of this period were not in relative wages among schooling groups but in wage structures within schooling group, and, I think, increased new-entrant cohort size is the most likely explanation of this change.

TABLE 4

WEEKLY WAGES OF NEW ENTRANTS RELATIVE TO PEAK EARNERS BY YEARS OF SCHOOLING, 1967–75

YEARS OF SCHOOL COMPLETED	YEAR								
	1967	1968	1969	1970	1971	1972	1973	1974	1975
Grade school:									
8–11 years	.56	.52	.50	.46	.41	.45	.44	.47	.48
12 years	.65	.63	.62	.58	.56	.55	.54	.55	.55
College:									
1–3 years	.59	.62	.58	.53	.50	.51	.49	.53	.55
4 or more years	.63	.63	.63	.59	.58	.55	.54	.54	.54

How Does Cohort Size Affect Earnings?

Only if all workers, regardless of experience, substitute perfectly for each other is the structure of earnings independent of cohort size, of the number of workers at a particular experience level. If perfect substitution were to hold, then the only feasible interpretation of life-cycle profiles would be one of purely physical aging. The investment views, that age profiles are products of learning and depreciation, all suggest that people at different stages of the career do different things. If so, then the value of each thing would reasonably depend on the number of people doing it, and cohort size matters.

But as quickly as we admit this possibility, we are left with the thorny problem of specifying such an effect. At issue is the question of the way the number of workers in one particular class affects their own productivity and that of all other classes.[5] This is a question of substitutability between groups, and we know too little about the nature of these relationships for easy inference.

With workers classified by schooling and experience or date of entering the work force, the number of specifications of substitution patterns is too large to expect unstructured data to be able to sort through them. For example, there may be asymmetries. Young high school and college graduates may be better substitutes in jobs ordinarily performed by high school graduates than in jobs ordinarily performed by college graduates. If so, large entering classes of college graduates may partly ratchet into typical high school jobs when options for entering cohorts of high school jobs do not include switching into jobs ordinarily performed by college graduates.

If job experience congeals initially malleable skills, then substitutability across activities may erode as experience accrues. At the other extreme, if what distinguishes workers is the skills acquired in school, then as these skills erode with work experience, substitutability among schooling groups may increase.

The approach I follow here is to ignore substitution between schooling classes in favor of a sharpened focus within classes. The structure is as though each school-completion group forms a separable branch of an aggregate production process and substitution among schooling classes is independent of levels of experience. Within each schooling group relative wages (productivities) are de-

[5] There have, of course, been several attempts to estimate substitution relationships for worker groups segregated on the basis of age and other things. Recent papers by Anderson (1977) and Freeman (1978) are examples. I avoid this kind of specification for two reasons. First, I do not know how many age groups to specify, but I do know that many inputs are generally not empirically manageable. Second, the abrupt now-you're-in-now-you're-out implications of rigid age demarcations that are usually imposed are unappealing.

termined by numbers of workers at each experience level. I assume that these productivity effects depend only on ratios of number of workers, so that the structure of relative wages across experience levels (the wage profile) depends only on the experience distribution within the group.

The empirical specification I use is to construct a measure of own-cohort size and to estimate own-wage elasticities for this measure. Estimated elasticities are interacted with work experience in an attempt to see if effects dilute as time since entry increases. I think it likely that if larger cohorts have a more difficult start, these effects will erode as the career unfolds.

Career Phases

Perhaps the simplest view of the way cohort size affects earnings follows from the notion that work careers consist of a series of more or less distinct phases. A new job-market entrant arrives fresh from school and enters his profession as a trainee, apprentice, or learner. Only rarely, if his school training is narrowly applied or if the tasks of his profession are very simple, will he immediately become a full-fledged member of the profession. More generally, he enters as a raw recruit or learner, first achieves junior membership, and somewhat later senior membership in the profession.

Just how many phases there are does not really matter. What does matter is that at each phase members of the profession do different things and, vis-à-vis aggregate product, these things are not perfect substitutes. Each activity is productive and marginal productivities are determined, as for any factor, by numbers of workers engaged in all activities. In this view, a profession is an ordered series of worker types. At any moment in the career, a member of the profession is in transit between two of these types and can be viewed as a (convex) combination of them.

This view is essentially identical to the optimal life-cycle configuration suggested by Rosen (1972). In his statement of the problem, a career consists of a continuum of occupations and a worker solves for an optimal occupational sequence by recognizing that each occupation corresponds to learning options that affect performance in subsequent occupations. Rosen allowed productivity in each occupation to depend on number of workers in that and other occupations, and it is clear that had he considered cohort size, the theory would have predicted adverse effects on earnings. To highlight effects of cohort size, I abstract from questions of optimal rates of progression, of transit between career phases, and take them as exogenous. I also abstract from depreciation or skill obsolescence. Presumably the skills possessed on job-market entry are more conducive to learning (think of schooling as learning to learn) and are depleted as the career progresses, so that comparative advantage switches from learning to more directly productive activities. As such, progression is toward higher realized wage activities.

Consider an aggregate production function of the form:

$$y = f(N, Z), \tag{1}$$

where N refers to the productive effort of persons in a given profession (characterized by a given level of schooling). Those things contained in Z include other schooling composites and, like N, each is assumed to form a (weakly) separable branch of the aggregate process, $f(\cdot)$, so that N is only illustrative.

The total effort, N, is itself a function of numbers of workers in each of several worker types,

$$N = g(N_1, N_2, \ldots), \tag{2}$$

where the number of workers of each type is the number of members of the profession devoting their effort to that type of activity. A career phase involves transition between two types such that members of the profession in their first x_1 years on the job are in transition between the first two activities or worker types, in their next $x_2 - x_1$ years transition is between activities two and three, and so on. The ith career phase is passed in experience year, x_i.

If $n(x)$ refers to the number of members of the profession with x years of work experience, then the number of workers of type j is given by:

$$N_j = \int_{x_{j-1}}^{x_j} [1 - p_{j-1}(x)]n(x)dx + \int_{x_j}^{x_{j+1}} p_j(x)n(x)dx. \tag{3}$$

where $p_j(x)$ refers to the part of a worker's time spent in activity j and

$$p_j'(x) > 0;\ x_j \leq x \leq x_{j+1};\ \text{with } p_j(x_j) = 1 \text{ and } p_j(x_{j+1}) = 0.^{6}$$

That is, as a worker enters the ith career phase he initially devotes full time to the ith activity and at that moment begins transition into the $i + 1$st activity. As the ith phase progresses the proportion of time spent in the ith activity decreases until at the end of the phase all of his time is devoted to the next activity and a new phase begins.

The wage of those with x years of experience, their marginal product, is

$$w(x) = \frac{\partial f}{\partial n(x)} = f_1[p_i g_i + (1 - p_i)g_{i+1}], \tag{4}$$

[6] In expression (3), the first (RHS) term is omitted for the first career phase since negative experience has no meaning.

where x falls in the ith career phase. Notice in this phase,

$$\frac{\partial N_i}{\partial n(x)} = p_i \text{ and } \frac{\partial N_{i+1}}{\partial n(x)} = 1 - p_i. \tag{5}$$

Since $w_i = f_1 g_i$ is the wage of activity i workers, the wage of persons in the ith career phase is the combination,

$$w(x) = p_i(x)w_i + [1 - p_i(x)]w_{i+1}, \tag{6}$$

and wage growth during this phase, $[\partial w(x)]/\partial x$, follows from the presumption that the fraction of time allocated to activity i is falling and that realized wages rise with activity level, $w_{i+1} > w_i$.

An individual's wage consists of two parts, the price or marginal product of the profession, f_1, and the individual's own contribution to the level of effort of his profession,

$$\frac{\partial N}{\partial n(x)} = w(x)/f_1 = p_i g_i + (1 - p_i)g_{i+1}. \tag{7}$$

Changes in f_1 are neutral across experience groups and f_1 determines levels but not shapes of wage profiles. In analyzing cohort size effects, I abstract from f_1 which is determined, among other things, by aggregate factor ratios and in empirical analysis over fairly short periods is unlikely to be distinguished from pure trend.

Effects of cohort size on (own) wages are given by the quadratic form,

$$\frac{\partial w(x)/f_i}{\partial n(x)} = \frac{\partial^2 N}{\partial n(x)^2} = (p_i, 1 - p_i)\{G_{jk}\}(p_i, 1 - p_i)' < 0, \tag{8}$$

where

$$G_{jk} = \begin{pmatrix} g_{ii} & g_{i,i+1} \\ g_{i,i+1} & g_{i+1,i+1} \end{pmatrix}$$

and, not surprisingly, if $g(\cdot)$ is (quasi-) concave, the effect of larger cohort size is to reduce wages if there are more than two factors in $g(\cdot)$.

For simplicity consider the two-factor constant elasticity of substitution case,

$$g = (\delta_1 N_1^{-\beta} + \delta_2 N_2^{-\beta})^{-1/\beta}, \tag{9}$$

where $\sigma = 1/(1 + \beta)$ is the elasticity of substitution between N_1 and N_2. In this case there are only two activities, learner (N_1) and worker (N_2), and the life cycle can be viewed first as one of transition from learner to worker followed by a period as a fully vested worker. In this example,

$$\frac{\partial w(x)/f_1}{\partial n(x)} = -\frac{1}{\sigma}\theta N_1 N_2 \left(\frac{p}{N_1} - \frac{(1-p)}{N_2}\right)^2, \tag{10}$$

where $\theta = g_1 g_2/N$ and $p = p(x)$ is the fraction of time, at x, spent as a learner.

The profile implied by equation (10) is illustrated in figure 1. The difference between the normal wage profile and that for an illustratively large cohort is never positive. There is, however, a neutrality point where the cohort's division between worker and learner is the same as for all members of the group, and since at that point, the example cohort has no effect on factor ratios, it has no effect on wages.[7]

In this example, new entrants are exclusively learners, and at point of entry they not only draw all their wages as learners, but have the greatest depressing effect on learner wages. As experience accrues, the cohort transits to the worker phase, drawing an increasingly larger share of a wage being depressed by their arrival. In the early career as the cohort is disproportionately involved in the learning phase, transition implies faster-than-normal wage growth to the neutrality point. Afterward, the depressant effect on worker productivity dominates and wage growth is slower than normal. Finally at the point indicated as $p = 0$ in figure 1, when the cohort is fully vested in worker status, the process is completed. Thereafter, wages are depressed and the extent of the depression remains constant.

Several points deserve note. Effects of increased cohort size are inversely proportional to the elasticity of substitution. The substitution elasticity indexes worker-learner differences in the nature of jobs performed. Greater similarity of activities implies greater substitutability. It is likely that the substitution elasticity is related to the transition function, $p(x)$. Rapid transition from learner to worker status implies that learners can easily adapt to worker tasks. I expect that when transition occurs easily, worker-learner tasks are more similar, that is, workers and learners are better substitutes.

This leads immediately to predictions across schooling groups of differences in worker-learner substitution elasticities. It is a near

[7] This is, of course, an artifact of the two-factor assumption. If there were three or more factors and if $g(\cdot)$ were linear homogeneous with a two-factor branch like that of eq. (9), eq. (10) would partition into two effects, one always negative and the other never positive. Equation (10) captures this second effect only, and it vanishes when the cohort being considered divides its time such that it has no effect on the N_1/N_2 ratio. With more than two factors, the cohort being considered would necessarily increase both N_1 and N_2 relative to other factors (regardless of whether it changed the N_1/N_2 ratio) and would therefore reduce wages for the N_1-N_2 composite.

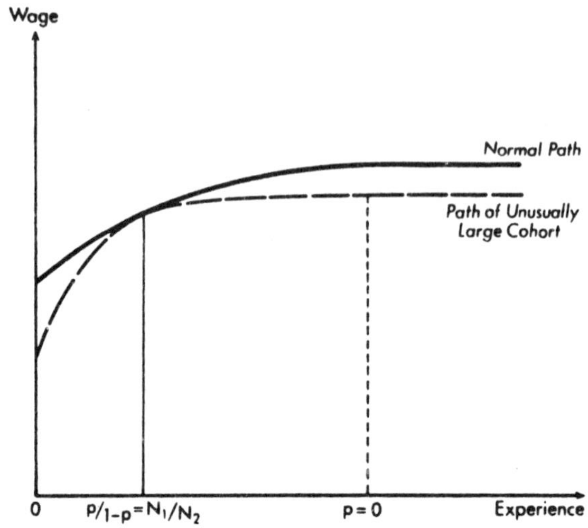

FIG. 1.—Hypothetical contrast between career wage paths of normal and unusually large cohort.

tautology that those who acquire more schooling ultimately perform tasks requiring more training. As total training increases, a balance is reached between learning in the isolation and abstraction of schools and learning on the job. If so, then those having more schooling transit less rapidly from learner to worker status after beginning work, and it is likely that worker-learner substitution elasticities are smaller than for those with less schooling. I will not pretend that I have not seen the data; I do contend, however, that the story the data tell of cohort-size effects increasing with schooling is highly plausible.

Worker/learner wage ratios are determined by three factors in this model. Two of these are treated as parameters in the intermediate process forming the schooling composite. The first refers to the distribution parameter, δ_2/δ_1, and the second refers to the elasticity of substitution. The third is the worker/learner ratio, N_2/N_1.

The normal wage path depicted in figure 1 holds these three factors constant and only describes transition from learner to worker status. If the experience distribution were uniform, that is, if $n(x) = n$ for all x, then the worker/learner ratio is the ratio of the fraction spent in learner status. But a uniform experience distribution implies no growth. Each year the number of new entrants equals the number of retirees. If steady growth occurs, the experience distribution is a negative exponential of the form $q(x) \propto e^{-\rho x}$, such that the ratio, $\ln [n(x-1)/n(x)] = \rho$, is constant. If growth remains steady, the ratio N_2/N_1 is constant, and the more rapid the growth, the lower the ratio.

TABLE 5

ESTIMATED AVERAGE ANNUAL GROWTH RATES IN NUMBERS OF WHITE MALE WORKERS BY SCHOOLING CLASS, 1967–75

	YEARS OF SCHOOL COMPLETED			
	8–11	12	13–15	16 or More
Estimated growth rate as a percentage	−.31	2.89	4.59	6.25
SE	.07	.09	.11	.17

NOTE.—Numbers of people observed are scaled to take account of the declining size of *Current Population Surveys* relative to the total U.S. population.

Thus, in a regime of steady growth, for other things equal, the wage ratio W_2/W_1 is a positive function of the growth rate.

This is an obvious point which has been ignored in the literature of income returns to schooling. A common finding of such estimates is that life-cycle earnings profiles are more concave for higher levels of schooling, which has been interpreted as implying that early career investments in training (investments in human capital), expressed as a fraction of income potential, increase with the level of schooling. Such a view has obvious intuitive appeal, but greater concavity is just another way of saying that new-entrant wages are reduced relative to those of peak earners. And the reported positive association between concavity of the wage profile and schooling may partly be an artifact of rising average education levels: this, because growing school-completion levels imply positive association between schooling and the learner/worker employment ratio within schooling level which, in turn, implies lower learner/worker wage ratios.

As a crude approximation to average growth rates among schooling groups, I calculated regressions of the form:

$$\ln n(x)_{it} = a_i + \rho_i(t - x) + u_{xit}, \tag{11}$$

where t indicates survey year, x is experience, and i refers to schooling group.[8]

Implied growth rates are summarized in table 5 and tell an unsurprising story of rising average educational levels. What may be surprising is that the number of persons with 8–11 years of schooling is actually falling while the number of college graduates is averaging an annual growth of over 6 percent.[9]

[8] There are nine surveys and 44 experience levels for a total of 396 observations for each schooling group.

[9] Recall that table 3 shows a rising new-entrant share of the work force with 8–11 years of schooling. The observation in table 5 of negative average growth for this group

Before examining the evidence of cohort size effects on earnings, a few other features of the career-phase model should be considered. First, recall the difference between the normal wage path and that of a large cohort illustrated in figure 1. Relative to the normal path, earnings for the large cohort grow more rapidly before the neutrality point is reached and less rapidly thereafter. Although this model ignores individual optimization concerning on-the-job training, its predictions are similar to what we might expect from optimizing behavior. If large entering cohorts depress wages, then the opportunity cost of on-the-job training is depressed on entry and cost incentives are to speed learning.

In this model, the depressant effect on entry wages diminishes as the N_1/N_2 ratio rises.[10] This follows from the observation that the higher is N_1/N_2, the smaller is the effect of a given size cohort, $n(x)$ on factor ratios at point of entry, $x = 0$.

The level of experience when wage neutrality is reached occurs earlier, the higher is N_1/N_2 and later in the career as the transition process is itself delayed. The existence of a fully neutral point is an artifact of the simplification that the career consists of only two phases, a transitional one and a worker phase. If the career structure is fully hierarchical such that individuals are continuously transiting between adjacent stages, then there would be a series of neutrality points or points of minimum depressant effect, but at no point would wage depression vanish altogether.

Regardless of whether a point of full neutrality exists, any career-phase model will predict that wage depressant effects on job-market entry erode in the early career as transition spreads the cohort bulge among more than one activity. This kind of result is intuitively appealing and (largely) supported by the data.

The Regression Analysis

Before turning to regressions it may be useful to review the underlying data. There are nine surveys referring to earnings years 1967 to

---

only demonstrates that in the cross-section number of workers increases with experience *on average* and this effect dominates shifts between years. Actually, by 1975 the experience distribution in this group is bimodal. Contrary to earlier trend, the baby boom entry bulge has its impact on high school dropouts as well as for those with more schooling.

[10] Actually, there is some ambiguity on this score. There is none if the worker share of the composite product exceeds one-half or if the worker-learner substitution elasticity exceeds two. Otherwise, if $\delta_2 < 1/2 - [\sigma/(1 - \sigma/2)]$ (where δ refers to worker share) the entry effect increases, in absolute value, as N_1/N_2 increases. There is no ambiguity about the size of the entry effect ($p = 1$) relative to the persistent effect once transition is complete, $p = 0$. That ratio is $(N_2/N_1)^2$.

1975 and, although there is some overlap between adjacent years resulting from the *CPS*'s in 4-out to 8-in 4-month rotation, overlapping observations are not identified. Thus the surveys are treated as though they are statistically independent. All observations refer to white males who presumably are out of school and not retired and are between 14 and 65 years old. Individuals are placed in four school-completion groups.

For each individual, j, work experience is estimated in the form of a full density, $p_{ij}: i = 1{,}45$, where p_{ij} corresponds to the individual's estimated probability of being in the ith year on the job and p_{45} refers to the open-end class, more than 44 years. Experience probabilities are conditional on age, schooling, and year of birth as described in Welch and Gould (1976). These data are aggregated (within schooling group) based on single years of job-market experience, and the total number of persons with i years of experience in a particular survey year is simply the aggregate of the individual probabilities, that is, $n_i = \Sigma_j p_{ij}$.

Within each experience interval two proportions are calculated. One refers to the fraction of observations lost due to failure to report earnings for those who worked (i.e., those individuals in families for which *CPS* imputes earnings) and the other refers to the fraction of observations who did not work and therefore have no reported earnings. Conditional on observations of earnings, (geometric) means of annual and average weekly earnings are then computed within experience interval.

The regression observations refer to means computed within survey year for single-year experience intervals. The open-end interval (more than 44 years of experience) is omitted and observations are pooled across surveys. There are therefore 396 (44 experience levels × 9 surveys) observations for each schooling group.

The objective is to estimate effects of own cohort size on earnings. The first step in computing cohort size involves normalization by the size of the work force. It seems likely that wages of a particular cohort are affected both by its own size and by the size of surrounding cohorts as well. Furthermore, calculated proportions include sampling errors, so for estimation the proportion of group members at each experience level is smoothed by computing a moving average with inverted V weights. Cohort size is then defined as

$$c(x) = \sum_{i=-2}^{2} \alpha_i n_{x+i}, \tag{12}$$

where n_x is the fraction of those in the group who are in their xth year of work experience. The α weights are: $\underline{\alpha} = \frac{1}{3}(\frac{1}{3}, \frac{2}{3}, 1, \frac{2}{3}, \frac{1}{3})$, except for recent entrants where succeeding cohort fractions are not defined.

In this case, the α distribution is truncated and remaining weights are scaled accordingly to sum to one.

The objective is to estimate wage elasticities with respect to cohort size and to allow these elasticities to vary over the career. In fact, only one form of experience interaction is examined. It is a spline of the form:

$$\frac{Ew(x)}{Ec(x)} = \gamma_0 S + \gamma_1, \tag{13}$$

where $EZ = \partial Z/Z$ and where $S = \max\{0, 1 - x/\bar{x}\}$. The wage elasticity begins at an entry ($x = 0$) value of $\gamma_0 + \gamma_1$ and then declines linearly (at a rate $-\gamma_0/\bar{x}$) to a permanent level, γ_1 in $\bar{x}$ years, and remains at γ_1 thereafter. Experimentation with alternative values of $\bar{x}$ (the duration of the unique initial effect) over the four schooling groups suggests that it increases with schooling. The estimates reported impose $\bar{x}$ = (6, 7, 8, and 9 years), respectively, for those with 8–11, 12, 13–15, and 16 or more years of schooling.

One characteristic noted in Smith and Welch (1978) is that for the *CPS* data, wage profiles are not adequately described by the commonly used quadratic, experience and experience squared. When estimated profiles are restricted to this form, they consistently overestimate early career earnings. Although we suggested an alternative specification, in this case I have added S (as defined above) to experience and experience squared to allow more flexibility to the wage path. This (splined) experience profile is itself continuous but its derivative is discontinuous at $\bar{x}$.

In addition to the cohort and experience variables, a linear trend term is included along with the national aggregate unemployment rate for white males. The two variables for proportions of observations excluded (see the discussion of eqq. [12] and [13]) also appear as explanatory variables. One is called the exclusion rate due to income imputation. It is the fraction of observations lost in computing mean earnings because of the imputation problem. Inclusion of this variable represents a straightforward attempt to control for selectivity bias in reporting income. If those not reporting have above-average earnings, then the higher the proportion of those not reporting, the lower will be the mean wage of those who do.

The other is called the exclusion rate due to nonwork. It refers to those without valid income observations. Most of those excluded on this basis either are not in the labor force or did not work. Others who appear to have worked were coded as having no earnings. Still others show reported earnings that are so low that I presume they are coded incorrectly. Therefore I exclude from earnings comparisons all who either did not work or had calculated weekly earnings of less than

$10. The variable describing proportions of observations within each experience and survey year lost on this basis is viewed as a composite of selectivity and cyclical effects. Presumably those who are excluded on this basis have below-average earnings so that as this proportion increases, the mean wage of those included should also increase. But, to the extent that the proxy variable used for business cycles (the national average unemployment rate for white males which varies between but not within surveys) controls imperfectly for them, it seems likely that cyclical effects which drive this measure of exclusion may imply that as conditions worsen to increase proportions not working, they also reduce mean earnings of those who do work.

Tables 6, 7, and 8 summarize regression results for mean earnings within schooling class. The regressions reported are weighted by numbers of earners in each experience cell.

Table 6 contains regressions for (ln) annual earnings, table 7 refers to weekly wages, and table 8 refers to weekly wage with the list of explanatory variables being augmented by a part-time variable indicating the proportion of persons in an observational cell who "usually" worked less than 35 hours per week. The part-time variable is viewed as partial control for hours worked. It is not perfect (and if hourly wages were observed, I would have used them), but it is more than "just a dummy" variable. With individual observations, a dummy for less than 35 hours only controls for variation between those working less and those working more than 35 hours leaving within-group variance uncontrolled. But with grouped data, this variable is the proportion of people working less than 35 hours, and with it, there is more effective control for average hours. Consider, for example, an hours-worked distribution over a limited range of, say, 0–70 hours. As work experience changes or as cyclic conditions change, the hours density shifts, and as it does the frequency of hours less than 35 changes. In general, for well-behaved functions we would presume that average hours and the frequency of hours less than 35 move closely together, and if they do, the part-time variable is a "good" control for average hours.[11]

In examining the estimates of tables 6, 7, and 8, notice that calculated standard errors for coefficients understate estimation error.

[11] The type of variation that this measure misses stems from compensated shifts in the density that hold the part-time frequency constant and changes the mean. Such motion seems unlikely. More importantly, by forcing the part-time measure to have only one parameter it captures only average covariation between part-time frequency and mean hours. Since covariance from changes in levels of economic activity is probably different than covariance resulting from changes, say, in potential experience, the forced average effect is incorrectly specified. In any case, in these data the part-time variable is the best available adjustment for hours worked short of resorting to an instrument between it and the hours worked last week for the March survey.

TABLE 6

REGRESSION ESTIMATES OF DETERMINANTS OF ANNUAL EARNINGS OF WHITE MALES, 1967–75

	YEARS OF SCHOOL COMPLETED			
	Grade School		College	
INDEPENDENT VARIABLES	8–11	12	1–3	4 or More
Cohort size:				
Main effect	−.252	−.120	−.194	−.204
	(12.3)	(6.7)	(13.5)	(11.3)
Interaction with early career spline	.0140	−.302	−.365	−.791
	(.33)	(6.7)	(7.3)	(12.0)
Experience:				
Early career spline	−.690	−1.46	−1.52	−2.71
	(4.2)	(9.7)	(9.9)	(12.7)
Experience	.0428	.0393	.0374	.0600
	(43.2)	(32.7)	(21.7)	(36.9)
Experience squared	−.00073	−.00083	−.00086	−.00146
	(31.8)	(28.3)	(21.6)	(28.0)
Exclusion rate due to nonwork	−.647	.472	−.745	.622
	(4.7)	(2.2)	(2.2)	(2.1)
Exclusion rate due to income imputation	−.231	−.430	−.249	−.855
	(3.1)	(5.6)	(2.8)	(12.7)
Unemployment rate	−.0270	−.0360	−.0287	−.0176
	(10.7)	(16.9)	(13.4)	(8.4)
Trend	.0137	.0137	.0108	.0131
	(10.5)	(11.1)	(7.8)	(12.1)
Intercept	7.3	8.25	8.14	8.23
R^2	.989	.983	.984	.985
SE of estimate	.034	.033	.035	.030

NOTE.—Number of observations = 396; the dependent and cohort size variables are in (natural) logarithms; the exclusion and unemployment rates are expressed as fractions; absolute values of t-statistics are in parentheses.

With the data arrayed across experience levels and across years, there is probably nontrivial positive serial correlation which I ignored in the calculations reported. Furthermore, residuals are probably (positively) correlated across equations (schooling groups) so that estimates should not be viewed as independent. A preferred estimation procedure to gain efficiency would have recognized both contemporaneous and serial correlations, but software for this kind of procedure is not available to me. As is always true in such cases, estimates may be unbiased but are inefficient, and computed standard errors are biased.

Notice that the three sets of regressions in tables 6, 7, and 8 can be

TABLE 7

REGRESSION ESTIMATES OF DETERMINANTS OF WEEKLY EARNINGS OF WHITE MALES, 1967–75

	YEARS OF SCHOOL COMPLETED			
	Grade School		College	
INDEPENDENT VARIABLES	8–11	12	1–3	4 or More
Cohort size:				
Main effect	−.161	−.080	−.163	−.194
	(9.4)	(6.5)	(12.4)	(11.6)
Interaction with early career spline	−.072	−.237	−.278	−.591
	(2.0)	(7.0)	(6.1)	(9.6)
Experience:				
Early career spline	−.849	−1.156	−1.180	2.010
	(6.2)	(10.2)	(8.4)	(10.1)
Experience	.033	.033	.037	.050
	(40.2)	(36.9)	(23.5)	(39.4)
Experience squared	−.00055	−.00067	−.00080	−.00143
	(28.8)	(30.3)	(22.1)	(29.4)
Exclusion rate due to nonwork	−.615	+.103	−.751	+.744
	(5.3)	(.64)	(2.5)	(2.7)
Exclusion rate due to income imputation	−.338	−.441	−.366	−.924
	(5.4)	(7.7)	(4.5)	(14.7)
Unemployment rate	−.0117	−.0184	−.0197	−.0121
	(5.6)	(11.5)	(10.2)	(6.2)
Trend	.0172	.0147	.0129	.0130
	(15.8)	(15.9)	(10.2)	(12.9)
Intercept	3.90	4.47	4.33	4.33
R^2	.988	.986	.984	.985
SE of estimate	.028	.025	.032	.028

NOTE.—Number of observations = 396; the dependent and cohort size variables are in (natural) logarithms; the exclusion and unemployment rates are expressed as fractions; absolute values of t-statistics are in parentheses.

contrasted for implications on hourly wages, hours per week, and weeks per year. The dependent variable in table 6 is the logarithm of annual earnings and is therefore the sum of the logarithms of the weekly wage and of weeks worked per year. Coefficient differences, table 6 less 7, are then coefficients for weeks worked. Similarly, if the part-time variable effectively controls for hours, differences between tables 7 and 8 refer to hours worked, while table 8 coefficients refer to the hourly wage.

These distinctions are useful in contrasting cohort effects, since if larger entering cohorts imply increased job competition, effects

TABLE 8

REGRESSION ESTIMATES OF DETERMINANTS (including Part-Time Status) OF WEEKLY EARNINGS OF WHITE MALES, 1967–75

Independent Variables	Years of School Completed: Grade School 8–11	12	College 1–3	4 or More
Cohort size:				
Main effect	−.181	−.096	−.168	−.218
	(12.6)	(8.7)	(14.0)	(13.7)
Interaction with early career spline	.118	−.193	−.141	−.503
	(3.5)	(6.4)	(3.2)	(8.6)
Experience:				
Early career spline	.184	−.860	−.596	−1.620
	(1.3)	(8.3)	(4.1)	(8.5)
Experience	.035	.033	.0367	.0581
	(49.4)	(41.9)	(25.6)	(40.8)
Experience squared	−.00058	−.00067	−.00080	−.00141
	(35.9)	(34.5)	(24.1)	(31.2)
Exclusion rate due to nonwork	−.274	+.266	−.517	.608
	(2.7)	(1.9)	(1.9)	(2.4)
Exclusion rate due to income imputation	−.516	−.498	−.457	−.915
	(9.5)	(9.8)	(6.1)	(15.7)
Unemployment rate	−.0139	−.0163	−.0170	−.0095
	(7.9)	(11.5)	(9.4)	(5.1)
Part-time	−.905	−1.113	−.869	−1.400
	(12.8)	(10.7)	(8.8)	(7.8)
Trend	.0172	.0149	.0124	.0136
	(18.9)	(18.3)	(10.8)	(14.4)
Intercept	3.84	4.41	4.32	4.27
R^2	.99	.989	.987	.987
SE of estimate	.024	.022	.029	.026

NOTE.—Number of observations = 396; the dependent and cohort size variables are in (natural) logarithms; the exclusion and unemployment rates are expressed as fractions; absolute values of t-statistics are in parentheses.

should emerge not only for wages but also for labor-utilization rates (weeks and hours worked). Before examining cohort elasticities, consider other implications of these estimates. As is common for this kind of analysis, there is evidence that early-career wage growth is more rapid for those with more schooling. The splined experience coefficients generally imply more rapidly early-career earnings growth than can be captured in the experience quadratic alone.

Evidently, earnings are very sensitive to aggregate unemployment. This perhaps is not surprising for annual earnings where weeks worked are free to vary but may be for weekly earnings holding part-time status constant (table 8). There is at least some support for notions of wage flexibility. In general, wage sensitivity to aggregate unemployment falls with increased schooling, so that these data continue to support the idea that more schooled workers are less affected by swings in aggregate labor demand.

Coefficients on the exclusion rate due to income imputation refer to adjustments in mean earnings of those reporting income associated with variations in proportions reporting. These coefficients are consistently negative to suggest that those with the highest wages are the most likely to not report earnings. In fact, mean rates for income not reported together with these coefficient estimates imply average annual earnings for the combined total of those who do and do not report that exceed the average of those reporting by 3–5 percent in the first and fourth schooling groups and by 6 percent for high school and 14 percent for college graduates. This is important especially for income comparisons across schooling groups, as, for example, in rate-of-return calculations. The implication of table 6 is that annual earnings of college relative to high school graduates are 8 percent higher in the total population than in the reporting population. This could result in underestimates of rates of return that as an order of magnitude would approach 2 percentage points, about 20 percent of most current estimates.

Notice also that magnitudes of coefficients on this variable increase as control for labor utilization increases (in tables 7 and 8), so that the problem of understatement due to nonreporting seems more severe in weekly wage comparisons.

There is an often-stated belief that the annual *Current Population Surveys* are more reliable than the decennial census data mainly because of greater effort to ensure reporting. Evidently, nonreporting remains a serious problem even for *CPS*. Furthermore, analysts using *CPS* data should be aware that when missing observations are filled with imputations, the assumption of the procedure used is that nonreporters are representative of reporters. Unless my estimates are completely wrong, they are not.[12]

[12] To impute missing income observations, the census bureau uses what it calls a "hot deck" procedure. Briefly, this procedure fills a matrix stratified on various characteristics with the "last" valid observation and uses that observation to fill in the blanks. Aside from convenience there is little to recommend this approach, especially in light of the emerging literature on selectivity biases. The number of strata on which imputations are based was expanded for the 1976 survey to include schooling, labor-force status of spouse, marital status, region, and type of residence, and more detail was introduced for age, family relationship, occupation, class of worker, weeks worked, race, etc. For a description of this procedure and for contrasts with earlier imputations, see U.S. Department of Commerce, Bureau of the Census (1976).

Coefficients on exclusions due to nonwork do not have consistent sign patterns across schooling groups but are consistent across income definition. As such, unambiguous interpretation is not easy. In any case the overall average exclusion rate due to nonwork is less than 3 percent, so that this correction has little effect on estimated mean earnings.

In these data, dependent variables are measured in constant (CPI) dollars and the evidence is of very low rates of growth in real earnings or wages. Since the unemployment rate is held constant, it is tempting to argue that growth implied by the year variable reflects cyclic corrected longer-run trends, but in my opinion it would be a mistake to do so. Recall that the observation period is itself strongly trended vis-à-vis aggregate economic activity. The first 3 years, 1967–69, were more robust than any to follow, and 1975 was by far the most depressed. The question relevant to trend comparisons is whether the unemployment rate alongside the nonwork exclusion rate adequately controls for cycles so that the residual trend can be taken as a secular one.

In these data, there are a variety of indexes of labor utilization rates which are themselves indexes of labor demand. In addition to weeks worked and the part-time variable, the most obvious is weeks unemployed or looking for work and the exclusion rate itself. In auxiliary calculations (not reported here), I regressed each of these variables on the same set of independent variables as those of tables 6 and 7.[13] The result in every schooling group is that even though the aggregate unemployment rate is taken into account, weeks worked are negatively and weeks looking for work are positively trended through the period. Except for college graduates, the exclusion rate due to not working is also positively trended. Part-time status alone seems devoid of trend. Evidently, the unemployment rate is too imperfect an instrumental predictor of labor demand for the implied trend rates of earnings to be taken as estimates of long-run patterns. In any case, estimated trend growth rates show little evidence of differences among schooling groups.

Estimated Cohort Effects

Table 9 summarizes cohort elasticities from regressions reported in tables 6–8. The entry elasticity is the respective wage or earning elasticity evaluated for those in their first year on the job ($x = 1$), and the persistent elasticity is the main effect, copied from tables 6–8.

[13] Of course when the exclusion rate is the dependent variable, it is not included as an independent variable. It is included, however, for other dependent variables.

TABLE 9

ESTIMATED ELASTICITIES OF ANNUAL AND WEEKLY EARNINGS WITH RESPECT TO COHORT SIZE

	Years of School Completed			
	Grade School		College	
Estimated Elasticity	8–11	12	1–3	4 or More
A. Annual earnings:				
Entry	−.240	−.369	−.514	−.907
	(8.8)	(10.9)	(12.7)	(12.1)
Persistent	−.252	−.080	−.194	−.204
	(112.3)	(6.6)	(13.5)	(11.3)
B. Weekly wages, part-time status excluded:				
Entry	−.221	−.283	−.406	−.720
	(9.8)	(11.2)	(11.1)	(14.8)
Persistent	−.161	−.080	−.163	−.194
	(9.4)	(6.6)	(12.4)	(11.6)
C. Weekly wages, part-time status included:				
Entry	−.082	−.261	−.291	−.665
	(3.8)	(11.6)	(8.1)	(14.5)
Persistent	−.181	−.096	−.168	−.218
	(12.6)	(8.7)	(14.0)	(13.7)

NOTE.—Absolute values of *t*-statistics in parentheses.

Only those with 8–11 years of schooling show persistent elasticities exceeding entry elasticities (in parts *A* and *C*). This result is anomalous, and I have no explanation for it. Each of the other schooling groups shows that entry effects exceed persistent ones.

Aside from high school dropouts, wage and earning elasticities rise with level of schooling and most of the discrepancy occurs in the early career. The career-phase model predicts that effects are inversely proportionate to worker-learner substitution elasticities. Thus the finding of effects increasing with schooling level suggests that worker-learner substitution elasticities fall with increased schooling.

One of the most interesting patterns exhibited in table 9 is that entry elasticities fall between part *A*, where weeks worked are free to vary, and part *B*, where they are not. These elasticities also fall between part *B*, where hours worked are variable, and part *C*, where they are partially controlled. The evidence then is that large entry cohorts depress not only wages but also hours and weeks worked. In contrast, persistent elasticities are much less sensitive to control for weeks and hours. Evidently, although new-entrant labor-utilization rates are depressed, this effect is transient.

It may be surprising that wage effects have as large a persistent component as they do. I, for one, would not have been surprised to find no persistent elasticity, an indication that cohort size effects are restricted to congestion at point of entry. Nonetheless, career-phase models suggest that although entry effects may exceed persistent ones, it is imperfect substitution between work activities performed at different phases of the career that generates both entry and persistent effects. From this perspective, the existence of an entry effect implies a persistent effect and vice versa. It is important, however, in assessing the size of persistent effects to keep in mind the operational definition of cohort size as the share of the current total work force. Through time as the working population expands, the share accounted for by a particular cohort declines.

How Large Are the Estimated Effects?

Are the estimated effects presented in table 9 large enough for those interested in earning patterns to view fluctuations in cohort size as a legitimate concern? We know from table 3 that the age or experience composition of the work force changed significantly in an 8-year interval. And table 4 shows falling relative earnings of new entrants that are coincident with increasing new-entrant shares of the total work force.

There are two obvious ways to try to get an intuitive feel for orders of magnitude of earnings changes implied by the parameter estimates in table 9. The first is to examine predicted changes in the range of the data used here, that is, for the 1967–75 interval. The second is to examine the historical record for longer periods to see what patterns of shifting cohort size have been and to combine them with parameter estimates for implications of effects on lifetime earnings.

For the *CPS* data, among new entrants (those in their first 5 years on the job) 1967–75 growth in cohort size yields predicted reductions in weekly wages ranging from a low of 6 percent for those with 1–3 years of college to a high of 13 percent for college graduates. Implied reductions are 8 percent for high school graduates and 12 percent for those with 8–11 years of schooling.

For all but college graduates, relative cohort size of peak earners (23–27 years of work experience) fell over the period, and resultant predictions of wage growth range between 3 and 5 percent. For college graduates, relative cohort size of peak earners did not change. Thus, new-entrant weekly earnings are predicted to have fallen relative to wages of peak earners by 15 percent for those with 8–11 years of schooling, by 10 percent both for high school graduates and for those who attended but did not finish college, and by 13 percent for college graduates. These predictions, which ignore changes other than cohort size, are reasonably close to the observations reported in table 4, especially for those with 8–11 years of grade school and for college graduates. Predicted changes understate observations for high school graduates and for those with 1–3 years of college.

In comparing wages across schooling groups, between 1967 and 1975 the observed college/high school graduate new entrant weekly wage ratio fell something less than 3 percent. The change predicted by cohort growth with larger wage responses for college graduates is 5 percent. If these estimates are correct, then what has passed for a new depression in higher education may be unique to the entrants of the early 1970s. For them, as effects erode over the career, the future is brighter, and for subsequent arrivals who themselves will be members of smaller cohorts, the future is also brighter.

The story of large swings in total numbers of births and of secular drift in average schooling levels is well known. To get a rough idea of how these changes affect cohort shares of the work force, and therefore lifetime earnings, I have merged the historical record of number of births with what evidence I could find for school-completion distributions to construct cohort shares similar to those used in the regressions described above.

I have proceeded under the assumption that after 1975, the number of births in the United States will stabilize at 2.5 million per year (roughly the level maintained from 1971–75) and that average levels of school completion will continue their upward drift for a few years and then stabilize. For each level of school completion, I assume that all members of a birth cohort who attain that level begin work at the same age and retire after 45 years. With these assumptions, I construct a "guesstimated" work experience × schooling distribution for each calendar year, 1940–2035. The final year corresponds to retirement for new entrants of 1990, so that the constructed distributions permit estimates of lifetime earnings for cohorts joining the work force over the half-century 1940–90.

For each market-entering cohort, work-force shares are calculated for every year from entry to retirement, and these shares are the raw input for calculations of cohort size effects on lifetime earnings. Aggregation of a particular entering cohort's shares over its career gives a crude basis for measuring total cohort size.

As expected, these aggregates show extreme swings in cohort size. For example, the group with 8–11 years of schooling has a minimum average cohort share for 1953 entrants and a maximum for 1977 entrants, and the average share of the largest cohort exceeds that of the smallest by 62 percent. For high school graduates, the smallest cohort entered in 1954 and the largest in 1975, and the largest accounts for a 55 percent greater lifetime average work-force share than the smallest. Those with 1–3 years of college have even greater variation in lifetime cohort shares. The minimum for 1956 entrants is only 45 percent of the maximum (for 1967 entrants). For college graduates, the smallest cohort entered in 1962 and the largest in 1970, and the largest has a lifetime average share 51 percent bigger than the smallest. In general, these patterns reflect the depression-related trough in number of births and the late 1950s culmination of the postwar baby boom. Timing differentials reflect delayed entry for those with more schooling and swings about trend in school completion.

It is of course obvious that cohort size effects on life earnings do not correspond perfectly to the average lifetime shares just described. Cohorts that are large as they enter the work force and small as they leave it are penalized relative to those with similar average shares but with more uniform career representation. In a sense, something analogous to double-discounting is involved. First there is time preference, and I assume a 5 percent discount rate to represent it. Second, there is the fact that, aside from high school dropouts, estimated cohort size effects erode over the career.

In view of the extraordinarily large swings in cohort size, the estimates for effects on life earnings are not massive but, to the cohorts most affected, they may not be trivial. Using coefficient estimates for part *C* of table 9, which refer to my best estimates of hourly wage effects and presumably, therefore, correspond more closely to full incomes, variations for high school graduates are restricted to a 4 percent range. Not surprisingly, there is more action for college graduates where a 10 percent range is implied.

Calculations for college graduates suggest that, in terms of pure cohort size alone, the most favored generation entered the work force in 1962 and the least favored entered only 8 years later. As noted, life earnings for 1970 entrants (ignoring secular real wage growth) are estimated to be about 90 percent of the level for 1962 entrants. This focus on extremes omits much that is of interest in comparisons across entering cohorts.

For example, if the presumptions of future birthrates and school-attainment levels are at all accurate, then the wage depression for college graduates implied by the arrival of baby boom cohorts that starts in the mid-1960s will begin to erode around 1980, and the estimates for 1990 entrants suggest career earnings equal to those of the "most favored" classes who enter between the mid-1950s and early 1960s. Although the baby boom cohorts seem to have the poorest career income prospects, my simulations suggest that their lifetime incomes will not be significantly below the life earnings of cohorts entering in the mid-1940s. These earlier entrants joined the work force during a period of rapid acceleration in numbers of college graduates. As such, they began their careers with very large cohort shares, and although these shares fell rapidly under continuing growth in numbers of entrants, the early career effects swamped the (double-discounted) late career effects. In comparison to the baby boom groups, the mid-1940 entrants have smaller average work-force shares but the shape of the career profile nullifies what would otherwise be an advantage.

It is not necessary to enumerate the heroic nature of these simulations. They are only an exercise to derive a "feel" for orders of magnitude of the estimated effects involved and to examine the historical record of swings in the experience composition of the work force. But, if these machinations reasonably describe cohort patterns in life earnings, then one final observation is in order: The depression in early career earnings of college graduates witnessed in the first part of this decade is not unique, and just as earlier depressions eroded into higher incomes, the recent depression will be followed by higher college-graduate earnings.[14]

Summary and Conclusions

Anyone working with wage and earnings data for the period 1967 to 1975 must be impressed by variability. Real annual earnings fell in 1971, in 1974, and again in 1975 for experienced workers. For new entrants, real earnings fell in 1970 and in 1972 and again in 1974 and 1975. College graduates are, however, somewhat atypical. Although they shared in the 1970–72 recession, effects were less severe. However, the foundering economy of late 1973 and 1974 affected college graduates more than others, and in 1975 when real income fell sharply for most schooling groups, income of college graduates, especially those with considerable work experience, actually rose.

This kind of variability challenges those concerned with wage behavior and gives much room for statistical exploration, yet so much happened during the period that any set of relatively simple explanations is likely to be confounded by competing explanations. Clearly business cycles should be taken into account, but the evidence is that the composition of the cycles that occurred was different enough to raise questions of "how."

Relative incomes changed among schooling groups, especially for

[14] In a recent paper, T. W. Schultz (1977) exhibits a variety of relative wage calculations for different times in the twentieth century. Working with four groups: unskilled, manufacturing production workers, teachers, and associate professors, Schultz describes four periods of rapidly declining relative wages of skilled workers (1915–19, 1932–35, 1940–42, and 1969–75). Since only the last two of these periods correspond to rapid cohort expansion, there would seem to be a real advantage to further exploration of the historical record. In particular, Schultz stresses that both inflation and levels of economic activity are candidates for further investigation.

new entrants. Why? Is it cycles or a longer-run depression in the market for college graduates? The hypothesis put forward here is that whatever it is, it is not long run. The 1975 data challenge any notions of persistence.

The most dramatic change in earnings structures witnessed during these 9 years was the drop in earnings of new entrants relative to more experienced workers, and this change coincided with the arrival of the peak-sized cohorts spawned by the post–World War II baby boom. How does a market digest an increasingly large number of new arrivals? As a device for describing effects of cohort size on earnings, I have explored a career-phase model in which activities performed at various phases are not perfect substitutes for activities performed at other phases. I then attempted to fit a (loosely specified) version of this model to earnings data taken from the March *Current Population Surveys* for 1968–76.

By conventional statistical standards, there is fairly strong evidence that large cohorts do depress earnings and that most of the effect comes early in the career. The evidence also suggests that cohort size effects increase with level of schooling. Whether these effects are real or just statistical illusions depends on what the future brings. Population age structures suggest that entering cohort sizes are probably already falling for lower levels of schooling and will do so soon for higher levels. The prediction of the estimates presented is that when this happens, wages of new entrants will rise relative to experienced workers and that, given similar reductions in cohort size, wages of new-entrant college graduates will rise relative to those of workers with less schooling.

Appendix

TABLE A1

Numbers of Individual Records Included for Estimation of Earnings Profiles and Cohort Sizes by Years of School Completed, 1968–76

Years of School Completed	Year								
	1968	1969	1970	1971	1972	1973	1974	1975	1976
Grade school:									
8–11 years	6,823	6,466	6,344	6,159	5,892	5,453	4,997	4,578	4,406
12 years	7,817	7,934	8,123	8,487	8,352	8,280	7,994	7,763	7,462
College:									
1–3 years	2,373	2,489	2,584	2,699	2,651	2,712	2,731	2,729	2,772
4 or more years	3,065	3,061	3,097	3,312	3,550	3,383	3,546	3,518	3,477

Source.—*Current Population Surveys* (March 1968–76).

TABLE A2

Percentages of Otherwise Valid Observations Lost due to Income Imputations by Years of School Completed and Survey Years, 1968–76

Years of School Completed	1968	1969	1970	1971	1972	1973	1974	1975	1976
Grade school:									
8–11 years	10.6	13.7	10.0	10.9	10.1	11.6	14.2	15.8	18.8
12 years	10.9	13.8	10.8	9.9	10.2	11.9	14.0	15.0	20.0
College:									
1–3 years	12.0	15.0	11.4	11.7	11.6	12.7	14.3	16.4	19.6
4 or more years	12.4	15.3	12.4	12.6	7.3	13.3	14.4	16.2	22.4

TABLE A3

Estimated Average Experience Profiles by Age (17–30) for High School Graduates, 1967–75

Age (Years)	Year at Work 1	2	3	4	5	6	7	8
17	.592	.276	.098	.029	.005	...	...	...
18	.535	.275	.128	.046	.014	.002	...	...
19	.458	.287	.151	.071	.025	.007	.001	...
20	.359	.290	.186	.097	.046	.016	.005	.001
21	.244	.259	.220	.146	.077	.036	.013	.004
22	.153	.201	.217	.189	.127	.067	.031	.011
23	.086	.136	.181	.198	.174	.119	.062	.029
24	.045	.083	.129	.173	.189	.166	.113	.060
25	.017	.044	.082	.127	.169	.186	.164	.112
26	.005	.017	.043	.080	.125	.168	.185	.164
27	.003	.007	.108	.043	.080	.124	.166	.183
28	.002	.004	.009	.020	.004	.079	.123	.165
29	.001	.002	.004	.010	.021	.044	.079	.122
30	.001	.002	.003	.005	.011	.021	.043	.077

References

Anderson, Joseph. "An Economic Demographic Model of the U.S. Labor Market." Ph.D. dissertation, Harvard Univ., 1977.

Becker, Gary S. *Human Capital.* New York: Columbia Univ. Press (for Nat. Bur. Econ. Res.), 1964.

Berndt, E. R., and Christensen, L. R. "Testing for the Existence of a Consistent Aggregate Index of Labor Input." *A.E.R.* 64, no. 3 (June 1974): 391–404.

Butz, William P., and Ward, Michael P. "The Emergence of Countercyclical U.S. Fertility." *A.E.R.* 69, no. 3 (June 1979): 318–28.

Easterlin, Richard A. "What Will 1984 Be Like? Socioeconomic Implications of Recent Twists in Age Structure." Presidential address to the Population Association of America, Atlanta, April 1978.

Easterlin, Richard A.; Wachter, Michael L.; and Wachter, Susan M. "Demographic Influences on Economic Stability: The United States Experience." *Population and Development Rev.* 4, no. 1 (March 1978): 1–23.

Freeman, Richard B. "Overinvestment in College Training." *J. Human Resources* 10, no. 3 (Summer 1975): 287–311.

———. *The Overeducated American.* New York: Academic Press, 1976.

———. "The Decline in Economic Rewards to College Education." *Rev. Econ. and Statis.* 59, no. 1 (February 1977): 18–29.

———. "The Effect of Demographic Factors on the Age-Earnings Profile in the U.S." Unpublished paper. Harvard Univ., Dept. Econ., August 1978.

Griliches, Zvi. "Capital-Skill Complementarity." *Rev. Econ. and Statis.* 51, no. 4 (November 1969): 465–68.

Oi, Walter. "Labor as a Quasi-fixed Factor." *J.P.E.* 70, no. 6 (December 1962): 538–55.

Rosen, Sherwin. "Short-Run Employment Variations on Class-I Railroads in the U.S., 1947–63." *Econometrica* 36 (July/October 1968): 511–29.

———. "Learning, Experience and the Labor Market." *J. Human Resources* 7, no. 3 (Summer 1972): 326–42.

Schultz, T. W. "Education in an Unstable Economy." Human Capital Paper no. 77:1, Univ. Chicago, Dept. Econ., January 1977.

Smith, James P., and Welch, F. "Local Labor Markets and Cyclic Components in Demand for College Trained Manpower." *Annales de l'INSEE* 30–31 (April-September 1978): 599–630.

U.S. Department of Commerce, Bureau of the Census. "Money Income and Poverty Status of Families and Persons in the United States: 1975 and 1974 Revisions (Advance Report)." *Current Population Reports.* Consumer Income Series P-60, no. 103. Washington: Government Printing Office, September 1976.

U.S. Department of Labor, Bureau of Labor Statistics. *Special Labor Force Report No. 186.* Washington: Government Printing Office, March 1975.

Wachter, Michael L. "Intermediate Swings in Labor-Force Participation." *Brookings Papers on Economic Activity*, no. 2 (1977), pp. 545–74.

Welch, F. "Education in Production." *J.P.E.* 78, no. 1 (January/February 1970): 35–59.

Welch, F., and Gould, W. "An Experience Imputation or an Imputation Experience." Mimeographed. RAND Corp., 1976.

[13]

European Economic Review 33 (1989) 355-366. North-Holland

UNEMPLOYMENT CONSEQUENCES OF AN AGING POPULATION:

An Application of Insider–Outsider Theory

Christopher A. PISSARIDES
London School of Economics, London WC2A 2AE, UK

1. Introduction

The first question that needs to be settled when investigating how unemployment responds to an aging population is why does the age composition of the population have any effect at all on unemployment? Undoubtedly more than one answer can be given to this question. Here I explore the assumption that different age groups are treated differently in union utility functions. In particular, I assume that although all workers care about the same things, unions attach greater weight to older workers' wishes than to younger workers' wishes.

Many reasons can be advanced to rationalise this preference for old age. To keep matters simple (and general), I do not derive the particular union utility function that I use. Seniority is probably the most important factor behind unions' preference for old age, though any insider–outsider argument can also justify my assumption [Freeman and Medoff (1984), Grossman (1983), Oswald (1985)]. Thus, the model that I develop can be thought of as a model of insider–outsider conflict, with insider status gained through seniority and aging on the job.

I use an equilibrium model of a decentralised but completely unionised economy. Wages and employment for young and old workers are determined by Nash bargains at the firm level. The model is closed by the assumption that equilibrium is symmetric. The union utility function is a weighted average of the utility functions of young and old workers, each of which is a utilitarian function. I show that in equilibrium the wages of old workers are always higher than the wages of young workers, and the differential is independent of relative group size. But the equilibrium unemployment rate of the old may be higher or lower than the equilibrium unemployment rate of the young, depending on how the rest of the model is specified; in particular, on what assumptions are made about the outside opportunities of old and young workers. The critical question turns out to be whether old workers can get senior jobs outside their firm, at the same rates of pay as old workers who are 'insiders'. If they can, the equilibrium unemployment rate of the old is higher than the equilibrium unemployment rate of the young. But if senior jobs are not open to outsiders the equilibrium unemployment rate of the old is below the rate of the young.

As with wage differentials, unemployment differentials are independent of group size under plausible conditions (but stronger ones than needed to establish the independence of wage differentials). But overall unemployment is not independent of the age composition of the labour force. An increase in the relative number of older workers for given labour force size can be shown to lead to a fall in both young and old unemployment. The wages of each group also fall.

In the next section we analyse the contract between the firm and the union, given outside conditions. In section 3 we consider the market outcome when outside conditions are also determined by firm–union contracts. In section 4 we study the role of the age composition of the labour force in the determination of equilibrium.

2. The partial model

The firm has a production function $F(N_1, N_2)$ defined over employment of the young, N_1 and employment of the old, N_2. The marginal products are both positive and denoted F_1 and F_2. The wages of young and old workers, w_1 and w_2 respectively, are negotiated between the firm and a single union. Employment levels are also negotiated by the firm and the union. We use the Nash solution that maximizes the product of each party's economic rent.

The firm's net return from production is the profit

$$\Pi = F(N_1, N_2) - w_1 N_1 - w_2 N_2. \tag{1}$$

Its alternative return (fallback) is some constant $\bar{\Pi}$. The union's utility function is the weighted average of the utility functions of young and old workers, V_1 and V_2 respectively

$$V = \alpha V_1 + V_2, \qquad \alpha \leqq 1. \tag{2}$$

The weight α is in general assumed to be less than one to show that the union attaches more weight to the wishes of old workers.

Each worker has a utility function $v(\cdot)$ defined over the wages that he receives. If he is not employed by the firm he can get $\bar{v}_1$ from outside when young and $\bar{v}_2$ when old. Hence, the union's rent from the employment relation is

$$V-\bar{V}=\alpha N_1[v(w_1)-\bar{v}_1]+N_2[v(w_2)-\bar{v}_2]. \tag{3}$$

Wages and employment for each group are determined by maximising the product

$$(V-\bar{V})^{\beta}(\Pi-\bar{\Pi})^{1-\beta}, \tag{4}$$

where in general $0<\beta<1$ but in the symmetric Nash case $\beta=\frac{1}{2}$.

The first-order conditions with respect to w_1 and w_2 are

$$\beta\alpha v'(w_1)(\Pi-\bar{\Pi})-(1-\beta)(V-\bar{V})=0, \tag{5}$$

$$\beta v'(w_2)(\Pi-\bar{\Pi})-(1-\beta)(V-\bar{V})=0. \tag{6}$$

From these we easily obtain

$$\alpha v'(w_1)=v'(w_2). \tag{7}$$

So, with concave utility functions and $\alpha<1$, the wages of older workers are always higher than the wages of younger workers. Moreover, the wage differential depends only on the structure of the utility function: neither marginal products nor relative group size have any influence on it.

The maximization conditions for employment are

$$\beta\alpha[v(w_1)-\bar{v}_1](\Pi-\bar{\Pi})+(1-\beta)(F_1-w_1)(V-\bar{V})=0, \tag{8}$$

$$\beta[v(w_2)-\bar{v}_2](\Pi-\bar{\Pi})+(1-\beta)(F_2-w_2)(V-\bar{V})=0. \tag{9}$$

From (5) and (8) and from (6) and (9) we obtain respectively the familiar conditions

$$F_1-w_1+\frac{v(w_1)-\bar{v}_1}{v'(w_1)}=0, \tag{10}$$

$$F_2-w_2+\frac{v(w_2)-\bar{v}_2}{v'(w_2)}=0, \tag{11}$$

If the utility functions $v(\cdot)$ are linear, (10) and (11) reduce to the efficient bargain conditions that marginal products are equal to the respective outside returns. With non-linear utility functions there is a distortion because we have not allowed severence payments to unemployed union members. The distortion in this case implies overemployment, i.e., marginal products fall below outside returns [see for example the argument in Pissarides (1981)].

An interesting feature of conditions (10) and (11) is that with linear utility functions (or with full severence payments) the weighting in favour of older workers in the union utility function does not influence relative employment levels. This, as we shall show below, is true only in the partial model. When $\bar{v}_1$ and $\bar{v}_2$ are endogenised to close the model, the result breaks down. Also, relative group size in (10) and (11) influences employment only to the extent that it influences marginal products. In the extreme but plausible case where junior and senior workers are indistinguishable, relative group size has no effect. Again this is a feature of the partial model only.

In what follows I shall assume that all workers are identical in production and write the production function as $F(N_1+N_2)$. Then

$$F_1=F_2=F'(N_1+N_2), \tag{12}$$

and any effect of relative group size disappears from (10) and (11). With (12), the only reason there may be different outcomes for young and old workers, either in the partial bargaining of this section or in the equilibrium outcomes of the next, is that young and old workers are treated differently by unions (i.e., $\alpha<1$).

3. General equilibrium

The critical step in going from the partial to the general equilibrium model is the endogenising of the outside returns $\bar{v}_1$ and $\bar{v}_2$. The approach I follow here is to assume that the economy consists entirely of firm-union pairs like the one analysed in the preceding section and that when a union member does not get a job at his union's firm, he searches for a job elsewhere. Search leads to employment with a positive probability that depends on equilibrium unemployment. For simplicity I assume that if unemployment of group i workers ($i=1$ for young and 2 for old) is u_i, the probability with which a job is found is the employment rate $1-u_i$. I consider briefly below a more general search environment.

Let $\bar{w}_i$ be the wage workers of group i are offered elsewhere and b_i be unemployment compensation. Then the outside return of group i workers is

$$\bar{v}_i=(1-u_i)v(\bar{w}_i)+u_iv(b_i), \qquad i=1,2. \tag{13}$$

For young workers it is natural to assume that $\bar{w}_1=w_1$; i.e., the young workers get junior jobs elsewhere (by junior jobs we simply mean jobs at young worker's rates of pay). Then the rent of young workers from working for their union's firm is

$$v(w_1)-\bar{v}_1=u_1[v(w_1)-v(b_1)]. \tag{14}$$

For older workers the specification of $\bar{w}_2$ is not as straightforward. One obvious possibility is to write $\bar{w}_2=w_2$; old workers get the same senior wage everywhere, regardless of whether they have come from outside or from inside the firm. But if the reason older workers carry more weight in the union's preference function is long tenure, it is more natural to assume that outsiders, even if old, are treated less favourably than senior insiders. I explore, as an alternative, the assumption $\bar{w}_2=w_1$; i.e. old workers unable to secure jobs with their own firm are offered the junior wage elsewhere.

It turns out that it makes substantial difference whether we assume $\bar{w}_2=w_2$ or $\bar{w}_2=w_1$. In the first case senior unemployment is higher than junior unemployment in equilibrium. In the second case it is lower. Before demonstrating this claim we offer some remarks about the determination of equilibrium unemployment in models with efficient bargains.

Consider, for purposes of illustration, the case of linear utility and the determination of junior unemployment. Then the efficient bargain implies that marginal product is equal to outside return $\bar{v}_1$. By contrast, a labour demand model (or 'right to manage') that gives exclusive rights of employment determination to the firm implies that marginal product is equal to the wage rate w_1. But if, as we argued, the outside return in equilibrium is given by (14), with linear utility the outside return is proportional to the wage rate w_1. The factor of proportionality is given by $(1-\rho_1)\ u_1$, where $\rho_1=b_1/w_1$ is the replacement ratio. Thus, marginal products in an efficient bargain model are effectively proportional to wages, and as shown in Pissarides (1986), if the production function is Cobb–Douglas the unemployment rates implied by the labour demand model and the efficient bargain model in this case are the same. Layard and Nickell (1988) offer a more general analysis with other production functions.

For senior workers, however, results could be different. In the case $\bar{w}_2=w_2$ the argument of the preceding paragraph holds and so the labour demand model and the efficient bargain model (with Cobb–Douglas production function) give the same employment level. If as we argued $w_2>w_1$, senior unemployment is higher than junior unemployment in equilibrium. But if $\bar{w}_2=w_1$, the two models give different results. The labour demand model again gives higher senior unemployment, since the inside wage w_2 is higher than w_1. But the efficient bargain model, as we show below gives lower senior than junior unemployment, even though the outside wage is equal to w_1.

We derive the full equilibrium results for the special case of Cobb–Douglas production function, logarithmic utility function and age-invariant replacement ratio, i.e., $b_t = \rho \bar{w}_t$. Then, for junior workers,

$$v(w_1) - \bar{v}_1 = -u_1 \ln \rho, \tag{15}$$

for senior workers when $\bar{w}_2 = w_2$,

$$v(w_2) - \bar{v}_2 = -u_2 \ln \rho, \tag{16}$$

and for senior workers when $\bar{w}_2 = w_1$,

$$v(w_2) - \bar{v}_2 = \ln w_2/w_1 - u_2 \ln \rho. \tag{17}$$

For logarithmic utility the wage condition (7) implies

$$w_1 = \alpha w_2, \tag{18}$$

so if $\bar{w}_2 = w_1$, (17) implies

$$v(w_2) - \bar{v}_2 = -\ln \alpha - u_2 \ln \rho. \tag{19}$$

We investigate the determination of equilibrium unemployment under the alternative pairs (15) and (16) or (15) and (19), and when the production function is given by

$$F(N_1 + N_2) = (N_1 + N_2)^\gamma, \qquad 0 < \gamma < 1. \tag{20}$$

First, we note that when the two types of labour are perfect substitutes and whatever the production function, (10) and (11) imply

$$w_1 - \frac{v(w_1) - \bar{v}_1}{v'(w_1)} = w_2 - \frac{v(w_2) - \bar{v}_2}{v'(w_2)}. \tag{21}$$

Substitute into this from (15), (16) and (18) to get

$$u_2 = \alpha u_1 - \frac{1 - \alpha}{\ln \rho}. \tag{22}$$

If $\alpha = 1$, $u_1 = u_2$ in equilibrium (since in this case old and young workers are treated identically in both the production function and the union utility function). But (22) implies

$$\frac{\partial u_2}{\partial \alpha} = u_1 + \frac{1}{\ln \rho} = \frac{F'}{w_1 \ln \rho} < 0, \tag{23}$$

so for $\alpha < 1$ we get $u_2 > u_1$. In this case the unemployment rate of old workers is higher than the unemployment rate of younger workers because their wages are higher, and because their outside wage is the same as their inside wage.

Alternatively, if we substitute from (15), (14) and (19) into (21), we get

$$u_2 = \alpha u_1 - \frac{1 - \alpha + \ln \alpha}{\ln \rho}. \tag{24}$$

Once again if $\alpha = 1$, $u_2 = u_1$, but now

$$\frac{\partial u_2}{\partial \alpha} = u_1 - \frac{1 - \alpha}{\alpha \ln \rho} > 0. \tag{25}$$

So now, if $\alpha < 1$, the unemployment rate of old people is less than the unemployment rate of young people.

Old workers in the second case face exactly the same outside opportunities as young workers. If utility functions are linear their unemployment rates would be equal, since then only outside opportunities matter in the determination of employment. But with non-linear utility and no severence payments the contract acts also to reduce the income fluctuation that is experienced when the insiders get employment outside. Since old people get higher wage inside the firm than the wage that young people get, the outside opportunities of old people should also be better under optimal contracts. In equilibrium, the only way this can be brought about is through lower senior unemployment, since the wages of outsiders are by symmetry the same in all firms.

To derive an expression for the unemployment rate of each group we need to use the production function. To begin with, we multiply through (8) by N_1 and through (9) by N_2 and add, to get

$$\beta(\Pi - \bar{\Pi}) + (1 - \beta)(N_1 F_1 + N_2 F_2 - N_1 w_1 - N_2 w_2) = 0. \tag{26}$$

Let $\bar{\Pi} = 0$, then given (1) and (20), we get

$$F = (N_1 + N_2)^{\gamma} = \frac{1}{\beta + \gamma(1 - \beta)}(N_1 w_1 + N_2 w_2). \tag{27}$$

Marginal products are given by

$$F' = \frac{\gamma}{\beta + \gamma(1-\beta)} \frac{N_1 w_1 + N_2 w_2}{N_1 + N_2}. \tag{28}$$

Now let L_1 be the number of young people and L_2 the number of old people in the population and let $\lambda = L_2/L_1$, a parameter. Then

$$N_i = (1-u_i)L_i, \qquad i = 1, 2, \tag{29}$$

and so

$$N_2/N_1 = \lambda(1-u_2)/(1-u_1). \tag{30}$$

Substitution into (28) gives

$$F' = \frac{\gamma}{\beta + \gamma(1-\beta)} \frac{(1-u_1)w_1 + \lambda(1-u_2)w_2}{1-u_1+\lambda(1-u_2)}. \tag{31}$$

Hence, condition (10) in general equilibrium and with the logarithmic utility function and Cobb–Douglas production function becomes

$$\frac{\gamma}{\beta + \gamma(1-\beta)} \frac{\alpha(1-u_1) + \lambda(1-u_2)}{1-u_1+\lambda(1-u_2)} - \alpha(1+u_1 \ln \rho) = 0. \tag{32}$$

(32) and (22) are solved for the equilibrium unemployment rates when $\bar{w}_2 = w_2$ and (32) and (24) give the solutions when $\bar{w}_2 = w_1$. Wages can then be obtained from (5) and (6).

4. Changes in the age composition of the labour force

We now have the full equilibrium model, with endogenous determination of the two wages and two unemployment rates, and with the age composition of the labour force as a parameter of the model. All we need do to obtain the effects of an aging population on unemployment is to differentiate with respect to the critical parameter, λ.

Intuitively what happens when the ratio of old to young workers rises is that if total employment remains unchanged, the two groups' unemployment differential changes. The optimal bargain requires that the unemployment rates of the two groups bear a certain relationship that is independent of group size. In general, the new differential at given overall employment does not conform to this relationship, so the firm and the union find a new point on the relationship that is consistent with the new ratio of old to young workers. This normally requires a change in the overall employment rate, with consequent changes in wage rates.

To find the effect of changes in λ on equilibrium unemployment we differentiate (32) totally with respect to λ, noting that regardless of whether (22) or (24) holds, $du_2/du_1=\alpha$. Hence

$$\left\{\frac{\gamma}{\beta+\gamma(1-\beta)}\frac{\lambda(1-\alpha)[1-u_2-\alpha(1-u_1)]}{[1-u_1+\lambda(1-u_2)]^2}-\alpha\ln\rho\right\}$$

$$\times\frac{du_1}{d\lambda}+\frac{(1-\alpha)(1-u_1)(1-u_2)}{[1-u_1+\lambda(1-u_2)]^2}=0. \tag{33}$$

In the case where $\bar{w}_2=w_1$, the derivative can be signed unambiguously, since then $1-u_2>1-u_1$, and the expression in the curly brackets is positive. In this case $du_1/d\lambda<0$ for all permissible values of the parameters, so an increase in the relative number of old workers unambiguously lowers both young and old people's unemployment.

But if $\bar{w}_2=w_2$, the sign of the effect may be reversed, though as we shall argue shortly it is not likely to happen. When $\bar{w}_2=w_2$, u_2 and u_1 are related by (22), so

$$1-u_2-\alpha(1-u_1)=(1-\alpha)\left(1+\frac{1}{\ln\rho}\right). \tag{34}$$

If the expression in (34) is positive we once again get $du_1/d\lambda<0$ but if it is negative the sign of the expression in the curly brackets of (33), and so the sign of the derivative, is ambiguous.

The expression in (34) is positive if $\ln\rho<-1$, i.e., if $\rho<0.37$. Although this range for the replacement ratio may seem low by European standards, one should not hastily apply a model with as special functional forms as ours to real-world situations. Simulations with expression (22) can easily show that even for values of α close to 1, values of ρ above 0.3 give implausibly high values for the differential between u_1 and u_2. So the specification of the model is such that at the range of the parameters that the final solutions for unemployment look plausible, there is no ambiguity and a rise in the ratio of old to young workers lowers unemployment for both groups.

With knowledge of u_1 and u_2, the solution for wages can be obtained from, say, the equilibrium version of (10),

$$\gamma(N_1+N_2)^{\gamma-1}=w_1(1+u_1\ln\rho). \tag{35}$$

Since when λ rises unemployment rates fall, the sum N_1+N_2 must rise. So the marginal product of labour falls. u_1 on the right-hand side of the equation also falls, so the wage rate unambiguously falls as well.

5. Some remarks on outside opportunities

We saw that the way outside opportunities of older workers are specified makes a substantial difference to the solution of the model. Which of the two alternative specifications that we have studied is more plausible and what are the implications of considering a more general search environment for outsiders?

If we judge our two assumptions in terms of the implications for the relation between junior and senior unemployment the assumption that senior workers do not have access to senior jobs outside appears to be more plausible. Under this assumption senior unemployment is less than junior unemployment, though as we argue below this point may not be very important. More relevant is the fact that expression (24) is generally more appealing than (22). The range of the parameters α and ρ for which (22) gives reasonable results is extremely limited and requires α to be close to unity (say above 0.9) and ρ close to zero (below 0.3). For example, for $\alpha=0.9$ and $\rho=0.3$ we get

$$u_2=0.9u_1+0.083, \tag{36}$$

an expression with an already high constant. Small reductions in α or small increases in ρ raise the constant substantially. By contrast, (24) for the same parameter values gives

$$u_2=0.9u_1-0.004. \tag{37}$$

The plausible range of the parameters with the assumption that old workers do not have access to senior jobs outside is much wider. In terms of the plausibility of our assumptions on a priori grounds, much of recent trade union theory argues that there is a sharp distinction between insiders and outsiders – established union members versus newcomers [see for example, Solow (1985), Blanchard and Summers (1986) and Lindbeck and Snower (1986)]. This view suggests that our second assumption, leading to (24), is a priori more plausible than the first. If we assume that older workers can get the same jobs in outside firms as inside their own firm, we lose the distinction between established workers and newcomers. The assumption that old workers carry more weight in union preference functions than young workers do is then difficult to justify.

We hinted in parts of the preceding discussion that our special functional forms may give absurd results at what one might consider 'plausible' values of the parameters. For example, suppose that $\gamma=0.7$, $\beta=0.5$, $\alpha=0.9$, $\lambda=0.9$ and $\rho=0.5$. All these are plausible, and possibly with the exception of α for which not much can be said, the others either conform to observation or are commonly used numbers. With these parameters, the unemployment implied by our models is 0.20 for u_1 and 1.02 for u_2 when $\bar{w}_2=w_2$, and 0.19 for u_1 and 0.16 for u_2 when $\bar{w}_2=w_1$. The numbers in the second case are not unreasonable, confirming our earlier claim that the assumption $\bar{w}_2=w_1$, gives a plausible outcome for a big range of the parameters. But in the first case ($\bar{w}_2=w_2$) senior unemployment falls outside the zero-one range. Does this imply that at least one of the models is useless?

The model would be useless if one wanted to use it to simulate (or calibrate) the path of unemployment over time. But if the purpose of the model is to illustrate the interactions between the two types of unemployment, and their sensitivity to parameters changes, the plausibility of the solution in terms of a priori information is irrelevant. For example, in the numerical example above, if ρ is re-interpreted as general well-being during unemployment relative to general well-being in employment, a seemingly small change from say 0.5 to 0.3 because of a 'psychic' cost of unemployment could have big effects on the equilibrium outcome. The models that we have developed are examples intended to illustrate one aspect of the role of the age composition of the labour force and it is on those grounds that they should be judged.

One of the critical assumptions that helps us go from the partial bargain to the equilibrium of the market is that the workers unable to get jobs with their firm find a job elsewhere with probability $1-u_i$. The results generalise in an appealing way if we consider a more general search environment, but our central comparative static result does not change.

Suppose for example that the probability that worker i finds a job elsewhere is p_i and that the jobs for group i turn over at the exogenous rate δ_i. Then in equilibrium unemployment satisfies the stock-flow condition

$$p_i u_i=\delta_i(1-u_i), \tag{38}$$

and so the probability that a worker finds a job elsewhere is

$$p_i=\delta_i\left[\frac{1}{u_i}-1\right]. \tag{39}$$

This falls as u_i rises – the critical property needed to derive our result – but if old workers have lower turnover rates than young workers we may get a prediction that in equilibrium p_1 exceeds p_2, as we would in the case $\bar{w}_2=w_2$, and yet $u_1 \geqq u_2$; i.e., older workers may experience lower unemployment rates than younger workers do and yet find it more difficult to find a job outside.

If in addition we generalise the search environment over time and consider discounting, the rent from staying with one's own firm becomes an increasing function of the rate of discount. Then given u_i, if older workers have higher discount rates than younger workers do, their rents from inside jobs might be higher than the rents of younger workers, as our theory requires, even if their chances of finding a job outside are as good as young workers' chances.

6. Conclusion

In the model of this paper unions attach greater weight to the wishes of old workers than to the wishes of young workers and wages and employment are determined by efficient bargains. Then, the wages of old workers are always higher than the wages of young workers regardless of productivity and relative supply. Employment is influenced mainly by outside opportunities. In the plausible case where old workers cannot easily get senior jobs outside their firm junior unemployment is higher than senior unemployment. A seemingly robust result is that an increase in the ratio of old to young workers (population aging) reduces the unemployment rate and wage rate of both groups in the population.

References

Blanchard, O. and L. Summers, 1986, Hysteresis and the European unemployment problem, NBER Macroeconomics Annual, Vol. 1 (MIT Press, Cambridge, MA) 15–77.

Freeman, R. and J. Medoff, 1984, What do unions do? (Basic Books, New York).

Grossman, G., 1983, Union wages, seniority and unemployment, American Economic Review 73, 277–290.

Layard, R. and S. Nickell, 1988, Is unemployment lower if unions bargain over employment?, Discussion paper no. 308, Centre for London Labour Economics, London School of Economics.

Lindbeck, A. and D. Snower, 1986, Wage setting, unemployment and insider–outsider relations, American Economic Review, Papers and Proceedings 76, 235–239.

Oswald, A., 1985, The economic theory of trade unions: An introductory survey, Scandinavian Journal of Economics 87, Symposium Issue, 160–193.

Pissarides, C., 1981, Contract theory, temporary layoffs and unemployment: A critical assessment, in: D Currie, D. Peel and W. Peters, eds., Microeconomic analysis (Croom Helm, London).

Pissarides, C., 1986, Equilibrium effects of tax-based incomes policies, in: D. Colander, ed., Incentive-based incomes policies (Ballinger, Cambridge, MA).

Solow, R., 1985, Insiders and outsiders in wage determination, Scandinavian Journal of Economics 87, no. 2, 711–728.

[14]

Applied Economics, 1986, **18**, 901–913

Labour force substitution and the effects of an ageing population

BRIAN S. FERGUSON

Department of Economics, University of Guelph, Guelph, Ontario N1G 2W1, Canada

I. INTRODUCTION

It is generally realized that the baby boom of the 1950s, combined with small birth cohorts that preceded and followed it, will lead to a significant ageing of the Canadian population over the next decades. Taken as a proportion of the population aged 20 and over, the population aged 65 and over is projected to rise from its current level of one in seven to one in three by 2030. In terms of the operation of a pay-as-you-go pension plan like the Canada Pension Plan (CPP) this means that while there are presently six working aged individuals to contribute to the support of one retired individual, there will eventually be only two. This has led to considerable concern about how a large retired population is to be supported at a socially acceptable level.

The standard of living that the baby boom group experiences in retirement will depend on its ability to finance its own retirement consumption and on the ability of the birth cohorts which follow it to contribute to CPP type pension plans, which in turn will depend on the lifetime income patterns experienced by the baby boom group and the following cohorts. One factor that may be important in determining income experience is relative cohort size. The only time, in fact, that cohort size would have no impact on relative cohort income is when all age groups of labour are perfect substitutes in production, but while this is unlikely, there is very little evidence about the actual degree of substitutability among different age groups. Some of this evidence is discussed in the next section.

In the remainder of this paper, substitutability between different age groups is investigated using data from Canada's Atlantic[1] region: the provinces of Newfoundland, Prince Edward Island, Nova Scotia and New Brunswick. The approach used is set out in Section III below and Section IV discusses the data. Estimation results are set out in Section V. Since the focus of the paper is on the effects of substitutability on the income experience of different birth cohorts, we estimate Hicks elasticities of complementarity, rather than the more usual elasticities of substitution. The elasticity of complementarity measures the effect of changes in relative factor quantities on factor prices.

Section VI, contains the results of simulations, based on estimates of the elasticities of

[1] Data from Atlantic Canada is used rather than national data for the sake of estimating a production relation on a reasonably homogeneous area.

0003–6846/86 $03.00 + .12

complementarity and projections of the Canadian population to the year 2026, designed to show the likely impact of population changes on the income of different birth cohorts. In the long run, feedback would be expected from economic factors to decisions about family formation which would affect population patterns. (See Easterlin, 1968, on long swings, for example). In the absence of a generally accepted estimate of the magnitude of such feedbacks it has been decided to work with population projections based strictly on demographic factors.

In this paper the impact of demographic factors is discussed in terms of their effects on average incomes. In fact, part of the effect is expected to show up in incomes and part to take the form of changing unemployment rates, with the distribution between the two to depend on the degree of wage flexibility in the economy.

II. LITERATURE REVIEW

On simple supply and demand principles the size of the baby boom group would lead us to expect that its income will be less than if the cohort were smaller. There have been a number of studies which support this proposition, in particular Welch (1979) and Freeman (1979), both of which conclude that the unfavourable labour force experience of the baby boom group in recent years was largely due to the relative cohort size. Welch and Freeman disagree, however, on whether the unfavourable experience is likely to continue. Welch suggests that age and experience increase substitutability so that the baby boom group should experience a fairly rapid catch-up, and that through the rest of its working life it is likely to have income levels similar to those of earlier birth cohorts. Freeman suggests that while some catch-up is likely, the baby boom group will probably continue to have lower earnings than the cohort which preceded them had and than the cohort which follows them will have.

The cohort that follows the baby boom was born during what is often referred to as the birth dearth of the 1960s and 1970s, and is much smaller than the baby boom group. On simple demand and supply principles we would expect young labour to acquire a scarcity value over the next years, its income to rise and its unemployment rate to fall. This has led analysts to suggest that youth unemployment is likely to cease to be a serious problem and that as the baby boom group enters its thirties, its unemployment rate is likely to fall to levels experienced by that age group of labour in the past.

It is also possible that while the baby boom group may continue to experience low incomes the cohorts that follow may benefit from the presence of the baby boom cohort. Suppose, for example, the aggregate production process can be represented by a Cobb–Douglas production function using capital and different ages of labour as inputs, and that factors are paid their marginal products. Then, although the baby boom group will depress its own marginal product, in the Cobb–Douglas function an unusual increase in the size of one input increases the marginal products of all of the other inputs. As a result, the cohorts following the baby boom group would experience higher incomes, and their capacity to support the baby boom group in retirement would be considerably increased.

On the other hand, if the birth cohort of the 1960s finds itself competing with unemployed members of the baby boom group for jobs, employers may prefer the older workers, so that youth unemployment rates will remain high and their incomes low. Clearly the degree to which different age groups are substitutes in production will be a major determinant of future income patterns.

There are only a limited number of studies of substitution among age groups of labour. In their survey of labour substitution, Hamermesh and Grant (1979) find only five studies dealing with age group substitution. Of those five, two use CES production functions, which do not allow for the possibility of different degrees of substitutability, nor the possibility of complementarity, among different age groups. In their summary of the results, Hamermesh and Grant describe the conclusions as very tentative, but suggesting that middle-aged workers are only slightly substitutable for capital while younger and older (over age 45) workers are more easily substituted for by capital. They also note that more skilled labour groups tend to be complements with capital, and jointly substitutable with capital for less skilled groups.

Of the five studies considering substitution among different age groups discussed by Hamermesh and Grant only that by Freeman (1979) considers substitutability between male and female labour. Freeman finds complementarity between female labour and capital, and weak complementarity between female and male labour. He finds that the number of female workers has a slight positive effect on the earnings of younger men and a slight negative effect on the earnings of older men, but argues that the magnitudes of these effects are so small that male and female workers apparently operate in what are essentially separate production processes. In a later study, Grant and Hamermesh (1981) find a high degree of substitutability between youths and adult women in US manufacturing in 1969, and suggest that the recent rapid growth in the female labour force hurt the earnings prospects of younger workers. Grant and Hamermesh also find that they are unable to reject the hypothesis of weak separability between youth labour (not differentiated by sex) and adult white women (aged 25 and over).

The only Canadian study in the literature, Merrilees (1982), reaches conclusions that are markedly different from those of most American studies. Merrilees uses aggregate Canadian data for 1957–78, and four broad labour force groups: adult male, adult female, youth male and youth female, plus capital. He concludes that there is virtually no substitutability among these broad groupings of labour, but rather a small degree of complementarity, and takes his results as support for the segmented labour market hypothesis. Freeman (1979) suggests a similar possibility on US data, but argues that problems of estimation are sufficiently severe that little weight should be given to this result.

The differences between Merrilees' results and those surveyed by Hamermesh and Grant (1979) do not appear to be due to the broad groupings Merrilees uses, since Grant and Hamermesh (1981) use similarly broad groupings and find a significant degree of substitutability. It may be due to the approach Merrilees takes to estimating the degree of substitutability, which will be referred to in the following section.

It is not unreasonable to expect some degree of complementarity among different age groups. Adult labour may be complementary with youth labour in a training relationship, as younger workers acquire labour force experience. The educational composition of the young labour force in recent years may also be a factor, as the increasing rate of post-secondary education may give recent young entrants skills different from those acquired by groups whose investment in human capital tended toward more on-the-job training. This might well reduce the substitutability among labour classified strictly by age relative to earlier periods when different age groups had all accumulated a higher proportion of their human capital in the labour force. Also, the different type of skills being brought into the labour force by young workers with longer schooling could well be complements to the skills acquired by the existing labour force.

III. ESTIMATION

The degree of substitutability between inputs in production can be determined from either a cost or a production function. Common practice among studies at the industry level is to use a cost function approach, treating factor prices as exogenous to the industry and input levels as endogenous, while at the national level it is more common to regard factor levels as exogenous and prices as endogenous. The size of different groups of labour inputs, for example, is generally regarded as being primarily demographically determined at the national level, with endogeneity entering only through the participation rate, which may itself be determined as much by social as by economic factors.[2]

At the provincial level the choice is not quite as clear, since a small province in an efficiently functioning national labour market might find itself a price taker, while migration might add another element of endogeneity to the input level. In general, however, it seems likely that the provincial case will be closer to the national than to the industry level, so an aggregate production function will be estimated in preference to a cost function.

Estimates are based on a translog form of aggregate production function for the Atlantic region. The translog is attractive since it allows for the possibility of differing elasticities of substitution between different pairs of inputs and because it allows the marginal rate of substitution between any pair of inputs to depend on the levels of the other inputs.

These considerations have made the translog an increasingly popular form for studies dealing with input substitutability, as can be seen from the discussions in Freeman (1979) and Hamermesh and Grant (1979). A dissenting view on its value can be found in Merrilees (1982), where it is argued that it is particularly vulnerable to multicollinearity between inputs. Merrilees prefers a constant difference of elasticity (CDE) form, in which elasticities of substitution are not required to be constant, as in CES forms, but in which the difference between elasticities is constant. In addition to this more restrictive form of production function, Merrilees finds support for further restrictions, which eventually constrain the elasticity of substitution to be equal for all pairs of labour inputs. This may account for the marked difference between Merrilees' results and those of the various American studies noted above.

The general form of the translog production function is

$$\ln Y = A + \Sigma_i \alpha_i \ln X_i + 1/2 \Sigma_i \Sigma_j \gamma_{ij} \ln X_i \ln X_j. \tag{1}$$

Here, Y is aggregate output and X_i and X_j are the factors of production. On the assumption of competitive input markets in which factors are paid their marginal products, differentiating Equation 1 with respect to $\ln X_i$ gives

$$S_i = \alpha_i + \Sigma_j \gamma_{ij} \ln X_j, \tag{2}$$

[2] There is clear evidence of the dependence of female participation, in particular on the level of economic activity, which it would be desirable to allow for. Ultimately, computational costs prevent this, a weakness shared by virtually all of the literature estimating share equations, forcing attention to be concentrated on only one side of the market.

where S_i is the share of input i in the value of output. With constant returns the shares sum to one, $\Sigma_i S_i = 1$, and the second order coefficients sum to zero across equations, $\Sigma_j \gamma_{ji} = 0 = \Sigma_i \gamma_{ij}$. Because of the adding-up constraints on the shares of the inputs, we also have $\Sigma_i \alpha_i = 1$.

From the derivation of Equation 2 from Equation 1 it is clear that the second order coefficients should be symmetric across equations in the system (Equation 2), $\gamma_{ij} = \gamma_{ji}$. Berndt and Christensen (1973) note that symmetry could be regarded as a test of constant returns, but suggest that it will generally have to be imposed. Most studies using translog forms impose symmetry and test other hypotheses conditional on symmetry, and we follow custom in this.

In the system (Equation 2), if none of the γ_{ij} terms are significantly different from zero the translog form collapses into a Cobb–Douglas, with constant shares. Thus we have a test of the usefulness of the Cobb–Douglas form as an approximation to the aggregate production function.

Because the effect of changes in the age structure of the labour force on the relative incomes of different birth cohorts is the matter in question, the estimated equations are used to calculate Hicks partial elasticities of complementarity between pairs of inputs, which measure the effect on relative factor prices of changes in relative factor quantities. These elasticities can be calculated from Equation 2 as

$$C_{ij} = (\gamma_{ij} + S_i S_j)/S_i S_j \tag{3a}$$

and

$$C_{ii} = (\gamma_{ii} + S_i^2 - S_i)/S_i^2. \tag{3b}$$

Inputs are referred to as q-complements or substitutes as C_{ij} is positive or negative.

IV. DATA

For the estimation, capital (k) and seven labour groups are chosen as inputs: male labour aged 15–24 (M1); male labour aged 25–34 (M2); male labour aged 35–64 (M3); female labour 15–24 (F1); females 25–34 (F2); females 35–64 (F3); and a combined male and female group aged 65 and over and still in the labour force (L6). The capital series is taken from Statistics Canada's (1982) estimates of provincial capital stock, and the labour series from Statistics Canada's estimates of provincial labour forces by age and sex. Shares in the value of output were calculated on the basis of the Provincial Income figure in Statistics Canada's (1981) published provincial economic accounts, using the share of wages and salaries in Provincial Income as the aggregate labour share, and disaggregating that by age on the basis of unpublished data from Revenue Canada, Taxation, on sources of income by province, age and sex. The remainder of provincial income in each province and year was allocated to capital. For New Brunswick, 1979, for example, the share of capital was approximately 25%, and (rounded) of M1 = 8.2%, M2 = 17.5%, M3 = 30.0%, F1 = 4.4%, F2 = 6.0%, F3 = 8.4% and L6 = 0.8%. We chose to omit the equation for the share of the over 65 group from the system in the estimation. The remaining equations were estimated using full information maximum likelihood, on data from each of the four provinces for the years 1966 to 1979 inclusive. While fourteen years is a relatively short period, these years cover the entry of the baby boom group into the labour force, and the ageing of much of that group as they moved from the first to the second of our 10-year age groups. Over the data set there was a strong negative correlation between the ratio of capital to aggregate labour and the relative share of capital, suggesting an elasticity of substitution between capital and aggregate labour of less than one.

V. ESTIMATION RESULTS

Maximum likelihood estimates of the translog share equations and associated t-statistics are shown in Table 1. On the whole the fit of the equations is reasonably good, although the share equation for the fourth labour class has an R^2 of only 0.375. On the 28 independent γ_{ij} coefficients shown, only 9 are not significantly different from zero. The remaining coefficients are not shown since they can be determined from the symmetry requirement. The coefficients for the L6 share equation were calculated from those of the remaining equations. The number of significant γ_{ij} coefficients indicates that we can reject the hypothesis that the true aggregate production relation is Cobb-Douglas.

The interaction terms in the translog production function frequently make it difficult to interpret the estimated coefficients. In Table 2 estimated elasticities of complementarity are presented, calculated using Equation 3, using the 1979 New Brunswick values for factor shares. Since $C_{ij} = C_{ji}$ only the upper triangular matrix of elasticities is shown.

The elements of the main diagonal of Table 2 are the own-elasticities, all of which have the correct negative sign. The largest single own-elasticity is that of the 65 + group, but because of the small size of this group and various institutional factors which may constrain people who

Table 1. *Estimated translog share equations*

		Input								
Share of	Constant	k	M1	M2	M3	F1	F2	F3	L6	R^2
k	0.272	−0.276	0.024	0.071	0.164	0.005	0.001	0.031	−0.020	0.702
	(57.04)	(−10.11)	(1.88)	(5.51)	(8.72)	(1.06)	(0.125)	(5.15)		
M1	0.078		0.048	0.001	−0.042	0.002	−0.015	−0.021	0.003	0.623
	(36.81)		(2.94)	(0.124)	(−3.52)	(0.432)	(−3.03)	(−3.60)		
M2	0.145			0.046	−0.092	0.005	0.001	−0.036	0.004	0.938
	(69.15)			(2.54)	(−9.96)	(0.677)	(0.197)	(−8.29)		
M3	0.326				0.012	−0.003	−0.019	−0.034	0.014	0.375
	(96.97)				(0.635)	(−0.83)	(−3.16)	(−5.15)		
F1	0.043					−0.001	0.003	−0.007	−0.004	0.709
	(43.35)					(−0.308)	(1.39)	(−2.65)		
F2	0.042						0.022	0.014	−0.007	0.788
	(39.68)						(8.09)	(4.86)		
F3	0.078							0.043	0.010	0.848
	(54.03)							(10.58)		
L6	0.016	−0.020	0.003	0.004	0.014	−0.004	−0.007	0.010	0	—

t-statistics in parentheses; critical $t(0.05) = 1.68$, $t(0.01) = 2.42$.

Table 2. *Estimated elasticities of complementarity*

Elasticity of	Change in quantity of							
	k	M1	M2	M3	F1	F2	F3	L6
k	−7.57	2.17	2.64	3.21	1.47	1.08	2.50	−9.11
M1		−4.02	1.05	−0.69	1.66	−2.03	−2.03	6.10
M2			−3.20	−0.76	1.68	1.14	−1.43	7.62
M3				−2.20	0.76	−0.06	−0.36	6.67
F1					−22.21	1.89	−0.81	−11.36
F2						−9.44	3.76	−12.50
F3							−4.84	16.34
L6								−125.00

wish to go on working after age 65 limited weight is placed on the results for this group. Of the other inputs, young female workers (F1) have the largest own-elasticity, more than twice the size of the next largest which is that for females aged 25–34. All of the labour inputs, with the exception of the oldest, are complementary with capital, with the more experienced groups showing greater complementarity than do the younger groups for both males and females. The first and second age groups of male labour are *q*-complements as are the first and second groups of female labour. The youngest group of female labour is complementary with the first and second male groups and the second age group of female labour is complementary with the second age group of male labour, but is a *q*-substitute for the youngest group of male labour. There also appears to be weak substitutability between the more experienced male and female groups.

One of the most interesting results shown in Table 2 is the substitutability between the third age group of female labour and the first age group of male labour. The third female age group is also a q-substitute the first female group, although complementary with the second, and the second female age group is a *q*-substitute for the first male group, with an elasticity of complementarity equal to that between F3 and M1. These results support the Grant and Hamermesh (1981) finding of a high degree of substitutability between adult (white) women and young labour, and the elasticity of complementarity they find between these groups is of the same order of magnitude as the elasticity we find between F3 and M1.[3]

The results in Table 2 do not present clear indications of the effect of the baby boom group on the following birth cohorts, although they suggest that the birth cohorts immediately following the baby boom will not find themselves in competition with the baby boom group.

To see more clearly what these elasticities imply for the income patterns of various groups, we have found elasticities of factor price with respect to changes in factor quantities, calculated as

$$\Theta_{ij} = S_j C_{ij} \tag{4}$$

[3]A referee has pointed out that the *q*-substitutability between women 35–64 and men 15–24 may reflect the relatively high proportion of married women in the older age group. Unfortunately, the data do not permit disaggregation of incomes by marital status nor by education, workforce experience or part time vs full time labour force attachments. Increasing female labour force participation rates suggest that in the future, older women will have accumulated greater work force experience and so should become closer substitutes for older age groups of men, rather than for men and women in the younger groups.

and defined as the change in the price of factor i in response to a 1 % change in the quantity of factor j, all else held constant. These elasticities are presented in Table 3, again using 1979 New Brunswick levels for factor shares. Because $S_i \neq S_j$ the matrix of elasticities of factor prices will not be symmetric.

The main diagonal of the matrix in Table 3 shows the effect on own price of a change in a factor quantity. All of these elasticities are negative, and the largest is that of capital. The first column of Table 3 shows that all of the labour groups with the exception of the oldest benefit from an increase in the capital stock, and that for all but the F1 and F2 groups the elasticity associated with a change in the capital stock is larger in absolute value than any of the other elasticities, including the own-elasticity. This supports the view that labour generally benefits from an increase in the capital stock.

If we consider the first and second male groups, we see that while their q-complementarity is apparent, the effect of a change in the level of the second group on the price of the first is twice the effect of a change in the level of M1 on the price of M2. For the corresponding female groups the difference is much smaller. The effect of an increase in the size of M3 on the price of M1 is much stronger than the effect of the quantity of M1 on the price of M3, but the elasticity of the price of M1 with respect to the level of F3 is equal to the elasticity of the price of F3 with respect to the quantity of M1. This supports the view that over the period from which our data is drawn, young male labour was in competition with older female labour. The elasticity of the price of F1 with respect to the quantity of F3 is twice the elasticity of the price of F3 with respect to the quantity of F1. Since the oldest of the baby boom group, those born at the end of the 1940s, are just beginning to move into our third age group, the pattern of q-substitutability suggests that youth incomes may remain depressed (and youth unemployment high) for some time to come, at least in the case of young males. Again, however, the pattern of elasticities does not yield unambiguous predictions.

VI. SIMULATION RESULTS

Because the elasticities in Tables 2 and 3 can be difficult to interpret, we have prepared some simple simulations suggesting the possible implications of the relationships we have found.

Table 3. *Elasticities of factor prices (New Brunswick, 1979)*

	Change in quantity of							
Price of	k	M1	M2	M3	F1	F2	F3	L6
k	−1.86	0.17	0.46	0.96	0.07	0.07	0.21	−0.07
M1	0.54	−0.33	0.18	−0.21	0.07	−0.12	−0.17	0.05
M2	0.65	0.09	−0.56	−0.23	0.07	0.07	−0.12	0.06
M3	0.79	−0.06	−0.13	−0.66	0.03	−0.004	−0.03	0.05
F1	0.36	0.14	0.29	0.23	−0.97	0.11	−0.06	−0.09
F2	0.27	−0.17	0.20	−0.02	0.08	−0.57	0.32	−1.10
F3	0.62	−0.17	−0.25	−0.11	−0.03	0.23	−0.40	0.13
L6	−2.25	0.50	1.33	2.00	−0.50	−0.75	1.37	−1.00

Table 4. *Labour force group of different birth cohorts, by year*

	Born in					
Year	1940	1945	1950	1955	1958	1965
1981	L_3	L_3	L_2	L_2	L_1	L_1
1986	L_3	L_3	L_3	L_2	L_2	L_1
1991	L_3	L_3	L_3	L_3	L_2	L_2
1996	L_3	L_3	L_3	L_3	L_3	L_2
2001	L_3	L_3	L_3	L_3	L_3	L_3
2006	L_6	L_3	L_3	L_3	L_3	L_3
2011	—	L_6	L_3	L_3	L_3	L_3
2016	—	—	L_6	L_3	L_3	L_3
2021	—	—	—	L_6	L_3	L_3
2026	—	—	—	—	L_6	L_3

L_i = age group *i*, male and female. 1 = 15–24; 2 = 25–34; 3 = 35–64; 6 = 65 +.

Consider individuals born in 1940, 1945, 1950, 1955, 1958 and 1965 respectively. In Table 4 their progress is charted through the labour force groups from 1981 to 2026, in five-year groupings.

Using Statistics Canada's Population Projection Number One (Statistics Canada, 1979), which gives annual population projections until the year 2000 and five-yearly projections beginning in 2001, and assuming labour force participation rates remain constant at the levels prevailing in New Brunswick in 1981, period-to-period percentage changes in the New Brunswick labour force are calculated and the results shown in Table 5.

Applying these percentages to the elasticities of price in Table 3, percentage changes in average factor prices being paid to each age class of labour over each 5-year period are calculated in Table 6. Thus the figure for M2 in 1986 represents the percentage change in the wage of the second male age group relative to what individuals who were in that age class in 1981 were earning. Because of the importance of capital in determining wages, we have had to include an assumption about capital growth. In the period 1976 to 1981, New Brunswick experienced a relatively rapid increase in its capital stock, with the ratio of capital to total labour force increasing after it had levelled off in the other three provinces. Instead of continuing this increase into the future there is a more conservative assumption that the capital stock would increase sufficiently in each 5-year period to maintain the ratio of capital to the total labour force constant at its 1981 level.

An individual born in 1955, midway through the baby boom, would be in the second age class of labour in 1981. Using the New Brunswick projections, male income would be 7 % higher than the average for an individual in that class in 1976, while female income would be 12 % lower. Table 5 shows a particularly large percentage increase in the F2 group from 1976 to 1981 (48 % over the 5-year period), due both to the ageing of the baby boom group and to the increase in the female labour force participation rate for that age group over that period (from 46 % in 1976 to 56 % in 1981). The participation rate for the first age group of female labour rose from 47 % to 55 % which, along with the high own-elasticity of complementarity for that group, accounts for

Table 5. *Projected percent change, New Brunswick labour force (by age/sex group, five-year intervals)*

	1976–81	1981–6	1986–91	1991–6	1996–2001	2001–6	2006–11	2011–6	2016–21	2021–6
M1	4.65	−11.76	−13.16	−1.23	7.14	7.64	0.23	−3.60	−0.58	4.67
M2	20.00	6.17	2.29	−9.88	−11.30	3.39	11.05	7.10	0.22	−3.37
M3	6.94	10.79	9.93	12.20	9.61	6.19	2.65	1.74	2.15	1.15
F1	18.75	−11.63	−13.16	−0.92	6.72	7.63	0.25	−3.60	−0.59	4.65
F2	47.80	5.47	1.10	−10.11	−11.42	3.26	11.26	7.11	0.23	−3.39
F3	20.20	9.89	9.90	11.41	9.50	6.29	2.77	1.51	1.68	0.86
L6	33.30	9.50	8.27	3.08	1.32	4.65	9.55	14.83	14.39	13.77
k^a	24.09	3.22	2.42	2.96	3.62	5.77	4.64	3.61	3.23	3.14

Source: Statistics Canada (1979) 1976–81 = actual, remainder = projected.
[a]Capital: 1976–81 = actual; remainder = change needed to maintain constant 1981 ratio of capital to total labour force.

Table 6. *Percent change in average income of labour force groups, over five-year intervals*

	1976–81	1981–6	1986–91	1991–6	1996–2001	2001–6	2006–11	2011–6	2016–21	2021–6
M1	7.08	1.79	1.65	−2.97	−4.16	−0.79	2.54	3.43	1.89	0.58
M2	7.27	−5.95	−4.71	2.58	5.72	1.40	−2.72	−1.40	2.06	4.90
M3	12.94	−4.87	−4.43	−4.53	−2.41	−0.17	0.82	1.56	1.79	2.70
F1	−0.54	14.22	13.52	−0.35	−7.22	−2.28	5.49	6.10	0.84	−5.10
F2	−12.39	2.05	3.81	7.82	7.26	1.11	−3.10	−2.37	−0.11	0.56
F3	14.26	0.15	−0.16	−3.29	−3.65	−0.64	2.50	3.95	3.08	2.40
L6	−59.50	22.42	21.93	24.58	16.52	5.43	−4.65	−13.29	−14.93	−19.29

Table 7. *Percent change in average income of labour force groups with total capital stock held constant, over five-year intervals*

	1976–81	1981–6	1986–91	1991–6	1996–2001	2001–6	2006–11	2011–6	2016–21	2021–6
M1	−5.92	0.05	0.35	−4.57	−6.12	−3.90	0.03	1.48	0.14	−1.11
M2	−8.39	−8.04	−6.29	0.66	3.37	−2.35	−5.73	−3.75	−0.03	2.85
M3	−6.09	−7.41	−6.34	−6.87	−5.27	−4.72	−2.84	−1.29	−0.76	0.21
F1	−9.21	13.06	12.65	−1.41	−8.53	−4.36	3.82	4.80	−0.32	−6.23
F2	−18.90	1.18	3.16	7.02	6.29	−0.44	−4.35	−3.34	−0.98	−0.29
F3	−0.67	−1.84	−1.66	−5.12	−5.90	−4.22	−0.38	1.71	1.07	0.45
L6	−5.30	29.67	27.37	31.24	24.66	18.42	5.78	−5.17	−7.66	−12.22

the drop in its average income between 1976 and 1981, while the average income of the first age group of male labour rose over the same period.

Between 1981 and 1986 the average income of males born in 1955 is projected to fall by 6%, while that of females is projected to rise 2% (after the 12% drop in the previous 5-year period for that female age group). In 1991 the 1955 cohort will be in the third age group, and both males and females will have lower average incomes than did the birth cohorts which preceded them in the third age group. Their incomes will decline through the first years they are in the third age group (until 2006 for both males and females) and then rise again until 2021. The 1955 birth cohort will be in the 65 + group beginning in 2021, and will, on these projections, find that their average labour income is 15% smaller than that of their predecessors in the 65 + group and that it continues to fall while they are in this labour force group.

An individual entering the labour force in 1981 (and so part of the birth-dearth cohort of the 1960s) will find, in the case of a male, that his average income is higher than that of the previous members of that age group, and that it continues to rise during the period he is in the first and second age groups, that it drops slightly during the first years he is in the third group and rises after that. The pattern for a female is similar. Individuals who are in the third age group in 1981 (and so were in the pre-baby boom birth cohort) however, are projected to experience depressed incomes through the remainder of their working lives, due first to the pattern of *q*-substitutability between the older and younger labour, particularly for males, and then to the own-substitution effect as the baby boom group enters the third age group. In the case of females in this birth cohort there is enough *q*-complementarity between older and younger workers to delay the depressing effect on incomes until the baby boom group enters the third age class. If the female labour force participation rate continues to increase, however, there may be a depressing effect on the incomes of older females through substitution.

It appears, therefore, that the baby boom group is likely to experience depressed incomes through most of its working life, and that the post-baby boom cohorts will experience higher incomes than will the baby boom group. While the effects reported in Table 6 may seem small for 5-year changes, it should be remembered that no allowance has been made for technological change and that it has been assumed that the ratio of capital to aggregate labour would remain constant. Calculations for capital similar to those in Table 6 show its marginal productivity rising at least until the end of the twentieth century. This should encourage investment, which in turn will increase the incomes of all but the oldest age group of labour, according to our estimates. As an indication of the significance of capital in determining labour income, the calculations for Table 6 have been repeated in Table 7 with the capital stock held constant at its 1976 level, so the capital–labour ratio is declining. In particular, the first column of Table 7 shows that in the absence of the rapid increase in capital stock that New Brunswick experienced between 1976 and 1981, the average incomes of all of the labour groups would have declined over that period.

VII. CONCLUSIONS

The chief implication of the estimation reported here is that demographically induced changes in the age structure of the labour force in Atlantic Canada may be of considerable economic importance for some time to come. While we have not attempted to make actual forecasts, the simulations do indicate something about the likely direction of the effects. In particular they suggest that the baby boom group is likely to find its relative size working to its disadvantage through the bulk of its working life. The post-baby boom groups appear to do better, suggesting that their capacity to support a large retired population may be somewhat greater than recent discussions have implied.

The results here seem generally reasonable, although *q*-substitutability between M3 and M1 and between F3 and F1 warrant further investigation. Results clearly indicate that the size of the capital stock will be an important factor in determining the time path of income for different birth cohorts, suggesting that it is important that the private pension system be improved, both to finance the retirement of a growing aged population and to finance additional capital stock to improve their income experience through their labour force years.

ACKNOWLEDGEMENTS

I am indebted for helpful comments on earlier versions of this paper to members of the Economics Department seminars at the University of Guelph and McMaster University, participants at the 1982 Atlantic Canada Economics Association Conference, and to an anonymous referee.

REFERENCES

Berndt, E. and Christensen, L. R. (1973) The translog function and the substitution of equipment, structures and labor in US manufacturing 1929-68, *Journal of Econometrics*, **1**, 81-114.

Easterlin, R. (1968) *Population, Labour Force, and Long Swings in Economic Growth: The American Experience*, Columbia University Press, for the National Bureau of Economic Research, New York.

Freeman, R. B. (1979) The effect of demographic factors on age-earnings profiles, *Journal of Human Resources*, **14**, 518-42.

Grant, J. H. and Hamermesh, D. S. (1981) Labour market competition among youths, white women and others, *Review of Economics and Statistics*, **63**, 354-60.

Hamermesh, D. S. and Grant, J. H. (1979) Econometric studies of labor-labor substitution and their implications for policy, *Journal of Human Resources*, **14**, 518-42.

Merrilees, W. J. (1982) Labour market segmentation in Canada: an econometric approach, *Canadian Journal of Economics*, **15**, 458-73.

Statistics Canada (1979) *Population Projections for Canada and the Provinces*, Ottawa, Catalogue No. 91-520, Occasional.

Statistics Canada (1981): *Provincial Economic Accounts Experimental Data 1964-1979*, Ottawa, Cat. No. 13-213, Annual.

Statistics Canada (1982) *Fixed Capital Flows and Stock*, 1955-82 uncatalogued series, by province.

Welch, F. (1979) Effects of cohort size on earnings: the baby boom babies' financial bust, *Journal of Political Economy*, **87**, S65-S98.

[15]

Jnl Soc. Pol., 18, 2, 211–233 1989

Dependency and Ageing in Britain: A Re-Examination of the Evidence*

JANE FALKINGHAM†

ABSTRACT
There has been growing concern over the consequences for public expenditure of an increasing number of elderly people dependent on a relatively diminishing working population. This concern stems largely from demographically determined dependency ratios and it is not necessarily the case that a change in the age profile of the population will lead to a greater burden of dependency. The 'engine of dependency' is shown to have at least two other cylinders—patterns of labour-force participation across age and gender, and levels of unemployment. Policy to date has had a surprisingly narrow focus in view of the dual role of economic and demographic forces in influencing the ratio of dependency. The economic and political feasibility of alternative policy options is discussed.

INTRODUCTION

The last decade has seen increasing interest in the future age structure of the population. Much of this has been fuelled by a concern with the implications for public expenditure of the anticipated rise in the number of elderly people. The resultant increase in the need for pensions, health and other services is believed to impose a growing burden on the working population, the size of which is expected to diminish relative to that of the dependent population. A central theme of the recent Green and White Papers on the reform of social security has been the Government's assessment of the level of expenditure on pensions which will be necessary to maintain an ageing population (Cmnd 9518, 1985; Cmnd 9691, 1985). Demographic indicators of the ratio of national insurance contributors to pensioners were presented to support the argument that

* This paper is based on research funded by the Economic and Social Research Council (ESRC) reference No. G00 23 2344. I am grateful to Nick Barr, Maria Evandrou, Chris Gordon, Paul Johnson and Julian Le Grand for their helpful comments on earlier drafts of this paper.

† Research Officer, London School of Economics.

the cost of the State Earnings Related Pension Scheme (SERPS) would be too high, and in the event the SERPS scheme was substantially modified by the Social Security Act of 1986. Nonetheless, it is not necessarily the case that a change in the age profile will lead to a greater burden of dependency.

This paper aims to show that the 'engine of future dependency' has at least two other cylinders in addition to demographic movements: namely, changing age–sex patterns of labour force participation and the level of unemployment. The first section provides the background to the debate, looking at how Britain's population is ageing and at the composition of its aged population. The second section then examines how demographic forces interacted with other, economic, forces to influence dependency between 1951 and 1981. It questions the usefulness of age-based dependency ratios, and suggests alternative ways of using demographic information to construct more meaningful measures of dependency. It then examines whether increased dependency has simply been the product of the ageing population or whether there have been other equally important labour market changes influencing dependency that have so far been given insufficient attention in the debate on dependency.

The paper is primarily concerned with measurement problems and how we can measure dependency ratios more realistically. However, the changing level of dependency also has implications for policy. It is argued that present policy proposals have been based on inadequately calculated ratios. The latter section of the paper, therefore, also surveys briefly the alternative policies which could be adopted as a means of stabilising the overall dependency ratio in the future. These include not only changes in the levels of female labour force participation and unemployment, but also changes in the retirement age, levels of immigration and, on the output side, labour productivity.

POPULATION AGEING

Since much of the debate over future levels of dependency has arisen through concern about the 'ageing of the population' it is instructive to look at the changing age structure of the population and the mechanics of that change.

First it is necessary to distinguish between individual and population ageing. Individual ageing is a continuous process, and a person ages inexorably from birth through to the moment of death. Populations, however, can become older or younger depending on changes in the proportion of people in different age groups. The 'age' of a population is normally measured in one of three ways: by the proportion of elderly people in the population, generally taken in Britain as those over age 60 for women and over age 65 for men; by the proportion of children in the population, usually taken as those under age 16; and by the median age of the population.

The age structure in any period is affected by the age structure of the previous period as peaks and troughs in the age distribution at a particular moment move forward in time. Thus the age composition of a population is determined by past changes in mortality, fertility, and net immigration. Fertility is the chief determinant of age structure in all but the highest mortality populations. The level of fertility determines the number of persons feeding into the population pyramid at its base. This cohort moves up through the pyramid with time, the size of the cohorts thus influencing the total age structure. Unless mortality levels are very unstable, they will affect each cohort in turn in a similar fashion leaving the underlying age structure relatively unchanged. Thus:

> ... the most important factor determining the proportion of elderly people in the population has been not the improvement in the capacity to survive to pension age but the changes in the sizes of generations available to survive (Benjamin *et al.*, 1985, p.4).

However, improvements in mortality at older ages can contribute significantly to the ageing of the elderly population itself. The recent increase in the numbers of very old people (85+) has been larger than expected because of unanticipated falls in mortality among the elderly, particularly the very old (Preston, 1984). It is now recognised that changes in mortality at older ages may influence both the size and the structure of the elderly population. Bourgeois-Pichat (1979) has suggested that, if fertility is at or below replacement level, mortality changes can cause population ageing from the apex rather than the base of the pyramid.

Since reductions in mortality alone are not able to bring about the ageing of the population from the base, demographic ageing begins only after mortality has fallen, rapid population growth has been established and the subsequent fertility decline already underway. The ageing process then continues beyond the end of the demographic transition.

> The period of the age transition therefore lags behind the transition in population vital rates and the main engine of ageing is fertility (Warnes, 1982, p.7).

This can be demonstrated using the British case. From Figure 1 it can be seen that the percentage of elderly persons in the population, defined

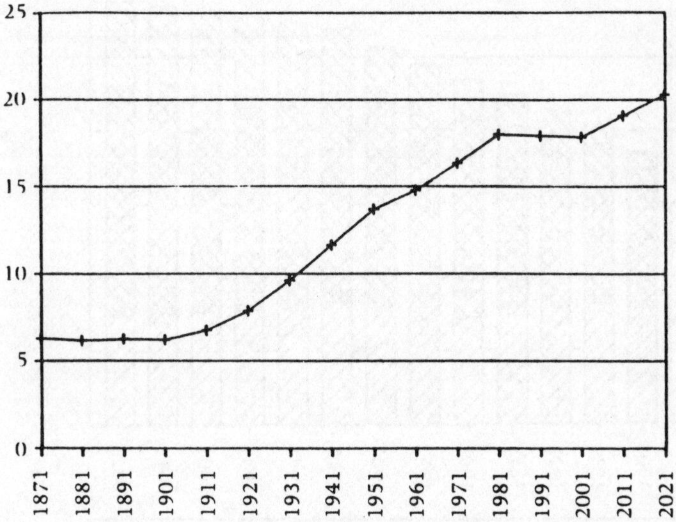

Figure 1. *Percentage of the population of pensionable age: Great Britain 1871–2021 (year 1941 interpolated, years 1991–2021 projected).* +,% 60/65 plus.

here as those of current pensionable age[1], was remarkably stable from 1840 to 1900 at around 6 per cent. It began to increase rapidly from 1911, and only recently has its growth rate begun to slow, the proportion of elderly persons in the population reaching a temporary plateau at 18 per cent this decade. The onset of the fall in mortality levels, however, began in the 1770s and fertility rates declined from the 1870s. The number of elderly people began to rise at a modest rate in the late nineteenth century, but its growth rate did not exceed that of the population in general, leaving the proportion of the elderly in the population unchanged. It was not until 1911 that the number of persons over 60/65 grew at a rate exceeding that of the rest of the population, the peak birth cohorts of mid-Victorian Britain moving into these age groups and 40 years of fertility decline reducing the numbers in the younger age groups. Figure 2a shows the absolute growth in the British population and the changing age structure of that population over time. As well as increasing the size in relative terms, the size of the elderly population has risen in absolute terms by over 300 per cent this century—from 2.2 million in 1901 to 9.7 million in 1981. The rate of increase of the elderly population has fallen off in the last decade, due to the small birth cohorts of World War I and (excepting the post-war baby booms of 1920–21) the inter-war years. However, the ageing of the population has continued with the ageing of the elderly population itself.

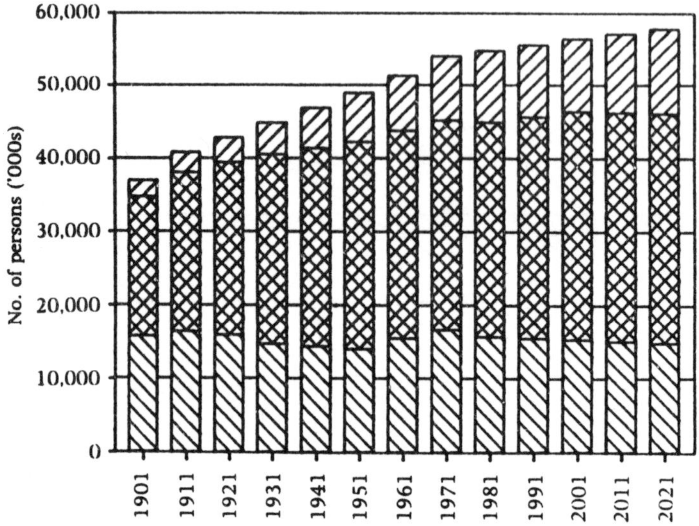

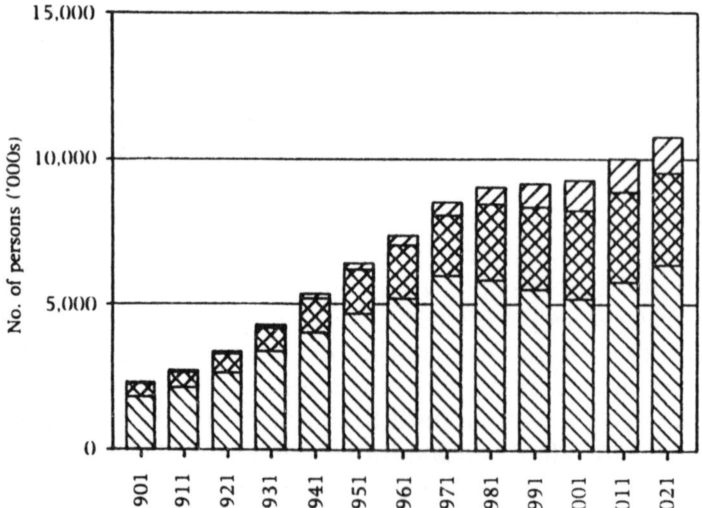

Figure 2*a*. *Age structure of the population: Great Britain 1901–2021 (year 1941 interpolated, years 1991–2021 projected).* ▨, 60/65 plus; ⊠, 20–59/64; ▧, 0–19.

Figure 2*b*. *Age structure of the elderly population: Great Britain 1901–2021 (year 1941 interpolated, years 1991–2021 projected).* ▨, 85 Plus; ⊠, 75–84; ▧, 60/65–74.

Sources for Figures 1, 2*a* and 2*b*. 'Sex and Age Structure Tables' published in the *Census of England and Wales* volumes produced by the Registrar General for the relevant Census years up to 1981; population projections of the gender–age structure of the population using 'OPCS Population Projections 1983–2023, prepared by the Government Actuary in consultation with the Registrars General, Series PP2 No. 13 (1985)'. The projections used were based on medium-level assumptions concerning future fertility and mortality trends.

The elderly population forms a broad age group which has itself changed in composition over time. The effective age range of individuals in statutory retirement is approximately 30–35 years, if the small numbers aged 95 plus are ignored. Because of the wide age span of the elderly population it is useful to divide them into two subgroups, with the 'young-elderly' consisting of those persons aged 60/65 to 74 and the 'old-elderly' of those aged 75 and above. This convention is a recent one, recognising the importance of distinguishing the separate needs and characteristics of the 'young-elderly' and 'old-elderly' due to the heterogeneity of this group as a whole (Taylor and Ford, 1983).

The composition of the elderly group is influenced by trends in births over a long period 60–80 years earlier, and, to a lesser extent, rises in life expectancy due to reductions in subsequent mortality rates at various ages. Figure 2b shows the age structure of the elderly population. From this it is apparent that Britain is currently experiencing a decrease in the number of young-elderly, a trend which will continue in the near future. Between 1981 and 1991 the number of people between ages 60/65 and 74 is expected to fall by 5 per cent. This is a consequence of both the falling number of births throughout the 1920s and 1930s, and the impact of the Second World War and the casualties inflicted on these and earlier birth cohorts. Post-war emigration, largely to the 'Old Commonwealth' countries of Canada and the Antipodes, also served to deplete the numbers in age groups now entering their sixties.[2] The full effect of this 'age trough' is more evident in the projected age distribution of 2001. This trend is not reversed until the survivors of the post World War II baby-boom start to reach their sixties in the 2010s.

In contrast, up until 1905 the number of births rose fairly steadily. With the progressive fall in deaths due to improvements in public health and nutrition in the late nineteenth century, the number of survivors of successive cohorts reaching old age was increasing over time. Those born at the turn of the century are the survivors of the first generation to benefit from the fall in the adolescent death rates in the first half of the century. The birth cohort of 1891–1901, which now accounts for the majority of the very old (85+), was the first in which over half lived to beyond age 65 (Grundy, 1986). Thus the number of those aged 75–84 and 85 plus increased throughout the 1970s and will continue to do so until the survivors of the trough in births during the First World War (partially offset by a peak in 1920) and those of the smaller birth cohorts of the 1920s and 1930s reach these ages.

Accordingly, the rate of increase of the group aged 74–84 will remain appreciable until the 1990s. At present 38.2 per cent of the elderly population are aged over 75 and 6.5 per cent are aged 85 years or more. Official population projections by the Government Actuary's Department (OPCS, 1985) suggest that by the beginning of the next century (2001) these proportions will have increased to 47.2 per cent and 12.1 per cent respectively.[3] The numbers aged 85 and over are expected to rise for the next 35 years (apart from a temporary decline in 15–20 years' time due to the trough of World War I) to account for 13 per cent of all elderly persons. The downward trend of births of the inter-war years will not lead to a downward trend in the population 85 plus until after 2030.

This ageing of the aged population itself has important policy implications for present and future levels of both social and economic dependency. The different age groups that comprise the elderly population exert differential demands on the health and social services, with those aged 85 and over being the most expensive group per capita, and over half of hospital beds now being occupied by those aged over 75. These age related differences in demand must be borne in mind.

It was noted earlier that the increase in the absolute numbers of elderly persons over time has recently become a cause for concern amongst ministers and their advisers. Much of this alarm has stemmed from work which has focused on the changing age structure and its implications for the ratio of 'dependants' to those of working age. So far little work has been done which has examined past trends, and that which has been done has taken at face value the estimates of dependency derived from the use of conventional dependency ratios. In the next section we go on to disaggregate these ratios in order to examine in greater depth the reasons for the apparent increase in dependency.

CHANGING DEPENDENCY RATIOS—A DEMOGRAPHIC OR AN ECONOMIC PHENOMENON?

Population ageing as an 'economic bad'?

On a macro level much of the literature and the debate on the economic consequences of the ageing of the population has centred on the concept of dependency. It is important to stress, however, that the concept is used not in the sense of the 'structural dependency' of the individual as developed in the writings on the political economy of ageing by social theorists such as Townsend and Walker[4], but in terms of the level of overall dependency on the state. It is the economic dependency of the elderly rather than their so-called social or 'structured' dependency that is of concern here.

Historically, both economists and demographers have used the dependency ratio of a population to measure the 'burden' on the economy. The dependency ratio is a measure of how many 'dependent' people there are in an economy. It is calculated as the number in the non-economically active population divided by the size of the economically active population. At the most simplistic level, and indeed the most widely used level, the dependency ratio is calculated as those aged 0–19 and 60/65 plus divided by the population aged 20–59/64. Thus age alone defines whether or not a person is to be treated as dependent or not.

Given this definition, an increase in the herontic (old age) dependency ratio which is calculated as the number of people of pensionable age (comprising the 'non-economically active' population) divided by the population aged 20–59/64 (comprising the 'economically active' population) is a simple demographic consequence of population ageing. As the relative number of aged persons in the population increases so too must the gerontic ratio.

The gerontic ratio has increased steadily during this century, reflecting the continuous ageing of the British population over this period. It has increased from 12 old persons per 100 in the working age ranges[5] in 1901 to 34 in 1981 and this figure is projected to reach 38 by 2021. These trends have given rise to the idea that an ageing population is an 'economic bad', imposing growing welfare burdens on a relatively diminishing working population. While an ageing population is normally accompanied by a decline in the child (neontic) dependency ratio, and the trend in the aggregate ratio may not be favourable, it is generally held that the public and private costs of an elderly person's maintenance are greater than those of a child. It is argued that the elderly have superior housing and income expectations and require more frequent medical services and thus the overall level of dependency increases.[6] Furthermore there is also the added dimension that expenditure on children is also investment in future human capital whilst expenditure on the aged is not.

These negative attitudes to population ageing are fairly recent. There was some recognition of the problem of population ageing prior to World War II. However, it was the effect of falling fertility and the decline in the rate of population growth, rather than the effect of the changing age structure, which dominated the debate. In the late 1940s attention was drawn to the dangers of an ageing population with the publication of the report of the Royal Commission on Population (1949). This suggested that an ageing population, with the concomitant decline in the proportion of young people, might become 'dangerously unprogressive, falling behind other communities in technical efficiency and economic welfare' (p.121). The early 1950s were also characterised by a growing alarm at the prospective cost of pensions, an alarm reflected in the recommendations of the Phillips Committee in 1954 (Cmnd 933).

These concerns have returned once more to the forefront of political debate in Britain with increasing apprehension as to the future cost of pensions. Projections of the ratio of national insurance contributors to pensioners show that this ratio will fall from 2.3 in 1985 to 2.2 in 2001 and 1.8 in 2025 (DHSS, 1984). In the Fowler Green Paper (Cmnd 9517, 1985; Cmnd 9518, 1985) these figures were used to argue that the economy would have been unable to support future pension payments under the system which then existed.

Nonetheless, it is not necessarily the case that a change in the age profile of a society leads to a greater (or lesser) burden of dependency. Demographic factors alone do not determine the ratio of workers and non-workers, and demographic ratios such as the simple age determined dependency ratios are unsatisfactory measures of the dependency burden within a society. Given the change in the structure of the labour market and the shifts in labour force participation that have taken place over the past two or three decades, it is necessary to rethink age based dependency ratios. With changing trends in the employment of women, and the rise of the spectre of unemployment, the validity of distinguishing between 'worker' and 'dependent' on the grounds of gender and age are increasingly questionable. The remainder of this section is concerned with recalculating the traditional age based dependency ratio to take account of differential labour force participation rates.

Dependency ratios re-examined

In Figure 3 the simple age dependency ratio is shown as RATIO A. This is the population under age 20 and over age 60/65 divided by the 'working population', that is, those aged 20–59/64. In this ratio economic activity status is defined in terms of age alone; this is unsatisfactory in that it ignores differences in economic activity rates. Therefore, the dependency ratio was recalculated using economic activity rates for five year age groups for the entire population drawn from census data. Age groups, by gender, were multiplied by their economic activity rate and summed to give the economically active population. These rates are given in the Appendix, Table 1. The results are illustrated in Figure 3 as RATIO B. This is the age–gender dependency ratio weighted for participation in the labour market. As can be seen it gives a higher level of ratio dependency than before, primarily due to the high level of non-activity of women in the middle age range.

Finally, unemployment was also taken into account giving rise to

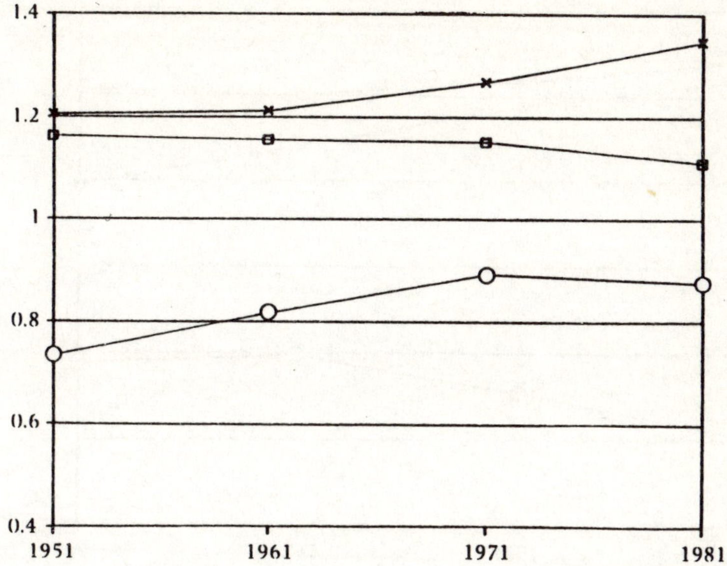

Figure 3. *Dependency ratios: All.* ⊖, ratio A; ⊟, ratio B; ×, ratio C.

RATIO C. People given as economically active in the census data are not necessarily in employment but rather are defined as available for work. However, those persons who are temporarily out of the labour force through sickness or unemployment are to a greater or lesser degree dependent on the state and so should be included in the numerator rather than the denominator of a 'dependency' ratio. Economically active here is now taken to mean in either full or part time employment. The age–sex specific economic activity rates used in calculating ratio C are given in the Appendix, Table 2. The difference between ratios B and C is purely that due to unemployment and temporary sickness leave.

It can be seen, then, that dependency levels are underestimated when calculated solely on an age basis. Nonetheless, it is necessary to disaggregate the dependency ratios by gender, in view of the very different labour market experiences of men and women over the post war period. Figures 4a and 4b show, respectively, the number of females and males dependent on the total 'working' population—the sum of the gender specific rates being equal to those shown in Figure 3. The ratios for women were much higher than for men in all cases. The effect of increasing female labour-force participation is evident in the downward slopes of both ratios B and C in Figure 4a, although its impact is offset in ratio C by rising unemployment, especially during the 1970s. Likewise, the impact of increasing levels of male unemployment on the level of total

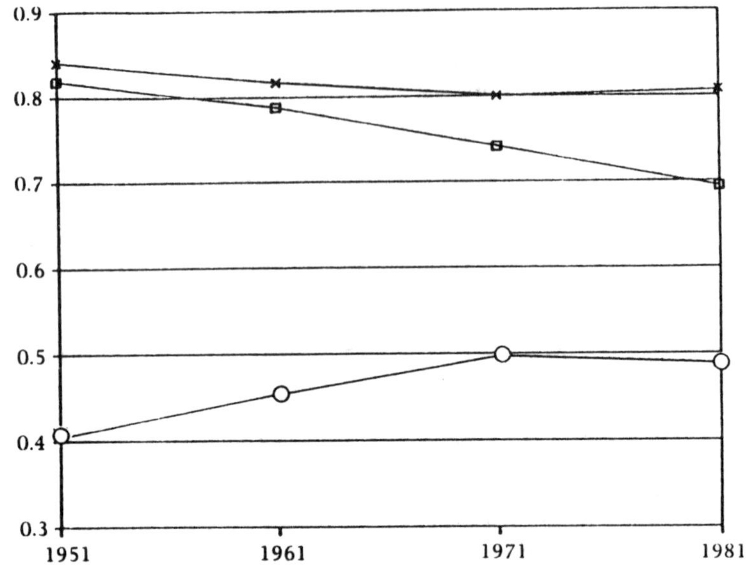

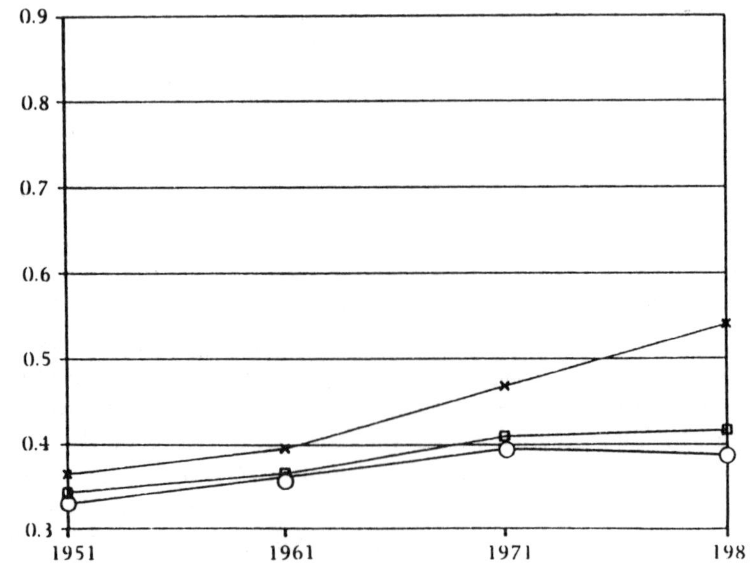

Figure 4*a*. *Dependency ratios: Females.* ⊖, Ratio A; ⊟, ratio B; ×, ratio C.
Figure 4*b*. *Dependency ratios: Males.* ⊖, Ratio A; ⊟, ratio B; ×, ratio C.

dependency is clearly visible in the sharp upward trend of ratio C in Figure 4b.

The overwhelming reason for the high rates of female dependency is that a large proportion of women are not active in the formal labour market and are therefore counted as economically inactive. The validity of including in the dependent population all 'economically inactive' women aged 20–59 is open to question. Prior to 1881 the Census of England and Wales included women's household chores in the category of productive work. In 1881, however, housewives were classified as 'unoccupied', the rationale being that many women would otherwise be counted twice—once as a housewife and again as engaged in a specific occupation (Lewis, 1984). Since the late nineteenth century women's work in the home has not been considered of economic value despite the fact that it frees their partners from laborious household tasks and in many cases also relieves the state from looking after an old, young or disabled person who would otherwise have been its responsibility.

It can be argued that in these instances women, by being economically inactive, decrease overall dependency on the state rather than increase it. Thus, whereas the traditional age based dependency ratio may underestimate the true level of dependency, calculations on a more sophisticated basis may in fact over-estimate dependency if they take all women not engaged in formal labour market activities as dependent. Falkingham (1987) recalculated the dependency ratio in an attempt to take account of the true economic contribution of women. To avoid counting all women who are not in the labour force as dependent (that is, in the numerator) an assumption based on data from the Women and Employment Survey (Martin and Roberts, 1984) and the 1981 General Household Survey (OPCS, 1983) was made that 50 per cent of these women were engaged in productive work, including looking after children and aged relatives. After adjustment ratio C was found to be of the magnitude of 1.1 in 1981.

However, this redefinition itself raises problems. If the dependency ratio is constructed with the aim of examining the problem of financing state transfer payments it has been argued that the numerator should only include those who are expected to be eligible beneficiaries of government schemes (Creedy and Disney, 1988). Furthermore, the denominator for women includes all part time workers and it may be preferable to produce a measure of 'full-time equivalent' persons in this instance.

A further note of caution is necessary in interpreting the figures presented. All of the above ratios weight all members of the population equally, whereas the average social costs of a 'dependent' school-child differ from those of an unemployed person and these differ in turn from those of a pensioner. Moreover, there is only limited homogeneity within these groups. Therefore one cannot ignore the effects of age structure within our society, although it is questionable which is the best means of weighting for the dependency costs of different segments of the population.

One final point is that, as with women, non-participation in paid employment by the elderly does not necessarily imply 'dependency'. Many elderly people are active in the informal labour market and in voluntary work as well as in making important contributions within the family and the wider community.

Despite these deficiencies the above ratios show that changes in the labour market potentially have a strong effect on the level of dependency. It is appropriate, then, to attribute rising dependency ratios to the phenomenon of the ageing population and to treat ageing as an economic bad which increases dependency independently of other economic forces? The level of labour force participation of different groups of the population and the rate of unemployment also affect dependency. The next section uses a decomposition analysis to examine the relative importance of economic and demographic factors.

What's driving dependency?

Taking the most sophisticated ratio, C, as the original non-adjusted rate, an attempt was made to disaggregate it to ascertain what was the driving force behind its change over time—labour market forces or changes in age structure. Earlier in the century a sizeable proportion of those beyond current retirement age continued to work in paid occupations. Activity rates of those aged 60/65 plus have decreased over time. In 1881 nearly three-quarters of all men aged over 65 were classified as economically active. This figure had fallen to just under 50 per cent by 1931 and by 1961 only a quarter of elderly males were still in the paid labour force (Johnson, 1985). In 1981 only 10 per cent of men aged 65 and over and 8 per cent of women aged 60 and over were still in paid employment (OPCS, 1984). The social and economic factors that have reduced these rates might be expected to have had as much influence on dependency ratios as the growth in the size of the elderly population itself. Given the numerous other drastic changes that the labour market has experienced over recent years we expected to find that this would be the major mover in any changes in dependency. Thus the hypothesis was that economic forces would exercise a greater influence than demographic trends over the dependency ratios.

To disaggregate the trend over time of the 'employed participation

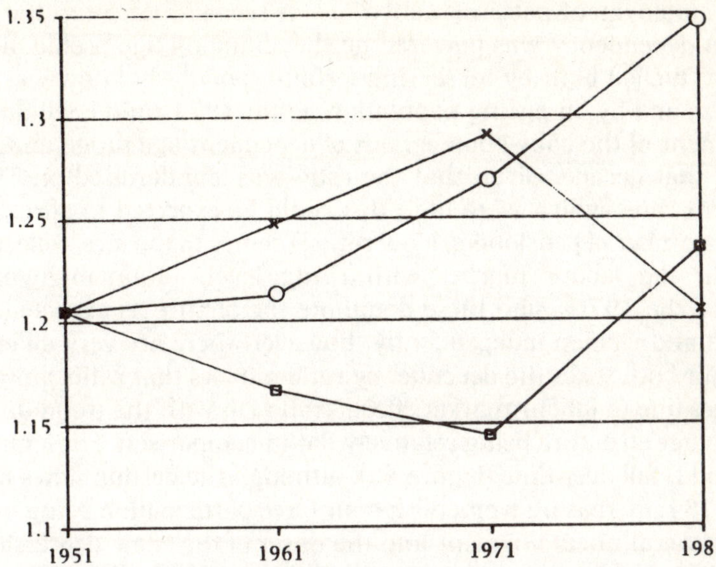

Figure 5. *Standardised ratios: All.* ⊖, Ratio C; ⊟, ratio D; ×, ratio E.

weighted' dependency ratio into that part due to changes in the age structure of the population, and that part due to changes in the labour market, it was necessary to standardise the ratio in order to net out the other effects in turn. The dependency ratio C can be written as

$$\text{Dep} = \frac{\Sigma P_x - \Sigma P_x . E_x}{\Sigma P_x . E_x}$$

where P_x is the size of the population in age group x, and E_x is the real economic activity rate (taking into account sickness and unemployment) of the population age group x. By keeping either of the component parts constant over time it is possible to see the effect on the ratio of the change in the component allowed to vary. Firstly, the ratio was standardised over time on the 1951 age structure, keeping P_x constant. Ratio D in Figure 5 thus shows the influence of changing labour force participation (changing E_x), on the dependency ratio. Then the ratio was standardised on 1951 economic activity rates with E_x constant and P_x allowed to vary. Therefore ratio E shows the effect of changing age structure over time on the total dependency rate.

For the total population the results, as shown in Figure 5, were not as clear-cut as expected. From 1951 to 1971 the dependency ratio, C, followed the same trend as ratio E: that is, the ratio with the effect of changing employment patterns netted out. It seems, therefore, that the increase in dependency was powered by the changing age profile of the population, fuelled both by increasing fertility (popularly known as the Baby Boom) and by an ageing population. From 1971 ratio E fell due to the movement of the baby boomers out of dependent age range and low fertility in that decade. Given that the ratio was standardised on 1951 employment rates which were high this could be expected to offset any rise in the number of pensioners. Now ratio D comes to the fore, reflecting changes in the labour market with rising levels of unemployment throughout the 1970s, and these dominate the picture as expected.

For men and women independently, however, there are very different pictures. For both sexes the dependency ratio mirrors that ratio showing the changes due to labour market effects (ratio D), with the trend due to changes in age structure being relatively flat in comparison. For females, ratios C and D fall over time (Figure 6a), although the decline slows from 1971 to 1981, increasing women's labour force participation being offset by rising general unemployment and the onset of the 'new depression'. The strength of labour market effects is highlighted by the fact that after 1971 ratio C rose slightly (still following the trend of ratio D) despite falling dependency levels due to changes in age structure reflected by ratio E. Meanwhile, the ratios for men are rising (Figure 6b), primarily due to increasing levels of employment. Again ratio C mirrors the trend of ratio D, labour market effects being strong enough to outweigh the predicted downturn in dependency levels from 1971 onwards due to a more favourable age structure.

The combination of male and female pictures in Figure 5 is therefore confusing as it is made up of two conflicting gender trends in dependency levels. Taking men and women separately it has been found that changes in the labour market are more important in influencing dependency than demographic trends, although in the aggregate the demographic variations were more important before 1971. This finding comes as no surprise in view of the changes in aggregate economic activity over the period. However, it does serve to remind us of the importance of economic movements, and of the sensitivity of the dependency ratio to them.

In contrast, the Green Paper on social security (Cmnd 9517, Cmnd 9518, 1983) based its proposals for the reform of SERPS on the ratio of national insurance contributors to pensioners. However, the projections used by the government took no account of changing rates of labour force participation over time, while unemployment was assumed to remain at a constant rate of 6 per cent. It is felt that those assumptions

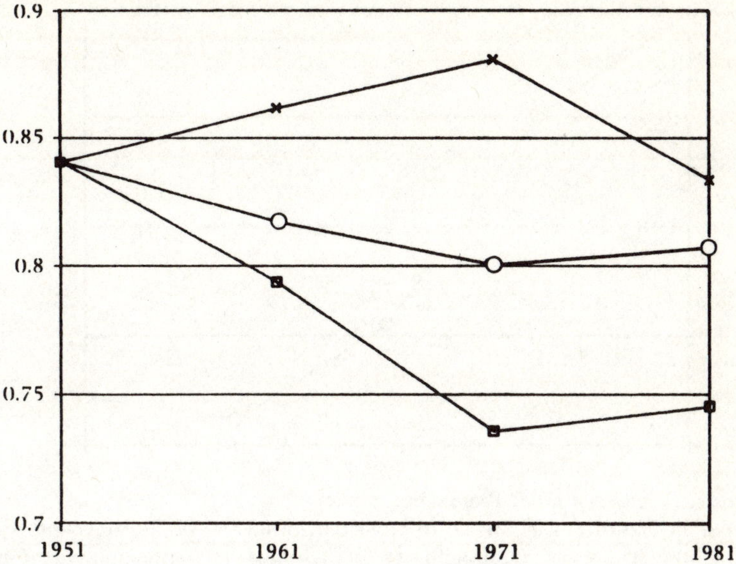

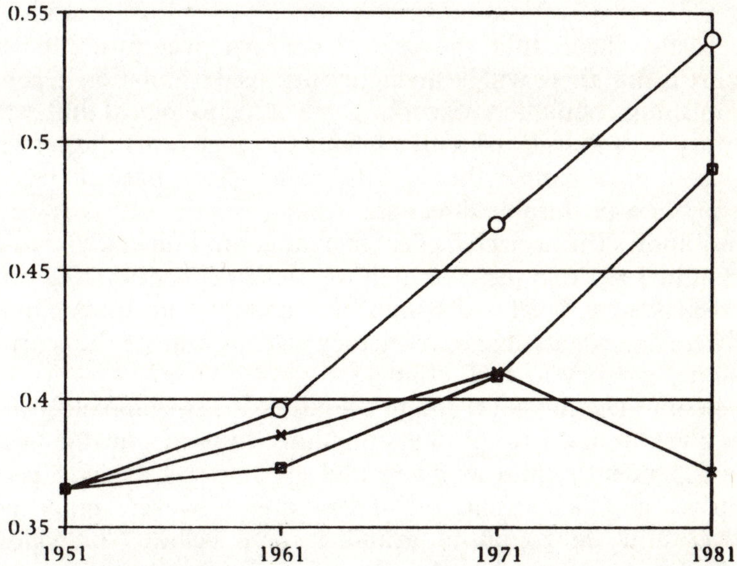

Figure 6*a*. *Standardised ratios: Females.* ⊖, Ratio C; ⊟, ratio D; ×, ratio E.
Figure 6*b*. *Standardised ratios: Males.* ⊖, Ratio C; ⊟, ratio D; ×, ratio E.
Sources for Figures 3–6*b*. 'Sex and Age Structure Tables' and 'Economic Activity Tables' or 'Occupational Tables' from the Census volumes 1951–1981.

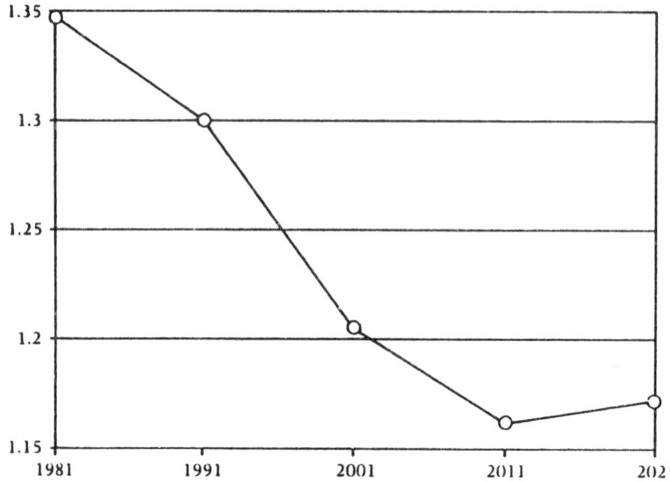

Figure 7. *Dependency ratio: Projection.*
Sources for Figure 7. Age Structure projections from the OPCS Projection (*op. cit.*); economic activity rates adjusted for assumed 10% unemployment in 1991, 5% in 2001 and 2% in 2021.

are unrealistic. Given that the central concern over future pensions expenditure is that there will be an increasing aged population dependent on a diminishing population of working age, it seems logical that into the next century we will be faced with a labour shortage or, at the very least, falling rates of unemployment. This will affect overall levels of dependency in a favourable direction.

Figure 7 shows the projected effect of changes in unemployment from 10 per cent in 1991 to 5 per cent in 2001 and 2 per cent in 2021 on the overall dependency level. Although the changes in unemployment depicted here are essentially arbitrary they do demonstrate the sensitivity of overall dependency to such changes.

Thus, in our view the government's analysis was incomplete as it was based on a very narrow range of assumptions. In particular the analysis took the dependency ratio as given and did not look beyond pension reduction as a possible solution. There are, however, other policy alternatives and we go on to examine these below. The following discussion does not aim to be exhaustive, but merely to point out certain potential policy options that we feel have been relatively ignored in the debate so far.

Alternative policy options

There are three possible approaches to the pension problem in the face of a decline in the population of working age: (1) reducing benefits (thereby reducing the demand of pensioners); (2) increasing contributions (thereby reducing the demand of workers); and (3) increasing output sufficiently to meet the demands of both workers and pensioners. Most analysis to date has concentrated on (1), that is, pension reduction, as also has government policy as set out in the White Paper (Cmnd 9691, 1985) and implemented in the 1986 Act. This question can, however, be addressed from an alternative viewpoint, focusing directly on the determinants of output, namely the size of the working population and labour productivity.

The above results suggest that the pensions problem is amenable to alternative policy intervention. The sensitivity of the dependency ratio to changes in rates of labour force participation and unemployment has been demonstrated. Given this, a variety of policies exist to prevent the (recalculated) dependency ratio from rising, counteracting wholly or in part the effect of changing age structure. These include: (a) reducing unemployment; (b) increasing female labour force participation; and (c) importing labour, for example, immigration and 'guestworkers', all of which would increase the denominator in the redefined dependency ratio. Additionally it is possible (d) to increase the age of retirement. This last policy would simultaneously increase the denominator and reduce the numerator. Furthermore, if later retirement involved no entitlement to a larger pension, then (d) would also lead to an implicit reduction in benefits by reducing the duration of retirement.

As yet these alternative avenues have received little attention in the policy debate. It is beyond the scope of this paper to address the multiplicity of ethical questions that a policy of encouraging 'guestworkers' would raise, but some of the difficulties implicit in implementing the other policies merit further, albeit brief, comment. It is open to question what impact each of them would have, or indeed how feasible they are as policy options. Certainly a reduction of unemployment is both desirable and possible in the future. The other options, however, are more ambiguous.

With the increase in the elderly population pensioners now constitute a large, and growing, proportion of the electorate. This increase in political power may make untenable such policies as raising the age of retirement or reducing benefits. Furthermore, the present trend is towards earlier rather than later retirement; and as trade unions, employers and workers all co-operate on this, it will be a difficult trend to reverse (Laczko *et al.*, 1988). It is not clear what policy instruments could be used to implement an increase in the age of retirement. Even if statutory retirement age was increased by law, its impact on the size of the workforce would be tempered as people could 'voluntarily' remove themselves from the market earlier, either through disability pensions—as is happening in France (Guillemard, 1988)—or through private pension schemes. However, this avenue is already being explored in the US where the age of retirement has been raised to 67 and a further rise to age 70 is being considered.

Another potential avenue is an increase in female labour force participation. However, it is questionable how much further participation rates will and can increase. Heather Joshi's work (1986) demonstrates that lifetime participation rates for women are now as high as those for men in the younger age cohorts, excluding 4–5 years out of the labour market for child bearing. An increase in female labour force participation in the absence of a coherent child care policy will be difficult.

Children are not the only group for which provision for care is necessary. The elderly themselves, with a rising number of frail elderly, exert increasing demands on the caring capacities both of the state and of individuals. Care of the elderly is provided primarily within the family (Family Policy Studies Centre, 1984). Therefore, a policy of increased female labour force participation may conflict with the government's increasing emphasis on community care. Although of immediate and pressing concern, the pension debate is only one implication of an ageing population. There are two sides to the 'cost of an ageing population' coin: income support and care. If a coherent approach to the problem of population ageing is to be found then economists must not ignore 'tails', just as those concerned with social policy cannot ignore 'heads'.

CONCLUSION

We have illustrated that changing economic activity rates (particularly those of women), together with changing levels of unemployment, have had a significant effect on overall levels of dependency. Furthermore, dependency levels have been generally underestimated when calculated solely on an age basis. If economic activity—excluding unemployment—is taken into account, some people previously defined as dependent on age criteria now fall into the non-dependent category, this is far outweighed by transfers in the reverse direction. However, calculations on this more sophisticated basis may now in fact overestimate the level of dependency if they take all women of conventional working ages (20–59) who are not engaged in formal labour market activities as dependent. Earlier work (Falkingham, 1987) has attempted to compensate for this and found overall dependency rates of approximately 1.1 dependent person to 1 non-dependent person in 1981, compared to 0.85 in 1951.

These factors have received scant attention in the debate concerning the demographic crisis facing the welfare state, and in particular the discussion over future levels of old age dependency and pension expenditure. The Green and White Papers based their proposals for the reform of SERPS on the ratio of national insurance contributors to pensioners. Although projected levels of dependency will rise due to the increase in the number of elderly people, and an increase in the number of these holding pension entitlements, it is likely that these levels have been overestimated.

The fallacy of the approach in the Green and White Papers is that it took the dependency ratio as given and viewed levels of pensioner dependency in isolation from the rest of the economy. However, pensioner dependency is only a fraction of total dependency and viewing society as a whole the outlook is less pessimistic than predicted. It has been demonstrated that the overall level of dependency is at present higher than has been recognised. So far this level has been accommodated without bringing the economy to crisis point. If we are able to cope with such high levels of total dependency now, it is reasonable to speculate that the economy will continue to do so. Furthermore, dependency ratios in the future may not be comparable with those of today as technological advances continue to decrease the number of workers needed to produce goods and services. Thus levels of consumption may well be sustainable and the burden of the elderly 'baby boom' lighter than expected.

This is not to say that we should be complacent over future dependency levels, but rather that the degree of scaremongering over the ageing of the population that has been prevalent in the last few years has been unfounded. In fact, a breathing space exists with respect to increasing age dependency until c.2020. Current and short-future problems regarding dependency levels are likely to relate to the state of the economy rather than to age pyramids.

Given the dual role of economic and demographic forces in influencing dependency, policy concerned with retirement provision has had, to date, a surprisingly narrow focus. It has concentrated almost entirely on pension reduction. However, if the problem is addressed from a different angle, namely that of output, alternative options present themselves which have been relatively ignored in the debate to date. Several policy options are available to government to deal with increasing economic dependency apart from tinkering with pensions. Policies such as intervention in the labour market, via the adjustment of labour force participation rates through increased female participation and raising the age of retirement, have yet to be fully explored. They may seem politically infeasible in a period of high employment but we should not wait for labour shortage before we begin to evaluate them as realistic policy options for the future.

However, in discussing policies to maintain the level of dependency we should also be careful not to overlook another aspect of the ageing population—namely, the cost of caring for the population. Increased female labour force participation may have a trade-off effect in decreasing the pool of 'informal carers' and increasing the cost of formal care to the state. At present the government is pursuing a policy of promoting 'community care'—care in and by the community. It may be the case that policies proposed to deal with one side of the cost equation will necessarily clash with those to deal with the other. We will need a coherent approach to deal with both if we are to avoid women being the losers in the 'ageing game', faced with the triple burden of work, housewife and mother, and carer.

NOTES

1 Current pensionable age is 60 plus for women and 65 plus for men. However this has not always been the case. Pensionable age for both sexes was established at 70 by the 1908 Old Age Pensions Act, and it was only from 1925 through the Contributory Pensions Act that the male pensionable age was reduced to its present level. A pensionable age of 60 for women was effected in 1940 by the Old Age and Widows' Pension Act (1940).
2 This was to some extent offset by immigration in the late 1950s and 1960s. However, the majority of these immigrants were only in their 20s and early 30s on arrival and so form part of the next age cohort, entering the elderly population at the end of this decade.
3 It needs to be emphasised that any population projection is subject to uncertainty due to the necessary assumptions about future fertility and mortality trends that have to be made. Comparisons between new and preceding projections 'should be made with care, both as regards the total population and specific age groups within due to their discontinuity' (OPCS, 1985). The effect of various changes in assumptions from 1979 to 1983 has been to increase the projected number of persons of pensionable age in 2011 by 800,000 (that is, by 9 per cent). A reduction of 25 per cent in mortality rates for ages over 65 is assumed in the 40 year period up to 2021. This is a larger reduction than assumed in previous projections and has 'regard to the lower levels of mortality achieved at those ages in a number of other countries'.
4 Apart from an interest in SERPS and its impact on future tax burdens, economists have largely ignored the issues of the elderly and of ageing. It has been left to social policy analysts to deal with economic questions. Writers such as Peter Townsend, Alan Walker and Chris Phillipson perceive these questions as having an explicitly political nature. They argue that the dependent status of the elderly has been deliberately structured by the state and society. The state is seen as being the major determinant of the economic status of the elderly and as such has promoted the marginalisation of the elderly. At present this concept of structured dependency is a matter of controversy, but this debate need not concern us here.
5 In our calculations the 'working age ranges' were taken to be 20–64 inclusive for men and

20–59 inclusive for women. Although these ranges were felt to be applicable to the present day, when the majority of young persons aged 16–19 are either in full time education or on 'Youth Training Schemes', they become more unrealistic as one moves back through time. At the beginning of this century it was common for the majority of children to leave school and enter full time employment at the age of 12. Furthermore, a significant number of persons aged over 65 continued to work. Thus any comparison of dependency rates over time must take these factors into account. This is a further indication of the inadequacies of simple age based dependency ratios.

6 As early as 1954 Parish and Peacock calculated that twice as much was spent by the five major social services per capita on pensioners as on children and three and a half as much as on the active population. However, as Thane (1986) points out, their calculations were based on a series of fairly pessimistic demographic assumptions. Decreasing child dependency does provide some latitude for redeployment of resources towards the elderly.

REFERENCES

B. Benjamin *et al.* (1985), *Pensions, the Problems of Today and Tomorrow*, City University, London.

J. Bourgeois-Pichat (1979), 'La transition demographique', in *Population Science in the Service of Mankind*, IUSSP, Liege.

Census of Population for England and Wales (1911, 1921, 1931, 1951, 1961, 1971, 1981), HMSO, London.

Cmd 7695 (1949), *Final Report*, HMSO, London.

Cmd 933 (1954), *Report of the Committee on the Economic and Financial Problems of the Provision for Old Age*, HMSO, London.

Cmnd 9517 (1985), *Reform of Social Security*, HMSO, London.

Cmnd 9518 (1985), *Reform of Social Security: Programme for Change*, HMSO, London.

Cmnd 9691 (1985), *Reform of Social Security: Programme for Action*, HMSO, London.

J. Creedy and R. Disney (1988), *Population Aging and Social Security*, Research Paper No. 195, University of Melbourne.

Department of Health and Social Security (1984), *Population, Pension Costs and Pensioners' Incomes*, HMSO, London.

J. Falkingham (1987), *Britain's Ageing Population: the Engine Behind Increasing Dependency?*, Welfare State Programme Discussion Paper No. 17, London School of Economics.

Family Policy Studies Centre (1984), *The Forgotten Army: Family Care and Elderly People*, Briefing Paper, London.

E. Grundy (1986), *Age Related Change in Later Life*, Prepared for the BSPS Conference, September 10–12 1985, University of East Anglia.

A-M. Guillemard (1988), 'The International Trend Towards Early Withdrawal from the Workforce', presented at CEPR Conference on 'Work, Retirement and Intergenerational Equity, 1850–2050', 19–21 July 1988, St. John's College, Cambridge.

P. Johnson (1985), *The Economics of Old Age in Britain: A Long Run View 1881–1981*, Centre for Economic Policy Research Discussion Paper No. 47, London.

H. Joshi (1986), 'Participation in Paid Work: Evidence from the Women and Employment Survey', in R. Blundell and I. Walker (eds), *Unemployment, Search and Labour Supply*, Cambridge University Press, Cambridge.

F. Laczko, A. Dale, S. Arber and G. Gilbert (1988), 'Early retirement in a period of unemployment', *Journal of Social Policy*, 17:3, 313–334.

J. Lewis (1984), *Women in England 1870–1950*, Wheatsheaf Books, Brighton.

J. Martin and C. Roberts (1984), *Women and Employment: A Lifetime Perspective*, HMSO, London.

OPCS (1983), *General Household Survey 1981*, HMSO, London.

OPCS (1984), *Census Guide 1: Britain's Elderly Population*, HMSO, London.

OPCS (1985), *OPCS Population Projections 1983–2023 Prepared by the Government Actuary in Consultation with the Registrar General*, Series PP2 No. 13, HMSO, London.

S. Preston (1984), 'Children and the elderly: divergent paths for America's dependents', *Demography*, 21, 435–457.

R. Taylor and G. Ford (1983), 'Inequalities in old age: an examination of age, sex and class differences in a sample of community elderly', *Ageing and Society*, 3:2, 183–208.
P. Thane (1987), Address to CEPR/BSPS Lunchtime Meeting Series, Chatham House, 23.2.87, London.
A. Warnes (1982), *Geographical Perspectives on Ageing*, John Wiley and Son Ltd, London.

APPENDIX

TABLE 1. *Economic activity rates for men and women, Great Britain 1951, 1961, 1971, 1981*

	Men				Women			
Age group	*1951*	*1961*	*1971*	*1981*	*1951*	*1961*	*1971*	*1981*
15–19	83.9	74.4	60.9	51.2	78.4	70.4	55.9	48.8
20–24	95.3	93.3	89.9	89.1	65.5	62.6	60.1	69.3
25–29	98.1	97.8	97.0	96.5	37.1	39.9	43.0	55.3
30–34	98.1	98.7	98.0	95.4	37.1	37.1	45.1	53.5
35–39	98.7	98.8	98.3	97.9	34.4	43.0	54.4	62.6
40–44	98.7	98.8	98.3	97.8	34.4	43.0	60.3	68.6
45–49	97.9	98.6	98.0	97.8	34.0	43.8	62.0	68.5
50–54	97.9	98.6	97.2	95.7	34.0	43.8	59.1	63.5
55–59	95.4	97.1	95.3	91.5	27.7	37.2	51.1	52.0
60–64	87.8	90.9	86.6	74.6	14.4	20.5	28.2	22.5
65–69	48.7	39.7	30.1	17.0	9.0	10.4	12.9	7.5
70 plus	20.9	12.5	11.0	6.9	3.2	2.6	3.1	2.0

TABLE 2. *Employment rates for men and women, Great Britain 1951, 1961, 1971, 1981*

	Men				Women			
Age group	*1951*	*1961*	*1971*	*1981*	*1951*	*1961*	*1971*	*1981*
15–19	82.3	72.5	55.4	41.3	76.9	68.6	51.9	36.9
20–24	93.8	91.1	84.3	74.4	64.4	60.9	57.1	61.3
25–29	96.7	95.9	92.3	85.0	36.4	38.9	40.8	50.4
30–34	96.7	96.8	93.5	86.4	36.4	36.3	42.8	50.2
35–39	97.2	96.8	94.2	89.5	33.9	42.3	52.1	59.6
40–44	97.2	96.8	94.2	89.2	33.9	42.3	58.0	65.6
45–49	95.7	96.1	93.9	88.9	33.5	42.8	59.5	65.5
50–54	95.7	96.1	93.1	87.2	33.5	42.8	56.5	60.4
55–59	92.0	93.2	90.3	81.9	26.9	35.8	48.5	49.2
60–64	83.1	84.1	78.1	62.8	14.2	20.1	27.1	22.1
65–69	47.9	38.9	29.7	16.7	8.8	10.2	12.3	7.4
70 plus	20.5	12.3	10.7	6.7	3.1	2.5	2.8	1.9

Sources:
1951 Census of England and Wales Occupation Tables, Census of Scotland Volume 4.
1961 Census of Great Britain Occupation Tables.
1971 Census of Great Britain Economic Activity Tables.
1981 Census of Great Britain Economic Activity Tables.

Part III
Ageing and Social Insurance

[16]

THE JOURNAL OF
POLITICAL ECONOMY

Volume LXVI DECEMBER 1958 Number 6

AN EXACT CONSUMPTION-LOAN MODEL OF INTEREST WITH OR WITHOUT THE SOCIAL CONTRIVANCE OF MONEY*

PAUL A. SAMUELSON
Massachusetts Institute of Technology

MY FIRST published paper[1] has come of age, and at a time when the subjects it dealt with have come back into fashion. It developed the equilibrium conditions for a rational consumer's lifetime consumption-saving pattern, a problem more recently given by Harrod the useful name of "hump saving" but which Landry, Böhm-Bawerk, Fisher, and others had touched on long before my time.[2] It dealt only with a single individual and did not discuss the mutual determination by all individuals of the market interest rates which each man had to accept parametrically as given to him.

Now I should like to give a complete general equilibrium solution to the determination of the time-shape of interest rates. This sounds easy, but actually it is very hard, so hard that I shall have to make drastic simplifications in order to arrive at exact results. For while Böhm and Fisher have given us the essential insights into the pure theory of interest, neither they nor other writers seem to have grappled with the following tough problem: in order to define an equilibrium path of interest in a perfect capital market endowed with *perfect certainty*, you have to determine *all* interest rates between now and the end of time; every finite time period points beyond itself!

Some interesting mathematical boundary problems, a little like those in the modern theories of dynamic programming, result from this analysis. And the way is paved for a rigorous attack on a simple model involving money as a store of value and a medium of exchange. My essay concludes with some provocative

* Research aid from the Ford Foundation is gratefully acknowledged.

[1] "A Note on Measurement of Utility," *Review of Economic Studies*, IV (1937), 155–61.

[2] As an undergraduate student of Paul Douglas at Chicago, I was struck by the fact that we might, from the marginal utility schedule of consumptions, deduce saving behavior exactly in the same way that we might deduce gambling behavior. Realizing that, watching the consumer's gambling responses to varying odds, we could deduce his numerical marginal utilities, it occurred to me that, by watching the consumer's saving responses to varying interest rates, we might similarly measure his marginal utilities, and thus the paper was born. (I knew and pointed out, p. 155, n. 2; p. 160, that such a cardinal measurement of utility hinged on a certain refutable "independence" hypothesis.)

remarks about the field of social collusions, a subject of vital importance for political economy and of great analytical interest to the modern theorist.

THE PROBLEM STATED

Let us assume that men enter the labor market at about the age of twenty. They work for forty-five years or so and then live for fifteen years in retirement. (As children they are part of their parents' consumptions, and we take no note of them.) Naturally, they want to consume in their old age, and, in the absence of comprehensive social security—an institution which has important bearing on interest rates and saving—men will want to consume less than they produce during their working years so that they can consume something in the years when they produce nothing.

If there were only Robinson Crusoe, he would hope to put by some durable goods which could be drawn on in his old age. He would, so to speak, want to trade with Mother Nature current consumption goods in return for future consumption goods. And if goods kept perfectly, he could at worst always make the trade through time on a one-to-one basis, and we could say that the interest rate was zero ($i = 0$). If goods kept imperfectly, like ice or radium, Crusoe might have to face a negative real interest rate, $i < 0$. If goods were like rabbits or yeast, reproducing without supervision at compound interest, he would face a positive rate of interest, $i > 0$. This last case is usually considered to be technologically the most realistic one: that is, machines and round-about processes (rather than rabbits) are considered to have a "net productivity," and this is taken to be brute fact. (Böhm himself, after bitterly criticizing naïve productivity theorists and criticizing Thünen and others for assuming such a fact, ends up with his own celebrated third cause for interest, which also asserts the fact of net productivity. Contrary to much methodological discussion, there is nothing circular about assuming brute facts—that is all we can do; we certainly cannot deduce them, although, admittedly, we can hope by experience to refute falsely alleged facts.)

For the present purpose, I shall make the extreme assumption that nothing will keep at all. Thus no intertemporal trade with Nature is possible (that is, for all such exchanges we would have $i = -1$!). If Crusoe were alone, he would obviously die at the beginning of his retirement years.

But we live in a world where new generations are always coming along. Formerly we used to support our parents in their old age. That is now out of fashion. But cannot men during their productive years give up some of their product to bribe other men to support them in their retirement years? Thus, forty-year-old A gives some of his product to twenty-year-old B, so that when A gets to be seventy-five he can receive some of the product that B is then producing.

Our problem, then, is this: In a stationary population (or, alternatively, one growing in any prescribed fashion) what will be the intertemporal terms of trade or interest rates that will spring up spontaneously in ideally competitive markets?

SIMPLIFYING ASSUMPTIONS

To make progress, let us make convenient assumptions. Break each life up into thirds: men produce one unit of product in period 1 and one unit in period 2; in period 3 they retire and produce nothing. (No one dies in midstream.)

In specifying consumption preferences,

I suppose that each man's tastes can be summarized by an ordinal utility function of the consumptions of the three periods of his life: $U = U(C_1, C_2, C_3)$. This is the same in every generation and has the usual regular indifference-curve concavities, but for much of the argument nothing is said about whether, subjectively, men systematically discount future consumptions or satisfactions. (Thus Böhm's second cause of interest may or may not be operative; it could even be reversed, men being supposed to overvalue the future!)

In addition to ignoring Böhm's second cause of systematic time preference, I am in a sense also denying or reversing his first cause of interest, in that we are *not* supposing that society is getting more prosperous as time passes or that any single man can expect to be more prosperous at a later date in his life, since, on the contrary, during his years of retirement he must look forward to producing even less than during his working years.

Finally, recall our assumption that no goods keep, no trade with Nature being possible, and hence Böhm's third technological cause of interest is being denied.

Under these assumptions, what will be the equilibrium time path of interest rates?

INDIVIDUAL SAVING FUNCTIONS

The simplest case to tackle to answer this question is that of a stationary population, which has always been stationary in numbers and will always be stationary. This ideal case sidesteps the difficult "planning-until-infinity" aspect of the problem. In it births are given by $B_t = B$, the same constant for all positive and negative t.

Now consider any time t. There are B men of age one, B men of age two, and B retired men of age three. Since each producer produces 1 unit, total product is $B + B$. Now, for convenience of symbols, let $R_t = 1/(1 + i_t)$ be the discount rate between goods (chocolates) of period t traded for chocolates of the next period, $t + 1$. Thus, if $R_t = 0.5$, you must promise me two chocolates tomorrow to get me to part with one chocolate today, the interest rate being 100 per cent per period. If $R_t = 1$, the interest rate is zero, and tomorrow's chocolates cost 1.0 of today's. If $R_t > 1$, say $R_t = 1.5$, the interest rate is negative, and one future chocolate costs 1.5 of today's. (Clearly, R_t is the price of tomorrow's chocolates expressed in terms of today's chocolates as numeraire.)

We seek the equilibrium levels of . . . R_t, R_{t+1}, . . . , that will clear the competitive markets in which present and future goods exchange against each other.

At time t each man who is beginning his life faces[3] the budget equation,

$$C_1 + C_2R_t + C_3R_tR_{t+1} = 1 + 1R_t + 0R_tR_{t+1}\,. \qquad (1)$$

This merely says that the total discounted value of his life's consumptions must equal the discounted value of his productions. Subject to this constraint, he will, for each given R_t and R_{t+1}, determine an optimal (C_1, C_2, C_3) to maximize $U(C_1, C_2, C_3)$, which we can summarize by the "demand" functions,

$$C_i = C_i(R_t, R_{t+1}) \qquad (i = 1, 2, 3)\,. \qquad (2)$$

[3] I rule out, as I did explicitly in my 1937 paper (p.160), the Ulysses-Strotz-Allais phenomenon whereby time perspective distorts present decisions planned for the future from later actual decisions. Thus, if at the end of period 1 his ordinal preference follows $V(C_1, C_2, C_3)$ rather than $U(C_1, C_2, C_3)$, I am assuming $(\partial V/\partial C_i)/(\partial V/\partial C_j) = (\partial U/\partial C\,)/(\partial U/\partial C_j)$. Hence all later decisions will ratify earlier plans. For a valuable discussion of this problem see R. H. Strotz, "Myopia and Inconsistency in Dynamic Utility Maximization," *Review of Economic Studies*, XXIII (1956), 165–80.

It might be convenient for us to work with "net" or "excess demands" of each man: these are the algebraic differences between what a man consumes and what he produces. Net demands in this sense are the negative of what men usually call "saving," and, in deference to capital theory, I shall work with such "net saving" as defined by

$$S_1 = S_1(R_t, R_{t+1}) = 1 - C_1(R_t, R_{t+1}),$$
$$S_2 = S_2(R_t, R_{t+1}) = 1 - C_2(R_t, R_{t+1}), \quad (3)$$
$$S_3 = S_3(R_t, R_{t+1}) = 0 - C_3(R_t, R_{t+1}).$$

In old age presumably S_3 is negative, matched by positive youthful saving, so as to satisfy for all (R_t, R_{t+1}) the budget identity,

$$S_1(R_t, R_{t+1}) + R_t S_2(R_t, R_{t+1}) + R_t R_{t+1} S_3(R_t, R_{t+1}) = 0. \quad (4)$$

Of course, these functions are subject to all the restrictions of modern consumption theory of the ordinal utility or revealed preference type. Thus, with consumption in every period being a "superior good," we can infer that $\partial C_3/\partial R_{t+1} > 0$ and $\partial S_3/\partial R_{t+1} < 0$. (This says that lowering the interest rate earned on savings carried over into retirement must increase retirement consumption.) We cannot unambiguously deduce the sign of $\partial S_1/\partial R_t$ and other terms, for the reasons implicit in modern consumption theory.

We can similarly work out the saving functions for men born a period later, which will be of the form $S_i(R_{t+1}, R_{t+2})$, etc., containing, of course, the later interest rates they will face—likewise for earlier interest rates facing men born earlier. Finally, our fundamental condition of clearing the market is this: Total net saving for the community must cancel out to zero in every period. (Remember that no goods keep and that real net investment is impossible, all loans being "consumption" loans.)

At any time t there exist B_t men of the first period, B_{t-1} men of the second period, and B_{t-2} men of the third period. The sum of their savings gives us the fundamental equilibrium condition:

$$0 = B_t S_1(R_t, R_{t+1}) + B_{t-1} S_2(R_{t-1}, R_t) + B_{t-2} S_3(R_{t-2}, R_{t-1}), \quad (5)$$

for every t. Note that in S_2 we have the interest rates of one earlier period than in S_1, and in S_3 we have still earlier interest rates (in fact, interest rates that are, at time t, already history and no longer to be determined.)

We have such an equation for every t, and if we take any finite stretch of time and write out the equilibrium conditions, we always find them containing discount rates from before the finite period and discount rates from afterward. We never seem to get enough equations: lengthening our time period turns out always to add as many new unknowns as it supplies equations, as will be spelled out later in equations (14).

THE STATIONARY CASE

We can try to cut the Gordian knot by our special assumption of stationariness, namely,

$$\ldots B_{t-1} = B_t = B_{t+1} = \ldots = B, \text{ a given constant for all time}$$
$$\ldots R_{t-1} = R_t = R_{t+1} = \ldots = R, \text{ the unknown discount rate.} \quad (6)$$

The first of these is a demographic datum; the second assumption of nonchanging interest rates is a conjecture whose consistency we must explore and verify.

Now substituting relations (6) in equation (5), we get one equilibrium equation to determine our one unknown R, namely,

$$0 = BS_1(R, R) + BS_2(R, R) + BS_3(R, R) . \tag{7}$$

By inspection, we recognize a solution of equation (7) to be $R = 1$, or $i = 0$: that is, zero interest must be one equilibrium rate under our conditions.[4]

Why? Because

$$B[S_1(1, 1) + 1S_2(1, 1) + 1S_3(1, 1)] = 0$$

by virtue of the budget identity (4).

Can a common-sense explanation of this somewhat striking result be given? Let me try. In a stationary system everyone goes through the same life-cycle, albeit at different times. Giving over goods now to an older man is figuratively giving over goods to *yourself* when old. At what rate does one give over goods to one's later self? At $R > 1$, or $R < 1$, or $R = 1$? To answer this, note that a chocolate today *is* a chocolate today, and when middle-aged A today gives over a chocolate to old B, there is a one-to-one *physical* transfer of chocolates, none melting in the transfer and none sticking to the hands of a broker. So, heuristically, we see that the hypothetical "transfer *through time*" of the chocolates must be at $R = 1$ with the interest rate i exactly zero.

Note that this result is quite independent of whether or not people have a systematic subjective preference for present consumption over future. Why? Because we have assumed that if *anyone* has such a systematic preference, *everyone* has such a systematic preference. There is no one any different in the system, no outsider—so to speak—to exact a positive interest rate from the impatient consumers.[5]

[4] We shall see that $R = 1$ is not the only root of equation (7) and that there are multiple equilibriums.

A BIOLOGICAL THEORY OF INTEREST AND POPULATION GROWTH

A zero rate of population growth was seen to be consistent with a zero rate of interest for a consumption-loan world. I now turn to the case of a population growing exponentially or geometrically. Now

$$B_t = B(1 + m)^t, \quad \text{with}$$

$$B_{t+1} = (1 + m)B_t = (1 + m)^2 B_{t-1} \ldots .$$

For $m > 0$, we have growth; for $m < 0$, decay; for $m = 0$, our previous case of a stationary population. As before, we suppose

$$\ldots R_{t-1} = R_t = R_{t+1} = \ldots = R, \text{ a constant through time.}$$

Now our clearing-of-the-market equation is

$$0 = B(1 + m)^t S_1(R, R) + B(1 + m)^{t-1} S_2(R, R) + B(1 + m)^{t-2} S_3(R, R) ; \tag{8}$$

or, cancelling $B(1 + m)^t$, we have

$$0 = S_1(R, R) + (1 + m)^{-1} S_2(R, R) + (1 + m)^{-2} S_3(R, R) . \tag{9}$$

Recalling our budget identity (4), we realize $R = (1 + m)^{-1}$ or $i = m$ is one root satisfying the equation, giving

$$0 = S_1(R, R) + RS_2(R, R) + R^2 S_3(R, R) .$$

We have therefore established the following paradoxical result:

[5] If productive opportunities were to exist, Mother Nature would operate as an important outsider, with whom trade could take place, and our conclusion would be modified. But recall our strong postulate that such technological opportunities are non-existent.

THEOREM: Every geometrically growing consumption-loan economy has an equilibrium market rate of interest exactly equal to its biological percentage growth rate.

Thus, if the net reproductive rate gives a population growth of 15 per cent per period, $i = 0.15$ is the corresponding market rate of interest. If, as in Sweden or Ireland, $m < 0$ and population decays, the market rate of interest will be negative, with $i < 0$ and $R > 1$!

OPTIMUM PROPERTY OF THE BIOLOGICAL INTEREST RATE

The equality of the market rate of interest in a pure consumption-loan world to the rate of population growth was deduced solely from mechanically finding a root of the supply-demand equations that clear the market. Experience often confirms what faith avers: that competitive market relations achieve some kind of an optimum.

Does the saving-consumption pattern given by $S_1(R, R)$, $S_2(R, R)$, $S_3(R, R)$, where $R = 1/(1+m)$, represent some kind of a social optimum? One would guess that, if it does maximize something, this equilibrium pattern probably maximizes the "lifetime (ordinal) well-being of a representative person, subject to the resources available to him (and to every other representative man) over his lifetime." Or, what seems virtually the same thing, consider a cross-sectional family or clan that has an unchanging age distribution because the group remains in statistical equilibrium, though individuals are born and die. Such a clan will divide its available resources to maximize a welfare function differing only in scale from each man's utility function and will achieve the same result as the biological growth rate.

To test this optimality conjecture, first stick to the stationary population case. The representative man is thought to maximize $U(C_1, C_2, C_3)$, subject to

$$C_1 + C_2 + C_3 = 1 + 1, \qquad (10)$$

$1 + 1$ being the lifetime product available to each man. The solution to this technocratic welfare problem (free in its formulation and solution of all mention of prices or interest rates) requires

$$\frac{\partial U/\partial C_2}{\partial U/\partial C_1} = \frac{\partial U/\partial C_3}{\partial U/\partial C_1}. \qquad (11)$$

But this formulation is seen to be identical with that of a single maximizing man facing market discount rates $R_1 = R_2 = 1$. Hence the solution of equations (10) and (11) is exactly that given earlier by equation (3): that is, our present welfare problem has, for its optimality solution,

$$1 - C_1 = S_1(1, 1),$$
$$1 - C_2 = S_2(1, 1),$$
$$0 - C_3 = S_3(1, 1).$$

Now that we have verified our conjecture for the stationary $m = 0$ case, we can prove it for population growing like $B(1+m)^t$, where $m \gtreqless 0$. As before, we maximize $U(C_1, C_2, C_3)$ for the representative man. But what resources are now available to him? Recall that in a growing population the age distribution is permanently skewed in favor of the younger productive ages: society and each clan has an age distribution proportional to $[1, 1/(1+m), 1/(1+m)^2]$ and has therefore a per capita output to divide in consumption among the three age classes satisfying

$$C_1 + \frac{1}{1+m} C_2 + \frac{1}{(1+m)^2} C_3 = 1 + \frac{1}{1+m}. \qquad (12)$$

By following a representative man throughout his life and remembering that there are always $(1+m)^{-1}$ just older than he and $(1+m)^{-2}$ two periods older, we derive this same "budget" or availibility equation. Subject to equation (12), we maximize $U(C_1, C_2, C_3)$ and necessarily end up with the same conditions as would a competitor facing the biological market interest rate $R_1 = R_2 = 1/(1+m)$: namely,

$$\begin{aligned} 1 - C_1 &= S_1(R,R)\,, \\ 1 - C_2 &= S_2(R,R)\,, \\ 0 - C_3 &= S_3(R,R)\,, \qquad (13) \\ R &= \frac{1}{1+m}\,. \end{aligned}$$

Hence the identity of the social optimality conditions and the biological market interest theory has been demonstrated.[6]

COMMON-SENSE EXPLANATION OF BIOLOGICAL MARKET INTEREST RATE

Productivity theorists have always related interest to the biological habits of rabbits and cows. And Gustav Cassel long ago developed a striking (but rather nonsensical) biological theory relating interest to the life-expectancy of men of means and their alleged propensity to go from maintaining capital to the buying of annuities at an allegedly critical positive i. I seem to be the first, outside a slave economy, to develop a biological theory of interest relating it to the reproductivity of human mothers.

Is there a common-sense market explanation of this (to me at least) astonishing result? I suppose it would go like this: in a growing population men of twenty outnumber men of forty; and retired men are outnumbered by workers more than in the ratio of the work span to the retirement span. With more workers to support them, the aged live better than in the stationary state—the excess being positive interest on their savings.

Such an explanation cannot be deemed entirely convincing. Outside of social security and family altruism, the aged have no claims on the young: cold and selfish competitive markets will not teleologically respect the old; the aged will get only what supply and demand impute to them.

So we might try another more detailed explanation. Recall that men of forty or of period 2 bargain with men of twenty or period 1, trying to bribe the latter to provide them with consumption in their retirement. (Men of over sixty-five or of period 3 can make fresh bargains with no one: after retirement it is too late for them to try to provide for their old age.) In a growing population there are more period 1 men for period 2 men to bargain with; this presumably confers a competitive advantage on period 2 men, the manifestation of it being the positive interest rate.

So might go the explanation. It is at least superficially plausible, and it does qualitatively suggest a positive interest rate when population is growing, al-

[6] If U has the usual quasi-concavity, this social optimum will be unique—whether U does or does not have the time-symmetry that is sometimes (for concreteness) assumed in later arguments. Not only will the representative man's utility U be maximized, but so will the "total" of social utility enjoyed over a long period of time: specifically, the divergence from attainable bliss

$$[U(C_1, C_2, C_3) - U^*] + [U(C_1, C_2, C_3) - U^*] + \ldots$$

over all time will be miminized, where U^* is the utility achieved when $R_1 = 1 = R_2$ and $S_i = S_i(1, 1)$. This theorem may require that we use an ordinal utility indicator that is concave in the C_i, as it is always open to us to do.

Of course, this entire footnote and the related text need obvious modifications if $m \neq 0$.

though perhaps it falls short of explaining the remarkable quantitative identity between the growth rates of interest and of population.

THE INFINITY PARADOX REVEALED

But will the explanation survive rigorous scrutiny? Is it true, in a growing or in a stationary population, that twenty-year-olds are, in fact, overconsuming so that the middle-aged can provide for their retirement? Specifically, in the stationary case where $R = 1$, is it necessarily true that $S_1(1, 1) < 0$? Study of $U(C_1, C_2, C_3)$ shows how doubtful such a general result would be; thus, if there is no systematic subjective time preference so that U is a function *symmetric* in its arguments, it would be easy to show that $C_1 = C_2 = C_3 = \frac{2}{3}$, with $S_1(1, 1) = S_2(1, 1) = +\frac{1}{3}$ and $S_3(1, 1) = -\frac{2}{3}$. Contrary to our scenario, the middle-aged are *not* turning over to the young what the young will later make good to them in retirement support.

THE TWO-PERIOD CASE

The paradox is delineated more clearly if we suppose but two equal periods of life—work and retirement. Now it becomes *impossible* for *any* worker to find a worker younger than himself to be bribed to support him in old age. Whatever the trend of births, there is but one equilibrium saving pattern possible: during working years, consumption equals product and saving is zero; the same during the brutish years of retirement. What equilibrium interest rate, or R, will prevail? Since no transactions take place, $R = 0/0$, so to speak, and appears rather indeterminate—and rather academic. However, if men desperately want *some* consumption at *all* times, only $R = \infty$ can be regarded as the (virtual) equilibrium rate, with interest equal to -100 per cent per period.[7]

We think we know the right answer just given in the two-period case. Let us test our previous mathematical methods. Now our equations are much as before and can be summarized by:

$$\text{Maximize } U(C_1, C_2) = U(1 - S_1, 0 - S_2)$$

$$\text{subject to } S_1 + R_t S_2 = 0\,.$$

The resulting saving functions, $S_1(R_t)$ and $S_2(R_t)$, are subject to the budget identity,

$$S_1(R_t) + R_t S_2(R_t) \equiv 0 \text{ for all } R_t\,. \quad (4')$$

Clearing the market requires

$$0 = B_t S_1(R_t) + B_{t-1} S_2(R_{t-1}) \quad \text{for} \quad t = 0, \pm 1, \pm 2, \ldots. \quad (5')$$

If $B_t = B(1 + m)^t$ and $R_t = R_{t+1} = \ldots = R$, our final equation becomes

$$0 = B\left[S_1(R) + \frac{1}{1+m} S_2(R)\right]. \quad (8')$$

The budget equation (4′) assures us that equation (8′) has a solution:

$$R = \frac{1}{1+m} \quad \text{or} \quad m = i\,.$$

$$\text{with} \quad 0 < S_1(R) = -RS_2(R)\,.$$

So the two-period mathematics appears to give us the same answer as before—a biological rate of interest equal to the rate of population growth.

Yet we earlier deduced that *there can be no voluntary saving in a two-period world*. Instead of $S_1 > 0$, we must have $S_1 = 0 = S_2$ with $R = +\infty$. How can we reconcile this with the mathematics?

[7] A later numerical example, where $U = \log C_1 + \log C_2 + \log C_3$, shows that cases can arise where no positive R, however large, will clear the market. I adopt the harmless convention of setting $R = \infty$ in every case, even if the limit as $R \to \infty$ does not wipe out the discrepancy between supply and demand.

We substitute $S_1 = 0 = S_2$ in equation (5′) or equation (8′), and indeed this does satisfy the clearing-of-the-market equation. Apparently our one equilibrium equation in our one unknown R has more than a single solution! And the relevant one for a free market is *not* that given by our biological or demographic theory of interest, even though our earlier social optimality argument does perfectly fit the two-period case.

THE PARADOX CONTEMPLATED

The transparent two-period case alerts us to the possibility that in the three-period (or n-period) case, the fundamental equation of supply and demand may have multiple solutions. And, indeed, it does.[8] We see that

$$0 = S_1(\infty, \infty) = S_2(\infty, \infty) = S_3(\infty, \infty)$$

is indeed a valid mathematical solution. This raises the following questions:

Is a condition of no saving with dismal retirement consumption and interest rate of -100 per cent per period thinkable as the economically correct equilibrium for a free market?

Surely, the non-myopic middle-aged will do almost anything to make retirement consumption, C_3 non-zero?[9]

One might conjecture that the fact that, in the three-period model, workers can always find younger workers to bargain with is a crucial difference from the two-period case.[10] To investigate the problem, we must drop the assumption of a population that is, always has been, and always will be stationary (or exponentially growing or exponentially decaying). For within that ambiguous context $R = 1(R < 1,\ R > 1)$ was indeed an impeccable solution, in the sense that no one can point to a violated equilibrium condition. (Exactly the same can be said of the two-period case, even though we "know" the impeccable solution is economically nonsense.)

We must give mankind a beginning. So, once upon a time, B men were born into the labor force. Then B more. Then B more. Until what? Until . . . ? Or until no more men are born? Must we give mankind an end as well as a beginning? Even the Lord rested after the beginning, so let us tackle one problem at a time and keep births forever constant. Our equilibrium equations, with the constant B's omitted, now become

$$\begin{aligned}
&S_1(R_1, R_2) + 0 + 0 = 0\,,\\
&S_2(R_1, R_2) + S_1(R_2, R_3) + 0 = 0\,,\\
&S_3(R_1, R_2) + S_2(R_2, R_3)\\
&\qquad\qquad + S_1(R_3, R_4) = 0\,,\\
&S_3(R_2, R_3) + S_2(R_3, R_4)\\
&\qquad\qquad + S_1(R_4, R_5) = 0\,,\\
&\dots\dots\dots\dots\dots\dots\,,\\
&S_3(R_{t-2}, R_{t-1}) + S_2(R_{t-1}, R_t)\\
&\qquad\qquad + S_1(R_t, R_{t+1}) = 0\,,\\
&\dots\dots\dots\dots\dots\dots
\end{aligned} \tag{14}$$

We feel that $S_1 \equiv 0 \equiv S_2 \equiv S_3$, while a mathematical solution, is not the economically relevant one. Since $S_1(1, 1)$, $S_2(1, 1)$, and $S_3(1, 1)$ do satisfy the last

[8] There is nothing surprising about multiple solutions in economics: not infrequently income effects make possible other intersections, including the possibility of an infinite number where demand and supply curves coincide.

[9] Before answering these questions, it would be well to decide what the word "surely" in the previous sentence means. Surely, no sentence beginning with the word "surely" can validly contain a question mark at its end? However, one paradox is enough for one article, and I shall stick to my economist's last.

[10] By introducing overlap between workers of different ages, the three-period model is essentially equivalent to a general n-period model or to the continuous-time model of real life.

of the written equations, we dare hope[11] that the Invisible Hand will ultimately work its way to the socially optimal biological-interest configuration—or that the solution to equation (14) satisfies

$$\lim_{t\to\infty} R_t = 1, \quad S_i(R_t, R_{t+1}) = S_i(1, 1), \; (i = 1, 2, 3) . \tag{15}$$

THE IMPOSSIBILITY THEOREM

But have we any right to hope that the free market will even ultimately approach the specified social optimum? Does not the two-period case rob us of hope? Will not all the trade that the three-period case makes possible consist of middle-aged period 2 people giving consumption to young period 1 people in return for getting consumption back from them one period later? Do not such voluntary mutual-aid compacts suggest that, if R_t does approach a limit x, it must be such as to make $S_1(x, x) < 0$? Whereas, for many men[12] not too subject to systematic preference for the present over the future (not too affected by Böhm's second cause of interest), we expect $S_1(1, 1) > 0$.

A colleague, whose conjectures are often better than many people's theorems, has suggested to me that in the three-period or n-period case I am taking too bilateral a view of trade. We might end up with $S_1 > 0$ and encounter no contradictions to voluntary trade by virtue of the fact that young men trade with *anyone* in the market: they do not know or care that all or part of the motive for trade with them comes from the desire of the middle-aged to provide for retirement. The present young are content to be trading with the present old (or, for that matter, with the unborn or dead): all they care about is that their trades take place at the quoted market prices; and, if some kind of triangular or multilateral offsetting among the generations can take place and result in $S_1(R_t, R_{t+1})$ positive and becoming closer and closer to $S_1(1, 1) > 0$, why cannot this happen?

I, too, found the multilateral notion appealing. But the following considerations—of a type I do not recall seeing treated anywhere—suggest to me that the ultimate approach to $R = 1$ and $S_1(1, 1) > 0$ is quite impossible.

List all men from the beginning to time t. All the voluntary trades ever made must be mutually advantageous. If A gives something to B and B does nothing for A directly in return, we know B must be doing something for some C, who does do something good for A. (Of course, C might be more than one man, and there might be many-linked connections within C.)

Now consider a time when $S_1(R_t, R_{t+1})$ has become positive, with $S_2(R_{t-1}, R_t)$ also positive. Young man A is then giving goods to old man B. Young man A expects something in return and will actually two periods later be getting goods from someone. From whom? It certainly cannot be directly from B: B will

[11] Our confidence in this would be enhanced if the linear difference equation relating small deviations $r_t = R_t - 1$ had characteristic roots all less than 1 in absolute value. Thus $a_0 r_{t+3} + a_1 r_{t+2} + a_2 r_{t+1} + a_3 r_t = 0$, where the a_i are given in terms of the $S_i(R_t, R_{t+1})$ functions and their partial derivatives, evaluated at $R_t = 1\, R_{t+1}$. Logically, this would be neither quite necessary nor sufficient: not sufficient, since the initial R_0, R_1, R_2 might be so far from 1 as to make the linear approximations irrelevant; not necessary, since, with one root less than unity in absolute value, we might ride in toward $R = 1$ on a razor's edge. In any case, as our later numerical example shows, our hope is a vain one.

[12] There is admittedly some econometric evidence that many young adults do dissave, to acquire assets and for other reasons. Some modifications of exposition would have to be made to allow for this.

be dead then. Let it be from someone called C. Can B ever do anything good for such a C, or have in the past done so? No. B only has produce during his first two periods of life, and all the good he can do anyone must be to people who were born before him or just after him. That *never* includes C. So the postulated pattern of $S_1 > 0$ is logically impossible in a free market: and hence $R_t = 1 = R_{t+1}$, as an exact or approximate relation, is impossible. (Note that, for some special pattern of time preference, the competitive solution *might* coincide with the "biological optimum.")

A NUMERICAL EXAMPLE

A concrete case will illustrate all this. The purest Marshallian case of unitary price and income elasticities can be characterized by $U = \log C_1 + \log C_2 + \log C_3$, where all systematic time preference is replaced by *symmetry*.

A maximum of

$$\sum_1^3 \log C_i \text{ subject to} \quad C_1 + R_1C_2 + R_1R_2C_3 = 1 + R_1 \tag{16}$$

implies

$$R_1 = \frac{\partial U/\partial C_2}{\partial U/\partial C_1} = \frac{1/C_2}{1/C_1},$$

$$R_1R_2 = \frac{\partial U/\partial C_3}{\partial U/\partial C_1} = \frac{1/C_3}{1/C_1};$$

and, after combining this with the budget equation, we end up with saving functions,

$$\begin{aligned} S_1(R_1, R_2) &= \frac{2}{3} - \frac{R_1}{3}, \\ S_2(R_1, R_2) &= \frac{2}{3} - \frac{1}{3R_1}, \\ S_3(R_1, R_2) &= 0 - \frac{1}{3R_1R_2} - \frac{1}{3R_2}. \end{aligned} \tag{17}$$

Equations (14) now take the form

$$\begin{aligned} &\frac{2}{3} - \frac{R_1}{3} + 0 + 0 = 0, \\ &\frac{2}{3} - \frac{1}{3R_1} + \left(\frac{2}{3} - \frac{R_2}{3}\right) + 0 = 0, \\ &-\frac{1}{3R_1R_2} - \frac{1}{3R_2} + \left(\frac{2}{3} - \frac{1}{3R_2}\right) + \left(\frac{2}{3} - \frac{R_3}{3}\right) = 0, \\ &\left(-\frac{1}{3R_2R_3} - \frac{1}{3R_3}\right) + \left(\frac{2}{3} - \frac{1}{3R_3}\right) + \left(\frac{2}{3} - \frac{R_4}{3}\right) = 0, \\ &\cdots\cdots\cdots\cdots \\ &\left(-\frac{1}{3R_{t-1}R_{t-2}} - \frac{1}{3R_{t-1}}\right) + \left(\frac{2}{3} - \frac{1}{3R_{t-1}}\right) + \left(\frac{2}{3} - \frac{R_t}{3}\right) = 0, \\ &\cdots\cdots\cdots\cdots \end{aligned} \tag{18}$$

Aside from initial conditions, this can be written in the recursive form,

$$R_t = 4 - \frac{1}{R_{t-1}R_{t-2}} - \frac{2}{R_{t-1}}. \tag{19}$$

Note that $\partial S_1(R_1, R_2) \equiv 0$ made our third-order difference equation degenerate into a second-order difference equation.

If we expand the last equation around $R_{t-2} = 1 = R_{t-1}$, retaining only linear terms and working in terms of deviations from the equilibrium level, $r_t = R_t - 1$, we get the recursive system,

$$r_{t+2} = 3r_{t+1} + r_t. \tag{20}$$

which obviously explodes away from $r = 0$ and $R = 1$ for all small perturbations from such an equilibrium. This confirms our proof that the *social optimum configuration can never here be reached by the competitive market, or even be approached in ever so long a time.*

Where does the solution to (18) eventually go? Its first few R's are numerically calculated to be $[R_1, R_2, R_3, \ldots] = [2, 3\frac{1}{2}, 3\frac{2}{7}, \ldots]$. It is plain that the limiting R_t exceeds 1; hence a negative interest rate i is being asymptotically approached. Substituting $R_{t+2} = R_{t+1} = R_t = x$ in equation (19), we get the following cubic equation to solve for possible equilibrium levels:[13]

$$x = 4 - \frac{1}{x^2} - \frac{2}{x} \quad \text{or} \qquad (21)$$
$$x^3 - 4x^2 + 2x + 1 = 0 .$$

We know that $x = 1$, the irrelevant optimal level, is one root; so, dividing it out, we end up with

$$(x-1)(x^2 - 3x - 1) = 0 .$$

Solving the quadratic, we have

$$x = \frac{3 \pm \sqrt{9+4}}{2}$$

or

$$x = \frac{3}{2} + \frac{\sqrt{13}}{2} = 3.297 \text{ approx}.$$

for the asymptote approached by the free competitive market. The other root, $(3 - \sqrt{13})/2$, corresponds to a negative R, which is economically meaningless, in that it implies that the more we give up of today's consumption, the more we must give up of tomorrow's.

Our meaningful positive root, $R = 3.297$, corresponds to an ultimate negative interest rate,

$$i = \frac{1-R}{R} = -\frac{2.297}{3.297},$$

which implies that consumption loans lose about two-thirds of their principal in one period. This is here the competitive price to avoid retirement starvation.[14]

RECAPITULATION

The task of giving an exact description of a pure consumption-loan interest model is finished. We end up, in the stationary population case, with a negative market interest rate, rather than with the biological zero interest rate corresponding to the social optimum for the representative man. This was proved by the impossibility theorem and verified by an arithmetic example.

A corresponding result will hold for changing population where $m \gtrless 0$. The actual competitive market rate i_m will always be negative and always less than the biological optimality rate m.[15] And

[13] Martin J. Bailey has pointed out to me that the budget equation and the clearing-of-the-market equations do, in the stationary state, imply $S_1 = RS_2$ whenever $R \neq 1$, a fact which can be used to give an alternative demonstration of possible equilibrium values.

[14] In other examples, this competitive solution would not deviate so much from the $i = m$ biological optimum. But it is important to realize that solutions to equations (14) that come from quasi-concave utility functions—with or without systematic time preference—*cannot* be counted on to approach asymptotically the biological optimum configuration of equation (13).

In this case the linear approximation gives for $r_t = R_t - 3.297$ the recursion relation

$$r_{t+2} = \frac{1}{(3.297)^3} r_{t+1} + \frac{2}{(3.297)^2} r_t .$$

This difference equation has roots easily shown to be less than 1 in absolute value, so the local stability of our competitive equilibrium is assured.

[15] Writing $\lambda = 1/(1+m)$, our recursion relation (14) becomes

$$0 = S_1(R_t, R_{t+1}) + \lambda S_2(R_{t-1}, R_t) + \lambda^2 S_3(R_{t-2}, R_{t-1}) .$$

For the case where $U = \Sigma \log C_i$, our recursion relation (18) becomes

$$R_t = 2(1+\lambda) - \frac{\lambda^2}{R_{t-1}R_{t-2}} - \frac{\lambda^2}{R_{t-1}} - \frac{\lambda}{R_{t-1}} .$$

Then $x = R_t = R_{t-1} = R_{t-2}$ gives a cubic equation with biological root corresponding to $x = \lambda$ and

increasing the productive years relative to the retirement years of zero product would undoubtedly still leave us with a negative interest rate, albeit one that climbs ever closer to zero.

Is this negative interest rate a hard-to-believe result? Not, I think, when one recalls our extreme and purposely unrealistic assumptions. With Böhm's third technological reason for interest ruled out by assumption, with his second reason involving systematic preference for the present soft-pedaled, and with his first reason reversed (that is, with people expecting to be *poorer* in the future), we should perhaps have been surprised if the market rate had not turned out negative.

Yet, aside from giving the general biological optimum interest rate, our model is an instructive one for a number of reasons.

1. It shows us what interest rates would be implied if the "hump saving" process were acting alone in a world devoid of systematic time preference.[16]

2. It incidentally confirms what modern theorists showed long ago but what is still occasionally denied in the literature, that a zero or negative interest rate is in no sense a *logically* contradictory thing, however bizarre may be the *empirical* hypotheses that entail a zero or negative rate.

3. It may help us a little to isolate the effects of adding one by one, or together, (*a*) technological investment possibilities, (*b*) innovations that secularly raise productivity and real incomes, (*c*) strong biases toward present goods and against future goods, (*d*) governmental laws and more general collusions than are envisaged in simple laissez faire markets, or (*e*) various aspects of uncertainty. To be sure, other orderings of analysis would also be possible; and these separate processes interact, with the whole not the simple sum of its parts.

4. It points up a fundamental and intrinsic deficiency in a free pricing system, namely, that free pricing gets you on the Pareto-efficiency frontier but by itself has no tendency to get you to positions on the frontier that are ethically optimal in terms of a social welfare function; only by social collusions—of tax, expenditure, fiat, or other type—can an ethical observer hope to end up where he wants to be. (This obvious and ancient point is related to 3*d* above.)

5. The present model enables us to see one "function" of money from a new slant—as a social compact that can provide optimal old age social security. (This is also related to 3*d* above.)

For the rest of this essay, I shall develop aspects of the last two of these themes.

SOCIAL COMPACTS AND THE OPTIMUM

If each man insists on a *quid pro quo*, we apparently continue until the end of time, with each worse off than in the social optimum, biological interest case. Yet how easy it is by a simple change in the rules of the game to get to the optimum. Let mankind enter into a Hobbes-Rousseau social contract in which the

---

$i = m$. The relevant competitive market root is given by

$$x=\frac{2+\lambda}{2}+\sqrt{\frac{(2+\lambda)^2+4\lambda}{2}}.$$

Where $m = 0$, $\lambda = 1$, we have $x = 3.297$; for $m \rightarrow \infty$, $\lambda \rightarrow 0$, $x \rightarrow 2$ and $i \rightarrow -\frac{1}{2}$; for $m \rightarrow -1$, $\lambda \rightarrow \infty$, $x \rightarrow \infty$ and $i \rightarrow -1$. Thus the market rate of interest is always between -1 and $-\frac{1}{2}$, growing as m grows, in agreement with the small husk of truth in our earlier "common-sense explanation."

[16] T. Ophir, of the Massachusetts Institute of Technology and Hebrew University, Jerusalem, has done unpublished work showing how systematic time preference will tend to alter the equilibrium interest rate pattern.

young are assured of their retirement subsistence if they will today support the aged, such support to be guaranteed by a draft on the yet-unborn. Then the social optimum can be achieved within one lifetime, and our equations (14) will become

$$S_1(1, 1) + S_2(1, 1) + S_3(1, 1) = 0$$

from $t = 3$ on.

We economists have been told[17] that what we are to economize on is love or altruism, this being a scarce good in our imperfect world. True enough, in the sense that we want what there is to go as far as possible. But it is also the task of political economy to point out where common rules in the form of self-imposed fiats can attain higher positions on the social welfare functions prescribed for us by ethical observers.

The Golden Rule or Kant's Categorical Imperative (enjoining like people to follow the common pattern that makes each best off) are often not self-enforcing: if all but one obey, the one may gain selfish advantage by disobeying—which is where the sheriff comes in: *we* politically invoke force on *ourselves*, attempting to make an unstable equilibrium a stable one.[18]

Once social coercion or contracting is admitted into the picture, the present problem disappears. The reluctance of the young to give to the old what the old can never themselves directly or indirectly repay is overcome. Yet the young never suffer, since their successors come under the same requirement. Everybody ends better off. It is as simple as that.[19]

The economics of social collusions is a rich field for analysis, involving fascinating predictive and normative properties. Thus, when society *acts as if* it were maximizing certain functions, we can predict the effect upon equilibrium of specified exogenous disburbances. And certain patterns of thought appropriate to a single mind become appropriate,

[17] D. H. Robertson, *What Does the Economist Maximize?* (a keynote address at the Columbia bicentennial celebrations, May, 1954), published by the Trustees of the University in the *Proceedings of the Conference, 1955* (New York: Doubleday & Co.) and reprinted as chap. ix in D. H. Robertson, *Economic Commentaries* (London: Staples, 1956).

[18] Now, admittedly, there is usually lacking in the real world the axes of symmetry needed to make all this an easy process. In a formulation elsewhere, I have shown some of the requirements for an optimal theory of public expenditure of the Sax-Wicksell-Lindahl-Musgrave-Bowen type, and the failure of the usual voting and signaling mechanisms to converge to an optimum solution (see "The Pure Theory of Public Expenditure," *Review of Economics and Statistics*, XXXVI [November, 1954], 387–89, and "Diagrammatic Exposition of Public Expenditure," *ibid.*, XXXVII [November, 1955], 350–56). Such a model is poles apart from the pure case in which Walrasian laissez faire happens to be optimal. I should be prepared to argue that a good deal of what is important and interesting in the real world lies between these extreme poles, perhaps in between in the sense of displaying properties that are a blending of the polar properties. But such discussion must await another time.

[19] How can the competitive configuration with negative interest rates be altered to everyone's advantage? Does not this deny the Pareto optimality of perfect competition, which is the least (and most) we can expect from it? Here we encounter one more paradox, which no doubt arises from the "infinity" aspect of our model. If we assume a large finite span to the human race—say 1 million generations—then the final few generations face the equations

$$S_1(R_{T-1}, \infty) + S_2(R_{T-2}, R_{T-1}) + S_3(R_{T-3}, R_{T-2}) = 0\,,$$

$$S_2(R_{T-1}, \infty) + S_3(R_{T-2}, R_{T-1}) + 0 = 0\,,$$

$$S_3(R_{T-1}, \infty) + 0 + 0 = 0\,,$$

$$\text{where} \quad T = 1{,}000{,}000\,.$$

If we depart from the negative interest rate pattern, the final young will be cheated by the demise of the human race. Should such a cheating of one generation 30 million years from now perpetually condemn society to a suboptimal configuration? Perfect competition shrugs its shoulders at such a question and (not improperly) sticks to its Pareto optimality.

even though we reject the notion of a group mind. (Example: developed social security could give rise to the same bias toward increasing population that exists among farmers and close family groups, where children are wanted as a means of old age support.)

The economics of collusion provides an important field of study for the theorist. Such collusions can be important elements of strength in the struggle for existence. Reverence for life, in the Schweitzer sense of respecting ants and flowers, might be a handicap in the Darwinian struggle for existence. (And, since the reverencer tends to disappear, the ants may not be helped much in the long run.) But culture in which altruism abounds—because men do not think to behave like atomistic competitors or because men have by custom and law entered into binding social contracts—may have great survival and expansion powers.

An essay could be written on the welfare state as a complicated device for self- or reinsurance. (From this view, the graduated income tax becomes in part a device for reducing *ex ante* variance.) That the Protestant Ethic should have been instrumental in creating individualistic capitalism one may accept; but that it should stop there is not necessarily plausible.[20] What made Jeremy Bentham a Benthamite in 1800, one suspects, might in 1900 have made him a Fabian (and do we not see a lot in common in the personalities of James Mill and Friedrich Engels?).

Much as you and I may dislike government "interferences" in economic life, we must face the positive fact that the motivations for higher living standards that a free market channels into Walrasian equilibrium when the special conditions for that pattern happen to be favorable —these same motivations often lead to social collusions and myriad uses of the apparatus of the state. For good or evil, these may not be aberrations from laissez faire, but theorems entailed by its intrinsic axioms.

[20] Recall the Myrdal thesis that the austere planned economies of Europe are Protestant, the Catholic countries being individualistic.

CONCLUSION: MONEY AS A SOCIAL CONTRIVANCE

Let me conclude by applying all these considerations to an analysis of the role of money in our consumption-loan world. In it nothing kept. All ice melted, and so did all chocolates. (If non-depletable land existed, it must have been superabundant.) Workers could not carry goods over into their retirement years.

There is no arguing with Nature. But what is to stop man—or rather men—from printing oblongs of paper or stamping circles of shell. These units of money can keep.[21] (Even if ink fades, this could be true.) With ideal clearing arrangements, money as a medium of exchange might have little function. But remember that a money medium of exchange is itself a rather efficient clearing arrangement.

So suppose men officially through the state, or unofficially through custom, make a grand consensus on the use of these greenbacks as a money of exchange. Now the young and middle-aged do have something to hold and to carry over into their retirement years. And note this: as long as the new current generations of

[21] I have been asked whether introducing durable money does not violate my fiat against durable goods and trades with Nature. All that I must insist on is that the new durable moneys (or records) be themselves quite worthless for consumption. The essence of them as money is that they are valued only for what they will fetch in exchange.

workers do not repudiate the old money, this gives workers of one epoch a claim on workers of a later epoch, even though no real *quid pro quo* (other than money) is possible.

We then find this remarkable fact: without legislating social security or entering into elaborate social compacts, society by using money will go from the non-optimal negative-interest-rate configuration to the optimal biological-interest-rate configuration. How does this happen? I shall try to give only a sketchy account that does not pretend to be rigorous.

Take the stationary population case with $m = 0$. With total money M constant and the flow of goods constant, the price level can be expected very soon to level off and be constant. The productive invest their hump savings in currency; in their old age they disinvest this currency, turning it over to the productive workers in return for sustenance.

With population growing like $(1 + m)^t$, output will come to grow at that rate. Fixed M will come to mean prices falling like $1/(1 + m)^t$. Each dollar saved today will thus yield a *real* rate of interest of exactly m per period—just what the biological social-optimality configuration calls for. Similarly, when $m < 0$ and population falls, rising prices will create the desired negative real rate of interest equal to m.

In short, the use of money can itself be regarded as a social compact.[22] When economists say that one of the functions of money is to act as a store of wealth and that one of money's desirable properties is constancy of value (as measured by constancy of average prices), we are entitled to ask: How do you know this? Why *should* prices be stable? On what tablets is that injunction written? Perhaps the function of money, if it is to serve as an optimal store of wealth, is so to change in its value as to create that optimal pattern of lifetime saving which could otherwise be established only by alternative social contrivances.[23]

I do not pretend to pass judgment on the policies related to all this. But I do suggest for economists' further research the difficult analysis of capital models which grapple with the fact that each and every today is followed by a tomorrow.

[22] In terms of immediate self-interest the existing productive workers should perhaps unilaterally repudiate the money upon which the aged hope to live in retirement. (Compare the Russian and Belgium calling-in of currencies.) So a continuing social compact is required. (Compare, too, current inflationary trends which do give the old less purchasing power than many of them had counted on.)

[23] Conversely, with satisfactory social security programs, the necessity for having secular stable prices so that the retired are taken care of can be lightened. Even after extreme inflations, social security programs can re-create themselves anew astride the community's indestructible real tax base.

[17]

THE SOCIAL INSURANCE PARADOX

Henry Aaron *Harvard University*

In 1958 Professor Samuelson demonstrated that social insurance could improve the lot of each person in society.[1] Each person could support a portion of the

[1]Paul A. Samuelson, "An Exact Consumption-Loan Model of Interest with or without the Social Contrivance of Money," *Journal of Political Economy*, LXVI (Dec. 1958), 467–82.

XXXII, no. 3, August/août, 1966

cost of maintaining the retired population in return for which future generations would support him during his retirement. The return on this form of saving would exceed the real rate of interest which was in turn a function of population growth. In this note I present a proof of a related theorem: that social insurance can increase the welfare of each person if the sum of the rates of growth of population and real wages exceeds the rate of interest. I call this theorem, after Samuelson, the social insurance "paradox." This theorem does not conflict with Samuelson's because nothing is assumed here about the level of the interest rate or its determinants, other than that it equals both the marginal rate of time preference and the marginal rate of transformation between present and future goods.

I / The paradox stated

Ideally, private insurers set premiums to equalize the present expected value of benefits and the present expected value of premiums.[2] A reserve is accumulated for each person. As the number of people covered by insurance increases, the total reserves for all people increase. If the age composition of the insured population remains the same, the rate of increase of total reserves is the same as the rate of growth of the insured population. If the same procedure were followed in social insurance, and if the covered population increased, then the total reserves would likewise increase. In a mature system the amount of reserves would increase at the same rate as population grows if the age composition of the population remains constant. If social insurance premiums were set below the level which would equalize the present expected value of benefits and premiums, the rate of increase of the social insurance trust fund could be reduced. In an extreme case, no social insurance reserves at all might be accumulated. It follows, that if the covered population increases and if no reserve is accumulated, the present expected value of premiums is less than the present expected value of benefits for each person, although for the group as a whole viewed in perpetuity, the equality will be maintained.

The logical implication of the above remarks is that, if no reserve is accumulated in the financing of old age pensions, each person will receive a larger pension than he has paid for. Or put another way, the present value of his lifetime income, earnings plus pension, will be higher if no reserves are accumulated than if they are. This fact holds for every person. Consequently, *for the nation as a whole, the present expected value of the sum of real net lifetime receipts is greater when reserves are not accumulated than when they are, although the national income at each point in time is unaffected.* Has a fallacy crept in?

From an insurance equity standpoint it has. The fact that the same pension is paid under the pay-as-you-go assessment system and the reserve system, although premiums are higher in the latter case than in the former, means simply that a higher interest rate is implicitly being paid on contributions

[2]I am abstracting here from profits, commissions, and other administrative expenses.

under the "no reserve" system than under the reserve system. If this higher interest rate is used in calculating each person's implicit fund under assessment financing and in discounting social insurance benefits to the present, the equality between expected present values of premiums and benefits is restored.

II / The paradox demonstrated

On the macro-economic level, however, the paradox remains intact. This section will be devoted to a rigorous demonstration of this proposition. Assume that, upon reaching a particular age A, all people enter the labour force and that the number reaching this age each year grows at the rate of g per cent. Assume that average real wages grow at the rate of h per cent and that the interest rate is i per cent. Let $t = 1 + g$, $s = 1 + h$, and $r = 1 + i$. Each person works m years and then retires. He lives in retirement for $n - m$ years dying at the age of $A + n$. During each year of retirement each person receives a pension equal to the average wage then prevailing among active workers.

After k years (where $k < n$), the total population, P, will be:

$$(1) \quad P = P_0 t^k[(t^m + t^{m-1} + \ldots + t) + (1 + t^{-1} + t^{-2} + \ldots + t^{-n+m+1})],$$

where P_0 is the population at time 0. The first parenthetical expression inside the brackets, multiplied by $P_0 t^k$, gives the total working population; the second parenthetical expression, multiplied by $P_0 t^k$, gives the total retired population.

The total wages any worker receives during his working life, w, will be:

$$(2) \quad w = w_0 s^k (s^{-m} + s^{-m+1} + \ldots + s^{-1}),$$

where the worker retires in year k, and w_0 is the wage prevailing in year 0.

During retirement the same worker will receive pensions, p, indicated by:

$$(3) \quad p = w_0 s^k (1 + s + s^2 + \ldots + s^{n-m-1}).$$

During his working life, each pension recipient had paid taxes to support pensions. Assuming that taxes were just sufficient to cover pension costs, i.e. that no reserve was accumulated, each worker paid a fraction of his wage, f, equal to the ratio of the retired to the active population. This fraction, f, is equal to the ratio of the second parenthetical expression in equation (1) to the first. Assuming that these taxes had been invested, as they would be in private insurance or in funded social insurance, they would have a present value, PV_T, at the time the worker retires shown by equation (4).

$$(4) \quad PV_T = f w_0 s^k (s^{-m} r^m + s^{-m-1} r^{m-1} + \ldots + s^{-1} r).$$

Assuming that at retirement the worker discounts future benefits at the interest rate i, the present value of pensions, benefits PV_B, is shown by equation (5).

$$(5) \quad PV_B = w_0 s^k = (1 + s r^{-1} + s^2 r^{-2} + \ldots + s^{n-m-1} r^{-n+m+1}).$$

The paradox presented in section I states that $PV_B > PV_T$ when r is below some value. I shall now show that the critical value of r occurs approximately when $i = g + h$, i.e., where the rate of interest equals the sum of population growth and the increase in real wages. To do so it is necessary to establish the precise conditions under which $PV_B > PV_T$. Writing both out in full, moving the numerator of f to the left of the inequality sign, and cancelling where possible, the inequality may be written as follows:

$$(6) \quad \frac{(1 + sr^{-1} - s^2r^{-2} + \ldots + s^{n-m-1}r^{-n+m+1})}{(1 + t^{-1} + t^{-2} + \ldots + t^{-n+m+1})} > \frac{(s^{-m}r^{m} + s^{-m+1}r^{m-1} + \ldots + s^{-1}r)}{(t^{m} + t^{m-1} + \ldots + t)}.$$

Now, the right and left expressions are equal when $r = st$. In that case the numerator on each side becomes identical, term for term, with the denominator. The derivative of the left(right)-hand expression with respect to r is clearly negative (positive). Consequently for smaller values of r, the inequality holds. For larger values, it does not. When r, s, and t differ only slightly from unity, the condition that $r = st$ can be approximated by the condition that $i \approx g + h$.

III / Welfare implications

The results of section II show that if the sum of the rates of growth of per capita wages and of population exceeds the rate of interest, and if the rate of interest equals the marginal rate of time preference and the marginal rate of transformation of present into future goods, then the introduction of some social insurance pensions on a pay-as-you-go basis will improve the welfare position of each person. If saving and, hence, investment and, hence, the rate of growth of income are reduced as the level of social insurance increases, this conclusion does not necessarily follow. If the rate of growth is unaffected, the effective rate of return on premiums paid for such social insurance will exceed the marginal rate of time preference, and, consequently, people in the active labour force would willingly forego some current consumption in order to obtain such returns. Individually they are unable to do so; collectively they can.

If a small trust fund is accumulated, the proceeds from which are invested, the addition to welfare will be smaller than if no fund is accumulated, and in the limiting case of a full reserve, no increase in welfare will occur.

If the rate of interest exceeds the sum of the rate of growth of real wages and the rate of growth of population, then introduction of social insurance either on a pay-as-you-go or a funded basis will reduce welfare, unless (*a*) market imperfections render the pre-existing situation suboptimal, (*b*) the social welfare function calls for income redistribution, or (*c*) there are economies of scale in social insurance; none of these factors will be discussed here.

[18]

INTERNATIONAL ECONOMIC REVIEW
Vol. 16, No. 3, October, 1975

OPTIMUM SOCIAL SECURITY IN A LIFE-CYCLE GROWTH MODEL*

BY PAUL A. SAMUELSON[1]

INTRODUCTION

AN EXACT MODEL OF STEADY-STATE, exponential-growth social security, characterized by two parameters of benefit levels and real-capital owned, is introduced into the life-cycle model of Modigliani, Diamond, Cass and Yaari, and Samuelson. Its incidence is shown to be such that, by an infinite number of different combinations of its parameters, the optimal social security program can be found to convert laissez faire equilibrium into golden-rule equilibrium that maximizes lifetime wellbeing of every subsequent generation. The infinity of optimal patterns results from the fact that greater public thrift will rationally lower the need for private thrift and, uncertainty aside, the precise allocation between the two is a matter of indifference. Indeed, "fully-funded social security," in this model always drives out an equivalent amount of "private saving," only the total mattering. However, once elements of private myopia are introduced into the model, it can be shown that a social security program that is second-best in its induced real capital formation can still add much to true citizenry wellbeing.

SANS SOCIAL SECURITY

Let the wellbeing of the representative person who works for a period when young and retires for a period when old be $u[c^1, c^2]$ as in Samuelson [7, 8, 9]. Let labor grow forever like $(1 + g)^t$, and output be given neoclassically by $L_t f[K_t/L_t]$, as in Solow [6]. Then the two-part golden rule to achieve, at growth rate g, maximum steady-state lifetime wellbeing is given by

$$c_g^1 + \frac{c_g^2}{(1+g)} = f(k_g) - gk_g \tag{1}$$

$$f'[k_g] = g \tag{2}$$

$$\frac{\partial u[c_g^1, c_g^2]/\partial c^1}{\partial u[c^1, c^2]/\partial c^2} = 1 + g\,. \tag{3}$$

However, unless g happens to equal the optimum population growth rate g^*, that maximizes $u[c_g^1, c_g^2]$ with respect to g and ensures the goldenest golden rule of Samuelson [8], the laissez faire life-cycle saving model of Modigliani [4, 5], Diamond [2], Tobin [10], Cass and Yaari [1], and von Weizsäcker [11] will not

* Manuscript received April 17, 1975.

[1] I owe thanks to the National Science Foundation and to the National Institute of Health for financial aid, and to Lynn Mary Karjala for editorial assistance.

asymptotically evolve into $u[c_g^1, c_g^2]$, but rather into $(k_!, c_!^1, c_!^2, r_! \gtreqless g)$, the roots of

$$(4) \qquad c^1 + \frac{c^2}{(1+r)} = f[k] - rk$$

$$(5) \qquad f'[k] = r$$

$$(6) \qquad \frac{\partial u[c^1, c^2]/\partial c^1}{\partial u[c^1, c^2]/\partial c^2} = 1 + r$$

$$(7) \qquad (f[k] - rk) - c^1 \equiv \frac{c^2}{(1+r)} = k(1+g)\,.$$

This last equation states the equality of saving when young with the system's productive capital (and out of which, interest and principal, the retired consume).

If $r_!$ of (4)–(7) happens to equal g, we are in the golden-rule state satisfying (1)–(3) and, as shown by the Samuelson **[8]** Serendipity Theorem, we are then at the goldenest g^*.

WITH SOCIAL SECURITY

We can now add a social security program to the system and endeavor to convert laissez faire's $u[c_!^1, c_!^2]$ into the higher $u[c_g^1, c_g^2]$.

A steady-state social security system taxes each worker τ and pays benefits to each retired person of β, while owning k^s of real capital per laborer. Private owned capital per capita is then $k - k^s$. The budget identity of the steady-state social security program is given as

$$\beta L_{t-1} \equiv \tau L_t + r_t k_t L_t - (k_{t+1}L_{t+1} - k_t L_t)$$

or, when L_t grows like $(1+g)^t$ and we are in the steady state

$$(8) \qquad \frac{\beta}{(1+g)} \equiv \tau + (1+r)k^s - (1+g)k^s\,.$$

We may use this identity to eliminate β as an unknown, thereby characterizing each steady-state social security program by its two independent parameters, τ and k^s. (Note: the transient burden of building up to k^s involves straightforward dynamic analysis that casts no new light on the comparative statics of steady states; it is reserved for explicit analysis elsewhere.)

Now we generalize (4)–(7) to the following four equations to determine the four unknowns, $k(\tau, k^s)$, $c^1(\tau, k^s)$, $c^2(\tau, k^s)$, $r(\tau, k^s)$:

$$(9) \qquad c^1 + \frac{c^2}{(1+r)} = f[k] - rk - \tau + \frac{\beta}{(1+r)}$$

$$= f[k] - rk - \tau + (1+r)(1+g)^{-1}[\tau + (r-g)k^s]$$

$$(10) \qquad f'[k] = r$$

$$(11)\qquad \frac{\partial u[c^1, c^2]/\partial c^1}{\partial u[c^1, c^2]/\partial c^2} = 1 + r$$

$$(12)\qquad \frac{c^2}{(1 + r)} - (1 + r)(1 + g)^{-1}[\tau + (r - g)k^s] = (1 + g)(k - k^s)\,.$$

The incidence of a change in either τ or k^s can be worked out by straightforward total differentiation of (9)–(12) with respect to either of those parameters, giving linear relations to solve for $\partial c^i(\tau, k^s)/\partial\tau$, $\partial c^i(\tau, k^s)/\partial k^s$, etc.

OPTIMUM SOCIAL SECURITY

But to solve the problem of achieving the golden-rule state, we need not go through that analysis. Instead, we can force $r = g$ in (9), (10), (11), and note what values of (τ, k^s) are then needed to satisfy (12), namely (τ_g, k^s_g) in the following

$$(13)\qquad \frac{c^2_g}{(1 + g)} = \tau_g + (1 + g)(k_g - k^s)\,.$$

THEOREM 1. *By an appropriate steady-state, life-cycle social security system, we can support a golden-rule state instead of bearing with a laissez faire equilibrium that is not in that state. And that golden-rule steady state can be supported by an infinity of different social security programs (some involving more rather than less social capital, k^s, and less rather than more current taxing, τ_g). It is really indifferent in the steady state whether we are doing much or little of lifetime saving in our purely private capacities or via our democratic social security system.*

Obviously in applying an abstract theorem like this, the severe idealizations of the model will have to be qualified. (Thus, private savings may be channeled under uncertainty in a qualitatively more efficient way; or, in a system of depression rigidities, when private thrift becomes abortive, public thrift may be more effective.) Also, when private myopia is deemed to require merit-want intensification of social security, the fuller analysis will need to take into account that private $k - k^s$ will be displaced in some degree by an increase in β and τ, and this quite aside from induced longer retirement analyzed in Feldstein [3].

It should also be obvious that "ever-fully-funded" social security, so beloved by actuaries and so necessary in a voluntary system, can accomplish nothing in this model.

THEOREM 2. *Any increase in "fully-funded" social security merely displaces exactly as much private capital as the public capital it brings into being.*

Thus, by definition of full funding,

$$\beta L_{t-1} = \tau L_{t-1}(1 + r)$$
$$= k^s L_t(1 + r)$$

or

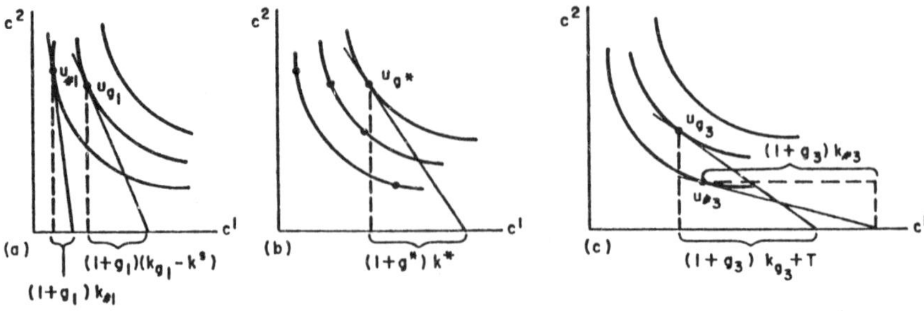

FIGURE 1

IN 1(b) WHERE THE GROWTH RATE IS JUST AT THE OPTIMUM POPULATION GROWTH RATE, HIGHEST WELLBEING IS AT u_{g^*}; PRIVATE SAVING WITH ZERO SOCIAL SECURITY OR WITH "FULLY-FUNDED SOCIAL SECURITY" CAN SUPPORT THIS GOLDENEST STATE.

IN 1(a) WHERE THE GROWTH RATE g_1 EXCEEDS THE OPTIMUM RATE g^*, LAISSEZ FAIRE WILL LEAD TO $u_{\S_1}$ WHERE LIFETIME SAVINGS JUST MATCH THE $k_{\S_1}$ LEVEL OF PER CAPITA CAPITAL AND WHERE $r_{\S_1}$ FALLS SHORT OF g_1. AN OPTIMAL SOCIAL SECURITY PROGRAM THAT IS "OVER-FUNDED" CAN GENERATE ONE OF THE SET OF k^s SOCIALLY-OWNED REAL CAPITAL WHICH CAN SUPPORT PERMANENTLY THE GOLDEN-RULE LIFETIME WELLBEING OF u_{g_1}.

IN 1(c) WHERE THE SOCIAL RATE IS BELOW THE OPTIMUM RATE g^*, LAISSEZ FAIRE WILL LEAD TO THE PERMANENTLY INEFFICIENT POINT $u_{\S_3}$, WITH $r_{\S_3}$ BELOW g_3. A PAY-AS-YOU-GO PONZI-LIKE PROGRAM CAN RAISE THE PERMANENT LEVEL OF THE SYSTEM TO THE GOLDEN-RULE POINT u_{g_3}. ALWAYS AN INFINITE NUMBER OF DIFFERENT BLENDS OF PAY-AS-YOU-GO AND OVER-FUNDING CAN ACHIEVE ANY DESIRED STATE.

$$\tau = k^s(1 + g) = \frac{\beta}{(1 + r)} \,. \tag{14}$$

If we put (14) into (9)–(12), that system degenerates into the laissez faire equilibrium of (4)–(7): then large τ merely lowers private $k - k^s$ as much as k^s rises, a trivially obvious result once we realize that the representative man is no different off if much or little of his "spontaneous" thrift is embalmed in private or public capital.

If $k_{\S} < k_g$ and $c_g^2/(1 + g) < k_g(1 + g)$, it is obvious that $gk^s - \tau_g$ in (13) must be positive—which can happen only if $k^s > 0$ and social security is *more* than fully funded (as that term is defined in (14)). If, as in Cass and Yaari [**1**], $k_{\S} > k_g$, as when growth rates become very low or very negative, $c_g^2/(1 + g) > k_g(1 + g)$ and $\tau_g - gk^s$ must be positive, which can be salubriously realized under pay-as-you-go social security with

$$k^s = 0$$

and

$$\tau_g = \frac{c^2}{(1 + g)} - (1 + g)k_g \,.$$

Increases in g so long as $k_{\S}$ remains above k_g will improve lifetime wellbeing and reduce the τ_g of pay-as-you-go social security, until at the Samuelson [**8**] optimum growth rate g^*, *no* social security program is needed (and the only optimal ones have to be fully-funded).

A concluding warning is in order. Reserved for later treatment is the analysis needed for transient analysis out of steady states. Thus, begin with laissez faire equilibrium at too high an interest rate. If we now aim to attain golden-rule steady state with positive social capital, it is clear that (with β and τ non-negative!) ever-pay-as-you-go social security cannot be utilized to accomplish this; but this truth does not deny that, *after* enough k^s has been built up and can be maintained out of its own earnings, the requisite steady-state social security program could forever after be a purely pay-as-you-go one with $\beta_g = (1+g)\tau_g$.

Figure 1 illustrates how optimal social security programs can convert private life-cycle saving into golden-rule states.

FINAL REMARKS

1. Just because a system is observed in a permanent steady-state equilibrium, $u[c^1, c^2]$, which is lower than the golden-rule $u[c_g^1, c_g^2]$ by virtue of the fact that the interest rate exceeds the growth rate, $r > g$, this does not mean that it will necessarily wish to move toward the higher u_g level; for to do so, must necessarily imply transient sacrifice of utility by some generations, and society's systematic rate of time preference might reckon this to be a bad bargain. In short, the hypothesized non-golden-rule steady state is not (repeat, not) *intertemporally* inefficient.

2. Many social security systems, like the New Deal U.S. system, may be deemed most valuable precisely because the myopia ignored by the present models does in fact prevail. People live miserably in old age because they do not realize when young what are the consequences of their private saving habits. So by democratic fiat, they paternalistically impose on themselves a within-life pattern of consumption that favors old age at the expense of young. Precisely because of the myopia that makes paternalism optimal, once citizens are subject to social security taxation and benefits they do not see clearly how they can undo by private-saving offsets what the mandatory system is doing to them. So, both because of themselves and yet despite themselves, they contrive social security that makes them better off.

This can be formalized by a model in which the $u[c^1, c^2]$ function "upon which people act" is different from the "true" $v[c^1, c^2]$ in terms of which they definitely wish to be guiding their decisions. Subject to (9)–(12), we pick (τ, k^s) to maximize $v[c^1(\tau, k^s), c^2(\tau, k^s)]$.

Massachusetts Institute of Technology, U.S.A.

REFERENCES

[1] CASS, D. AND YAARI, M., "Individual Savings, Aggregate Capital Accumulation, and Efficient Growth," in K. Shell, ed., *Essays on the Theory of Optimal Economic Growth* (Cambridge, Mass: MIT Press, 1967), 233–268.

[2] DIAMOND, P., "National Debt in a Neoclassical Growth Model," *American Economic Review*, LV (December, 1965), 1126–1150.
[3] FELDSTEIN, M., "Social Security and Private Savings: International Evidence in an Extended Life Cycle Model," unpublished Discussion Paper Number 361, Harvard Institute of Economic Research, Harvard University, (May, 1974).
[4] MODIGLIANI, F., "The Life-Cycle Hypotheses of Saving Twenty Years Later," in M. Parkin, ed., *Contemporary Issues in Economics* (Manchester: Manchester University Press, 1974).
[5] ——— AND R. BRUMBERG, "Utility Analysis and the Consumption Function: An Interpretation of Cross-Section Data," in K. K. Kurihara, ed., *Post Keynesian Economics* (New Brunswick, N. J.: Rutgers University Press, 1954).
[6] SOLOW, R. M., "A Contribution to the Theory of Economic Growth," *Quarterly Journal of Economics*, LXX (February, 1956), 65–94.
[7] SAMUELSON, P. A., "An Exact Consumption-Loan Model of Interest with or without the Social Contrivance of Money," *Journal of Political Economy*, LXVI (December, 1958), 467–482. Reprinted in Joseph E. Stiglitz, ed., *The Collected Scientific Papers of Paul A. Samuelson*, Volume I (Cambridge, Mass: MIT Press, 1966), Chapter 21.
[8] ———, "The Optimum Growth Rate for Population," *International Economic Review*, XVI (October, 1975), 531–538.
[9] ———, "The Two-Part Golden Rule Deduced as the Asymptotic Turnpike of Catenary Motions," *Western Economic Journal*, VI (March, 1968), 85–89. Reprinted in Robert C. Merton, ed., *The Collected Scientific Papers of Paul A. Samuelson*, Volume III (Cambridge, Mass.: MIT Press, 1972), Chapter 138.
[10] TOBIN, J., "Life Cycle Saving and Balanced Growth," in W. Fellner *et al.*, eds., *Ten Economic Studies in the Tradition of Irving Fisher* (New York: John Wiley and Sons, Inc., 1967), 231–256.
[11] VON WEIZSÄCKER, C. C., *Steady State Capital Theory* (Berlin: Springer Verlag, 1971).

[19]

Journal of Public Economics 8 (1977) 275–298. © North-Holland Publishing Company

A FRAMEWORK FOR SOCIAL SECURITY ANALYSIS

P.A. DIAMOND*

M.I.T., Cambridge, MA 02139, U.S.A.

Received April 1977, revised version received June 1977

The public provision of pensions in the U.S. by means of the Social Security system is examined relative to conventional arguments for public intervention. The system is analysed in terms of income redistribution, the provision of insurance where private markets are not efficient, and the compelling of saving by individuals.

1. Introduction

The U.S. Social Security program is a large one.[1] Being explicitly intertemporal in nature and concerned with individual risks, analysis of the program does not fit comfortably in the framework conventionally used to examine the income tax. In the next section, the basic structure of the retirement portion of the current Social Security program will be presented, including the over-indexing feature which has received much attention recently. Then, we shall inquire into the justifications for a program roughly of this sort. This discussion will also spell out the functions that Social Security can play in the current economy.[2]

2. Present structure

At the present time, earnings of employees up to the maximum taxable

*This paper was prepared for presentation at the NSF–NBER conference on taxation at Stanford in January 1976. The paper has benefited from comments at that conference and at seminar presentations at MIT, Wisconsin, and Yale. The author is also grateful for the help received in discussions with Henry Aaron, Michael Boskin, Frank Griffin, Jay Helms, James Hickman, William Hsiao, James Mirrlees, E. J. Moorhead, Alicia Munnell, Aaron Prero, Michael Rothschild, Bernard Saffran, Eytan Sheshinski, Robert Solow, and Peter Temin. Financial support from the National Science Foundation is gratefully acknowledged.

[1]In fiscal year 1975, the Old Age and Survivors program received $56 billion in contributions and $2 billion in interest. Benefit payments were $55 billion, with another billion for railroad retirement. For comparison, the U.S. individual income tax collected $122 billion in the same year.

[2]This paper does not contain a detailed discussion of policy recommendations for the Social Security system. For a discussion of such reforms, including the views of the author, see Consultant Panel on Social Security to the Congressional Research Service (1976).

earnings base are subject to a tax of 9.9% for OASDI,[3] half levied on the employer and half on the employee.[4] The self-employed are taxed on all earnings to the same maximum, but at the rate[5] of 7%. The maximum taxable earnings base is $15,300 in 1976 and increases automatically with increases in average covered wages in the economy. The Social Security trust funds are invested in regular Treasury securities, special ones issued to Social Security which pay an interest rate equal to the average rate on Treasury debt of more than four years, and obligations of federally sponsored agencies. Except for some small items, this completes the revenue side of the system.

To examine the payment of benefits to retirees let us consider a single worker of either sex, age 65, who is receiving a first benefit check.[6] To determine his benefit, the system examines the history of his earnings which have been subject to Social Security tax (not the history of taxes paid on this earnings record). From his earnings record is calculated an average monthly wage (AMW) counting only his best years. The number of years included will eventually be 35, 5 less than the number between 21 and 62, the age at which retired workers may first claim benefits.[7] At present no earnings before 1951 affect benefits for most workers, and a much shorter averaging period is used to reflect this cutoff. To determine benefits that will be paid in any future year, one takes a function[8] of the AMW and multiplies the result by the growth in the consumer price index from 1974 until the year of benefits:

$$B_t = f(AMW) \times CPI_t / CPI_{1974}. \tag{1}$$

Since the AMW is in nominal terms and the result is multiplied by CPI growth

[3]Old-Age, Survivors, and Disability Insurance. There is an additional payroll tax at present for health insurance. Current law legislates a 9.9% rate until 2010 and an 11.9% rate thereafter. The tax rate for the self-employed is not presently scheduled to change at the same time.

[4]Because the employee half, but not the employer half, of this tax is included in taxable income for the federal income tax, this distinction is not irrelevant.

[5]The self-employed get no deduction on the income tax for the payment of Social Security taxes. Until 1972, the self-employed tax rate was 75% of the combined employer and employee rates. Given the differences in deductibility on personal income tax and full deductibility of taxes on the corporate income tax, the historic 75% rule is a not unreasonable approximation to taxing different workers similarly.

[6]For simplicity I omit the rules determining the achievement of insured status, and so eligibility for benefits.

[7]For someone with fewer years of positive earnings, an appropriate number of zeros is included in calculation of the average wage.

[8]At present the function is defined up to the maximum AMW which a worker could possibly have. Whenever the maximum taxable earnings base is increased the function acquires a new piecewise linear segment with a lower slope. These slopes are not yet determined, depending on the inflation rate up to the time of wage base increase. The function is piecewise linear. After a horizontal section, the slope of the first increasing section is 1.2. Remaining slopes are lower and tend to decrease, reaching 0.2 for the last section determined in 1974. Assuming continued inflation the slope will approach zero as wages increase.

from a fixed calendar date (not the date of retirement), benefits are overindexed if one looks across successive generations of retirees. This overindexing and the expected level of inflation give rise to a major portion of the long range deficit projected for the system.

To complete this rough picture we need to consider the age at which benefits are collected, the definition of a retired worker, and the effects of the presence of dependents of the worker. Should a worker claim benefits between 62 and 65 the benefits are reduced by 5/9 of 1% for each month before age 65. Should a worker first claim benefits after age 65, the benefits are increased by 1/12 of 1% for each month after 65 (up to a maximum of 7%, since all workers 72 and over are entitled to benefits independent of retirement).

A worker is considered retired if he earns less than the allowed amount ($2760 per year in 1976). This allowed amount is indexed and increases according to the same index of average annual wages used for increasing the maximum taxable earnings base. For each dollar of earnings above the allowed amount, benefits are decreased by $0.50, until benefits are reduced to zero.[9]

Independent of adjustment for the age at which benefits are claimed, dependents can receive benefits which are functions of the benefits defined in equation one, called the primary insurance amount (*PIA*). An eligible spouse receives one-half the *PIA*. To be eligible, a spouse must be over 62, retired, and not entitled to a larger benefit on his or her own earnings record.[10] In addition, dependent children, mothers of dependent children even if younger than 62, grandchildren, and parents can also collect on a worker's earnings record, all benefits being subject to a family maximum. Further, divorced wives can also collect benefits in some circumstances.

The Social Security system is generally described as being on a pay as you go basis. There are two senses in which this is correct, although the automatic provisions do not adjust benefits to the available level of revenues. One sense in which this is true is that at present there is a trust fund of approximately $45 billion, very small relative to the estimated liabilities of $2.4 trillion. A second sense in which the system is on a pay as you go basis is that Congressional attitude appears to be that it is appropriate to increase benefits whenever the system can finance such an increase over the following 75 years,[11] independent of any perceived need for a substantial fund at the end of the planning horizon.

In considering the system, benefits do depend on individual earnings histories. Benefits also depend on the financial balance of the system since Congress

[9]A worker can also collect in a month of low earnings independent of his earnings in other months.

[10]This isn't quite accurate in that the spouse receives the difference between ½ the *PIA* of the worker and the *PIA* based on the spouse's own record. This distinction matters in complicated cases. In addition there is a decrease if the spouse is younger than 65.

[11]Projections of the system for the next 75 years are made annually by the Board of Trustees of the Federal Old-Age and Survivors Insurance and Disability Insurance Trust Funds.

regularly alters some of the parameters of the system. Thus using either the cash flow of a single year across all workers or the cash flow of a single worker over his full (expected) lifetime based on current law is an inaccurate picture of the entire system. I will argue that it makes more sense to view the system on an individual lifetime basis with some adjustments for short-run considerations rather than as an annual tax transfer system with lifetime considerations.

3. Reasons for a Social Security program

Before considering how to modify the present Social Security program, it seems appropriate to ask why one should have a program with a shape roughly like that describeed above. Conventionally, there are four reasons for government tax-transfer programs – raising revenue, redistributing income, correcting market failures, and paternalism. The Social Security system is not being used as a significant net revenue generating device, so I shall consider the other three reasons. In addition, since the system has considerable insurance aspects, we shall consider the possibility that the government can provide insurance more efficiently than the private market. (The macro effects of the system will not be considered.)

3.1. Income redistribution

There are two different ways in which the Social Security system serves a redistributive function. Within generations, the benefit formula given in (1) yields a relationship between expected benefits and taxes paid which implies redistribution.[12] Since an annual income tax plus estate taxes do not result in ideal (second-best) income redistribution, there is room for an additional device to redistribute incomes. The progressive income tax uses a very imperfect measure of who is rich and who poor. It is imperfect in its measure of income and imperfect in concentrating on a year rather than a longer time in defining need or ability to pay. A measure of lifetime earnings is also imperfect, ignoring capital income and individual planning that is shorter than a lifetime (and thus failure to use full lifetime opportunities). However, the imperfections are different

[12] As a crude indication of the magnitude of redistribution at the margin, it is generally estimated that approximately half the revenue generated by an increase in the maximum taxable earnings base (with continued automatic adjustments) is returned in higher benefits to workers subjected to the higher tax. There are many complicating features in evaluating the actual degree of redistribution including expected length of life, age at entry into covered employment, presence of dependents, age of claiming benefits. For an examination of internal rates of return on taxes and benefits for different individuals, see Freiden, Leimer and Hoffman (1976).

and this seems likely to be a case where two instruments, both redistributing, will do better than either one alone,[13]

The second redistributive function is between generations. The increase in benefits associated with a small trust fund (relative to full funding) represents redistribution to earlier generations from later ones. The bulk of the anticipated redistribution has occurred in the start up of the system. This can be viewed as appropriate either because earlier generations are expected to be poorer on average or because the particular generations involved experienced the depression of the 1930s, making them particularly needy.

Both of these redistributive purposes appear fully legitimate, but neither, standing alone could justify a Social Security system like the current one. On purely redistributive grounds there is no reason to be paying any benefits to the wealthiest (i.e. those contributing most to the redistribution) much less giving them the largest pensions.[14] Thus, we need to look further for justifications. Within a lifetime perspective, we will find reasons for benefit payments to those deemed most well off. My preference for a lifetime rather than annual perspective rests in part on the fact that the annual perspective makes very little sense of the redistributive pattern. To tax all workers, rich and poor, to give benefits to retirees both rich and poor would make little sense. Similarly to give larger benefits to those with less need (as measured by their lifetime earnings) would also make little sense. The lifetime perspective, viewing individuals both as taxpayers and benefit recipients will make sense of these patterns, as we will see below.

3.2. *Market failure*

Judged by the standard of an ideal market system covering all eventualities and all future periods, there are a number of market failures in the present US economy which a Social Security system could help alleviate. There are three such failures which will be discussed – the absence of safe investment opportunities (in real terms), the absence of real annuities, and the problems in insuring the risk associated with a varying length of working life.

Someone seeking to accumulate funds for retirement has an array of investment opportunities which do not appear to give a combination of a reasonable yield and a safe real rate of return. Particularly for the small investor who cannot develop a diversified portfolio of real investments, this shortcoming limits the ability to save for a relatively guaranteed consumption level in retirement.

[13]Of course one would expect to do even better by a suitable integration of the income tax and Social Security system, for example by subjecting benefits to income taxation. A priori, one cannot rule out the possibility that the optimum involves using one tool to redistribute to the rich so as to use the other one to redistribute more heavily to the poor.

[14]Arguments for the avoidance of the stigma of welfare might support a uniform pension, but not one with the appearance of the present system.

Even a mutual fund is subject to large value changes in a short time when the individual might want to convert wealth into an annuity. If this problem alone were felt to be the main issue, the answer would obviously be the issuance of indexed bonds by the government rather than the development of a large Social Security system. However, having the system lessens the importance of the absence of such bonds.[15]

Someone reaching retirement age with a capital sum might reasonably want to purchase a real annuity. While the annuity market is very well developed, it is not possible to purchase real annuities (i.e. annuities indexed to the *CPI*) in today's market. If this were the only reason for a Social Security program, the problem could well be more easily handled by having the government make this market or provide investment opportunities (indexed bonds) which would induce insurance companies to provide this asset. Once one has a Social Security program, it seems appropriate to have benefits paid as an indexed annuity.

The next risk to be discussed is a very large one for individual workers and not easily handled by alternative institutions. It is the risk associated with the length of working life. The risk comes from two sources – a possible decline in earning abilities (due to declining skills or health, for example) or a possible large increase in the disutility associated with working (again possibly from poor health or just general decline in strength or energy). The rough magnitude of the risk can be viewed by examining the large spread in retirement ages (in 1970 male labor force participation rates declined from 72.7 for 62 year olds to 47.1 for 65 year olds to 22.1 for 72 year olds) [U.S. Bureau of the Census (1973, pp. 31–32)]. Of course, without a theory of financial incentives for retirement these figures don't give the magnitude of the risks involved but do show that a wide variation must be present in the economy.[16] The importance of the risk is increased by the double nature of the implications of an early need for retirement.[17] By shortening the working life, early retirement shortens the period during which individuals accumulate savings out of earnings to finance retirement. Insofar as early retirement is not associated with an event that shortens life expectancy or insofar as there are dependents, early retirement lengthens the period of retirement which needs to be financed out of accumulated savings.

This risk is clearly very large. In addition any attempt to insure the risk faces severe moral hazard and adverse selection problems. Health itself is often difficult to monitor accurately. Inability to obtain a suitable job is also difficult

[15]Conventionally, market failures are identified by description of their cause. The cause of the absence of indexed investments is not clear to me. One possibility is the recentness of the increase in inflation rates and the presence of a lag in market development. Another is the desirability of intertemporal risk pooling for uncertainties in inflation rates. The absence of a conventional cause does not necessarily imply the absence of this market failure.

[16]To pursue the magnitude of the risk one would also want to examine the shift from full to part time labor.

[17]I will use the word retirement very loosely to represent both a full or nearly full cessation of work and a sharp decline in earnings even when their level remains high.

to monitor. Much of the need for retirement probably comes from an interaction of events without a single sharp health or unemployment problem, making monitoring far more difficult, being dependent on feelings of fatigue and interest in labor. Thus a private market cannot do very well with this problem.[18] Social Security as insurance against declines in earnings is the natural social tool for dealing with the problem. Of course, this implies that a proper design of the regulations relating benefits to current earnings, past earnings, and age at retirement is a major part of the design of a good Social Security system. Such regulations must trade off the advantages of insurance (paying larger benefits when needed more) against the work disincentives thus created.[19]

3.3. Paternalism

A third line of justification for Social Security is that many individuals will not save enough for retirement if left to their own devices.[20] There are a number of different possible strands to this argument, all leading to roughly the same conclusion. One could peg the argument on the difficulty in obtaining suitable information for informed judgement on the need for savings for retirement. (One might argue that people severely overestimate the likelihood that they will be able and interested in working at full earnings level right up to death.) Citing the evidence on the difficulties people have in making decisions under uncertainty [e.g. Tumerin and Resik (1972), Tversky and Kahneman (1974), Kun-

[18]Compulsory insurance clearly avoids part of the adverse selection problem. (Part of the problem remains as long as different options are available, for example early retirement.) Collection of information for tax purposes and use of other tax tools create differences between public and private abilities to deal with the moral hazard problem of the financial incentive to retire early. This moral hazard problem is a necessary part of insuring the decline in earnings without full measurement of the causes of such a decline.

[19]This is a topic which clearly needs considerable research. On the theoretical side there has been little analysis of tax systems that simultaneously insure and redistribute. On the empirical side little is known of the response of labor supply to the different parameters that could be used in relating benefits to earnings and age. The use of some earnings test transfers an individual's income from the state of nature where he does earn to one where he doesn't. This is an essential element of insuring this risk. (Another element comes from basing benefits on average earnings over a fixed number of years rather than cumulated contributions or all earnings.) Since some of the risks involved lessen earnings without making full retirement desirable, perhaps the earnings test should be related to the decline in earnings (current earnings relative to *AMW*) as well as the absolute level of earnings.

[20]Welfare has been available for a long time. At present the U.S. has the Supplemental Security Income Program, essentially a negative income tax for the elderly. The program has a 100% tax rate on unearned income and a limitation on wealth for eligibility. It is reasonable that people planning to collect SSI will have little incentive to save. Thus, to look for evidence of undersaving we should look to those with sufficiently high income that a decline to the standard of living financed by welfare is very large. Also a forced savings program would be a way of making those with large lifetime incomes but small retirement incomes pay for their own welfare payments when old.

reuther et al. (1977)], one could base the argument on efficiency in decision making rather than in information gathering. Third one might simply fall back on the factors that lead people to spend more now and less later than seems sensible. Some individuals might be aware of these factors and therefore not object to this compulsion (self-paternalism). Whatever the tack taken in explaining the phenomenon, the main line of this argument is insufficient individual savings. Before proceeding to the obvious conclusion that Social Security can play an important role as a forced savings program, let us examine the definition of and some evidence for the argument of inadequate private savings for retirement.[21]

In the static model of individual choice, a person makes a single selection of his entire consumption basket. Lack of rationality is normally associated with intransitivity of preferences in response to alternative choice situations. Thus, if a person prefers A to B, B to C, and C to A, we are suspicious of his ability to make decisions for himself. This sort of irrationality does not seem central for the savings issue. A somewhat simpler type of irrationality to observe would be a situation where decisions are made at several points in time and these decisions appear to be inconsistent with a single maximization procedure (and we have reason to think that circumstances have not changed sharply). For example, one-fifth of ordinary life insurance policies in force fewer than two years voluntarily lapse.[22] This results in individuals having purchased exceptionally expensive one or two year term insurance policies unless the commission to the agent benefits the purchaser.[23] Unless there is reason to believe that this large a fraction of purchasers have significantly changed economic or family circumstances or close relations with the agent, it seems appropriate to conclude that some irrationality is present either at the first purchase date or the date when the policy is allowed to lapse. In the savings area, however, it is difficult to find pairs of inconsistent decisions.[24]

A third approach to the question is methodologically sharply different from the other two. The first two situations did not involve enquiry into the preferences being exhibited but rather into the consistency of their maximization. A third approach to this issue is to ask whether any sensible person would act in a

[21]To analyze this question properly, longitudinal data on individual savings should be subjected to detailed analysis. For an argument that rule of thumb behavior explains aggregate data as well as lifecycle theories, see Marglin (1975).

[22]Life Insurance Fact Book (1975, p. 52). This behavior is probably affected by the way individual life insurance is sold.

[23]This example reflects decisions which are part of a long-run plan, not repeated opportunities to make the same decision which might reasonably result in different decisions since past consumption might affect current preferences, even if in a fully foreseen manner.

[24]One not terribly good indicator of the situation is whether people regret earlier decisions (with regret suitably reflecting knowledge available at the earlier decision date). It would be interesting but not necessarily conclusive to interview the retired to inquire whether they wished they had saved more. (And to interview the young on the extent of their awareness of later needs.)

particular way. This line of approach seems to be behind some attitudes toward some consumer product safety issues – no sensible person would buy a crib with a noticeable probability of strangling a baby. In addition to being foreign to conventional economic methodology, this line of argument standing alone is unappealing in that it is lacking any natural limits on the policies one suspects could be justified.[25] I do not propose to enter into a discussion of the appropriate use of paternalism arguments. It seems to me that they are occasionally appropriate and that this may be one of those cases.

To use this third line (since I have little evidence on the applicability of the first two), I need to argue that the savings patterns of a sizeable fraction of Americans do not seem to be sensible.[26] Ideally one would like to examine individual income, wealth, and savings histories. I know of no empirical studies on savings using longitudinal data and so shedding light on the fraction of the population for whom a life-cycle model seems appropriate.[27] As an easily available substitute we shall argue that many persons do little saving in absolute terms by examining the various Social Security surveys which show a very large fraction of the aged population with little income from assets and small or no holdings of financial assets (although home ownership is widespread). This evidence is suggestive; however, in the absence of income figures it is not clear how many people ought to have very little wealth. Therefore we will also examine the distribution of wealth-income ratios for different income brackets, based on data from the Longitudinal Retirement History Survey of 1969 and the Parnes data for those near retirement age.

Table 1 reports on older surveys giving the percentage of aged beneficiary units reporting receipt of income from financial assets and retirement pensions other than OASDHI. As can be seen, a large fraction of the aged (generally at least 20%) do not report any such income. It is also interesting to note that the overwhelming majority (on the order of 80%) report no contributions from relatives. While one would expect Social Security to displace such contributions,

[25]Of course a similar situation holds with the fundamental welfare theorem which shows the equality of the sets of competitive equilibria and pareto optima. Currently the theorem is normally interpreted as describing a set of circumstances where no government action (other than income redistribution) is warranted. The theorem can equally well be read the other way, as showing that the market can't do better than a planner, so why bother with markets? Just to be clear, I don't think the theorem contains everything relevant to a choice between market and nonmarket solutions. I am merely indicating the use that could be made of the theorem as conventionally presented and in the absence of further discussion. Similarly in any particular situation one would want more discussion than merely the conclusion that paternalism can be justified in some circumstances.

[26]Someone accepting the conclusion but not liking raw paternalism can, of course, interpret the results as showing a lack of information on the nature of the risks that individual earners face and an enormous difficulty in conveying the magnitude of the risks in a convincing manner. The policy conclusions of this tack would be roughly the same.

[27]Of course, the model may be appropriate for most wealth without being appropriate for most persons. The former may reflect on the efficiency of capital markets while the latter is relevant for the need for Social Security.

these figures from the early 1940s suggest that there was not very much in the way of such contributions to be displaced.[28]

The Social Security system conducted a survey of the aged in 1968 asking questions about conditions in 1967 [Bixby et al. (1975)]. The sample (of 8,248 interviewees) represents an estimated 15,800,000 aged units where a unit is a single person or a couple with at least one member at least 65 years old.[29] In the survey 40% of couples and 56% of nonmarried persons reported no money[30] income from assets.[31] Income flows from sources other than assets, OASDHI, and earnings[32] are not widely reported (other public pensions were reported by 10% of units, private pensions and annuities by 14%, veterans benefits by 10% unemployment insurance and public assistance by 13%). Thus, it seems natural to conclude[33] that a large fraction of units have little more than Social Security or are relying on a continued ability to earn throughout their lifetimes. One would expect that rational lifetime accumulation patterns would give much

[28]One is naturally suspicious of answers to questions about whether one is receiving financial support from one's relatives. There is less reason to be suspicious about the question: do you give support to your relatives? The Longitudinal Retirement History Survey asked this question in 1969 to households aged 58–63. While the survey was sufficiently recent that the presence of Social Security may well have affected the answers, the ages of the parents of 58–63 year olds are sufficiently great that the availability of Social Security for the children may be more important than its availability for their parents. Without details on the number of children per parent, the comparison of these numbers with those in table 1 is not immediate. Nevertheless they are supportive of the conclusion that Social Security transfers are only offset in small part by decreases in private transfers. The results are summarized in the following table. The percentages are percentages of households with living parents.

	% with parent living in household	% with parent not in household and giving some support*
Married couples		
Men	5	12
Spouse	9	13
Men, no spouse present	35	19
Women, no spouse present	31	12

*A small number report complete support; about one-half of remainder report making regular contributions and one-half giving occasional support.
Source: Janet Murray (1976, table 75, p. 92).

[29]38% of the units are couples; 15%, nonmarried men; and 47%, nonmarried women.
[30]Over 75% of couples and 35–40% of nonmarried persons do own their own homes (Bixby et al., p. 105).
[31](Bixby et al., table 2.2, p. 14). The pattern was the same for 65–72 year olds and for those 73 and over (table 2B).
[32]27% of units - 46% of couples and 15% of nonmarried persons reported earnings.
[33]It seems unlikely that a great deal of the wealth of the aged (other than houses) is in a form which does not generate income.

Table 1
Percent of units with income from specified sources.

Type of beneficiary unit and survey	Earnings[a]	Retirement pensions other than OASDHI	Interest, dividends, rents	Unemployment insurance[a]	Public assistance	Contributions by relatives[b]
Married couples						
1941–42 surveys:						
Philadelphia–Baltimore	24	25	44	25	7	9
St. Louis	38	18	42	13	7	9
Birmingham–Memphis–Atlanta	44	15	33	18	3	13
Los Angeles	39	12	52	14	21	15
1944 middle-sized Ohio cities	57	16	56	2	7	16
1946 Boston	27	22	70	2	16	17
1949 Philadelphia–Baltimore	24	24	55	5	6	22
1951 National Beneficiary Survey	36	23	50	4	12	6
1957 National Beneficiary Survey	38	25	59	2	7	5
1963 Survey of the Aged	33[c]	27	65	2	6	3
Nonmarried men						
1941–42 surveys:						
Philadelphia–Baltimore	28	21	35	26	10	5
St. Louis	36	21	31	7	11	7
Birmingham–Memphis–Atlanta	52	8	23	16	4	16
Los Angeles	32	7	34	12	39	7
1944 middle-sized Ohio cities	48	15	40	2	9	14
1946 Boston	20	22	61	1	22	9
1949 Philadelphia–Baltimore	23	25	43	6	17	14
1951 National Beneficiary Survey	28	16	34	2	22	5
1957 National Beneficiary Survey	29	19	38	2	14	5
1963 Survey of the Aged	24	18	50	1	10	2
Nonmarried retired women						
1941–42 surveys:						
Philadelphia–Baltimore	21	20	51	28	8	7
St. Louis	30	22	37	11	7	10
Birmingham–Memphis–Atlanta	39	6	44	6	4	22
Los Angeles	35	5	50	9	32	13
1944 middle-sized Ohio cities	41	2	45	1	14	27
1946 Boston	22	21	60	1	24	10
1951 National Beneficiary Survey	27	12	45	2	20	9
1957 National Beneficiary Survey	36	11	53	1	13	12
1963 Survey of the Aged	34	15	56	2	10	4
Widows						
1941–42 surveys:						
Philadelphia–Baltimore	17		56		6	11
St. Louis	9		44		5	16
Birmingham–Memphis–Atlanta	36		46		0	21
Los Angeles	17		72		10	17
1944 middle-sized Ohio cities	35		58		5	34
1946 Boston	15		69		18	18
1951 National Beneficiary Survey	14	2	49		13	10
1957 National Beneficiary Survey	15	2	52		12	11
1963 Survey of the Aged	17	3	58	d	8	5

Source: U.S. Department of Health, Education and Welfare, (1970, table 7, p. 61).
[a]For married couples, percent of married men.
[b]Relatives and friends outside the household.
[c]Including couples with either or both members reporting earnings: 50 percent.
[d]0.5 percent or less.

wider financial asset holding in the economy since models of lifetime accumulation do not ordinarily imply savings for retirement which is this small except with very large discount factors. We will return to the appropriate size of accumulated wealth below. Another measure of the magnitude of private accumulation is that only 17% of the aged units report that they receive at least 20% of their income from assets. 44% of couples and 54% of the nonmarried report receipt of at least half their income from OASDHI (Bixby et al., table 2.6, pp. 19 and 20). Given the relatively small size of the Social Security system in 1967,[34] it seems unlikely this pattern would have evolved from sensible savings and normal risks. Considering reported financial assets, 55% of all units reporting reported less than $1000 in financial assets (approximately 75% of interviewees reported on their financial assets (Bixby et al., table 6.9, p. 115)).

The Social Security Administration has surveyed a sample of 20,260 individuals who applied for benefits between January and June 1970 [U.S. Department of Health, Education and Welfare (1973)]. The sample was analyzed separately for those whose benefits were payable at award and those who had benefits postponed (i.e. those applying primarily for Medicare, but not eligible for benefits, presumably because of earnings). Of those with payable benefits 45% of couples, 69% of nonmarried men and 53% of nonmarried women did not report any asset income. Of those with postponed benefits 40% of couples, 53% of nonmarried men and 42% of nonmarried women did not report any asset income.[35]

Next we shall turn to data of individual wealth–income ratios to examine the accumulation patterns by income class. There are two points to be gathered from this examination. Inadequate savings appears to be a phenomenon which is widespread, not confined to the bottom of the income distribution. Secondly, insofar as wealth–income ratios do rise with income level there may be a declining need for Social Security in the future if real as well as relative position in the income distribution affect private accumulation.[36]

Before considering the data let us briefly consider the wealth–earnings level which would be sensible for a 60 year old. The central case we'll analyze is that of an individual who works and saves for 30 years[37] (ages 35–64) and is then retired for 15 years, dying precisely on schedule. We will relate the wealth–

[34]In 1967 average monthly retirement benefits for male workers only were $92.50, for female $71.90, and for couples $144.20. By 1973 these numbers had increased to $180.10, $146.00, and $276.70. Source: Social Security Bulletin (1973, table 29, p. 59).

[35](USDHEW, table 1, p. 20). These numbers are restricted to those reporting on all sources of income.

[36]One complication in examining individual choice of current savings patterns is the presence of Social Security. Thus, this quick look at earlier asset and income levels gives some perspective on the possibility that Social Security is responsible for a very large fraction of the low savers which is present.

[37]Longer periods of savings would give higher wealth–earnings ratios at age 60 to finance a given replacement of net earnings with a constant savings rate.

earnings ratio at age 60 to savings rates, interest rates, and earnings growth rates (all calculations in real terms). Then we can relate different parameters (and their implied wealth–earnings ratios) to the replacement ratio (annuity/earnings) that can be financed.

To start, let us consider a world of no wage growth and no interest. Since there are two working years for every retirement year, a savings rate of 1/3 would finance a constant income flow net of savings. However, this ignores earnings costs and income taxes. A savings rate of 1/4 would give an annuity equal to 2/3 the level of gross income less savings. That probably corresponds fairly closely to a steady net income pattern, allowing for taxes and the costs of earning. With 25 years of acccumulation of 1/4 of income, the wealth–earnings ratio at age 60 would be 6.25. Continuing with the assumption of constant earnings, let us now consider the case of positive interest. If saving is going on continuously (at a constant rate s) and interest is compounded continuously at rate i, we have wealth at age t satisfying

$$W_t = \frac{sY}{i}\left(\mathrm{e}^{(t-35)i}-1\right), \tag{2}$$

where Y is earnings. If we consider the constant annuity that can be financed for 15 years out of W_{65},we have

$$A = iW_{65}\frac{\mathrm{e}^{15i}}{\mathrm{e}^{15i}-1}. \tag{3}$$

Combining these equations we can relate both the replacement ratio $(A/(1-s)Y)$ and the wealth income ratio at 60 to the interest rate,

$$\frac{A}{(1-s)Y} = \left(\frac{s}{1-s}\right)\mathrm{e}^{15i}\left(\frac{\mathrm{e}^{30i}-1}{\mathrm{e}^{15i}-1}\right), \tag{4}$$

$$\frac{W_{60}}{Y_{60}} = \frac{s}{i}\left(\mathrm{e}^{25i}-1\right). \tag{5}$$

To achieve a replacement ratio of $\frac{2}{3}$ we would need a savings rate satisfying

$$s = \frac{2}{2+3\mathrm{e}^{15i}\left(\dfrac{\mathrm{e}_{30}{}^{i}-1}{\mathrm{e}^{15i}-1}\right)}. \tag{6}$$

c

The matching savings rates and wealth income ratios are shown in the following table.

interest rate	0	0.01	0.02	0.03	0.04
savings rate	0.25	0.21	0.17	0.14	0.12
wealth/income at 60	6.3	6.0	5.6	5.3	4.9

Next let us consider the effect of growing earnings. Assume that earnings have grown at the rate g. With a fixed savings rate consumption grows at the same rate. If consumption after retirement were to grow at this rate also, then the above calculations are unchanged, with i being the excess of the interest rate over the growth rate of wages. While this pattern might come from some optimal savings formulations, there are reasons to consider slower growing consumption after retirement. In any case we are interested in examining assumptions which yield low levels of desired wealth. As an example of this, let us assume that consumption is constant after retirement. Since consumption has grown steadily in the past, there is now a problem in finding a benchmark level of consumption with which to compare postretirement income. One possible value, which (given smooth earnings growth) captures a sense of the standard of living in the period before retirement, is net earnings at age 60. Thus, we now have the following relations between the annuity, wealth, and income: first, the size annuity that can be financed out of wealth at retirement, which remains (2) above; second, the growth of wealth based on savings out of growing income (with $i > g$),

$$W_t = \frac{sY_{35}}{(g-i)} e^{-35g} e^{it}[e^{(g-i)t} - e^{(g-i)35}]; \tag{7}$$

and third the desired level of A,

$$A = \tfrac{2}{3} Y_{60} (1-s). \tag{8}$$

Combining these we can again calculate the savings rate and wealth–income ratios for different interest rates assuming a 2% growth rate for earnings.[38]

interest rate	0.02	0.03	0.04
savings rate	0.21	0.17	0.14
wealth/income at 60	5.2	4.9	4.6

[38] Analysis of Social Security data in Consultant Panel on Social Security (1976) found earnings growth for an individual between ages 35 and 60 approximately equal to the growth of average earnings in the economy.

The calculations in the two tables above suggest that an individual with a known 2% earnings growth pattern and a plan to retire at 65 and die at 80 should have a wealth–earnings ratio in the neighborhood of 5 to have a postretirement consumption level roughly equal to his preretirement consumption level. However, some individuals won't like this plan and all individuals are eligible for Social Security, welfare and (presently) SSI benefits after 65 and are subject to considerable uncertainties. The presence of welfare and SSI means that low income people might reasonably plan to have low wealth to collect welfare or SSI. Thus, any test of the hypothesis that sensible savings patterns are absent for a large fraction of the population will have to consider income levels before retirement sufficiently high that a plan to have a living standard which falls to the level supported by welfare and SSI does not seem reasonable (i.e. this result is unlikely to be the outcome of a careful plan). The presence of Social Security benefits does decrease the needed wealth to carry out the plan described above. The earlier the observations on the population, the smaller the Social Security system has been. The observations discussed below are from 1969 and 1971, before the large increase in 1972, although some increase might reasonably have been foreseen. In 1976 single workers with steady earnings history and income between median earnings and the taxable maximum commonly received a benefit equal to 30 to 40% of earnings at age 65 [Consultant Panel on Social Security (1976, p. 8)]. Those above the taxable maximum receive a smaller percentage of total earnings. A married couple with just one worker receives a 50% higher percentage of previous wage. Since Y_{65}/Y_{60} is about $(1.02)^5$ or 1.10, expectations of this level of benefits would approximately halve the wealth need of a single person (or two-worker couple) and decrease by $\frac{2}{3}$ the need of a one-worker couple. Before 1972, Social Security benefits were approximately 20% smaller, in real terms. They were even smaller in earlier years when accumulation was going on. It is not clear how optimistic one should expect savers in their 50s to have been in the 1960s. From these considerations, ratios in the range of 2 to $2\frac{1}{2}$ seem possibly reasonable. Similar arguments imply that private pensions, especially when vested, significantly reduce the amount of wealth an individual needs. Since data on expected pension benefits were not available, calculations are done separately for those with and without pensions.

Now let us turn to the uncertainties. The most obvious one is uncertainty about length of life. While Social Security is indexed to the *CPI*, annuities indexed to the *CPI* are not available in the market. Variable annuities are available, but anyone familiar with recent stock market history recognizes these as an imperfect hedge against inflation for time periods on the order of a few years. This greatly increases the desirable wealth level. For example, someone planning on a sufficient annuity for precisely 20 years, rather than 15, needs a 25% higher wealth at retirement. Someone also hedging against inflation would presumably (but not necessarily) increase wealth further. One hedge against inflation is the holding of consumer goods. In the ownership of homes this is common. However, it is difficult to draw down much of the equity in a house to finance consumption during retirement.[39] A second element to be considered with couples is that it is not twice as expensive for two to live as for one. Thus, the likelihood of a significant period with a single survivor raises the necessary wealth to finance a given standard of living (relative to the same aggregate expected years of life with simultaneous deaths). From Social Security, the one worker couple receives one and a half times the real benefit they will receive when there is a single survivor. These considerations probably increase the sensible ratio at least into the range of 2½ to 3, with the ratio increasing as one moves above the taxable maximum for Social Security.

The second major uncertainty is over length of working life. Unfortunately, this issue is very complicated to analyze for purposes of this argument. There are two elements at work. One is that there is considerable uncertainty for any individual about the length of his desired or feasible working life.[40] Generally we would expect this uncertainty to noticeably increase planned wealth at age 60. The second is that individuals differ in the risks that they face and some of these differences would reasonably be known well before age 60 and so capable of affecting savings decisions.

Many elements in addition to a steady consumption level after retirement enter into a sensible wealth accumulation pattern. In addition to redistributing planned consumption, wealth serves to cushion unexpected large expenditures (for example, legal or medical expenses not covered by insurance) and unexpected decreases in earnings (from unemployment or disability). The presence of the former after retirement raises the desired wealth. The presence of both risks before retirement raises desired savings rates, but depending on the actual occurrence of these events, may raise or lower the level of wealth an individual has at age 60. The discussion above has omitted early working years (before age 35), inheritances received or expected, planned bequests, and expenses for children.[41] All of these elements add uncertainty to the interpretation of the data.

[39]I have been told that in England one can readily sell ownership of a house conditional on one's death.

[40]The large decline in labor force participation of 62–65 year olds when retirement benefits became available is an indication of sizeable risk or lack of planning. Because of actuarial reduction, there is little substitution effect associated with the choice of early retirement over retirement at age 65. In 1975, 61 % of all benefit awards moving to payment status were reduced for early retirement. Source: Social Security Bulletin (1976, table Q5, p. 83).

[41]Consideration of these various functions served by accumulated wealth makes clear that an individual would not want all his planned retirement consumption in a wealth form which was inaccessible before retirement. As the level of Social Security benefits gets close to the optimal retirement consumption level, Social Security becomes an inefficient way to hold wealth. Thus, there is a clear efficiency justification for the conventional description of Social Security as aiming for a floor on retirement income rather than the optimal individual level. Variation across individuals in the desired level of savings for retirement and the greater ease of additional positive savings rather than negative savings is a second reason for Social Security to be a floor.

Serious consideration of these issues needs to be based on individual savings patterns described in longitudinal data. Here we can only be suggestive.

Thus, in examination of the data it should be rememberd that it is reasonable for some fraction of the population to have low wealth-earnings ratios even at age 60. Perhaps the reader should form an opinion on a plausible fraction of the population below different wealth-income ratios before looking at the data.

Now let us consider two bodies of data[42] shedding light on this issue. Here we will consider the percentages of married men in an income bracket with wealth-income ratios below 2 and below 1.[43] To set the discussion, in table 2 are presented the percentages of males aged 58–63 in 1969 by marital status and private pension coverage. Considering only married men, we will be considering over

Table 2
Distribution of 58–63 year old males by marital status and private pension coverage, 1969.

	Married	Not married
Covered	46.0%	5.9%
Not covered	40.1%	7.9%

Source: Longitudinal Retirement History Survey. Those listed as not covered answered 'no' to questions of pension coverage based on present, previous, and longest jobs.

85% of the males in this age group, slightly more than half of whom have some coverage in pensions other than OASI. We will consider the groups with and without pensions separately since the data do not contain the size of the anticipated pension. There are three complications in performing this analysis – the definition of wealth, the definition of income, and the treatment of those for whom either income or wealth datum is not available.[44] For wealth, the data report net worth including all assets (except, of course, the value of public and private pensions).[45]

Ideally one would want a measure of lifetime earnings. Since this ideal was

[42]I am grateful to Joseph Quinn for providing the data from the Longitudinal Retirement History Survey and to Alicia Munnell for that from the Parnes data.

[43]The nonmarried men report considerably lower wealth-earnings ratios to the Longitudinal Retirement History Survey.

[44]In addition there is the difficulty in interpretation from the under-reporting of wealth in addition to nonreporting by a fraction of the population.

[45]The measure which excludes net equity in a house is in some ways more relevant. For most categories the fraction with a wealth net of house-income ratio below one is very similar to the fraction with a wealth-income ratio below two.

not available, the tables report on calculations with three different income definitions. In tables 3 and 4, two different definitions are provided. Earnings 1968 is the sum of reported earnings for husband and wife in 1968.[46] Full earnings 1969 is an estimate of earnings obtained from whatever earnings rate figure for the man was given (hourly, weekly, monthly, or annually) by multiplying by the number of full-time units in a year. This significantly decreases the number for which an income figure is unavailable and sharply raises the percentage with low wealth in the bottom income category. A third measure, reported in table 5, is based on family income rather than earnings. (Given an assumed interest rate, the wealth–income ratio can be converted to a wealth–earnings ratio.) This disadvantage is somewhat offset by having up to six years of income observations, 1965–1970, on the individuals. The income figure reported is the average of these nominal income figures, using only those that are positive and available.

For some individuals, income data are not available. In tables 3 and 4 these individuals are reported separately. In table 5 they have been excluded from the data set.[47] For some individuals a wealth estimate is not available. In constructing tables 3 and 5 these individuals are excluded from the data set. This produces the same answer as would the assumption that the distribution of wealth–income ratios for those out of the sample is the same as those in the sample. This seems the most appropriate assumption. In constructing table 4, all those without wealth estimates were assumed to have wealth–income ratios in excess of two to generate a lower bound.

If we consider the central 60% of the population in terms of annual earnings in table 3 something on the order of 10–15% of the population have a wealth–earnings ratio below one and on the order of 30% have a ratio below 2. Considering the six year average income measure, about 20–30% have a wealth–income ratio below 1 and 40–50% have a ratio below two.[48] These calculations are very crude. In the absence of more thorough analysis of individual savings, they are suggestive that a sizeable fraction of American workers would not follow sensible savings plans in the absence of Social Security.[49]

Forcing individuals who are saving rationally to save a little more has little welfare cost by the usual envelope argument.[50] Forcing those saving too little to save more would have a large effect since the envelope argument is not

[46]Those reported as being out of the labor force in early 1969 when interviewed have been put in the not available category.

[47]The sample used to construct table 5 excluded men for whom the data set was not complete on other variables too.

[48]The presence of considerable random variation in individual earnings may be a part of the differences in these estimates.

[49]The desirability of individual savings at higher levels than would occur without government action does not necessarily imply the desirability of higher aggregate capital accumulation, since the intergenerational redistributive aspects of the program will naturally have capital accumulation implications.

[50]I am considering efficiency given income distribution. Even with individual rationality aggregate savings may not be optimal if it is desired to transfer resources between generations.

Table 3
Percentage of married men 58–63 with low wealth–earnings ratios in 1969 by earnings level and private pension coverage status.
(Numbers in parentheses are percentage of population in earnings bracket; those for whom wealth information is not available are excluded from calculations)

	Full earnings 1969[a]						Reported earnings 1968[a]					
	Not covered[b]			Covered[b]			Not covered			Covered		
Earnings level	≤1[c]	≤2[c]		≤1	≤2		≤1	≤2		≤1	≤2	
Under 2500	74.7	76.4	(28.3)	88.0	88.3	(16.5)	28.5	33.7	(8.6)	10.2	15.9	(1.8)
2500–4999	26.4	29.6	(20.6)	20.0	38.1	(8.4)	25.2	42.4	(14.8)	23.3	37.1	(5.8)
5000–7499	14.6	30.0	(21.1)	15.3	31.3	(27.4)	21.4	38.0	(17.7)	19.4	38.0	(16.9)
7500–9998	13.1	26.8	(10.3)	9.4	22.4	(21.4)	14.5	33.9	(11.7)	13.3	31.8	(18.6)
10000–12499	7.7	17.6	(6.2)	5.3	18.6	(11.8)	14.9	30.7	(8.1)	13.2	35.1	(15.0,
12500–14999	0.0	11.8	(1.7)	5.0	18.0	(4.2)	7.8	29.4	(3.4)	5.8	25.2	(8.3)
15000–24999	2.7	13.7	(3.7)	0.8	6.5	(5.2)	5.9	15.6	(4.7)	2.1	18.8	(9.7)
25000 and up	2.6	13.1	(2.2)	2.2	6.6	(2.0)	5.8	22.7	(2.0)	1.5	9.3	(2.8)
Not available	–	–	(6.0)	–	–	(3.2)	–	–	(29.0)	–	–	(21.1)

Source: Longitudinal Retirement History Survey.
[a]Earnings measure.
[b]Pension coverage
[c]Wealth–earnings ratio

Table 4

Percentage of married men 58–63 with low wealth–earnings ratios in 1969 by earnings level and private pension coverage status.

(Numbers in parentheses are percentage of population in earnings bracket; those for whom wealth information is not available are included in the calculations, and assumed to have wealth exceeding twice income)

	Full earnings 1969[a]						Reported earnings 1968[a]					
	Not covered[b]			Covered[b]			Not Covered			Covered		
Earnings level	≤1[c]	≤2[c]		≤1	≤2		≤1	≤2		≤1	≤2	
Under 2500	53.2	54.4	(28.3)	57.4	57.9	(16.5)	20.2	23.9	(8.6)	7.6	11.8	(1.8)
2500–4999	19.5	21.9	(20.6)	15.8	30.0	(8.4)	19.4	32.6	(14.8)	18.9	30.1	(5.8)
5000–7499	10.3	21.2	(21.1)	10.8	22.0	(27.4)	15.4	27.3	(17.7)	13.7	26.8	(16.9)
7500–9998	8.0	16.3	(10.3)	6.6	15.7	(21.4)	10.1	23.6	(11.7)	9.7	23.2	(18.6)
10000–12499	4.5	10.2	(6.2)	3.5	12.2	(11.8)	9.7	19.9	(8.1)	9.3	24.8	(15.0)
12500–14999	0.0	8.5	(1.7)	3.7	13.3	(4.2)	4.5	16.8	(3.4)	4.2	18.4	(8.3)
15000–24999	1.7	8.7	(3.7)	0.5	4.1	(5.2)	3.9	10.3	(4.7)	1.4	12.3	(9.7)
25000 and up	1.3	6.6	(2.2)	1.3	3.9	(2.0)	3.0	11.8	(2.0)	0.9	5.7	(2.8)
Not available	–	–	(6.0)	–	–	(3.2)	–	–	(29.0)	–	–	(21.1)

Source: Longitudinal Retirement History Survey.
[a]Earnings measure.
[b]Pension coverage.
[c]Wealth–earnings ratio.

Table 5

Percentage of married, nonretired men 58–63 with low wealth–income ratios in 1971 by average income level 1965–70 and private pension coverage status.

(Numbers in parentheses are percentage of covered or not covered sample population in earnings bracket; those for whom wealth information is not available are excluded from the calculations)

	Not covered[a]			Covered[a]		
Income level	≤1[b]	≤2[b]		≤1	≤2	
Under 2500	43.9	52.6	(13.9)	66.7	66.7	(0.8)
2500–4999	42.7	57.3	(28.5)	43.5	60.9	(5.9)
5000–7499	32.6	55.0	(21.7)	41.3	58.7	(16.2)
7500–9999	25.4	41.3	(15.3)	23.9	50.0	(23.6)
10000–12499	15.8	50.0	(9.2)	20.3	36.2	(17.7)
12500–14999	13.0	21.7	(5.6)	9.8	31.1	(15.6)
15000–24999	10.0	20.0	(4.9)	7.8	34.4	(16.4)
25000 and up	0.0	0.0	(1.0)	13.3	33.3	(3.8)

Source: Parnes data.
[a]Pension coverage.
[b]Wealth–income ratio.

applicable. Thus, 20% of the population with inadequate savings seems to leave room for a considerable gain in social welfare.

3.4. Efficiency[51]

As with any other industry, the costs of providing insurance can be conceptually divided into those of providing the product and those of convincing would-be purchasers to buy. When selling costs are large and a relatively easy device (payroll tax) for government compulsion is available, having a compulsory program may save a significant portion of the total costs of the product.[52] Before turning to the costs of compulsion let us briefly consider the potential for benefits.

In the Social Security Program, administrative costs normally run about 2% of receipts or payments, which are both about the same size [Board of Trustees of the Federal Old-Age and Survivors Insurance and Disability Insurance Trust Funds (1967, table 3)]. Of course, this doesn't include the costs to employers self-employed, and IRS in handling their sides of the financial transactions. At a guess, total transaction costs are probably less than twice the costs to the Social Security Administration. In contrast, in 1974 17% of total outgo of the life insurance industry was for operating expenses, with 10.1% for home and field offices and 6.9% for commissions to agents [Life Insurance Fact Book (1975, p. 58)]. These numbers represent an averaging of much higher numbers for individual policies and much lower numbers for group policies, with the latter probably comparable to Social Security. For example, for 8 leading companies expenses as a percentage of premiums averaged 6% for group policies and 27% for ordinary policies [Ralph Nader (1973, table C, p. 18)]. For a compulsory program to represent a gain in transaction costs, the compulsory program must be sufficiently close to the desired package that a sizeable fraction of the population does not purchase private insurance policies in addition. If the public program displaces no group plans and displaces individual policies for at least 15% of the population then there will be a gain in transaction costs[53] (ignoring the differences in policies selected and the provision of policies to those previously without policies). Given these numbers on transactions costs, let us consider the full range of efficiency issues.

Among the costs of a compulsory insurance scheme there are three aspects of efficiency to examine – the provision of different commodities to different buyers, the development of new products, and the levels and changes in efficiency in production. Let us consider these in reverse order. Given the large

[51]Considerations of efficiency in the provision of insurance are relevant for several parts of the program, even if not for all parts.

[52]The argument for efficiency gains of compulsion does not imply any superiority of public management of the compulsory program over private management of such a program.

[53]Since (0.15) times (0.27) equals 0.04, the assumed transaction cost of Social Security.

size of selling costs relative to other costs and the easily understood technology there is little reason to expect that the absence of competition would seriously affect the relative cost-effectiveness of Social Security and private insurance. Second, the nature of insurance makes the introduction of new products a not terribly important issue. While there may be new types of policies introduced, these may often be due to changes in demand rather than inventions of previously unthought of policies.

Thus we are left with the issue of public choice of policy relative to private choice. There are two separate issues here – the provision of a relatively uniform public program where a private program would show more variation in either choice of policy or quantities purchased and the selection of a public program which might not be the optimal public program.

It is difficult to easily assess the importance of these items, but their size is kept limited by three factors. One is that the private market continues to exist. This doesn't help those compelled to have more than they should. It does help those provided with significantly too little insurance, although in this case the efficiency gains from public provision may be largely (or fully) lost. Second, a large part of the private market is in group policies which have limited individual variation, although they can differ from group to group. Third, the selection of an optimal insurance package is a difficult and complicated matter, requiring sophisticatication in both data evaluation and decision making.[54] Insofar as this is not reasonably well done by individuals, a sensibly chosen public program may do better and may economize on decision making. These are issues that are impossible to settle a priori and would require detailed examination of individual insurance portfolios to evaluate properly. This consideration of the narrowly economic aspects of compulsory savings and insurance does not mean that the issues associated with the presence of compulsion per se are uninteresting or unimportant.

4. Concluding remarks

The discussions of the previous section seem to me to justify a program which would combine forced savings, insurance of earning capabilities, and redistribution. Such a program could be achieved by limited modification of the existing Social Security system. This is not the place for a detailed analysis of particular suggestions to change Social Security. However, let us briefly consider a few proposals to indicate the relevance of the three aspects we have identified.

Discussion of the optimal size of the Social Security program needs to relate the efficiency of forced savings to that of private savings, recognizing that some people may save too little but that for those with adequate savings having the wealth unavailable for other uses will generate some inefficiency. Proposals to

[54]The same problems also arise in the selection of a savings rate.

allow individuals to opt out of Social Security must decrease its redistributive purposes or continue taxation for redistributive purposes of those who do opt out. Dropping the earnings limitation for workers over 65 decreases the ability of the system to provide insurance for the random length of working life. Of course the moral hazard (or adverse incentive) aspect of these taxes is relevant for design of the optimal retirement test, with a balancing required between the decrease in risk bearing and the adverse incentives generated.

Reform of the Social Security system seems to me to be an important policy question. Such reform would benefit from expansion of the ongoing theoretical and empirical work on intertemporal equilibria with uncertainty.

References

Bixby, L. et al., 1975, Demographic and economic characteristics of the aged, 1968 Social Security Survey (U.S. Government Printing Office, Washington).

Board of Trustees of the Federal Old-Age and Survivors Insurance and Disability Insurance Trust Funds, Annual Report (U.S. Government Printing Office, Washington).

Consultant Panel on Social Security to the Congressional Research Service, 1976, Report (U.S. Government Printing Office, Washington).

Frieden, A., D. Leimer and R. Hoffman, 1976, Internal rates of return to retired worker-only beneficiaries under social security, 1967–70, Studies in Income Distribution 5, U.S. Department of Health, Education, and Welfare, Social Security Administration, Office of Research and Statistics.

Kunreuther, H. et al., 1977, Limited knowledge and insurance protection: Implications for natural hazard policy, Report to NSF–RANN.

Life Insurance Fact Book, 1975 (Institute of Life Insurance, New York).

Marglin, S., 1975, What do bosses do?, Part II, Review of Radical Political Economics 7, 20–37.

Murray, J., 1976, Family structure in the preretirement years, in: U.S. Department of Health, Education, and Welfare, Almost 65: Baseline data from the retirement history study (U.S. Government Printing Office, Washington).

Nader, R., 1973, Testimony at Hearings before U.S. Senate, Subcommittee on Antitrust and Monopoly of the Committee of the Judiciary, 93rd Congress (U.S. Government Printing Office, Washington).

Social Security Bulletin, 1973, Annual statistical supplement.

Social Security Bulletin, September 1976, vol. 39.

Tumerin, J.D. and H.L.D. Resik, 1972, Risk taking by individual option: Case study – Cigarette smoking, in: National Academy of Engineering, Perspective on benefit–risk decision making (Washington) 73–84.

Tversky, A. and D. Kahneman, 1974, Judgment under uncertainty: Heuristics and biases, Science, 1124–1131.

U.S. Bureau of the Census, 1973, Census of Population PC(2)–6A (U.S. Government Printing Office, Washington).

U.S. Department of Health, Education, and Welfare, Social Security Administration, Office of Research and Statistics, 1970, Resources after retirement (U.S. Government Printing Office, Washington).

U.S. Department of Health, Education, and Welfare, Social Security Administration, Office of Research and Statistics, 1973, Income of newly entitled beneficiaries, 1970 (U.S. Government Printing Office, Washington).

[20]

SOCIAL SECURITY AND RETIREMENT DECISIONS

MICHAEL J. BOSKIN*
Stanford University and
National Bureau of Economic Research

One of the most striking features of the postwar U.S. economy has been the rapid decrease in the labor force participation of the elderly at a time when the health of this group has been improving. In spite of this, previous research, based on retrospective interviews with the retired population, usually concludes that poor health accounts for the overwhelming majority of retirements. This paper suggests that nothing could be further from the truth. Using data from the Panel Study of Income Dynamics, we follow a cohort of white married males through their sixties to estimate a model of retirement behavior. Using several definitions of retirement suggested in the literature, we find that the two key policy parameters of the social security system — the income guarantee and the implicit tax on earnings — exert an enormous influence on retirement decisions. For example, our results suggest that a decrease in the implicit tax rate on earnings from one-half to one-third would reduce the annual probability of retirement by about fifty percent! Applying the coefficient estimates to time series data on the labor force participation of the elderly implies that the social security system has been the major factor in the explosion in earlier retirement.

The rapid growth of the social security system in recent years has been one of the most important developments in the United States' economy: social security benefits and taxes are each the second largest — and fastest growing — item on their respective side of the federal government budget and will soon exceed $100 billion. For a large fraction of all U.S. families, social security taxes exceed their income taxes and expected social security benefits are the major item in their retirement portfolio. The system has become so large that even modest changes in benefits or their method of finance may have important impacts on the entire economy. While the social security system is widely heralded by politicians and the public as a vital element of our income security system, it recently has come under increased criticism from economists.

*I am indebted to William Barsky, Louis Garrison and Henry Moore for research assistance, and participants at various seminars plus T. Connor, M. Feldstein, V. Fuchs, J. Heckman, L. Lillard, F. Nold, J. Pechman, J. Ross, L. Thompson, P. Van de Water, and F. Welch for useful suggestions. This paper should not be considered an official NBER publication, as it has not undergone the full NBER review.

Economic Inquiry
Vol. XV, Jan. 1977

For example, Pechman, Aaron and Taussig (1968) and Brittain (1971) object to payroll tax finance as inequitable; Buchanan (1968) and Campbell (1969) would like to see the transfer, or anti-poverty goal of the system separated from the income replacement, or annuity, goal; and Feldstein (1974a) estimates a huge substitution of expected social security benefits for private savings, which in turn leads him to question whether the system should be financed on a pay-as-you-go basis (Feldstein, 1974c).

The primary objective of social security is to replace income during retirement (or disability); in so doing, social security benefits supplement — and potentially substitute for — prior savings (including private pensions, equity in a home, savings accounts, stocks and bonds, etc.), intrafamily transfers of income and, perhaps most importantly, continued earnings. The purpose of the present paper is to focus on the potential inducement to retire earlier in the presence of social security than in its absence, and the corresponding substitution of social security benefits for potential earnings. Toward this end, section I reviews some previous attempts to study retirement behavior. Section II presents a simple theoretical model which explains the ways in which the current social security system affects labor supply and retirement decisions. Section III details the data used in the analysis. Section IV reports the empirical results — primarily probability of retirement equations which relate retirement decisions to parameters of the social security system and other financial and demographic variables. Section V concludes with a discussion of some of the implications of the results for social security policy, as well as some suggestions for future research.

I. A CURSORY REVIEW OF THE LITERATURE ON RETIREMENT

Social security guarantees elderly retired persons a certain income based upon their previous covered earnings and taxes some of these benefits back if earnings exceed a modest amount. Hence, both the income and wage effects of the system operate to reduce labor supply. Since some workers achieve a preferred consumption bundle by working enough so that they receive no benefits (i.e., they elect not to be covered currently by the system), others would retire independently of their social security benefits, and the sizes of the income — or benefit guarantee — and wage — or earnings test — effects are unknown, the overall effect of social security on retirement is primarily an empirical question.

Previous research on retirement decisions may be divided into three types corresponding to the type of data used: retrospective studies of retired workers, prospective studies of workers approaching retirement age, and studies of the labor force participation rate of the elderly.

In an early and frequently cited study, Steiner and Dorfman (1959) report the results of a special 1952 Follow-Up Survey of the Aged to the Current Population Survey. In particular, all men not in the labor force were asked why they stopped working. They conclude that "... only a small proportion of the older population had been driven out of the labor force by retirement systems."[1] Thus, the overwhelming majority retired "voluntarily"; further, ". . . in 79 per cent of all voluntary retirements poor health was the major reason for retirement."[2] While it is undoubtedly correct that some people retire because of poor health, accepting the conclusion that most do so from retrospective surveys of retired workers is hazardous: poor health is certainly the most socially acceptable reason for retirement and, on average, the health of those interviewed had probably deteriorated since retirement. Yet retrospective studies invariably conclude that poor health is the primary reason for retirement.

For example, Wentworth (1968) summarizes a series of Social Security Administration surveys of the aged in the years 1941-1963 by noting that ". . . approximately 88 percent of the beneficiaries queried in the 1941-51 surveys and 74 percent of those in the 1963 survey had their jobs terminated by their employer or were forced to quit because of ill health."[3] Thus, the conclusion usually reached in these studies is that social security benefits cushion income declines beyond the control of the individual worker and that relatively few workers are induced to retire to receive benefits. On the other hand, the 1963 Social Security Survey of the Aged also found that a substantial fraction of those non-beneficiaries reporting an inclination to retire soon intended to do so to obtain retirement (public and/or private) benefits. Further, a considerable shift into partial retirement — reduced hours of work and changes in occupation — was noted. Finally, Epstein and Murray (1967) note an increase in the number of aged men ". . . who might get some kind of job if they were interested, but prefer the leisure of retirement."[4]

Barfield and Morgan (1969) conducted an interesting study of prospective retirement plans; in particular, they focused on the decision to retire before age 65. Analyzing data from a national sample collected in 1966, they report ordinary least squares regressions of whether or not early retirement was planned on a variety of variables. The most important result was that planned early retirement was strongly and positively related to expected pension income (government and private) and negatively associated with a subjective evaluation of health. While these results are both intriguing and suggestive, relying on reported plans for retirement — in an uncertain world where expectations may not be realized — is hazardous at best. A preferable alternative is to analyze actual retirement decisions.

1. Steiner and Dorfman, p. 49.
2. Steiner and Dorfman, p. 49.
3. Wentworth, p. 5.
4. Epstein and Murray, p. 105.

In his classic study, Long (1958) notes the decline in the labor force participation rate of older workers in the U.S. and elsewhere since 1890. He examines a variety of types of data, and concludes that neither the growth of pension programs — public and private — nor the general increase in personal disposable income accounts for the sharp decline. Indeed, Long's major conclusion is that jobs have been competed away from older workers by younger women.

Pechman, Aaron and Taussig (1968) were the first to present evidence that social security accelerates retirement; they report the results of an international cross-sectional regression on aggregate data for 1960 from 19 countries of the labor force participation rate of the population over age 65 on the ratio of per capita benefits to the average wage in manufacturing and other variables. Their results suggest that the higher this replacement ratio, the lower the labor force participation rate of the elderly, i.e., the more generous the social security system, the lower the labor supply of the elderly. Whether this is caused by the income effect of high benefit guarantees, the wage effect of rigid earnings tests in countries with generous benefits or even the wage effect of higher social insurance taxes to finance the higher benefits is impossible to tell from their results. Feldstein (1974b) reports a similar result, also based on an international cross section, on his way to estimating private savings functions. He also notes a negative effect on labor force participation of men over 65 of retirement tests. While these studies are open to the usual criticisms of international cross sections, the results do suggest that higher social security benefits do induce a withdrawal from the labor force.

Thus, there are two competing conjectures concerning the effects of social security on retirement. On the one hand, a group of studies suggest that the social security system plays a relatively passive and minor role, the major reason for retirement being poor health. On the other, evidence from international cross-sections — albeit hardly the type of data upon which one would like to place exclusive reliance — suggests that social security induces — or enables — elderly men to withdraw from the labor force.

Aggregate time series data for the United States reveal that the labor force participation rates of elderly males have fallen dramatically in the postwar period. These data are presented in Table 1.1. The rate for both whites and nonwhites is currently less than half of the rate in the late nineteen forties.[5] In the 55-64 age bracket, the rates have fallen thirteen and twenty-one percent for whites and nonwhites, respectively. The decline in this age group, of course, is heavily concentrated in the rates for men in their early sixties; more men now claim initial social security benefits at age sixty-two than at age sixty-five.

5. These data slightly overstate this decline since the average age of males over 65 has risen somewhat.

TABLE 1.1

Labor Force Participation Rates for Elderly Males, 1948-74

	WHITE		NONWHITE	
	55-64 years	65 and over	55-64 years	65 and over
1948	89.6	46.5	88.6	50.3
1949	87.6	46.6	86.0	51.4
1950	87.3	45.8	81.9	45.5
1951	87.4	44.5	84.6	49.5
1952	87.7	42.5	85.7	43.3
1953	87.7	41.3	86.7	41.1
1954	89.2	40.4	83.0	41.2
1955	88.4	39.5	83.1	40.0
1956	88.9	40.0	83.9	39.8
1957	88.0	37.7	82.4	35.9
1958	88.2	35.7	83.3	34.5
1959	87.9	34.3	82.5	33.5
1960	87.2	33.3	82.5	31.2
1961	87.8	31.9	81.6	29.4
1962	86.7	30.6	81.5	27.2
1963	86.6	28.4	82.5	27.6
1964	86.1	27.9	80.6	29.6
1965	85.2	27.9	78.8	27.9
1966	84.9	27.2	81.1	25.6
1967	84.9	27.1	79.3	27.2
1968	84.7	27.3	79.6	26.6
1969	83.9	27.3	77.9	26.1
1970	83.3	26.7	79.2	27.4
1971	82.6	25.6	77.8	24.5
1972	81.2	24.4	73.6	23.6
1973	79.0	22.8	70.7	22.6
1974	78.1	22.5	70.2	21.7

Source: Manpower Report of the President, 1975.

This sharp secular decline in the labor force participation came during a period when the economy was relatively healthy and the health of the elderly on average improved; it also came during a period of broad extension of social security coverage and sharp increases in benefits. While these correlations may be merely a coincidence, they should make us skeptical of the survey data alleging social security had no effect and poor health was the prime mover in retirement decisions. We shall present and analyze below evidence from an entirely different — and in many ways superior — type of data: a panel study of a cohort of elderly men. Before doing so, it is worthwhile to examine in somewhat more detail the ways in which social security affects labor supply.

II. SOCIAL SECURITY AND LABOR SUPPLY

The social security system has three basic features which afect life-cycle labor supply and saving decisions: the benefits, the social insurance contributions, and the earnings test. The social security system imposes a tax for old age (and disability) insurance of approximately 6 percent each on employees and employers[6] on the first $14,100 of earnings; it provides benefits during retirement based in part on previous taxes; and potential benefits are reduced if earnings exceed a certain modest amount. Thus, throughout one's working life the social security tax reduces the after-tax wage rate. Once one retires, the system provides an income flow, but imposes an implicit tax on earnings beyond a certain amount.

Focusing on a year during which a worker eligible for social security benefits is contemplating retirement, and ignoring life cycle phenomena,[7] we may characterize the effect of the system on labor supply and retirement decisions in the usual way. Before accounting for the social security system, the budget constraint of the individual is

$$(1) \qquad (1+r)K + W(T-L) = PX + \Delta K.$$

Assets plus earnings equals consumption of goods plus saving.

With a tax rate of t, benefits of B when no earnings are made, and an implicit tax under the earnings test of α, the budget constraint becomes

$$(2) \qquad B + K(1+r) + W(1-t-\alpha)(T-L) = PX + \Delta K.$$

Graphically (ignoring saving), the budget constraint changes as in Figure 1, where we see that the worker, in attempting to maximize utility, must choose which arm of the budget constraint he wishes to be on. Since for the period we will be studying, the earnings test had two components (a 50 cent reduction per dollar of earnings over a certain range, then increasing to a dollar), the effective budget constraint has three arms: the parts AB, BC and CD. Hence social security creates a situation where

6. It is usually argued that employees bear both parts of the tax (see Brittain); however, Feldstein (1972) has called this assertion into question when the system affects saving. If we argue that the benefits would be financed by some other tax (which may itself affect saving and/or labor supply), the employee burden argument is probably a good approximation.

7. A simple discussion of life-cycle effects is presented in Appendix B.

FIGURE 1

Social Security and Labor Supply

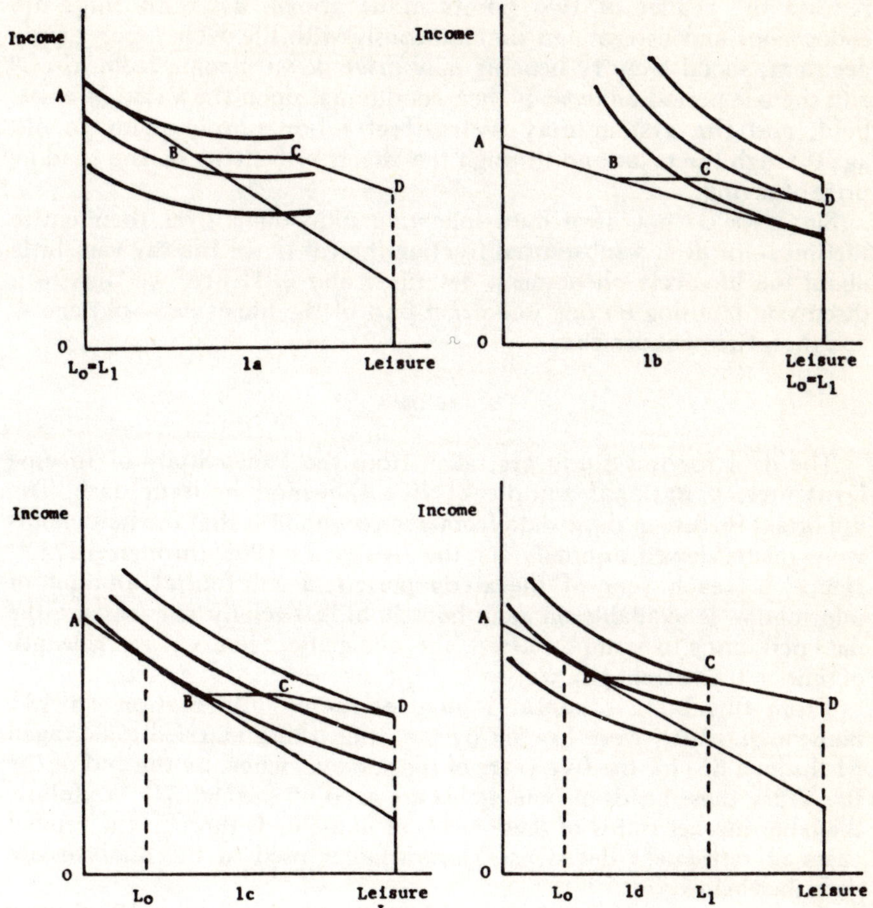

workers face a kinky budget constraint. In some cases social security will not affect labor supply during part of old age. In Figure 1a, the worker works full time regardless of the social security system; in Figure 1b, the worker retires completely regardless of the social security system. However, many workers may be in the situation depicted in Figures 1c and 1d: in the former, the worker works a substantial amount of time in the absence of the social security system, but retires completely in its presence; in the latter, social security induces partial retirement.[8]

These effects — providing an income support and taxing earnings with the earnings test — both operate to reduce the labor supply of some elderly workers. Before turning to an attempt to estimate them, we remind the reader of two points made above: asset holdings are endogenous and determined simultaneously with life-cycle labor supply decisions; social security benefits may drive down income from assets[9] and the one-period analysis is then conditional upon the value of assets held; and the system may well affect labor supply prior to old age through the taxes and through the effects of benefits on the shadow price of saving.

Since we do not have data following individuals over their entire lifetime — or even a substantial fraction thereof — we can say very little about the life-cycle phenomena described above. Hence, we turn to a discussion focusing on one important part of the life-cycle — old age — and the retirement decision.

III. THE DATA

The data for this study are taken from the Panel Study of Income Dynamics, a national sample of five thousand households.[10] The important feature of these data from our viewpoint is that the households were reinterviewed annually for the five years 1968 through 1972.[11] Hence, for each year of the study period, a substantial amount of information is available on each household. Especially relevant are the data pertaining to earnings, assets, age, occupation, hours of work, length of time on the current job, etc.

From this body of data, I have extracted information on 131 households which were headed by the same white married male, aged 61 through 65, for the five years of the survey. Hence, by the end of the five years, these heads of households are aged 66 through 70. We follow the labor market status of these heads of households through the crucial years of retirement decisions. The variables used in the analysis are described below.

Retirement. A study by the Social Security Administration (1972) notes

8. This multi-armed budget constraint produces certain econometric problems in estimating labor supply functions. The density of labor supply piles up at several discrete values; hence we must estimate the probability the worker will choose to be on one of the three arms of the budget constraint simultaneously with hours worked conditional upon being on a particular arm. I am currently working on a generalization of Tobit analysis to deal with this problem. The estimates presented below, in part, skirt this issue. See Hall (forthcoming) for a discussion of this problem in the two-armed case.

9. See Feldstein (1974a) for evidence this indeed occurs.

10. These data are described in detail in Survey Research Center.

11. The annual reinterviewing is still in progress.

no less than six definitions of retirement in common use. Among these are zero hours of work per year, less than 35 hours per week of work, saying that one is retired, etc. The common perception of retirement is a stepping-down from normal career patterns — leaving the main job or occupation, working less and earning less. A substantial number of people say they are retired while working several hundred hours per year for several years. Several definitions of retirement were tried in the estimation of the probability of retirement equations: less than quarter-time work, less than half-time work, less than one-tenth time work, and the individual worker's statement that he was retired. The results using all four definitions are similar, and only those for quarter-time work are presented below.[12] This definition corresponds roughly to the point where most of the sample becomes subject to the earnings test. A state of quasi-retirement was also defined for use in following a pattern of gradual stepping-down from full-time work. Again, similar results were obtained for several definitions mapping hours of work, wages, and occupation into quasi-retirement. The definition used in the results presented below was less than half-time work (or earnings less than half of full-time earnings on the job previously held).

The distribution of actual hours and earnings — as we would suspect from the discussion above — tends to pile up in certain ranges, roughly corresponding to full-time work, work not subject to the earnings test, etc. Further, about 40 percent of the sample retired before age 65, while slightly under 40 percent were still working at age 66 and beyond. Of the latter, two-fifths were working very few hours.

Social security benefits. The maximum social security benefits obtainable for the couple are based on the primary insurance amount from estimated average monthly earnings. Average monthly earnings are estimated as the social security maximum for those earning the maximum or receiving the maximum benefit during the survey period and imputed either from a regression of earnings on education, occupation, and other personal characteristics or from actual benefits received and information on age, earnings, etc. The benefits formula for each year is used and benefits are adjusted downward for each year from age 62 to 64, and, of course, are zero for age 61. It is worth pointing out that the group under study received social security benefits which are a large multiple of their taxes paid in plus interest. This occurs both because of the blanketing in of all existing workers each time benefits are increased and the large increase in legislated benefits, which bear little relation to taxes paid in plus interest (see Campbell (1969) and Brittain (1971)).

Income from assets. Income from assets include the usual rents, pensions,[13] dividends, interest and asset part of business income. Also

12. The other results are available upon request.

13. Lack of complete information on pension rights of those still working is a problem with these, as well as most other, household data.

included are the imputed income to home ownership (at 6 percent of equity) and to automobiles (at 12 percent of value). Experiments with a two-year average yielded results virtually identical to use of current income from assets.

Net earnings. Net earnings refers to earnings net of earnings-tested decreases in social security benefits. They are calculated in two ways — using actual earnings and using expected earnings at full-time or part-time work, i.e., for different measures of a standardized number of hours.[14] While the former is potentially endogenous, it reflects the actual point chosen on a particular arm of the budget constraint. In any event, the results are quite similar regardless of the definition used. We standardize at 1750 hours for those not working in defining potential net earnings for full-time work, and at 875 hours for quasi-retirement. Changing these indexes of a standard number of hours by modest amounts does not affect the results.[15]

Age dummies. A variable taking the value one when the worker is 65, zero otherwise; and likewise when the worker is 62.

Education. Years of schooling.

Spouse's earnings. Only infrequently does the spouse's earnings amount to a substantial share of total earnings. The actual figures are used. Were our data set much larger, we would have attempted to build a simultaneous husband-wife retirement model. Since only a small fraction of these wives worked any appreciable amount, we eschew any such attempt here.

Hours ill. Total hours of illness estimated for the year. In light of the conjecture reported above that poor health is the primary cause of retirement, it is interesting to note that for those people in the sample who retired, the average hours of illness the year prior to retirement was 59.2; for the entire sample of work years, the average was 84.5!

All dollar values are adjusted for inflation by deflating by the consumer price index.

IV. EMPIRICAL RESULTS

As mentioned above, there are many different definitions of retirement which have been used by various researchers. Generally, retirement entails a stepping down from a normal career and employment pattern. The stepping down may entail an abrupt reduction of hours of work to zero, a change of job or occupation, a gradual reduction of hours of

14. Potential full-time earnings are imputed on the basis of a regression of earnings on education, occupation, location, union membership, health, etc.

15. Again, results are available upon request. Variables referring to the specific year were also included (year dummies, unemployment rate, etc.), but their coefficients were small and not statistically different from zero.

work, etc. We may conceive of the worker as being in one of N labor market states (e.g., state 1 may be full-time work on the career job, state 2 part-time work on the same job, state 3 full-time work on a different job, . . . , state N zero hours of market work, etc.). Observing individual workers for a sequence of years, we may characterize this stepping down process by an $N x N$ matrix of transition probabilities. $P = (P_{ij})$, where P_{ij} is the probability that the worker moves from state i (e.g., full-time work) to state j (e.g., part-time). These probabilities, in turn, depend on a vector of variables such as earnings, social security benefits, age, health and education, some of which depend upon which state the worker chooses to occupy.

As a simple example, consider a two-way partition of labor market states into working and retired. Then P_{12} is the probability a worker retires in a given period. P_{12} may depend upon social security benefits and earnings, which differ dramatically if he works or retires. Of course, once we know P_{12}, we also know P_{11}, the probability the worker keeps working. Finally, there is a duality between the transitions among states[16] and the distribution of the elderly population among the various labor market states.

A full derivation of this model as the multinomial logistic parameterization of a multi-state Markov chain is presented in Appendix A.

As mentioned above, we have experimented with different numbers of states defining employment status as well as different definitions of the states. The results are rather robust against modest changes in the definition of the states. Our data limit us to a two-state (working/retired) and a three-state (close to full-time, quasi-retirement, retirement) parameterization. We examine the effect on the probability of retirement of several types of variables: health (hours ill), wage effects (net earnings), income effects (social security benefits and income from assets), cross-wage effects (spouse's earnings), and institutional retirements tests (represented by a dummy variable for age 65). Conjectures on the signs and magnitudes of these effects were discussed above in the review of the literature. Briefly, one school of thought would expect the effects of the age dummy and hours ill to be large and positive, and most other effects to be small. As we shall see, nothing could be further from the truth.

Table 4.1 presents our basic probability of retirement equation. We note first that the sign of the health effect is opposite to that conjectured in numerous previous studies. This effect, however, is not estimated very precisely. While some workers undoubtedly do retire for reasons of poor health and the measure of health is open to question, these data provide no support for the conjecture that poor health is the prime mover in

16. Note that some transitions may have probabilities of zero or close to zero, i.e., it may be rare to observe certain transitions.

TABLE 4.1

Probability of Retirement Equation

Variable	Coefficient ($\times 10^3$)[a]
Social Security benefits	0.917 (0.288)
Income from assets	0.135 (0.051)
Net earnings	−1.49 (0.39)
Age = 65 dummy	1248.7 (307.6)
Spouse's earnings	−0.218 (0.093)
Hours ill	−1.38 (1.21)
log likelihood = −141.026	

a. Asymptotic standard errors in parentheses.

retirement decisions.

The effects of all of the other variables are measured quite precisely, and operate in the expected direction. The probability of retirement in a given year at mean values of the right hand variables is about eight percent.

There is clearly a large increase in the probability of retirement at age 65. Whether this is due to social custom or institutionalized retirement rules within firms is difficult to judge. It is not uncommon for workers to change occupations in their sixties — stepping down from their normal career to a lower wage part-time job.

There is a small negative effect of the spouse's earnings on the probability of retirement.[17] Thus, leisure of husbands and wives appear to be complements in old age.

Turning attention to income from assets, we note that the effect of an increase in asset income is a modest increase in the probability of retirement. At mean values of the other variables, a $1,000 annual increase

17. Were our data set larger, we would have attempted to examine the retirement decisions of husbands and wives simultaneously.

in income from assets increases the probability of retirement by 15 percent.

The effect of the income guarantee in social security on the probability of retirement is large and, as expected, positive. Indeed, it is seven times as large as the effect of income from assets. An increase in social security benefits from $3,000 to $4,000 per year per couple *raises the annual probability of retirement from 7.5 percent to 16 percent.* Viewed another way, the expected number of work years in the 61-70 age interval declines from between five and six to less than four. Why is the effect of social security benefits so much more important than the effect of income from assets? Social security benefits are guaranteed for the remainder of one's life and are indexed against inflation.[18] Further, to the extent bequests are planned, personal wealth may be transferred to one's heirs, whereas social security benefits cannot. Also, income from assets includes the imputed income to owner-occupied housing; the elderly may be reluctant to borrow against their equity for fear of living so long as to have to vacate the house and pay capital gains taxes.

Finally, net (after tax and earnings test) earnings has the predicted negative effect; indeed, it is large and measured quite precisely. The negative effect of net earnings is roughly half again as large as the positive effect of the income guarantee. A $1,000 increase in net earnings reduces the probability of retirement by about 60 percent. Since the earnings test reduces net earnings substantially for some fraction of elderly workers, it clearly dramatically increases the probability of retirement.[19] A reduction of the implicit tax on earnings from one-half to one-third cuts the annual probability of retirement in half for typical workers. The relationship between benefits and the earnings test is also important. In the example given above, a $1,000 increase in social security benefits which exposed more earnings to the earnings test would have only about one-fourth the impact on retirement as a pure increase in benefits (i.e., a $1,000 increase combined with a $1,000 increase in earnings exempted from the earnings test).

Since no serial correlation structure was imbedded directly in the model, we report here the results of running the regression reported in Table 4.1 on the first transition only, i.e., on a single cross-section. While, of course, the estimated coefficients are measured less precisely in this case, their signs and magnitudes are quite similar to those reported for the full set of transitions: social security benefits, 1.49 (0.85); income from assets, 0.26 (0.12); net earnings −2.59 (1.08); hours ill, −334.8 (453.3); age = 65, 790.6 (768.1); spouse's earnings, −1.56 (1.40).

Note the larger coefficients on the two social security variables; this

18. Benefits are now indexed directly; previously, they were implicitly indexed — with a lag — by periodic Congressional review.

19. See the discussion in section V below.

suggests that there may be some self selection of those with larger wage and income elasticities retiring first and hence causing our estimates to be weighted more heavily toward those with less wage and income guarantee sensitivity. Thus our coefficients may be biased downwards.

Note also that this same weighting problem may cause us to underestimate standard errors. With a larger and richer data source, we could deal with these problems more directly.

Thus, the overall impact of the social security system, through the income guarantee and the earnings test, is clearly to induce earlier retirement for a substantial fraction of the elderly population.

We noted above that the coefficient for social security benefits was much larger than the coefficient for income from assets. We may make a formal test of the equality of these two coefficients by the likelihood ratio method. Table 4.2 reports the results of a regression in which the coefficients of social security benefits and income from assets are constrained to be equal. The quantity $-2 \ ln \ \lambda$, where λ is the ratio of the constrained to the unconstrained maximum of the likelihood function is a χ^2 variable. In this case, our χ^2 statistic of 7.23 exceeds the critical value at conventional levels and we reject the hypothesis that the effects of social security benefits and income from assets are equal. This conclusion has a startling implication if Feldstein's (1974a) result is correct that

TABLE 4.2

Probability of Retirement Equation

Variable	Coefficient ($\times 10^3$)[a]
Social Security benefits + income from assets	0.160 (0.049)
Net earnings	−1.203 (0.169)
Age = 65 dummy	1248 (300)
Spouse's earnings	−0.178 (0.090)
Hours ill	−1.595 (1.273)
log likelihood = −144.742	
$\chi^2(1) = 7.23$	

a. Asymptotic standard errors in parentheses.

private savings substitute virtually dollar for dollar with social security savings. Even in an actuarily sound program, the net impact of this substitution is an inducement to retire![20]

In Table 4.3, we present results from a logistic regression expanded to include education, age sixty-two, and year dummies. Mincer (1974)

TABLE 4.3

Probability of Retirement Equation

Variable	Coefficient ($\times 10^3$)[a]
Social Security benefits	0.893
	(0.353)
Income from assets	0.132
	(0.051)
Net earnings	−2.048
	(1.028)
Age = 65 dummy	1189.5
	(313.1)
Spouse's earnings	−0.225
	(0.099)
Education	−0.036
	(0.053)
Age = 62 dummy	−774.3
	(2202.3)
Year 1	−1962.0
	(709.8)
Year 2	−2534.4
	(760.5)
Year 3	−1985.1
	(783.9)
Year 4	−1502.9
	(862.0)
Log likelihood	−136.02

a. Asymptotic standard errors in parentheses.

20. Even once account is taken of the using up of social security capital.

notes the positive correlation between education and retirement age. This simple correlation may disguise the influences of other variables associated with increases in education (such as higher earnings). The estimated coefficient has the expected negative sign, but is quite small and not measured very precisely.

Since the worker may retire and commence receiving social security benefits at age sixty-two, we include a dummy variable for age equals sixty-two. The estimated coefficient is negative, and not measured at all precisely.

To see if there is a general age effect on retirement (in addition to the age equals sixty-five effect) over *this* age range, dummy variables for each year were included. If there is a general age effect, the coefficients should increase year by year. In fact, this is not the case.[21] Hence, in this age range, age does not appear to affect retirement probabilities except indirectly through its effect on the other variables. At later ages there well may be a pure age effect.

The coefficients of the original variables change only slightly with the introduction of these additional variables. The most notable change is the slight increase in the absolute value of the coefficient on net earnings. These results suggest that our results are not at all due to a spurious correlation through time among age, retirement and social security benefits.

Finally, we present in Table 4.4 the results of a slightly more general model — one with three labor market states: regular work, quasi-retirement, and retirement, as defined above in section 3.[22] The estimated coefficients are quite similar to those in Table 4.1, all coefficients having the same sign as the simpler model, and most are measured relatively precisely.

Again, we note the positive inducement to retire at age 65 and the negative effect of spouse's earnings.

The effect of income from assets on the probability of either retiring or quasi-retiring is positive, but modest.

The effect of social security benefits on the probability of either retiring or quasi-retiring is positive and much larger than that of income from assets. At mean values of the independent variables, a $1,000 increase in social security benefits is associated with an increase of 40 percent in the probability of quasi-retirementn and of 60 percent in the probability of retirement.

Again, the negative effect of net earnings — modest in the case of

21. A formal likelihood ratio test of the equality of these coefficients passes easily at conventional levels. Of course, these dummy variables also reflect year to year variation in labor market conditions.

22. We noted a small amount of "unretirement" in the data and tried to estimate probability of unretirement equations. The small sample size prevented us from noting any general tendencies.

TABLE 4.4

Probability of Retirement Equations

Variable	Coefficient (× 10³)[a]	
	Quasi-Retire	Retire
Social Security benefits	0.470 (0.250)	0.497 (0.204)
Income from assets	0.107 (0.064)	0.125 (0.060)
Net earnings	−1.95 (0.47)	−1.37 (0.49)
Age = 65 dummy	1720 (408)	617 (317)
Spouse's earnings	−0.121 (0.101)	−0.390 (0.194)
log likelihood = −200.136		

a. Asymptotic standard errors in parentheses.

quasi-retirement and large in the case of retirement — is measured quite precisely. The earnings test induces both quasi-retirement and complete retirement.

Of course, there are also movements out of quasi-retirement (part-time work), usually into complete retirement. We present in Table 4.5 estimates of the probability of such movements.[23] Combined with the results from Table 4.4 they reveal a picture of gradual (perhaps stepwise is more accurate) retirement; movements from full-time to part-time work (perhaps in a different occupation) to complete retirement over a number of years are not uncommon.

Again, the effects are those we have come to expect — strong negative net earnings effects, strong positive social security income and age equal to 65 effects, and modest income from asset effects. Because of the smaller number of potential observations, the individual coefficients are not measured as precisely as those reported above. Hence, we have somewhat more confidence in the empirical results reported above. It is worth noting that for many elderly persons working part time, social security

23. Infrequent movements from quasi-retirement back to full-time work also occur; our estimates for this movement were very imprecise and are not reported here.

TABLE 4.5

Probability of Movement from Quasi-Retirement to Complete Retirement

Variable	Coefficient (× 10³)[a]
Social Security benefits	0.355 (0.188)
Income from assets	0.150 (0.095)
Net earnings	−1.66 (0.45)
Age = 65 dummy	806 (359)
Spouse's earnings	−0.255 (0.153)
log likelihood = −103.57	

a. Asymptotic standard errors in parentheses.

benefit increases may not be earnings tested over a modest range.

Thus, the results reported above describe a complete stochastic structure of retirement decisions — including the stepping-down gradually phenomenon described above. The estimates may be used to estimate the effects of alternative policies on retirement decisions and their time path.

What do these results imply for the time series decline in the labor force participation rates of elderly males? Of the variables affecting retirement, the effect of the growth in spouse's earnings would be to reduce the probability of retirement; so, perhaps, would the improved health of the elderly (despite our unreliable negative coefficient!). Certainly the growth of after-tax real earnings would do so. Of these three effects, the effect of net earnings is the only one which would be very important given our coefficients. Hence, we must seek an explanation for the decline in the labor force participation in the tremendous increase in social security benefits[24] and the negating of part of the effect of net earnings increases by the earnings test and expansion of social security coverage. Indeed, assuming on average that one-half of the real

24. The modest growth in income from assets combined with the small coefficient account for only a very small increase in the annual probability of retirement.

increase in earnings has been offset by reduced social security benefits and allowing for the growth in real "full" social security benefits, using the coefficients in Table 4.1 suggests that the social security system has increased the annual probability of retirement by some forty percent! Since the actual reduction in labor force participation (refer back to Table 1.1) appears to be about fifty percent for the over sixty-five group and perhaps half of that for the 61-65 age cohort, we see that social security has been the prime mover in the acceleration of retirement![25]

We turn next to a discussion of some overall implications of these results and some suggestions for future research.

V. CONCLUSION

If the results reported above are at all accurate, they suggest that recent increases in social security benefits and coverage, combined with the earnings test are a significant contributor to the rapid decline of the labor force participation of the elderly in the United States. The social security system is inducing (or enabling) a substantial fraction of the elderly population to retire earlier than they would have in the absence of the system. While a general analysis of the welfare economics of such movements is beyond the scope of this paper, a few comments are worth making.

First, the earnings test creates a huge distortion in the labor supply decisions of a large number of elderly workers. The distortion of this work-leisure choice produces the usual dead-weight loss of the analysis of the effects of taxes on labor supply (see Harberger (1964)). Liberalization of the earnings test would dramatically reduce the probability of retirement and improve the allocation of resources.[26] However, the flow of funds through the social security system probably would have to be increased. This has led many researchers (e.g., Pechman, et. al. (1968)) to argue that reduction of the implicit tax in the earnings test is too costly. Two provisos need to be added to this allegation.

First, the only real resource cost would be any *additional* distortions resulting from increased taxes to finance the change in the earnings test (and these are likely to fall well short of the *marginal* gain in welfare of reducing the earnings test tax both because the labor supply of the elderly is much more elastic than that of the general population and because the marginal welfare cost is a function of the marginal tax rate on earnings,

25. Of course, with much more data we could try to track retirement by age, marital status, occupation, etc. The aggregate figures may cover up important differences among different groups!

26. One can also imagine a wide variety of external economies *and* diseconomies associated with driving the elderly out of the labor force. We are ignoring intertemporal cross-substitution effects of the earnings test on labor supply earlier in life; if such effects are important the welfare analysis becomes much more complex. I know of no empirical evidence which deals with this issue.

which for many elderly persons substantially exceeds the rate for the non-elderly).

Second, the large labor supply elasticity itself would substantially reduce the net impact on the flow of funds required to finance the additional benefits for two reasons: the increased labor supply of the elderly would increase the direct social security taxes paid by the elderly and the decreased earnings tested rate would apply to a larger earnings base.

Second, while we have produced no direct evidence relating to the effects of social security on saving or labor supply prior to old age, our results are certainly consistent with the induced retirement effect discussed by Feldstein (1974a) in his analysis of social security and saving. Thus, any substitution of social security for private saving is in spite of induced retirement working to increase saving.[27]

Finally, let me conclude by noting that the conclusions above are based on a single source of data and a modest sample size. Further analysis of panel studies[28] is certainly in order to help confirm or reject these conclusions; indeed, I hope that the entire subject of social insurance will begin to receive the attention it deserves.

APPENDIX A: THE STATISTICAL MODEL

We observe an individual's labor market behavior for five consecutive years. Let the individual be in one of N states (e.g., full-time work, quasi-retirement, retirement), choose the conditional logit parametrization of the probabilities of movements among states,[29] and focus for the moment on transitions out of a single state, say state l; we have the following Markov model of retirement behavior:

$$P_{ll,st} = \frac{1}{1 + \sum_N e^{\beta_n' X_{nst}}}$$

(A.1)

$$P_{1l,st} = \frac{e^{\beta_l' X_{lst}}}{1 + \sum_N e^{\beta_n' X_{nst}}}$$

27. Indeed, the results of Munnell (1974) suggest that the induced retirement effect thus far has offset the asset substitution effect. She suggests the net effect eventually will be a decrease in saving.

28. Once the mature males sample of the Parnes data reaches retirement age and once the Retirement History Survey records several more years of information, we will have two large samples with which to address the questions raised in the current paper.

29. Conditional logit estimation is developed in McFadden (1973).

where $P_{1\ell st}$ is the probability individual s will move from state 1 (e.g., full-time work) to state ℓ (e.g., retirement) in period t, X_{nst} is a vector of variables for individual s in time t in state n, and the β's are unknown parameters to be estimated. The β's may be interpreted as relative shadow weights or prices attached to the variables in choosing which state to move to each period. We choose the maximum likelihood method of estimating β.[30] The part of the likelihood function referring to a single state i may be written as:

$$\mathscr{L}_i = \prod_{s=1}^{S} \prod_{t \varepsilon T_{is}} P_{iv,st} \qquad v \, \varepsilon \, [1, N] \tag{A.2}$$

where T_{is} is the set of time individual s is in state i. The entire likelihood function, of course, is $\prod_i \mathscr{L}_i$. To maximize the likelihood of observing our sample in the sequence of states they occupy, given their right-hand variables in each state in each period, we take logarithms

$$ln \, \mathscr{L}_i = \sum_s \sum_{t \varepsilon T_{is}} ln \, P_{iv,st} \tag{A.3}$$

and differentiate with respect to the unknown β,

$$\frac{\partial \, ln \, \mathscr{L}_i}{\partial \, \beta_{\ell q}} = \sum_s \sum_{t \varepsilon T_{is}} \frac{\partial \, ln \, P_{iv,st}}{\partial \, \beta_{\ell q}} \tag{A.4}$$

where ℓ denotes possible states and q indexes right hand variables. Hence, we have as many first-order derivatives as the product of the number of right hand variables and one less than the number of states. Now

$$\frac{\partial \, ln \, P_{ivst}}{\partial \, \beta_{\ell q}} = -X_{\ell q,st} P_{i\ell,st} \qquad \text{if } v \neq \ell \tag{A.5.i}$$

and

$$\frac{\partial \, ln \, P_{i\ell,st}}{\partial \, \beta_{\ell q}} = X_{\ell q,st}(1 - P_{i\ell,st}) \qquad \text{if } v = \ell. \tag{A.5.ii}$$

Equations (A.5) may be substituted into (A.4). To maximize the likelihood

30. See Kendall and Stuart (1969-73) for a discussion of the properties of maximum likelihood estimators and Kemeny and Snell for an introduction to Markov chains.

function, these first derivatives must be set equal to zero and the resulting system of equations solved. We use Newton's method, which requires information on the second partial derivatives of the likelihood function. The iterative procedure is defined by

$$\beta_{\tau+1} = \beta_{\tau} - [B]^{-1}_{\beta_{\tau}} A_{\beta_{\tau}} \tag{A.6}$$

where τ refers to iteration number, B is the matrix of second partial derivatives, and A is the vector of first partial derivatives, each evaluated at the β vector obtained in iteration τ. Typical elements of the matrix of second partial derivatives are

$$\frac{\partial^2 \ln \mathcal{L}_i}{\partial \beta_{un} \partial \beta_{lq}} = \sum_s \sum_{t \epsilon T_u} \frac{\partial^2 \ln P_{iv,st}}{\partial \beta_{un} \partial \beta_{lq}} \tag{A.7}$$

where

$$\frac{\partial^2 \ln P_{iv,st}}{\partial \beta_{un} \partial \beta_{lq}} = \begin{cases} X_{lqst} X_{unst} P_{ilst} P_{iust} & \text{if } u \neq l \\ -X_{lqst} X_{unst} P_{ilst}(1 - P_{ilst}) & \text{if } u = l \end{cases} \tag{A.8}$$

The iterative process is said to converge when successive iterations yield sufficiently similar estimates of β. Further, the square roots of the negative of the diagonal elements of B may be used as estimated standard errors of the estimated coefficient vector β.

The important thing to note about the model is that it enables us to capture the stochastic structure of retirement decisions — retirement may take place gradually as potential retirees pass through a series of labor market states (full-time work, part-time work, complete retirement, etc.), perhaps even moving back and forth among several. Our model potentially enables us to capture such movements through their dependence on a series of variables which may in turn depend upon time. Thus, if accurate estimates of the coefficients are found, the effects of alternative policies, such as the provision of social security benefits and the earnings test under social security, which affect the variables influencing retirement decisions, on the time structure and extent of retirement may be estimated.

APPENDIX B: A LIFE CYCLE LABOR SUPPLY MODEL

Consider an individual planning his lifetime consumption of goods, X, and leisure, L. We assume the individual acts to maximize discounted lifetime utility subject to a budget constraint, i.e., he

(B.1) maximizes $\int_{t=0}^{T} e^{-rt} U(X, L) dt$

subject to

(B.2) $\dot{K} = rK + W(t)(T - L(t)) - P(t)X(t)$,

where T is time available, K is assets, $\dot{K}$ saving, and $W(t)$ and $P(t)$ are the wage rate (after-tax) and price of consumption goods.

Form the Hamiltonian

(B.3) $\mathscr{H} = e^{-\delta t} U(X, L) + P_K(t)[rK + W(t)(T - L(t)) - P(t)X(t)]$

where $P_K(t)$ is the shadow price of saving. Necessary conditions for an optimum are then

(B.4)
$$\begin{cases} \dot{P}_K(t) = \dfrac{-\partial H}{\partial K} = -r P_K(t), \\ \dfrac{\partial H}{\partial C} = e^{-\delta t} \dfrac{\partial U}{\partial X} - P_K(t) P(t) = 0 \\ \dfrac{\partial H}{\partial C} = e^{-\delta t} \dfrac{\partial U}{\partial L} - P_K(t) P(t) = 0. \end{cases}$$

Rearranging, and dividing, we see that

(B.5) $(\partial U/\partial X)/(\partial U/\partial L) = P(t)/W(t)$;

i.e., the consumer workers equate the instantaneous marginal rate of substitution between goods and leisure to their relative prices. Further

(B.6) $P_K(t) = e^{-\delta t}(\partial U/\partial X)/P(t) = e^{-\delta t}(\partial U/\partial L)/W(t)$

the shadow price of saving is equal to each of the time discounted marginal utilities of consumption and leisure, divided by their respective prices. From this set of optimum conditions, we may derive the consumer-worker's optimal lifetime pattern of consumption of leisure and goods, as well as the comparative dynamic effects on the consumption of goods and leisure of changes in wages, prices and assets. Since explicit solutions require specific functional forms for utility functions, we present here only a heuristic discussion of these effects. The general labor supply function may be written as

$$LS = f(P, W, K_0) \tag{B.7}$$

where the coefficients on the price, wages and assets depend upon age, the interest rate and the initial shadow price of saving as well as upon parameters of the utility function.

First, compared to the usual comparative static result that labor supply may be an increasing or decreasing function of wage rates, depending upon whether the income or substitution effect dominates, the wage elasticity of labor supply now also depends upon the sensitivity of the shadow price of saving to wage changes. A permanent increase in wage rates makes the individual wealthier and is most likely to decrease the shadow price of saving. Second, the time pattern of labor supply also depends upon the shadow price of saving. An increase in this initial shadow price will accelerate the time rate of change of leisure consumption. Thus, any program which alters the wage rates or assets of individuals potentially affects labor supply and saving over the entire life cycle.

REFERENCES

Barfield, Richard, and Morgan, James. *Early Retirement: The Decision and the Experience*, Survey Research Center, University of Michigan, Ann Arbor, Michigan, 1969.

Brittain, John A. "The Incidence of Social Security Payroll Taxes," *American Economic Review*, 61(1), March 1971.

__________, *The Payroll Tax for Social Security*, The Brookings Institution, Washington, D.C., 1972.

Buchanan, James M. "Social Insurance in a Growing Economy: A Proposal for Radical Reform," *National Tax Journal*, XXI(4), December 1968.

Campbell, Colin. "Social Insurance in the United States: A Program in Search of an Explanation," *Journal of Law and Economics*, XII(2), October 1969.

Epstein, Lenore A., and Murray, Janet H. *The Aged Population of the United States*, U.S. Government Printing Office, Washington, D.C., 1967.

Feldstein, Martin S. "Social Security, Induced Retirement and Aggregate Capital Accumulation," *Journal of Political Economy*, 82(5), September 1974a.

__________, "Social Security and Private Capital Accumulation: International Evidence in an Extended Life-Cycle Model," Harvard Institute of Economic Research Discussion Paper, Harvard University, Cambridge, Massachusetts, 1974b.

__________, "Optimal Financing of Social Security," unpublished mimeograph, 1974c.

__________, "The Incidence of the Social Security Payroll Tax: Comment," *American Economic Review*, LXII(4), September 1972.

Hall, R. "An Analysis of the Labor Supply Results," in M. Timpane (ed.), *An Evaluation of the New Jersey-Pennsylvania Negative Income Tax Experiment*, The Brookings Institution, Washington, D.C., forthcoming.

Harberger, Arnold C. "Taxation, Resource Allocation, and Welfare," in *The Role of Direct and Indirect Taxes in the Federal Revenue System*, Princeton University Press, Princeton, N.J., 1964.

Kemeny, John G., and Snell, J. Laurie. *Finite Markov Chains*, Van Nostrand, Princeton, N.J., 1963.

Kendall, Maurice G., and Stuart, Alan. *The Advanced Theory of Statistics*, 2nd ed. (3 vol.), Hafner, New York, 1963-68; 3rd ed., 1969-73.

Long, Clarence. *The Labor Force under Changing Income and Employment*, Princeton University Press, Princeton, N.J., 1958.

McFadden, Daniel. "Conditional Logit Analysis of Qualitative Choice Behavior," in Paul Zarembka (ed.), *Frontiers in Econometrics*, Academic Press, New York, 1973.

Mincer, J. *Schooling, Experience and Earnings*, NBER, 1974.

Munnell, A. "The Impact of Social Security on Personal Savings," in *National Tax Journal*, December 1974.

Pechman, Joseph A., Aaron, Henry J., and Taussig, Michael K. *Social Security: Perspectives for Reform*, The Brookings Institution, Washington, D.C., 1968.

Steiner, Peter, and Dorfman, Robert. *The Economic Status of the Aged*, University of California Press, Berkeley, 1959.

Survey Research Center. *A Panel Study of Income Dynamics*, Institute for Social Research, The University of Michigan, Ann Arbor, Michigan, 1972.

U.S. Department of Health, Education, and Welfare. *The 1963 Social Security Survey of the Aged*, Social Security Administration, Washington, D.C.

Wentworth, Edna C. *Employment after Retirement*, U.S. Department of Health, Education, and Welfare, Social Security Administration, Office of Research and Statistics, Research Report 21, 1968.

[21]

Social Security, Induced Retirement, and Aggregate Capital Accumulation

Martin Feldstein

Harvard University

For the great majority of Americans, the most important form of household wealth is the anticipated social security retirement benefits. In 1971 the aggregate value of these annuities was approximately $2 trillion or some 60 percent of other household assets. This paper uses an extended life-cycle model to analyze the impact of social security on the individual's simultaneous decision about retirement and saving. Econometric evidence, using an estimated time series of "social security wealth," indicates that social security depresses personal saving by 30–50 percent. Implications of this research for the theory of consumption and for the level and distribution of income are discussed.

For the great majority of Americans, the most important form of household wealth is the anticipated social security retirement benefits. In 1971 the aggregate value of these annuities was approximately $2 trillion or some 60 percent of other household assets. Neither the theoretical nor the empirical analysis of household consumption behavior has given adequate attention to the existence and growth of social security.

This paper shows that the effect of social security is very important and is more complex than previous discussions have recognized. Section 1 presents a theoretical analysis that emphasizes the impact of social security on the individual's simultaneous decision about retirement and saving. In contrast to previous models of life-cycle saving, the extent of retirement is endogenous. Section 2 discusses the use of an aggregate consumption

This paper is part of a larger study of the effects of fiscal policies on capital formation and income distribution. I am grateful to the National Science Foundation for financial support, and to Roger Gordon, Alicia Munnell, and Anthony Pellechio for assistance with this research. I have also benefited from discussions and comments on a previous draft by Henry Aaron, John Flemming, Milton Friedman, Thomas Mayer, Franco Modigliani, Richard Musgrave, and the referees of this *Journal*.
[*Journal of Political Economy*, 1974, vol. 82, no. 5]

function to assess the effect of social security. A key variable in the analysis is an estimated time series of "social security wealth," that is, the present value of the social security annuities to which individuals are entitled. The data sources are described in Section 3, and the parameter estimates are presented in Section 4. The evidence indicates that social security has substantially decreased aggregate capital accumulation; specific estimates are presented in Section 5. A final section discusses some of the implications for the level and distribution of income.

I. A Life-Cycle Model with Induced Retirement

Ever since Harrod's (1948) discussion of "hump saving," economists have recognized the importance of saving during working years for consumption during retirement.[1] Although there are a variety of other motives for saving, the life-cycle hypothesis provides a particularly suitable framework for discussing the effects of social security. The most obvious implication of this familiar model is that social security, by providing income during retirement, reduces the amount of saving during the working years. More specifically, if the combination of social security tax and benefits has no net income effect, that is, if the individual's lifetime budget constraint is unchanged, savings will be reduced by just enough to leave consumption during retirement unchanged.

The possible importance of social security has been recognized but has never been formally incorporated into the theoretical or empirical analysis of the life-cycle model. Friedman (1957, p. 123) noted that social security "would clearly tend to reduce the need for private reserves and so to reduce private savings" but made no allowance for this in his analysis of both aggregate and cross-section savings. The potential effect of social security has also been ignored in Modigliani's own tests of the life-cycle hypothesis using time-series data for the United States (Ando and Modigliani 1963) and aggregate data for a cross-section of countries (Modigliani 1970). Mayer's (1972) recent book provides an extensive review of previous studies of the life-cycle hypothesis but no examples of studies in which the effect of social security had been considered.[2]

[1] As Harrod explicitly recognized, Fisher (1930) provided the basic model of consumption behavior from which his own analysis is derived. Harrod's contribution was to relate Fisher's two-period model to the stages of the life cycle and to explore some of its implications for Keynesian macroeconomics. The Modigliani-Brumberg (1954) paper extended this to a more general multiperiod analysis and derived the implications for the effects of wealth on consumption.

[2] In a cross-section study of savings in different countries, Aaron (1967) found evidence that higher social security benefits decreased private saving. His basic equation is inconsistent with the life-cycle hypothesis, ignoring variables such as the growth rates of income and of population that would be important determinants of intercountry differences in savings (see Modigliani 1970). This may explain why Aaron later reported that,

In contrast to the implications of the life-cycle theory, students of social security have generally argued that social security is not likely to have a substantial effect on personal savings and that it might even cause such savings to increase.[3] This conclusion is based largely on the evidence of Katona (1964) and Cagan (1965) that persons covered by private pensions do not save less and may save more than those persons not covered by pensions. More specifically, Cagan analyzed data generated by a mail survey of *Consumer Reports* subscribers and found that the average savings rate was slightly higher for those with pensions than for those without and was also higher for those with vested pensions than for those whose pensions were not vested. A regression equation implied that an increase in the individual's rate of pension contribution was associated with a higher level of direct ("discretionary") saving. Katona analyzed data collected by a University of Michigan survey of randomly selected households and also found that participation in a pension plan raised savings rates when age and current income were taken into account.

Cagan explained his surprising results in terms of a "recognition effect": when an individual is forced to participate in a pension plan, he recognizes for the first time the importance of saving for his old age. Participation in a pension plan has an educational effect; more formally, it changes the individual's utility function as he perceives it ex ante during his working years. Katona added to this a second explanation: the "goal gradient" hypothesis borrowed from psychological research on the forming of aspirations. According to this theory, "effort is intensified the closer one is to one's goal" (Katona 1964, p. 4). In more conventional economic terms, this would imply that individual preferences are themselves a function of the opportunity set or of the initial position, a dramatic departure from the usual assumption of economic analysis.

The findings of Cagan and Katona can be explained without invoking a recognition effect or a model of changing preferences by extending the life-cycle model to make the extent of retirement endogenous. Workers who are covered by pensions have an incentive to retire earlier than they otherwise would. To receive a pension requires retiring from a current job and generally involves loss of union seniority. Even if the individual is permitted to draw the pension after taking a new job, the loss of

---

when his equation was reestimated with data for a different year, the earlier effect of social security was no longer significant (Aaron 1968). A more recent international study using an extended life-cycle model to assess the impact of social security found that higher social security benefits and broader coverage do substantially reduce private savings (see Feldstein 1974).

[3] See, e.g., Pechman, Aaron, and Taussig (1968). Ever since Harris's (1941) study, estimates of the effect of social security on savings have concentrated on the impact of the reduction in disposable income (because of the payroll tax) rather than the life-cycle wealth effect of social security. For a more recent example of this, see Tax Foundation (1967).

seniority and of job-specific skills generally entails a substantial fall in the available wage. The pension therefore acts as a combination of an annual lump sum grant and a tax on earnings after the standard retirement age. The result is to reduce the labor supply of pension recipients, generally through earlier retirement. The pension, therefore has two effects on personal savings: (1) it reduces personal saving because it substitutes for household assets, but (2) it also increases personal saving because it lengthens the period of retirement over which accumulated assets will be spread. The net effect of the pension depends on the relative strength of these two forces.

Social security has a similar dual impact. The "tax" on earnings after age 65 is higher and even more obvious than with private pensions. The "earnings test" in the current social security law provides that a potential recipient loses his social security benefits if he earns more than $2,400 per year, thus requiring retirement from regular employment as a condition of receiving benefits. For an individual who in the absence of social security would have retired at age 65 to consume the income and principal of his accumulated assets, the social security benefits have the unambiguous effect of reducing saving. For those who would otherwise have worked beyond age 65, social security would generally (but not always) induce retirement at an earlier age. For such individuals, the effect of social security on savings is uncertain. In the extreme case of the individual who planned to work as long as he was able and then to be supported by his children or at public expense, the inducement to plan an early retirement could only increase savings. Although additional cases could be distinguished, it is already clear that the two countervailing effects make the net impact of social security ambiguous.[4]

The dual effect of social security is illustrated in figure 1. The horizontal axis measures income and consumption before age 65 (Y_1 and C_1), and the vertical axis measures income and consumption after that age (Y_2 and C_2). For simplicity, pretax income before age 65 is assumed to be unaffected by the introduction of social security. Consider first an individual who in the absence of social security would be fully retired after age 65. His earnings are described by point A: Y_{1A} in period 1 but zero in period 2. Faced with an opportunity to save at the rate of interest implied by the budget line through point A, the individual chooses the pair of consumption levels denoted by point I. During his preretirement period, he

[4] The introduction of social security also had the effect of removing a peculiar "tax" on savings by low-income individuals. Before social security, an individual could generally receive support at public expense only after he had exhausted all of his own assets. For the individual whose income was so low that a reasonable rate of saving during working years permitted a level of retirement consumption little better than that provided by public assistance, there would be a strong incentive to save nothing. In the same way, aged persons who lived with their children might find that their own assets, if any, did not alter retirement conditions and, therefore, were in effect taxed away.

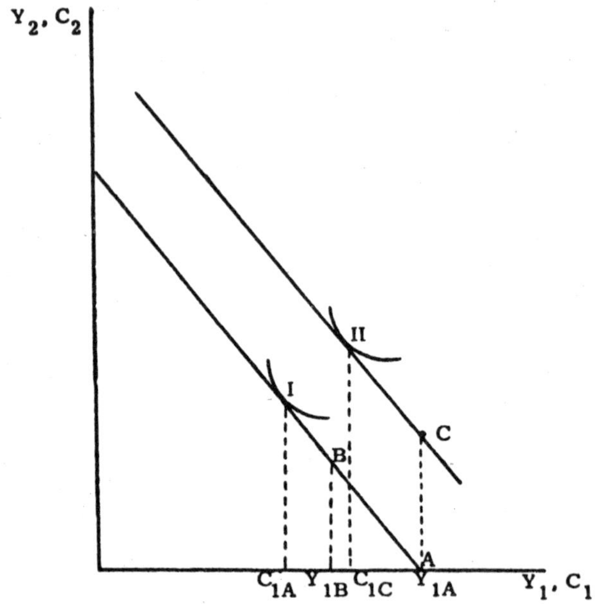

FIG. 1

consumes C_{1A} and saves $Y_{1A} - C_{1A}$. Point B describes that individual's initial position after the introduction of a social security tax; his second-period income is raised by the amount of the benefit, and his first-period income is reduced by the payroll tax to Y_{1B}; the difference between Y_{1A} and Y_{1B} is just sufficient to finance the benefits at the market rate of interest. Since the introduction of social security does not alter this individual's budget line, he retains the original equilibrium consumption point (I). The reduction in disposable income implies that saving is reduced from $Y_{1A} - C_{1A}$ to $Y_{1B} - C_{1A}$, that is, by the amount of the tax $(Y_{1A} - Y_{1B})$.

This reduction in saving can be contrasted with the experience of an individual who in the absence of social security would continue to work for some time after age 65. Point C indicates an initial position with positive earnings in the second period and the same level of first-period earnings as point A. The new equilibrium consumption pair is denoted by point II; first-period consumption is C_{1C}, and the corresponding saving is the relatively small amount $Y_{1A} - C_{1C}$. If the social security program induces him to retire completely at age 65, his initial position shifts from C to B, that is, his period 1 disposable income is reduced by the amount of the payroll tax, while his period 2 disposable income falls because earnings are reduced to zero and not fully replaced by social security benefits. With initial position B, the individual chooses consumption pair I.[5] The effect of introducing social security is, therefore, to change savings from $Y_{1A} - C_{1C}$ to $Y_{1B} - C_{1A}$. The current figure is constructed to make $Y_{1B} - C_{1A} > Y_{1A} - C_{1C}$, that is, the introduction of social security increases saving. Alternative assumptions about the consumption-expansion path could yield different results.

These two examples are sufficient to illustrate how social security will increase savings by some and decrease savings by others. A more general mathematical analysis of the effect of social security in the extended life-cycle model shows[6] that, *if the labor supply is fixed in both periods*, the introduction of a social security program reduces personal saving even if there are positive second-period earnings. When the labor supply in the second period is endogenous, social security benefits reduce second-period labor (i.e., induce earlier retirement), but the effect on savings is ambiguous.

As is so often the case, a theoretical analysis can illuminate the ways in which a public policy affects individual behavior, but it cannot yield an estimate of the magnitude of the effect nor even an unambiguous conclusion about its sign. For this we must turn to an empirical investigation. A full study of this issue would require examining the effect of social security on retirement plans in different circumstances and of the dependence of individual savings on both the retirement plans and the expected social security benefits. The task of the current study is more modest: to assess how the introduction and growth of social security have affected aggregate personal saving and the national accumulation of capital.

II. An Aggregate Consumption Function with Social Security Wealth

To assess the effect of social security, I have adapted the specification of the consumption function used by Ando and Modigliani (1963) and have added a social security wealth variable. The starting point for the analysis is thus:

$$C_t = \alpha + \beta_1 Y_t + \gamma_1 W_{t-1}, \tag{1}$$

where C_t is consumer expenditure, Y_t is permanent income (specified below as a distributed lag on past values of disposable income),[7] and W_t

[5] The indifference curves through points I and II are not comparable. The second individual prefers point I to point II because I is associated with not working after age 65.

[6] This analysis is presented in Feldstein (1974).

[7] Ando and Modigliani originally used *labor* income only but, because of the difficulties of defining and measuring disposable labor income, Modigliani (1971) has more recently abandoned labor income and used total disposable income. Ando and Modigliani also introduced an adjustment for unemployment. Although the use of a permanent income variable can serve this purpose, the unemployment rate will be examined explicitly.

is the stock of household wealth at the end of year t (excluding social security wealth).

Equation 2 introduces the social security wealth variable (SSW_t) into this consumption function:

$$C_t = \alpha + \beta_1 Y_t + \gamma_1 W_{t-1} + \gamma_2 SSW_t. \quad (2)$$

Two different definitions of SSW are used in the current study. Gross social security wealth ($SSWG_t$) is the present value in year t of the retirement benefits which could eventually be claimed by all those who are either in the labor force or already retired in year t. The calculation of these present values reflects survival probabilities as well as the discounting of future receipts. Net social security wealth ($SSWN_t$) equals gross social security wealth minus the present value of the social security taxes to be paid by those who are currently in the labor force. Net social security wealth is positive because the social security program involves a transfer to those who are currently working or retired from those who are yet to enter the labor force.

Since disposable income already excludes social security taxes, the gross social security wealth variable is probably the correct specification. Using the net social security wealth is equivalent to taking into account not only the current payroll tax but the present value of all future taxes. This is more appropriate if one views the social security program as creating for each individual an amount of wealth equal to the present value of the difference between his future benefits and his future taxes. The consumption function has been estimated with both definitions. Fortunately, both sets of estimates have the same implications.

The basic logic of the calculations used to evaluate $SSWG$ and $SSWN$ can be explained briefly.[8] Consider an unmarried worker who is age a in year t. If he remains single and survives to age 65, he will be entitled to an annual social security benefit in the amount $b_{a,t}$. In estimating the average value of future benefits for a single surviving annuitant, it would be wrong to assume that the schedule of benefits provided by law in year t would remain in effect. The history of social security shows continually rising benefit levels, a fact that individuals no doubt perceive when they contemplate the order of magnitude of their own benefits at retirement age. The ratio of annual benefits for retired workers (excluding dependents' benefits) to per capita disposable income has varied without any trend around a mean level of 0.41. The current calculation assumes that $b_{a,t}$ is 0.41 times per capita disposable income in year $t + 65 - a$ when the individual retires, Y_{t+65-a}. Finally, this future value of disposable income is estimated by projecting the current level at a constant rate of growth of disposable per capita income, $Y_{t+65-a} = Y_t(1 + g)^{65-a}$.

[8] A full description of the algorithm used is available from the author.

The anticipated benefits at age 65 are thus $b_{a,t} = 0.41\ Y_t(1 + g)^{65-a}$. During his retirement, the annual benefit will continue to grow. For simplicity we assume that this growth also occurs at rate g; thus at age $n > 65$, his annual benefit is $b_{a,t}(1 + g)^{n-65}$.

Let $S_{i,j}$ denote the probability that a man age i survives to at least age j, and let d be the rate at which the individual discounts expected future benefits. At age 65, his social security annuity will have a value of

$$\sum_{n \geq 65} S_{65,n} b_{a,t}(1 + g)^{n-65}(1 + d)^{-(n-65)};$$

for practical purposes the sum may be truncated at age 100. At time t (when the individual is age a) the future annuity has value:

$$A_{a,t} = S_{a,65}(1 + d)^{-(65-a)} \sum_{n \geq 65} S_{65,n} b_{a,t}(1 + g)^{n-65}(1 + d)^{-n+65}.$$

After substituting for $b_{a,t}$ we obtain:

$$A_{a,t} = 0.41\ Y_t S_{a,65}[(1 + g)/(1 + d)]^{65-a} \times \sum_{n \geq 65} S_{65,n}[(1 + g)/(1 + d)]^{n-65}. \quad (3)$$

Analogous calculations are done for single women, for working wives, and for married couples in which only the husband works. The special benefit rules for wives and for working women are reflected in these calculations. In particular, the value of the annuity for a married worker includes the benefits paid to his surviving spouse. The value of $SSWG_t$ is the weighted sum of the $A_{a,t}$ values for each type of worker and for each age group, weighting by the numbers of workers of that type and age covered by social security in year t.[9]

The present value of future social security taxes is obtained by a similar method. A worker who contemplates his future social security taxes recognizes that they will rise because of increases in both the tax rate and the level of taxable earnings. For simplicity, we combine these and assume that the individual forecasts the ratio of social security taxes per covered worker to per capita disposable income, θ_t. An average worker who is age a in year t pays a tax of $T_t = \theta_t Y_t$, independent of his age. He expects that at age m he will pay a tax of $T_{t+m-a} = \theta_{t+m-a} Y_t(1 + g)^{m-a}$. The present value of all his future taxes until age 65 is thus:[10]

$$\text{TAX}_{a,t} = \sum_{m=a}^{64} S_{a,m} \theta_{t+m-a} Y_t[(1 + g)/(1 + d)]^{m-a}. \quad (4)$$

[9] An adjustment is made for those who are not currently labor-force participants but can be expected to draw social security benefits at some time in the future.

[10] A special adjustment is made for those over age 65 who are still employed.

The value of 0_t has been rising in an irregular pattern since the introduction of social security and in 1971 reached approximately 0.15 for males and 0.07 for females. The current calculations assume that the individuals correctly foresaw the changes in 0_t before 1971 and assumed that after 1971 the 0_t's would remain at the 1971 levels. The total present value of expected future taxes is a weighted sum of the $TAX_{a,t}$ values for different employee types (single men, married men, etc.) and age groups, weighting by the numbers of covered workers in each group in year t. The net social security wealth value in each year is the difference between $SSWG_t$ and this aggregate tax value.

Despite the complexity of these calculations, the values of $SSWG_t$ and $SSWN_t$ do not have the precision of actuarial estimates. For example, there is no adjustment for future marriages and divorces or for remarriages by surviving beneficiaries. But an exact actuarial estimate is not required for the current analysis. The *SSW* variable should reflect the magnitude of the effect of social security to which households respond. The household's implicit evaluation of social security benefits is likely to reflect their perception of the current standard of living among social security annuitants and of the way in which this has changed in the past. Note that households may therefore be able to respond appropriately to changes in social security without being able to calculate or articulate the value of benefits.

The *SSW* variable values the benefits for which individuals are *eligible* at age 65: there is no reduction for the individuals who can be expected to continue to work beyond age 65. In this way, the *SSW* variable represents both the "substitute asset" effect that would reduce savings and the "inducement to retire" effect that would increase savings. The estimate of γ_2, therefore, measures the net effect of the introduction and growth of the social security program. It therefore underestimates the effect on saving of the increasing number of individuals who already plan to retire at 65.

The consumption function of equation 2 should be extended to reflect the impact of corporate saving on household consumption. During the period since the introduction of social security in 1937, the growing tax incentive associated with rising marginal personal income tax rates has induced companies to increase the fraction of total earnings that is saved.[11] The traditional specification of equation 1 implies that dividends have a much greater effect on concurrent consumption than retained earnings. This implies that the tax-induced substitution of retained earnings for dividends during the past 30 years has reduced household consumption. I believe that this is an unintended result of specifying

[11] See Brittain (1966) for evidence that this has occurred. Feldstein (1970) found that British firms also varied their savings rate in response to tax-induced changes in the opportunity cost of retentions in terms of foregone dividends.

consumer behavior without considering the implication of the corporate form of business. The current paper, therefore, relaxes this restrictive assumption and uses a model developed in Feldstein (1973) and Feldstein and Fane (1973) in which retained earnings have a short-run effect on consumption in addition to their long-run wealth effect. More specifically, the basic specification used in this paper is:

$$C_t = \alpha + \beta_1 Y_t + \beta_2 RE_t + \gamma_1 W_{t-1} + \gamma_2 SSW_t. \quad (5)$$

Separate estimates with the retained earnings variable excluded show that this does not substantially affect the estimated impact of social security wealth.

III. The Data

The estimates presented below are based on aggregate U.S. data for the periods 1929 through 1971, excluding the years 1941 through 1946. Separate analyses for the postwar period, 1947 through 1971, are also presented.

Consumer expenditure (C) and disposable personal income (YD) are the usual national income account values, deflated to constant 1958 dollars and divided by population. The measurement of retained earnings raises a problem because of inadequate data on true economic depreciation. Undistributed profits as reported in the national income accounts are equal to gross profits minus an estimate of corporate capital consumption. Because of the accounting conventions used to calculate capital consumption, this measure of net retained earnings is likely to be an underestimate of true net corporate saving. Gross retained earnings is obviously an overestimate. Separate equations have been estimated with each specification. The similar implications of the results with both measures indicates that further work to improve the measurement of retained earnings would not alter any conclusions. Only the equations with gross retained earnings are reported.

The wealth variable is the per capita net worth of households at market value expressed in 1958 dollars. The series was estimated by Ando and Modigliani (1963) based on Goldsmith's (1956) earlier study and updated for the FRB-MIT econometric model.[12] The variable W_t refers to the wealth at the end of year t.

The basic data required to calculate the social security wealth variable are published in the annual statistical supplements of the *Social Security Bulletin*. Each year the average level of benefits for retired workers is published as well as the average payroll tax per covered employee and

[12] I am grateful to Franco Modigliani for making available the unpublished data.

TABLE 1

SOCIAL SECURITY WEALTH
(BILLIONS OF CONSTANT 1971 DOLLARS)

Year	Gross Wealth SSWG1 (1)	Gross Wealth SSWG5 (2)	Net Wealth SSWN1 (3)	Net Wealth SSWN5 (4)	GNP (5)
1940	235	70	145	25	321
1950	442	153	227	36	503
1955	690	270	366	81	620
1960	917	380	493	122	691
1965	1,397	596	805	234	875
1971	2,029	875	1,162	342	1,050

the number of covered employees and annuitants by age and demographic group (single men, etc.). Separate survival probabilities ($S_{i,j}$'s) for men and women are obtained from the life tables published by the U.S. Department of Health, Education and Welfare (1968).

The formula for *SSW* also contains the rate of growth of real per capita disposable income (g) and the individual's rate of discount for future real income (d). For the 35 years from the introduction of the social security program to 1972, real per capita disposable income grew at a rate of 2 percent per year. The value of d can be considered the average real rate of interest after tax that was available to savers during the period since the introduction of social security. The nominal rate of interest on Moody's Baa bonds averaged 5.0 percent from 1937 to 1972. The average inflation of consumer prices was 3.0 percent. The real yield before tax was, therefore, 2.0 percent. The yield on bank deposits and savings bonds was lower. Although the return on common stocks and private homes was much higher, investment in common stocks has been relatively unimportant for low- and moderate-income households, and the scope for additional saving in owner-occupied housing is obviously limited. A value of $d = 0.03$, therefore, appears to be an appropriate estimate. Equations 6 and 7 show that g and d always enter together in the form $(1 + d)/(1 + g)$. What matters, therefore, is only this net discount ratio and not the individual values of g and d. The values $g = 0.02$ and $d = 0.03$ imply a ratio of 1.01. To test the sensitivity of the regression analysis to this value, estimates were also made with *SSW* calculated with the very high ratio of 1.05. Although 1.05 produces much smaller values of *SSW*, the choice of discount ratio does not alter the implications of the regression estimates.

Table 1 presents values of gross and net social security wealth at six dates; the *SSW* values are converted to constant 1971 dollars by the implicit price deflator for personal consumption expenditures. The choice of discount factor is indicated by a final number in the name of the variable, for example, *SSWG*1 refers to the gross social security variable computed using a net discount ratio of 1.01. Note that by 1971 the value of *SSWG*1 was more than $2.0 trillion in constant 1971 dollars, and the value of *SSWN*1 was more than $1.1 trillion. This compares with total household assets of $3.5 trillion. The social security wealth increases household assets by 60 percent according to the gross definitions and 30 percent according to the net definition.[13]

A comparison of the *SSW* variables with real GNP (presented in col. 5 of table 1) shows that social security wealth has grown much more rapidly. This reflects a substantial aging of the population and, more important, an increase in the proportion of workers covered by social security from 58 percent of paid employees in 1940 to 89 percent in 1971.

For the regression analysis the *SSW* values are all divided by population. By construction they are already in constant 1958 dollars.

IV. Estimates of the Effect of Social Security Wealth

The estimates presented below support the conclusion that social security substantially depresses personal savings. The marginal propensity to consume social security wealth is generally statistically significant and slightly larger than the propensity to consume ordinary wealth. This difference probably reflects the fact that a large portion of ordinary wealth is held by a small fraction of households for whom bequests and the accumulation of larger fortunes are more important than saving for retirement. Although the coefficient of *SSW* depends on the choice of definition and discount rate, Section 5 will show that nearly all of the estimates imply that, in the absence of social security, personal savings would be at least 50 percent higher than they are now and probably closer to 100 percent higher.

Equation 2.1 of table 2 presents an estimate of the consumption function with gross social security wealth and a discount ratio of 1.01 (*SSWG*1).[14] The marginal propensity to consume *SSWG*1 is 0.021 with a standard error of only 0.006. The other coefficients are of the expected size: 0.650 for disposable income[15] and 0.014 for household wealth. The marginal propensity to consume gross retained earnings (0.36) is approximately equal to the value of 0.50 reported in Feldstein (1973) for an

[13] Although the other measures of *SSW* are lower, they are based on less acceptable assumptions about the valuing of *SSW*.

[14] Recall that the discount ratio is defined as $(1 + d)/(1 + g)$, where d is the individual's rate of discount and g is the rate of growth of real per capita income.

[15] The value of 0.650 may appear low as an estimate of the long-run marginal propensity to consume. It should be remembered, however, that the equation contains wealth and retained earnings variables. If these are omitted, the coefficient of income rises substantially.

TABLE 2

Consumption Functions with Social Security Wealth

Eq.	Period*	*SSW* Definition	*YD*	YD_{-1}	*RE*	W_{-1}	*SSW*	*RU*	Const.	*SSR*	D-W Statis.
2.1	1929–71	*SSWG*1	0.530	0.120	0.356	0.014	0.021	...	228	3,618	1.82
			(0.047)	(0.035)	(0.074)	(0.004)	(0.006)		(31)		
2.2	1929–71	*SSWN*1	0.528	0.137	0.376	0.013	0.032	...	218	3,548	1.85
			(0.047)	(0.034)	(0.073)	(0.004)	(0.009)		(27)		
2.3	1929–71	*SSWG*5	0.530	0.136	0.400	0.008	0.051	...	244	3,714	1.82
			(0.048)	(0.035)	(0.075)	(0.005)	(0.016)		(37)		
2.4	1929–71	*SSWN*5	0.538	0.163	0.432	0.009	0.075	...	204	3,944	1.71
			(0.049)	(0.037)	(0.079)	(0.006)	(0.027)		(29)		
2.5	1929–71	*SSWG*1	0.675	0.046	...	0.009	0.024	...	204	6,289	1.43
			(0.047)	(0.041)		(0.005)	(0.008)		(40)		
2.6	1929–71	*SSWG*1	0.553	0.154	0.436	0.013	0.010	1.170	155	3,422	1.80
			(0.050)	(0.043)	(0.096)	(0.004)	(0.011)	(0.892)	(64)		
2.7	1929–71	*SSWG*1	0.549	0.149	0.423	0.012	0.012	1.020	169	3,430	1.82
			(0.047)	(0.037)	(0.079)	(0.004)	(0.004)	(0.663)	(30)		
2.8	1947–71	*SSWG*1	0.535	0.139	0.414	0.015	0.014	...	193	3,087	1.63
			(0.097)	(0.097)	(0.163)	(0.009)	(0.030)		(159)		
2.9	1947–71	*SSWN*1	0.535	0.119	0.349	0.014	0.035	...	232	2,926	1.78
			(0.084)	(0.085)	(0.170)	(0.007)	(0.030)		(104)		
2.10	1947–71	*SSWG*1	0.531	0.106	0.423	0.008	0.029	2.786	252	2,965	1.80
			(0.098)	(0.105)	(0.164)	(0.012)	(0.035)	(3.237)	(175)		

* The years 1941–46 are excluded from the sample. The Durbin-Watson statistic is adjusted for this gap. Standard errors are shown in parentheses.

equation that ignored the effect of social security and that was limited to the period 1929 through 1965.[16]

Using the *net* definition of social security wealth or a higher discount ratio strengthens these conclusions. Equations 2.2 through 2.4 show that alternative measures of *SSW* leave the other coefficients unchanged but increase the size of the propensity to consume social security wealth. These differences in the coefficient of *SSW* are primarily due to differences in the magnitudes of the *SSW* measures. Comparing these coefficients with the *SSW* values presented in table 1 shows that all four equations imply approximately the same effect of security wealth on consumption.

Although the retained earnings variable has a stable and statistically important coefficient, its novelty in the consumption function may raise doubts about its effect on the coefficients of the other variables. Equation 2.5 shows that excluding *RE* causes a slight increase in the coefficient of the *SSW* variable. The results are similar when a higher discount ratio is used.

Equations 2.1 through 2.5 were estimated by ordinary least squares and are therefore subject to possible simultaneous equation bias. Reestimating these equations with a consistent instrumental variable procedure confirmed the original ordinary least-squares results.[17] For example, with *SSWG*1 the coefficient of *SSW* was increased from 0.021 in equation 2.1 to 0.033 with the instrumental variable estimator. The coefficient of the retained earnings variable also rose, from 0.356 in equation 2.1 to 0.501 with the instrumental variable estimator. There was some indication of substantial simultaneous equation bias in the estimated effect of disposable income; the sum of the coefficients fell from 0.650 in equation 2.1 to 0.561 with the instrumental variable estimator.

An alternative dynamic specification of permanent income also leaves the other coefficients unchanged. More specifically, a permanent income variable was defined by the recursive relation $YP_t = (1 - \mu)YD_t + \mu YP_{t-1}$. A maximum-likelihood estimate was obtained by doing ordinary least squares conditional on values of μ between zero and one and selecting that value of μ that minimizes the sum of squared residuals. For a specification analogous to equation 2.1, the maximum-likelihood estimate of μ was 0.18, implying a rapid response that can be well represented by the 2-year distributed lag. The long-run marginal propensity to consume disposable income was 0.65, and the other coefficients were almost unchanged from the 2-year distributed lag specification of equation 2.1: 0.35 for retained earnings, 0.014 for wealth, and 0.021 for *SSWG*1.

[16] Since the R^2 values are extremely high for all equations ($R^2 \geq .99$), only the sum of squared residuals and the Durbin-Watson statistic are presented.

[17] The instrumental variables were government expenditure, exports, money supply, household wealth, and the social security wealth variable.

While the use of a distributed lag on past incomes is the most common way of relating consumption to "permanent" income, the rate of unemployment has often been included in the consumption function to adjust for the cyclical variation in the relation of consumption and income.[18] Introducing the unemployment rate (*RU*) in equation 2.6 lowers the coefficient of *SSW* and increases its standard error. However, the coefficient of *RU* is not statistically significant and is absolutely very small. More specifically, the coefficient implies that even a 5-percentage-point increase in *RU* would raise consumption by less than $6.00, that is, doubling the unemployment rate would raise consumption by much less than 1 percent.[19] Equation 2.7 shows that the insignificance of the unemployment coefficient is not merely due to its collinearity with the social security wealth variable. Instead of estimating separate coefficients for personal wealth and *SSW*, the two coefficients are constrained to be equal; the coefficient of *RU* is still insignificant, while the coefficient of the total wealth variable is more than three times its standard error.

The apparent collinearity of the *RU* and *SSW* variable also raises the possibility that the social security variable (which is zero before 1937) is only a reflection of the shift in consumption behavior from the prewar to the postwar period. To test this possibility, the consumption equations have been reestimated with data restricted to the postwar period (1947 through 1971). The results reject this explanation and support the original conclusion that social security substantially depresses personal savings. In equation 2.8, the coefficient of *SSWG*1 is somewhat smaller than the corresponding coefficient for the entire period, while in equation 2.9 the coefficient of *SSWN*1 is somewhat larger than for the entire period; comparing the residual sums of squares again indicates a slight preference for the net worth measure and, therefore, the larger coefficient. Introducing the unemployment rate (eq. 2.10) substantially raises the estimated effect of *SSWG*1, while the coefficient of the unemployment variable is itself statistically insignificant. In short, although the smaller variation of *SSW* in the postwar period than in the entire sample raises the standard errors of its estimated coefficient, these coefficient estimates are similar to the values for the entire interval.

V. The Impact on Aggregate Saving

While the coefficients of table 2 must be regarded with caution, it is interesting to examine the implications of these parameter values for aggregate savings. In equation 2.1, the marginal propensity to consume disposable income is 0.650, and the marginal propensity to consume social

[18] See Ando and Modigliani (1963) for the rationale for using the unemployment rate and the recent level of income to represent expected future income.

[19] Real per capita consumption rose from $1,145 in 1929 to $2,393 in 1971.

security wealth is 0.021. In 1971, social security taxes and contributions reduced disposable income by $51 billion in 1971 prices. The corresponding reduction in personal savings is, therefore, $18 billion. The social security wealth (*SSWG*1) for 1971 was $2,029 billion, implying a reduction in saving of $43 billion. The wealth effect is, therefore, more than twice as important as the tax effect through the reduction in disposable income. The total fall in personal saving was therefore $61 billion in 1971 prices.[20] Since personal saving in 1971 was also $61 billion, the implied effect of social security is to reduce personal saving to half of what it otherwise would be.[21] Repeating these calculations for each of the other three definitions of social security wealth yields similar estimates of the reduction in personal savings, ranging from $44 billion with *SSWN*5 to $63 billion with *SSWG*5.

The implication that social security halves the rate of personal saving is startling but not unreasonable. For middle- and low-income families, social security is a complete substitute for a substantial rate of private saving.[22] The asset-substitution effect is, therefore, likely to be very significant. Although social security induced retirements that would otherwise have been postponed, a substantial fraction of older men were already retiring before the introduction of social security. In 1930, 46 percent of men over 65 were retired, while in 1971 this was 75 percent. For the original 46 percent, social security has only an asset-substitution effect. Only for the remaining 25 percent does social security have a stimulating "retirement effect" as well as a depressing asset-substitution effect.[23] The estimates imply that any additional savings that result from induced retirement among this group have been outweighed by the asset-substitution effect among all social security beneficiaries.

Although the coefficient of social security wealth has been treated as a constant in estimating the consumption function, it is more appropriate

[20] This slightly overstates the effect on saving because the social security taxes and contributions include funds for Medicare and disability insurance. The calculations implicitly assume that the parameters of the consumption function would be unchanged if consumer expenditure were replaced by the sum of consumer expenditure, interest paid by consumers, and personal transfers to foreigners; the two additional items were only 3 percent of 1971 consumer expenditure.

[21] Personal saving in 1971 was 9.2 percent of disposable income and thus substantially higher than other years in the postwar period. For the postwar sample period, the average was 6.4 percent. The choice of 1971, therefore, substantially understates the relative impact of social security. Note, however, that the assumption that all social security benefits are consumed may overstate the effect of the program on saving. If instead the propensity to consume these benefits is assumed to be the same as for other forms of disposable income, only the wealth effect would remain. This implies that saving would be reduced by $43 billion to 59 percent of what it would otherwise be.

[22] For an individual with earnings below the covered maximum ($9,000 in 1972), social security can replace personal savings of at least 10 percent of disposable income.

[23] Note that the 46 percent and 25 percent refer to man-years and not to individuals.

to regard the estimate as an average of the different propensities to consume that prevailed during the sample period. Moreover, it seems likely that the marginal propensity to consume increases in *SSW* will be higher in the future than it has been in the past. The coefficient of *SSW* reflects both the asset-substitution effect and the inducement-to-retire effect. The relative importance of these two countervailing effects will change as the social security program matures. Until recently, social security has been increasing the frequency of retirement among men over age 65. These induced retirements led to additional saving and, therefore, partly offset the asset-substitution effect that gives the *SSW* coefficient its positive sign. Since 75 percent of men and 91 percent of women over 65 were retired in 1971, there is now much less scope for a proportional increase in retirement, and the asset-substitution effect can be expected to dominate even more strongly in the future.[24]

VI. Some General Implications

The model and empirical estimates presented in this paper have wide-ranging and important implications. Although these cannot be explored here in any detail, the following section will provide some brief remarks about three different issues.

The Theory of Consumption

The analysis lends support to the general idea of life-cycle saving while indicating the importance of extending the traditional model by making the age of retirement an economic decision. The substantial estimated effect of social security wealth on consumption is consistent with this life-cycle hypothesis. By taking into account the effect on saving of induced retirement, the generalized life-cycle model can also explain previous survey evidence on the relation between pensions and household saving without recourse to Cagan's "recognition effect" or Katona's "goal gradient" hypothesis.

Previous tests of the life-cycle model should be reconsidered within this more general framework and with explicit recognition of the role of social

[24] Munnell (1973) independently recognized the important effect of changing retirement behavior on aggregate savings. Her study examines the various forces that have altered retirement rates since 1900 and provides an explicit estimate of the positive effect of increasing retirement on personal saving. By using national balance-sheet data to construct savings series, she is able to separate savings in the assets that are most important for the families with low and moderate incomes for whom social security is a primary source of retirement income. Her analysis using the *SSW* series of the current paper provides strong support for the conclusion of this section.

security.[25] A measure of social security wealth should also be included in future tests of other hypotheses about consumption behavior.

One of the most firmly established facts about consumer behavior is the long-run constancy of the aggregate savings rate (Kuznets 1946; Denison 1958; David and Scadding 1972). Much of modern consumption theory arose in the attempt to reconcile this fact with other observations about aggregate and individual consumption. The substantial depressing effect of social security on the postwar savings rate raises a serious question about the *behavioral* significance of the observed constancy of the savings rate. The evidence presented in this paper seems more consistent with the Keynesian view that the aggregate rate of saving would increase as income rose if there were no offsetting government policies.

Capital Accumulation and National Income

The evidence that the social security program approximately halves the personal savings rate implies that it substantially reduces the stock of capital and the level of national income. During the 1960s, personal saving accounted for 60 percent of total private saving. By halving personal saving, social security reduced total private saving by 38 percent. In the long run, this decrease in the rate of private saving would also decrease the private capital stock by 38 percent.[26]

These estimates are consistent with the magnitude of the social security wealth derived in Section 3. The 1971 value of gross social security wealth with the most plausible value of the relative discount ratio (*SSWG*1) was $2,029 billion in 1971 prices. Total household assets (*W*) in that year were $3,474 billion in 1971 prices. The actual level of assets was, therefore, 37 percent less than if all of the social security wealth had instead been saved privately. This is remarkably close to the predicted long-run effect of 38 percent, in spite of conceptual differences between household assets and real capital stock.

A 38 percent decrease in the capital stock implies a substantial reduction in GNP. If this asset substitution had not occurred, the long-run capital stock would be some 60 percent higher.[27] A rough approximation of the effect that this greater capital stock would have on national income

[25] The possibility that the generalized life-cycle model is appropriate for most of the population but not for the very wealthy should be examined. See Tobin (1967) for an interesting simulation approach to testing the consistency of the life-cycle hypothesis with actual savings, and Mayer (1972) for a survey of previous econometric estimates.

[26] Since the social security system is not "funded" but operates on a pay-as-you-go basis, the reduction in private saving is not offset by any increase in public saving. Note that if the tax-transfer process does not reduce saving so that saving falls only because of the wealth effect of the social security program, the decrease in the rate of private saving and therefore in the private capital stock is 29 percent.

[27] In providing a "fiat" asset as a substitute for real capital formation, social security is similar to absorbing saving by a growing money supply (see Tobin 1965).

can be obtained by assuming a Cobb-Douglas technology and a capital coefficient of 0.3. With this assumption, GNP is multiplied by $(1.6)^{0.3}$, that is, income would rise by 15 percent. A more conservative assumption of a 40 percent increase in the capital stock implies that GNP would rise by 11 percent. For 1972, this implies that GNP would be increased by more than $127 billion.

The lower level of GNP reflects the pay-as-you-go nature of our social security system. Because social security contributions are used to pay concurrent benefits, the capital stock is smaller and income is less.[28] This result should be contrasted with Samuelson's (1958) important and much misinterpreted analysis of the effect of social security in a "consumption loan" model. Samuelson considered an economy in which real capital accumulation was physically impossible. In his analysis, all commodities were like "chocolates" that melted and could not be stored through time. Private saving required finding a borrower who wished to consume more than his income and could repay at a later time. In this situation, life-cycle saving cannot be carried out efficiently. Samuelson showed that a pay-as-you-go social security system could lead to an unambiguous improvement in welfare; each generation would prefer the social security system to the alternative equilibrium. In this analysis, the assumption that there is no store of value or method of real accumulation is crucial. As Samuelson notes, simply introducing a stock of fiat money to provide a store of value makes it unnecessary to create a social security system in order to achieve intertemporal efficiency. Allowing for the accumulation of productive capital goods makes the analysis more complex and, as shown here, implies that a pay-as-you-go social security system reduces aggregate saving and lowers the level of real income.[29]

The Distribution of Income

Analyses of the distributional impact of social security have focused on two questions. First, how do the taxes nominally paid by persons at different income levels compare with the benefits that are eventually received?[30] Second, how does the payroll tax affect gross factor prices,

[28] Note that this lower level of income does not measure lost welfare because some additional consumption was obtained at an earlier date. An analysis of the welfare loss would require a cardinal social utility function capable of intergenerational calculations of time preference.

[29] As Aaron (1966) has noted, a pay-as-you-go social security system can lead to an unambiguous welfare increase in an economy that would otherwise save too much, that is, in the unlikely case of an economy that is so capital intensive that the rate of return is less than the rate of growth of real output.

[30] The system has been shown to pay a rather high implicit rate of interest on these taxes, with relatively higher yields going to those at lower income levels (see Brittain 1972). The redistributive impact is generally understated by ignoring the fact that higher-income individuals are much less likely to retire at age 65.

that is, what is the incidence of the tax? This paper indicates that the benefits side of the social security program also has important effects on the distribution of income. Two separate issues can be distinguished: the changes in factor prices, and the effects on the income of the aged.[31]

The substantial reduction in the capital stock that results from the current social security program decreases wage rates and increases the rate of profit. To obtain an order of magnitude for these effects, I will again assume a Cobb-Douglas technology with a capital elasticity of 0.3. With a fixed labor supply, the wage rate is proportional to $K^{0.3}$ (where K is the capital stock), and the rate of interest is proportional to $K^{-0.7}$. If, in the absence of the current social security system, the capital stock were 60 percent greater, the wage rate would rise by 15 percent and the rate of interest would fall by 28 percent. Although the Cobb-Douglas technology implies that factor shares would be unchanged, there would be a substantial redistribution of capital income to those who, because of the social security system, now save very little.

The induced retirement implies that the labor supply is also decreased by the social security system. Less labor raises the wage rate and lowers the rate of return.[32] This partly offsets the distributional effect of the change in the capital stock. But even if all of the increase in retirements since 1930 were attributed to social security, the reduction in the labor supply would be quite small in comparison to the reduction in the capital stock. More specifically, if the labor force participation rates of those over 65 were at the 1930 values, the labor force in 1970 would be increased by less than 3 percent.[33] The net effect of the changes in capital and labor has clearly been to raise the rate of profit and lower the wage rate.

Although the social security program was intended primarily as a system of income maintenance for the aged, it may now have the effect of reducing the levels of income and consumption for many of those over 65. Those who are induced by the combination of available benefits and the "earnings test" to retire earlier than they would otherwise have done generally receive substantially less in social security benefits than they would have earned if they had continued to work. As the analysis of Section 1 showed, even with optimal savings during the preretirement years, the level of consumption is likely to fall at retirement. The income-

[31] By replacing individual saving, social security also has a substantial effect on the distribution of wealth. If each household's social security wealth were added to its other assets, the distribution of total wealth would be much more equal than the distribution of wealth as traditionally defined.

[32] A reduction in labor supply through earlier retirement has a different long-run effect on factor prices than a proportional reduction in the quantity of labor supplied each year with no change in retirement. In particular, these two changes in labor supply have different effects on savings behavior (see Feldstein 1972).

[33] Future increases in the level of social security benefits will have relatively little effect on the labor supply since 74 percent of men over 65 are already retired.

maintenance goal of the social security program is thus partly vitiated by imposing an earnings test as a condition for receiving benefits.[34]

VII. Conclusion

It is best to conclude this paper with a caveat. The substantial estimated effect of social security on personal savings is based on aggregate time-series data for a single country. The results are consistent with the generalized life-cycle hypothesis but require further analysis with different sets of data. Work is currently in progress to examine household data for the United States and aggregate data for a cross-section of countries. Additional studies for individual countries, using both aggregate time series and household surveys, could be of great value in testing the current conclusions.

References

Aaron, Henry. "The Social Insurance Paradox." *Canadian J. Econ. and Polit. Sci.* 33 (August 1966): 371–74.

———. "Social Security: International Comparisons." In *Studies in the Economics of Income Maintenance*, edited by Otto Eckstein. Washington: Brookings Inst., 1967.

———. "International Comparisons," appendix D. In *Social Security: Perspectives for Reform*, by J. A. Pechman, H. J. Aaron, and M. K. Taussig. Washington: Brookings Inst., 1968.

Ando, Albert, and Modigliani, F. "The 'Life Cycle' Hypothesis of Saving: Aggregate Implications and Tests." *A.E.R.* 53 (March 1963): 55–84.

Brittain, John A. *Corporate Dividend Policy*. Washington: Brookings Inst., 1966.

———. *The Payroll Tax for Social Security*. Washington: Brookings Inst., 1972.

Cagan, Phillip. *The Effect of Pension Plans on Aggregate Savings*. New York: Nat. Bur. Econ. Res., 1965.

David, P., and Scadding, J. L. "What You Always Wanted to Know about 'Denison's Law' But Were Afraid to Ask." Memorandum no. 129, Stanford Center for Research, 1972.

Denison, Edward F. "A Note in Private Saving." *Rev. Econ. and Statis.* 40 (August 1958): 261–67.

Feldstein, M. S. "Corporate Taxation and Dividend Behavior." *Rev. Econ. Studies* 37 (January 1970): 57–72.

———. "Tax Incidence in a Growing Economy with Variable Factor Supply." Harvard Institute of Economic Research Discussion Paper no. 263, 1972. Forthcoming in *Q.J.E.*

———. "Tax Incentives, Corporate Saving, and Capital Accumulation in the United States." *J. Public Econ.* 2 (April 1973): 159–71.

———. "Social Security and Private Savings: International Evidence in an Extended Life Cycle Model." Harvard Institute of Economic Research Discussion Paper, 1974. Forthcoming in *The Economics of Public Services: Proceedings*

[34] There is also an important loss of economic welfare due to induced retirement. The earnings test and the social security benefits imply a very high marginal rate of tax on earnings after age 65.

of an International Economics Association Conference, edited by Martin Feldstein and Robert Inman.

Feldstein, M. S., and Fane, George. "Taxes, Corporate Dividend Policy and Personal Savings: The British Postwar Experience." *Rev. Econ. and Statis.* 55 (November 1973): 399–411.

Fisher, I. *The Theory of Interest*. New York: Macmillan, 1930.

Friedman, Milton. *A Theory of the Consumption Function*. Princeton, N.J.: Princeton Univ. Press, 1957.

Goldsmith, R. W. *A Study of Saving in the United States*. Vols. 1–3. Princeton, N.J.: Princeton Univ. Press, 1956.

Harris, Seymour. *Economics of Social Security*. New York: McGraw-Hill, 1941.

Harrod, R. F. *Towards a Dynamic Economics*. London: Macmillan, 1948.

Katona, George. *Private Pensions and Individual Savings*. Ann Arbor: Survey Research Center, Institute for Social Research, Univ. Michigan, 1964.

Kuznets, Simon. *National Product since 1869*. New York: Nat. Bur. Econ. Res., 1946.

Mayer, Thomas. *Permanent Income, Wealth and Consumption*. Berkeley: Univ. California Press, 1972.

Modigliani, Franco. "The Life Cycle Hypothesis of Saving and Intercountry Differences in the Saving Ratio." In *Induction, Growth, and Trade: Essays in Honour of Sir Roy Harrod*, edited by W. A. Eltis, M. FG. Scott, and J. N. Wolfe. Oxford: Clarendon, 1970.

———. "Monetary Policy and Consumption: Linkages via Interest Rate and Wealth Effects in the FMP Model." In *Consumer Spending and Monetary Policy*. Monetary Conference Series no. 5. Boston: Fed. Res. Bank Boston, 1971.

Modigliani, F., and Brumberg, R. "Utility Analysis and the Consumption Function: An Interpretation of Cross Section Data." In *Post Keynesian Economics*, edited by K. Kurihara. New Brunswick, N.J.: Rutgers Univ. Press, 1954.

Munnell, Alicia. *The Effect of Social Security on Personal Savings*. Ph.D. dissertation, Harvard Univ., 1973.

Pechman, Joseph A.; Aaron, Henry; and Taussig, Michael K. *Social Security: Perspectives for Reform*. Washington: Brookings Inst., 1968.

Samuelson, Paul. "An Exact Consumption Loan Model of Interest with or without the Social Contrivance of Money." *J.P.E.* 66 (December 1958): 467–82.

Tax Foundation. *Economic Aspects of the Social Security Tax*. New York: Tax Foundation, Inc., 1967.

Tobin, James. "Money and Economic Growth." *Econometrica* 33 (October 1965): 671–84.

———. "Life Cycle Saving and Balanced Growth." In *Ten Economic Studies in the Tradition of Irving Fisher*, edited by W. Fellner et al. New York: Wiley, 1967.

U.S. Department of Health, Education and Welfare. *Life Tables: 1959–61*. PHS Publication no. 1252. Vol. 1, no. 1. Washington: Government Printing Office, 1968.

[22]

Population Aging and Security of the Aged

JOSEPH J. SPENGLER*

"Consideration of alternatives that would tend to extend worklife . . . and a reexamination of financial arrangements under which old age is presently managed are essential."

Juanita M. Kreps

Population aging–i.e., increase in a population's median age and fraction over 59 or 64 years of age–has become a matter of concern because of its supposed implications for social security and ostensibly pay-as-you-go pension programs. In this essay I show that the basic source of concern is likely to remain labor force participation rather than age structure as such. I shall indicate also that the security of the aged depends largely upon the avoidance of early retirement along with extension of the normal age of retirement.

I. The Demographic Prospect

A variety of forces that seem to be weakening the family as a stable institution, together with circumstances favorable to control of reproduction, make uncertain the prospective course of population growth. As a basis for discussion I shall use three projections made by the Bureau of the Census [*Current Population Reports*, (A), pp. 1-7, 21-26, 31].

According to the first projection, Series II, cohort fertility settles at the replacement level 2.1 and net legal immigration continues at 400,000 per year. In contrast, Series IIx assumes cohort fertility at the replacement level, but with *no* net immigration. Series III assumes that cohort fertility declines below replacement (i.e., 2.1) to 1.7, but with net legal immigration continuing at 400,000 per year. Under Series II, the annual rate of population growth rises slightly to a peak of 1.0 percent in 1980-05 and then declines slowly while under Series III the rate of increase begins to decline in 1985-90, sinking to − 0.1 percent in 2020-25 [*Current Population Reports* (A), p. 3; Tables 8-9, 11-12, F-1, F-2]. No allowance is made for illegal immigration which at times may have exceeded 200,000 annually.

Whether U.S. total fertility will descend below the replacement level and remain there is uncertain. In a number of European states (see *Demographic Yearbook of the United Nations*), the net reproduction rate already is slightly below the replacement level. In the United States, the total fertility rate had declined to 1.760 by 1976 after finally moving below replacement to 1.994 in 1972–to a level much below the 3.606 rate attained in 1960. Yet, since wives 18-24 years old have been reporting that they expect to average 2.1 or slightly more births in their lifetimes, the total fertility rate would move into the neighborhood of replacement should these expectations be realized [*Current Population Reports* (C), pp. 1-4; (A), pp. 22-25; (D)]. Expectations may, however, prove instable with the result that fertility settles below replacement (e.g., Series III in Table 1).

II. Age Structure

A population's age structure is determined almost entirely by its fertility. This is particularly true of modern societies that have attained levels of life expectancy at birth and at later years that are susceptible of very little increase [*Statistical Bulletin*, pp. 8-9; Preston, ch. 1, pp. 4, 30-42]. While immigration may temporarily affect a population's

*Duke University. Presidential address of the Fifth Annual Atlantic Economic Conference, October 12-15, 1977, Washington, D.C. This paper has been facilitated by a Ford-Rockefeller Foundation population grant.

age structure slightly, its effect will not be permanent unless the fertility and mortality pattern of the immigrant population modifies that of the immigrant-receiving country. We may assume, therefore, that the age structure of the American, Canadian, and other modern populations will be dominated by the behavior of fertility in the course of the next 75 years [Coale; Keyfitz; *Current Population Reports* (D)].

TABLE 1

POPULATION PROJECTIONS, 1975-2050

	1974-75	1990	2000	2025	2050
		Series II			
0-17	67.3	67.7	71.1	74.8	78.7
18-64	122.8	148.5	160.8	176.8	188.5
65 & over	21.8	28.9	30.6	48.1	51.2
Total	211.9	245.1	262.5	299.7	318.4
18-64/total	0.58	0.61	0.61	0.59	0.59
18-64/65 & over	5.7	5.1	5.25	3.7	3.7
Median Age	28.8	32.3	34.8	36.9	37
		Series IIx			
0-17	67.3	64.8	66.5	65.9	65.6
18-64	122.8	143.8	152.4	154.7	158.6
65 & over	21.8	28.8	30.2	45.7	45.8
Total	211.9	237.4	249.1	269.3	270.0
18-64/total	0.58	0.61	0.61	0.57	0.59
18-64/65 & over	5.7	5.0	5.0	3.38	3.46
Median Age	28.8	32.6	35.4	37.7	37.8
		Series III			
0-17	67.3	58.2	57.3	49.9	44.1
18-64	122.8	148.5	157.2	152.4	135.6
65 & over	21.8	28.9	30.6	48.1	47.0
Total	211.9	235.6	245.1	250.4	226.7
18-64/total	0.58	0.63	0.64	0.61	0.6
18-64/65 & over	5.7	5.1	5.1	3.17	2.89
Median Age	28.8	33.4	37.0	41.8	42.6

Source: Series P-25, No. 601, Tables 8-11, F-2. Series II assumes fertility at 2.1 and immigration at 400,000 per year; Series IIx assumes fertility at 2.1 and immigration at 0; Series III assumes fertility settles at 1.7 while immigration remains at 400,000.

We may divide a near stationary population into those of conventional working age—say 18-64—and those of dependent age, under 18 and over 64 as in Table 1. Then, given replacement fertility and 400,000 net immigration annually (Series II) the number of dependents under 18 would increase about one-sixth between 1975 and 2050 while that of dependents over 64 would increase about 135 percent. Meanwhile, the population of working age would increase enough to constitute about 60 percent of the total population and to maintain the ratio of persons 18-64 to those under 18 and over 64 at roughly 1.5. Even (see Series IIx) should net immigration approximate zero instead of 400,000, the *relative* number of young and old dependents would be little affected and the ratio of those of working age to those of dependent age would remain in the neighborhood of 1.5.

Should fertility settle below the replacement level at 1.7 (Series III), the ratio of persons of working age to the population would remain in the neighborhood of 0.6, in part because annual net immigration of 400,000 is assumed. Of course, the total population would eventually begin to decline–after 2020–and the median age of the population would rise, moving to 42.6 years by 2050 compared with medians of between 37 and 38 years in Series II and IIx.

Of especial significance for the present discussion, of course, is the age composition of the population defined as of dependent age (i.e., below 18 and over 64). For since the cost of supporting dependents varies with age, the public, the private, and the total cost of supporting a society's dependents will be affected by the age structure of this segment of the population [Clark; Clark and Spengler]. Moreover, as the percentages presented in Table 2 indicate, the fraction of the dependent population that is over 64 rises until the declining population becomes stable, but at a higher level than when a population is stationary. For example, 52 percent of the dependents in Series III are over 64 compared with 39-40 percent in Series II and IIx. Average support cost per dependent under similar conditions will be higher, therefore, when a population is declining than when it is stationary or near stationary (cf. III with II and IIx) [Clark; Clark and Spengler].

TABLE 2

PERCENT OF DEPENDENTS (0-17 + 65 AND OVER) OVER 64

	1990	2050
Series II	29.9	39.4
Series IIx	30.8	41.1
Series III	33.2	51.6

Source: Series P-25, No. 601, Oct., 1975.

III. Ratio of Persons of Non-Dependent Age to Those of Dependent Age

Although, as noted, the ratio of *all* persons of dependent age (i.e., 0-17 and over 64) to those of non-dependent age (i.e., 18-64) declines as a population's fertility declines and its intrinsic growth rate approaches zero, the relative number of persons over 64 increases while that of persons under 18 decreases (see Series IIx in Table 1). On occasion economists have noted that when a population is growing, the number of working age may grow faster than that 65 and over, a movement favorable to systems such as the American Social Security System (OASDHI). This condition no longer obtains, however, when a population's age composition becomes stable, for then all age groups grow at the same rate. Moreover, when a *stable* population is not replacing itself, the ratio of persons of dependent to non-dependent age may settle at a level slightly above that in a stationary population [Coale and Demeny, p. 168].

Most critical in the course of the next 75 years may be the period 2010-2030 when the aging population will be echoing the post-war baby boom. For between 2010 and 2030, while older and presumably retired persons (i.e., those 65 and over) are increasing nearly 60 percent, the population of working age (i.e., 18-64) will remain virtually stationary and the total population will probably increase only about 10 percent.

Dependency-non-dependency ratios may be expressed in terms of life years for a stationary population as for an individual. To illustrate, if a white male with life expectancy as of 1974 (i.e., 68.9 years) enters the labor force at age 18 and survives to retire at age 65, he will have worked 47 years and may expect to live 13.7 years in retirement, or 4.4 years less than a female retiring at age 65. Should this white male have retired at age 55 or 60, he would have worked 37 or 42 years and face

20.4 or 16.8 years in retirement. Should he have retired at 65, he would have worked about 3.4 years per each year in retirement, whereas, if he retired at 55, he would have worked only about 1.8 years per each year in retirement. In the latter case, he would have imposed a much heavier burden upon the co-existing population of working age and earlier have contributed much less to the support of persons of dependent age. Of course, should he have deferred retirement to beyond 65, he would have worked more than 3.4 years per year in retirement.

With the ratios for this representative individual, we may compare a stationary population (see Table 3). Should 65 denote the age of retirement, the ratio of those in the labor force (i.e., aged 18-64) to those supposedly retired (i.e., 65 and over) would approximate 3.5, whereas, if 55 denoted the retirement age the ratio of those then in the labor force (i.e., 18-54) to those supposedly retired (i.e., 55 and over) would approximate only 1.7. Given retirement at an age intermediate between 55 and 65, the corresponding ratio would be in the neighborhood of 2.3. In sum, reduction of those enrolled in the labor force from all persons aged 18-65 to all aged 18-55 reduces the productive capacity of a population by something like one-fifth and its comparative capacity to support all dependents by about 37 percent.

TABLE 3

AGE STRUCTURE OF STATIONARY POPULATION

AGE GROUP	PERCENT
0-17	24.0
18-64	58.9
65 & over	17.1
Total	100.0
18-54	47.6
55 & over	28.4
55-64	11.3

Source: Series P-25, No. 601, Oct., 1975, p. 142.

While the claims to social security, pension payments, and similar payments have originated in the past, the capacity of the employed labor force to meet these claims originates in the present flow *0* of goods and services.[1] In a sense, therefore, these claims must be met on a pay-as-you-go basis, with the capacity to do so dependent on the size of the labor force L. For

$$0 = f(L, C)$$

where C denotes the current stock of capital or productive physical assets. Withdrawal unaccompanied by replacement of elements of the labor force L reduces *0* both directly and indirectly (i.e., by idling elements of C) [Sweezy and Owens, pp. 45-50, esp. p. 46]. Such withdrawal results, for example, when retirement age is reduced, or when workers migrate from a regional economy (e.g., New York City) and reduce its labor force. Deferment of retirement and prolongation of work life have an opposite effect in that they increase the ratio of workers to retirees as well as the ratio of the years a worker spends in the labor force to those he spends in retirement.

IV. Critical Age Group

Of critical importance, in view of what has been said, is the age group 55-64 or perhaps the age group 55-68. Over the long run the age of entry into the labor force has risen while that of withdrawal has fallen, particularly since World War II. The overall rate of labor force participation has remained relatively stable at around 60-61 percent because decline in male labor force participation has continued to be offset by increase in female labor force participation [*Statistical Abstract,* p. 355]. Of the age-group components of the labor force apparently most prone to shrinkage in recent years and in the near future is the group made up of persons 55-64. Moreover, this shrinkage,

[1] "Intergenerational transfers of income are, in fact, nothing more than an instance of debt finance shifting costs to future generations" [Browning, pp. 215-37].

if it should continue, can be only partly offset by a slight increase among those under (say) 19—for example, by reducing (say) one-fourth the years spent in primary, secondary, and college-level educational institutions—together with a further increase in female labor force participation.

The age group 55-64 constitutes 11.3 percent of the stationary population represented in Table 3 and Series IIx; it there amounts to about one-fifth of the age group 18-64 and nearly one-fourth of the age group 18-54. Should retirement begin at age 55 instead of at age 65, the ratio of persons supposedly in the labor force to that of retired persons (that is, 55 and over instead of 65 and over) would decline from 3.44 to 1.68.[2] Accordingly, the burden of supporting retirees incident on the average member of the labor force would be doubled under similar conditions.

The character of the burden is conditioned, of course, by the size of the fraction of the population of working age in the labor force and the degree to which all retired but formerly active members of the labor force are supported. In general, the larger this fraction, the greater will be both the annual contribution per worker to the support of retirees and the amount distributed annually to the retirees. Always at issue, therefore, is the ratio of contributors to retirees, together with the magnitude of contribution and benefit.[3]

There is a limit to how large a retirement and related burden will be tolerated by the active work force—a limit not yet reached in 1975 when social security, together with other federal benefits, amounted to nearly \$86 billion and private benefits approximated \$13 billion, \$99 billion in all compared with a national income of about \$1,208 billion [*Statistical Abstract*, pp. 297, 305, 307]. Given retirement at 65 and the appropriation of 15 percent of the national income for the support of retirees 65 and over, the amount received per retiree in a stationary population would approximate 60 percent of the average amount remaining in the hands of labor-force members who supply the support of those 65 and over. It is questionable, therefore, if the active labor force would long tolerate surrendering much above 15 percent of their pre-tax income to support those 65 and over. It is evident that shrinkage of the fraction 55-64 in the labor force would make this burden intolerable. Presumably, a tolerable set of retirement systems for a country entails continuation in the labor force until in the middle 60's and probably longer unless workers and/or retirees are satisfied with lower incomes than they currently anticipate.

The burden incident upon the work force is subject to increase not only as a result of early retirement and increase in retirement allowances (e.g., of government employees, legislators, and such) but also as a result of rising expenditure on the part of federal, state, and local legislative bodies. For the goods and services commanded by these expenditures are produced by the work force and withdrawn from the resulting flow of goods and services, but not always entirely offset by governmental production of goods and services should these not meet the test of the market. Accordingly, the only way the burden on the work force can be limited is by increasing the ratio of the work force to the dependents and by curbing the production of goods and services that do not meet the test of the market.

A high ratio of the work force to dependents

[2] Recall that in a stationary population 58.9 percent are aged 18-64 and 17.1 percent over 64, whereas 47.6 percent are aged 18-54 compared with 28.4 percent over 54.

[3] In general, $r/y = (L/R)\,t$ when r denotes average retirement income, y denotes average current income, L denotes the labor force, R denotes retirees, and t denotes the contribution or tax utilized to collect social security or to appropriate the proportion of gross corporate and other income required to meet current and/or prospective pension commitments. Then given a value for r/y, the value of t varies inversely with L/R, given full employment. Given some unemployment, the value of $(L/R)t$ is reduced.

can best be realized by so ordering arrangements governing retirement income that it depends mainly upon the number of years worked, together with income and savings profiles, and the return on savings or contributions. For then the incentive to remain in the labor force will be strengthened, particularly if the income expected in retirement bears a close relation to the incomes enjoyed by the retirees' cohort.

V. Inequality

The value of a tolerable *r/y* or ratio of retirement pay to output per employed member of the labor force, would stay put in real terms in a stationary population only if *y* remained constant in real terms, a condition not likely to hold. In a modern society—at least in a proleterian-oriented democracy such as dominates the West—prices now tend to rise 3-5 percent annually even when output per worker increases 2 or 3 percent per year. The recipient of *r*, therefore, suffers a decrease of 3-5 percent in the purchasing power of his money income; at the same time he fails to share in the increase in output per head unless he is under a retirement system that corrects for loss of purchasing power *and* increase in output per head. Accordingly, should prices rise 5 percent annually and the retiree also be denied a share in the increase in average output, then, at the end of ten years, the comparative value of his retirement pay, initailly *x* percent of that received by a member of the labor force, might have declined to about 0.46*x* percent.

In a stationary population, therefore, inequality will develop among those over 50 or 60 years old even though inequality should diminish somewhat within the group of persons under 50 or 60 years old. The ratio of average real retirement pay to the average pay of non-retirees tends to be below the initial value of the ratio *r/y* for reasons already indicated. Moreover, between 16 and 21 percent of a near stationary or declining population may be in the relatively poor age group, 65 and over, compared with about 10 percent in 1970. Of course, should retirement pay be indexed against inflation and should retirees share equitably in the increase of average output, essentially the product of increase and/or improvement in capital per head and relevant technology, *r* might increase nearly commensurately with *y*. Under present conditions, however, average income is much lower among those in and beyond their 60's than among those in their 50's [Bixby; *Current Population Reports* (B), pp. 31-40]. It will continue so as long as inflation persists and retirees do not share with others in the fruits of income-increasing forces.

The inequality-producing forces described could be intensified in the long run should dysgenic selection continue to increase. For a decline in the quality of the nation's gene pool would eventuate in a decrease in the relative number of high-level producers and, given the current tendency to provide abundant state support for incompetents, impose ever heavier economic and other burdens upon the productive elements in a stationary or declining population. This trend could continue should the ratio of the expected utility of children to their expected disutility continue to decrease as a result of parents' increasing loss of control over their children, together with deterioration of the components of a child's environment.

VI. Future

The future of security of the aged will depend upon the age structure, labor force participation on the part of those over (say) 17 years of age, and the character of the system of arrangements whereunder intergenerational transfer of support is attempted. As has been suggested cohort fertility is unlikely to rise above the replacement level in the absence of changes conducive to increase in fertility, particularly in that of the more competent components of the population.[4] Labor force participation rates can be increased by associating relative retirement pay closely with years spent in the labor force, by dissipating current barriers to employment issuing from private labor and business monopolies and government regulations, and by removing employer and government incentive to permit or promote "early retirement" (sometimes to reduce employeemnt costs). Finally the system of arrangements facilitating intergenerational transfer of support requires to be made secure against inflation and to allow retirees to share in the increase of income per worker imputable to public and eleemosynary investment in human capital, scientific progress, and physical capital.[5]

We have implied that it will suffice to meet retirement costs should age of retirement approximate 65 years. In reality this will not suffice if the required ratio of retirement benefits to pay in later years is too high. Indeed, deferment of retirement to age 68 or 69 may be essential to support a generally desired ratio of retirement pay to pre-retirement earnings.[6] A white male retiring as late as at age 70 may look forward on an average to at least 10.9 more years of life, and a white female to 14.4 more years. Many, of course, may look forward to even more years.

REFERENCES

[1] Lenore E. Bixby, et al., *Demographic and Economic Characteristics of the Aged. 1968 Social Security Survey*, Washington, D. C., 1975.

[2] E. K. Browning, "Social Insurance and Intergenerational Transfers," *Journal of Law and Economics*, XVI, October 1973.

[3] Robert Clark, "The Influence of Low Fertility Rates and Retirement Policy on Dependency Costs," prepared for The American Institutes for Research in the Behavioral Sciences under a study funded by the Ford and Burden Foundations, 1976.

[4] Robert Clark and Joseph J. Spengler, "Changing Demography and Dependency Costs: The Implications of New Dependency Ratios and Their Composition," presented to Support for the Aged: Policy Options and Research Needs, a conference sponsored by the Gerontological Society, April 1976.

[5] A. J. Coale, *The Growth and Structure of Human Populations. A Mathematical Investigation*, Princeton: Princeton University Press, 1972.

[6] A. J. Coale and Paul Demeny, *Regional Model Life Tables and Stable Populations*, Princeton: Princeton University Press, 1966.

[7] Nathan Keyfitz, *Introduction to the Mathematics of Population*, Reading, MA: Addison-Wesley Publishing Co., 1968.

[8] Juanita M. Kreps (A), "Age, Work, and Income," *Southern Economic Journal*, XLIII, April 1977, pp. 1423-37.

[9] ———, (B), "Social Security in the Coming Decade: Questions for a Mature System," *Social Security Bulletin*, March 1976, pp. 21-29.

[10] Martin O'Connell and Maurice J. Moore, "New Evidence on the Value of Birth Expectations," *Demography*, XIV, August 1977.

[11] Alfred M. Pitts, "Social Security and Aging Populations," prepared for a Conference on the Economic Consequences of Slowing Population Growth, sponsored by the Center for Population Research, National Institute of Child Health and Human Development, Washington, D. C., May 1977.

[12] Samuel H. Preston, Nathan Keyfitz, and Robert Schoen, *Causes of Death. Life Tables for National Populations*, New York: Seminar Press, 1972.

[13] Alan Sweezy and Aaron Owens, "The Impact of Population Growth on Population," *American Economic Review, Papers and Proceedings*, LIV (2), May 1974.

[14] Unsigned, "Potential Gains in Longevity After Midlife," *Statistical Bulletin*, Metropolitan Life Insurance Company, 56, September 1975.

[15] U. S. Bureau of the Census, "Projections of the Population of the United States: 1975 to 2050," *Current Population Reports* (A), Series P-25, No. 601, Washington, D. C., October 1975.

[16] ———, "Social and Economic Characteristics of the Older Population: 1974," *Current Population Reports* (B), Special Studies, Series P-23, No. 57, Washington, D. C., 1975.

[17] ———, "Fertility of American Women, June 1976," *Current Population Reports* (C), Series P-20, No. 308, Washington, D. C., June 1977.

[18] ———, "Projections of the Population of The United States: 1977 to 2050," *Current Population Reports* (D), Series P-25, No. 704, Washington, D. C., July 1977.

[19] ——— , *Statistical Abstract of the United States, 1976*, Washington, D. C., 1976.

[4] Factors affecting the predictive value of reported birth expectations have been discussed frequently [O'Connell and Moore, pp. 255-64, and bibliography].

[5] The significance of fertility behavior for the American Social Security System has been carefully analyzed by Alfred M. Pitts.

[6] Juanita M. Kreps has dealt with most relevant aspects of this issue in [Kreps, (A) and (B)].

[23]

SOME REDISTRIBUTIONAL ASPECTS OF THE NATIONAL SUPERANNUATION FUND

BY A. R. PREST
University of Manchester

THE *National Superannuation and Social Insurance Bill*, published on 17th December 1969 and debated by Parliament during the first few months of 1970 was a massive affair of 129 clauses and 9 schedules. It was preceded by one bevy of White Papers;[1] and accompanied by another.[2] Nor is that all: quite apart from a good deal of contemporary discussion, those who really wish to understand the origins of the proposals must go back some ten years – to the Labour Party's publication *National Superannuation*[3] and the controversies surrounding it at the time.

It is obviously impossible to discuss all the important features of this legislation adequately in one article. We shall therefore outline the main features very briefly in Section I; and in Section II we shall concentrate on one particular feature – the redistributional aspects of the superannuation part of the scheme. We concentrate on this because it would appear to be an extremely important, and, as yet, relatively little understood feature of the new arrangements.

---

[1] *National Superannuation and Social Insurance*, Cmnd. 3883, January 1969; *Social Insurance*, Cmnd. 4124, July 1969; *National Superannuation*, Cmnd. 4195, November 1969 (all HMSO).
[2] *Explanatory Memorandum on the National Insurance and Social Insurance Bill*; and *Report by the Government Actuary on the Financial Provisions* (both HMSO December 1969).
[3] Transport House, Smith Square, London S.W.1 (undated).

I. Main Features of the Legislation

Although there is a common theme running through the new legislation – that of both contributions and benefits being on an earnings-related, rather than a flat rate, basis – two separate schemes are being established. The first is the National Superannuation Fund into which payments will be made on the basis of earnings both by employees (up to a ceiling) and employers (no ceiling), as well as by the Exchequer; similarly pensions will be earnings-related, though flat-rate death grants will continue to be paid. The old system of contributions will be superseded in 1972; and the new style pensions will be introduced slowly over the years, full entitlement being possible from 1992. There are many other changes, for example, the introduction of pensions for married women on the basis of their own contributions whilst at work, as distinct from entitlement on the basis of their husbands' contributions; and entirely new arrangements for partial contracting out.

The second scheme is the Social Insurance Fund. This will be concerned with such benefits as those for short- and long-term sickness, unemployment, attendance on the severely disabled, maternity and the like. Earnings-related contributions will be paid in essentially the same way as on the superannuation side; and most (though not all) of these benefits will be earnings-related too.

There are various features common to both schemes. Stamp-licking will go and contributions are to be collected through the PAYE mechanism. And the Government has been at great pains to state that the new system will be on a Pay as You Go, rather than a funded, basis. To make our task manageable, we shall say nothing more at all about the Social Insurance part, but concentrate entirely on the National Superannuation side. This should not be interpreted to mean that we regard the Social Insurance part as unworthy of discussion. It does after all represent something like one-third of total contributions at the outset (including those destined for the National Health Service and industrial injuries benefits) but simply that we cannot discuss both sides of the legislation with any pretence at adequacy.

Leading Issues

The following questions, not all independent of one another, arise with the Superannuation Fund proposals.

(1) *The optimum role of the public sector in pension provision.* A large number of different views can be held about this. To take the two extreme cases, one could argue for complete reliance on private provision or for complete supersession of private provision. Most people are likely to come down somewhere between these limits, their exact attitude depending on, for example, views about the need for income redistribution between different groups. It should be noted that one argument sometimes made for public provision – that the improvident should be compelled to save more than they otherwise would, so as to prevent them from being a liability in old age to their more provident fellows – is weak. All that this argument establishes is that everyone should be compelled to save, but not necessarily through a public, rather than a private, institution. If saving via private institutions could be made compulsory without too much administrative fuss, this problem would be solved.[1] On the other hand, protection against inflation, and *a fortiori* securing increases in real incomes, after retirement is by no means certain under a purely private system. So although many will wish to argue for a certain element of contracting out from a public scheme if there is an adequate private

[1] Cf. J. M. Buchanan, 'Social Insurance in a Growing Economy: a Proposal for Radical Reform', *National Tax Journal*, December 1968, and A. R. Prest, 'Comments on Social Insurance in a Growing Economy: a Proposal for Radical Reform', *ibid.*, December 1969.

alternative, most people are likely to take the view that there is room for both public and private provision. The precise terms for contracting out can, nevertheless, be a matter for great controversy, as we have seen in the last few months.

(2) *The form of public sector provision.* There are three major controversies here. The first is whether public pension provision should be part of the general budget or whether there should be a separate earmarked fund. Support for the first alternative may be based on grounds of administrative simplicity or the proposition that special contributions will probably be a more regressive form of tax than the most likely alternative sources of general revenue. Earmarking is supported by those who believe that a system of compulsory lending, with ultimate prospects of repayment, has less disadvantageous effects than outright taxation. Given the Government's insistence in its various White Papers on retaining the contributory principle and feeding such revenues into a special fund, it would not seem that this issue is currently a very live one in the U.K., whatever the position in other countries.

The second area of controversy is the form to be taken by an earmarked scheme. Should it be on a 'Pay as You Go' basis, with current incomings matching current outgoings? Or should it be funded like a private pension scheme which at any one time will have sufficient in the way of accumulated funds to meet all its likely future liabilities? Thirdly, there is ample scope for disagreement about the basis of contributions – whether they should be related to payrolls or not, for instance; and about whether contributions and/or benefits should be on a flat rate or earnings-related basis. We shall have more to say about these matters later.

(3) *Macroeconomic aspects.* There are some major issues here too. One, which has led to some argument in recent months in Britain is the effect of a major new scheme, such as the one before Parliament in early 1970, on the level and

composition of saving in the years ahead. This means considering whether any displaced private schemes would have been running a larger excess of receipts over disbursements than the public scheme; whether people cut current consumption to the same extent if paying exactly the same contributions to public and private schemes; and whether additional public sector saving is an acceptable substitute for private saving. Another, which goes back to the 1944 White Paper on *Employment Policy*, is the extent to which contributions should be varied between one year and another in order to offset excesses or deficiencies of demand. We shall not do more than touch on these topics here, important as they are.

(4) *Efficiency aspects*. Pensions plans have to be rated by their relative effects on incentives to work and the like; and on the possible substitution of more for less capital-intensive methods of production. There are some aspects of the new scheme which are of importance in this context (e.g. the earnings rules for pensioners, the preservation of pension rights when changing jobs), but we shall have no space to deal with them here.

(5) *Redistribution aspects*. We propose to concentrate on this subject in the rest of this article. We hope to show that it is an extremely important, but not, as yet, a very fully explored, aspect of the new legislation. Where our discussion does impinge on the other issues outlined above, we shall draw attention to the connections.

II. Types of redistribution

First of all, we must specify the basic redistribution issues. We should like to know what differences are likely to be made to the distribution of income by size as a result of introducing a scheme of contributions and benefits, such as is now proposed. In other words, we start with the assumption that the alternative is *either* no public superannuation scheme at all *or* one which is, in the relevant sense, distributionally neutral. We shall allow for qualifications at a later stage.

Redistribution can take many dimensions but, for the most part, we shall concentrate on two of them. First, we have to think about *intra-generation redistribution.* We can think of two individuals of a given generation (let us call it generation A) who, in the absence of the scheme, would have had incomes bearing a particular relation to one another over the years. The scheme, by exacting contributions which are not exactly proportional to lifetime incomes or by paying out benefits which are not proportional (or, by a mixture of both), may make for a markedly different relation between lifetime incomes, when measured on a post-contribution and post-benefit basis. The second fundamental concept is *inter-generation redistribution.* Here the point is that at one time generation B (the active one) is supporting generation A (the retired one); later, generation C is supporting generation B and so on.[1] The basic question then is whether C's support of B is greater than B's support of A; if so, we may say that B gains in the inter-generational redistribution process.

It may help if we construct a hypothetical example to illustrate the way these processes interlock.

MODEL OF INTRA-GENERATION AND INTER-GENERATION TRANSFERS

Generation	*Representative Individuals' Incomes* (Before contributions and benefits)	*Sums transferred* (− = payment; + = receipt) 'Year' 1	'Year' 2	'Year' 3
A	(i) $1\frac{1}{4}$ × mean income	−$66\frac{2}{3}$	+75	—
	(ii) $\frac{3}{4}$ × mean income	−$33\frac{1}{3}$	+75	—
B	(i) $1\frac{1}{4}$ × mean income	—	−100	+100
	(ii) $\frac{3}{4}$ × mean income	—	−50	+100
C	(i) $1\frac{1}{4}$ × mean income	—	—	−$133\frac{1}{3}$
	(ii) $\frac{3}{4}$ × mean income	—	—	−$66\frac{2}{3}$

[1] 'Supporting' in the sense that A's consumption, when retired, will be met from the excess of B's output over B's consumption.

Generation A is at work in 'year' 1 and retired in 'year' 2; Generation B is at work in 'year' 2 and retired in 'year' 3 etc. We assume that the man with income equal to 1¼ times the average in each generation makes a contribution equal to twice that of the man with an income equal to ¾ of the average; pensions are distributed equally between the two; and the money income of any one generation is so much more than that of the preceding one, that the sum collected in contributions increases by 50 each 'year' even though contribution rates are unchanged. Total contributions are exactly equal to total pensions in each and every 'year'.

Intra-generation transfers can be deduced from looking at the *rows* in the table; *inter*-generation transfers from looking at the *columns*. Or putting it another way, in the first case, one can think of contributions as a compulsory loan to be repaid (with interest) when retired; and in the second, as a tax on those currently working to finance the pensions of those currently retired.

Intra-generation redistribution takes place because, for instance, contributions by the two members of the A-generation are disproportionate to incomes but benefits are the same for each; so by this double process the worse-off man has gained relatively to the better-off over the period of the two 'years' taken together. And the same holds for the two members of generation B. *Inter*-generation redistribution also takes place in that whereas the B-generation can be said to support the A-generation to the tune of 150 (the total of contributions payable in 'year' 2), the C-generation transfers 200 to B; so B is a net gainer. It should be particularly noted that one cannot reach any conclusions about inter-generation redistribution simply by looking at the transfer from B to A; one must also look at that from C to B to see the whole picture about B.

Although this example brings out the difference between the two primary concepts of redistribution, it nevertheless remains artificial. We are guilty of drastic over-simplification in confining ourselves to three generations, each with two individuals, and three 'years'; we have also assumed that nothing else happens which might modify the redistributional effects of such a scheme (e.g. the intra-generation picture would be affected if there were a reduction of pre-existing welfare payments to the poorer man and a consequent reduction of the richer man's general tax burden; similarly, in the *inter*-generation case the amount of capital privately bequeathed from one generation to the next may differ from what it would have been in the absence of the scheme). So the most we can claim is that we are illustrating these concepts in a rudimentary form.

The New Scheme and Intra-Generation Redistribution

To assess the redistributional aspects of the new superannuation scheme in detail, it seemed best to work out the consequences which would have resulted if such a scheme had been in operation in this country from 1948 to 1969 (inclusive). This is roughly the period over which the Beveridge scheme has operated and it is not too drastic a simplification to say that we can neglect any pension rights obtained during the pre-1948 period in the case of people imagined to be in the new scheme from 1948–69 and then retiring. We also have the very great advantage that we are applying the scheme to a known series of yearly earnings rather than having to guess what they might be for the rest of the century. We also have a period of over 20 years – just long enough for the full consequences of the new scheme to work themselves out.

Details of the method of calculation are given in the Appendix – and this *must* be read if the process is to be completely understood – but an outline of the procedure is as follows:

(1) Annual employee and employer contributions were calculated on the basis of earnings each year for some representative individuals.
(2) Allowances were made for Exchequer contributions, interest on accumulated funds etc.
(3) The total contribution over the period for each representative individual was estimated in end-1969 terms by compounding earlier payments forward to that year.
(4) The pension entitlement at end-1969 was calculated for each individual.
(5) On the basis of life-expectancy tables and assumptions about price rises and personal tax rates in the years immediately following 1969, the whole series of annual pension entitlements was estimated for each individual.
(6) Each of the series estimated in (5) was discounted back to end-1969 to obtain a lump sum equivalent.

Table 1 (opposite p. 19 for convenience) shows the basic results. Let us look at the intra-generation aspects first and the *inter*-generation ones later.

The most important single set of figures to look at is that relating to a married couple (not abated) under the 6 per cent discount rate heading. It seems to us more important to look first at married couples than at single people; and also to take the case of someone fully within the scheme rather than someone partially contracted out because of membership of an occupational scheme. (The new national scheme allows members of approved occupational schemes to be partially contracted out; in this case both contributions and benefits are abated compared to the full rate.) And 6 per cent would seem to be the best single interest rate to take; it does, in fact, roughly correspond to the annual growth rate of average manufacturing earnings over the period. Concentrating on these figures, we find that the relative size of the capital value of pensions to that of contributions would have been very much greater for lower than for higher income groups, e.g. a ratio of 4·3 for the lowest group and only 1·3 for the top one. In other words, the scheme would have implied 'presents' of thousands of pounds over the period from better off to worse off members of the community. Taking the discount rate as 4 or 8 per cent would modify the details but not the overall picture.

Turning to Part A of the table relating to a single man, we find that, as might be expected, ratios of pension entitlements to contributions would have been lower in all cases than for the married couple. Nevertheless, redistribution from richer to poorer would still have been very substantial. In the case of Part C (married couples partially contracted out) the ratios of pensions entitlements to contributions would have been greater than in the married couple (non-abated) case;[1] and the size of lifetime 'presents' from richer to poorer would have been greater. In none of these cases do we possess sufficient information to say what the *total* amount redistributed from one income group to another would have been; but the general nature of the process, as exemplified by these representatives of different income and marital groups, is perfectly clear.

One or two other aspects of the intra-generation redistributional process need emphasis. There are many ways in which government intervention favours particular groups at particular times in their lives, e.g. family allowances benefit mothers with children, maternity allowances benefit women giving birth to children and so on. Now it can be said in the case of many such benefits that any given family may gain from them at the appropriate stage in its life-cycle; but it will

[1] This seems to weaken the case of those who have argued, with more passion than accuracy, that the terms for partial contracting out of the new scheme are onerous; the converse would have held for the period under examination.

bear the burden of financing such benefits to other families at other stages. So the *net* amount of redistribution towards a family over its whole lifetime may be much less than appears from looking at individual benefits in isolation. Such an argument does not hold for the new superannuation scheme. It is designed in such a way as to redistribute income over the whole life span and so is a very much more powerful agent of redistribution. Furthermore, it should be emphasised that the absolute gains by lower income groups will be *very* much greater in the years to come than over the 1948–69 period, because the redistribution mechanism will operate on levels of earnings which are likely to be considerably higher in the future than in our test period, due to productivity gains as well as inflationary tendencies.

So far, we have simply considered the effects of superimposing the new scheme on the 1948–69 period, and traced the primary distributional consequences. We must now dig a little deeper. In so far as one assumes that the National Insurance scheme, as we have known it in the post-war world, would have been superseded this does not alter the picture in any essential way. By and large, that scheme – or at least the pensions aspects of it – did not provide for any measure of intra-generation redistribution; flat-rate contributions earned flat-rate pensions and graduated additions were exactly proportional to additional contributions.[1] The more important point is that if the new scheme had been operating in the post-war period, presumably the need for supplementation of pensions would have been less; and this would have meant less necessity to raise taxes to finance such benefits. Therefore the *net* effects of introducing the new scheme would presumably have been less – and will, for the same reason, be less in the years ahead when it is in

[1] This is not true after the changes of November 1969; but these should be thought of more as a stepping stone to the new scheme rather than as being in conformity with the old one.

operation – than would appear from the tabulations. Unfortunately, this is as far as we can go in that we have no means whatever of knowing exactly which taxes might have been reduced and exactly which income groups would have benefitted from any such reductions in general revenue needs.

Some further complications should be noticed. It might be argued that poorer people would be likely to start to earn sooner and/or die earlier than richer people; if so, the calculations of transfers from richer to poorer would be biased upwards. However, it is worth noting that even if we try to allow for this by taking an 8 per cent discount rate for the lowest income group and a 4 per cent rate for the top one, the ratio of benefits to contributions is higher for the lowest income group, irrespective of whether we take the A, B or C cases. It must also be emphasised that we have concentrated on one or two particular aspects of redistribution. There are many other dimensions to the discussion: redistribution between males and females, between occupations, between regions etc. etc. which are not touched on at all here.[1] It is to be hoped that someone at official level has gone into all this; it would be more reassuring if there had been the slightest indication that this was so.

The New Scheme and Inter-Generation Redistribution

It is time to look at the inter-generation redistributional aspects of the statistical exercises in Table 1. The central case – the married couple (not abated) with a 6 per cent discount rate – shows that in all cases the value of pension entitlement

---

[1] It is perhaps worth mentioning that one implication of the scheme is redistribution from better off to worse off employees, but not at all from property income to labour income recipients.

Also, it has been argued that the new scheme will be more unfavourable to single women than to widows (cf. A. B. Atkinson, *Poverty in Britain and the Reform of Social Security* (Cambridge University Press, Cambridge, 1969), p. 113.

would have been greater than that of accumulated contributions, implying a substantial handover from those currently at work to those retiring at the end of 1969. In fact, the same conclusion holds for most of the cases illustrated; the main ones where the handover would have been substantially negative (i.e. capital value of contributions exceeding that of pensions) are the single man earning three times the national average and subject to discount rates of 6 and 8 per cent. So the overall preliminary impression must be that over this period the scheme would have been a 'good buy' for most of the contributors. And it must be remembered in this context (see Appendix A) that we have allocated both employers' contributions and the finance met from general revenue, as well as employees' contributions, to the various participants and so cannot in any way be accused of underestimating contributions.

However, there are some complications to take into account. Even though the great majority of those retiring at end-1969 would have been receiving capital sums much larger than the accumulated value of their contributions, this only shows the average 'handover' from one generation to another whereas, as shown earlier,[1] we need to know the difference between such 'handovers' from generation 2 to generation 1 and from generation 3 to generation 2 before we can have any certainty about the net sums involved. Information is also needed about the relative numbers involved in the succeeding generations. And even when we know all this, there is another, even more formidable question to answer: we need to know whether the scheme results in a smaller (or larger) addition to the wealth privately inherited by each generation than would have been the case in its absence. Only then could we tell whether the size of the primary 'handover' should be adjusted upwards or downwards to find the true inter-generation transfer.

[1] See p. 9, *supra*.

We have no means of making such calculations with any pretence of accuracy either for our 1948–69 test period or for the years ahead during which the scheme will actually operate.[1] Nevertheless, there is one overriding consideration which should make it *possible* for each generation to receive more from the next than it handed over to its predecessor: the simple fact of growing real income per head over time. This is not the occasion for going into details but it is now a well-established proposition that a Pay as You Go social security scheme with a fixed rate of contribution can yield a high implicit rate of return to its contributors, the exact figure depending on the growth rates of population and real income.[2] Provided that the social compact is kept between the generations to use contributions from the currently active to pay the pensions of the currently retired, the lack of the funding arrangement normally found in private pension arrangements is of no consequence. Instead, a pensioner in year *n* has the protection afforded by the State's power to exact contributions compulsorily from the work-force in year *n*.

At the same time, one must note that such an outcome is dependent on the observance of the social compact. Some may very well feel safer with a fund (with their names inscribed on it, so to speak) behind any pensions promises. But they might be unwise to feel too safe even then – tax laws can always be changed adversely, pension funds might at some stage be compelled to invest a minimum proportion

[1] The bald statement in the January 1969 White Paper (Cmnd. 3883) that the new scheme will not impose 'an excessive burden on future generations of contributors' (para. 43) is so vague as to be completely empty of meaning.

[2] Cf. P. A. Samuelson, 'An Exact Consumption-Loan Model of Interest With or Without the Social Contrivance of Money', *Journal of Political Economy*, December 1958; J. A. Pechman, H. J. Aaron and M. K. Taussig, *Social Security* (Brookings Institution, Washington, D.C., 1968); C. D. Campbell, 'Social Insurance in the U.S.', *Journal of Law and Economics*, October 1969.

of their funds in gilt-edged and so on. All that is really relevant here is the *net* additional safety in a funding arrangement and it is by no means clear that this is very great.

So we conclude that, as far as the limited evidence goes, the inter-generation transfer during the 1948–69 period would have been substantial, had the new scheme been operating then. Indeed, this is the normal thing to expect from social security pension arrangements.[1]

Conclusions

All in all, the critics of the new scheme would have been better advised to concentrate their fire on the intra-generation aspects, for this is where the break with the past is really decisive. In effect, we are moving from the former system of compulsory lending with repayments proportionate to contributions to one where repayments are expressly and designedly non-proportional; or, to put the same point in another way, the importance of the loan element in our arrangements is being reduced and that of the compulsion element is being increased.

As a minimum, one might ask that this feature of the new scheme should be openly and publicly admitted, instead of being concealed by such evasive half-truths as the proposition[2] that 'rights to benefits must be earned by the payment of contributions', when this will simply not be true in the vast majority of cases. Unless the redistributional aspects are clearly and fully set out, it is totally impossible to discuss

[1] The benefit/contribution ratio stemming from the U.K. flat rate basis between 1948 and 1969 seems to have been very high (Hansard, 10th June 1969, Written Answers, cols. 186–187). And calculations on the U.S. system have shown similar results (cf. J. A. Brittain, 'The Real Rate of Interest on Lifetime Contributions Towards Retirement under Social Security' in *Old Age Income Assurance*, Compendium of Papers on Problems and Policy Issues in the Public and Private Pension System, Pt. III, Washington D.C., 1967; and C. D. Campbell, *op. cit.*).
[2] Cmnd. 3883, p. 12.

with any semblance of rationality whether such changes should be additional to, or in substitution for, the various other redistributional activities of the public sector.

But this is only a minimum. Many may feel that the attempt to build a large redistributional element into a superannuation scheme is misconceived. The Government itself has made great play with the fact that people are more willing to pay over the sums of money called 'contributions' than those called 'taxes'. But such willingness may very rapidly disappear in the case of those who realise that what they are really doing is contributing substantially towards the pensions of their contemporaries and not just towards their own.

Large-scale alterations in the new system could take many forms. One view is that of Sir Paul Chambers.[1] His main proposals are that earmarking of specific government revenues for pensions should be abolished, that employer and employee contributions should be eliminated and more revenue raised from income taxation and that the state should confine itself to paying flat rate pensions out of general revenue. Objections could be raised to each of these ideas: (1) The first is tantamount to saying that there is no distinction between a tax and a compulsory loan. (2) The second ignores the fact that the economic effects of income taxation and payroll taxation may be very different. (3) The third assumes that private pension schemes are an adequate substitute under *all* circumstances for public earnings-related schemes. The view here is rather that one could do very much worse than look at the arrangements in Canada. (It is, incidentally, more than disturbing that the Government's scheme is fundamentally the same as the Labour Party proposals of some ten years ago, without any overt recognition of the many changes which have occurred in arrangements

[1] Cf. Sir Paul Chambers, 'Forward from Beveridge' (Institute of Statisticians, Beveridge Memorial Lecture, 1969).

in other countries in the meanwhile. Perhaps it is not only the Bourbons who learned nothing and forgot nothing.) Essentially, the Canadian system consists of two parts – a flat-rate pension (with a minimum income guarantee added recently) financed from a variety of tax sources rather than from contributions; and an earnings-related contributions and pension component. Obviously, the details of any such system might need to be very different in Britain, but the general principles are appealing, especially if coupled with such ideas as changes in flat-rate pensions in line with price changes, insistence on membership of an earnings-related pension scheme but allowing reasonable freedom of choice between private schemes meeting minimum requirements (e.g. of pension preservation) and the public one, deductibility of employee contributions to the earnings-related scheme for income tax and surtax purposes,[1] fixing a ceiling for employer as well as employee contributions and so on. The result could be a system which achieves both redistributional and retirement provision objectives, but at the same time distinguishes clearly between them. No doubt there would be cases where supplementary benefits in one form or another would still be needed. But anyone who believes that this will not be the case with the new superannuation system – well, he would believe anything.

[1] Was the 1965 abolition of the (partial) allowance of National Insurance contributions against income tax and surtax entirely disconnected with the possibility of introducing the new National Superannuation System?

APPENDIX

Details of 1948–69 Calculations

(1) *Earnings data.* Department of Employment and Productivity earnings data for adult males in manufacturing industry were available for April and October in each year. It was assumed that the April figure in any year could be taken as ⅙ of earnings in the first half of the year and the October figure as ⅙ of earnings in the second half.

(2) *Representative individuals* were taken at points equal to ½ national earnings, to national earnings, 1½ times that figure and 3 times that figure. It is important to take ½ earnings as one fixed point, as the pension formula changeover point comes here; and 1½ times earnings is the ceiling for contributions and pensions.

(3) *Contributions.*

(a) *Employee's contribution.* 4¾ per cent of annual earnings for the lower three incomes; 4¾ per cent of earnings in the first half of the year for the 3 times national earnings individual.

(b) *Employer's contribution.* Controversy has raged for years on the exact working of this tax – whether it is effectively passed on to employees, whether it is passed forward in prices or whether it reduces profits below what they would otherwise be. Indeed, the Government itself at the moment subscribes to two opposite views: the *National Income Blue Book* would appear to assume that employees bear the tax whilst the main Superannuation White Paper assumes the tax is passed forward – perhaps a case of the right hand not knowing what the left hand doeth.

We assume here that the tax is borne by employees. This is not such an extreme assumption as it may sound at first sight in that, even if the tax is passed forward entirely on to consumer goods prices, the percentage error in attributing it to employees is likely to be much the same at the various points on the income scale. And although there may be over-attribution to the employee class as a whole, relatively to, say, people living on income from property, this makes our calculation of returns on contributions an under- rather than an over-estimate. The fact that employer contributions are a deductible item against taxes on business profits is irrelevant for the calculations.

(c) *Exchequer contribution.* This was taken (as is proposed under the new scheme) as amounting to 18 per cent of the sum of employee and employer contributions in each year; it was assumed to rest on employees proportionately to incomes. Although we do not know which taxes would be remitted (and hence who would benefit) if there were no Exchequer contribution, any over-attribution to employees on this score is offset to some extent by not counting in the taxes needed to finance the interest on the accumulated reserves. This is clearly a crude approximation but it is unlikely to introduce errors into the calculations.

(4) *Compounding and discounting.* The choice of appropriate discount rates is always difficult. Although one can argue for taking 6 per cent as the main figure on the grounds that this was more or less the rate at which money earnings grew each year over the period, it was thought advisable to apply 4 and 8 per cent rates as well. Compounding forward was done on a half-yearly basis.

(5) *Pensions.* Assuming retirement at age 65 on 31st December 1969, the pension payable to a single man can be calculated by applying the formula (60 per cent of earnings up to ½ national average earnings and 25 per cent of the remainder up to 1½ average earnings) to October 1969 earnings figures. We are told that pensions will be raised every second year in accordance with price rises; and perhaps more, to allow real incomes to increase. We therefore

assumed that there would be a 10 per cent rise in pension entitlement every second year. (Once again, this figure may be wrong; but it will not alter the relative position of people at different points on the income scale.) Income tax rates were assumed to stay unchanged at 1969/70 rates; by applying these, net annual pensions receipts were obtained. The cut-off point was determined by reference to life-expectancy tables; and a death grant of £30 was added in each case.

The final stage was to discount this series, again on a half-yearly basis, back to 1969 at rates of 4, 6 and 8 per cent, thus obtaining a capital value for the pension stream, for each of our four representative individuals.

(6) *Further calculations.* Further calculations were made, on the same general principles as above, in relation to married couples fully in the scheme and also to those partially contracted out. In the former case, it was assumed that wives had the same age as their husbands, that they had no earnings record of their own but simply drew a flat rate supplement while the husband was alive, reverting to the pension appropriate to the husband's contribution position etc. after his death. In the latter case, contributions and pensions were abated according to the principles set forth in the various White Papers.

[24]

Guns vs. Canes: The Fiscal Implications of an Aging Population

By BARBARA BOYLE TORREY*

The share of the federal budget devoted to the older population (defined in this paper as people who are 65 and above) has expanded substantially from approximately 2 percent in 1940 to 25 percent today. Over the next fifty years this older population is expected to more than double in size and increase from 11 percent of the population to between 20 and 26 percent. These increases will come in two distinct periods, the 1980's and the twenty years beginning in 2010. Even if no further responsibilities are assumed by the federal government, this population increase alone will put inexorable fiscal pressure on future federal budgets.

I. Federal Outlays for the Older Population: 1980–86

Based on budget estimates presented in the Office of Management and Budget's 1981 *Mid-Session Review*, federal outlays for the older population will increase substantially as a percentage of total federal outlays from 1980 to 1986. However, as shown in Table 1, federal outlays for this group are estimated to rise very little relative to *GNP*.

The share of federal outlays going to the older population increases in the near term partly because the proposed budget cuts reduce other federal programs disproportionately. In addition, older people are the fastest growing recipient group for federal programs, and most of the federal outlays for this group increase with inflation.

The two programs for the older population that are projected to grow the fastest between 1980 and 1986 are Medicare and veterans programs. The projected growth in Medicare alone is responsible for over half (58 percent) of the increase in the share of the federal budget that is devoted to this population. The Old Age and Survivors Insurance program (OASI), in contrast is projected to grow at only half the rate of Medicare. There is also an unprecedented near doubling (95 percent) increase in federal outlays for older veterans as a result of the aging of the World War II veterans.

The effect of an aging population on federal revenues is less certain than its effect on outlays. There are specific tax expenditures for the aged, such as the exclusion of Social Security benefits, the additional exemption, and the tax credit for the elderly. These tax expenditures have increased from 1.6 percent of total federal revenues in 1976 to an estimated 2.4 percent in 1982, and are estimated to increase to 2.8 percent by 1986. However, the "middle-aging" of the rest of the population is likely to increase revenues and, therefore, partially offset the revenue loss resulting from the increase in the elderly.

II. Federal Outlays for the Older Population: 1990–2035

Between 1980 and 1990 the number of people who will be 65 and over is expected to increase at an average annual rate of 2.3 percent. Over the following twenty years, however, this growth is expected to slow to an average annual rate of only 1.2 percent. Then, between 2010 and 2030, as the post-World War II baby boom retires, this population will increase at the average annual rate of 2.0 percent. This increase will pose renewed fiscal challenges for the federal

*Fiscal economist, Office of Management and Budget. The opinions in this paper are my own and do not necessarily reflect the views of the Office of Management and Budget. I would like to thank Robert Kilpatrick, Darwin Johnson, John L. Palmer, and John Wilkens for their comments on earlier versions of this paper.

TABLE 1—FEDERAL OUTLAYS FOR PEOPLE 65 AND OLDER; BY FISCAL YEARS

	1980	1981	1982	1983	1984	1985	1986
As a Percentage of Federal Outlays	24.8	25.4	26.6	27.4	28.9	29.3	30.1
As a Percentage of *GNP*	5.6	5.8	5.9	5.8	5.8	5.8	5.9

Source: The estimates are based on projections in *Mid-Session Review of the 1982 Budget*. The outlays are based on agency estimates of the proportion of program outlays that go to people 65 and older. They include proposed legislation, but not the unspecified savings to be proposed for fiscal years 1983–86. These percentages would, therefore, change, depending on how additional savings affect the older population.

TABLE 2—OUTLAYS FOR THE OLDER POPULATION AS A PERCENT OF TOTAL FEDERAL OUTLAYS

Calendar Year:	Clark-Menefee	O'Neill	Califano	Torrey[c]
1990	–	29.8[a]	–	32.4
2000	29.5	31.6	33.9	34.1
2010	30.5	33.2[b]	36.4	36.2
2025	41.5	46.3	50.8	49.6
2030	–	–	–	49.5

[a]Interpolated from data for 1985 and 1995.
[b]Interpolated from data for 2005 and 2015.
[c]The detailed calculations of these projections are in an unpublished appendix that is available on request from the author.

government that can, to some degree, be anticipated.

Four recent studies[1] summarized in Table 2 estimate the outlay effects of the future increase in the older population. Since official budget estimates beyond 1986 do not exist, most of these longer-term projections rely heavily on actuarial projections of the retirement systems and Medicare, which together comprise 90 percent or more of the outlays for the older population after 2000. The outlays for other programs such as Medicaid and SSI are projected using economic and demographic assumptions consistent with the Social Security actuarial projections. The outlay effects are shown in terms of federal budgets that are assumed to be 20 percent of *GNP*; therefore the increased share of federal spending for the older population is offset by an equal reduction in the share of other federal outlays.

[1]See Robert Clark and John Menefee, Joseph Califano, June O'Neill, and my 1981 paper.

The Clark-Menefee projection is different from the other three because it assumes that the older population continues to receive the same relative per capita share of *GNP* as it did in 1977, although this is an unlikely assumption for Medicare. All of the projections use the intermediate economic assumptions of the annual Social Security Trustees' *Report*. O'Neill projected the major federal programs for the older population; Califano's and my projections are estimates of growth in both the major and minor programs. The latter three estimates suggest that if the budget is constrained to 20 percent of *GNP*, outlays for the present programs for the older population will become about half of the federal budget by 2025. My projections also suggest that federal outlays as a percentage of the budget will not continue to grow indefinitely, but will peak around 2025.

Alternatively, if it is assumed that future outlays for other programs remain a constant share of *GNP* at the 1980 level (17 percent), then total federal outlays would increase as a percentage of *GNP* to 26.9 percent by 2030.

TABLE 3—SENSITIVITY OF OUTLAY PROJECTIONS: PERCENTAGE DIFFERENCE IN OUTLAYS FOR THE OLDER POPULATION

Assumption	1990	2000	2010	2020	2030
More Pessimistic Economic Assumptions	+23.8	+49.1	+46.7	+53.8	+63.8
Historical Improvement in the Mortality Rate	+3.0	+8.7	+13.4	+15.4	+17.4
Constraint on Medicare Growth in 1990 instead of 2005	-	−12.4	−18.0	−18.3	−18.9

The potential increase in federal outlays as a percentage of *GNP* would require correspondingly higher federal taxes in order to avoid a permanent and large increase in the federal deficit. If outlays remained 20 percent of *GNP*, then higher taxes would not be needed. However, if Social Security and Medicare continue to be financed by payroll taxes, then in this case over 40 percent of the federal receipts would come from payroll taxes by 2030. This increase from the present level of 29 percent would make the total tax system less progressive and would increase the cost of labor relative to other factors of production.

III. The Sensitivity of the Projections

Projections of future outlays as a percentage of the budget suggest a false sense of inevitability, since even modest differences in the assumptions can substantially change the outcomes. The effects of three major factors that can significantly change my results—economic conditions, the mortality rate, and the constraints on Medicare costs—are summarized in Table 3.

Economic Assumptions. My base projection assumes a long-term average annual increase of 1.5 percent for the real wage rate, 2.7 percent for real *GNP*, and 4.0 percent for the price level (the alternative IIB economic assumptions in the 1981 OASDI Trustees' *Report*). Alternative assumptions used to indicate the sensitivity of the projection to economic factors assume 1.0, 2.2, and 5.0 percent, respectively (the alternative III "pessimistic" assumptions of the Trustees' *Report*). These alternative assumptions would increase the outlay projection for the older population by 64 percent in 2030. This is because higher inflation rates increase postretirement benefits and higher nominal wage rates increase the initial annuity.

Mortality Rate Assumptions. The base projection assumes that the improvement in the mortality rate will be half the average annual improvement that occurred from 1900 to 1978. The alternative projection assumes that the improvement continues at the historical average (1.2 percent per year). International comparisons and biological research both suggest that potential changes in life styles could make this assumption realistic. If mortality rates do continue to improve at their historical rate, then the number of older people in the future would be higher than assumed above, which in turn would increase the projections of federal outlays for this population by 17 percent for 2030.

Medicare Growth Constraints. My projections of Medicare, which are based on the estimates in the Hospital Insurance Trustees' *Report*, grow faster than *GNP* through 2005 due in large part to increased utilization rates and increased use of technology. This rate of growth is not sustainable indefinitely because it assumes a continual increase in the relative price of health services without an offsetting change in the demand. Consequently, Medicare's growth after 2005 is assumed to be constrained to the OASI growth rate. If it were constrained fifteen years earlier, outlays for the older population would be reduced 19 percent by 2030. The risk, however, is more likely that they will not be constrained by 2005. O'Neill estimated that if medicare outlays continue to

TABLE 4—SHARE OF THE FEDERAL BUDGET DEVOTED TO THE ELIGIBLE POPULATION
(In Percentages)

Age of Eligibility	1990	2000	2010	2020	2030
65	32.4	34.1	36.2	43.8	49.5
68	26.5	29.0	29.8	35.6	41.7
70	23.4	26.1	26.6	31.5	37.3

increase at the historical rate, outlays for the older population by 2025 would become 63 percent of a federal budget that was 20 percent of *GNP*.

IV. Implications for Policy

While specific outlay projections for the older population depend heavily on the assumptions made, the trend of increasing outlays and the pressure on the budget are obvious under all the alternatives. The increase in the outlays for the older population implies that, unless the deficit is increased, either outlays for non-aged programs will have to decrease substantially in the future or total taxes will have to increase. In fact, it is likely that the fiscal burden would be shared by both, rather than borne solely by either. The projected increase in outlays for the older population as a share of the federal budget raises several other policy questions.

What should be the federal responsibilities for the older population? Today the federal government pays 78 percent of all the retirement and survivors benefits in the United States and 54 percent of the medical care costs of people 65 and over. The private sector pays an estimated 15 and 37 percent, respectively, not including personal savings and intrafamily transfers, with the state and local sector paying the rest. The effect on *GNP* is the same whether transfers for the aged go through the public or the private sector. But the size of the federal budget as a share of *GNP* would, of course, be affected if the responsibilities shifted. The potential fiscal pressures in the twenty-first century should focus more attention on the division of responsibility between the public and private sectors.

Should the age of eligibility for federal benefits be increased? Increasing the age of eligibility would be one way to reduce the Federal responsibility for the older population. Table 4 shows how higher eligibility ages for government programs would reduce my estimated share of the budget devoted to the eligible population if the budget were constrained to 20 percent of *GNP* and people retired when they were eligible.

The potential length of retirement has increased from 7 percent of adult life expectancy in 1940 to 23 percent today. Future increases in life expectancy will cause higher federal outlays for the older population unless average monthly benefits are reduced or the age of eligibility is raised.

Alternatively, shouldn't the aged-dependency question be placed in the broader context of the total dependency burden for the society? Although the aged-dependency ratio is estimated to peak in 2035, the total dependency burden for the society as a whole may never again be as high as in 1965. The total dependency burden is rarely emphasized at the federal level because young dependents are primarily the responsibility of the private and state and local sectors. Yet the effect of the total dependency burden on the economy will help determine the amount of resources available to the federal government to meet the aged dependency burden.

Finally, how can medicare costs be effectively controlled? Projections based on the 1981 OASDI and Hospital Insurance Trustees' *Reports* suggest that Medicare (HI and SMI) outlays for older people will be larger than OASI outlays by 2005. The projections in this paper assume constraints on the growth of Medicare costs after 2005. But the nature of these constraints is left unspecified.

Constructing them is one of the most important public policy challenges today.

V. Conclusion

The fiscal sociology of the aged suggests that the traditional tradeoff between guns and butter may in the future be better characterized as a tradeoff between guns and canes. The increase in the older population is likely to generate an increasingly powerful fiscal interest group, concentrating its attention on the federal government. The estimated outlay increases that could be expected in the future because of the increases in the older population are not insupportable. In fact, the relative increase in outlays is likely to be consistent with the changing priorities of an aging population in general. It does, however, represent a clear shift in future priorities for the federal government that will need to be confronted.

REFERENCES

Califano, Joseph A., "The Aging of America: Questions for the Four Generation Society," *The Annals of American Academy of Political and Social Science*, July 1978, *438*, 97–107.

Clark, Robert L. and Menefee, John A., "Federal Expenditures for the Elderly: Past and Future," *The Gerentologist*, 1981, No. 2, *21*, 132–37.

Musgrave, Richard A., "Theories of Fiscal Crises: An Essay in Fiscal Sociology," in *The Economics of Taxation*, Washington: Brookings Institution, 1980.

O'Neill, June, unpublished material prepared for the Congressional Budget Office, 1978; Estimates summarized in James Storey and Gary Hendricks, "Retirement Income Issues in an Aging Society," unpublished paper, Urban Institute, December 1979.

Torrey, Barbara Boyle, "Technical Details on the Projection of Federal Outlays for the Older Population," Office of Management and Budget, Washington 1981.

U.S. Board of Trustees, Federal Hospital Insurance Trust Fund, *1981 Annual Report*, Washington 1981.

______, Federal Old-Age and Survivors Insurance and Disability Insurance Trust Funds, *1981 Annual Report*, Washington, 1981.

U.S. Department of Health and Human Services, Social Security Administration, unpublished materials, March 30, 1978, and July, 1981.

Office of Management and Budget, Executive Office of the President, *Mid-Session Review of the 1982 Budget*, July 15, 1981.

[25]

The Impact of Demographic Change on Social Security Financing

WILLIAM A. HALTER and RICHARD HEMMING*

The relationship between prospective demographic changes and social security tax rates over the long term is examined for four countries—the Federal Republic of Germany, Japan, the United Kingdom, and the United States. Through use of a simple projection model it is shown that, without significant reform, social security programs as constituted in 1980 would have implied substantial increases in social security tax rates by the year 2025 in all four countries. The model is then used to explore how a range of policy options would affect the evolution of tax rates. Recent policy measures taken in each of the countries can be summarized in terms of the model, and it is shown that these measures lead to markedly lower tax rates than with unreformed programs, although the tax rate in Germany will remain high.

DEMOGRAPHIC PROJECTIONS suggest that the aging of the general population in many industrial countries will continue into the foreseeable future, and that in some countries the elderly will become, during the lifetime of today's young, a large proportion of the total population. Given the existing structure of social support in many of these countries, the elderly are likely to command an increasing share of available resources. Many countries have recognized that the tax rates

* Mr. Halter, who holds degrees from Stanford and Oxford Universities, works for McKinsey and Company, Inc. This paper was written while he was an intern in the Fiscal Affairs Department of the Fund.

Mr. Hemming, Senior Economist in the Fiscal Affairs Department when this paper was written, is now Senior Economist in the Asian Department of the Fund. He holds degrees from Sussex and Stirling Universities.

An earlier version of this paper was prepared for the Joint Japanese/OECD Conference on Health and Pension Policies in the Context of Demographic Evolution and Economic Constraint, Tokyo, November 25–28, 1985.

required to finance social security pensions for the retired will increase substantially, and several countries have begun to face up to the issues raised by this prospect.[1]

The purpose of this paper is to examine the relationship between population aging and social security financing in the context of prospective developments in four countries—the Federal Republic of Germany, Japan, the United Kingdom, and the United States. In each of these countries the financing of social security has been widely discussed, and, to varying degrees and in different ways, programs have been, or are in the process of being, restructured so as to cushion against future financial pressures.

Section I of the paper describes projected demographic developments through 2025. In Section II these developments are incorporated into a simple model of a social security program. Although the model requires that actual programs be described only in terms of their essential characteristics, the model nevertheless embodies the principal trade-offs facing policymakers. Section III looks at how the model can be used to assess the implications of reform strategies that do not imply a radical departure from existing financing mechanisms. The section also discusses more radical reform that breaks with existing financing mechanisms. Section IV describes and analyzes recent policy developments in the four countries covered; Section V summarizes the discussion and draws some conclusions.

I. Demographic Trends Through 2025

The analysis that follows is, for the most part, based on a single demographic projection for each of the four countries. These projections share certain characteristics as regards future trends in fertility, mortality, and immigration.[2]

Demographic Assumptions

In all four countries the fertility rate (the average number of children per woman) has recently been below replacement level, which is around 2.1. The 1980 fertility rates were 1.42 for Germany, 1.75 for Japan, 1.78

[1] Throughout this paper, the term "social security" is used to refer only to a pension program, as is the practice in the United States. In many other countries, the term is used to describe a wider range of programs.

[2] These projections have been chosen because of their shared characteristics. They correspond to the baseline demographic projection described in Heller, Hemming, and Kohnert (1986), where a fuller description of the underlying assumptions can be found. These assumptions are broadly similar to those used to produce recent official mid-range population projections in the countries concerned.

for the United Kingdom, and 1.86 for the United States. In Japan and the United Kingdom, the fertility rate is projected to return to replacement level between 2010 and 2025. In the United States, the fertility rate is expected to increase but not quite reach replacement level. The fertility rate in Germany is expected to increase by as much as in the other three countries; however, because the 1980 fertility rate was relatively low, the rate of 1.65 projected for 2025 remains well below replacement level.

Mortality rates are expected to fall so that, between 1980 and 2025, male life expectancy increases by about 5 percent on average, whereas female life expectancy increases by about 3 percent. Improvements in life expectancy are greatest in the United Kingdom and the United States and smallest in Japan, although the range is narrow.

The projections for immigration differ widely because quite different patterns are expected in each country. For Germany, net emigration of about 1 million people before 1990 is anticipated; for the United Kingdom, steadily declining net emigration through 2015 is expected; for Japan, no immigration or emigration is anticipated; and for the United States, the steady net immigration of about 400,000 people a year is expected.

Population Structure

The assumptions about fertility, mortality, and immigration described above, combined with the 1980 population structures, suggest markedly different demographic developments for each of the four countries through 2025. These developments are summarized in Table 1. Total

Table 1. *Demographic Structure, 1980–2025*

Country	1980	2000	2010	2025
Index of total population				
Germany, Fed. Rep. of	100.0	94.6	94.1	87.0
Japan	100.0	109.8	112.9	112.9
United Kingdom	100.0	101.8	102.9	104.7
United States	100.0	117.4	124.3	132.9
Population aged 65 and over[a]				
Germany, Fed. Rep. of	15.5	17.0	20.7	23.6
Japan	9.0	14.9	18.2	21.2
United Kingdom	14.8	15.1	15.8	18.5
United States	11.2	13.0	13.8	19.4

Source: Heller, Hemming, and Kohnert (1986).
[a] As a percentage of total population.

population is projected to fall steadily in Germany and will be 13 percent smaller by 2025 than in 1980. In Japan, total population is projected to increase by 10 percent between 1980 and 2000, then to increase a little further by 2010, and to be at that same level in 2025. Total population is projected to increase steadily in the United Kingdom, although the overall increase will be less than 5 percent. In the United States, total population is projected to grow fairly rapidly, with an overall increase of 33 percent.

Table 1 shows how population aging is projected to occur in each country. Between 1980 and 2000, the increase in the proportion of the population aged 65 and over is minimal in the United Kingdom, modest in Germany and the United States, and much larger in Japan. As a result, by 2000 a considerable part of the difference in age structure observed among the four countries in 1980 will have been eliminated. After 2000, aging in Japan slows down, whereas the populations of Germany and the United States age more rapidly than previously. Aging also accelerates in the United Kingdom, but still remains relatively slow. By 2025, close to 21 percent of the population in these countries, on average, is 65 and over, compared with 17 percent in 2010, 15 percent in 2000, and 13 percent in 1980.

Figure 1 places the aging pattern for 1980–2025 in some historical perspective. It is clear that the population of Japan will continue to age faster than at any time in the recent past, at least up until 2020. The population of the United States will begin to age more rapidly from about 2005, after aging slowly between 1980 and 2005. But population aging in both Germany and the United Kingdom is expected to occur, except for a brief period in Germany (between 2000 and 2005), at a slower rate than at any time between 1950 and 1980.[3]

In light of this historical perspective, why is concern about the implications of the aging of the populations of industrial countries emerging so widely and strongly in the 1980s? Everywhere except in Japan, aging is taking place at a slower rate than at any time since World War II. Clearly, a rapidly aging population poses more difficult problems of adjustment than a more slowly aging one, although rapid aging may be quite manageable when there are relatively few elderly to begin with. Once the elderly have become more numerous, however, even fairly slow aging can begin to look unmanageable. The current concern is not about rapid aging—although this is certainly of some immediate importance in Japan—so much as about the problems that may be created by

[3] These statements are based on the rate of change of the proportion of the population aged 65 and over, represented by the slopes of the curves in Chart 1.

Figure 1. ***Percentage of Total Population Aged 65 or Over, Four Industrial Countries, 1950–2025***

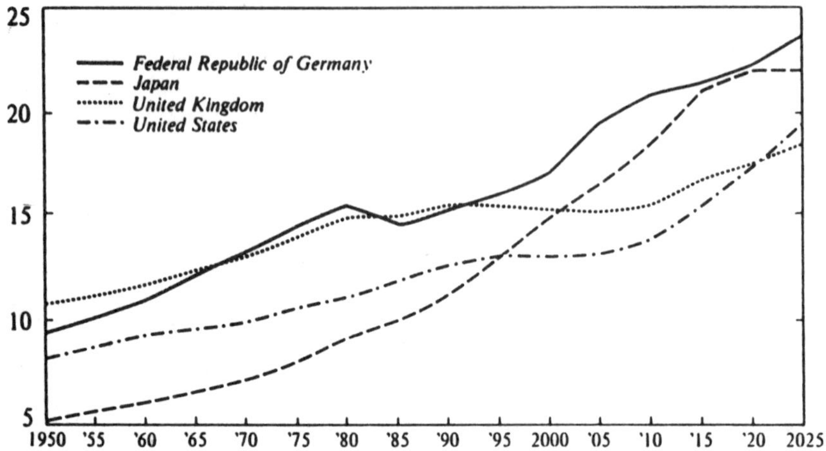

Sources: OECD (1980); Heller, Hemming, and Kohnert (1986); and authors' estimates.

half a century or more of continuous aging. One particular fear emerges from the way in which the financing of social security is affected by aging of the population.

II. Population Aging and Social Security Financing

This paper takes what Aaron (1986) refers to as a "nation-as-a-whole" view of social security financing. Programs are assumed to operate on a pay-as-you-go basis—as for the most part they do in the four countries covered—with all pensions being paid out of current revenue. If a social security financing problem arises, it is likely to take the form of conflict about how current resources are split between workers and pensioners. In particular, demographic developments imply that the financing of social security, as currently constituted, may require tax rates that are unacceptable to the working population.[4]

[4] Note, however, that the social security financing issue can be viewed in other ways. For example, it may be that a relatively large age cohort retires after having saved and added more to productive capacity than smaller cohorts, and so has at least partially financed its apparently unacceptable claim to current resources (see Aaron (1986)).

Methodology

The relationship between population aging and social security financing will be examined in the context of a simple model of a pay-as-you-go social security program. It is assumed that the average social security pension and the average social security tax payment are a fixed proportion of the same average earnings base, y. If there are R retirement pensioners and the average pension is $p = \beta y$, then total pension expenditure is $R\beta y$, where β is the average replacement rate.[5] This pension program is financed on a pay-as-you-go basis, so that a social security tax is levied on the working population at a rate α to meet concurrent pension expenditure. If there are W workers, then total social security tax revenue is $W\alpha y$, with the pay-as-you-go rule requiring that the tax rate be given by

$$\alpha = \beta R/W = \beta/S, \tag{1}$$

where $S = W/R$ is the support ratio; that is, the number of workers per pensioner. With the replacement rate β fixed, the social security tax rate is inversely proportional to the support ratio. Thus, if projected demographic shifts can be transformed into changes in the support ratio, the implications of these shifts for social security tax rates follow directly.

Equation (1) forms the basis of the first set of social security tax rate projections—which may be thought of as the "1980 status quo"—reported in this paper. These projections take as their starting point social security pension expenditure in 1980 and the pay-as-you-go tax rate needed to finance it, which in turn reflects the demographic structure, age-specific labor force participation rates, and unemployment rates. The social security programs included are the old-age component of the social insurance program in Germany, the old-age component of the full range of public programs in Japan, the flat-rate and earnings-related state pensions in the United Kingdom, and the old-age and survivors' component (OASI) of the social security program in the United States.[6] From published information on these programs, it is reasonably straightforward to calculate the 1980 values of α.[7] The vari-

[5] The *average* replacement rate, which is the ratio of the average pension to average earnings at the same point in time, should be distinguished from the more widely referred to *marginal* replacement rate, which is the ratio of the full pension to average earnings (or an average of previous earnings) on retirement. From now on, the term "replacement rate" will refer to the average rate.

[6] A brief description of these programs is contained in Appendix II to Heller, Hemming, and Kohnert (1986).

[7] Social security tax rates are levied on both employees and employers; α refers to the sum of the employees' and employers' rates. For Germany and the United

Table 2. *Social Security Tax Rates, Replacement Rates, and Support Ratios, 1980*

Country	Tax Rate (α)[a]	Replacement Rate (β)[b]	Support Ratio (S)[c]
Germany, Fed. Rep. of	14.6	40.2	2.75
Japan	6.4	35.9	5.61
United Kingdom	10.5	28.7	2.73
United States	9.4	42.2	4.49

Source: Authors' estimates.
[a] In percent.
[b] In percent. Derived by using equation (1) of the text; that is, $\beta = \alpha S$.
[c] Workers per pensioner.

ables R and W reflect the age structure of the population, pension age, and the labor market factors noted above. Then, from equation (1), β is derived as a residual. The 1980 values of α, β, and $S = W/R$ are shown in Table 2.[8]

With β fixed, a projection of α requires a projection of the support ratio S. This projection in turn is derived from the demographic projections, under the assumptions that pension age and age-specific labor force participation rates remain at their 1980 values and that unemployment reverts to 1980 rates (or below) by 2000.[9] The resultant support ratios are shown in Table 3. The fall in support ratios in each country by 2025 mirrors the increase in the proportion of the total population aged 65 or over shown in Table 1, although the decline differs

Kingdom, where the social security programs are run on a purely pay-as-you-go basis, these rates are the actual tax rates associated with the programs concerned. The U.S. program is backed by a trust fund, but in 1980 the actual tax rate was close to the pay-as-you-go rate. In Japan, the multiplicity of programs with widely ranging characteristics, and the fact that social security is partially funded, make estimation of the pay-as-you-go tax rate difficult. The assessed rate is well below the actual rate, which in 1980 was 10.6 percent for men in the largest program, the Employees' Pension Plan. In all cases, the pay-as-you-go tax rates have been calculated net of any government subsidy to the social security program, and such subsidy is assumed to remain unchanged in percentage terms over the projection period.

[8] When one takes into account differences in coverage, the different bases used to compute taxes and pensions, and government subsidies, the estimated average replacement rates reported in Table 2 are not obviously inconsistent with the marginal replacement rates reported in Aldrich (1982). We do not have sufficient information to make a more careful comparison of the two sets of replacement rates.

[9] The assumed unemployment rates from 2000 onward are 3.0 percent in Germany, 2.0 percent in Japan, 6.0 percent in the United Kingdom, and 5.5 percent in the United States.

Table 3. *Support Ratios, 1980–2025*
(Workers per pensioner)

Country	1980	2000	2010	2025
Germany, Fed. Rep. of	2.75	2.35	1.95	1.56
Japan	5.61	3.59	2.77	2.38
United Kingdom	2.73	2.81	2.69	2.18
United States	4.49	3.99	3.78	2.53

Source: Authors' estimates.

among countries because pension age and labor force participation rates (and hence retirement age) also differ.[10] The most dramatic decline occurs in Japan, where the number of workers per pensioner drops by more than half, and the most modest decline occurs in the United Kingdom, where the support ratio remains between about 2.0 and 3.0 for the entire projection period. This is the range ultimately reached in Japan and the United States, whereas in Germany the support ratio falls below 2.0 between 2000 and 2010 and then falls significantly thereafter.

In moving from projections of the support ratio to projections of social security tax rates, one must take into account an additional factor not reflected in equation (1). In each of the four countries discussed in this paper, pensions are related to some measure of a workers' previous earnings and to the number of working years spent in the program. Such programs have a maturation period during which average replacement rates increase as people approach retirement, having spent an increasing share of their working life in the program. Well-established programs, such as that in Germany, are fully mature. The program in the United States is newer but is nearly mature because of its relatively short qualifying period (ten years). Like the U.S. program, Japan's major programs are newer, but the Japanese programs are still immature because of their much longer qualifying period (35 years in the case of the Employees' Pension Plan). In the United Kingdom, the earnings-related program only came into effect in 1978 and will not fully mature until halfway through the twenty-first century. Because of the immaturity of the programs in Japan and the United Kingdom, the average replacement rate β for these countries is allowed to grow steadily between 1980 and 2025. Thus, if the subscript zero indicates 1980 and the subscript t indicates any future year (so that $t = 45$ indicates 2025), then

[10] Pension ages are 63 for Germany, 60 for Japan, 65 for the United States, and 65 for men and 60 for women in the United Kingdom. In Japan different schemes have different pension ages. For example, the Employees' Pension Plan has pension ages of 60 for men and 55 for women, whereas the National Pension Plan has pension ages of 65 for both men and women.

Table 4. *Social Security Tax Rates, 1980–2025: Pensions Fixed Relative to Average Gross Earnings*

(In percent)

Country	1980	2000	2010	2025
Germany, Fed. Rep. of	14.6	17.1	20.6	25.7
Japan	6.4	11.2	15.4	19.5
United Kingdom	10.5	11.5	12.7	17.2
United States	9.4	10.6	11.2	16.7

Source: Authors' estimates.

Note: Rates are derived by using equation (2); that is, $\alpha_t = \alpha_0(1+b)^t S_0/S_t$, with $b = 0.00572$ for Japan, $b = 0.00595$ for the United Kingdom, and $b = 0$ for Germany and the United States.

$$\alpha_t = \beta_0(1+b)^t/S_t\,,$$

where b is the rate at which the replacement rate is assumed to grow. Given that $\beta_0 = \alpha_0 S_0$,

$$\alpha_t = \alpha_0(1+b)^t S_0/S_t\,, \qquad (2)$$

with $b = 0$ for Germany and the United States and $b > 0$ for Japan and the United Kingdom. The growth rates in the latter two countries have been derived from the maturity adjustment implicit in official projections.[11] These growth rates are a little less than 0.6 percent a year in each case, and they imply that the average replacement rate will increase from 35.9 percent in 1980 to 46.4 percent by 2025 in Japan, and from 28.7 percent in 1980 to 37.5 percent by 2025 in the United Kingdom.

Results

Projected social security tax rates implied by the changes in support ratios shown in Table 3 are reported in Table 4. In all four countries, the "1980 status quo" projections suggest that social security tax rates will be markedly higher in 2025 than they were in 1980, with much larger increases after 2000 than before. Overall, the tax rate less than doubles in Germany, the United Kingdom, and the United States, whereas it more than triples in Japan. From being the lowest in 1980, the tax rate in Japan increases to nearly 20 percent by 2025, a figure that is exceeded only in Germany, where the tax rate rises to over 25 percent by 2025. In

[11] For Japan, the official projection relates to only one program, the Employees' Pension Plan, as reported in Takayama (1982). For the United Kingdom, the official projection is taken from United Kingdom (1982).

Figure 2. *Ratio of Social Security Pension Expenditure to GDP, Four Industrial Countries, 1960–2025*

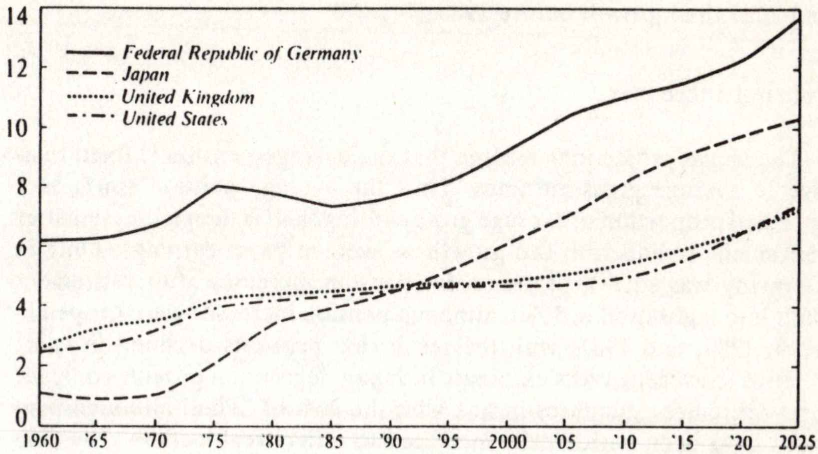

Sources: OECD (1985) and authors' estimates.

Note: The 1960–80 data relate to the OECD definition of social expenditure on pensions, which is somewhat broader than the definition of social security pensions used in this paper. The OECD definition includes all benefits paid to the elderly, the disabled, and survivors, as well as government employee pensions.

the United Kingdom and the United States, the social security tax rate increases to about 17 percent.

As with demographic developments, it is interesting to compare prospective changes with past ones. Although a time series of pay-as-you-go tax rates is not readily available, the Organization for Economic Cooperation and Development (OECD (1985)) reports the ratio of social security pension expenditure to gross domestic product (GDP) for the period 1960–80. The projections in Table 4 can be converted to a similar base, which has been done in Figure 2.[12] This chart provides little indica-

[12] It has been assumed that real GDP growth reflects changes in employment, as assumed in the support ratio projections, and the following annual rates of growth of average productivity: 2.0 percent for Germany, 3.0 percent for Japan, 1.4 percent for the United States, and 1.6 percent for the United Kingdom (see Heller, Hemming, and Kohnert (1986) for further details and discussion). Note that the OECD definition of pension expenditure is broader than that used in this paper. The two series of expenditure to GDP ratios have been integrated by using the 1980 ratio implied by the social security tax rates reported in Table 2 as a base.

tion that the ratio of social security pension expenditure to GDP will, in general, grow faster after 1980 than before; indeed, in each country future growth is markedly slower over much of the period between 1980 and 2025 than growth before 1980.

Pension Increases

The above projections assume that the average pension is fixed relative to average gross earnings. Thus the average pension starts as a specified proportion of average gross earnings and is then increased after retirement in line with the growth in average gross earnings. Only in Germany was such a provision for pension increases after retirement built into legislation in 1980, although pension increases were capped in 1979, 1980, and 1981, with the result that pensions declined in value relative to average gross earnings. In Japan, legislation provides only for post-retirement increases in line with the cost of living, although pensions have been periodically increased to reflect real income growth in the economy as a whole. The United Kingdom and the United States appear to be more firmly committed to, at the most, increasing pensions to reflect price movements. In the United Kingdom, however, pension increases have been more generous in the past, reflecting in part periods with less restrictive legislation and in part government discretion. In the United States, pension increases have also been more generous in the past, although this was due in part to an error in the pension formula, now corrected, that provided for double indexation (relative to price changes) between 1972 and 1977 (see Munnell (1977) for more details).

In terms of a "1980 status quo," it would appear that fixing pensions relative to earnings is more reasonable in Germany and Japan than in the United Kingdom and the United States. Table 5 illustrates the potential effects that breaking the link between pensions and earnings can have on social security tax rates. If pensions are fixed at their real 1980 levels, other than for increases to reflect the maturing process, then in all countries the social security tax rate will be lower in 2025 than in 1980. Because the programs in each country relate starting pension levels to previous earnings, however, pensions can only be held constant in real terms after retirement, in which case the future tax rate will reflect the demographic and labor market characteristics of the retired population. There is no straightforward way of capturing this type of provision in the model used in this paper. Official U.K. projections, however, suggest that, in the long term, maintaining the real value of pensions after retirement significantly reduces future social security tax rates compared with linking pensions to earnings. In terms of the projections reported

Table 5. *Social Security Tax Rates, 1980–2025: Pensions Fixed at 1980 Real Levels*

(In percent)

Country	1980	2000	2010	2025
Germany, Fed. Rep. of	14.6	11.5	11.4	10.5
Japan	6.4	6.2	6.3	5.2
United Kingdom	10.5	8.7	8.4	9.2
United States	9.4	7.7	6.9	8.2

Source: Authors' estimates.

Note: Rates are derived from the equation $\alpha_t = \alpha_0[(1+b)/(1+g)]^t S_0/S_t$, where g is the assumed rate of growth of real earnings. This rate of growth has been equated with the rate of growth of productivity. Thus $g = 0.02$ for Germany, $g = 0.03$ for Japan, $g = 0.014$ for the United Kingdom, and $g = 0.016$ for the United States.

in Table 4 for the United Kingdom, if pensions were increased after retirement by 1 percentage point less than the growth rate of earnings (with earnings growing at 8 percent a year in nominal terms), the 2025 social security tax rate would be about 13.5 percent rather than the reported 17.2 percent.[13]

The significant effect on social security tax rates of alternative provisions relating to pension increases after retirement gives rise to the question of whether long-run projections based on pension increases that are linked to average earnings—especially if the legislated provision diverges from actual changes in average real earnings—provide a true guide to future tax rates. The answer depends on whether a deviation from what has happened in the past can be sustained. This paper assumes that if changes in average real earnings are not reflected in pension levels, divergences and mismatches in living standards will result—between workers and pensioners and between older and younger pensioners—that are probably not sustainable in the long run.

Sensitivity to Principal Assumptions

The preceding analysis is based on a single, probably optimistic, demographic projection that corresponds to the baseline projection reported in Heller, Hemming, and Kohnert (1986). That study also made use of a less optimistic "greater-aging" demographic projection, which we have also used here. Under these "pessimistic" demographic assumptions,

[13] Based on the estimates in Table 14 of United Kingdom (1982).

fertility rates are expected to remain at their 1980 levels except in the United States, where a small decline is assumed. Life expectancy is assumed to increase by a little less than twice as much as in the baseline case; that is, average male life expectancy increases by 9 percent, average female life expectancy by 6 percent. It is also assumed that the number of immigrants to the United States is reduced by 25 percent in the greater-aging case. These revised assumptions yield both lower projections of total population in each country and lower support ratios; the consequences of these lower projections for social security tax rates are indicated in Table 6. By 2025, tax rates will be significantly higher in Germany, Japan, and the United States; in the United Kingdom, the difference between the baseline and greater-aging population projections will be relatively small.

In addition to the demography, the economic environment may turn out somewhat less favorably than allowed for in the projections. Lower productivity growth than expected would have no impact on the projections, however, since pensions are assumed to increase in line with average earnings. Only if the link between pensions and earnings is severed will higher or lower average productivity growth affect the projections. The assumed unemployment rate, in contrast, has a direct effect on the projections because a higher unemployment rate reduces the size of the working population.

Table 6. *Support Ratios and Social Security Tax Rates, 1980–2025: Pessimistic Demographic Assumptions with Pensions Fixed Relative to Average Gross Earnings*

Country	1980	2000	2010	2025
Support ratios[a]				
Germany, Fed. Rep. of	2.75	2.35	1.93	1.47
Japan	5.61	3.10	2.38	2.06
United Kingdom	2.73	2.81	2.69	2.12
United States	4.49	3.80	3.46	2.14
Social security tax rates[b]				
Germany, Fed. Rep. of	14.6	17.1	20.8	27.4
Japan	6.4	12.8	17.7	22.3
United Kingdom	10.5	11.5	12.7	17.6
United States	9.4	11.1	12.2	19.8

Source: Authors' estimates.

Note: For these "pessimistic" assumptions, see Section II (under "Sensitivity to Principal Assumptions").

[a] Workers per pensioner.

[b] In percent. See Table 4 for derivation.

III. Social Security Reform

The foregoing analysis is fairly mechanical and makes no attempt to assess whether the social security tax rates generated by the projection exercises are sustainable, from either an economic or a political point of view. The economic arguments—which revolve around the supply-side effects of high tax rates—cannot be resolved. In any event, political considerations are likely to dominate economic considerations, and the consensus emerging among today's politicians is that future generations of workers will find the currently projected social security tax rates unacceptable. Thus social security reform is again a topical subject, with the focus of attention on how to accommodate the financial pressures associated with population aging.

In the existing pay-as-you-go programs, the range of broad policy options is limited. In terms of the model used above, the trade-off is between social security tax rates and pension levels (as reflected in the average replacement rate) and pension age. Before exploring this trade-off further, however, we will outline an alternative approach to pension reform in the face of demographic pressure. A pay-as-you-go pension program can be viewed as an implicit intergenerational contract, under whose terms each working generation supports the retired—and expects to be supported in turn by future working generations. Musgrave (1981) has examined how contracts with different terms divide demographic and economic risks between working and retired generations and has assessed the effect of amending the terms of the existing contract in various ways.

Changing the Pension Contract

With respect to demographic change, under pay-as-you-go arrangements the cost of adjustment falls on the working population.[14] The rules determining pensions tend to be fixed, and the tax rate is adjusted to guarantee that income matches expenditure. With pensions fixed relative to average gross earnings, population aging results in continuously increasing tax rates, with a corresponding decrease in the relative net incomes of workers. According to Musgrave (1981), this type of contract "contains a built-in potential for collapse" (p. 103). Continuously in-

[14] Although Musgrave's analysis is in terms of risk bearing (that is, who pays if demographic developments are less favorable than expected?), this paper focuses on the burden of costs (that is, who pays for given specific demographic developments?). The difference between these two approaches relates only to whether a particular change is anticipated or unanticipated.

creasing tax rates without any compensating reduction in relative pension levels may induce a future generation of workers to renege on the contract. An alternative intergenerational contract, where the cost of aging is shared more evenly by working and retired generations, could reduce the likelihood of such an outcome.[15]

One way to achieve fairer cost sharing is to fix the average pension not as a proportion of average gross earnings, but as a proportion of average net earnings. If the social security tax is the only tax, then average net earnings are given by $n = (1 - \alpha^*)y$, where α^* is the social security tax rate. The average pension is then $p = \beta^* n = \beta^*(1 - \alpha^*)y$, where β^* is the average replacement rate defined relative to net earnings, and total pensions expenditure is $R\beta^*(1 - \alpha^*)y$. Social security tax revenue is again $W\alpha^* y$, with pay-as-you-go financing now requiring that

$$\alpha^*/(1 - \alpha^*) = \beta^*/S. \tag{3}$$

The social security tax rate α^* is inversely related to the support ratio, and average net earnings and the average pension change in the same proportion, reflecting the change in the retention rate $(1 - \alpha^*)$, as the support ratio worsens. This is the sense in which cost sharing is equitable.[16]

Taking into account increasing maturity, the future social security tax rate can be written (using the notation employed in Section II) as follows:

$$\begin{aligned}\alpha_t^*/(1 - \alpha_t^*) &= \beta_0^*(1 + b)^t/S_t \\ &= [\alpha_0/(1 - \alpha_0)](1 + b)^t S_0/S_t,\end{aligned}$$

since $\beta_0^* = \alpha_0 S_0/(1 - \alpha_0)$. It then follows from equation (2) that $\alpha_t^*/(1 - \alpha_t^*) = \alpha_t/(1 - \alpha_0)$,[17] and therefore that

$$\alpha_t^* = \alpha_t/(1 - \alpha_0 + \alpha_t), \tag{4}$$

[15] A similar problem arises when pensions after retirement are increased in line with prices rather than earnings. Adverse demographic developments do not affect real pension levels; therefore, the full cost of adjustment is borne by workers.

[16] As well as the costs (risks) associated with demographic developments, those associated with economic developments—for example, an anticipated or unanticipated slowdown in productivity growth—are also of interest. If pensions are fixed relative to either gross or net earnings, then workers and pensioners share economic costs and risks. If pensions are fixed in real terms, however, such costs and risks are borne by workers.

[17] For Japan and the United Kingdom it is assumed that the replacement rate defined in terms of average net earnings, β^*, increases at the same rate as the replacement rate defined in terms of gross earnings, β; that is, b. Since b reflects the increase in the average length of the working life spent in a program, this assumption seems appropriate.

Table 7. *Social Security Tax Rates, 1980–2025: Pensions Fixed Relative to Average Net Earnings*
(In percent)

Country	1980	2000	2010	2025
Germany Fed. Rep. of	14.6	16.7	19.4	23.1
Japan	6.4	10.7	14.1	17.2
United Kingdom	10.5	11.4	12.5	16.1
United States	9.4	10.5	11.0	15.6

Source: Authors' estimates.
Note: Rates are derived by using equation (4); that is, $\alpha_t^* = \alpha_t/(1 - \alpha_0 + \alpha_t)$.

which is the equation used to derive the social security tax rates reported in Table 7.

A comparison of the tax rates in Table 7 and the rates reported in Table 4 reveals that the reduction in social security tax rates implied by the switch in pension contracts taking effect in 1980 is between 2 and 3 percentage points by 2025 in Germany and Japan, and about 1 percentage point by 2025 in the United Kingdom and the United States. If the definition of net earnings were to take into account not only the social security tax but all direct taxes on income—a procedure that can be justified if it is believed that pensioners should share the costs of all government activities, and not just the costs of pension provision—the 2025 tax rate would be a little lower; that is, about 1 percentage point in Japan, about ¾ of 1 percentage point in Germany, and about ½ of 1 percentage point elsewhere.[18] But the effect of the fairer cost-sharing formula remains modest and suggests that, although such a switch may be desirable in itself, it may not shift enough of the burden of population aging to the retired so as to guarantee the survival of the pension contract. More direct intervention is then required.

Pension Levels and Pension Age

In the context of a pay-as-you-go social security system, any attempt to contain the growth of pension expenditure so as to limit the increase in tax rates must focus on pension levels or pension age.

[18]These estimates are based on the assumption that the overall rate of income tax increases only as a result of increasing social security taxes. But other public expenditure programs—in particular health care—are affected by demographic developments, with the result that the financing of nonpension expenditure will also require higher tax rates (see Heller, Hemming, and Kohnert (1986)).

Pension Levels

Pension levels are a function of replacement rates, and the focus of attention will now shift from average to marginal rates (that is, the proportion of earnings, appropriately defined, that are replaced by a pension at the date of retirement) and to the provision for pension increases after retirement. Among the ways in which marginal replacement rates could be changed, two would directly affect social security tax rates: the number of pensionable years of employment could be limited, or accrual rates could be reduced. Alternatively, the pension base could be changed: for example, qualifying earnings could be reduced through the use of floors and ceilings, or, where past earnings were taken into account in determining a pension, intervening inflation and real earnings growth could be either partially compensated for or ignored. The above changes need not be applied uniformly. Rather, replacement rates could be made a decreasing function of earnings, with a view to targeting social security expenditure more directly at pensioners who need income support.

As noted above, altering pension levels by limiting pension increases after retirement has potentially large financial impact. We have argued, however, that pension levels are unlikely, in the long run, to move vastly out of line with earnings; nor is it desirable that they do so. One argument against linking pensions to earnings is that the real incomes of pensioners will fall when real earnings fall. But it seems more reasonable to argue that pensioners should not be afforded more inflation protection than workers themselves can secure. If pensions are to be linked to earnings, however, there is a compelling case for linking them to some measure of *net* earnings. In response to the financial pressures created by demographic change, there is a strong case for having the fortunes of the retired population linked directly to those of the working population that is paying its pensions. Linking pensions to net earnings, on retirement and thereafter, achieves this objective.

Pension Age

Pension age is different from retirement age in that there is early or late retirement, a difference that is reflected in the participation rates of those in the labor force close to pension age. Pension age and other provisions of the pension program necessarily affect participation rates, as do a range of other factors that could themselves be influenced by policy so as to increase the size of the work force (for example, the availability of child-care facilities). We will focus, however, on the effects of changes in pension age.

Table 8. *Support Ratios and Social Security Tax Rates, 1980–2025: Phased Increase in Pension Age of Two Years with Pensions Fixed Relative to Average Gross Earnings*

Country	1980	2000	2010	2025
Support ratios[a]				
Germany, Fed. Rep. of	2.75	2.35	2.05	1.78
Japan	5.61	3.59	2.86	2.49
United Kingdom	2.73	2.81	2.84	2.44
United States	4.49	3.99	3.96	2.79
Social security tax rates[b]				
Germany, Fed. Rep. of	14.6	17.1	19.6	22.6
Japan	6.4	11.2	14.9	18.6
United Kingdom	10.5	11.5	12.1	15.3
United States	9.4	10.6	10.7	15.1

Source: Authors' estimates.

Note: Pension age is assumed to increase by one year in 2000 and by one year in 2010.

[a] Workers per pensioner.

[b] In percent. See Table 4 for derivation.

Increasing pension age has a direct effect on the support ratio—because it increases the number of workers and reduces the number of pensioners—and on social security tax rates. In this paper the effects of two alternative pension-age scenarios are considered. In the first scenario, pension age is increased by one year in 2000 and by one year in 2010, with adjustments to labor force participation rates close to pension age made to reflect the implied disincentive for a worker to retire.[19] The impact of this change is shown in Table 8. In the second scenario, pension age is assumed to increase by one year every five years, starting in 1995 and ending in 2015. The impact of this change is shown in Table 9.

To compare these alternative pension-age scenarios with the 1980 status quo position shown in Table 4 and with the effect of a revised pension contract as shown in Table 7, Figure 3 combines these four separate projections for each of the four countries. As outlined above, the revised pension contract has limited financial effect and, with the exception of Japan, a two-year increase in pension age is of greater benefit. By 2025, social security tax rates would be about 3 percentage points lower in Germany than in the 1980 status quo, about 2 percentage points lower in the United Kingdom, between 1 and 2 percentage points

[19] These adjustments are fairly arbitrary, involving no more than an extension of the age range over which participation rates immediately prior to the original pension age are applied.

Table 9. *Social Security Tax Rates, 1980–2025: Phased Increase in Pension Age of Five Years with Pensions Fixed Relative to Average Gross Earnings*

Country	1980	2000	2010	2025
Support ratios[a]				
Germany, Fed. Rep. of	2.75	2.71	2.49	2.13
Japan	5.61	3.82	3.17	2.68
United Kingdom	2.73	3.00	3.14	2.65
United States	4.49	4.31	4.55	3.26
Social security tax rates[b]				
Germany, Fed. Rep. of	14.6	14.8	16.1	18.9
Japan	6.4	10.5	13.3	17.3
United Kingdom	10.5	10.8	10.9	14.1
United States	9.4	9.8	9.3	13.0

Source: Authors' estimates.

Note: Pension age is assumed to increase by one year every five years, starting in 1995 and ending in 2015.

[a] Workers per pensioner.

[b] In percent. See Table 4 for derivation.

lower in the United States, and about 1 percentage point lower in Japan. A five-year increase in pension age implies significantly lower social security tax rates in all countries, again with the exception of Japan, where the tax rate is reduced by less than 3 percentage points. The reduction is between 3 and 4 percentage points in the United Kingdom and the United States, and nearly 7 percentage points in Germany.

The Funding Option

The preceding analysis has been set in the framework of a pay-as-you-go social security program, which is the norm throughout the developed world. The alternative—actuarial funding—is common in the private sector and is also used in the public sector (in public enterprises and local government) but has been little used as a means of social security financing. There are three main reasons why pay-as-you-go programs have proved so popular. First, in a funded system, where pensions are paid out of accumulated savings, it takes many years to build up a claim to a reasonable pension. In contrast, under a pay-as-you-go system, a full pension can be paid immediately, with a transitional gain to retirees and some older workers. Second, because pensions are paid out of workers' earnings, they can be increased to reflect changes in prices or earnings without claiming an increasing share of these earnings. It is difficult—

Figure 3. *Impact of Alternative Policy Measures on Social Security Tax Rates, Four Industrial Countries, 1980–2025*

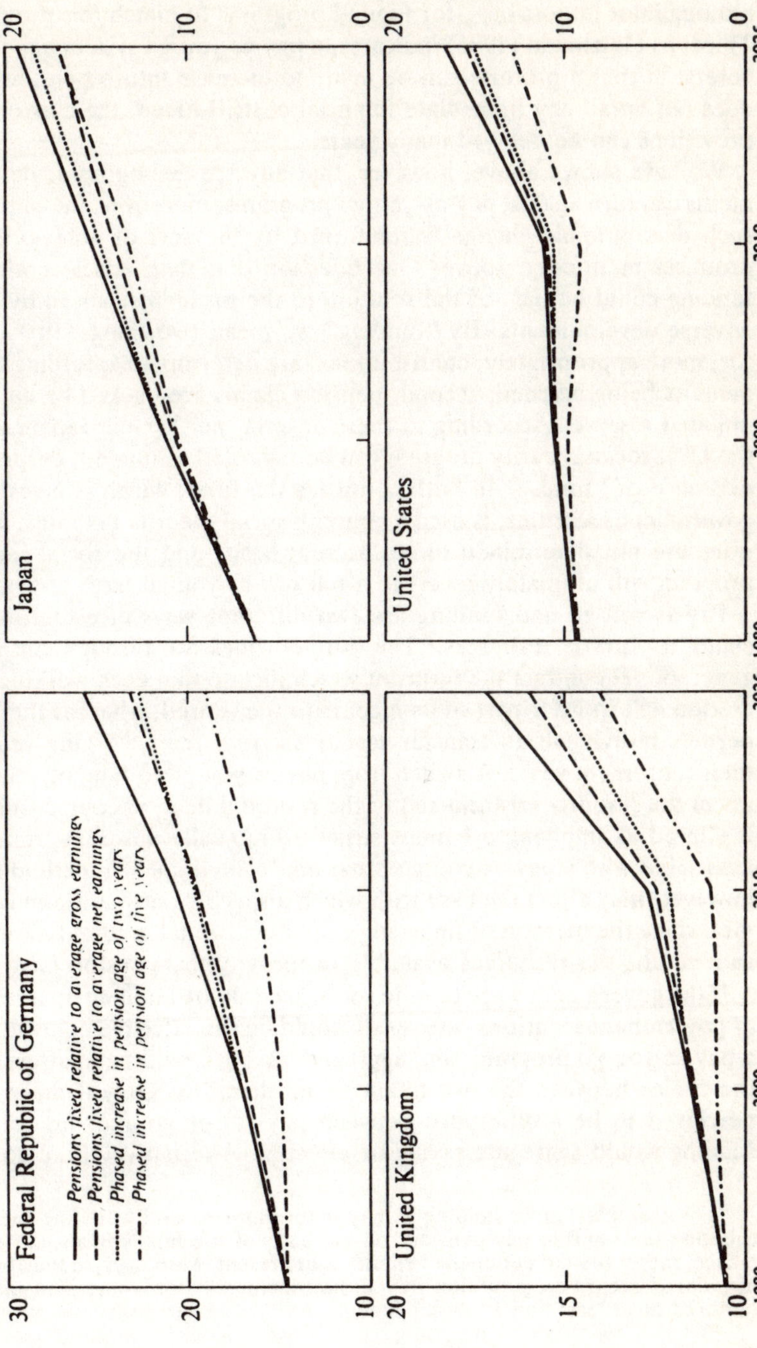

although not impossible—for funded programs to match this provision. Third, as Holzmann (1986) indicates, a pay-as-you-go system appeals to voters, in that a promise can be made to increase future pensions that does not entail any immediate financial costs. Indeed, the cost of such provisions can be delayed many years.

We have shown above, however, that adverse demographic developments can turn against pay-as-you-go programs; moreover, the impact of such demographic change is reinforced by the sort of voter-oriented promises mentioned above. One question that then arises is whether funding could be part of the solution to the problems caused by these adverse developments. By "funding" we mean two things: first, taxes (or, more appropriately, contributions) are determined according to the benefits being accrued; second, pension claims are backed by an accumulated reserve. According to these criteria, neither the Japanese nor the U.S. social security program can be regarded as funded, despite the existence of "funds." In both countries the fund, which is invested in government securities, is used to smooth social security tax rates. These rates are not determined on an accrual basis, and the social security program will ultimately revert to a full pay-as-you-go basis.

Pay-as-you-go and funding are two different ways of establishing a claim to future resources. The former does so through an intergenerational contract the terms of which dictate that each working generation will transfer part of its income to the retired, whereas the latter permits individuals to transfer resources from their working years to their retirement years. A switch from pay-as-you-go to funding does not affect the resources transferred to the retired unless, of course, funding is viewed as implying a benefit structure radically different from that associated with a pay-as-you-go program.[20] The financing method used, however, may affect the ease with which a specific pension claim can be met, since the method of financing can affect capital accumulation and, as a result, the resources available to meet future pension payments.

If the government were to fund social security by building up a reserve of government securities, the result would be the effective equivalent of a pay-as-you-go program, and aggregate saving would be unaffected by the choice between the two financing mechanisms. Only if there were perceived to be a difference between pay-as-you-go and this form of funding would aggregate saving be affected. Alternatively, the govern-

[20] For example, under funding it may seem more natural to define the contribution level and to pay pensions on the basis of the fund's financial performance, rather than to define the benefits as at present. Moreover, in the absence of indexed securities, provision for pension increases after retirement may be removed or at least limited under funding.

ment could accumulate private sector assets, although the extent to which this action contributes to an increase in the capital stock would depend on the reactions of private investors and the corporate sector to the resultant change in the structure of asset demand and supply.[21] Clearly, the effects of alternative social security financing methods on aggregate saving and capital accumulation cannot be determined a priori. Moreover, where aspects of these relationships have been subjected to empirical investigation, few clear and uncontroversial conclusions have been produced.[22] Thus, it cannot be concluded that there are strong grounds for substituting funding for pay-as-you-go because of the beneficial effect of the former on the capital stock; even if there were, other fiscal and monetary policy instruments probably provide the government with more direct means of influencing both public and private saving. Furthermore, any shift from pay-as-you-go to funding would involve transitional losses, since at least one generation has to pay for the pensions of a previous generation (under pay-as-you-go) while providing for its own pensions (under funding).

Although funding offers the private sector several advantages—the most important are tax concessions and a measure of financial security for program members—its signaling function is of clear value to both the private and public sectors. The accrual basis requires that taxes (or contribution rates) reflect the liabilities that are being incurred. This is not a feature of the pay-as-you-go system, although such a link could be established without resorting to funding; rather than building up a fund, government could levy higher taxes than under pay-as-you-go and reduce current borrowing. The result would be that, if compensating deficits did not build up on other programs, increases in future tax rates would be correspondingly contained. This principle underlies the notional funding practice common in the public sector in the United Kingdom (see Kay (1983)). It is also partially reflected in the current trust fund arrangement in the United States, in that between 1987 and about 2025 workers will be paying more than is necessary under pay-as-you-go while, for a number of years, future generations will be paying less. In the interests of equity between generations, however, the taxes paid and pensions received by each generation should ideally bear a fixed relationship to that generation's earnings (Aaron (1985)).[23] In effect, and in

[21] A question may also arise about the justification for heavy public investment in the private sector, which would certainly rest uneasily with widely held misgivings about public ownership.

[22] For a review of this evidence, see Thompson (1983) and the references cited therein.

[23] Such an outcome would only emerge under pay-as-you-go if the *aggregate* earnings of each successive generation were to increase at a constant rate.

contrast to current arrangements in the United States and elsewhere, the rate of return successive generations receive under the social security program would be brought into line.

IV. Social Security Policy

The preceding analysis makes it clear that pay-as-you-go social security programs, as currently constituted, will come under severe pressure from the forces of demographic change. Many countries have recognized this, including the four examined in this paper. But countries have also recognized that pay-as-you-go financing has limited potential for flexibility in response to demographic change. As reflected in the model used in this paper—the issue of the appropriate basis for pension increases aside—the social security tax rate, the replacement rate, and pension age are the only direct policy instruments. Expenditure control requires either lower replacement rates, a higher pension age, or some combination of the two. If social security expenditure does not fully adjust, then tax rates must inevitably increase.

Recent Policy Responses

This trade-off is exemplified in the policy responses that have occurred in Germany, Japan, the United Kingdom, and the United States.

Germany

The early 1970s was a period of rapid expansion of the social security system in Germany that was marked by extensions in coverage to groups outside the work force and by the introduction of generous early retirement provisions that brought pension age and effective retirement age down to 63 (and later to 60 for unemployed men). During the period social security expenditure as a percentage of GDP increased rapidly, reflecting in part this expansion, and in part demographic developments and real wage growth, with real growth in wages affecting both starting pension levels and pension increases that were linked to increases in average earnings (see Figure 2).

As we pointed out earlier, by the beginning of the 1980s Germany was relying on ad hoc post-retirement pension increases in place of the specific indexation mechanism previously used—increasing pensions in line with average gross earnings (averaged over the previous three years)—to control the growth of social security pension expenditure in response to the pressures of an aging population, increasing unemployment, and a falling retirement age (itself largely a response to increasing unemployment). The capping of pension increases during 1979–81 led to a drop in pensions (not only relative to average earnings, but also in real terms; see Cumming (1983)) and to a decline in social security expenditure as a percentage of GDP (see Figure 2). After 1981, pensions were again increased in line with average gross earnings, but this practice was soon abandoned with the onset of recession, and ad hoc procedures (in particular, delayed increases) were reinstated. At the end of 1984, however, these procedures were replaced by a formal arrangement when the authorities decided, in a supplementary law to the 1985 budget, that, in principle, pensions would be adjusted in line with average net earnings.[24]

Japan

The social security system in Japan underwent rapid expansion throughout the 1970s as coverage grew, pension levels improved as the programs matured, and the population aged. Social security expenditure as a percentage of GDP increased correspondingly (see Figure 2). The prospect of still larger expenditure increases after 1980 made social security reform a central issue in Japan.

The 1985 Pensions Reform Act represents a comprehensive plan to restructure the Japanese social security program. There are two principal elements to the reform. The first is the integration of the two largest public programs, the National Pension Plan and the Employees' Pension Plan. Because the first of these pays flat-rate pensions and the second pays earnings-related pensions, the integrated program will pay a combination of the two. There will also be some extensions of coverage, an aspect of the plan that brings about a significant rationalization of the existing system. The second element of the reform attempts to tackle the financial difficulties created by rapid population aging.

As pointed out earlier, the Japanese social security program is still immature. The integrated system, however, will cap earnings-related benefits at their current levels in real terms for single-earner couples and reduce them for single people or two-earner couples, effectively eliminating any further maturation of the program. The average new pensioner has now been in the program about 32 years, compared with the maximum of 40 years. The long-run average replacement rate has therefore been reduced by about 20 percent. Significant increases in contributions are also proposed, some to take effect immediately and some in

[24] Based on information reported in Germany (1984). No further details relating to this change are available.

the future. Although the growth in benefits will be moderated, by 2025 social security tax rates will still be more than twice as high as they are now. Thus the government has also indicated that the pension age may have to be increased at some time in the future and that the basis for pension increases may have to be changed.

The United Kingdom

Social security expenditure as a percentage of GDP grew slowly but steadily in the United Kingdom between 1960 and 1980 and is expected to continue, although at a slightly slower rate, through 2000 (see Figure 2). Thereafter, as demographic pressures mount and the costs of the earnings-related component of the social security program—introduced in 1978—build up, the ratio of social security expenditure to GDP will increase more rapidly, although not as fast as in Japan and Germany.

After only a few years of operation the new earnings-related program was being criticized—in particular, the detailed workings of the scheme, its long-run costs, and the structure of pension provision as a whole that it implied (see, for example, Hemming and Kay (1982)). The government, sharing misgivings about the scheme (its costs in particular), developed a reform strategy.

The government's initial proposal to counter cost increases was to phase out earnings-related pensions and to make occupational pension coverage mandatory. In response to criticism of this proposal, however, the government decided to retain the earnings-related pension scheme but to eliminate some of its more costly and less essential provisions.[25] These include switching from the highest-earning 20 years to a lifetime basis for pension determination, changing the replacement rate from 25 percent to 20 percent, shifting a larger part of the responsibility for pension increases for employees who are not full members of the scheme (by virtue of the quality of their private pension) to the private sector, and reducing widows' pensions. The pension changes are to be phased in beginning in 1988. In the long run (by about 2033 in official projections), and without reform, earnings-related pensions would have accounted for about half the total costs of social security pension provision; the reforms described above will reduce these costs by about half. Rather than making occupational pension schemes mandatory, the government is now going to provide incentives to encourage the growth of this sector.

[25] For a description of these reforms, see United Kingdom (1985).

The United States

The future growth of social security expenditure relative to GDP in the United States, with an unreformed social security program, would also be modest (see Figure 2). But social security reform in the United States has proceeded faster than in any of the other countries analyzed in this paper; the program was substantially reformed in 1983, with the result that future expenditure growth will be slower than under the 1980 status quo. The major changes can be divided into those of a short-term nature and those of a long-term nature. For the short term, it was decided to increase the social security tax rate, to delay annual benefit increases by six months, to bring new federal employees and all employees of nonprofit organizations into the program, and to tax half of the benefits received by high-income individuals. For the long term, an increase in pension age—from 65 to 67—is to be phased in between 2000 and 2027, while early retirement benefits are to be lowered, and delayed retirement credits increased, so as to promote later retirement.[26]

Assessment

Section III described the alternative approaches that might be taken to social security reform within a pay-as-you-go framework; it is clear that the four countries examined in this paper have followed different courses. In Germany, the basis for pension increases has been switched from gross to net earnings; in Japan, replacement rates are to be held constant or reduced, and it looks as though social security tax rates will be deliberately allowed to increase markedly, at least at present; in the United Kingdom, replacement rates will rise less than initially envisaged; and in the United States future increases in social security tax rates are to be limited by an increase in the retirement age.

Table 10 attempts to capture the financial impact of the reforms described above. The estimates shown relate, for the most part, to the principal features of reform packages as they are best reflected in the projection model described earlier. Thus, in the case of Germany, the 2025 social security tax rate—with recent reforms—of 23.1 percent allows for pension increases related to changes in earnings net of social security taxes. If all direct taxes on income are taken into account, the corresponding estimate would be 22.4 percent.[27] In Japan the replace-

[26] These reforms are described in *Social Security Amendments of 1983* (April 1983).

[27] If account were taken of the impact of demographic change on other social programs, the reduction in future tax rates would be larger; see Heller, Hemming, and Kohnert (1986, p. 35).

Table 10. *Social Security Tax Rates, 1980 and 2025, Under 1980 Status Quo and with Recent Reforms*

(In percent)

Country	1980	2025: 1980 status quo	2025: With recent reforms
Germany, Fed. Rep. of	14.6	25.7	23.1
Japan	6.4	19.5	13.6
United Kingdom	10.5	17.2	14.4
United States	9.4	16.7	15.1

Source: Authors' estimates. For assumptions underlying the estimates, see Section IV (under "Assessment").

ment rate has been frozen at its 1985 level. For the United Kingdom, the full impact of the 1985 reforms on social security expenditure is reflected in the reported estimate; this estimate, not surprisingly, coincides with the official estimate adjusted to the same basis. Recall that the reported estimate assumes that pension increases are linked to average earnings; if pensions are increased in line with prices, the 2025 U.K. social security tax rate is close to that prevailing in 1980. In the United States, the reported tax rate takes into account a two-year increase in pension age (up to 2025 rather than 2027). Official projections (United States (1985)) indicate that the pay-as-you-go rate for OASI in 2025 will be about 12.5 percent rather than the 15.1 percent reported in Table 10. This difference reflects several factors: the assumed link between pension increases and average earnings as opposed to cost-of-living increases; the impact of the 1983 amendments other than the phased increase in pension age; and differences in modeling (in particular, the fuller analysis of behavioral responses to the social security amendments contained in the official projections).

For the present, the current arrangements in the United States look stable, as do those provisions in the United Kingdom that reflect the 1985 reforms. The arrangements in Japan are also probably sustainable, although with the relatively low pension age there is scope to limit future increases in tax rates by increasing pension age, which is under consideration. The German situation is the most intriguing. Even with pensions linked to net rather than gross earnings, the social security tax rate (or at least the part that pays for pensions) is set to increase to well over 20 percent by 2025. This increase may well combine with other social security taxes and the income tax to produce a total personal tax burden that would be judged unsustainable.[28] If this possibility is soon recognized, then recent developments in the other three countries are certainly instructive, since those countries acknowledge what is widely regarded as a crucial requirement of pension reform: the need to announce future changes well in advance.

Major pension reforms cannot be introduced in haste. Many older workers and pensioners make irreversible labor market and savings decisions on the basis of expectations set up by prevailing social security arrangements. To violate these expectations may undermine the contractual basis of social security pension programs and diminish the widespread support that such programs have attracted in the past. But social security pension schemes have weaknesses, one clear example of which is the way they are affected by demographic change. Reform in this area, and in others, is manifestly desirable. Change must be gradual, however, to give people time to adjust. Because demographic pressures will not really begin to be felt until after the turn of the century, there is time for the necessary reforms to be phased in.

V. Summary and Conclusions

Expenditure on social security pensions is expected to grow rapidly between 1987 and the end of the first quarter of the twenty-first century, principally because of population aging. Demographic trends imply a substantial increase in the number of retired people as the baby-boom generation—born between 1945 and 1960—reaches retirement age. This generation is currently in the work force and is sharing the cost of a relatively modest pension burden. For the next 30 years or so, the net effect of having this large birth cohort move through the population age structure will be to contain the growth of social security tax rates. Thereafter, social security taxes will begin to escalate and in some countries may reach a level that, it is widely felt, would be unsupportable.

In this paper we have not attempted to explore the full range of equity and efficiency issues associated with demographic change and social

[28] Heller, Hemming, and Kohnert (1986) reported that payroll tax rates in Germany will have to rise by about 15 percentage points between 1980 and 2025 to pay for projected increases in government social expenditure, and that payroll taxes will reach about 43 percent. This figure is nearly double the corresponding social security tax rate. Note also that in Japan payroll tax rates are projected to increase by over 20 percentage points (with social security tax rates projected to increase by about 7 percentage points). In the United Kingdom payroll tax rates are projected to increase by about 6 percentage points, whereas in the United States the projected increase is only 3 percentage points.

security financing. Although these are important issues, they would take us into the areas of the distributional characteristics of alternative programs, the interaction of the social security system with tax or transfer systems, and the appropriate role of the public and private sectors in pension provision. Our purpose has been more modest: to examine the effect that some modifications to existing social security programs would have on future social security tax rates.

We have focused on four industrial countries in which policy developments are of particular interest (the Federal Republic of Germany, Japan, the United Kingdom, and the United States). Our analysis of each is for the most part based on a single, probably optimistic, demographic projection. Although, by historical standards, populations will not age particularly quickly between 1980 and 2025, the share of the elderly in the population of these countries will rise, on average, from 12.5 to 20.5 percent. It is assumed that social security is financed on a pay-as-you-go basis, with pensions initially fixed relative to average gross earnings. Demographic developments then govern the projections. Under such an assumption, social security tax rates will increase significantly in each country, but more so in Germany and Japan than in the United Kingdom and the United States.

A feature of pay-as-you-go financing, as reflected in these projections, is that the burden of adjustment to adverse demographic developments falls on the working population, whose tax rates adjust to pay for the benefits that the pension programs define. It is this feature that has led some observers to conclude that the implicit pension contract that exists between successive generations contains the seeds of its own destruction. One generation of workers will ultimately walk away from its obligation to provide the preceding generation with pensions. How can such an eventuality be avoided? This paper explores some possible solutions. One involves letting pensions automatically adjust as the population structure changes, in a way that apportions the adjustment costs equally between the working and retired populations. Fixing pensions relative to net earnings achieves this; however, the impact of such a switch on future tax rates is limited. Another possibility is to adjust retirement age, and in each of the four countries a two-year or, more significant, a five-year increase in pension age has a marked effect on tax rates. Within the framework developed in this paper, if expenditure growth is not controlled in one of these ways, then the replacement rate has to be reduced directly. The alternative is to let tax rates rise.

Having presented the basic model and results, we should emphasize that the exercise we have described is wholly mechanical. It does not point to the need for expenditure control, nor does it provide a guide to appropriate policy responses, although it *can* indicate how effective certain policies might prove. Presenting policy choices quite starkly—as the model does—and then trying to summarize actual policy responses so that they can be analyzed in terms of the model plainly does not do full justice to the reforms undertaken in the countries examined. Even though the model is not all-embracing, it does still embody the trade-offs facing the policymakers charged with controlling the growth of social security expenditure, and therefore the model provides a guide to the implications of choosing between broad alternative strategies. In this context, two concluding comments should be made.

By linking pensions to earnings and by equating increases in earnings and productivity, the possibility that economic growth will provide the means to support the retired has been ruled out. To the extent that pensions are not indexed to earnings but are instead designed to preserve pensioners' real income levels, economic growth can provide the means to support current pension arrangements. But this possibility does not make reform any less urgent; indeed, it compounds the problems. Our concern in this paper has been the costs (or risks) associated with demographic change. Because existing programs do not have any built-in capability to adjust in response to these costs (and risks), reform is needed. As we emphasized earlier, whatever adjustment is planned, preparations have to be made well in advance so that, if major structural changes are involved, people are given the time to make appropriate behavioral adjustments. Taking account of the costs (and risks) associated with future economic developments reinforces the need for advance preparation.

A final comment should be offered on the pay-as-you-go financing mechanism itself. We again emphasize that the choice between pay-as-you-go financing and funding depends on the respective effects of these arrangements on the real economy, as well as on aspects of monetary and fiscal management. A switch to funding may affect the ability of the economy to support a particular level of pension expenditure. Given the social security benefit structure, however, the switch cannot affect the required level of expenditure and, as a result, the resources transferred to the elderly. But this does not preclude the possibility that introducing an element of funding—either because it will contribute to capital accumulation or, more realistically, because it will endow a pay-as-you-go scheme with greater intergenerational fairness—will help accommodate demographic and economic developments in a way that secures the future of existing social security programs.

REFERENCES

Aaron, Henry J., "Social Security: Problems of Maturity," paper presented at the Fourth Congress of the International Institute of Public Finance, Madrid, August 1985 (Saarbrücken, Germany; forthcoming in congress proceedings).

———, "When Is a Burden Not a Burden? The Elderly in America," *The Brookings Review* (Washington), Vol. 4 (Summer 1986), pp. 17–24.

Aldrich, Jonathan, "The Earnings Replacement of Old-Age Benefits in 12 Countries, 1969–80," *Social Security Bulletin* (Washington), Vol. 45 (November 1982), pp. 3–11.

Cumming, Christine, "Social Security in Germany and the United Kingdom," *Federal Reserve Bank of New York Quarterly Review* (New York), Vol. 8 (Spring 1983), pp. 13–25.

Germany, Federal Republic of, *Haushaltsbegleitgesetz,* Sections 79 AVG and 1271 RVD (Bonn, December 22, 1984).

Heller, Peter S., Richard Hemming, and Peter W. Kohnert, *Aging and Social Expenditure in the Major Industrial Countries, 1980–2025,* Occasional Paper 47 (Washington: International Monetary Fund, September 1986).

Hemming, Richard, and John A. Kay, "The Costs of the State Earnings-Related Pension Scheme," *Economic Journal* (London), Vol. 92 (June 1982), pp. 300–19.

Holzmann, Robert, "Pension Reform: Sharing the Burden," *OECD Observer* (Paris), No. 138 (January 1986), pp. 3–10.

Kay, John A., "The Finance of Public Sector Pension Schemes," Panel Paper 20, in Bank of England Panel of Academic Consultants, *The Economics of Pension Arrangements* (London, March 1983).

Munnell, Alicia H., *The Future of Social Security,* Brookings Studies in Social Economics (Washington: The Brookings Institution, 1977).

Musgrave, Richard A., "A Reappraisal of Social Security Financing," in *Social Security Financing,* ed. by Felicity Skidmore (Cambridge, Massachusetts: MIT Press, 1981).

Organization for Economic Cooperation and Development, *OECD Demographic Trends, 1950–1990* (Paris, 1980).

———, *Social Expenditure, 1960–1990: Problems of Growth and Control* (Paris, 1985).

Social Security Amendments of 1983, P.L. 98-21 (Washington, April 1983).

Takayama, Noriyuki, "Japan," *The World Crisis in Social Security,* ed. by Jean-Jacques Rosa (San Francisco: Institute for Contemporary Studies, 1982; Paris: Bonnel, 1982).

Thompson, Lawrence H., "The Social Security Reform Debate," *Journal of Economic Literature* (Nashville, Tennessee), Vol. 21 (December 1983), pp. 1425–67.

United Kingdom, *National Insurance Fund: Long-Term Financial Estimates,*

Report by the Government Actuary on the First Quinquennial Review Under Section 137 of the Social Security Act 1975 (London: H.M. Stationery Office, 1982).

———, *Reform of Social Security: Programme for Action*, Cmnd. 9691 (London: H.M. Stationery Office, 1985).

United States, Department of Health and Human Services, Social Security Administration, Board of Trustees of the OASDI Trust Funds, *1985 Annual Report of the Old-Age, Survivors Insurance and Disability Insurance Trust Funds* (Washington: Government Printing Office, March 1985).

[26]

INCREASING INCOME TRANSFERS TO THE ELDERLY IMPLIED BY ZERO POPULATION GROWTH

By ROBERT CLARK*
North Carolina State University at Raleigh

The financial plight of America's aged population has been well documented in recent years. [Bixby, G. Thompson, U. S. Congress, 1968] While few people would deny the need to improve the standard of living of many elderly persons, the method of financing their transfer payments calls for constant scrutiny. In particular, the question of who bears the final incidence of these payments continues to command attention. The proportion of an average worker's income that is currently being transferred to finance support programs for the elderly is estimated to exceed 12 percent. If fertility rates continue at their current low levels, the magnitude of this compulsory transfer or support burden may be significantly higher in the future.

This paper develops a model through which the magnitude of the compulsory intergenerational transfer of income required by social and private assistance programs to the elderly can be appraised. Intergenerational transfers of income are defined as that portion of a current worker's income that is withdrawn to finance programs benefiting current retirees. To discover the aggregate size of this transfer, we examine first the amount of Social Security taxes that supports current retirement benefits; second, the transfers inherent in private pension plans; and finally, the transfer that occurs through other governmental taxing and expenditure decisions. Using this model, we then show the effect of the change in age structure that accompanies zero population growth on the size of each of these intergenerational transfers. We also examine the impact of changes in retirement policy, increases in replacement rates, and increases in pension coverage on the distribution of income in old age.

Of course, these are not the only intergenerational transfers that occur in our society. They do, however, represent the major compul-

* Assistant Professor of Economics and Business, North Carolina State University. This investigation was supported in part by NIH Training Grant No. HD00164 from the National Institute of Child Health and Human Development and by National Science Foundation Grant No. GI41002. I am grateful to Professors Juanita Kreps and J. S. Spengler for many helpful comments.

sory flow of income from workers to retirees. A complete model of intergenerational transfers would include: private financing of the retirement years of one's parents and charitable gifts that support the aged. On the other hand, the elderly give their assets to members of younger cohorts—voluntarily or perhaps involuntarily at death—through private transfers or through compulsory public transfers by means of gift and inheritance taxes. In addition, each cohort receives transfers of human capital, maintenance support in early life, and claims on public assets from its predecessors. Thus, there may be an implied social contract of the intergenerational transfer of income over the life cycle of each cohort. This paper analyzes only one phase of these intergenerational transfers and attempts to measure the potential increase as a percentage of a worker's income. The relevant political question may be how large can this transfer become without producing major objections to the transfer programs by workers.

I. THE MODEL

Through Social Security, expenditures financed by general governmental revenues and private pensions, society exacts an intergenerational transfer of income from current workers to retirees. Each worker contributes a certain percentage of his income each year to the support of the elderly, in return for which he expects to be similarly supported during his own retirement.[1] Assuming that there are n retired individuals in the economy and m workers, the system-wide transfer in any period can be represented by equation (1):[2]

$$\sum_{i=1}^{n} Tr_i \cdot A_i = \sum_{j=1}^{m} R_j \cdot Y_j \cdot W_j \qquad (1)$$

[1] In a different cultural context, the elderly might be supported through private channels by the extended family. Within the framework of this model, such private support would not be considered a compulsory transfer; however, in such a society, cultural and social pressure may be equally as demanding and certain as are federally imposed taxes in the United States.

[2] There may be a lag between the payments by workers and the receipt of benefits by the elderly. Such a lag should be short in the case of Social Security, but may be quite long for private pensions and general fund expenditures. Throughout this paper, however, we assume that the payment of taxes and contributions and the receipt of benefits occur in the same period.

where A_i = i^{th} retired individual receiving benefits,
Tr_i = the transfer (in dollars) received by A_i,
W_j = j^{th} worker,
R_j = proportion of W_j's income that goes to finance transfer payments, and
Y_j = W_j's total income which is equal to earnings plus any nonwage income that a worker may receive.[3]

The transfer ratio, R, can be divided into the following three effects: b_1 represents the percentage of a worker's income paid in Social Security taxes to finance benefit payments to the elderly; b_2 is the proportion of pension payments that is used to increase the benefits of current retirees rather than being placed in a trust fund for the individual worker; and b_3 is the percentage of a worker's structure that is transferred intergenerationally through the income tax structure and government spending on programs that primarily benefit the aged; hence, $R = b_1 + b_2 + b_3$. To discover the magnitude of R, we first examine the size of the transfer systems.

A. *The Social Security Transfer*

Funds are collected for Social Security benefits through payroll deductions of a certain percentage of income, T_1, and similar employer contributions, T_2. In 1976, T_1 and T_2 were both 5.85 percent of the first $15,300 of individual's earnings. To determine the magnitude of the intergenerational transfer for each worker we need to know what percentage of the payroll tax finances benefit to the aged, α_1 (as opposed to survivors and disability payments to younger individuals) and also, what portion of the employer's tax is borne by the worker, α_2. Our general formula for b_1 would be:

$$b_1 = \alpha_1 [T_1 + \alpha_2 T_2] (Y_0 \div Y), \quad (2)$$

where Y_0 represents that portion of a worker's total income that is subject to the payroll tax. Currently, the worker who has no nonwage income and whose earnings are $15,300 or less (approximately the median income for the nation) pays the maximum percentage of his

[3]Thus the transfer is shown as a percentage of an individual's observable income, Y_j. This does not include income that is kept from the worker to finance the employer Social Security tax, private pensions, other social insurance programs and other fringe benefits. Therefore, Y_j is not an accurate measure of a worker's "real" income and R would overstate the transfer as a percentage of "real" income.

wages in payroll taxes, whereas the one whose earnings are above the median pays a lower payroll tax rate.

The Social Security Administration and other investigators have estimated that α_1 is approximately 80 percent of revenues derived from the payroll tax.[4] The final incidence of the employer portion of the payroll tax has long been debated and is still subject to review. However, many researchers believe that the employee bears the entire burden of this tax [Brittain, Ch. II, III], *i.e.,* $\alpha_2 = 1$. For the average American described above, Y_0 is approximately equal to Y and therefore,

$$b_1 \cong .8\ [.0585 + 1\ (.0585)] \cdot (Y/Y)$$
$$= .0936 = 9.36\%.$$

Of course, lower estimates of the portion of the employer tax borne by the worker would decrease the transfer. For example $\alpha_2 = 0$ implies $b_1 = 4.68$ percent while an $\alpha_2 = .5$ would result in a transfer of 7.02 percent. By incorporating the above assumptions, including $\alpha_2 = 1$ we estimate that the intergenerational transfer of income through the Social Security System is approximately 9 percent of an average worker's income.

B. *Private Pensions*

While Social Security payments are almost universal, contributions to pension funds cover only about 50 percent of the private nonfarm, civilian workforce. If a worker is not in a job covered by a pension system, neither he nor his employer makes a payment in support of current pensioners. However, a portion of the contributions of those workers currently covered by a pension plan may be transferred to retired workers. We postulate the following equations to estimate the value of this intergenerational transfer as a percentage of a worker's

[4] While discussing the related problem of whether an individual worker receives benefits equal to his lifetime payments, Robert Myers, then chief actuary for the Social Security Administration, stated "about 20 percent of the OASDI contributions should be eliminated because the individual has had certain survivor benefit protection before attaining retirement age." [U. S. Congress, 1967, p. 331] Thus, the remaining 80 percent of tax payments go to finance current retirement benefits. The present distribution of benefits by type of recipient is shown in Board of Trustees. [OASDI Funds, pp. 20-21, 33] To the extent that health insurance benefits go almost exclusively to the elderly, our estimate of the total payment may underestimate the intergenerational transfer of this system.

wage income.

$$b_2 = s\ [\lambda \cdot V \cdot P + (1\text{-}\lambda \cdot r \cdot P],\qquad (4)$$

where s = the percentage of pension payments that are borne by employees (assumed to be 1),
λ = the probability of termination,
r = proportion of contributions that fund current retirement benefits; *i.e.*, do not fund future benefits for current workers,
P = percentage of employee compensation that goes for pension contributions, and
V = 1 — (the proportion of benefits that are vested).

Although the recent pension reform bill attempts to protect the rights of workers, millions of employees within pension systems still will have no vested right to future benefits. Paul Douglas estimated in the early 1960s that "only from one-third to one-half of those ostensibly covered, and for whom contributions were made, will actually benefit at journey's end." [Douglas, p. iii][5] Thus, loss of job in many cases means that the portion of the terminated worker's salary that was contributed to the pension fund is lost to him forever. Full vesting, however, implies that $V = 0$ and that loss of job results in no transfer because the benefits accrued will still be paid to the worker upon retirement. To a certain extent, the fact that terminated workers lose benefits makes it possible to pay higher benefits to current pensioners; an intergenerational transfer from one set of workers to retirees occurs.

The crucial variable for many workers is λ, the probability of layoff or voluntary job change. For each worker, λ is a function of age, tenure, position in the firm, and market conditions. It does not seem unreasonable to hypothesize that for young workers the cumulative probability of leaving their current job prior to vesting is very near 1, perhaps .9. If this is true for all young workers, then 90 percent of the pension contributions of the "average" young worker can be viewed as a potential intergenerational transfer through this mechanism. *Ex post*, of course, the worker either retained his job or left

[5] Verifying the loss of benefits, the February 1973 Interim Report on Pension Reform by the State Subcommittee on Labor stated ". . . 92 percent of all participants who left plans which required 11 or more years of service for vesting and 73 percent of all participants in plan with 10 years or less for vesting . . . did not qualify for benefits."

his employer, making λ either one or zero.[6]

Even if the worker remains on the job and receives full vesting, some portion of his pension contributions, r, may be transferred to current retirees. This occurs in part because as benefits are raised, retirement age is lowered, or as a new plan is initiated and past service credited, unfunded benefits are created. Those workers and retirees who benefit from expansion of pension plans are supported by the current workforce. In other words, current workers contribute a greater percentage of their income than the present benefit schedules require for their pensions in order to fund benefits now being paid.[7]

In those companies which have pension plans, contributions range from 1.8 percent to 11.9 percent of total compensation with an average of around 4 percent. [U. S. Senate, 1973, p. 3] Thus, for the young worker with no vesting covered by an average pension plan, the expected value of b_2 ranges between 3 percent ($r = 0$) and 4 percent ($r = 1$). Thus, over 3 percent of this worker's income may be being transferred to the company's retirees through the pension system, and for any individual worker, the transfers would range between zero and a potential maximum of almost 12 percent.

C. *Governmental Activities*

The final transfer mechanism is the general fund expenditures which are financed primarily by income and sales taxes. Assume that the following conditions describe the economy: 1) workers pay a higher percentage of their income in taxes than do retirees; 2) due to programs designed for the elderly and other programs aimed at conditions prevalent among the elderly (poverty for example), the aged population receives a net benefit greater than could be financed by its own tax revenues. Under these conditions, there would be an intergenerational transfer of income by general fiscal policies, even without the Social Security System. Thus, we assert that b_3 is positive, but its magnitude remains undefined; any estimate of the size of

[6] Employers rely on the loss of benefits of workers who leave their company to lower the costs of their pension system. This, in part, explains the strong lobbying efforts of employer associations against the recent pension reform legislation and specifically the clauses lowering the requirements for vesting and the proposed portability of pension credits.

[7] Professor J. J. Spengler argues that $r \leqq 1$ for the additional reason that pension funds are usually invested in a manner that makes the size of the fund dependent on current market conditions, *i.e.*, stock market has a prolonged decline, pension funds decrease, thus requiring greater contributions to support present benefit levels.

the intergenerational transfer based on $b_1 + b_2$ would, therefore, underestimate the value of R. It should be noted that the abolition of the Social Security tax in favor of a financing of benefits from the general fund would represent an increase in b_3 while b_1 would become zero. The size of the intergenerational transfer in the economy would remain the same but the incidence would be shifted from low to middle and high income recipients.

Our model indicates that the current intergenerational transfer of income from the average young worker whose full income is subject to the Social Security tax and who is covered by an average private pension plan is greater than 12 percent: R = 9.36 percent due to payroll tax; more than 3 percent is paid under a private pension system; and some positive level of tax liability is associated with general governmental spending on behalf of retirees.

II. TRENDS IN SOCIAL SECURITY AND PENSION PAYMENTS

The Social Security System operates on a pay-as-you-go basis—payroll tax revenues collected from workers are paid to retirees in benefits. This can be illustrated by using equation (5), similar to equation (1).

$$\sum_{i=1}^{n} SS_{it} \cdot A_{it} = \sum_{j=1}^{m} (b_1 \cdot Y_{jt}) \cdot W_{jt}, \tag{5}$$

where SS_{it} = Social Security benefit to the ith retiree in period t,
A_{it} = the ith retiree,
b_1 = the tax rate on the jth worker in period t,
Y_{jt} = income of the jth worker, and
W_{jt} = the jth worker.

This equation shows that workers contribute different portions of their incomes to support retirees, but the sum of the contributions is roughly the equivalent of total benefits paid in any year. In actual practice, revenues may not exactly equal payments in any one year. Thus, the relatively small trust fund may be enlarged or depleted from year to year.

To simplify projections of payroll tax rates, we make the following assumptions: 1) all retirees receive the same benefit; 2) all workers earn the per capita income in the income; 3) the economy grows at a constant rate, g; *i.e.*, $Y_2 = Y_1 \cdot 1{+}g$). These assumptions allow us to write equation (5) in the following form:

$$SS_t \cdot A_t = (b_{1,t} \cdot Y_t) \cdot W_t. \tag{6}$$

Using equation (6), it can be shown that a country with a growing population (W_t increasing faster than A_t), an expanding economy, or a combination of both of these factors could continually raise the benefit level to its retirees without increasing the tax rate. Paul Samuelson describes such a growing economy as "the greatest Ponzi game ever contrived," since its growth, both economic and demographic, makes possible ever-increasing retirement benefits. [Samuelson, p. 88]

An often used measure of the economic adequacy of pension plans is the replacement ratio, *i.e.*, the benefit paid to a retiree divided by his preretirement income. Let $B_{It} = \frac{SS_{It}}{Y_{It-1}}$ represent the replacement ratio for the ith individual retiring in time t. Then employing the above assumptions and equation (6), we can indicate potential changes in the replacement ratio for given changes in population and the tax rate.

The average replacement ratio would be:

$$B_t = \frac{SS_t}{Y_{t-1}}$$

Employing our assumption of a constant rate of economic growth we can show that

$$B_t = b_{1,t} \cdot (\frac{W_t}{A_t}) \cdot (1 + g). \tag{7}$$

Although benefits have increased greatly, steady increases in the replacement ratio have not occurred over the twenty-year period, 1952 to 1972. Table 1 shows replacement ratios for six earnings histories. These ratios are calculated by comparing the Social Security benefit of a 65-year-old person applying for initial retirement benefits in a given year, with his or her previous year's earnings. These replacement ratios fluctuate from year to year but have exhibited no trend over the twenty-year period. In support of this premise, Feldstein finds that the "ratio of annual benefits for retired workers (excluding dependent's benefits) to per capita disposable income has varied without any trend around a mean level of 0.41." [Feldstein, p. 911]

With a growing population, the model implies that a constant replacement ratio could be financed by a constant or falling tax rate. But in fact, the tax rate has risen steadily since 1950. Table 2 indicates the effective tax rate on a worker with median earnings from wages and salaries, for selected years. Thus, the maintenance of a replacement ratio that has fluctuated around a constant mean has required a rising tax rate, with intergenerational transfers increasing from 2.1 percent in 1950 to approximately 9.4 percent in 1974.

From these estimates, it appears that the average worker has paid a steadily rising portion of his income to finance retirement benefits that have remained a constant fraction of wages. Several changes in the system have necessitated higher taxes. First, over the years new groups (such as farmers and domestic workers) have become eligible for benefits. Second, there have been substantial increases in the

TABLE 1

SOCIAL SECURITY BENEFITS (PRIMARY INSURANCE AMOUNTS) AS A PERCENTAGE OF EARNINGS IN YEAR PRIOR TO RETIREMENT, SIX EARNINGS HISTORIES, SINGLE MAN 65 YEARS OLD, 1952-72

Retirement date (January 1)	Low earnings model	Retail trade	Services	Manufacturing	All private industry	Construction
1952	38	30	29	22	23	19
1953	42	36	34	28	29	24
1954	41	35	33	28	28	23
1955	44	39	36	32	32	26
1956	43	38	36	31	31	26
1957	42	37	35	31	31	26
1958	41	37	34	30	30	25
1959	43	38	36	32	31	26
1960	41	37	35	31	30	25
1961	40	36	34	31	30	24
1962	39	36	33	30	29	24
1963	38	35	32	29	29	23
1964	37	35	31	28	28	22
1965	38	36	32	29	29	23
1966	37	35	31	28	28	22
1967	36	35	30	27	27	21
1968	35	34	29	27	26	21
1969	38	37	31	29	28	22
1970	43	40	34	32	31	24
1971	46	43	36	35	33	25
1972	45	42	34	34	32	24

Source: Peter Henle, "Trends in Retirement Benefits Related to Earnings," *Monthly Labor Review*, June 1972.

TABLE 2

AVERAGE TAX RATE ON WORKER EARNING THE MEDIAN INCOME FOR VARIOUS YEARS

Year	Median income of families	Statutory income ceiling subject to tax	Tax rate (rate by each of the employer and employee)	Tax rate financing retirement benefits as a percentage of total compensation[a]
	(dollars)		(percent)	
1950	3,319	3,000	1.5	2.17
1951	3,709	3,600	1.5	2.33
1955	4,421	4,200	2.0	3.04
1959	5,417	4,800	2.0	2.84
1960	5,620	4,800	3.0	4.1
1965	6,957	4,800	3.625	4.03
1966	7,500	6,600	3.625[b]	5.1
1967	7,974	6,600	4.40	5.83
1968	8,632	7,800	4.40	6.36
1969	9,433	7,800	4.40	5.82
1970	9,867	7,800	4.40	5.57
1971	10,285	7,800	5.2	6.31
1972	11,116	9,000	5.2	6.74
1973	12,051	10,800	5.85	8.4
1974	12,835	13,200	5.85	9.36
1975	•	14,100	5.85	9.36•

[a] Assumes worker bears incidence of both employer and employee tax and that 80 percent of funds finance retirement benefits.

[b] Health insurance was added to the Old-Age, Survivors, and Disability Insurance System (OASDI) in 1966 which resulted in a new allocation of the funds between OASI, DI and now HI.

• If the median income for 1975 is less than $14,100, the effective tax rate will be 9.36 percent.

Source: Bureau of the Census, Current Population Reports, *Money Income in 1973 of Families and Persons in the United States,* Series P-60, No. 97, p. 25.

minimum benefits. Moreover, earnings of the self-employed are taxed at only three-fourths the rate of employers; yet they are eligible for similar benefits. Finally, the lowering of the retirement age has had considerable impact on the system. [Eckstein]

Since 1940, the number of workers covered by private pension plans has increased from four million to a 1973 level of over 30 million. During this same period, assets of these funds have grown from $2.4 billion to $151.8 billion, with annual employer contributions now exceeding $15 billion. Employer and employee contributions for retirement plans as a percentage of wage and salaries in private industry have increased from 1.67 percent in 1950 (84 percent of total paid directly by the employer) to 3.7 percent in 1971 (91 percent of total paid directly by the employer). [Koladrubetz] This growth in pensions makes it more likely that a worker in the private sector will make an intergenerational transfer of income to retirees. In addition, the magnitude of his contributions has risen in accordance with the continued rise in the benefits and in the replacement rate. [See Table 3]

III. PROJECTIONS OF THE FUTURE

It is important to consider the probable changes in the Social Security tax rate and in private pension contributions that may ensue under conditions of zero population growth. To illustrate the changes in the age structure of the population, we use the Bureau of the

TABLE 3

DISTRIBUTION OF REPLACEMENT RATES FOR 28 PRIVATE PENSION PLANS, 1953 AND 1969

Item	Low-earnings worker		Average-earnings worker		High-earnings worker	
	1953	1969	1953	1969	1953	1969
			(dollars)			
Previous year's earnings	2,400	4,200	3,600	6,600	6,600	12,000
Number of plans with replacement rates (percent):						
Under 15	9	—	13	3	18	14
15-24	8	10	12	19	7	8
25-34	7	10	2	5	3	4
35 or more	4	8	1	1	—	2
Median replacement rates	19	28	15	21	10	15

Source: Peter Henle, "Trends in Retirement Benefits Relative to Earnings," *Monthly Labor Review*, June 1972.

Census's population series W, without immigration. The assumption of this series is that the fertility rate drops immediately to the replacement rate (2.11 births per woman) and remains there. [Bureau of Census, 1972] For the purpose of making projections, we will assume that all individuals aged 20-64 are productive workers while everyone over age 65 is retired.[8]

If we allow $S_t = \frac{A_t}{W_t}$, that is, the ratio of elderly retirees to current workers, equation 7 becomes

$$B = \frac{b_{1t}}{S_t} \cdot (1 + g). \tag{8}$$

Now, if we assume a constant replacement rate, and a constant rate of growth in income, changes in age structure will necessitate changes in the tax rate. Using series W, S = .188 in 1970 if 65 is the retirement age and people enter the labor force at age 20, if retirement age and age of entry remain constant, S will equal .282 in 2050, the year a stable population is reached. This would require an increase of 50 percent in the Social Security tax, due solely to changes in the age structure in 2050; no future increases in the transfer rate would be required under our assumptions.

During the twentieth century, however, there has been a steady decline in retirement age. If the retirement age continues in its course—dropping to age 60 by 2050 for example—more than a two-fold increase will be needed in b_1 during this 80-year period. If, by the middle of the next century, the retirement age has fallen to 55, S = .601 and the payroll tax would have to be 3.2 times its present level to maintain the same replacement rate. If, however, the retirement age rises—as some researchers are projecting—with the advent of a stable population, the ratio of retirees to the working population would not rise as significantly. In fact, if the retirement age were raised to 70, S would equal .180 and b_1 could be slightly reduced. Table 4 shows the implied tax rates at several points in time under differing retirement ages. To the extent that the age of entry is rising, these estimates understate the future need for higher taxes.

The replacement ratio is a key variable in determining the required level of financing for the Social Security System. Table 1 shows that replacement rates have remained relatively stable during the last 20

[8] This assumption could be relaxed to allow for differential patterns of labor force participation. However, as long as participation rates do not change, the percentage increases in the transfer rate would remain unchanged. Upward shifts in market activity rates—say, increased female participation—lower the required tax burden while decreases—for example, decline in the labor force participation rate of married males—will increase the transfer necessary to sustain the system.

TABLE 4

INCREASE IN TAX RATE UNDER VARYING RETIREMENT PATTERNS AND REPLACEMENT RATIOS

Retirement age	1985 S	1985 b_t[a]	1985 b_t^{I}[b]	1985 b_t^{II}[c]	2000 S	2000 b_t	2000 b_t^{I}	2000 b_t^{II}	2025 S	2025 b_t	2025 b_t^{I}	2025 b_t^{II}	2050 S	2050 b_t	2050 b_t^{I}	2050 b_t^{II}
		(percent)				(percent)				(percent)				(percent)		
55	.418	222	333	444	.400	213	319	426	.592	315	473	630	.602	320	480	640
60	.294	156	234	312	.274	146	219	292	.422	225	338	450	.423	225	338	450
65	.192	102	153	204	.192	102	153	204	.274	146	219	292	.282	150	225	300
70	.119	63	94.5	126	.128	68	102	136	.161	86	129	172	.174	93	140	186

[a] b_t represents the tax rate necessary in year t as a percentage of b_1 in 1970 holding the replacement rate constant.

[b] b_t^{I} represents the tax rate necessary in year t as a percentage of b_1 in 1970 with a 50 percent increase in the replacement ratio; *i.e.*, if B = .4 in 1970, B of the appropriate year would be .6.

[c] b_t^{II} represents the tax rate necessary in year t as a percentage of b_1 in 1970 with a 100 percent increase in the replacement rate.

years but have varied between 20 percent and 40 percent, depending on occupational classification. Are these replacement rates adequate?

One's concept of adequacy of benefits depends on what he views as the function of the social insurance system. Should benefits enable retirees to eke out a minimum subsistence? To maintain a modest standard of living? Or to maintain the same standard of living that they enjoyed just prior to retirement? Present benefits tend towards levels that permit a minimum subsistence. James Schulz has estimated that a replacement level of 60-65 percent would be needed to enable a retired couple to maintain the same standard of living in retirement as existed just prior to retirement. He arrived at this rate by lowering preretirement income by 13.5 percent, the difference between expenditure needs (as estimated by the Bureau of Labor Statistics) of a childless couple aged 55-64 and a similar couple aged 65 or more. This income level was then reduced by lower tax burdens and an end to the need to save for retirement. [Schulz, p. 41] He then recommends that the minimum guarantee should be about 55 percent. [Schulz, p. 231]

Schulz also makes an international comparison of replacement rates as shown in Table 5. These are replacement levels under existing pension regulations that will be provided to an "average" worker who begins work in 1960 and retires in the year 2000. The three European countries in Table 5 have especially high replacement rates, ranging from 55 percent to 84 percent. In comparison with these countries, he finds the United States falls short of providing relative benefit levels. "It is projected, for example, that in 1980 the overwhelming proportion of couples in the United States will have pensions that

TABLE 5

REPLACEMENT CHARACTERISTICS FOR THE AVERAGE WORKER RETIRING IN THE YEAR 2000 OF OLD AGE PENSION PROGRAMS IN VARIOUS COUNTRIES UNDER DIFFERENT RATES OF GROWTH

	Percent of Final Earnings	
Country	3 Percent Annual Growth in Wages	5 Percent Annual Growth in Wages
Sweden	69	55
Germany	72	81
Belgium	73	84
Canada	39	39

Source: James Schulz, *et al.*, *Providing Adequate Retirement Income* (The University Press of New England: Hanover, New Hampshire, 1974), p. 212.

represent less than half their pre-retirement average earnings." [Schulz, p. 213]

The cost to the worker of raising the replacement ratios to these higher standards would, in our model, be an equal percentage increase in the tax rate for a constant age distribution.

$$\text{Recall that } B = \frac{b_1}{S} \cdot (1+g).$$

If the replacement ratio, B, is doubled with S and g constant, the transfer rate b_1 must also be doubled. Thus, if the present replacement rate is approximately .4, taxes would have to rise by 50 percent to raise this rate to .6 and by 100 percent to allow a replacement rate of .8. Table 4 shows the percentage tax increase necessary to support these higher replacement rates at various years prior to the attainment of a stable population. Our model projects that maintaining a constant replacement ratio and holding the retirement age at 65 would entail an increase in the tax rate to 17.55 percent by 2050. In our framework, this implies an intergenerational transfer of more than 14.04 percent. Any decline in the retirement age or increase in the replacement rate will entail an even greater transfer burden.

The Social Security Administration (SSA) has made its own long-range projections, assuming that benefits will be adjusted to reflect increases in the Consumer Price Index (CPI) while the taxable earnings base will rise in accordance with the increase in average incomes. Adopting a fertility rate similar to the one we used earlier, SSA estimated that with an annual increase of 3 percent in the CPI and 5 percent in average earnings "the annual costs of Old-Age, Survivors, and Disability Insurance System is projected to increase slowly throughout the remainder of this century and after the turn of the century it will increase rapidly until leveling at about 17-18 percent of taxable payroll after the year 2025." [Board of Trustees, OASDI Funds, p. 63]

The automatic adjustment provisions included in the 1972 and 1973 amendments to the Social Security Act provide that the computational formula used to calculate the Primary Insurance Amount for each worker is adjusted to keep up with increases in the CPI and that the taxable earnings base be adjusted to keep up with increases in average earnings. This type of automatic adjustment procedure has the effect of raising a worker's potential benefits because of both the adjustment to the benefit formula and the increases in his credited earnings. He is therefore doubly compensated for inflation and this may in turn have the effect of raising replacement rates over time.

An annual increase of 3 percent in the CPI combined with a 5 percent growth in average earnings would result in an increase in the replacement ratio of a male earning the median wage from .425 in 1974 to .515 in 2045. [Thompson, p. 25] A higher inflation rate would increase the replacement ratio while greater growth in earnings would lower it.[9] Since these projections do not include costs for Health Insurance, they underestimate the total payroll tax for OASDHI. It would thus appear that even with our minimum assumptions, the projected intergenerational transfer of approximately 14 percent in 2050 (through the Social Security System) understates the probable magnitude of the transfer.

The trend in the size of the transfer associated with the private pension system is more difficult to analyze.[10] If unfunded benefits are increased by lowering retirement age and/or increasing benefits, then the portion of total compensation going to pension contributions will continue to rise. Since current workers must pay for these unfunded benefits, the size of the intergenerational transfer would grow. Recent pension reforms, including early vesting, decrease the probability of older workers losing all their pension contributions. For young workers, however, contributions still imply lower wages and a relatively high probability of losing all contributions through the loss of job when no vested rights are held. In addition, the trend toward an increase in the proportion of firms adopting pension plans increases the probability of a worker making contributions to such plans. The long-term effects of the 1974 pension reform law on the growth in coverage of pension plans are unknown. However, tentative first reports indicate an increase in the termination of plans and a decrease in the number of new plans since the passage of the act. ["Pension Reform," pp. 73-74]

[9] Thompson [p. 33] shows that a 1 percent annual growth in real wages combined with a 3 percent increase in prices would raise the replacement ratio to .743 in 2045 and require a combined employer-employee tax rate of 26.74 percent. However, if real wages and the CPI both rose at an annual rate of 2 percent, the replacement ratio would fall slightly to .416 and the required combined tax rate would be 14.95 percent in 2045.

[10] The combination of inflationary pressures on retirement benefits and a declining stock market have sent pension costs skyrocketing. For recent evidence on the surging costs and their relationship to profits and net equity of individual firms, see Faltermayer [p. 21].

Growing concern over poverty and other social problems has stimulated increased federal and state expenditures that may entail intergenerational transfers. Appropriations for social services have continued their upward spiral in recent years even in the presence of calls for controlling government spending to fight inflationary pressures in the economy. In a society where the changing age structure implies an increase in the percentage of older citizens, political pressures may mount to reorder spending priorities to provide even greater assistance to the elderly. Therefore, the transfer of income through general governmental revenues may also be rising as we approach a stable population.

In summary, we find that a significant portion of a worker's income is compulsorily transferred to elderly citizens. For the average worker covered by a private pension, we estimate that his transfer currently may represent over 12 percent of his income. The magnitude of the transfer has risen over threefold since the early 1950s. All of our projections indicate that the movement toward zero population growth will require even greater transfers of income to support the elderly, with the Social Security System being forced to bear much of the burden.

REFERENCES

Bixby, Lenore. "Income of People Aged 65 and Older: Overview from 1968 Survey of the Aged," *Social Security Bulletin*, 33, No. 4 (1970), pp. 3-34.

Brittain, John, *The Payroll Tax for Social Security*, Washington, D. C., 1974.

Ceccarelli, Jane, and Skolnick, Alfred. "Wage Replacement Rates Under the OASDHI Retirement Provisions," *Research and Statistical Note No. 18*, Department of Health, Education and Welfare, Washington, D. C., 1973.

Douglas, Paul. "Introduction," in *The Future of Private Pensions*, by Merton Bernstein, London, 1964.

Eckstein, Otto. "Financing the System of Social Insurance," in *The American System of Social Insurance*, edited by William Bowen *et al.*, New York, 1968.

Faltermayer, Edmund. "A Steeper Climb Up Pension Mountain," *Fortune*, Jan. 1975.

Feldstein, Martin. "Social Security, Induced Retirement, and Aggregate Capital Accumulation," *J. of Polit. Econ.*, Sept.-Oct. 1974.

Henle, Peter. "Trends in Retirement Benefits Related to Earnings," *Monthly Lab. Rev.*, June 1972.

Kolodrubetz, Walter. "Employer-Benefit Plans, 1971," *Social Security Bulletin*, April 1973.

Samuelson, Paul. "On Social Security," *Newsweek*, 13 February 1967.

Schulz, James, *et al. Providing Adequate Retirement Income*, Hanover, New Hampshire, 1974.

Thompson, Gayle. "Income of the Aged Population: 1971 Money Income and Changes from 1967," *Research and Statistical Note No. 14*, Social Security Administration, Office of Research and Statistics, Washington, D. C., 1973.

Thompson, Lawrence. *An Analysis of the Factors Currently Determining Benefit Level Adjustments in the Social Security Retirement Program*, Technical Analysis Paper No. 1, Department of Health, Education and Welfare, Washington, D. C., 1974.

Board of Trustees of the Federal Old-Age and Survivors Insurance and Disability Insurance Trust Funds. *1974 Annual Report of the Board of Trustees of the Federal Old-Age and Survivors Insurance and Disability Insurance Trust Funds*, Washington, D. C., 1974.

"Pension Reform — A 'Boom' That's Backfiring for Many," *U. S. News and World Report*, 16 June 1975.

U. S. Bureau of the Census. "Illustrative Population Projections for the United States: The Demographic Effects of Alternative Paths to Zero Growth," *Current Population Reports*, Series P-25, No. 480, Washington, D. C., 1972.

———. "Money Income in 1973 of Families and Persons in the United States," *Current Population Reports*, Series P-60, No. 97, Washington, D. C., 1974.

U. S. Congress, House Committee on Ways and Means. *President's Proposals for Revision in the Social Security System*, 90th Congress, 1st Session, Hearings, Part I, Washington, D. C., 1967.

U. S. Congress, Joint Economic Committee. *Old Age Income Assurance*, 90th Congress, 1st Session, Washington, D. C., 1968.

U. S. Senate, Subcommittee on Labor of the Committee on Labor and Public Welware. *Study of the Cost of Mandatory Vesting Provisions for Private Pension Plans*, Washington, D. C., 1973.

"When Pension Liabilities Damper Profits," *Business Week*, 16 June 1975.

[27]

Population Age Structure and the Size of Social Security*

JOHN A. TURNER
U.S. Department of Labor
Washington, D.C.

I. Introduction

In 1980, 35 million beneficiaries were receiving social security benefits at year-end and 115 million workers paid social security payroll taxes. The old-age dependency ratio is projected to increase from the current level of roughly 30 retirees per 100 workers to more than 50 retirees per 100 workers when the baby-boom generation is retired. With an increase in dependency of this magnitude, large increases in the payroll tax rate or large decreases in the benefit level (relative to the earnings of workers) must occur to maintain the solvency of the system. How will this question of intergenerational equity—payroll tax rate increases versus relative benefit level decreases—be resolved?

A number of models have been developed to explain the existence and size of the social security system.[1] The Samuelson [18] and Aaron [1] overlapping generations model indicates that when the growth rate of population and per capita earnings exceeds the real interest rate, at least one generation can be made better off (with none worse off) by a pay-as-you-go social security system.

In a more general framework, rate of return considerations are only one aspect of the demand for social security. Portfolio theory suggests that social security wealth may be held to diversity risk in retirement income [13]. Social security may be a means by which the older generation receives a return on its investment in the human capital of the younger generation [16]. Social security could be a form of "Depression bonds" by which a generation is compensated for an income loss suffered earlier in life [12]. These models, which focus on intertemporal price and income variables, have provided little guidance in analyzing the actual financing of social security.

Voting models are a second type of model that has been used to explain the size of social security. In a democracy, social security expenditures are affected by the preferences of voters as politicians attempt to maximize their probability of being elected. Voting

* I am indebted to Gary Becker, Tahitha Doescher, Richard Ippolito, participants at seminars at Vanderbilt University and the U.S. Department of Labor, and to an anonymous referee for helpful comments. Lori Foster has provided research assistance.

1. See Hagens [12] for a brief review of several models not discussed here. Aaron [2] has estimated regressions for aggregate old age benefits using cross-country data. Parsons [15] empirically examines determinants of old-age benefits using state data for 1934 and 1940.

models generally assume that voters selfishly maximize their own utility with the consumption of others not being an argument of their utility functions. These models predict that the larger is the beneficiary population, the higher is the payroll tax rate and the higher is total benefits [6]. Their implications for changes in the average benefit level have not been as clearly drawn, but it is generally assumed that they predict that the average benefit level will also increase. Neither the voting models nor the intertemporal models have led to empirical testing.

Myopic saving behavior provides another rationalization for a social security system [10]. This type of model assumes that at least some individuals do not save sufficiently to provide for their retirement. Perhaps because of altruism, the government provides old-age benefits for these myopic savers.

This paper uses a general overlapping generations model to analyze social security. Rather than focusing on intertemporal price and income considerations, however, the paper focuses on the effect of contemporaneous (same period) prices and income. The analysis shows that the old-age dependency ratio acts as a shadow price for old-age benefits. With this new shadow price, the equilibrium price and quantity of social security benefits and the level of the payroll tax rate are determined in a demand-supply framework with individual utility maximization. Three explicit demand functions (intergenerational contracts) are analyzed. The model is tested using time series data for the social security Old-Age and Survivors (OASI) program.

Intertemporal price and income effects suggested by earlier research can be incorporated in the model. Their treatment elsewhere, plus the failure of that literature to lead to empirical testing (perhaps because of the difficulty in measuring the intertemporal variables), suggests that in the initial development of the model for empirical testing they should be excluded. Myopia could readily be incorporated as a reason for making intergenerational transfers and the extent of transfers so motivated would presumably be affected by the shadow prices considered here.

A voting model could easily be developed producing implications consistent with those of this model. Nevertheless, the implications of this model differ to some extent from those of standard voting models. While voting models are commonly assumed to imply increases in average benefits with a larger old-age population, this model shows that the shadow price of benefits increases with the size of the old-age population, suggesting that average benefits would fall. In the empirical section, the old-age population is seen to have a negative effect on average social security benefits.

Most intergenerational transfers to old-age retirees are made publicly through social security, but before the social security legislation was enacted in the 1930s most of these transfers were made privately. The question of why intergenerational transfers to old-age retirees are now primarily made publicly rather than privately underlies the research cited earlier as well as research on social security's effects on labor supply and saving. This paper accepts the presence of a public social security program as given, and analyzes the effect of marginal changes in income and prices on the size of that program.

The question of the size of social security is an important aspect of the general question of the size of government transfer and subsidy programs and of the aggregate size of government. The theoretical model developed here is generally applicable for analyzing the size of government programs with distinct beneficiaries: the shadow price of government programs is the ratio of beneficiaries to taxpayers.

II. The Age Structure, Shadow Prices, and Intergenerational Transfers

The Model

In setting future social security benefit levels and payroll tax rates, policy makers must forecast various economic and demographic variables. To simplify the analysis, policy makers are assumed to forecast accurately, to react without lag to contemporaneous variables, and to carry out the desires of the populace.

It is assumed that the individual's labor supply is fixed. This assumption rules out distortionary effects on labor supply while young or on the retirement decision when old. Such distortions may affect the optimal level of social security benefits. Likewise, it is assumed that social security does not distort the consumption-savings decision. While welfare cost considerations may affect the optimal size of social security [10], the present analysis focuses on price effects associated with the age structure of the population.

The model presented here is a version of the overlapping generations model developed by Samuelson [18], Diamond [8], Barro [3] and others. Each individual lives three periods, which will be distinguished by the superscripts y (young), v (working), and o (old). Generations are numbered consecutively beginning with the generation which is currently old (subscript 1), followed by the current working generation (subscript 2), followed by the current young generation (subscript 3). Each of the N_1 members of the old generation is retired and receives social security benefits B_1. Each of the N_2 members of the working generation inelastically supplies L_2 hours of labor at a wage rate of w_2. Each of the N_3 members of the younger generation receives transfer payments D_3. It is assumed that all individuals are identical in terms of tastes. Asset holdings A take the form of equity capital K. The rate of return on assets is denoted by r and is assumed to be paid once per period. A member of the ith generation holds A_i^v assets while working which he consumes during his retirement period. For simplicity, it is assumed that there are no net bequests[2] and that all net intergenerational transfers are made *inter vivos* by the working generation. It is assumed that an individual's social security benefits received while old are independent of his own contribution while young.[3]

Using the letter c to denote consumption, and assuming that consumption, receipt of interest income, and receipt of wage payments occur at the start of the period, the budget equations for an individual of generation 2 during his young, working, and old periods are respectively

$$c_2^y = D_2 \tag{1}$$

$$L_2 w_2 = c_2^v + (1-r)A_2^v + p_{B1}B_1 + p_{D3}D_3 \tag{2}$$

$$c_2^o = A_2^v + B_2 . \tag{3}$$

The individual receives transfers D_2 when young which are assumed to be totally con-

2. "Gross" bequests can occur in this model through the reduction in the level of social security benefits received.

3. Feldstein [11] has argued that social security may reduce the capital stock. Barro [3] has countered that this would not occur because the older generation would leave larger benefits rather than consuming more when benefits rose.

sumed.[4] The individual during his working period allocates his earnings $L_2 w_2$ between consumption c_2^y, saving $(1 - r) A_2^y$, social security transfers $p_{B1} B_1$, and transfers to youth $P_{D2} D_2$. The price of the consumption good is the numeraire, and p_{B1} and P_{D3} are the shadow prices to the working generation of providing an additional dollar of transfers to the older[5] and younger[6] generations, respectively. The derivation of explicit expressions for these shadow prices is perhaps the key theoretical insight of the paper.

A portion of the lifetime resources of a member of generation i goes to social security transfers B_{i-1} to generation $i - 1$ and to transfers D_{i+1} to generation $i + 1$. These transfers are assumed to be motivated by a concern for members of generations $i - 1$ and $I + 1$.[7] This concern could be modeled by introducing either the consumption levels or the attainable utilities of generations $i - 1$ and $i + 1$ into the utility function for a member of the ith generation. So long as the intergenerational transfers are made only through the transfer of unrestricted purchasing power, the two types of models of interdependent preferences are equivalent in the sense of indirectly implying a concern for the endowments of members of generations $i - 1$ and $i + 1$.

For present purposes, it is convenient to assume that the utility of a member of generation i depends solely on own consumption, and on the attainable utility of his immediate descendants and ancestors, those utilities being U_{i-1}^* and U_{i+1}^* respectively [3].[8] The asterisks denote the maximum value of utility, conditional on given values of endowment and prices. The utility function for a member of the ith generation has the form[9]

$$U_i = U(c_i^y, c_i^v, c_i^o, U_{i-1}^*, U_{i+1}^*). \tag{4}$$

As well as facing his own budget constraint, the individual faces constraints affecting his intergenerational transfers. First, the individual's total expenditures on social security old-age transfers must equal his total payroll tax liability

$$p_{B1} B_1 = w_2 L_2 t_{B2} \tag{5}$$

where t_{B2} is the payroll tax rate paid by generation 2. (The payroll tax rate is endogenously determined in this model by the demand for providing social security benefits B_1.)

Second, the individual is constrained by the social security pay-as-you-go budget constraint. That constraint can be written

$$w_2 L_2 t_{B2} = N_1 B_1 / N_2 \tag{6}$$

which for the representative individual taxpayer states that his social security tax payments must equal total social security benefits divided by the number of taxpayers. This expression indicates that total benefits in a period must equal total payroll tax payments.

4. The model can be expanded to allow for human capital investment. For example, the amount of human capital transfers received while young could be incorporated to affect the earnings while working and the social security benefits received by the older generation who had financed that human capital investment.

5. As well as the contemporaneous price P_{B1}, there is a life-cycle price $\pi_{B1} = P_{B1} - dB_2/dB_1$. It is assumed that $dB_2/dB_1 = 0$ [6]. The effect of current earnings on future benefits is also ignored [7].

6. As well as the contemporaneous price P_{D3}, there is a life-cycle price $\pi_{D3} = p_{D3} - dB_2/dD_3$. It is assumed that $dB_2/dD_3 = 0$ [16].

7. Myopic savings behavior by the older generation could be a motivation for these transfers [10]. Alternatively, the model could be formulated as in Samuelson [18] where the utility of each generation depends only on that generation's own consumption, but where due to population and income growth, it is optimal for intergenerational transfers to successive older generations to occur based on the intergenerational contract.

8. The model could be extended by entering number of children as a parameter of the utility function [17].

9. It is assumed that a member of generation i can attach a metric to the indifference surfaces of generations $I-1$ and $i+1$ which makes those surfaces comparable to own consumption in terms of generating own utility.

Equations (5) and (6) imply that the shadow price p_{B1} of social security transfers is equal to the old-age dependency ratio

$$p_{B1} = N_1/N_2. \tag{7}$$

In general, for government programs where there is a distinct group of beneficiaries the shadow price of the program can be shown to be the ratio of beneficiaries to taxpayers. This result is similar to that for the shadow price of child quality derived by Becker and Lewis [5] in their model of the quantity-quality interaction, and this similarity is exploited later.

Similarly, it can be shown that the price p_{D3} of intergenerational transfers to the young is equal to the youth dependency ratio

$$p_{D3} = N_3/N_2. \tag{8}$$

Each member of generation 2 determines his allocation of resources to maximize U subject to equations (1)–(4), (7), and (8); to the budget constraints for generations 1 and 3 (corresponding to equations (1)–(3)), and to the inequality conditions $(c_i^y, c_i^w, c_i^o, B_i, D_i) > 0$ for all i. The choice of intergenerational transfers takes into accounts the effect of B_1 and D_3 on generation 1's and generation 3's resources, the impact of U_1^* and U_3^* on U_2 and the chain dependence of U_3 on U_4^*, etc.

The solution to this problem takes the general form

$$\begin{aligned}
c_2^y &= D_2 \\
c_2^v &= c^v(w_2 L_2, r, B_2, p_{B1}, p_{D3}) \\
c_2^o &= c^o(A_2^v + B_2, w_2 L_2, r, p_{B1}, p_{D3}) \\
A_2^v &= (1/(1-r))(w_2 L_2 - c_2^v - p_{B1} B_1 - p_{D3} D_3) = A^v(w_2 L_2, r, B_2, p_{B1}, p_{D3}) \\
D_3 &= D(w_2 L_2, r, B_2, p_{B1}, p_{D3}) \\
B_1 &= B(w_2 L_2, r, B_2, p_{B1}, p_{D3}).
\end{aligned} \tag{9}$$

The model can be closed, as in Diamond [8], by specifying a constant-returns-to-scale production function that depends on the amounts of capital and labor input, and by equating the marginal products of capital and labor to r and w, respectively. The value of r for the current period would then be determined in order to equate the supply of assets to the demand.

Restrictions on Elasticities

The payroll tax rate in this model is determined by the demand for social security benefits by the working generation for the retired generation. Let ϵ_B be the uncompensated own-price elasticity of the working generation for transferring social security benefits to retirees and let ϵ_t be the associated uncompensated price elasticity for the current payroll rax rate. Similarly, let η_B and η_t be the benefit and payroll tax rate income elasticities, and let Ω_B and Ω_t be the uncompensated benefit and payroll tax rate cross-price elasticities with respect to youth transfers. By making the assumption that the age structure does not affect the earnings level, the following restrictions on the demand elasticities can be derived from the social security budget constraint (eq. (6)):

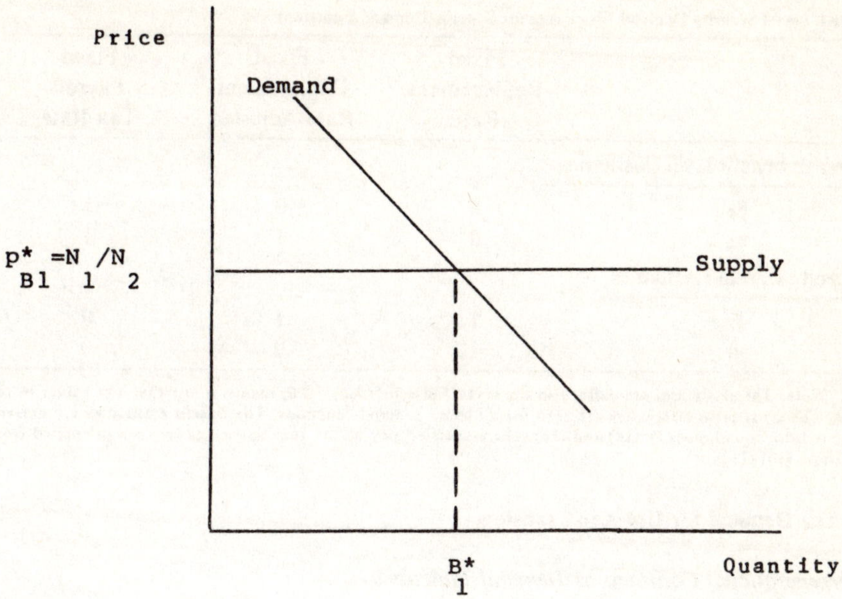

Figure 1

$$\epsilon_B = \epsilon_t - 1 \tag{10}$$

$$\eta_B = \eta_t + 1 \tag{11}$$

$$\Omega_B = \Omega_K. \tag{12}$$

These restrictions are used in subsequent sections.

The Marginal Cost of Social Security Benefits

In this simple model, the marginal cost of raising the level of social security benefits is determined solely by the age structure. In actuality, not all older persons receive social security benefits. For empirical estimation, the model is modified in a later section so that the shadow price of social security is the ratio of beneficiaries to covered workers. This modification introduces the complication that the equilibrium shadow price becomes endogenous since the decision to retire is affected by the level of benefits. When there is zero elasticity of beneficiaries with respect to the benefit level, the associated marginal cost curve of the benefit level is infinite. The greater is the elasticity of beneficiaries with respect to the benefit level, the less elastic is the associated supply curve. A full treatment of that problem is outside the scope of this paper.

The model is presented graphically in Figure 1. The demand curve is identified since both income and the price of youth transfers affect its position but do not affect the supply curve. The supply (or marginal cost) curve is determined by the old-age dependency ratio and is infinitely elastic.

Table I. Social Security Demand Elasticities for Specific Demand Functions

	Fixed Replacement Rate	Fixed Replacement Rate Adjusted	Fixed Payroll Tax Rate
Average benefit level elasticities			
ξ_B	0	0	−1
η_B	0	1	1
Payroll tax rate elasticities			
ξ_t	1	1	0
η_t	−1	0	0

Note: The elasticities are defined in the text. If $\partial(w_2L_2)/\partial(N_2) < 0$, then ϵ_t is less than the values in the table. The cross-price elasticities are zero for all three demand functions. The benefit elasticities are derived directly from equations (13), (14) and (15). The associated payroll tax rate elasticities are then calculated from equations (10) - (12).

III. The Demand for Old-Age Transfers

Intergenerational Contracts as Demand Functions

The idea that the social security program represents an intergenerational contract by which "the young are assured of their retirement subsistence if they will today support the aged" has been suggested by Samuelson [18], Musgrave [14] and others. The intergenerational contract reflects the underlying value judgements in society concerning the equitable distribution of benefits and tax burdens between generations given differing intergenerational patterns of lifetime income and prices.

The concept of a social security intergenerational contract is equivalent to the concept of the demand function for social security that is developed here.[10] Musgrave [14] has suggested three intergenerational contracts that may apply for social security. These three contracts are presented and the demand elasticities implied by them are derived (see Table I).[11] The elasticities are then estimated in the following section.

Three Specific Demand Functions for Social Security

The fixed replacement rate contract entitles retirees to receive a fixed fraction b of their pre-retirement earnings in benefits

$$B_1 = bw_1L_1. \tag{13}$$

This intergenerational contract states that social security should replace some portion of the earnings loss at retirement. With the fixed replacement rate adjusted contract, the replacement rate b is fixed, but the earnings base to which this rate is applied is adjusted

10. In principle, the demand function for social security benefits could be determined by examining the social security benefit formula. However, the causes of the ad hoc legislated increases in benefits must be known to determine the true benefit formula.

11. The three contracts are all consistent with the Samuelson-Aaron model. That model determines the conditions under which a pay-as-you-go social security system is favorable, but it does not determine the benefit formula that system will use. The fixed replacement rate demand function is a generalization of equation (9) since it incorporates the earnings of the older generation.

upward to allow for productivity gains after retirement. The replacement rate for this intergenerational contract is applied to the earnings of the subsequent working generation

$$B_1 = bw_2 L_2. \tag{14}$$

With the fixed payroll tax rate, the average benefit level increases with the rate of population growth and of earnings growth which can be expressed approximately in terms of the price p_{B1} and the earnings of the current working generation $w_2 L_2$ as[12]

$$B_1 = (b/p_{B1}) w_2 L_2. \tag{15}$$

These three demand functions represent testable alternative hypotheses about determinants of intergenerational transfers, but they also imply alternative hypotheses about the intergenerational sharing of risk due to macroeconomic and demographic fluctuations. The fixed replacement rate contract implies that the working generation entirely bears the risk of fluctuations in contemporaneous economic and demographic variables. It states that benefits should be predictable earlier in life and should not be affected by short run economic and political pressures. Retirees cannot adjust their labor supply as easily as workers and thus their consumption is more vulnerable to income fluctuations. The fixed replacement rate adjusted contract implies a sharing of risk so that if average earnings of current workers do not keep pace with inflation, then neither would average benefits. The fixed payroll tax rate contract implies that current retirees share economic risk as above but entirely bear the risk of demographic fluctuations. Any change in the size of the working population or the retirement population under this contract affects the level of benefits but has no effect on the payroll tax rate. Thus, as the old-age population increases under this contract (holding income and the working age population constant) the payroll tax payments per worker would be constant but benefits per retiree would fall.

IV. Empirically Implementing the Model

The Basic Regression Model

The demand for social security benefits can be written (9) as

$$B_1 = B(w_2 L_2, r, B_2, P_{B1}, p_{D3})$$

and the demand for the payroll tax rate is a function of the same variables

$$t_{B2} = t(w_2 L_2, r, B_2, p_{B1}, p_{D3}). \tag{16}$$

These demand functions can be written for empirical estimation as

$$\ln(B_1) = a_0 + a_1 \ln(p_{B1}) + a_2 \ln(p_{D3}) + a_3 \ln(w_2 L_2) \tag{17}$$

$$\ln(t_2) = b_0 + b_1 \ln(p_{B1}) + b_2 \ln(p_{D3}) + b_3 \ln(w_2 L_2) \tag{18}$$

12. Equation (15) is derived from the following equation

$$B_1 = b(1 + g + z) w_1 L_1,$$

where g is the rate of population growth and z is the rate of earnings growth.

where

$$a_1 = \epsilon_B, \quad a_2 = \Omega_B, \quad a_3 = \eta_B$$

$$b_1 = \epsilon_t, \quad b_2 = \Omega_t, \quad b_3 = \eta_t.$$

The effects of r and B_2 are ignored. The regressions are estimated in both log-log and linear forms.

The expected signs and magnitudes of the coefficients in the estimated regressions depend on the hypothesized form of the demand function. For example, if it is hypothesized that the demand function is for a fixed replacement rate (eq. (13)), in the benefit regression all the coefficients would be expected to be zero; while in the payroll tax rate regression the own-price coefficient b_1, the cross-price coefficient b_2, and the income coefficient b_3 would be 1, 0, and -1 respectively (see Table I).

The Empirical Variables

The payroll tax rate and benefit level regressions can be estimated once empirical counterparts for the theoretical variables are determined. In the simple theoretical model, it was assumed that all members of the old generation were retired and all members of the middle generation were workers. The appropriate empirical counterpart for the shadow price of social security is thus the ratio of old-age beneficiaries to covered workers rather than the associated age structure ratio. The beneficiary-covered worker ratio will be affected by changes in the age at which retirement benefits can be received.

OASI retired worker beneficiaries and OASI employed covered workers are used as the empirical counterparts for N_1 and N_2. This choice for N_1 excludes all OASI beneficiaries who are not receiving old-age benefits. The population aged 5 to 15 is used for N_3. Real average OASI covered earnings is used for w_2L_2. The OASI payroll tax rate (employee plus employer) is used for t. Average OASI retired worker benefits is used for B_1. Each of these empirical variables is subject to criticism because of differences between the simple theoretical model and the actual OASI system, and because of the limitations of the available data. For some of the key variables, alternative empirical representations are also used as is reported in the discussion of the regressions.

The sample period is 1947–77. The data sources, provided in the Appendix, are primarily published OASI statistics. The simple theoretical model produces weak empirical results. Those least squares regressions are shown in Tables II and III (equation (1)), but are not discussed.[13] For further estimation, a mathematically equivalent but economically and statistically superior model is developed.

The Extended Model

The model can be extended by analyzing the components of the social security price variable. The number of OASI beneficiaries N_1 is determined by the benefit acceptance rate N_1/G (where G is the number of eligible people eligible to receive benefits), the benefit

13. The results for the cross-price effect are the only ones that are plausible. Other regressions were estimated in linear form and with the age structure ratios but the results were similar. The positive autocorrelation in the payroll tax rate regression suggests the possibility of an omitted variable problem, and that hypothesis is supported by the Durbin-Watson statistic in the other payroll tax regression.

Table II. Payroll Tax Rate OLS Regressions, 1947-77

	(1)**	(2)**	(3)	(4)**	(5)**	(6)	(7)**
(a)* Earnings $w_2 L_2$	2.194	−1.279	−1.279	−1.046	−1.446	−.978	−1.593
	(15.02)	(1.62)	(2.33)	(1.76)	(1.73)	(1.65)	(2.19)
(c/b) Old-Age Dependency Ratio N_1/N_2	.028						
	(.91)						
(d/b) Youth Dependency Ratio N_3/N_2	.035						
	(.13)						
(b,e) Working Pop. $N16$		3.043	.021	2.839	1.948	.161	2.141
		(1.53)	(2.08)	(1.50)	(2.36)	(2.30)	(3.30)
(b) Labor Force Part. Rate $L/N16$		−4.011	−.239	−4.607	−3.537	−.127	−3.006
		(1.95)	(1.57)	(2.92)	(1.72)	(.79)	(2.00)
(b) Employment Rate M/L		2.089	.149	2.175	2.774	.016	2.636
		(1.23)	(1.74)	(1.31)	(1.75)	(.21)	(1.74)
(b) SS Coverage Rate N_2/M		−1.332	−.078	−1.389	−1.221	.006	−1.230
		(2.30)	(1.98)	(2.49)	(1.87)	(.29)	(1.91)
(c) Benefit Elibigility Rate $G/N65$		.970	.119	1.004			
		(3.03)	(1.67)	(3.28)			
(c) Benefit Acceptance Rate N_1/G		.503	.056	.613			
		(.88)	(1.34)	(1.21)			
(c) Old-Age Pop. $N65$		.042	−.300	.112			
		(.02)	(.52)	(.06)			
(c) Beneficiaries N_1					−.321	.327	.886
					(.39)	(.21)	(4.49)
(d) Youth Pop. N_3		.318	.052		.973	.188	
		(.46)	(.58)		(3.22)	(2.08)	
Constant	−17.56	−19.41	−10.11	−14.74	−13.58	7.93	−18.45
R^2	.945	.985	.987	.985	.982	.983	.982
F	116	137	156	159	160	166	187
Durbin-Watson	.95	2.03	2.14	2.06	2.02	1.78	2.02

Note: t-statistics in parentheses.

* The notation (a) indicates the earnings variable. (b) indicates an own-price (denominator) variable, (c) indicates an own-price (numerator) variable, (d) indicates a cross-price (numerator) variable, (e) indicates the cross-price (denominator) variable.

** Regression in log-log form.

eligibility rate $G/N65$,[14] and the population aged 65 and older $N65$

$$N_1 = (N_1/G)(G/N65)\,N65. \tag{19}$$

Not all eligible persons accept benefits because of the associated tax on earnings (the earnings test).

14. For simplicity, the extension of benefit eligibility to persons aged 62 to 64 is ignored.

Table III. Average OASI Benefit OLS Regressions, 1947-77

	(1)**	(2)**	(3)	(4)**	(5)**	(6)	(7)**
(a)* Earnings w_2L_2	−.027	.437	−.035	−.996	.722	.086	−1.522
	(.10)	(.70)	(.92)	(1.68)	(.89)	(.74)	(.95)
(c/b) Old-Age Dependency	.422						
Ratio N_1/N_2	(5.59)						
(d/b) Youth Dependency	−1.122						
Ratio N_3/N_2	(5.74)						
(b,e) Working Pop. $N16$		4.375	.056	5.635	−.927	.011	1.387
		(2.79)	(3.85)	(2.97)	(1.10)	(.61)	(1.75)
(b) Labor Force Part.		−2.859	−.027	.801	−1.730	.013	3.416
Rate $L/N16$		(1.75)	(1.25)	(.51)	(.88)	(.39)	(1.77)
(b) Employment Rate		−.464	.009	−.991	1.955	−.016	1.970
M/L		(.34)	(.74)	(.60)	(1.41)	(.99)	(1.10)
(b) SS Coverage Rate		−.970	−.012	−.620	−.959	.013	−.458
N_2/M		(2.11)	(2.20)	(1.12)	(1.63)	(2.65)	(.62)
(c) Benefit Elibigility		1.885	.057	1.675			
Rate $G/N65$		(7.44)	(5.54)	(5.49)			
(c) Benefit Acceptance		.633	.017	−.044			
Rate N_1/G		(1.41)	(2.75)	(.09)			
(c) Old-Age Pop. $N65$		−3.103	−.311	−3.539			
		(2.13)	(3.56)	(1.96)			
Beneficiaries N_1					1.038	.002	.532
					(5.32)	(.04)	(2.76)
(d) Youth Pop. N_3		−1.957	−.064		−2.878	−.0183	
		(3.58)	(5.02)		(4.06)	(1.23)	
Constant	−2.430	−9.611	.029	−24.812	8.123	−.579	−28.441
R^2	.948	.983	.980	.973	.967	.948	.944
F	171	114	114	89	89	76	63
Durbin-Watson	2.11	1.55	1.90	1.57	1.70	1.74	1.82

Note: see notes for Table II.

The number of employed covered workers N_2 is determined by the labor force coverage rate N_2/M, (where M is the employed labor force) the employment rate M/L, the labor force participation rate $L/N16$, and the size of the working age population (aged 16 to 64, $N16$)

$$N_2 = (N_2/M)(M/L)(L/N16)\,N16. \tag{20}$$

With the expansion of the own-price variable by the expansion of the beneficiary and covered worker variables, the benefit regression equation can now be written

$$\ln(B_1) = a_0 + a_1 \ln(N_1/G) + a_2 \ln(G/N65) + a_3 \ln(N65) - a_4 \ln(N/M) - a_5 \ln(M/L) - a_6 \ln(L/N16) - a_7 \ln(N16) + a_8 \ln(p_{D3}) + a_9 \ln(w_2 L_2). \quad (21)$$

and similarly for the payroll tax rate regression (not shown).

In comparison to the simple empirical model ((9) and (16)), the empirical results favor the more complex model of social security where the components of the social security price variable are separated (21). When the components of the price variable are separated, it is seen in the discussion of the results that not all components are expected to have the same coefficient, and that result is verified by the estimates. Nonetheless, the majority of the price estimates are expected to be the same and there is a general consistency among them.

V. The Regression Results

The primary results of the empirical work are estimated income and price elasticities for social security. If the legislated changes in social were ad hoc with no systematic relationship to changes in the economic and demographic environment, the predicted coefficients in the regressions would be zero. The empirical results, however, support the utility maximizing model development here. Reasonable estimates are produced for the income, price and cross-price elasticities. Regressions are estimated in both log-log and linear forms.

Payroll Tax Rate Regressions

The payroll tax rate regressions are discussed in some detail while the benefit regressions, which are similar, are summarized.

Earnings (a).[15] The estimated earnings coefficients are negative and sometimes significant. This result implies a negative income elasticity for the payroll tax rate. A negative income elasticity is predicted by the fixed replacement rate hypothesis.

The measured income elasticities of the payroll tax rate and the benefit level are biased towards zero because an increase in income with a positive income elasticity of benefits causes increased benefits and a higher acceptance rate. Since increases in the number of beneficiaries cause the shadow price p_{B1} to rise, real full income rises by a smaller percentage than real income, which biases towards zero the income elasticities as measured here [5].

Own-Price (Denominator, b). There are four components in the denominator of the social security price variable. The fixed replacement rate and fixed replacement rate adjusted hypotheses predict a positive price elasticity for the payroll tax rate which implies negative coefficients for these variables. The coefficient for the work-age population $N16$ is

15. The letter notation of subsections (e.g., "Earnings (a)") corresponds to the notation in the regression tables (Tables II and III). None of the regressions considered (i.e., excluding eq. (1)) has significant autocorrelation in either Table II or Table III. In regressions where the Durbin-Watson statistic is in the indeterminent range, the autocorrelation coefficient (not shown) is estimated using the Cochrane-Orcutt procedure. There is significant autocorrelation in one equation—Table III eq. (6)—but the Cochrane-Orcutt correction produces a Durbin-Watson statistic even further from 2 than the original statistic.

positive and sometimes significant. This result could be due to a strong time trend for this variable.

The labor force participation rate variable $L/N16$ for the work-age population is negative as expected and sometimes significant. The employment rate variable M/L is insignificant. This result is not surprising since the OASI trust fund is used to buffer the benefit level and the payroll tax rate against cyclical variation in employment rates.[16] Omitting the employment rate from regressions not shown did not affect the sign nor greatly affect the significance level of any of the remaining variables.

The coverage rate variable N_1/M is negative as expected and is frequently significant. Thus, the results for the own-price (denominator) variables generally suggest a positive price elasticity for the payroll tax rate.

Own-Price (Numerator, c). Positive coefficients for the own-price (numerator) variables imply a positive price elasticity for the payroll tax rate.

The benefit eligibility rate variable is positive as expected and generally significant. The beneficiary acceptance rate variable is insignificant. This insignificance may be due to reverse causality. The higher the benefit acceptance rate, the higher is the price of social security benefits, causing lower benefits and a lower benefit acceptance rate. The variable for the population aged 65 and older $N65$ is insignificant. In some regressions, total OASI beneficiaries is entered instead of the components of retired worker beneficiaries. The total beneficiaries variable is significantly positive in one regression as predicted by the fixed replacement rate hypotheses.

Cross-Price (Numerator, d). A positive coefficient for the cross-price (numerator) variable implies a positive cross-price elasticity for old-age benefits with respect to youth benefits. The variable for the population aged 5 to 15 is significantly positive in some regressions. The cross-price (denominator) is represented by the work-age population variable which was discussed earlier.

Benefit Regressions

The benefit regessions provide an alternative source of estimates for the social security demand elasticities. Their consistency with the payroll tax rate regressions provides a check on the model.

Three results from the benefit regressions are important for understanding social security financing. First, there is a negative effect of the size of the old-age population on its own benefit level. Second, there is a positive effect of the size of the working-age population. Third, there is a negative effect of the size of the young population. This last result suggests that the financing for the baby-boom generation's social seurity will be eased if there is a relatively low youth dependency rate at that time.[17]

To further investigate the determinants of the social security benefit level, several other measures of the benefit level were tried. These measures include total OASI benefits divided by total OASI beneficiaries, average Primary Insurance Amount (PIA) per new

16. The trust fund shields both the payroll tax rate and the average benefit level from the short run economic and demographic fluctuations [19].

17. Other results are briefly summarized here. The wage estimates are insignificant. They may be biased downwards as discussed earlier for the payroll tax rate regressions. The benefit eligibility rate and benefit acceptance rate variables are sometimes significantly positive, but this is arguably due to reverse casuality (higher benefits cause higher acceptance rates).

retired worker beneficiary, and average benefits per new retired worker beneficiary.[18] Each of these measures has distinctive strengths and weaknesses. The results can be summarized as follows. For all of these measures, positive autocorrelation, as indicated by the Durbin-Watson statistic, was potentially a problem, and thus the t-statistics may be overstated. Yet, the results for the estimated coefficients were similar to those in Table III. The old-age and youth population variables were generally significantly negative and the working-age population variable was significantly positive. The one exception was the earnings coefficients which were insignificant in the reported benefit level regressions, but were frequently significantly positive in the new regressions. As indicated in the discussion of the payroll tax rate regressions, the estimated income elasticities are biased towards zero due to an associated increase in the shadow price of benefits.

The empirical finding of perhaps most policy importance is that there is a negative effect of the old-age population on its own benefit level: total benefits rise, but average benefits fall. This finding is counter to the prediction commonly drawn from voting models that increases in the size of a voting group will increase the average benefits received by members of the group.

The finding of a negative effect of the old-age population on its own benefit level is consistent with the prediction that average benefits would decline due to the increase in the shadow price of benefits. It is also consistent with at least two other hypotheses. Becker [4] argues that since deadweight costs to taxpayers increase as the tax per person rises, the opposition of taxpayers to subsidies increases as the number of taxpayers relative to beneficiaries grows. Therefore, groups obtain smaller subsidies per beneficiary when they are large relative to the number of taxpayers. The Samuelson [18]-Aaron [1] model can also be interpreted to predict that the higher the ratio of beneficiaries to taxpayers, the lower would be average benefits. In a regime of slow population growth, not only is the price of providing benefits to current beneficiaries high, the rate of return on one's own tax payments will be relatively low. These behavioral models are not mutually exclusive but may all capture important elements of the transfer process.

VI. The Social Security Demand Function

The magnitudes of the estimated social security demand elasticities place restrictions on the form of the implied demand function. The empirical estimates suggest a negative income elasticity for the payroll tax rate and a zero or possibly positive income elasticity of the benefit level. They suggest a positive price elasticity for the payroll tax rate and a negative price elasticity for the benefit level; and they suggest a positive youth dependency cross-price elasticity for the payroll tax rate and a negative cross-price elasticity, for the benefit level.[19] A possible general form for the social security benefit demand function would be a CES demand function with a positive income elasticity, a negative price elasticity, and a positive cross-price elasticity for the youth dependence rate.

18. Average PIA per new male retired worker and average benefits per new male retired worker were also tried.

19. One test of the model is whether the estimated elasticities in the payroll tax rate and benefit regressions satisfy the restrictions of equations (10)-(12). For application to the regressions, the restrictions should be generalized so that the average wage decreases with the size of the work-age population and so that a larger young population is associated with women leaving the labor force. While not all the results are consistent, there is general consistency between the estimates in the payroll tax rate and benefit regressions.

These results imply that the effects of adverse changes in income and economic dependency are not entirely borne by the working generation but are shared by the working generation and the retired generation. For example, an increase in old-age dependency would cause both an increase in the payroll tax rate and a decrease in the level of benefits per beneficiary.

VII. Conclusions

This model shows that age structure ratios—the old age dependency ratio and the youth dependency ratio—act as shadow prices in a model of intergenerational transfers. Making use of these new shadow prices, social security can be analyzed by determining the equilibrium price and quantity of social security benefits and the level of the payroll tax rate in a demand-supply model with individual utility maximization. Three explicit demand functions are considered.

Though previous models of the size of social security have not led to empirical testing, this model is tested using time series data for the Old-Age and Survivors Insurance program. Both payroll tax rate and average benefit level regressions are estimated yielding the first price, cross-price, and income elasticities for social security. While voting models are commonly interpreted to predict that average benefits increase with the size of the old-age population due to its increased political power, these estimates suggest that average benefits on net decrease due to the increased shadow price of benefits. These results suggest that when the baby boom generation retires, benefits will be higher in real terms than currently, but benefits will be lower relative to earnings.

This model represents a first attempt at empirically analyzing the size of social security, and a number of difficult issues have been left untouched. A full treatment of the endogeneity of the equilibrium shadow price should be undertaken. The empirical analysis should be extended to incorporate some of the intertemporal effects suggested by previous studies.

Extensions of this model may lead to a better understanding of intergenerational transfers, the size of government expenditures, the level of tax rates, and the effect of demographic variables on the economy. The size of other government programs with clearly defined beneficiaries can be analyzed using this approach.

Appendix: Data Sources

Covered workers and covered earnings are from *Social Security Bulletin, Annual Statistical Supplement, 1977–79* (*SSB*), p. 84. The labor force and labor force participation data are from *Economic Report of the President, 1979* (*ERP*), p. 214. Data on the population aged 5 to 15, aged 15 to 64, and aged 65 and older are from *ERP*, p. 213. The payroll tax rate is from *SSB*, p. 35. The employment rate is calculated from the unemployment rate for the civilian labor force. Those data are from *ERP*, p. 214. Total OASI benefits are from *SSB*., p. 80. Retired worker benefits is from *SSB*, p. 142. The number of OASI beneficiaries is from *SSB*, p. 105, and retired worker beneficiaries is from *SSB*., p. 104. The number of people aged 65 and older who are eligible to receive OASI benefits and the percent of those people accepting benefits are from *SSB*, p. 101. The price deflator used is the consumer price index. All data are in millions except for the rate variables which are in percent.

References

1. Aaron, Henry, "The Social Insurance Paradox." *Canadian Journal of Economics and Political Science*, August 1966, 371-74.

2. ______. "Social Security: International Comparisons," in *Studies in the Economics of Income Maintenance*, edited by O. Eckstein. Washington, D.C.: Brookings Institution, 1967, pp. 13-48.

3. Barro, Robert J., "Are Government Bonds Net Wealth?" *Journal of Political Economy*, November/December 1974, 1095-117.

4. Becker, Gary S. "Competition Among Pressure Groups for Political Influence," University of Chicago, Center for the Study of the Economy and the State, Working Paper No. 23, 1982.

5. Becker, Gary S. and H. Gregg Lewis, "On the Interaction Between the Quantity and Quality of Children." *Journal of Political Economy*, March/April 1973, S279-88.

6. Browning, Edgar K., "Why Social Insurance Budget is Too Large in a Democracy." *Economic Inquiry*, September 1975, 373-88.

7. Burkhauser, Richard V. and John A. Turner. "Is the Social Security Payroll Tax a Tax?" Vanderbilt University, 1981.

8. Diamond, Peter A., "National Debt in a Neoclassical Growth Model." *American Economic Review*, December 1965, 1126-150.

9. *Economic Report of the President, 1979*. Washington, D.C.: United States Government Printing Office, 1979.

10. Feldstein, Martin. "The Optimal Level of Social Security Benefits." National Bureau of Economic Research Working Paper No. 970, August 1982.

11. ______, "Social Security, Induced Retirement, and Aggregate Capital Accumulation." *Journal of Political Economy*, September/October 1974, 905-26.

12. Hagens, John B. "A Re-examination of the Link Between Social Security and Saving." Office of Research and Statistics Working Paper No. 1. Washington, D.C.: Social Security Administration, February 1979.

13. Merton, Robert C. "On the Role of Social Security as a Means for Efficient Risk-Bearing in an Economy where Human Capital is not Tradeable." National Bureau of Economic Research Working Paper No. 743, September 1981.

14. Musgrave, Richard A. "A Reappraisal of Financing Social Security," in *Social Security Financing*, edited by F. Skidmore. Cambridge, Mass.: MIT Press, 1981.

15. Parsons, Donald O., "Demographic Effects on Public Charity to the Aged." *Journal of Human Resources*, Winter 1982, 144-52.

16. Pogue, T. and L. Sgontz, "Social Security and Investment in Human Capital." *National Tax Journal*, June 1977, 157-69.

17. Razin, Assaf and Uri Ben-Zion, "An Intergenerational Model of Population Growth." *American Economic Review*, December 1975, 923-33.

18. Samuelson, Paul A., "An Exact Consumption-Loan Model of Interest With or Without the Social Contrivance of Money." *Journal of Political Economy*, December 1958, 467-82.

19. Turner, John A. "Financing Social Security." *Review of Social Economy*, 1984 (forthcoming).

20. U.S. Department of Health and Human Services, Social Security Administration. *Social Security Bulletin, Annual Statistical Supplement, 1977-79*. Washington, D.C.: Government Printing Office, 1980.

[28]

Bulletin of Economic Research 44:1, 1992, 0307-3378 $2.00

FINANCING STATE PENSIONS IN ALTERNATIVE PAY-AS-YOU-GO SCHEMES*

John Creedy and Richard Disney

I. INTRODUCTION

Serious concern has been expressed in recent years over the projected high cost of state pension schemes, thought to be a consequence of population aging. Some authors have even referred to a 'world crisis' in social security.[1] In discussing alternative policies, major emphasis has usually been placed on the perceived need to reduce pensions because the tax rate required with an aging population and a pay-as-you-go state scheme would otherwise be unacceptably high. This view is often based on a very simple statement of the accounting relationship involved, in terms of the dependency ratio, the replacement ratio and a single rate of tax applied to the working population. This basic formulation is described in the following subsection.

The major purpose of this paper is to argue that many important elements of the problem of financing state pensions are ignored by such a simple approach. Not only are more policy options available, but rational policy making should also consider the redistributive implications of each policy. First, however, it is necessary to clarify the nature of the issue debated. If it is required to transfer a fixed amount of real resources to each retired person, financed by taxing the working population, then it is

*We should like to thank two referees for very helpful comments on an earlier draft of this paper.

[1] The phrase is that of Rosa (1982). Concern over the excess cost of state pension schemes led to a plethora of reports by international institutions (such as OECD, 1985 and Heller *et al.*, 1986), conferences (such as Campbell, 1984) and official working parties and reports (such as HMSO (1985a) and Foster (1988)).

obvious that a higher dependency ratio will raise the tax 'burden' faced by the current labour force. It is of course well known that the true 'burden' can only be assessed by considering three, rather than just two, generations. But if such transfers are required then it is equally obvious that alternative tax structures can influence only the distribution of the tax 'burden'. However, if the objective of the social insurance system is to provide a basic level of income support, the range of choices is much wider. In particular, a basic pension can be financed by taxes imposed not only on workers but also on those who are retired with relatively high incomes from other sources.

Section II therefore examines the tax structure in more detail, allowing not only for consumption taxes paid by those in receipt of a state pension but also the taxation of other income received by the retired population. This section also examines the question of the specification of the replacement ratio to allow for income taxation, compared with the taxation of the pension. Section III then considers the dependency ratio in more detail, concentrating on the importance of labour force participation.

The Simple Formula

The basic approach usually considers a pay-as-you-go pension scheme in which a non-taxed pension benefit per dependent person is denoted b, the number of retired persons and the labour force are respectively P and L, and pensions are financed using a constant proportional income tax at the rate t (the percentage tax rate is $100t$ %).[2] Average income of the working population is denoted by $\bar{y}$. For the tax revenue to finance pensions:

$$bP = t\bar{y}L \tag{1}$$

and

$$b/\bar{y} = t(L/P) \tag{2}$$

This may be rewritten in general terms as

$$R = \tau/D \tag{3}$$

where R is the 'replacement ratio', τ is the 'tax rate' and D is the 'aged dependency ratio', P/L. With this simple formula, it is easy to emphasize the importance of the ratio of workers to beneficiaries. For any given replacement ratio, an increase in the aged dependency ratio must be matched by a corresponding increase in the tax rate. With a 50 per cent replacement rate, the tax rate would need to increase from 12.5 per cent of income to 25 per cent as the ratio L/P falls from 4 to 2. This fall in the

[2] The formula is used by, for example, Clark and Spengler (1980) and underpins many official projections, such as HMSO (1985b). Some reservations about the use of such a formula are expressed by Wilson and Wilson (1982) who do not, however, develop the analytical framework further.

aged dependency ratio is representative of that occurring in many western industrialized countries in the next half century; see Heller *et al.* (1986). But it is also clear that the level of real benefits can be maintained with a constant tax rate so long as the increase in the dependency ratio is matched by a similar increase in average income. A desire to increase the real value of benefits, in order to allow pensioners to 'share' in the growth of real incomes of those in work, will require the tax rate to increase as the aged dependency ratio increases. Recognition of the extent to which the industrialized countries would experience increasing aged dependency ratios therefore led to widespread retrenchment in the indexation regulations of public pension schemes.

II. THE TAX STRUCTURE

A General Approach

The simple approach ignores a number of important practical features of social transfer systems. For example, it fails to acknowledge that the extent of such transfer payments is overstated when indirect taxes are also used to raise revenue. Some of the pensions are returned to the state in the form of indirect taxes. In general the direct and indirect tax systems can interact in quite complex ways. In addition, some state schemes, such as that operating in Australia, are means-tested.[3] This section begins by presenting a completely general analysis in terms of average tax rates; it can therefore apply to any type of tax schedule. Some special practical cases are then discussed.

Suppose that the average tax rate applied to the pension is τ_b. Furthermore, those in receipt of the pension may also receive income from other sources, such as interest payments, rents and other (private) pensions. Suppose that the average other income of those who are retired is equal to $\bar{w}$ and that this attracts an average tax rate of τ_r. This tax rate can differ from the average rate applied to the income of the working population, say τ_L. The difference may arise because of the imposition of additional taxes, such as payrolll taxes or National Insurance contributions on income from employment. Furthermore, in a progressive tax system τ_L will exceed τ_r when $\bar{y} > \bar{w}$ even if the applicable tax structure is similar.

The government's budget constraint requires that total pension payments, less the tax paid by pensioners, is equal to the tax paid by the working population. Then:

$$P(b - \tau_b b - \tau_r \bar{w}) = L\tau_L \bar{y} \tag{4}$$

[3] Means-testing of the basic state pension is used in Australia; see Creedy and Disney (1989) for further details.

which can be rearranged into the form $\tau = RD$ of equation (3), but with τ now taking the form:

$$\tau = \frac{\tau_L + D(\bar{w}/\bar{y})\,\tau_r}{1 - \tau_b} \qquad (5)$$

Hence the average tax rate applied to the working population is:

$$\tau_L = D\{(1 - \tau_b)\,R - (\bar{w}/\bar{y})\,\tau_r\} \qquad (6)$$

These results clearly show the extent to which the value of τ_L, for given D and R, is reduced as either τ_b, $\bar{w}$ or τ_r are increased. As with the simple framework of Section I, the need to raise additional revenue for other purposes has been ignored, but can easily be added. For example, if it is required to raise an amount, E, per person (including both retired and working) for non-pension purposes, then it is necessary to add the term $E(D+1)/(1-\tau_b)$ to the right-hand side of (5).

A Proportional Income Tax with Value Added Tax

The more general framework may easily be used to examine some special cases. Suppose first that there is a proportional income tax with rate τ, along with a Value Added Tax with a fixed rate of v applied to the tax-exclusive price of all goods. In this case the average tax rate τ_L is given by:

$$\tau_L = t + (1 - t)\,v/(1 + v) \qquad (7)$$

Equation (7) can be explained as follows. Each extra unit of income produces an increase in disposable income of $(1 - t)$ units. The VAT rate of v on the tax-exclusive price of goods translates into a rate of $v/(1 + v)$ when applied to the tax inclusive price, and assuming that all disposable income is spent means that the extra unit of income leads to additional VAT payments of $(1 - t)\,v/(1 + v)$, which is also the average consumption tax rate since both taxes are directly proportional. This must then be added to the income tax rate. Suppose also that the pension is non-taxable. This means that b is only subject to VAT, so that $\tau_b = v/(1 + v)$. Since $\tau_r = \tau_L$, appropriate substitution into (5) gives:

$$\tau = (v + t)\{1 + D(\bar{w}/\bar{y})\} \qquad (8)$$

If the basic pension, b, is instead included in the taxable income of the retired, then all three average rates are equal and $\tau_r = \tau_b = \tau_L$. Substitution and rearrangement then gives:[4]

$$\tau = \left\{\frac{v + t}{1 - t}\right\}\{1 + D(\bar{w}/\bar{y})\} \qquad (9)$$

Allowing for savings of the working population, with an average propensity to save of s, leads to a simple modification of equation (9). It is

[4] Substituting $\bar{w} = 0$ in equation (9) gives the result given in Creedy and Disney (1989a, p. 370).

only required to subtract vs from the right-hand side of (9), thereby raising the value of t required to finance a given value of $R = b/\bar{y}$ for a given value of v.

This approach also provides a simple demonstration that the inclusion of the pension in taxable income is equivalent to basing the replacement ratio, R, in terms of the post income-tax income of the working population, while leaving the basic pension untaxed. The value of R now becomes $b/\{(1-t)\bar{y}\}$, that is, the previous value divided by $(1-t)$. But it has been seen that (9) is just (8) divided by $(1-t)$, so it does not matter which system is used. It will, however, be shown below that this result does not hold with a non-proportional income tax system.

Some idea of the effect of very minor modification to the framework may be seen from numerical examples, assuming for convenience that $\bar{w}=0$ so that comparison may be made with the examples given in Section I. When $v=0$, a replacement rate of 50 per cent of post-tax income now requires a tax rate t, of 11.1 per cent of income when $L/P=4$; a halving of the latter ratio now raises the tax rate to 20 per cent. When $v=10$ per cent and $L/P=2$, a 50 per cent replacement rate in terms of post-income tax income can be financed with an income tax rate of 12 per cent; however, a VAT rate of 13 per cent would be required if the replacement rate were defined in terms of gross income. If the income tax rate is reduced to 10 per cent the required VAT rate is 12.5 per cent. The reason why the sum of the two rates is not constant is that in this context a lower income tax rate raises the ratio of b to $\bar{y}$ for any given value of R, when the latter is defined in terms of after-tax income.

Further comparisons are shown in Figure 1, which clearly demonstrates the effect of allowing for a consumption tax and the taxation of the pension as part of taxable income. Figure 1 shows the relationship between the 'replacement rate' and the income tax rate required, with $\bar{w}=0$. The line marked A is obtained from equation (3) and therefore has a slope equal to the reciprocal of the dependency ratio. As the latter ratio increases, the slopes of all the lines in Figure 1 are reduced, indicating the need for higher income tax rates. The line marked A^T applies to a system in which the replacement rate is defined in terms of the after-tax average income. The line marked B applies when a VAT is used in addition to income tax (with $v=0.10$); it is thus line A shifted to the left by an amount vL/P. Similarly B^T applies when after-income tax average income is used to specify the replacement rate; notice that in this case B^T is flatter than A^T. The latter two curves would also apply if pensions were subject to income tax (they must of course pay VAT).

A Non-Proportional Income tax

A proportional income tax has so far been used, whereas a policy decision must usually be made about the way in which tax thresholds are to be adjusted. A tax threshold introduces a powerful additional degree of

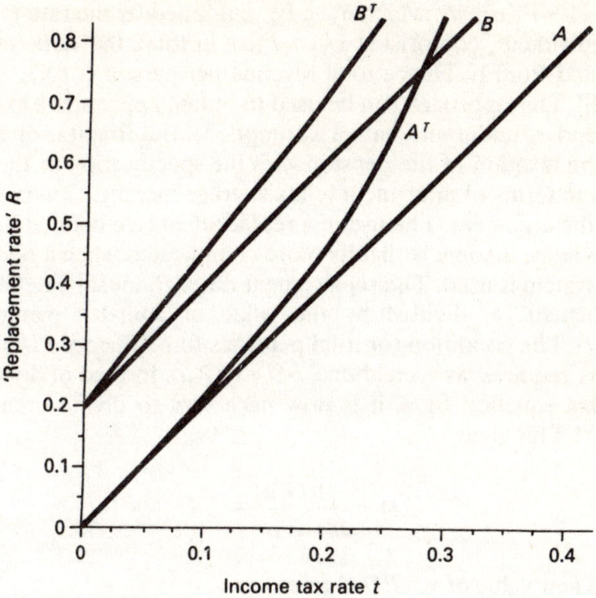

Notes: *A*: Proportional income tax
A^T: As *A* but with *R* in terms of after tax income
B: As *A* but with VAT
B^T: As *B* but with *R* in terms of after tax income

Fig. 1. Some policy alternatives.

freedom in policy choices. Suppose, for example, that the income tax system is such that the tax, $T(y)$, on an income of y is zero when $y < a$ but is equal to $t(y-a)$ when $y \geq a$. A multi-rate structure could be examined along the lines used below, but it is sufficient for present purposes to consider the simpler case of a single 'step' in the income tax schedule.

In order to obtain an expression for total income tax revenue from the working population, the distribution function of income, $F(y)$, is now required rather than simply the arithmetic mean income. It can be shown that the corresponding value of τ_L is equal to $tG(a)$, rather than simply t, where the function $G(a)$ is given by:

$$G(a) = \{1 - F_1(a)\} - (a/\bar{y})\{1 - F(a)\} \qquad (10)$$

and F_1 is the first moment distribution function of y, defined by $F_1(y) = \int^y u\,dF(u)/\bar{y}$, and interpreted as the proportion of total income obtained by those with incomes below y; see Creedy (1985, p. 135). The value of $G(a)$ declines from unity (where $a = 0$) to zero as the threshold increases. This result can be explained as follows. First, write the tax paid on an income of y as $ty - at$. Hence total revenue is expressed in terms of two components. The total income of those liable to tax, that is for whom $y > a$, is equal to $\{1-F_1(a)\}\,\bar{y}L$, which must be multiplied by the rate t. For each of these individuals, comprising $L\{1-F(a)\}$ in total, the value of at must be subtracted from ty. Hence total revenue per person is $t[\bar{y}\{1-F_1(a)\}-a\{1-F(a)\}]$. This approach can be used to obtain appropriate expressions for τ_L, τ_r and τ_b under alternative assumptions. But first it is of interest to compare the taxation of the pension with the specification of the replacement ratio in terms of after-income-tax average income. Complexity does not affect the argument. The use of a replacement rate defined in terms of after-tax average income is slightly more complicated when a non-proportional tax system is used. The replacement ratio, R, must be defined as the flat-rate benefit, b, divided by the value of after-tax mean income, $at+\bar{y}(1-t)$. The condition for total pensions to be financed from income tax revenue requires, as seen above, $bD=t\bar{y}G(a)$. Instead of dividing both sides of this equation by $\bar{y}$, it is now necessary to divide both sides by $at+\bar{y}(1-t)$. This gives:

$$RD=\frac{t\bar{y}G(a)}{at+\bar{y}(1-t)} \tag{11}$$

So that the new value of $\tau=RD$ is given by:

$$\tau=tG(a)/\{1-t(1-a/\bar{y})\} \tag{12}$$

rather than $t/(1-t)$ for the proportional tax. This can be compared with the result obtained when the pension is subject to income taxation, with $b>a$. It can be seen that the budget constraint for financing requires:

$$\{at+b(1-t)\}\,D=t\bar{y}G(a) \tag{13}$$

So that, with $R=b/\bar{y}$, it can be seen that:

$$\tau=\frac{t}{1-t}\{G(a)-D(a/\bar{y})\} \tag{14}$$

Hence a higher different tax rate, t, is required for any given replacement ratio compared with the situation in which pensions are specified as a proportion of after-tax mean income, using equation (12).[5]

Income and Value Added Taxes with National Insurance Contributions

Many countries combine the use of income taxation and a Value Added Tax with some type of hypothecated social security contribution. In the

[5] A basic reason for the difference arises because after-tax mean income, which is equal to $at+\bar{y}(1-t)$, is not the same thing as mean after-tax income. Since the tax revenue per person has been shown to equal $t\bar{y}G(a)$, the average value of after-tax income is simply $\bar{y}\{1-tG(a)\}$. This may usefully be rearranged, for direct comparison with after-tax mean income, as $at+\bar{y}[1-t\{G(a)+(a/\bar{y})\}]$.

UK this is known as the National Insurance Contribution. For example, suppose that this involves contributions at a constant proportional rate, c, on gross earnings up to an upper limit, y_2, but that no contributions are paid until a lower limit, y_1, is reached. A multi-rate system was used for a brief period in the UK; other countries have a similar system but often with $y_1 = 0$. For present purposes it is convenient to treat earnings and income as synonymous. The total value of NIC contributions is therefore the rate, c, multiplied by the total income of those with incomes between the lower and upper limits, plus the product of c and the value of the upper limit multiplied by the number of people with incomes above the upper limit. The total income of those with $y_1 \leq y \leq y_2$ is $\bar{y}\{F_1(y_2) - F_1(y_1)\} L$. Since there are $\{1 - F(y_2)\} L$ people with incomes above y_2, it can be shown that the total value of the National Insurance Contributions is equal to:

$$c\bar{y}\{1 - F_1(y_1) - G(y_2)\} L \tag{15}$$

The total tax paid by workers is equal to the sum of income tax, VAT and National Insurance Contributions, remembering that VAT is based on income after the deduction of direct taxes. Total tax revenue is thus:

$$L\bar{y}\left[tG(a) + c\{1 - F_1(y_1) - G(y_2)\} + \frac{v}{1+v}\{1 - tG(a) - c\{1 - F_1(y_1) - G(y_2)\}\right]$$

which can be simplified to give

$$L\bar{y}\left[\frac{v}{1+v} + \{tG(a) + c\{1 - F_1(y_1) - G(y_2)\}\frac{1}{1+v}\right] \tag{16}$$

If the pension is treated as taxable income, and the additional income of pensioners follows the distribution function $H(w)$, the total amount of income tax paid by pensioners, if $a > b$, is equal to

$$Pt\int_{a-b} (w + b - a)\,\mathrm{d}H(w) \tag{17}$$

Then (17) can be expressed as:

$$Pt\bar{w}\left[\{1 - H_1(\mathrm{a} - \mathrm{b})\} - \left(\frac{a-b}{\bar{w}}\right)\{1 - H(a-b)\}\right] \tag{18}$$

$$= Pt\bar{w}G^* \tag{19}$$

where G^* is the term in square brackets in (18). Alternatively, if $a < b$, all pensioners pay tax and $G^* = 1 + (b - a)/\bar{w}$.

Pensioners do not of course pay the National Insurance Contribution, so that the total VAT payments of those retired is given by:

$$\frac{v}{1+v}\,\bar{w}\left[1+\frac{b}{\bar{w}}-tG^*\right] \tag{20}$$

The budget constraint therefore requires that the gross transfer of Pb, less income tax (given by (19)) and VAT (given by (20)) paid by pensioners, is equal to the total tax paid by the working population (given by (16)). After some tedious manipulation it can be found that the income tax rate, t, required to finance any given system is, with $R = b/\bar{y}$, equal to:

$$\frac{RD(1-v)-v\{1+D(R+\bar{w}/\bar{y})\}-c\{1-F_1(y_1)-G(y_2)\}}{G(a)+D(\bar{w}/\bar{y})\,G^*} \tag{21}$$

It is easily confirmed that the various special cases considered earlier can be obtained from (21) after appropriate substitution. For example if pensioners receive no additional income, $y_1 = a = 0$ and $y_2 = \infty$, then τ becomes simply $(v+c+t)/(1-t)$. Policy choice in general requires decisions to be made regarding the six tax parameters t, a, v, c, y_1 and y_2, though of course there are only five degrees of freedom. The tax treatment of the basic pension is also subject to policy choice. It is important to recognize that alternative choices carry different implications for income distribution. Furthermore, the recognition of additional earnings of pensioners brings into consideration the dispersion of incomes among pensioners. The basic pension can be financed with the help of relatively richer pensioners, rather than relatively poorer workers (those below the tax thresholds).

It must be stressed that this section has concentrated on the basic accounting relationships involved in a static framework, while significantly extending the simple approach often used to highlight the problems arising in an aging population. A more complete treatment of the issues would have to consider some of the general equilibrium implications involved. However, the modelling of such endogeneity is outside the scope of the present paper. But it is necessary to consider the nature of the dependency ratio in more detail. This is the subject of the following section.

III. THE DEPENDENCY RATIO

In discussing demographic projections it is conventional to define aged dependants as the group including all those over pension age (usually 65 for men and 60 for women). The denominator in calculating the aged dependency ratio is usually the number of those between 20 and retirement age. It is often assumed that movements in such a ratio, defined only according to the age distribution of the population, will accurately reflect movements in 'true' dependency ratios. However, such an assumption is too simplistic as allowance must be made for factors such as labour force participation.[6] Many official projections have assumed constant participation rates, yet reduced fertility is likely to be associated with a movement towards higher female participation rates. This section extends the model of Section II to consider the relationship between 'demographic' dependency and 'economic' dependency, the latter taking account of changes in the labour force participation rate of workers and other dynamic factors.

A Dynamic Formulation

It is useful first to put the model in dynamic terms, extending somewhat the model in Creedy and Disney (1989). For this purpose it is convenient to work in terms of 'generations' of workers and retirees. The relationship between current dependents, P, and current workers, E, is determined by two parameters. The first, μ, is a survival parameter governed by the expected average duration of retirement of each retiring cohort. The second, θ, is the proportion of the labour force, L, that chooses to participate in paid work. Thus:

$$P = \mu L_{-1} \tag{22}$$

and

$$E = \theta L \tag{23}$$

The size of the current and previous generations of the labour force L and L_{-1}, are linked by the rate of population growth. n:

$$L = (1+n) L_{-1} \tag{24}$$

Substituting (23) into (24) and then using (23) lagged one generation gives:

$$E = (1+\varepsilon)(1+n) E_{-1} \tag{25}$$

where $(1+\varepsilon)$ denotes (θ/θ_{-1}) and ε is thereby the growth of the labour force participation rate. Equation (25) has a straightforward interpretation. Similarly, substituting for L_{-1} from the lagged form of (23) into (22) gives:

$$P = (\mu/\theta_{-1}) E_{-1} \tag{26}$$

Then dividing (26) by (25):

$$P/E = (\mu/\theta_{-1})/\{(1+\varepsilon)(1+n)\} \tag{27}$$

which is a more appropriate measure of dependency than P/L. However, equation (22) assumes that all members of the potential labour force, L, receive a pension, whether or not they participate in paid work. An alter-

[6] See, for example, Falkingham (1988).

native and simpler formulation is that where:

$$P = \mu E_{-1}$$

This case typifies a 'pure' social insurance system in which pensions are only received by those who participate. The model in this case is considerably simplified as all terms in θ drop out including ε, and $(1+n)$ combines the effects of both population growth and any changes in the participation rate. Although in theory this case may be thought to correspond more closely to insurance schemes in developed countries, in practice 'pure' insurance schemes are hard to find given the presence of additional non-insurance benefits such as dependant's allowances and means-tested benefits. For this reason (16) is preferred here.

The components of the replacement ratio, b and w, are also related Suppose that the benefit, b is set as a proportion, β, of the wage earned by the retirees in their work life, z. Then:

$$b = \beta z_{-1} \tag{28}$$

The average wages of the current and previous generation are also linked by the rate of growth of real wages, g, so that:

$$z = (1+g)\, z_{-1} \tag{29}$$

Dividing (28) by (29) gives the replacement ratio in terms of β and the growth of real earnings:

$$b/z = \beta/(1+g) \tag{30}$$

In the general formulation of the basic model in equation (3), the composite 'tax rate' τ is equal to RD. Substituting for R and D using (30) and (27) respectively gives:

$$\tau = \frac{\beta(\mu/\theta_{-1})}{(1+n)(1+g)(1+\varepsilon)} \tag{31}$$

This formula has an intuitive rationale. The average tax rate needed to finance pensions, given the tax formula, is determined by the fraction of earnings replaced, β, and by the ratio of survivors to previous workers (μ/θ_{-1}). Clearly, the higher this last ratio, the higher the current tax rate needed to finance the pension of survivors.

The value of τ is reduced if any of the three growth rates in the denominator are positive. The equation can again be simplified where pensions are only paid to retired workers, when θ_{-1} and $(1+\varepsilon)$ drop out. Furthermore not only is there an upper bound on $E = L$ which ultimately constrains ε, but in a 'steady state' $(1+\varepsilon)$ must be exactly offset when pensions are only paid to retired workers, as these extra workers will ultimately receive the pensions which are accrued. However, many of the issue of pension policy that arise are better suited to the above dynamic framework, in which the growth rate of participation may be non-zero, than to comparative statics of various steady states.

Finally, for generality, it can be noted that (31) can be simplified if it is assumed that benefits are indexed to earnings, which is less common, and not prices as in (30). In this case $(1+g)$ drops out of the denominator and one more degree of policy flexibility is lost. The derivation of more complex indexation arrangements is discussed by Rosen (1984).

A policy issue stemming from this model concerns the interdependence of the growth rates g, n and ε. The interrelationship among them is one of the most interesting and complex issues in this framework. For example, the growth of the labour force and productivity may be interdependent, although the form of the relationship is not clear *a priori*; see Creedy and Disney (1989). Furthermore, the growth of labour force participation may be affected by the growth of real wages: this relationship might be expected to be positive in the short run if real wage rises induce greater participation, especially among married women. On the other hand, a higher rate of population growth may be associated with lower labour force participation especially among women of child bearing age.

The growth rate of the composite tax rate τ as the population ages will be alleviated significantly if a falling population growth rate leads to an increase in real wages. This will stimulate participation both indirectly by lower non-participation due to childrearing and directly by raising real wages if labour supply curves are forward sloping. This might be regarded as a 'virtuous circle' associated with population aging, but other outcomes are of course possible.

Some Numerical Examples

To illustrate the magnitudes involved, this subsection presents some numerical examples. A problem is that the growth rates in the denominator of (31) are defined over 'generations' without any specification of the duration of a 'generation' in years. Suppose therefore that the working life is 40 years and the expected average duration of retirement is 15 years. The survival parameter μ is therefore 0.375. If it is assumed that all men and half the women were employed in their working life, θ is 0.75. Finally, assume that β is 0.5. If there is no growth in the population, in labour force productivity or in labour force participation, the required 'tax rate' τ is 25 per cent.

Now consider the dynamic aspect of the pension financing problem. Assume initially that the population grows at 1 per cent per annum through labour force entry, productivity grows at 2 per cent per annum, and that participation rates are constant. If discrete generations are considered, the tax rate needed to finance the retirement of a given generation declines exponentially in line with population and productivity growth. The 'length' of this retired duration can be considered to be the expected duration of retirement which, in this example, is 15 years. Thus the average tax rate needed to fund the pensions of this retired generation is:

$$\frac{0.5(0.375/0.75)}{(1.01)(1.02)(1.00)^{15}}=0.16 \tag{32}$$

This gives a rate of 16 per cent, considerably lower than in the static case. It can be noted that this result is equivalent to that obtained from an overlapping generation model in steady state growth where the size of the cohort does not enter (31) directly. The tax rate will vary out of steady state as changes in the population growth rate work their way through the age distribution of the working life and retirement.

An interesting result is that a change in the survival parameter, μ, affects both the numerator and the denominator. Thus a rise in the expected duration of retirement, say from 15 to 20 years, raises the tax rate needed to finance the scheme through the change in the numerator, but lowers it through the denominator, since the growth rates are now compounded over a longer period. In fact the former effect dominates (with $\beta=0.5$, the required tax rate rises from 16 per cent to 18.4 per cent), but the relationship between the tax rate and increasing longevity is non-linear, for the simple reason that the increased longevity occurs at the end of the life! In contrast, changes in β have linear effects on the tax rate. These implications are illustrated in Figure 2, which shows the impact on τ of variations

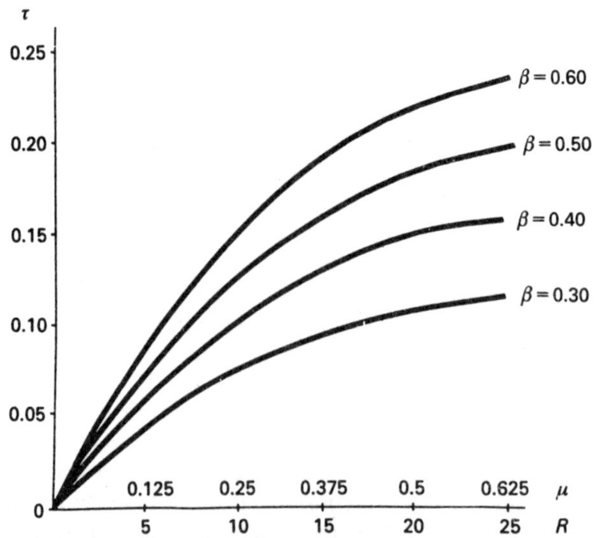

Fig. 2. Effects of variation in expected duration of retirement and replacement ratio on tax rate.

in μ, for different values of β. As explained, the variations in μ induce a non-linear response in τ, whereas changes in β (the shift factor) induce proportionate changes. Similar results would occur from variations in the length of the working life, such as changes in the rules governing early retirement, or even a change in the state pensionable age.

It is also useful to consider the case where the growth rates are interdependent. Suppose that the population growth rate falls by the one percentage point from the previous example, to zero growth. Also assume that the elasticity of productivity growth with respect to population growth is -1, of participation with respect to population growth is -2, and of participation with respect to productivity growth is $+1$ (this is the 'virtuous circle' case described earlier). This reduction in population growth reduces the tax rate needed to finance pensions by stimulating productivity growth and labour force participation growth. The consequent average tax rate in this case is 10.2 per cent.

In contrast, suppose the elasticity of productivity growth with respect to population growth is $+1$, with the other elasticities as before. Here the various effects of changes in population growth counteract each other, but the net effect is to raise the necessary tax rate slightly from the base-line case slightly to 18.6 per cent. Thus the tax rate is sensitive to the assumptions made concerning the relation between population growth and productivity growth; a topic of which insufficient is still known; see OECD (1988, chap. 7).

V. CONCLUSION

This paper starts from the standard model of pension financing in which the tax rate needed to finance a pay-as-you-go state pension is determined by the interaction of the replacement ratio and the demographically defined aged dependency ratio. It has been argued that projections of future pension costs on the basis of such a simple model are seriously misleading. The scope for flexibility within each of the three components of the model (the tax function, the replacement ratio, the aged dependency ratio) was then considered in turn.

The analysis suggests that the combination of direct and indirect taxes and the significant non-linearities in the system of direct taxation, along with additional incomes of the retired, permit a wide range of policy responses to rising pension costs. Similarly the replacement ratio can be measured in a number of ways, with the pension based on after-tax earnings or treated as taxable income.

The final section considered a dynamic version of the model, which took account of the possibility of changes in participation rates as well as population and productivity growth. Variations in longevity and the replacement ratio were examined and the interrelationships between population growth, productivity growth and labour force participation were explored.

The University of Melbourne and The University of Kent at Canterbury

Received November 1989, revision accepted October 1990

REFERENCES

Campbell, C. D. (ed.) (1984). *Controlling the Cost of Social Security*, Lexington, for American Enterprise Institute, Massachusetts.

Clark, R. I. and Spengler, J. J. (1980). *The Economics of Individual and Population Aging*, Cambridge University Press, Cambridge.

Creedy, J. (1985). *Dynamics of Income Distribution*, Basil Blackwell, Oxford.

Creedy, J. and Disney, R. (1989). 'The Australian State Pension Scheme: Some Basic Analytics', *Economic Record*, Vol. 65, pp. 357–68.

Creedy, J. and Disney, R. (1989a). 'Can We Afford to Grow Older? Population Aging and Social Security', *European Economic Review*, Vol. 33, pp. 367–76.

Falkingham, J. (1988). 'Dependency and Ageing in Britain: A Re-examination of the Evidence', *Journal of Social Policy*, Vol. 18, pp. 211–33.

Foster, C. (1988). *Towards a National Retirement Incomes Policy*, Issue Paper No. 6, Social Security Review, Department of Social Security, Canberra.

Heller, P. S., Hemming, R. and Kohnert, P. W. (1986). *Aging and Social Expenditure in the Major Industrial Countries 1980–2025*, Occasional Paper No. 47, International Monetary Fund, Washington DC.

HMSO (1985a). *Reform of Social Security*, Cmnd. 9517, HMSO, London.

HMSO (1985b). *Reform of Social Security, Background Paper No. 2, Volume 3*, Cmnd9519, HMSO, London.

OECD (1985). *Social Expenditure 1960–1990: Problems of Growth and Control*, OECD, Paris.

OECD (1988). *Ageing Populations: The Social Policy Implications*, Paris.

Rosen, S. (1984). 'Some Arithmetic of Social Security', In C. D. Campbell (ed.), *Controlling the Cost of Social Security*, American Enterprise Institute, Lexington, MA, pp. 233–55.

Rosa, J. J. (ed.) (1982). *The World Crisis in Social Security*, Bannel, Paris.

Wilson, T. and Wilson, D. J. (1982). *The Political Economy of the Welfare State*, George Allen and Unwin, London.

[29]

POPULATION AGING AND SOCIAL SECURITY: A POLITICO-ECONOMIC MODEL OF STATE PENSION FINANCING*

ROBERT K. VON WEIZSÄCKER**

I. INTRODUCTION

Most developed countries are currently facing great financial difficulties in maintaining public redistribution programs. Particularly endangered is the financing of the state pension system. One of the main reasons for this situation is a shift in the age structure of the population. The post-war baby boom has been followed by a rapid decline in birth rates; at the same time, mortality rates have continued to fall. As a consequence, the relative population share of those receiving public transfers has dramatically increased and will continue to do so in the future. This development must have an impact on public policy actions. But how should the government adjust to the demographic change? In which way should the key parameters of a pay-as-you-go financed state pension system be corrected to cope with the solvency problem? None of the two extreme variants, i.e., lowering the pension level while holding the contribution rate constant or increasing the social security tax rate while holding the replacement rate constant, seems politically acceptable. *Both* groups, pensioners and workers, should play some part in bearing the demographic burden. However, how can society compromise on the distributional dilemma?

The model designed in the present paper attempts to describe some aspects of the *politico-economic* process leading to a solution of the distributional problem. A conventional budgetary analysis, a widely used tool in the institutional public finance literature, clearly is not sufficient to determine the trade-off between workers' taxes and retirees' benefits. Indeed, an aging population does not only affect the financial relations of the state pension system; it also changes the relative number of *votes* cast by workers and pensioners. This puts conventional conclusions drawn from pure budgetary analyses in a different light. If the responsible policymakers aim at being reelected then fiscal adjustments of the state pension budget will depend on *political* factors determined by the *age structure* of the population.

The political economy of social security is a fairly young area of economic research. Most of the sparsely existing literature on the decision-making process with respect to the size and structure of public pensions deals with the case of direct democracy, i.e., with the median voter model. In this paper the median voter model is no longer adhered to. In fact, in most western industrialized countries the institutional form of the voting process is not of a direct but of a representative kind. Economic decisions are taken by politicians within a government organization. Individual voters do not have a direct influence on specific issues. However, the ruling political bodies are not autonomous in their decisions. They have to take into account a number of factors, like the pressure of political parties, the power of certain interest groups in the society (in our case, the working versus the retired generation), and last not least, the compulsion of being re-elected. This view is formalized by an explicit optimizing calculus. It is assumed that the government's objective is to choose the level of pension expenditure and social security taxation so as to maximize effective expected support by workers and pensioners, subject to the government budget constraints, the voter's utility-maximizing responses, as well as the just mentioned politico-economic influences. Given that no single voter has a direct impact on economic decisions, that different groups in the population exercise different political power, and that governmental actions are driven by reelection-motives, a solution to the distributional problem can be derived which deviates from standard budgetary considerations: The design of old-age pensions will be related to a *demographic politico-economic* interplay which has been neglected so far.

The paper is organized as follows. Section II presents the model. This is done in two steps. First, the individual utility-maximizing process is described (Subsection II.A), and second, the rational optimizing behaviour of the government is developed (Subsection II.B). This sets the stage for the main results of the paper presented in Section III. While theoretical implications for the state pension policy are derived in Subsection III.A, quantitative illustrations are given in Subsection III.B.

II. THE MODEL

Given the problem outlined in Section I, a decision has to be made on how the financial burden of an aging population is to be divided up between the old and the young. In deriving an objective function for the government which may serve this purpose, the present paper integrates certain observed characteristics of representative democracies. Adding hitherto unconnected factors like population age structure and political power distribution an exploratory framework is designed in Subsection II.B which allows for a demographic impact on a politico-economic trade-off between the level of contribution payments and the level of pensions. Three factors shape the division of the financial cake: individual maximizing responses (Subsection II.A), the institutional and financial constraints of the state pension system, and the optimizing behaviour of the government (Subsection II.B). The politically optimal state pension policy derived in Subsection III.A and illustrated in Subsection III.B hence explicitly results from rational, self-interested behaviour both in the private *and* public sector.

II. A. The Individuals

Economic life extends over of two periods. In the first period individuals work, in the second they retire. At start of economic life each individual faces the problem of how to allocate consumption between the two periods and how to decide on the supply of labour. The more labour the individual supplies, the higher his disposable income and thus his opportunities to consume; on the other hand, a higher labour supply entails less leisure. Most pay-as-you-go financed state pension systems relate the level of retirement incomes to the level of contributions, i.e., a higher labour income implies a higher pension when old (ceteris paribus). This institutional provision is also adapted here. Public policy parameters enter the individual decisions via the intertemporal budget constraint. The maximizing problem of a representative individual of generation t may formally be written as:

$$\max_{\{c_{1t}, c_{2t+1}, h_t\}} \quad U = u_1(c_{1t}, 1 - h_t) + u_2(c_{2t+1}, 1)$$

subject to

$$c_{1t} + \frac{c_{2t+1}}{1+r} = Y_t + \frac{P_{net,t+1}}{1+r}, \tag{1}$$

where:

$$Y_t = (1-\tau)(1-\theta)A_t,$$
$$P_{net,t+1} = (1-\tau)P_{t+1},$$
$$P_{t+1} = pA_t,$$
$$A_t = w_t h_t.$$

Hence, the individual acts as if he wants to maximize his lifetime utility U subject to the budget constraint (1). Arguments of the strictly quasi-concave utility function are first-period consumption c_{1t}, second-period consumption c_{2t+1}, and labour supply h_t. The latter is restricted to the working period. The fraction of time not spent working represents leisure ℓ; let $\ell_t + h_t = 1$. In the second period, $h = 0$ or $\ell = 1$. Gross earnings A_t result from $w_t h_t$, where w_t depicts the real wage rate. Three different policy instruments enter the constraint of the above maximization problem: the tax rate τ, the rate of contributions to the state pension fund θ, and the retirement benefit rate p. Individual earnings are subject to both taxation and compulsory pension contributions. The latter are directly proportional to earnings and tax-deductible, so taxable labour income is $(1-\theta)A_t$. In the present model the tax system only serves to finance a public grant to the pension fund. For illustrative purposes the simple case of proportional taxation at a constant marginal tax rate τ is assumed. Accordingly, it is net labour income Y_t which enters (1). Next-period pension P_{t+1} is linked to gross

earnings A_t through the retirement benefit rate p. P_{t+1} is subject to taxation. Finally, present values are determined by discounting second-period quantities at the market interest rate r.

Given the above assumptions, necessary *and* sufficient conditions for the utility-maximizing allocation of consumption and the optimal work/leisure-choice are:

$$\text{(2)} \qquad \frac{\partial u_1/\partial c_{1t}}{\partial u_2/\partial c_{2t+1}} = 1 + r,$$

$$\text{(3)} \qquad \frac{\partial u_1/\partial \ell_t}{\partial u_1/\partial c_{1t}} = \left(1 - \theta + \frac{p}{1+r}\right)(1-\tau)w_t.$$

Thus, in order to maximize lifetime utility, the individual should equate the ratio of the marginal utilities of first-period and second-period consumption to the ratio of discounted prices [eq. (2)], and the ratio of the marginal utilities of leisure and first-period consumption to the net-wage total given in eq. (3).

(1), (2), and (3) constitute three equations for three unknowns. For a given utility function U the individual demand functions c^*_{1t}, c^*_{2t+1}, and h^*_t can be derived. The numerical calculations of Subsection III.B call for *explicit* solutions. This requires an explicit functional specification of the utility function. A conventional and sufficiently flexible functional form is a constant elasticity of substitution utility function which may be expressed as:

$$\text{(4)} \qquad U = \left[\mu c_{1t}^{-\rho} + \nu(1-h_t)^{-\rho} + \xi c_{2t+1}^{-\rho}\right]^{\frac{-1}{\rho}},$$

$$0 < \mu, \nu, \xi < 1, \qquad -1 < \rho < 0.$$

Maximizing (4) subject to the intertemporal budget constraint (1) yields a closed parametric form solution for a representative individual's optimal labour supply:

$$\text{(5)} \qquad h^*_t = \left[1 + \frac{\left[(1-\tau)\left(1-\theta+\frac{p}{1+r}\right)w_t\right]^{\frac{\rho}{1+\rho}}}{\left(\frac{\mu}{\nu}\right)^{\frac{1}{1+\rho}} + \left(\frac{\xi}{\nu}\right)^{\frac{1}{1+\rho}}\left(\frac{1}{1+r}\right)^{\frac{\rho}{1+\rho}}}\right]^{-1}$$

To all parameters in (5) the period-index t could be affixed. The individual's calculations are based on parameter values which he can observe at the beginning of economic life. To determine tomorrow's net pension the individual uses today's policy parameters. The individual has no intertemporal information. His knowledge about tax and pension rates is restricted to period t. If in the second period the individual's

expectations, i.e., $E(\tau_{t+1}) = \tau_t$ etc. such that $P_{net,t+1} = [1 - E(\tau_{t+1})]E(P_{t+1})$ $A_t = (1 - \tau_t)p_t A_t$, turn out to be incorrect, then this has to be accepted. Behaviour remains unaffected since, by assumption, nothing is to be decided in the retirement period.

Utilizing (5) together with $A_t^* = w_t h_t^*$ gives the behavioural reactions of optimal gross earnings:

$$A_t^* = A_t^* \langle \overset{+}{\mu}, \overset{-}{\nu}, \overset{+}{\xi}, \rho; \overset{+}{w_t}, r; \overset{-}{\theta}, \overset{+}{p}, \overset{-}{\tau}, \rangle, \tag{6}$$

reflecting, among other things, the utility-maximizing responses to changes in the policy variables θ, p, and τ.

II. B. The Government

The present analysis is set in an overlapping generations framework.[1] Individuals born at the beginning of period t constitute generation t. Each individual lives for two periods, working in the first and retiring in the second. In period t the young of generation t overlap with the old of generation $t - 1$. The number of workers in period t is L_t, the number of retirees is R_t. The labour force grows at rate n per period, implying: $L_t = (1 + n)L_{t-1} = (1 + n)R_t$.

The policy instruments introduced in Subsection II.A are all part of a pay-as-you-go financed state pension system. In each period the policymaker has to assure the financing of old-age pensions by adjusting his instruments to the prevailing economic and demographic conditions.[2] But how are the retirement benefit rate p, the contribution rate θ, and the tax rate τ related to each other? How are they adjusted, e.g., to an aging population? The present paper tries to answer these questions in an exploratory way by devising an explicit optimizing calculus for the policymaker. All three instruments will be *endogenously* determined.

Whatever the government's objective function, its optimization is subject to certain financial constraints. In each period the expenditure side of the pension fund has to be matched with the revenue side. Expenditures are represented by total pension payments RP,[3] revenues by total contributions $L\theta A$ plus a state subsidy G. The latter is financed by a proportional tax on labour and retirement incomes. In this way, pensioners contribute to a small extent to the financing of old-age pensions. The state pension system at hand thus is not of a pure pay-as-you-go type; realistically, it is supplemented by a public grant financed by all taxpayers. In sum, the budget constraints are:[4]

$$RP = L\theta A + G, \tag{7}$$

$$G = L\tau(1 - \theta)A + R\tau P. \tag{8}$$

These restrictions are still incomplete, since no account is taken of the institutional details determining P and G. As already indicated in the foregoing section, the individual pension is related to the level of income earned in the working period, i.e., $P = pA_{-1}$; hence, p may be interpreted as the gross replacement rate. All countries employing a tax-financed state subsidy link this quantity in some way to the size of social security or to gross earnings. In Germany, for example, the new Pension Reform Act intends to combine both aspects by including the rate of contributions and gross wage income. This may be formalized by $G = \gamma\theta A$, where γ stands for a fixed subsidy rate.[5] Using both institutional details,

(9) $$P = pA_{-1}, \qquad p > 0,$$

and

(10) $$G = \gamma\theta A, \qquad \gamma > 0,$$

together with (7) and (8) gives:

(11) $$\tau = \frac{\gamma\theta}{\gamma\theta + L},$$

(12) $$p = \frac{L+\gamma}{R}(1+g)\theta,$$

where $g := A/A_{-1} - 1$. Relations (11) and (12) will be employed to express the tax rate τ and the retirement benefit rate p as (implicit) functions of the contribution rate θ.

Given (11) and (12), the question is of course: how is θ determined? The model designed in the present paper tries to answer this question in an exploratory manner by referring to the *politico-economic theory of old-age insurance*, a surprisingly neglected area of economic research.[6] The institutional form of the political decision-making process is indeed an important determinant of its outcome. In a direct democracy, each individual has the same weight in determining the result; size and structure of the state pension scheme only depend on the demand side of the political market. In a representative democracy, however, voters no longer have a direct influence on specific decisions; factors shaping the supply side of the political market come into play. In fact, combining the model set out above with the concept of a direct democracy would not yield any far-reaching results, since in a two-generation context the decision on the level of the social security tax rate simply depends on the old-age dependency ratio: if $R/L < 1$, workers are in the majority and the single decision-maker is the representative labourer; in the reverse case ($R > L$), the representative retiree decides on the level of the contribution rate ($\Rightarrow \theta = 1$).

The assumption that individual voters exercise a direct influence upon specific governmental decisions will be replaced by a broader perspective.[7] Before going into details, it should be pointed out that the model developed below studies the implications of different political equilibria, not the consequences of political processes. Questions concerning the existence and stability of political equilibrium are left out of consideration, so are explicit game-theoretic derivations of the governmental objective function.[8] Political equilibria are interpreted as the result of a competitive process. It is assumed that political competition is sufficiently strong to enforce convergence to an optimal strategy and that the resulting political equilibrium is stable.[9]

The present paper assumes that the government's objective is to set the policy instruments of the public pension system so as to maximize expected political support by workers and pensioners. This hypothesis rests on Anthony Downs' *homo politicus*; starting from a 'self-interest axiom', Downs presumes: "Politicians act solely in order to attain the income, prestige, and power which come from being in office. Thus they never seek office as a means of carrying out particular policies; their only goal is to reap the rewards of holding office *per se*. They treat policies purely as means to the attainment of their private ends, which they can reach only by being elected. ... This in turn implies that democratic governments act rationally to maximize political support" [1957, p. 28]. Effective individual support, as seen by the government, depends on three factors. First, on the level of old-age pensions received, and the loss in earnings resulting from taxation. Second, on characteristics which determine how a particular individual's net economic benefit from the social security system is translated into a probability of voting for the government. And third, on the individual's relative political influence. The latter alludes to the fact that in the real world equality of franchise differs from equality of influence; individuals (or groups of individuals) with greater political power are able to exercise greater political support. Taking these three factors into account, the government's behaviour can be interpreted as the maximization of a *weighted sum of expected votes*.

Effective political support of a representative worker can be formalized as follows. The probability of voting for the government is denoted by π_L. This probability is a monotonically increasing function of S_L, the index of support:

$$S_L = B_L(P^*_{net,+1}) - \Omega_L(Q^*), \tag{13}$$

where:

$$P^*_{net,+1} = (1-\tau)pA^*,$$
$$Q^* = [\theta + \tau(1-\theta)]A^*.$$

Thus, the probability of voting for the government is the higher, the smaller the loss in earnings from taxation Q^* and the smaller the resulting effective opposition Ω_L, and the greater the net pension $P^*_{net,+1}$ expected for tomorrow and the larger the benefits B_L associated with it. Marginal opposition to taxation increases with loss in earnings ($\partial^2\Omega_L/\partial Q^{*2} > 0$), while marginal benefits decline with net retirement income ($\partial^2 B_L/\partial P^{*}_{net,+1}{}^2 < 0$). The support index S_L is a function of A^* and hence explicitly takes into account the utility-maximizing reactions of a representative worker to changes in the policy parameters θ, τ, and p. From the government's point of view, not only the *economic* responses Q^* and $P^{*}_{net,+1}$, but also the *political* reactions $\Omega_L(\cdot)$ and $B_L(\cdot)$ are to be considered. Including as a final factor the relative political power of a representative worker, $1-\alpha$, the expected effective political support by the labourers can be expressed as: $L \cdot (1-\alpha)\pi_L\{S_L\}$.

Political support of a representative retiree differs in one important respect from S_L. While today's policy decisions directly affect lifetime utility maximization of the young (and thus concern both their net earnings of today and their net pensions of tomorrow), the old are only touched in the level of their net retirement incomes. Pension contributions devolve on the working generation. The index of support of a representative retiree, S_R, thus reduces to:

(14) $$S_R = B_R(P^{*}_{net}) = B_R[(1-\tau)pA^{*}_{-1}].$$

Let π_R denote the probability of voting for the government and α the relative political influence of a representative retiree, then the expected effective support by the group of pensioners is captured by: $R \cdot \alpha\pi_R\{S_R\}$.

Having introduced all components of the governmental objective function, the behaviour of the government can now be summarized: Given the two financial restrictions $RP - L\theta A - G = 0$ and $G - L\tau(1-\theta)A - R\tau P = 0$ and taking into account the individual reaction equation $A^*(\cdot)$, the government chooses the level of the retirement benefit rate p, the level of the rate of contributions to the state pension fund θ, and the level of the tax rate τ so as to maximize expected effective support Z, where:

(15) $$Z = L \cdot (1-\alpha) \cdot \pi_L\{S_L\} + R \cdot \alpha \cdot \pi_R\{S_R\}.$$

III. POLITICAL ECONOMY OF OLD-AGE SECURITY: RESULTS

III. A. Analytical Structure

Replacing the tax rate τ and the pension rate p by eqs. (11) and (12), the optimization problem of the government can be reduced to:

$$\max_{\{\theta\}} Z(\theta)$$

where:

(16) $$Z(\theta) = L \cdot (1-\alpha) \cdot \pi_L\{B_L[P^{*}_{net,+1}(\theta)] - \Omega_L[Q^*(\theta)]\} + R \cdot \alpha \cdot \pi_R\{B_R[P^{*}_{net}(\theta)]\}.$$

Realistically: $\partial Q^*/\partial\theta > 0, \alpha \neq 1$, and $\partial\pi_L/\partial S_L \neq 0$. Utilizing these relations, the first-order condition $\partial Z/\partial\theta = 0$ yields:[10]

$$\frac{L}{R}(1+g)\frac{\partial B_L}{\partial P^*_{net,+1}} + \frac{\alpha}{1-\alpha}\frac{\partial\pi_R/\partial S_R}{\partial\pi_L/\partial S_L}\frac{\partial B_R}{\partial P^*_{net}} = \frac{\partial\Omega_L}{\partial Q^*}. \tag{17}$$

Thus, following its optimizing calculus, the government has to adjust the social security tax rate so as to equalize marginal effective political return (resulting from a marginal increase of retirement income) and marginal political cost (resulting from an increased tax burden). The per-capita condition (17) for the optimal θ^* explicitly takes into account the political power distribution between workers and pensioners as well as the different voting reactions to changes in the politico-economic indices S_L and S_R.

Which are the properties of the optimal social security tax rate θ^*? Let us first consider the ceteris-paribus effect of a larger political power-share of a representative retiree. A higher α lends more weight to the expected marginal political benefit of a marginal rise in today's average pension; see (17). Since the retirees themselves do not pay for an additional retirement income, the rate of contributions to the state pension fund can be increased until the now larger politico-economic opposition to taxation by the workers again leads to an equalization of marginal return and marginal cost. Bearing in mind the second-order conditions for a unique solution to the government's problem, one may expect the politically optimal θ^* to grow with α; indeed, via the implicit function theorem:

$$\frac{\partial\theta^*}{\partial\alpha} = -\frac{F_\alpha}{F_\theta}, \tag{18}$$

where:

$$F_\alpha := \frac{\partial B_R}{\partial P^*_{net}}\frac{\Pi}{(1-\alpha)^2},$$

$$F_\theta := \frac{L}{R}(1+g)\frac{\partial^2 B_L}{\partial {P^*_{net,+1}}^2}\frac{\partial P^*_{net,+1}}{\partial\theta} + \frac{\alpha}{1-\alpha}\left(\frac{\partial\Pi}{\partial\theta}\frac{\partial B_R}{\partial P^*_{net}} + \Pi\frac{\partial^2 B_R}{\partial {P^*_{net}}^2}\frac{\partial P^*_{net}}{\partial\theta}\right)$$
$$-\frac{\partial^2\Omega_L}{\partial {Q^*}^2}\frac{\partial Q^*}{\partial\theta},$$

and:

$$\Pi(\theta) := \frac{\partial\pi_R\{S_R(\theta)\}/\partial S_R}{\partial\pi_L\{S_L(\theta)\}/\partial S_L}.$$

Stipulating $\partial\Pi/\partial\theta < 0$ (confirmed later), F_θ is unambiguously negative; together with $F_\alpha > 0$ this gives:

$$\frac{\partial\theta^*}{\partial\alpha} > 0, \tag{19}$$

i.e., the politico-economically optimal social security tax rate is an *increasing* function of a representative retiree's relative political power. This relation has often been alleged in political disputes and *exogenously* assumed in a number of studies. In the present case, it is an *endogenous* result of an explicit model based on economically *and* politically *rational* behaviour.

What about the politico-economic impact of a demographic change? How does a larger number of retirees affect the state budget constraints? How does this bear upon the allocational decisions of the workers, the individual economic net-positions, the expected political support- and opposition-weights, the optimizing responses of the government, and finally the politically optimal level of the social security tax? What is the effect of an aging population on the optimal levels of the replacement rate and the state subsidy, given that all policy instruments are endogenously determined?

Again applying the implicit function theorem to (17), one gets:

$$\frac{\partial\theta^*}{\partial R} = -\frac{F_R}{F_\theta}, \tag{20}$$

where:

$$F_R := \frac{L}{R}(1+g)\left(\frac{\partial^2 B_L}{\partial {P^*_{net,+1}}^2}\frac{\partial P^*_{net,+1}}{\partial R} - \frac{1}{R}\frac{\partial B_L}{\partial P^*_{net,+1}}\right)$$

$$+\frac{\alpha}{1-\alpha}\left(\frac{\partial\Pi}{\partial R}\frac{\partial B_R}{\partial P^*_{net}} + \Pi\frac{\partial^2 B_R}{\partial {P^*_{net}}^2}\frac{\partial P^*_{net}}{\partial R}\right) - \frac{\partial^2\Omega_L}{\partial {Q^*}^2}\frac{\partial Q^*}{\partial R},$$

$$F_\theta := \frac{L}{R}(1+g)\frac{\partial^2 B_L}{\partial {P^*_{net,+1}}^2}\frac{\partial P^*_{net,+1}}{\partial\theta} + \frac{\alpha}{1-\alpha}\left(\frac{\partial\Pi}{\partial\theta}\frac{\partial B_R}{\partial P^*_{net}} + \Pi\frac{\partial^2 B_R}{\partial {P^*_{net}}^2}\frac{\partial P^*_{net}}{\partial\theta}\right)$$

$$-\frac{\partial^2\Omega_L}{\partial {Q^*}^2}\frac{\partial Q^*}{\partial\theta}$$

The politico-economic impact of an aging population on the optimal rate of contributions is theoretically *unpredictable*, since the sign of F_R cannot be determined unambiguously. A larger number of pensioners (or a greater old-age dependency ratio) not only affects the level of retirement incomes [see (12)] and thus the expected political benefit, but via utility-maximizing labour supply responses it also changes the political opposition. If the marginal voting probability ratio between retirees and workers, Π, is a increasing function of the number of pensioners, R, and if the R-elasticity of the workers' marginal political benefit is greater than one, then the optimal social security tax rate increases with the number of retirees. In this case, the sought derivative corresponds with the well-known prediction of standard budgetary calculations. However, if the above conditions are *not* met, *both* derivative-signs are possible a priori.

Regarding the optimal state pension rate, one finds:

$$\frac{\partial p^*}{\partial R} = (L + \gamma)(1 + g)(\varepsilon_{\theta^*,R} - 1)\frac{\theta^*}{R^2}. \tag{21}$$

If the elasticity of the contribution rate with respect to the number of pensioners is negative, then the optimal retirement benefit rate p^* declines when the old-age dependency ratio goes up. On the other hand, if the mentioned elasticity is sufficiently large, the government, in order to maximize expected political support, ought to *raise* the level of pensions when the old-age dependency ratio *increases*. None of the public finance studies merely examining the budgetary restrictions of state pension schemes would permit such a conclusion. The actual size of the critical elasticity depends on a set of quite complex analytical conditions and thus on relations which can only be determined econometrically or by empirically founded numerical calculations. To this task the next section, i.e., the *quantitative* part of the paper, is devoted.[11]

III. B. Quantitative Analysis

In order to be able to characterize more closely the properties of the optimal rate of contributions θ^*, the optimal retirement benefit rate p^*, as well as the optimal size of the public grant G^*, an analytical link has to be established between the politico-economic support indices S_L and S_R on the one hand and the corresponding voting probabilities π_L and π_R on the other. The gap is closed by referring to the *logit model* of qualitative choice.[12] This device not only translates the support index into a voting probability in a rather flexible way, but it also allows for an integration of a fairly relevant, though widely neglected phenomenon. The public provision of social security is not simply an economic matter. A number of other factors come into play. There are social, redistributional, and legal reasons for the implementation of a pay-as-you-go financed state pension scheme. Financing aspects, economic profitability, and allocative efficiency are just partially decisive. In fact, polling evidence in a number of countries suggests that the social security system is broadly supported by the population, irrespective of the intergenerational redistribution problem raised by the demographic trend. Social custom, altruism, and confidence in political institutions increase the probability of voting for the government. Gallup polls in the United States and in Canada consistently indicate that the degree of support for social security is high and does not vary much by age; even the current young who are clear financial losers from social security in fact strongly support the programme.[13] In other words: There exists a *positive externality* of the state pension system which has been disregarded by the social security literature so far, which, however, can now be explicitly integrated using an extended version of the standard logit model:

$$\pi(S,\omega) = \frac{1}{1+\omega e^{-S}}, \tag{22}$$

where $1/\omega$ ($\omega > 0$) serves as a measure of the externality; the smaller ω, the larger the impact of the above-mentioned system-supporting factors. The present distinction between economic net-position, political evaluation, and individual support probability thus permits the inclusion of a quantity that bears upon the voting probability while leaving the allocational decisions untouched.

Numerical calculations necessitate a functional specification of $B_L(\cdot)$, $B_R(\cdot)$, and $\Omega_L(\cdot)$ [see (17)]. Here, the simplest functional form being consistent with all qualitative requirements formulated in Section III.A is chosen:

$$B_L(P^*_{net,+1}) = \frac{1}{x}P^{*\,x}_{net,+1}, \quad 0 < x < 1,$$

$$B_R(P^*_{net}) = \frac{1}{y}P^{*\,y}_{net}, \quad 0 < y < 1,$$

$$\Omega_L(Q^*) = \frac{1}{z}Q^{*z}, \quad z > 1.$$

The parameters x, y, and z can be interpreted as elasticities: $\varepsilon_{B_L}, P^*_{net,+1} = x$, $\varepsilon_{B_R}, P^*_{net} = y$, and $\varepsilon_{\Omega_L}, Q^* = z$. The given ranges for x, y, and z result from assumptions about derivatives made in preceding sections.[14] With these specifications the optimality condition (17) becomes:

$$\frac{L}{R}(1+g)P^{*\,x-1}_{net,+1} + \frac{\alpha}{1-\alpha}\frac{\pi_R(1-\pi_R)}{\pi_L(1-\pi_L)}P^{*\,y-1}_{net} = Q^{*z-1}. \tag{17a}$$

Utilizing a benchmark parameter set, the condition (17a) can be solved numerically by means of (5), (11), (12), and (22) in a recursive way.[15] The parameter values given below Table 1 are consistent with all theoretical restrictions and, as far as possible, empirically corroborated.[16]

III.B.1. Demographic Change, Individual Preferences, and Social Solidarity

Tables 1 – 3 concentrate on the policy instruments, since the comparative static reactions of θ^*, τ^*, G^*, and p^* reflect the complete structure of the model. To allow for comparisons of the orders of magnitude, the results are presented as elasticities.[17]

TABLE 1

Optimal State Pension Policy:
Demographic Change, Individual Preferences,
and Social Solidarity
(Ceteris-Paribus Sensitivities)

v	$\varepsilon_{\theta^*,v}$	$\varepsilon_{\tau^*,v}$	$\varepsilon_{G^*,v}$	$\varepsilon_{p^*,v}$
R	-0.074	-0.071	-0.214	-1.074
L	0.232	-0.729	0.371	1.032
μ	-0.558	-0.530	-0.028	-0.558
ν	0.771	0.732	0.039	0.771
ξ	-0.213	-0.202	-0.011	-0.213
x	0.254	0.241	0.266	0.254
y	0.229	0.218	0.240	0.229
z	-0.519	-0.492	-0.544	-0.519
ω	0.047	0.045	0.050	0.047
γ	-0.158	0.800	0.842	0.042
α	0.212	0.201	0.223	0.212

Benchmark Parameter Specification:
$\mu = 0.5, \nu = 0.5, \xi = 0.3, \rho = -0.5;$
$r = 0.06, \omega = 1; \gamma = 2.5; L = 10, R = 6;$
$\alpha = 0.4; \omega = 3; x = 0.5, y = 0.5, z = 1.5.$

In which way does the demographic change bear upon the politico-economically optimal state pension policy? How does a larger number of retirees affect the four policy instruments (ceteris paribus)? Inspecting the first line in Table 1, one comes across a surprise: The optimal rate of contributions θ^* is the *smaller* the *larger* the number of retirees; a counter-intuitive result, if one takes a pure budgetary analysis as a basis for intuition. What lies behind it? The partial derivatives given in (20) contain the answer: The R-elasticity of the workers' marginal political benefit is smaller than one; hence, the term in the first big parentheses in F_R is negative. Given the benchmark parameter set, this effect dominates all other effects in F_R. In order to reconcile marginal political return [which has been lowered by individual maximizing responses via the budget constraint (12)] with marginal political cost, the contribution rate has to be reduced [see (17)].[18]

The other three policy instruments also *fall* with R. Of particular interest is the optimal tax rate τ^*, since in budgetary equilibrium this rate reflects the distribution of the tax burden between workers and retirees; in fact, $1 - \tau^*$ gives the workers' share of rates and taxes.[19] How does the politico-economically optimal tax burden distribution react upon population aging? According to the quantitative sensitivity results presented in

Table 1, the pensioners' share of rates and taxes *decreases* with the number of retirees, while the workers' relative burden of payment goes *up*.

Since the model explicitly includes voters' utility-maximizing responses to public policy measures, the impact of individual preferences on the optimal state pension policy can be analyzed. A greater preference for leisure [$\nu \uparrow$, see (4)], for example, leads to a higher social security tax rate, a higher pension rate, as well as a higher state subsidy. A greater preference for consumption ($\mu \uparrow, \xi \uparrow$) has the opposite effects. Moreover, a larger opposition-elasticity z diminishes θ^*, τ^*, G^*, and p^*, while higher political benefit-elasticities x and y lead to opposite policy changes. Finally, the greater the social solidarity ($1/\omega \uparrow$), the higher the relative tax burden of the workers ($1 - \tau^* \uparrow$).

III.B.2. Population Age Structure and Political Power Distribution: Votes versus Dollar-Votes

In the preceding section the political power distribution $\{\alpha, 1-\alpha\}$ had been given exogenously. However, one could also think of linking the relative political influence of workers and retirees to other variables of the model, like, e.g., to the old-age dependency ratio. In this way, the *relative population shares* of both interest groups directly reflect their respective political powers; accordingly: $\alpha = R/(L+R)$.

TABLE 2

Optimal State Pension Policy:
Population Age Structure and Political Power Distribution
$\alpha = R/(L+R)$
(Ceteris-Paribus Sensitivities)

v	$\varepsilon_{\theta^*,v}$	$\varepsilon_{\tau^*,v}$	$\varepsilon_{G^*,v}$	$\varepsilon_{p^*,v}$
R	0.025	0.024	-0.109	-0.975
L	0.133	-0.824	0.267	0.933
μ	-0.558	-0.531	-0.028	-0.558
ν	0.771	0.733	0.038	0.771
ξ	-0.213	-0.202	-0.011	-0.213
x	0.263	0.250	0.276	0.263
y	0.215	0.205	0.226	0.215
z	-0.511	-0.486	-0.536	-0.511
ω	0.044	0.042	0.046	0.044
γ	-0.158	0.800	0.842	0.042

The impact of demographic shifts now gains in importance, since an increase in the old-age dependency ratio not only affects the financing constraints of the state pension system, but it also modifies the political power distribution. This leads to significant changes in the optimal level of all policy instruments. In particular, while in Table 1 the optimal social security tax rate declined with the number of retirees, it now *increases* with R — see Table 2. Responsible for the sign-reversal is an additional positive term in F_R [see (20)]. The retirement benefit rate still *decreases* with the old-age dependency ratio, though now *less* than before (see Tables 2 and 1). Note that the qualitative predictions of the present scenario are compatible with those drawn from a pure budgetary analysis — the widely used tool in the institutional public finance literature.

The relative population share, i.e., the relative number of voters in both interest groups, represents just one way to depict the relative political influence on government's decisions. Instead of the relative number of votes, it may very well be the relative number of *dollar*-votes, i.e., the *relative share of gross incomes*, which determines the political power distribution;[20] accordingly: $\alpha = RP^*/(LA^* + RP^*)$. The retirees' share of dollar-votes is smaller than their population share. The attribution of political influence to economic factors shifts the power distribution to the advantage of the workers.

TABLE 3

Optimal State Pension Policy:
Population Age Structure and Political Power Distribution
$\alpha = RP^*/(LA^* + RP^*)$
(Ceteris-Paribus Sensitivities)

v	$\epsilon_{\theta^*,v}$	$\epsilon_{T^*,v}$	$\epsilon_{G^*,v}$	$\epsilon_{P^*,v}$
R	-0.255	-0.243	-0.393	-1.255
L	0.414	-0.559	0.552	1.214
μ	-0.600	-0.572	-0.066	-0.600
ν	0.829	0.791	0.091	0.829
ξ	-0.229	-0.218	-0.025	-0.229
x	0.355	0.338	0.371	0.355
y	0.120	0.114	0.126	0.120
z	-0.490	-0.468	-0.513	-0.490
ω	0.023	0.022	0.024	0.023
γ	-0.159	0.803	0.841	0.041

In fact, the politico-economically optimal contribution rate now again *declines* as the number of retirees goes up, and it does so in an even *stronger* manner than before (compare Tables 3 and 1). Mainly responsible for this effect are individual disincentive reactions as reflected by respective changes in gross incomes, which now also affect the relative power weights.

These results suggest that, regarding the politico-economic impact of an aging population (and other factors), the integration and interpretation of the political power distribution between workers and retirees is of considerable importance for the practical design of a rational state pension policy.

IV. A FINAL REMARK

The main object of this paper has been to devise a conceptual framework for a consistent analysis of the question, which role *politico-economic* factors may play for the financing of state pension schemes and thus for the intergenerational distribution of the tax burden in view of the *demographic change*. The model designed here is intentionally simple to permit closed form parametric solutions which give an insight into the *structure* of the problem. The specific setup is more in the way of an illustration of the analytical framework, and the specific findings do no more than *warn* practitioners in this area not to rush to conclusions from simple budgetary analyses, rather than proclaim definitive answers or empirical truths.

NOTES

* Portions of this paper were presented at the Universities of Bonn and Hagen, as well as at the Annual Conference of the European Society for Population Economics in Paris, and at the Annual Congress of the German Economic Association in Vienna. Helpful comments from the participants at those meetings (especially from Dieter Biehl, Friedrich Breyer, Urs Schweizer, Harrie Verbon, and David Wildasin) and financial support from the Deutsche Forschungsgemeinschaft are gratefully acknowledged.

** The author currently is a Heisenberg Fellow of the German National Science Foundation. He is a member of the economics faculty at the University of Bonn and a DFG Research Associate (SFB 303, Bonn, Germany).

[1] See Samuelson [1958] and Diamond [1965].

[2] The continuance of the system as such is ensured and not under discussion. Political and economic arguments in favour of this presumption are provided by, e.g., Buchanan [1983] and Kotlikoff [1987].

[3] For ease of notation the period-index t is skipped.

[4] A and P denote labour and retirement incomes of a representative individual, which may be interpreted as per capita incomes.

[5] It would be of theoretical interest to extend the present model by looking at γ as an *endogenous* policy instrument determined by politico-economic forces in a similar way as θ, p, and τ are determined below. However, this would destroy the analytical tractability of the model unless some compensating simplifications are introduced — a price too high for the purposes of the present paper.

[6] Among the principal contributions are Browning [1975], Townley [1981], Hu [1982], Petersen [1984], Sjoblom [1985], van Velthoven and van Winden [1985], Verbon [1986, 1987], Breyer and Schulenburg [1987], as well as Boadway and Wildasin [1989a]. For partial surveys of the literature see Boadway and Wildasin [1989b] and Verbon [1988].

[7] The 'interest-function approach' developed by van Winden [1983] (and elaborated in van Velthoven and van Winden [1985], and in Renaud and van Winden [1987]) is a noteworthy possibility to formalize the mechanisms of a representative democracy in this context. This route, however, is not followed here.

[8] On this see e.g., Ordeshook [1986] and Coughlin [1986].

[9] This kind of approach has been followed by, among others, Stigler [1971], Peltzman [1976], Becker [1983], and Hettich and Winer [1988].

[10] Second-order conditions for a uniquely determined maximum of $Z(\theta)$ include (in addition to assumptions about derivatives made above): $\partial^2 B_L/\partial {P^*_{net,+1}}^2 < 0$, $\partial^2 B_R/\partial {P^*_{net}}^2 < 0$, $\partial^2 Q^*/\partial\theta^2 > 0$, $\partial^2 \Omega_L/\partial Q^* \partial\theta > 0$, and $\partial^2 A^*/\partial\theta^2 < 0$.

[11] For the sake of completeness it is mentioned that the reaction of the politically optimal state subsidy G^* to demographic shifts remains theoretically open; $G^*(R) = \gamma \cdot \theta^*(R) \cdot w \cdot h^*[\tau(\theta^*(R)), p(\theta^*(R)), \theta^*(R)]$. See the next section for further details.

[12] Careful reviews are provided by Amemiya [1981] and Kmenta [1986, Ch. 11–5].

[13] See Veall [1986, p. 238].

[14] Recall in particular: $B'_L > 0, B''_L < 0; B'_R > 0, B''_R < 0$, and $\Omega'_L > 0, \Omega''_L > 0$.

[15] The algorithm used is based on Broyden's secant method. See Dennis and Schnabel [1983, Ch. 8].

[16] The values listed below Table 1 roughly reflect the situation in Germany in 1986; see BMA [1988], BMI/Bundesregierung [1984], Statistisches Bundesamt [1986a, 1986b], and VDR [1988].

[17] The absolute values of the four instruments are, by the way: $\theta^* = 0.212$, $\tau^* = 0.050$, $G^* = 3.263$, and $p^* = 0.455$.

[18] This raises the marginal political benefit, while the marginal political opposition to taxation is decreased — note the second-order conditions listed in Section III.A.

[19] Total tax returns are: $L[\theta^* + \tau^*(1-\theta^*)]A^* + R\tau^* P^* = LQ^* + R\tau^* P^*$, see (7) and (8). Using (9) - (12), workers' relative tax contributions can be calculated as: $LQ^*/(LQ^* + R\tau^* P^*) = L/(\gamma\theta^* + L) = 1 - \tau^*$.

[20] This view is taken by, e.g., Stigler [1971] and Peltzman [1976].

REFERENCES

Amemiya, T., (1981), "Qualitative Response Models: A Survey", *Journal of Economic Literature*, Vol. 19, pp. 1483–1536.

Becker, G. S., (1983), "A Theory of Competition Among Pressure Groups for Political Influence", *Quarterly Journal of Economics*, Vol. 98, pp. 371–400.

BMA, (1988), *Arbeits- und Sozialstatistik: Hauptergebnisse 1988* (Bonn).

BMI/Bundesregierung, (1984), "Bericht über die Bevölkerungsentwicklung in der Bundesrepublik Deutschland, 2. Teil", *Bundestagsdrucksache*, 10/863.

Boadway, R. W., and Wildasin, D. E., (1989a), "A Median Voter Model of Social Security", *International Economic Review*, Vol. 30, pp. 307–28.

Boadway, R. W., and Wildasin, D. E., (1989b), "Voting Models of Social Security Determination", in: Gustafsson, B. A., and Klevmarken, N. A., eds., *The Political Economy of Social Security*, Contributions to Economic Analysis No. 179 (Amsterdam: North-Holland), pp. 29–50.

Breyer, F., and Schulenburg, J.-M. Graf von der, (1987), "Voting on Social Security: The Family as Decision-Making Unit", *Kyklos*, Vol. 40, pp. 529–47.

Browning, E. K., (1975), "Why the Social Insurance Budget is Too Large in a Democracy", *Economic Inquiry*, Vol. 13, pp. 373–88.

Buchanan, J. M., (1983), "Social Security Survival: A Public-Choice Perspective", *Cato Journal*, Vol. 3, pp. 339–53.

Coughlin, P. J., (1986), "Elections and Income Redistribution", *Public Choice*, Vol. 50, pp. 27–91.

Dennis, J. E., and Schnabel, R. B., (1983), *Numerical Methods for Unconstrained Optimization and Nonlinear Equations* (Englewood Cliffs, NJ: Prentice-Hall).

Diamond, P. A., (1965), "National Debt in a Neoclassical Growth Model", *American Economic Review*, Vol. 55, pp. 1126–50.

Downs, A., (1957), *An Economic Theory of Democracy* (New York: Harper & Brothers Publishers).

Hettich, W., and Winer, S. L., (1988), "Economic and Political Foundations of Tax Structure", *American Economic Review*, Vol. 78, pp. 701–12.

Hu, S. C., (1982), "Social Security, Majority-Voting Equilibrium and Dynamic Efficiency", *International Economic Review*, Vol. 23, pp. 269–87.

Kmenta, J., (1986), *Elements of Econometrics*, second edition (New York: Macmillan Publishing Company).

Kotlikoff, L. J., (1987), "Justifying Public Provision of Social Security", *Journal of Policy Analysis and Management*, Vol. 6, pp. 674–89.

Ordeshook, P. C., (1986), *Game Theory and Political Theory* (Cambridge: Cambridge University Press).

Peltzman, S., (1976), "Toward a More General Theory of Regulation", *Journal of Law and Economics*, Vol. 19, pp. 211–40.

Petersen, J. H., (1984), "The Political Economy of Financing Old-Age Pensions", *Zeitschrift für die gesamte Staatswissenschaft / Journal of Institutional and Theoretical Economics*, Vol. 140, pp. 430–47.

Renaud, P., and Winden, F. van, (1987), "Tax Rate and Government Expenditure", *Kyklos*, Vol. 40, pp. 349–67.

Samuelson, P. A., (1958), "An Exact Consumption-Loan Model of Interest with or without the Social Contrivance of Money", *Journal of Political Economy*, Vol. 66, pp. 467–82.

Sjoblom, K., (1985), "Voting for Social Security", *Public Choice*, Vol. 45, pp. 225–40.

Statistisches Bundesamt, (1986a), *Lange Reihen zur Wirtschaftsentwicklung 1986* (Stuttgart: Kohlhammer).

Statistisches Bundesamt, (1986b), "Sozialversicherungspflichtig beschäftigte Arbeitnehmer", *Bevölkerung und Erwerbstätigkeit*, Fachserie 1, Reihe 4.2 (Stuttgart: Kohlhammer).

Stigler, G. J., (1971), "The Theory of Economic Regulation", *Bell Journal of Economics*, Vol. 2, pp. 3–21.

Townley, P. G. C., (1981), "Public Choice and the Social Insurance Paradox: A Note", *Canadian Journal of Economics*, Vol. 14, pp. 712–17.

VDR, (1988), *Rentenversicherung in Zahlen 1988* (Frankfurt).

Veall, M. R., (1986), "Public Pensions as Optimal Social Contracts", *Journal of Public Economics*, Vol. 31, pp. 237–51.

Velthoven, B. van, and Winden, F. van, (1985), "Towards a Politico-Economic Theory of Social Security", *European Economic Review*, Vol. 27, pp. 263-89.

Verbon, H. A. A., (1986), "Altruism, Political Power, and Public Pensions", *Kyklos*, Vol. 39, pp. 343–58.

Verbon, H. A. A., (1987), "The Rise and Evolution of Public Pension Systems", *Public Choice*, Vol. 52, pp. 75–100.

Verbon, H. A. A., (1988), *The Evolution of Public Pension Schemes*, Microeconomic Studies (Berlin usw.: Springer-Verlag).

Winden, F. van, (1983), *On the Interaction Between State and Private Sector*, Contributions to Economic Analysis No. 146 (Amsterdam: North-Holland).

Summary: ***Population Aging and Social Security: A Politico-economic Model of State Pension Financing.*** **— The present paper attempts to provide a positive, politico-economic explanation of actual social security policies. A theoretical framework is devised which integrates individual utility maximization and governmental maximization of expected political support. Individual support depends on how net economic benefit from a pay-as-you-go financed state pension scheme is translated into a probability of voting for the government. The relation between net economic positions, public policy parameters, and voting probabilities is made explicit by referring to the logit model of qualitative choice. The analysis is set in an overlapping generations framework. Optimal state pension policies are characterized, relating such diverse factors as population aging, political power distribution, social solidarity, and income taxation.**

Part IV
Macroeconomic Effects

[30]

European Economic Review 6 (1975) 343–367. © North-Holland Publishing Company

INCOME TAX INCIDENCE IN AN AGEING POPULATION

An examination of the measurement of income redistribution

F.A. COWELL

University of Keele, Keele, Staffordshire, ST5 5BG, U.K.

Received December 1973, revised version received February 1975

The distribution of income in a population consists of the different distributions in the various age groups weighted by the age structure. In using inequality statistics to measure the redistributive effect of taxation, it is desirable to remove the arbitrary effect of the age-weighting. Formulae for 'conventional' and for 'correct' indices of incidence are given, and are evaluated in a stochastic-process model that captures many features of actual income distributions. For the lognormal distribution, the direction of bias of conventional incidence indices is determined simply by writing them as functions of the lognormal dispersion parameter.

1. Introduction

It is common practice to use inequality statistics as a basis for the measurement of 'incidence' of a tax programme when the number of agents in the economy is large. The use of such indices gives the observer an idea of 'how well' the tax programme is achieving the goal of mitigating inequality, and can facilitate comparison either between different countries' tax programmes, or between the tax programmes of one country at different points in time.

It is immediately apparent that the composition of the population over which these inequality statistics are defined is of crucial importance. This point has been implicitly recognised, for example, in empirical work where tax incidence has been measured for households of different sizes by considering the size-categories as separate subpopulations. Because of the heterogeneity of the population it may be misleading to aggregate separate groups in a simple fashion. For example, although there may be real differences in the level of well-being between single males and families with two children, a spurious component of 'inequality' will enter the index unless allowance is made for a relevant aspect of heterogeneity: households of different sizes have different needs.

This paper argues that age differences in the population are another vitally relevant aspect of heterogeneity. Such differences are important in inequality measurement in two ways. In the first place an individual's income is not constant over his lifetime. So, suppose a fantasy economy where all individuals of a given age receive the same income, but where the life cycle income profile has a typical 'hump' shape. It is easy to see that if we were uncritically to apply an inequality measure to this population's income we would find an apparently very unequal distribution. But this is simply a product of the non-constant lifetime income profile and the age structure. There is really no inequality whatever.[1] Misleading conclusions about income redistribution through taxation could be avoided were we to look at the age groups separately, or were we to normalise within each age group before aggregation. In the second place, income dispersion will typically change among the age groups, which may be the result of systematic influences on individual income variability that are uniform over the lifetime. It is with this feature that this paper is particularly concerned. Once again there is the problem that the apparent amount of inequality is affected by the arbitrary weighting of the age structure. Consider two societies alike in every respect other than the rate of growth of population. Income distribution of a given age group in each of the two societies is identical, and future income prospects facing an individual of given age and income in each society are likewise exactly the same. But in the conventional way of looking at inequality the society with the slower rate of population growth will appear to have income distributed more unequally than the other.[2] Without insisting that a method of inequality measurement should necessarily register these two societies as 'equally unequal', it is reasonable to suggest that we seek

(a) a way of looking at inequality that permits the explicit weighting of age groups as an alternative to the arbitrary weighting imposed by the age structure;
(b) a suitable method of aggregation over age groups;
(c) the relationship between such an aggregate index and conventional ways of looking at inequality.

There are three principal problems which need to be mentioned here.

I. What is an appropriate measure of 'well-being'? In a life cycle context, we might want to consider the life time aggregate of 'utility' for each man. However, apart from the problem of lifetime aggregation, we cannot in practice measure 'utility'. If we use 'income' as a surrogate, then insofar as (a) individuals' marginal utility of consumption, marginal utility of leisure and rate of time preference differ, and (b) facilities for borrowing, for varying the proportion of time worked, or for accumulating human capital vary from one person to

[1] I am not suggesting, of course, that there is no case for a policy which redistributes income among the age groups even when there is no inequality in the accepted sense. There may be a good argument for this, especially where capital market imperfections are important. But such redistribution should be sharply distinguished analytically from the usual notions of reduction of inequality.

[2] This assertion can easily be verified either by examining the formal model below, or by reflecting that under the process described, income dispersion will increase with age, and that in the slower-growing population there will be a higher proportion of old people.

another, then it is clear that an estimate of the effect of a tax programme where the Social Welfare Function is defined in terms of current income will differ from the ideal concept – an estimate where the SWF is defined in terms of individual utilities.[3] Since this problem is not central to the theme of the paper, I shall not pursue it farther here.

II. What Social Welfare Function should be used? This choice is implicit in the statistical measure of inequality used as a basis for computing tax incidence.[4] Many of the theorems which follow deal with a wide class of inequality measures (and hence SWFs), with examples from the commonly used types. This does not, of course remove the problem of selecting a satisfactory criterion in inequality.

III. The final problem is as follows. Apart from isolated case studies we do not have the detailed data concerning lifetime incomes which would be necessary for an accurate estimate of some measure of 'discounted lifetime income' or of 'lifetime utility'. Even if such data were available, we should still require a model of individual income dynamics in order to summarise this information in a model of tax incidence over the lifetime. Typically we have to hand 'macro data' only – that is income distributions by age groups rather than transitions from income class to income class over the life cycle. However it is possible to look at distribution of income cohort by cohort – i.e., as a set of subpopulations. By this we can remove the arbitrary weighting of cohorts' income distributions imposed by the birth and death process. If further we impose a particular model structure we can do more. Suppose that incomes are in fact generated according to a stochastic process. In particular it will be assumed here that there operates a simple Markov process in continuous time and continuous state space – i.e., continuous over the space of incomes. That is, a man's income in the next instant of time is a function only of his present income. Then we could compute expected future income, but more importantly we can see the family of cohorts' income distributions not as independent functions, but as being generated by the initial distribution (i.e., the distribution of incomes on entry to the model) and the parameters of the stochastic process. This device can be a useful way of formalising the relationship between the income distributions in different age groups.

[3]One rationalisation of the approach adopted is to suppose that individuals at different ages are regarded as members of different subpopulations that are not directly comparable, that all income is instantaneously consumed, and that no one can vary his working week. It is not in fact necessary to assume that there is no interest income, but that savings (and indeed work effort) should be inelastic w.r.t. individual income tax rates. Alternatively we can assume that we look at the ex post distribution of income (gross and net), that individuals have selected the optimum lifetime paths of consumption and leisure, everyone being faced with a perfect capital market (no instantaneous debt constraint) and a perfectly divisible labour market. Either way there will still be a built-in bias if utility is a nonlinear function of income.

[4]Once again it is beyond the scope of this paper to go into detail on this point. For a comprehensive introduction, see Atkinson (1970).

Given these 'macro data' and the model structure, we summarise the large number of actual forces that influence the development of individual incomes over the life cycle (such as seniority increases, promotion, windfall gains and losses, and job changes), by supposing that in the aggregate these are represented by random variables. As I have argued, we are likely to be far more interested in the impact that (for example) an income tax is likely to have on the income distribution in each cohort, rather than in the Observed Aggregate Income Distribution or OAID (which is an arbitrarily weighted aggregate of the cohorts' income distributions), and so one can also examine the direction and extent of 'aggregation bias' that there may be in measuring income redistribution on the basis of the OAID rather than for the separate subpopulations.

2. The model

I have chosen essentially the simplest model containing the three basic ingredients which I wish to examine: a population differentiated by age group as well by income class, an underlying stochastic process operating upon incomes, and a progressive income tax by which we propose to reduce inequality in each cohort. The most important factors that I shall omit are variations in personal incomes due to individual optimisation mentioned above the problem of formation of family units, and that of bequests and inheritances at different times over the life cycle. However the remaining features provide some useful lessons.

Suppose that incomes at 'age zero' (the age at which we consider the cohorts to enter our economic model) are distributed lognormally $\Lambda(\mu, \sigma^2)$;[5] suppose that in subsequent instants of time $(\theta, \theta+\delta\theta)$ incomes are subjected to a stochastic process; we shall assume, following Rutherford (1955), that this process is a series of normal shocks upon 'income power' (i.e., the logarithm of income) – incomes themselves then obey the familiar 'law of proportionate effect'; this shock system is assumed to be $N(0, v^2\delta\theta)$ where v^2 is constant $\forall\theta$. The population is assumed to 'decay' exponentially at a rate γ, which may be decomposed into $\gamma = \gamma_1+\gamma_2$. Here γ_1 reflects the probability of survival – an individual entering the system at age 0 can expect to live to age $1/\gamma_1$, γ_2 is the exponential rate of growth of new entrants at age 0 into the system.[6] We then have [see Rutherford (1955, pp. 281–283)] that income for the cohort of age θ is distributed

[5]This distribution has been widely used to describe income distributions – see Aitchison and Brown (1957) and Bjerke (1970) for a discussion of its empirical suitability. Note also that under the stochastic process described below, the central limit theorem will ensure that the income distribution in each cohort is *eventually* Λ.

[6]Notice that γ_2 should be distinguished carefully from the 'crude birth rate'. The latter expresses the fact that in the year t there were x births per thousand of the current population. We wish to draw attention to the fact that the number of 'births' (people of age zero) is growing at a rate γ_2.

The significance of the composite parameter $\gamma = \gamma_1+\gamma_2$ may be seen as follows. Draw a frequency curve of the population at any moment in time. Then this will be a negative exponential curve with parameter γ.

$\Lambda(\mu, \sigma^2+\theta v^2)$, and the total income distribution is described by the logarithmic transformation of the Gram Charlier Series of type A,

$$\sum_{i=0}^{\infty}\{[v^2/(2\sigma^2\gamma)]^i H_{2i}(\log z)\}\ \mathrm{d}\Lambda(z;0,1)/\mathrm{d}z,$$

where z is standardized income, and $H_{2i}(\cdot)$ is the Hermite polynomial of order $2i$. It is noted that the Gram Charlier itself has all odd moments zero (in this particular model) and nonzero even moments; thus it will be found that although the marginal distributions (i.e., income distributions of each cohort) are all lognormal, and although the distribution of income y [where $(\log y-\mu)/\sigma = \log z$] has as its first two moments expressions that approximate those one would expect from a lognormal [mean $= e^{\mu+1/2s^2}$, variance $=$ mean$^2\times(e^{s^2}-1)$, where $s^2 = \sigma^2+v^2/\gamma$] the distribution is *not* lognormal. As is demonstrated in fig. 1, for small values of v^2/γ, the Log Gram Charlier described above, which I shall denote here by LG(μ, σ^2, v^2/γ), approximates well to the lognormal, but that as v^2/γ approaches a critical value the curve ceases to be unimodal; beyond the critical value the series fails to converge, a finite number of terms yielding negative frequencies. In view of this behaviour, it may well be instructive to derive some preliminary results on the assumption that the Gram Charlier is approximately normal, before considering the importance of the divergent 4th and higher moments.

In order to arrive at an expression for income tax incidence in this model, we need to derive the distribution of net income. For the purposes of this illustrative example, it will be assumed that the tax function is of the following particular form:

$$T = y - Ay^b,$$

where A and b are constants. A discussion of the realism of this functional form will be found in appendix A; it is sufficient to note here that for $A > 0$, and $0 < b < 1$ the income tax is nominally progressive. It is then immediate that net income is given by $y-T = Ay^b$, and thus we know [see for example Aitchison and Brown (1957)] that if income for age cohort θ is distributed $\Lambda(\mu, \sigma^2+v^2\theta)$ then income net of tax in the same cohort is distributed $\Lambda(\mu+a, b^2[\sigma^2+v^2\theta])$, where $a = \log_e A$, and that net income in the total population is distributed LG($\mu+a$, $b^2\sigma^2$, b^2v^2/γ). We shall adopt the approximation that the disposable income of each cohort is distributed $\Lambda(\mu+a, b^2\sigma^2+v^2\theta)$, and for the total population as LG($\mu+a$, $b^2\sigma^2$, v^2/γ).[7]

[7]The importance of this approximation may be judged as follows. A typical value for v^2 (given that $\sigma^2 = 1$) is 0.005. Consider the second parameter of the lognormal distribution of the cohort at $\theta = 1/\gamma$, which is also the distribution of the lognormal approximation for the whole population. For $\gamma = 1/65$, and $b = 0.9$ (see the typical values found in appendix A) then

$$b^2[\sigma^2+v^2/\gamma] = 1.0733 \quad \text{and} \quad b^2\sigma^2+v^2/\gamma = 1.135$$

– i.e., an overestimate of the true value of the parameter by 5–6 percent. However, much of the analysis can be carried through without the approximation although the criteria in one or two of the theorems which follow need to be reinterpreted.

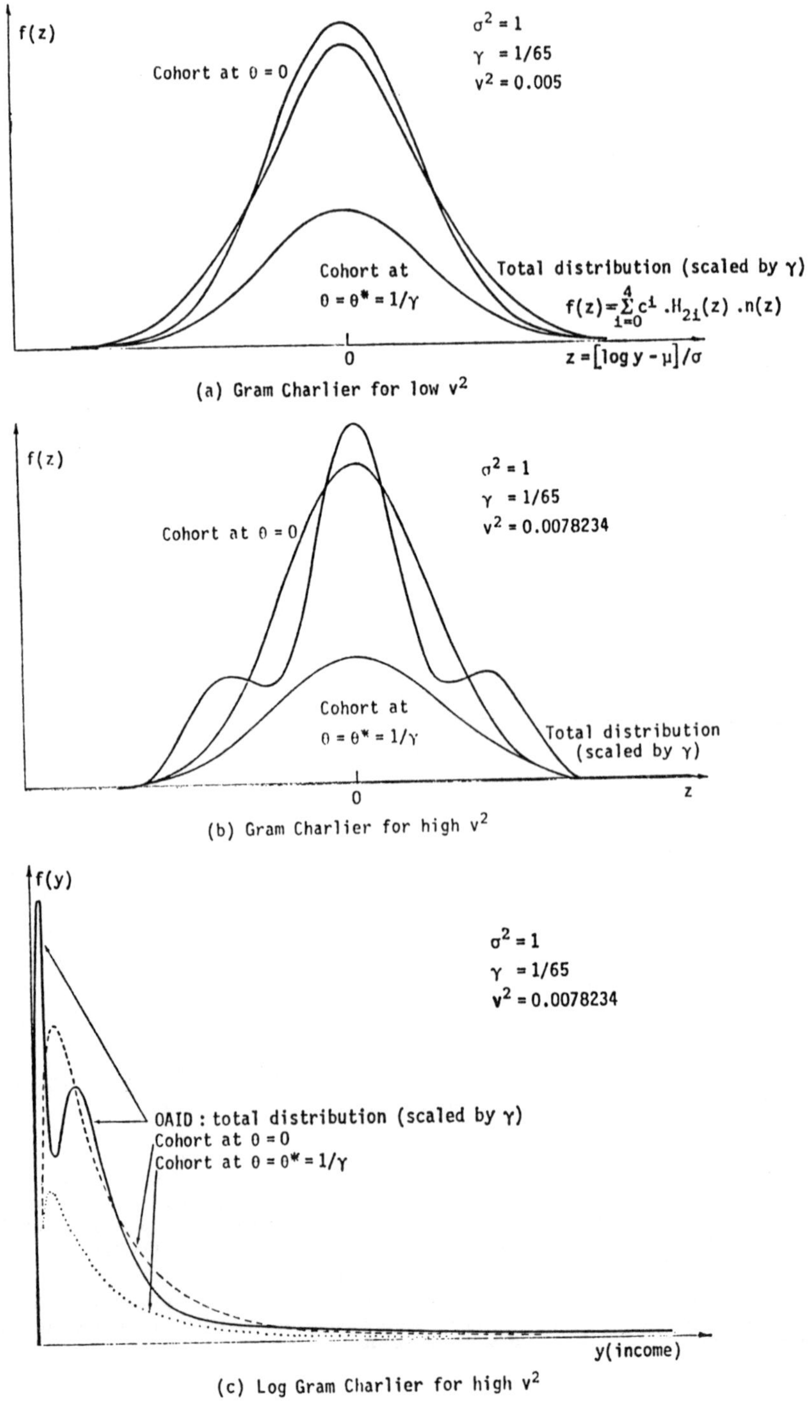

(a) Gram Charlier for low v^2

(b) Gram Charlier for high v^2

(c) Log Gram Charlier for high v^2

Fig. 1

We now need to define tax incidence, and in order to do this a measure of inequality will be required. Such a measure will be taken to mean a function $I(F(y), y)$ with domain a series of pairs $\{F(y), y\}$ where F is a distribution function defined on y, and with range a subset of the nonnegative real line.[8] If $F(\cdot)$ has a reasonably tractable functional form, then it may be possible to write I uniquely in terms of parameters of the distribution F. Within the scope of this paper, the form most frequently of interest will be the lognormal, and in this case for the distribution $\Lambda(m, s^2)$ the inequality measure will be written $I(m, s^2)$.

Definition 1. For a particular population, let the inequality measure (of arbitrary form within the class of admissible functions) for the distribution of gross income be I_G and that for net income be I_N, then for this inequality measure *the index of tax incidence* is defined to be $i = I_N/I_G$.

In order to obtain some preliminary results two further temporary assumptions will be made. Firstly it will be assumed that the OAID is approximately lognormal $\Lambda(\mu, \sigma^2 + v^2/\gamma)$ for gross income; secondly that the initial distribution is the ethically 'correct' basis for an assessment of tax incidence. It must be emphasised that this second point is only a temporary expedient, but a rough justification might run as follows: suppose that income generation for $\theta > 0$ is not just a quasi-random process – that ex post the combined effects of forces producing changes in income distribution act 'as though' a random process were at work – but that once an individual has started out in life with some inherited advantage (reflected in the income distribution at age zero) his income thereafter is determined by a purely random process, and thus in order to redistribute 'income opportunity', we should look at how the tax system can affect the distribution at ago 0. We are now in a position to prove the following theorem.

Theorem 1. (a) *Let i^0 denote incidence defined on the initial distribution as a basis, and i^T denote incidence defined on the OAID as a basis. Then for a lognormal structure of income $\Lambda(m, s^2)$ and for all $\gamma > 0$ and all multiplicatively separable measures of inequality $I(m, s^2)$, $i^T > i^0$ if I is concave in s^2.* (b) *The divergence between i^0 and i^T increases absolutely with v^2, decreases absolutely with γ.*

Proof. (a) We define

$$i^0 = \frac{I(\mu+a, b^2\sigma^2)}{I(\mu, \sigma^2)},$$

[8]Unfortunately, it does not appear to be possible to make the general definition more precise than this; in economic terms we should certainly like to restrict the class of admissible I by supposing that I should rank distributions F (weakly) in the same order as some pre-specified social ordering on the F, with $I = 0$ indicating the socially most preferred distribution, we should also perhaps like to standardise the range of admissible I's by transforming the function, but unfortunately it is not possible to reserve some of the essential features of the functions I which will be explored.

$$i^T = \frac{I(\mu+a,\, b^2\sigma^2+v^2/\gamma)}{I(\mu,\, \sigma^2+v^2/\gamma)}\,. \tag{1}$$

Multiplicative separability means that $I(\mu, \sigma^2) = \chi(\mu)\cdot\phi(\sigma^2)$.

Clearly $i^T \lesseqgtr i^0$ as [from (1)]

$$\frac{I(\mu+a,\, b^2\sigma^2+v^2/\gamma)}{I(\mu+a,\, b^2\sigma^2)} \lesseqgtr \frac{I(\mu,\, \sigma^2+v^2/\gamma)}{I(\mu,\, \sigma^2)}\,,$$

or, on account of separability,

$$\frac{\phi(b^2\sigma^2+v^2/\gamma)}{\phi(b^2\sigma^2)} \lesseqgtr \frac{\phi(\sigma^2+v^2/\gamma)}{\phi(\sigma^2)}\,. \tag{2}$$

If I is strictly concave in its second argument (and hence ϕ), then $\phi(x+\delta)/\phi(x)$ $\delta, x > 0$ strictly decreases with x. Now, in (2) σ^2 and v^2 are >0, and by assumption $\gamma > 0$, and $0 < b < 1$. Thus the arguments of the function ϕ are strictly greater on the RHS of the inequality than corresponding arguments on the LHS, all arguments being >0. Thus by strict concavity of ϕ '>' holds in relation (2). Thus for I strictly concave in s^2, $i^T > i^0$.

(b) For a strictly concave function $\phi(x)$, x, $\phi(x) > 0$, then $x\phi'(x)/\phi(x)$ decreases strictly with x. By the separability of I, it is found that

$$\frac{\partial i^T}{\partial v^2} \gtreqless 0$$

as

$$\frac{\partial}{\partial v^2}\log\left[\frac{\phi(b^2\sigma^2+v^2/\gamma)}{\phi(\sigma^2+v^2/\gamma)}\right] \gtreqless 0;$$

i.e., as

$$\frac{\sigma^2}{\gamma}\left[\frac{\phi'(b^2\sigma^2+v^2/\gamma)}{\phi(b^2\sigma^2+v^2/\gamma)} - \frac{\phi'(b^2\sigma^2)}{\phi(b^2\sigma^2)}\right] \gtreqless 0. \tag{3}$$

For ϕ strictly concave, $\gamma > 0$, and $b^2 < 1$, '>' holds in (3), and thus i^T increases with v^2. By a similar argument, it may be established that under the same conditions, i^T decreases with γ, as $\partial i^T/\partial\gamma$ is negative.

Recall that an approximation was made in assuming that disposable income was distributed $\Lambda(\mu+a,\, b^2\sigma^2+v^2/\gamma)$ rather than $\Lambda(\mu+a,\, b^2[\sigma^2+v^2/\gamma])$. To rephrase and reinterpret Theorem 1 without the use of this approximation, the following definition will be required.

Definition 2. Let a measure of inequality be described by $I(y;\alpha,\beta,\ldots)$ where α, β are parameters. The *elasticity* of the I w.r.t. parameter α is defined as $\eta(\alpha) = (\partial I/\partial\alpha)\cdot(\alpha/I)$.

Using this definition we may now restate theorem 1, where disposable income is supposed to be distributed $\Lambda(\mu+a, b^2[\sigma^2+v^2/\gamma])$.

Theorem 1.* (a) *Let i^0 denote incidence defined on the initial distribution, and i^T denote incidence defined on the OAID. Then for a lognormal structure of income and for all $\gamma > 0$ and all multiplicatively separable measures of inequality $I(m, s^2)$, $i^T \lesseqgtr i^0$ as I is strictly increasingly/decreasingly elastic in s^2.*

Proof. This follows lines very similar to the proof of theorem 1; however, instead of eq. (2) we now have the condition

$$\frac{\phi(b^2[\sigma^2+v^2/\gamma])}{\phi(b^2\sigma^2)} \lesseqgtr \frac{\phi(\sigma^2+v^2/\gamma)}{\phi(\sigma^2)}. \tag{2'}$$

For a decreasingly elastic function [that is $\eta'(s^2) < 0$], $\phi(x+\delta x)/\phi(x)$, $x, \delta > 0$ is strictly decreasing, and the theorem follows for this case. The proof for the increasingly elastic case follows by symmetry.

The relationship between concavity (resp. convexity) and decreasing (resp. increasing) elasticity is given by the following lemma.

Lemma 1. Let $\phi(x)$ be a non-negative, increasing differentiable function defined on the non-negative real line, and let $\eta(x) \equiv x\phi'(x)/\phi(x)$. If (i)

$$\eta(0) \leqq 1 \quad \textit{and} \quad \forall x \geqq 0, \eta'(x) \leqq 0,$$

then ϕ is concave. If (ii)

$$\eta(0) \geqq 1 \quad \textit{and} \quad \forall x \geqq 0, \eta'(x) \geqq 0,$$

then ϕ is convex.

Proof. We prove this for the case of concavity – the convexity case follows by symmetry.

Decreasing elasticity implies

$$\eta' = -x\phi'^2/\phi^2 + \phi'/\phi + x\phi''/\phi \leqq 0.$$

Rearranging, we find this implies

$$\phi\eta' = \phi'[1-\eta]+x\phi'' \leqq 0, \qquad x \geqq 0.$$

Suppose $\eta(0) \leqq 1$. Then if $\eta' \leqq 0$, for all non-negative x we have $\eta(x) \leqq 1$. Thus,

$$x\phi'' = \phi\eta'-\phi'[1-\eta] \leqq \phi\eta' \leqq 0$$

$$\Rightarrow \phi'' \leqq 0.$$

Q.E.D.

It happens that for the lognormal distribution either condition (i) or condition (ii) is satisfied for nearly every commonly-used measure of inequality. Thus it is almost true to say, for example, that we can take 'concave' and 'decreasingly elastic' as synonymous. The only commonly-used exception is the coefficient of variation, discussed below.

As an aid to further consideration of the significance of theorems 1 and 1*, the following definition will be required.

Definition 3. Suppose that i is some 'true' index of incidence, according to some prespecified criterion, and that another value i^* is used as an estimate of i. Then we shall say that i^* *understates the 'true' amount of income redistribution* or equivalently that it *understates the redistributive effect of the tax system* if $i^* > i$, and conversely that if $i^* < i$ then the estimate overstates the true amount of income redistribution.

The interpretation of Theorem 1* is then clear, if we accept that the measure of incidence derived for the first age cohort is the 'true' measure of incidence in Definition 3. A measure of incidence derived from the OAID, i^T, will under- or over-estimate the redistribution of income according as the measure of inequality from which the incidence measure is derived is concave or convex in its second argument (for the lognormal distribution). Part (b) shows that the bias increases absolutely as the variance of the underlying normal shock system on income power increases, and decreases as (i) the life expectancy at age 0 decreases or (ii) as the rate of growth of new-entrants increases.[9]

3. Some illustrations

Although it will be shown that the qualitative nature of the results of theorem 1 does *not* depend on the restrictive assumption that incidence as defined for the

[9]The conclusion as to whether there will be an under- or over-estimate is exactly reversed if γ is negative: this can only happen if the decline in the birth rate is greater than the rate of exponential decay represented by the death process (an unlikely event!).

initial cohort is the 'true' measure, for the purpose of maintaining mathematical simplicity it will be easier to work out one or two specific examples on the presumption that i^0 is the correct measure of tax incidence. It should be clear how individual examples can be generalised in the light of the ensuring results. Details of the derivations are to be found in appendix B.

3.1. Atkinson's inequality measure

Atkinson's (1970) measure of inequality depends on the prespecification of a non-negative parameter ε, which reflects 'inequality aversion'. For the distribution $\Lambda(m, s^2)$ this reduces to

$$I = 1 - e^{-1/2\varepsilon s^2}.$$

In this case I is in fact independent of m. We note further that

$$\partial I/\partial s^2 = \tfrac{1}{2}\varepsilon\, e^{-1/2\varepsilon s^2} \geqq 0 \qquad (\text{since } \varepsilon \geqq 0),$$

and

$$\partial^2 I/\partial s^4 = \tfrac{1}{4}\varepsilon^2\, e^{-1/2\varepsilon s^2} \leqq 0,$$

and thus I is concave in s^2 (strictly so for $\varepsilon > 0$). Thus I satisfies the conditions under which we would expect the measure of incidence derived from the OAID to understate the true amount of income redistribution (as defined by i^0). This underestimate we would expect to increase absolutely as v^2 increases. This is verified in the appendix.

3.2. Coefficient of variation

For the lognormal distribution $\Lambda(m, s^2)$, $I = [e^{s^2} - 1]^{-1/2}$. Once again I turns out to be independent of m. It is found that

$$\partial I/\partial s^2 = \tfrac{1}{2}\, e^{s^2}[e^{s^2} - 1]^{-1/2} > 0,$$

$$\partial^2 I/\partial s^4 = [\tfrac{1}{2}\, e^{s^2} - 1][e^{s^2} - 1]^{-3/2} \cdot \tfrac{1}{2}\, e^{s^2} \gtreqqless 0 \quad \text{as} \quad s^2 \gtreqqless \log_e 2,$$

an apparently awkward function! However, it can be shown that it is increasingly elastic since

$$\frac{\eta'(s^2)}{\eta(s^2)} = \frac{1}{s^2} - \frac{1}{e^{s^2} - 1} > 0.$$

Thus we will find $i^T < i^0$.

3.3. Variance

The standard result for the lognormal $\Lambda(m, s^2)$ is variance $= I = e^{2m}[e^{2s^2} - e^{s^2}]$. It is to be noted that I is multiplicatively separable in m, s^2 and that

$$\partial I/\partial s^2 = [2\,e^{2s^2} - e^{s^2}]\,e^{2m} > 0,$$

$$\partial^2 I/\partial s^4 = [4\,e^{2s^2} - e^{s^2}]\,e^{2m} > 0,$$

i.e., I is clearly convex in s^2 and therefore by theorem 1 variance will consistently overstate the true redistributive effect of the income tax, as comparing the OAID with the initial distribution.

3.4. Logarithmic variance

In appendix B a general definition of this inequality measure is provided, and it is shown that in this case of the distribution $\Lambda(m, s^2)$, it reduces to $I = s^2 + \frac{1}{4}s^4$. It is immediate that the first two derivatives are positive, and that thus I is once again strictly convex, this time independent of m. Again we shall expect an overstatement of the amount of income redistribution.

3.5. Relative mean deviation

It can be shown that for the lognormal this is simply $I = 2[2N(\frac{1}{2}s) - 1]$, where

$$N(x) = [2\pi]^{-1/2} \int_{-\infty}^{x} e^{-1/2 t^2}\, dt.$$

I is dependent of m and

$$\partial I/\partial s^2 = k_1 [2\pi]^{-1/2}\, e^{-1/8s^2} . 1/s > 0,$$

$$\partial^2 I/\partial s^2 = k_2 [2\pi]^{-1/2} [-\tfrac{1}{8}s^{-1} - \tfrac{1}{2}s^{-3}] < 0,$$

that is I is concave in s^2 and we expect that $i^T > i^0$.

3.6. Gini coefficient

The coefficient of concentration for the distribution $\Lambda(m, s^2)$ can be shown to result in the expression $I = 2N(s/\sqrt{2}) - 1$.[10] It is clear that this is independent of m, and analogously to the case of the Relative Mean Deviation, it is concave in s^2 and thus the true redistributive effect of the income tax is understated.

[10] Cf. Aitchison and Brown (1957, pp. 112–113).

3.7. Theil's measure

In Theil (1967) the inequality measure

$$\int_0^\infty y/\bar{y} \log (y/\bar{y})\, \mathrm{d}F(y)$$

is put forward on the basis of an information theoretic approach. It is shown there, that for the distribution $\Lambda(m, s^2)$, $I = \frac{1}{2}s^2$. Note that this means that I is both convex and concave in s^2 and is also increasingly and decreasingly elastic w.r.t. s^2. Thus this is one measure of inequality which, if used for determining tax incidence will lead to *no* bias if the OAID is used as a basis.

It is often the case that an inequality measure may be written in the mean-independent form

$$\int_0^\infty \Psi(y/\bar{y})\, \mathrm{d}F(y).$$

Then we may be interested in the following.

Theorem 2. Inequality measures of the form $I = \int_0^\infty \Psi(y/\bar{y})\, \mathrm{d}F(y)$, *where* Ψ *is concave (and has a positive first derivative) and has the elasticity of its first derivative bounded above by some* $\tilde{\varepsilon}$, $0 \geqq \tilde{\varepsilon} \geqq -1$, *for the distribution* $\Lambda(m, s^2)$ *are concave in* s^2.

Proof. It is sufficient to establish concavity in s. Differentiation twice gives us

$$\frac{\partial^2 I}{\partial s^2} = \int_{-\infty}^{+\infty} \left[\Psi''(z)\cdot z + \Psi'(z) \left[1 - \frac{1}{[x-s]^2} \right] \right] [x-s]^2 \cdot z \cdot \mathrm{d}N(x; 0, 1), \blacksquare$$

where $x = [\log(y) - m]/s$, $z = \mathrm{e}^{sx - 1/2s^2}$, and N is the normal distribution function. A *sufficient* condition for concavity of I in s^2 is then that

$$\forall x\colon \varepsilon = \frac{\Psi''(z)\cdot z}{\Psi'(z)} < -1 + \frac{1}{[x-s]^2}.$$

The extreme right-hand term is necessarily positive, and so the theorem is satisfied if $\varepsilon(z) < \tilde{\varepsilon}$, $0 \geqq \tilde{\varepsilon} \geqq -1$. In any case a concave function Ψ with a positive first derivative will have $\varepsilon \leqq 0$.

This is of use since the theorem can help us to determine which inequality measures are likely to fulfil the 'concavity' requirements for Theorem 1 and Theorem 3 (to follow).

4. Extensions

It is now time to drop the awkward practice of using simply the initial distribution as the criterion for 'true' tax incidence.

Corollary to Theorem 1. If I is concave (respectively convex) in s^2, then i^T understates the amount of income redistribution (respectively overstates . . .) not only in the first age cohort, but for all cohorts $\theta < 1/\gamma$.

This is evident once it is recalled that income in cohort θ is distributed $\Lambda(\mu, \sigma^2+v^2\theta)$ and that the OAID is assumed to be approximated by $\Lambda(\mu, \sigma^2+v^2/\gamma)$. The critical age $\theta^* = 1/\gamma$ is that at which numbers of the cohort which entered the system θ^* years previously are expected to have fallen to $1/e = 0.3679\ldots$ of the original numbers in the cohort, assuming a zero rate of growth of new entrants. For typical age structures, (for example the UK) this critical age is somewhere in the late 70's or the 80's – i.e., after most individuals' economic life span.

If the rate of growth of new entrants $\gamma_2 \neq 0$, then the critical age is reduced drastically. For example, assuming that $1/\gamma_1 = 65$ (assuming entry at age 20 years for example), and a 1 percent growth rate of entrants then $\theta^* \equiv 1/\gamma$ falls from 65 to about 39.4 – i.e., the critical age cohort is at 59.4 years. In this case, we may now face the problem that conclusions on the direction of bias of i^T will be ambiguous in the range of θ that is of interest – say up to retirement age. This problem will now be tackled.

Let us consider a 'weighted average' inequality measure, derived from the inequality measures for each age group, rather than weighting the distributions for each age group by the arbitrary age structure and then computing an inequality measure. The latter procedure, implicit in the use of OAID-based incidence indices, ignores the fact that one is aggregating in the same inequality measure individuals from different points in the life cycle. By adopting the former procedure we can explicitly incorporate society's sensitivity towards inequality within the different groups through an appropriate choice of weights. For a preliminary result, we may make these weights proportional to the numbers within each group. Thus we define a weighted inequality measure,

$$I_G^W = \int_0^\infty \gamma\, e^{-\gamma\theta} I_G(\mu, \sigma^2+v^2\theta)\,d\theta.$$

This composite inequality measure determines a 'representative age group' θ' such that $I_G^W = I_G^{\theta'}$. We then define a weighted incidence index,

$$i^W = I_N^{\theta'}/I_G^{\theta'},$$

where $I_N^{\theta'}$ is the inequality of net income in the representative age group. Naturally, the representative age group and the weighted incidence index are different for each set of weights.

Theorem 3. (a) *If the initial distribution is $\Lambda(\mu, \sigma^2)$ and the OAID is approximated by a lognormal distribution, given the same underlying stochastic process as* *before, then for all separable measures of inequality I, $i^T \lesseqgtr i^W$ as I is convex/concave in its second argument, where i^W is the weighted measure of incidence defined above.* (b) *The under-/over-estimate of incidence i^W/i^T increases with the variance of the shock system, v^2.*

Proof. (a) Let $I(m, s^2) = \chi(m)\cdot\phi(s^2)$. Suppose that ϕ is concave. Then for any set of weights $\{\xi_i\}$, $\xi_i > 0, \sum\xi_i = 1$, we have

$$\sum\xi_i\phi(s_i^2) < \phi(\sum\xi_i s_i^2).$$

Now for the cohort of age θ, $s^2 = \sigma^2 + v^2\theta$, and the age distribution is given by $g(\theta) = 1/\gamma\, e^{-\gamma\theta} > 0$, $\int_0^\infty g(\theta)\cdot d\theta = 1$. Thus in the limit, using $\{g(\theta)\}$ as a set of weights we have the inequality:

$$\int_0^\infty 1/\gamma\, e^{-\gamma\theta}\phi(\sigma^2 + v^2\theta)\, d\theta < \phi(\int_0^\infty 1/\gamma\, e^{-\gamma\theta}[\sigma^2 + v^2\theta]\, d\theta).$$

Denote the LHS by ϕ^W. Thus $\phi^W < \phi(\sigma^2 + v^2/\gamma)$, integrating the RHS; $\Rightarrow \phi^W < \phi^T$, where ϕ^T is the value of ϕ for the OAID. By the concavity of ϕ, it is now easy to see that

$$\phi_N^W/\phi_G^W < \phi_N^T/\phi_G^T \quad \forall b \in [0, 1)$$

$$\Rightarrow i^T > i^W.$$

A similar proof follows for convex ϕ.

(b) As for theorem 1.

Theorem 3 indicates that if we regard the OAID as a weighted sum of income distributions by age groups, and if we regard a suitable composite measure of inequality as a weighted sum (with the same age-distribution weights) of inequality measures for each of the age groups, then we can tell unambiguously whether the apparent amount of income redistribution is an over/under-estimate w.r.t. the weighted incidence index derived from this composite inequality measure.

Corollary to Theorem 3. For any *age distribution that has a mean, provided that the foregoing stochastic process operates, and that the resulting income distribution of the total population is approximately lognormal, then i^T under-/over-estimates the true amount of income redistribution according to i^W as a criterion as I is concave/convex in s^2, this bias increasing with v^2.*

It is easy to see that the proof of theorem 3 can be extended to general $g(\theta)$, where $\mathscr{E}(\theta) = \theta^*$, provided that the income distribution in each cohort is

$\Lambda(\mu, \sigma^2+v^2\theta)$ and that the OAID approximates to $\Lambda(\mu, \sigma^2+v^2\theta^*)$. In this case, we redefine I_G^W as $\int_0^\infty g(\theta)I_G^\theta \, d\theta$ and then redefine i^W accordingly.

It should be reasonably clear by this stage that the problem of ambiguity $i^T \gtrless i^\theta$ for $\theta < \theta^*$, $i^T \lessgtr i^\theta$ for $\theta > \theta^*$ can only be a significant one in practice if, loosely speaking, we attach unreasonably high weights to the older cohorts, when we attempt to derive a single composite index. In some sense we are weighting the welfare of an older generation more heavily than a younger generation when we try to construct a composite index of inequality that reflects social preferences. This can be illustrated quite straightforwardly with the aid of the above corollary. It is clear, that whatever weighting system one applied to the inequality measures in the various cohorts, provided that this could be represented by a frequency function with the same mean as the age structure, then for all concave inequality measures we would still get $i^T > i^W$. It is evident that (in the case of I concave in s^2) in order for us to have $i^T < i^W$ then we must have $\int_0^\infty \theta w^\theta \, d\theta > \theta^*$ – reflecting the heavier weights attached to the older cohorts. For easy comparison, let us restrict ourselves to sets of weights that can be represented by an exponential frequency function $\alpha \, e^{-\alpha\theta}$, where $1/\alpha$ is the 'centre of gravity' of the weights, and let us make the following definition.

Definition 4. The *critical weighting parameter*, α^* will denote the parameter of an exponential distribution, such that for the inequality measure $I(m, s^2) = \chi(m).\,\phi(s^2)$, and age structure with parameter γ,

$$\int_0^\infty \alpha^* \, e^{-\alpha^*\theta}\phi(\sigma^2+v^2\theta) \, d\theta = \phi(\sigma^2+v^2/\gamma).$$

Thus for all $\alpha^* < \gamma$, we will find $i^T < i^W$ and for $\alpha^* > \gamma$, $i^T > i^W$ where i is derived from I concave in s^2. It will be of interest to look at the critical weighting parameter for a particular I – Atkinson's inequality measure. For in this case we can relate the parameter α – which reflects the relative importance we attach to the inequality statistics for cohorts of different ages – to the parameter ε which reflects our aversion to inequality *within* cohorts. We find[11]

$$\alpha^* = \frac{\frac{1}{2}\varepsilon v^2}{e^{1/2\varepsilon v^2/\gamma} - 1}.$$

[11] From Definition 4 we get

$$\int_0^\infty \alpha^* \exp(-\alpha^*\theta) - \alpha^* \exp(-\tfrac{1}{2}\varepsilon[\sigma^2+v^2\theta] - \alpha^*\theta) \, d\theta = 1 - \alpha^* \exp(-\tfrac{1}{2}\varepsilon\sigma^2) \times \int_0^\infty \exp(-[\alpha^*\theta + \tfrac{1}{2}\varepsilon v^2\theta]) \, d\theta.$$

Thus we obtain

$$\exp(-\tfrac{1}{2}\varepsilon v^2/\gamma) = \int_0^\infty \exp(-[\alpha^*\theta + \tfrac{1}{2}\varepsilon v^2\theta]) \, d\theta,$$

and the result follows.

In general we expect $\alpha^* < \gamma$, that is $1/\alpha^*$ 'to the right' of θ^* – and we might suppose that $1/\alpha^*$ would be 'further to the right' the greater the absolute value of the second derivative of the inequality measure with respect to its second argument. In the case of Atkinson's inequality measure, this has a simple rationalisation in terms of the parameter ε, for treating I as a function of s^2 we find $\frac{1}{2}\varepsilon = -I''/I'$. Thus it is of interest to verify the above supposition by sketching $1/\alpha^*$ against ε. This is done in fig. 2.

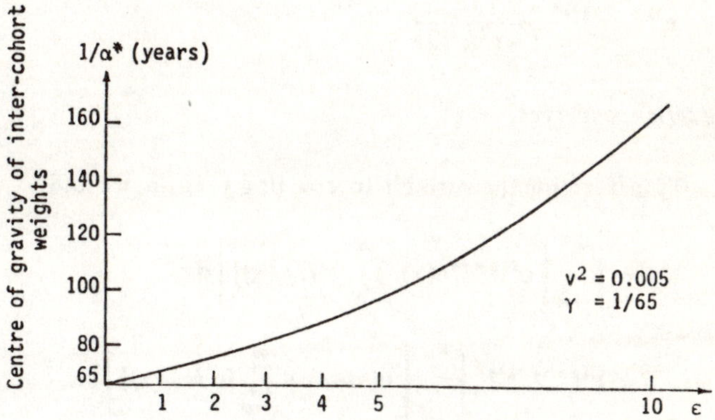

Fig. 2. The relationship between α and ε.

The significance of this is clear. It is only in the trivial limiting case of $\varepsilon = 0$ that the critical weighting parameter actually equals the parameter of the age distribution. As inequality aversion increases, then given the set of weights used to obtain a weighted index i^W will increase, unless at the same time the inter-cohort weighting is shifted in favour of the older age groups. From an inspection of fig. 2 it is apparent that unless the social welfare function happens to weight the older age groups heavily, the problem of ambiguity (i^T under- or over-estimating i^W) *cannot* arise for moderate or large values of inequality aversion.

5. General derivation for the LG distribution

If $c = v^2/2\gamma\sigma^2$ is large, then it has already been seen (cf. fig. 1) that the parent Gram Charlier series (if it converges) is only poorly approximated, and that thus incomes cannot be satisfactorily taken to be lognormal. In order to examine the properties of the general curve derived from the symmetrical Gram Charlier – that is the curve I have designated to be LG(μ, σ^2, v^2/γ) – the following lemma will be required.

Lemma 2. For the logarithmic transformation of the symmetric GC series

$$\frac{\mathrm{d}F(x)}{\mathrm{d}x} = n(x)\sum_{r=0}^{\infty} c^r H_{2r}(x),$$

where $x = [\log y - \mu]/\sigma$, *for all real* k, $\int_0^{+\infty} y^k \, \mathrm{d}LG(y; \mu, \sigma^2, v^2/\gamma)$, *the* kth *moment about the origin,* λ_k *can be expressed as*

$$e^{k\mu + 1/2k^2\sigma^2} \sum_{r=0}^{+\infty} \left[\frac{v^2 k^2}{2\gamma}\right]^r$$

or as

$$e^{k\mu + 1/2k^2\sigma^2} \frac{1}{1 - v^2k^2/2\gamma},$$

where the series converges.

Proof. Transforming the variable to $x = [\log y - \mu]/\sigma$, we find

$$\lambda_k = \int_{-\infty}^{\infty} \left[e^{xk\mu + k\sigma} n(x) \sum_{r=0}^{+\infty} [c^r H_{2r}(x)] \right] \mathrm{d}x$$

$$= e^{k\mu + 1/2k^2\sigma^2} \int_{-\infty}^{+\infty} \left[n(x - k\sigma) \sum_{r=0}^{\infty} [c^r H_{2r}(x)] \right] \mathrm{d}x.$$

Now for all ξ it is true that [see Kendall and Stuart (1958)]

$$n(x - \xi) = \sum_{j=0}^{+\infty} \frac{\xi^j}{j!} H_j(x)$$

from the definition of the Hermite polynomials. Thus

$$\lambda_k = e^{k\mu + 1/2k^2\sigma^2} \sum_{j=0}^{+\infty} \sum_{r=0}^{+\infty} \left[\left[\int_{-\infty}^{\infty} \left(n(x) H_j(x) H_{2r}(x) \frac{[\sigma k]^j}{j!} \right) \mathrm{d}x c^r \right] \right].$$

Using the orthogonality property of Hermite polynomials [see Kendall and Stuart (1958)] we find that the terms in the double infinite series are 0 for all $j \neq 2r$ and $j!([\sigma k]^j/j!)$ for all $j = 2r$, so that on substituting for $c = v^2/2\sigma^2\gamma$,

$$\lambda_k = e^{k\mu + 1/2k^2\sigma^2} \sum_{r=0}^{\infty} \left[\frac{v^2 k^2}{2\gamma}\right]^r,$$

and assuming $kc < 1$,

$$\lambda_k = e^{k\mu + 1/2k^2\sigma^2} \frac{1}{1 - k^2v^2/2\gamma}.$$

It is interesting to compare this with the kth moment about the origin for the lognormal, which is of course

$$\lambda_k = e^{k\mu + 1/2k^2[\sigma^2 + v^2/\gamma]} = e^{k\mu + 1/2k^2\sigma^2} \sum_{r=0}^{\infty} \left[\frac{v^2k^2}{2\gamma}\right]^r \frac{1}{r!}.$$

The nature of the approximation in assuming the first two moments to be identical, as was done above, can now clearly be seen – this is only true for small v^2/γ so that the higher terms in the series vanish rapidly.

Unfortunately the Log Gram Charlier itself is a cumbersome thing to work with for the purpose of deriving expressions for inequality measures in terms of the parameters. Indeed, there is apparently no simple generalisation of theorems 1 and 3 for all inequality measures, but the following has been established.

Theorem 4. Let i^T denote the incidence measure based on some I for the OAID using the lognormal approximation as before, and let i^T_+ denote the incidence measure derived for the Log Gram Charlier. Then whenever by theorem 1 *or* 3 *it is true that $i^T \gtrless$ some i^0, then for incidence measures derived from inequality measures A – D, $i^T_+ \gtrless i^0$ as $i^T \gtrless i^0$.*

The proof is in appendix B. The result is encouraging, since it suggests that generally speaking, by looking at the result for the lognormal approximation, we can draw inferences about the direction of bias of i^T as an estimate of the amount of income redistribution within any one cohort, or of some weighted index of incidence, that are robust in that the conclusions drawn are likely to hold for all admissible values of the variance of the shock system.

6. Summary

We have argued that a clearer picture of income redistribution through taxation is obtained from examining income distributions in each cohort rather than from examining the observed aggregate income distribution. In order to compare the two approaches we have had to use the following:

(i) a formal model of income generation incorporating the lognormal distribution, so as to relate the OAID to the income distribution in individual cohorts;
(ii) an 'index of incidence' defined in terms of inequality measures;
iii) a form of the tax function that simplifies the algebra.

We want to know whether incidence computed from the OAID under- or over-estimates incidence in the various cohorts. The principal result of the paper is that the issue can be settled simply by writing down the inequality measure as a function of σ^2 – the dispersion parameter in the Λ-distribution. One then checks whether this is concave or convex.

More generally important questions about the 'right' choice of income distribution are raised. Because of the arbitrary age-weighting, the OAID has been shown to be unsatisfactory. But how heavily should we weight inequality statistics relating to the old vis-à-vis those relating to the young? This seems to be as important a problem as that of determining the correct inequality measure in a homogeneous population. Finally, we must express the hope that more government statistical services will follow the practice of publishing income distribution statistics by age groups.

Appendix A

Clearly the tax functions that exist in the real world are not usually readily representable by simple mathematical expressions, the most common form being a step function. For this reason, it is common in analytical work to take as first approximation a particularly simple function – for example the proportional tax function or the linear progressive. In this respect then, the tax function used in the main text $T = y - Ay^b$ where T is the absolute tax liability, y is income before tax and A and B are parameters, is apparently no worse than many other commonly used rules-of-thumb that are available.

The function has the following properties:

(i) The marginal tax rate $(= 1 - bAy^{b-1})$ and the average rate $(= 1 - Ay^{b-1})$ are always strictly increasing, the former being greater than the latter, for all positive incomes.

(ii) For negative incomes the function is not defined, and for zero incomes both marginal and average rates are $-\infty$, the tax liability being 0. (This follows from $b < 1$.)

(iii) The tax liability is zero at $y_0 = A^{1/[1-b]}$ and is a minimum at $y_1 = [Ab]^{1/[1-b]}y_0$, so that in the interval $[0, y_0)$ the function operates as a form of negative income tax.

(iv) As $y \to \infty$, both marginal and average rates $\to 1$.

As an exercise, this functional form was fitted to the tax functions for France and Germany 1965 [see Tanzi (1969)]. The results are given in fig. 3 and suggest that this formalisation is a reasonable first approximation, since unlike the linear progressive form, this function can capture the effect of the rising marginal tax rates.

This functional form has also been suggested by Vickrey (1947).

Appendix B

We establish here a few of the formulae and results used in the main text.

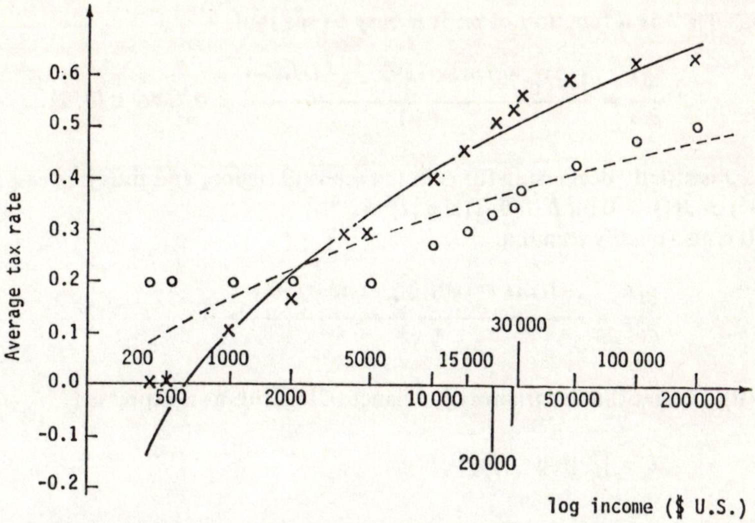

Fig. 3. Fitted function for France and Germany, 1965. Actual average tax rate for given income for couple+2 children (France and Germany, 1965). Parameter values for France: $A = 3.262$, $b = 0.8129$; for W. Germany: $A = 1.476$, $b = 0.9151$.

(A) For inequality-aversion parameter ε, Atkinson's inequality measure is defined as

$$I = 1-[\int_0^\infty [y/\bar{y}]^{1-\varepsilon}\,\mathrm{d}F(y)]^{1/[1-\varepsilon]}.$$

For the distribution $\Lambda(m, s^2)$, writing $x - \log_e y$, we find by virtue of the fact that the mean $\bar{y} = \mathrm{e}^{m+1/2s^2}$,

$$\begin{aligned} I &= 1-[\int_{-\infty}^{\infty} \mathrm{e}^{x[1-\varepsilon]}n(x; m, s^2)\cdot \mathrm{d}x]^{1/[1-\varepsilon]}.\mathrm{e}^{-m-1/2s^2} \\ &= 1-[\mathrm{e}^{[1-\varepsilon]m+1/2[1-\varepsilon]^2s^2}]^{1/[1-\varepsilon]}.\mathrm{e}^{-m-1/2s^2} \\ &= 1-\mathrm{e}^{-1/2\varepsilon s^2}. \end{aligned}$$

The result of theorem 1 in the text – i.e., that $i^T > i^0$ can be verified if we note that $i^T \gtrless i^0$ as

$$[1-\mathrm{e}^{-1/2\varepsilon b^2\sigma^2+v^2/\gamma}]/[1-\mathrm{e}^{-1/2\varepsilon\sigma^2+v^2/\gamma}] \gtrless [1-\mathrm{e}^{-1/2\varepsilon b^2\sigma^2}]/[1-\mathrm{e}^{-1/2\varepsilon\sigma^2}];$$

i.e., as $J(b^2) \gtrless J(1)$, where

$$J(\omega) = [1-\mathrm{e}^{-1/2\varepsilon[\omega\sigma^2+v^2/\gamma]}]/[1-\mathrm{e}^{-1/2\omega\varepsilon\sigma^2}].$$

C

Consider J as a function of ω. It is easy to see that

$$\frac{\partial J}{\partial \omega} = \frac{\frac{1}{2}\varepsilon\sigma^2[e^{-1/2\varepsilon[\omega\sigma^2+v^2/\gamma]} - e^{-1/2\varepsilon\omega\sigma^2}]}{(+)} < 0, \quad \forall\omega \in [0, 1].$$

I.e., J is strictly decreasing for ω in the relevant region, and thus it is easy to see $J(b^2) > J(1) > 0$ for $b \in (0, 1)$; i.e., $i^T > i^0$.

It is also readily seen that

$$\frac{\partial i^T}{\partial v^2} = \frac{e^{-1/2\varepsilon[b^2\sigma^2+v^2/\gamma]} - e^{-1/2\varepsilon[\sigma^2+v^2/\gamma]}}{(+)} > 0.$$

(B) Logarithmic variance or variance of logarithms is expressed

$$I = \int_0^\infty [\log(y/\bar{y})]^2 \, dF(y),$$

where again $\bar{y}$ represents the mean of the distribution. In the case of the lognormal $\Lambda(m, s^2)$, introducing the transformation $x = \log_e y$, we find that

$$I = \int_{-\infty}^{\infty} [x - m - \tfrac{1}{2}s^2]^2 n(x; m, s^2) \cdot dx = \int_{-\infty}^{\infty} [x-m]^2 n(x; m, s^2)\, dx$$
$$+ \int_{-\infty}^{\infty} [\tfrac{1}{4}s^4 + [x-m]s^2] n(x; m, s^2)\, dx = s^2 + \tfrac{1}{4}s^4.$$

(C) Relative mean deviation: $I = \int_0^\infty |y/\bar{y} - 1| \, dF(y)$: for the lognormal introducing the transformation $x = \log_e y$:

$$I = \int_{-\infty}^{\infty} |e^{x-m-1/2s^2} - 1| n(x; m, s^2)\, dx = -2\int_{-\infty}^{a} n(x; m+s^2, s^2)\, dx$$
$$+ \int_{-\infty}^{\infty} n(x; m+s^2, s^2)\, dx, + 2\int_{-\infty}^{a} n(x; m, s^2)\, dx - 1,$$

where $a = m + \frac{1}{2}s^2$, i.e.,

$$I = -2N(-\tfrac{1}{2}s) + 2N(\tfrac{1}{2}s)$$
$$= 2[2N(\tfrac{1}{2}s) - 1].$$

Proof of Theorem 4. Note that for this demonstration neither of the approximations involved in assuming that the OAID for disposable income is $\Lambda(\mu + a, b^2\sigma^2 + v^2/\gamma)$ is required. The distribution of disposable incomes is taken to be $LG(\mu + a, b^2\sigma^2, b^2v^2/\gamma)$.

(A) Atkinson's inequality measure may be written

$$I = 1 - \frac{1}{\bar{y}}[\int_0^\infty y^{1-\varepsilon}\,\mathrm{d}F]^{1/[1-\varepsilon]}.$$

By Lemma 2 of the text, assuming that ε is chosen to lie within a range that permits the series to converge, we find

$$I = 1 - \mathrm{e}^{-1/2\varepsilon\sigma^2}\Xi(1),$$

where I define

$$q = v^2/2\gamma,$$

$$\Xi(v) = [1-qv]/[1-[1-\varepsilon]^2 vq]^{-1/[1-\varepsilon]}.$$

Clearly $i_+^T > i^0$ if $I^T(v\sigma^2)/I^0(v\sigma^2)$ is an increasing function of v for $v \in [0, 1]$, since the tax parameter b is less than unity. In this case define

$$J(v) = \frac{1-\mathrm{e}^{-1/2\varepsilon v\sigma^2}\Xi(v)}{1-\mathrm{e}^{-1/2\varepsilon v\sigma^2}},$$

we wish to see if $J(v)$ is a strictly increasing function for $v \in [0, 1]$. It is evident that

$$J'(v) = [\tfrac{1}{2}\varepsilon\sigma^2[\Xi-1]+\Xi'[\mathrm{e}^{-1/2v\varepsilon\sigma^2}-1]]\mathrm{e}^{-1/2v\varepsilon\sigma^2}[1-\mathrm{e}^{-1/2v\varepsilon\sigma^2}]^{-2}.$$

This is clearly negative if (i) $\Xi(v) < 1$ and (ii) $\Xi'(v) > 0$. Condition (i) can be seen to be satisfied immediately by a series expansion of the divisor in the definition of $\Xi(v)$. Now differentiating Ξ, it is found that $\Xi'(v)$ has the same sign as $vq[1-\varepsilon]^2+[1-vq][1-\varepsilon]-1 = -\varepsilon[vq[1-\varepsilon]+1]$. Thus $\Xi'(v)$ can only be negative (since ε is restricted to be >0) if $\varepsilon > 1+1/vq$. However such values of ε are ruled out by the requirements for the geometrical series in the calculation of I to converge. Thus for the admissible range of ε, (ii) is also satisfied, and thus $J(v)$ is strictly increasing over [0, 1) resulting in $i_+^T > i^0$.

(B) Using a similar argument for the coefficient of variation, define

$$J(v) = \frac{\dfrac{e^{v\sigma^2}[1-vq]^2}{1-4vq}-1}{\mathrm{e}^{v\sigma^2}-1}.$$

This can be verified from Lemma 2 as being derived from the ratio of (c. of v.)^2 for the total population and for the initial cohort. It is to be expected on the basis of Theorem 1* that $i_+^T < i^0$. Again we check the behaviour of $J(v)$ for [0, 1).

$$J'(v) = (+)[[e^{v\sigma^2}-1][2+2vq-2v^2q^2]+[4v^2q^2+vq-2]v\sigma^2].$$

It may be easily verified that a sufficient condition for this to be positive is that $vq < 1$. Since in all practical cases $q = v^2/2\gamma \ll 1$, we find $J'(v) > 0$ and thus $i_+^T < i^0$.

(C) In (B) it has been established that in all practical cases,

$$\frac{[(\text{c. of v})_N^T]^2}{[(\text{c. of v})_G^T]^2} < \frac{[(\text{c. of v})_N^0]^2}{[(\text{c. of v})_G^0]^2}.$$

Now it can be shown that

$$\frac{e^{\mu+a+1/2b^2\sigma^2}\left(1-\dfrac{b^2v^2}{\gamma}\right)^{-1}}{e^{\mu+1/2\sigma^2}\left(1-\dfrac{v^2}{\gamma}\right)^{-1}} < e^a, \qquad \text{since} \quad b^2 < 1.$$

Multiplying the LHS of the first inequality of the LHS of the second, and similarly the RHS by the RHS it can be seen that $i_+^T < i^0$ for the variance as an inequality measure, since the LHS of the second inequality is clearly (from lemma 1) the ratio of post-tax and pre-tax means for the total distribution.

(D) For the Log Gram Charlier, using the transformation $x = [\log y-\mu]/\sigma$

$$I = \int_0^\infty [x-\mu-\tfrac{1}{2}s^2]^2 \,dG(x) = \sigma^2+v^2/\gamma+\tfrac{1}{4}s^4,$$

where s is defined by

$$e^{1/2s^2} = e^{1/2\sigma^2}\left(1-\frac{v^2}{2\gamma}\right)^{-1}.$$

We wish to check whether $i_+^T < i^0$.

Firstly, note that for $\omega < 1$, the following inequality holds

$$-\log\left(1-\frac{\omega v^2}{2\gamma}\right) < -\omega\log\left(1-\frac{v^2}{2\gamma}\right).$$

Substituting in the expression for s^2, it becomes clear that this means that

$$i^T < \frac{b^2\sigma^2+v^2/\gamma+\tfrac{1}{4}b^4s^4}{\sigma^2+v^2/\gamma+\tfrac{1}{4}s^4} = i_{++}^T \qquad \text{(say)}.$$

Now $i^T_{++} < i^0$ if

$$J(\omega) = \frac{\omega[\sigma^2 + v^2/\gamma] + \frac{1}{4}\omega^2 s^4}{\omega\sigma^2 + \omega^2 \frac{1}{4}\sigma^4}$$

is increasing over [0, 1). Differentiating J, it is found to have the same sign as $s^2 - \sigma^2 - v^2/\gamma$. Now from above, $s^2 - \sigma^2$ is found to be $-2 \log [1 - v^2/2\gamma]$. Expanding this as a series in $v^2/2\gamma$, it is readily seen that $s^2 - \sigma^2 - v^2/\gamma > 0$, and thus $J(\omega)$ is strictly increasing. Thus $i^T_{++} < i^0$, and $i^T_{+} < i^0$.

References

Aitchison, J. and J.A.C. Brown, 1957, The lognormal distribution (Cambridge University Press, Cambridge).

Atkinson, A.B., 1970, On the measurement of inequality, Journal of Economic Theory 2.

Bjerke, K., 1970, An analysis of the distribution of wages in Copenhagen in the second quarter of 1951, Review of Income and Wealth 16.

Kendall, M.G. and A. Stuart, 1958, The advanced theory of statistics, vol. I (Griffin, London).

Rutherford, R.S.G., 1955, Income distributions: A new model, Econometrica 23.

Tanzi, V., 1969, The individual income tax and economic growth (Johns Hopkins Press, Baltimore).

Theil, H., 1967, Economics and information theory (North-Holland, Amsterdam).

Vickrey, W., 1947, Agenda for progressive taxation (Ronald Press, New York).

[31]

IMF *Staff Papers*
Vol. 37, No. 3 (September 1990)

Macroeconomic Effects of Projected Population Aging in Industrial Countries

PAUL R. MASSON and RALPH W. TRYON*

The effects of population aging are examined with a theoretical model and simulations of MULTIMOD. An older population will consume more of aggregate disposable income, require higher government expenditure, and decrease labor supply. These effects should raise real interest rates and lower capital stock and output. Effects on current balances will depend on the relative speed and extent of aging. Simulations of projected demographic changes suggest that by 2025, real interest rates would be increased in all countries, and net foreign assets would be increased in the United States and decreased in the Federal Republic of Germany and Japan. [JEL 224, 421, 840]

IF CURRENT projections prove to be correct, the populations of most industrial countries will experience significant aging in the first few decades of the next century. Birthrates have already declined markedly from their high levels of the early postwar period, and are projected to decline further. Even though projections that far ahead are obviously subject to considerable uncertainty, a prospective increase in the average age of the population is to a large extent inevitable as the postwar "baby boom" generation moves through the age structure. Aging of the popu-

* Paul R. Masson, an Advisor in the Research Department, received his Ph.D. from the London School of Economics and Political Science.
Ralph W. Tryon, who holds a doctorate from the Massachusetts Institute of Technology, currently works at the Federal Reserve Board. This paper was written while he was an Economist in the Fund's Research Department.
The authors are grateful to A. Lans Bovenberg, William Branson, Ernesto Hernández-Catá, Andrew Dean, Robert Hagemann, Richard Hemming, Robert Holzmann, Yusuke Horiguchi, and Mark Lutz for comments, and to Warwick McKibbin, Torsten Persson, and Lars Svensson for useful discussion.

lation can be expected to bring about major changes in the economy, associated with an increase in the number of dependents relative to those that are employed (the dependency ratio), and in some countries with very low birthrates, projected declines in the population. An especially large element of uncertainty attaches to birthrate projections and to changes in population due to migration, but in any case, dependency ratios will almost certainly rise in the next three decades; a substantial rise in birthrates would, if anything, increase dependency ratios over this time period.

With the aging of the population, it is plausible to expect a decline in saving rates to the extent that "life-cycle" motives for saving operate—that is, individuals save for retirement during the years in which they are employed and dissave subsequently.[1] In addition, the demand for social services will change toward providing more medical services and pension benefits and away from spending on education. Finally, the presence of fewer individuals of working age will be associated with lower levels of employment and hence of output, other things being equal, than would otherwise be the case. What happens to per capita output will depend on the resulting capital stock per worker, as well as on the proportion of the population in the labor force.

The macroeconomic effects of these changes, which can be expected to be substantial, are the subject of this paper. Changes in saving propensities, government spending, and labor supply have implications for relative prices, real interest rates, and real exchange rates; these variables in turn feed back onto decisions to spend and produce. The paper is an attempt to gauge the global macroeconomic consequences of generalized aging of the population in industrial countries.

To understand these consequences requires a macroeconomic model. A multicountry context is also important because some of the effects—for example, on real exchange rates and on current account balances—depend crucially on the extent of aging in one country *relative* to that in other countries. In this paper, we use simulations of the International Monetary Fund's multiregion econometric model (MULTIMOD) in order to gauge the effects of the demographic developments described above.

[1] Saving may in fact be "hump-shaped"; that is, saving may be negative in the early years of adulthood, positive in the middle years, and negative again after retirement. Intergenerational transfers complicate the analysis of saving behavior, which should be modeled at the household level. Parents finance consumption for their children when young and may save for their college education. Moreover, the aged may also save in order to make bequests to their children (or to charity).

Aging of the population affects macroeconomic variables in the model through three channels.[2] First, aggregate consumption relative to income is increased by a rise in the dependency ratio. Second, higher dependency ratios lower the labor force, which is associated with a decline in potential output. Third, an older population requires larger government expenditures on medical services and on pension benefits; however, these may be partially offset by a decline in education expenditures.

To date, a macroeconomic framework has not been used to capture the general equilibrium, multicountry effects of demographic projections. There are a number of relevant studies of various features of the issue, however. Heller and others (1986) considered the effect of aging on social expenditures in seven major industrial countries (the so-called Group of Seven), and we will use their estimates below as input to our simulations. Heller (1989) examined the impact of aging on private saving, using several estimated consumption models; he also discussed implications for government budgets. The Organization for Economic Cooperation and Development (OECD) has produced several studies of saving behavior, including effects of demographic factors (Dean and others (1989) and Herd (1989)), and has examined implications of aging for public finances (Hagemann and Nicoletti (1989)). In addition, Auerbach and others (1989) studied the dynamics of the effects of aging on the economies of four industrial countries using a general equilibrium, overlapping-generations model; however, that model considered each country in isolation rather than as part of a closed world system. Ritzen and van Dalen (1989) considered the optimal fiscal policy in the transition to an older population, using a single-country theoretical model. Lee and Lapkoff (1988) looked at intergenerational transfer issues in an overlapping-generations context, but did not treat multicountry issues. Horne, Kremers, and Masson (1989) examined the long-run relationship between dependency ratios and net foreign asset positions for the United States, Japan, and the Federal Republic of Germany.

It is important to make clear at the outset the limitations of our study.[3] We do not examine issues related to intergenerational transfers—namely, questions of equity—since this would require a more detailed model. Furthermore, policy questions—for instance, how should increases in government spending be financed, or whether incentives for private saving should be put in place today—are not treated here.

[2] Another channel, through the rate of population growth, is ignored here; the population is taken to be exogenous in our simulations discussed below.

[3] Some of the issues mentioned in what follows are discussed in Bös and Weizsäcker (1989).

We have not attempted to incorporate projections for aging in developing countries. Finally, we do not take into account effects of the age structure on labor force participation due to endogenous participation or retirement decisions,[4] or to changes in the growth rate of the population.[5]

The plan of the paper is as follows. Section I discusses the OECD's demographic projections and presents the projections of expenditures on government services given in Heller and others (1986). Section II details the model of private consumption that is embodied in MULTIMOD and compares its estimate of the effect of demographic factors to those found in other studies. Section III presents simulations of the effects of aging using MULTIMOD; the results are compared to the long-run effects that can be derived from a simple theoretical model that is the prototype for MULTIMOD. (Derivations are detailed in the Appendix.) Finally, Section IV provides some concluding remarks.

I. Demographic Trends and Projections

In most industrial countries, the decade and a half following the end of World War II saw very high birthrates, which have since moderated. The early postwar generation—often termed the baby boom generation—is now 30–45 years old; as a result, a large fraction of the population is currently employed. However, when the baby boom generation retires in the years 2010–25, there will likely be large declines in the number employed relative to those that depend on them—or on their own savings.

A measure of the age structure of the population is the dependency ratio, which can be calculated in various ways. Table 1 gives historical data and projections for three measures—the ratios of the young and of the old to those of working age (assumed to be between 15 and 64), as well as their combined ratio.[6] The youth dependency ratio declined

[4] However, Table 8 below assesses the sensitivity of our results to these factors.

[5] Some theoretical effects of permanent changes in population growth are analyzed in the Appendix; other things being equal, a lower population growth rate would imply lower real interest rates.

[6] These projections of dependency ratios are substantially the same as those given in the *World Economic Outlook* (International Monetary Fund (1989)), with a few revisions. In particular, Japan's dependency ratio is projected here to be several percentage points higher in the 2010–20 period. However, the simulations discussed below extend the analysis in the *World Economic Outlook* by taking into account induced labor force and government spending changes. In International Monetary Fund (1990), some tax policy issues related to aging are also considered.

markedly from 1965 to 1985; that ratio is projected to decline further in some countries (the United States, France), but generally to remain constant through 2025, at least if birthrates do not change substantially. In contrast, the elderly dependency ratio—roughly constant since 1965—is projected to rise in all countries by 2025. However, the extent of the rise varies greatly across countries.

A summary statistic of the importance of the age structure is the overall dependency ratio, given in the bottom panel of Table 1. This ratio captures the labor force implications of the fraction of the population

Table 1. *Selected Demographic Variables, 1965–2025*
(In percent)

Country	1965	1975	1985	Projections 1995	2005	2015	2025
	Population under 15/population 15–64						
United States	51	39	33	34	29	29	30
Japan	38	36	32	25	28	28	27
Germany, Fed. Rep. of	35	34	22	23	22	19	23
France	41	38	32	31	28	26	28
Italy	—	—	—	25	25	22	24
United Kingdom	36	37	29	31	31	31	31
Canada	57	41	32	30	27	25	28
	Population 65 and over/population 15–64						
United States	16	16	18	19	18	21	29
Japan	9	12	15	19	26	33	32
Germany, Fed. Rep. of	18	23	21	24	29	31	37
France	19	22	20	22	24	27	33
Italy	—	—	—	22	25	28	32
United Kingdom	19	22	23	23	22	24	28
Canada	13	13	15	18	19	25	34
	Overall dependency ratio						
United States	67	55	51	52	47	50	59
Japan	48	48	47	44	54	61	59
Germany, Fed. Rep. of	54	56	43	47	51	51	60
France	61	60	52	53	52	53	61
Italy[a]	52	54	45	47	50	50	55
United Kingdom	55	59	52	54	53	55	59
Canada	70	54	48	48	46	50	61

Sources: Organization for Economic Cooperation and Development, *Labour Force Statistics, 1964–84, 1967–87;* and OECD Secretariat, Directorate for Social Affairs, Manpower, and Education, Demographic Databank projections.

[a] Fund staff estimates for 1965–85.

that is either too young or too old to work.[7] Whether the increase in the overall dependency ratio occurs because of an increase in the young or the old has implications for other variables, for instance medical care and education, as discussed below. It may also matter for the economy's saving propensity; however, consumption equation estimates reported in Section II below use the overall ratio, since there was no significant difference between the effects of youth and elderly dependency ratios.

With the year 1995 as a base (as is done in the simulations in Section III), changes in the overall dependency ratio to 2025 vary greatly across countries, though dependency ratios end up at similar levels in 2025. Increases of 13–15 percentage points are projected for Japan and the Federal Republic of Germany; moreover, a large part of the increase occurs by 2015 (especially in Japan). In contrast, the ratio for the United States increases by 7 percentage points by 2025, and is actually projected to be lower in 2015 than in 1995; the ratio for the United Kingdom increases by 5 percentage points. Canada is projected to have a large increase, but only in the 2015–25 period. France and Italy have increases on the order of 8 percentage points by 2025, with the changes occurring fairly gradually. Thus, both the extent of aging and the speed with which it occurs differ substantially among the major industrial countries. Projections for the smaller industrial countries (Hagemann and Nicoletti (1989)) also indicate significant increases in dependency ratios.

Heller and others (1986) projected the change of social expenditures by governments on the basis of demographic projections similar to those in Table 1. They included in their study expenditures on education, medical care, pensions, unemployment compensation, and income maintenance for the poor, at both the general and local government levels.

We focus in this paper on three components of government spending that are closely related to demographic developments: medical expenses, education expenses, and pension benefit payments. We do not attempt to disaggregate *revenues,* however—for instance, by separating social security contributions from other taxes. Whether social security programs are funded or unfunded and the resulting implications for the economy are beyond the scope of this paper. Instead, we simulate the model with a tax-rate reaction function that tends to resist movements

[7] Of course, in many countries secondary education extends beyond age 15, and in addition many students proceed to university before entering the labor force. Also, retirement age may not correspond to age 65; early retirement is possible; conversely, in most professions retirement at 65 is not compulsory. A more precise measure of dependency would adjust the denominator (the working-age population) by the participation rate, to obtain those actually in the labor force (see Hagemann and Nicoletti (1989)).

away from an exogenous government debt to gross national product (GNP) ratio. This rule prevents a snowballing accumulation of debt leading to eventual government default. Deficits do occur for a number of years as a result of demographic changes, but they are eventually eliminated.

Table 2 summarizes the projections in Heller and others (1986) for government spending on medical care, education, and pensions. The effects of demographic changes are calculated as the difference between the GNP share of spending on each category projected for 2000–25, and its value in 1980 (a more recent year of historical data was not available in their study). The increases in government expenditure on medical care (as a percent of gross domestic product (GDP)) are large but not enormous. Moreover, except in Germany and Japan, they are mostly offset by declines in projected education expenditures. In contrast, pension benefits (which are treated in the model as negative taxes) increase by between 5 percent and 10 percent of GDP for Germany, Italy, and Japan. By 2025, government spending in all three areas taken together increases by up to 10 percentage points of GDP; however, these increases differ markedly across countries. They are largest in Japan, Germany, and Italy, and smallest in the United States and Canada, as would be expected given the demographic trends discussed above.

II. Estimated Consumption Equation

This section describes the estimated consumption equation and compares the effect it attributes to the dependency ratio to effects found in other studies. The starting point for the consumption equation is the intertemporal optimizing model of Blanchard (1985), as extended by Buiter (1988). This model makes consumption a function of financial and "human" wealth—that is, the expected value of lifetime earnings, discounted to the present. It is a useful tool for analyzing fiscal policy because it allows for an effect of the government stock of bonds on interest rates (provided the birthrate is nonzero); the model allows simple aggregation because of the assumption that the probability of death is the same for individuals of all ages. However, as noted by Blanchard (1985, p. 235), the model is not convenient for rigorously treating "saving for retirement" or for allowing for a path of labor income that abruptly drops to zero at a certain point. Moreover, it does not allow for constraints that individuals face on their borrowing. In our estimated model, we implement liquidity constraints in an error-correction framework, as in Davidson and others (1978) and Hendry and von Ungern-

Table 2. *Changes in Government Expenditures Due to Demographic Changes, 2000–25*
(In percent of GDP)

Country	Medical Expenditures			Education			Pension Expenditures			Combined Effects of (1)–(3)		
	2000	2010 (1)	2025	2000	2010 (2)	2025	2000	2010 (3)	2025	2000	2010 (4)	2025
United States	0.01	0.15	1.06	−0.92	−1.14	−1.29	−0.50	−0.60	0.60	−1.41	−1.59	0.37
Japan	0.67	1.25	1.63	−1.00	−0.50	−0.70	5.41	8.69	9.20	5.08	9.44	10.13
Germany, Fed. Rep. of	0.43	0.92	1.59	−0.63	−0.88	−0.81	3.80	5.30	7.20	3.60	5.34	7.98
France	0.34	0.40	0.80	−0.46	−0.54	−0.51	1.00	1.50	3.00	0.88	1.36	3.29
Italy	0.20	0.49	0.88	−0.80	−0.90	−1.00	2.50	4.60	8.60	1.90	4.19	8.48
United Kingdom	0.05	—	0.66	−1.00	−1.00	−1.10	0.85	1.42	2.56	−0.10	0.42	2.12
Canada	−0.06	0.18	1.45	−1.91	−2.15	−1.87	−0.40	−0.40	0.80	−2.37	−2.37	0.38

Source: Heller and others (1986, Table 14).
Note: Figures represent the difference between the share of spending projected for 2000–25 and its 1980 value (the latest year of historical data available from the Heller study). Medical expenditure figures were obtained directly from Peter Heller.

Sternberg (1981). We also add a dependency ratio to capture effects of differences in age structure on consumption and saving, admittedly in an ad hoc fashion. The data for human wealth used to estimate the consumption equation do not include adjustment for future demographic changes; rather, human wealth is the discounted value of future net disposable income from production, the latter variable extrapolated from historical data.

We implement the consumption model by allowing a lagged adjustment to the long-run wealth/consumption ratio. The specification, in logs, forces that ratio to be constant in the steady state. The dynamics are affected by the change in the log of disposable income and the level of the real interest rate. The latter variable serves two purposes: it captures intertemporal substitution, and it serves to pick up effects on the discounted present value of future income not captured in our measure of human wealth, which uses a constant discount rate. In addition, the path of consumption (and the long-run wealth/consumption ratio) is assumed to be influenced by the dependency ratio.

The equation was estimated using ordinary least squares with annual data from 1969 to 1987 pooled across the Group of Seven countries and the "smaller industrial country" block. The estimated equation, which is used in the simulations described below, is as follows:

$$\Delta\log C = \text{country constants} + \underset{(3.5)}{.113} \log (W_{-1}/C_{-1}) - \underset{(4.0)}{.473}\, RLR$$

$$+\underset{(5.5)}{.408}\, \Delta\log YD + \underset{(1.5)}{.124}\, DEM3 + \underset{(2.2)}{.032}\, DEM3^{*}DUM80$$

$$\overline{R}^2 = .641, \qquad \text{SER} = .026,$$

where the numbers in parentheses are t-statistics ($\overline{R}^2$ is the coefficient of determination corrected for degrees of freedom and SER is the standard error), and where C is the real consumption expenditure, W is real wealth, RLR is the real long-term interest rate (expected inflation is proxied for estimation purposes by a centered ten-year moving average of actual inflation), YD is real, after-tax net domestic product, $DEM3$ is the overall dependency ratio (the ratio of dependents to the working age population),[8] and $DUM80$ is a dummy variable equal to 1.0 after 1980. This variable was included because visual inspection of our population data indicated a break in that year, perhaps because of imperfect splicing of census data with earlier estimates. It is important to note that wealth includes the discounted present value of future (noninterest)

[8] Expressed as a decimal fraction, rather than in percent as in Table 1.

disposable income, *WH*.[9] Total wealth *W* is the sum of *WH* and the real value of financial wealth, held in the form of domestic outside money *M*, government bonds *B*, and net claims on foreigners *NFA* (in U.S. dollars; *ER* is the exchange rate):

$$W = WH + (M + B + NFA/ER)/P.$$

The disposable income variable *YD* is constrained by the error-correction specification to have only transitory effects, because liquidity constraints are assumed to operate only in the short to medium term.

The estimated equation attributes a positive effect on consumption of an increase in the overall dependency ratio—significant at the 5 percent level when the product of the dependency ratio and the dummy variable is considered. Including the youth and elderly dependency ratios separately did not significantly increase the explanatory power of the equation; hence, they were constrained to have the same coefficient. The data also could not reject the constraint of a common coefficient on the overall dependency ratio across countries. Some further estimation was done, after the above equation was incorporated into the model, in order to examine the robustness of the results. Using instrumental variables to estimate the equation[10] yielded a somewhat larger and more significant effect of the dependency ratio, as well as a higher coefficient on *YD* and a lower one on *RLR* (in absolute terms).[11] Adding the inflation rate (as in Bovenberg and Evans (1990; this issue)) in place of the post-1980 dummy variable, however, decreased the value of the coefficient on the remaining dependency ratio. Also, differences in sample periods or countries included could make a nonnegligible difference to the results, and the sensitivity of our simulation results to this coefficient is discussed below. Nevertheless, there is some evidence from our results that increases in the dependency ratio may have been associated historically with increases in consumption relative to income and wealth, a conclusion that emerges more strongly from the quarterly estimation by Bovenberg and Evans (1990) using U.S. data of a specification similar to ours.[12]

From our equation, a 1 percentage point increase in the dependency ratio is estimated to cause an increase in consumption in the post-1980

[9] As defined, therefore, *WH* includes the discounted present value of income to both labor and capital.

[10] Instruments were the rate of money growth, the ratio of government spending to GDP, the lagged wealth/consumption ratio, the lagged change in disposable income, and the dependency ratio.

[11] Results from a similar specification are discussed in Masson, Symansky, and Meredith (1990).

[12] Their measure of wealth is household net worth, and they include separate population variables to capture dependents below age 20 and over age 65.

Table 3. *Long-Run Effects of an Increase in Elderly Dependency Ratio on Private Saving Rate in Various Models*

Model	Estimate
Modigliani	−0.88
Modigliani and Sterling	−0.51
Feldstein	−1.21
Horioka	−1.61
Memorandum item:	
MULTIMOD	−1.10

Source: Heller (1989).

period of 0.16 percent in the short run and 1.4 percent in the long run (equal to 0.124 plus 0.032, divided by 0.113). It is of interest to compare these results to those found in other studies. Heller (1989) surveyed saving equations that included estimated effects of dependency ratios. Though the definitions of variables differ, as do sample periods, a rough comparison can be made with the equation estimated for MULTIMOD, after converting it to a saving equation. The private saving rate (s) can be defined as C above, divided by private national income (Y), and subtracted from unity: $s = 1 - C/Y$. Therefore, MULTIMOD's equation implies that the saving rate responds to the dependency ratio in the long run (for a given real interest rate and wealth/income ratio) as follows:

$$\frac{ds}{dDEM3} = -\frac{d(C/Y)}{dDEM3} = -\frac{d \log C}{dDEM3} C/Y = \frac{(.124 + .032)}{.113} C/Y.$$

Table 3 gives estimates for MULTIMOD as well as four other models.[13] It can be seen that MULTIMOD is near the center of the range of available estimates. Each estimate shows a powerful effect on saving of an increase in the elderly as a proportion of the working-age population.[14] There thus appears to be considerable additional support for the hypothesis that the aging of the population projected for the next century is likely to increase consumption relative to income. However, it must be stressed that other studies (Aaron, Bosworth, and Burtless (1989), for instance, examining U.S. evidence), have failed to find a significant effect. The next section uses simulations of MULTIMOD to

[13] The estimate for MULTIMOD assumes a consumption income ratio (C/Y) of 0.8.

[14] These studies also estimate a separate effect of the proportion of the young in the population; in each case, this variable has the same sign but a smaller coefficient.

capture the implications of our estimated consumption equation for the effects of aging on macroeconomic variables, as well as effects through the other two channels mentioned above.

III. Simulation of the Effects of Population Aging

In order to study the macroeconomic effects of the demographic shifts discussed above, we use simulations of MULTIMOD, which is a macroeconometric model of the Group of Seven countries and the remaining industrial countries and of developing countries divided into capital exporters and capital importers (see Masson, Symansky, and Meredith (1990)). The simulations take place over a horizon from 1996 to 2025. The baseline simulation of the model is constructed by constraining growth rates of real variables to converge to current estimates of potential output growth, while private and government saving rates remain constant at their levels projected for 1995. With respect to the demographic variables, the dependency ratio and the labor force participation rate are assumed to remain constant in each country throughout the baseline. It should be emphasized that we are not attempting to construct an ex ante forecast for the Group of Seven countries through 2025—we are only attempting to quantify the macroeconomic effects of aging over that horizon.

Demographic effects are captured in MULTIMOD using the dependency ratio defined above. This variable appears in the model in two equations for each industrial country: in the consumption function, as described above, and in the production function, in which the total labor force is set equal to the working-age population times an exogenous participation rate. The working-age population is determined by the total population, which is exogenous, and the dependency ratio. The dependency ratio is also exogenous, but we simulate the model with an alternative path for this variable to quantify the effects of the projected aging of the population.

The alternative scenario we simulate with MULTIMOD allows the dependency ratio in each country to evolve along its projected path through 2025, rather than remaining constant as in the baseline scenario at its 1995 value. The labor force participation rate is, however, assumed to remain on its baseline path. As described more fully in Section I above, two different periods can be identified: in the first, through 2010, there is *differential* aging in the industrial countries, while the *average* dependency ratio remains roughly constant. In the second period, the populations in all industrial countries except Japan age steadily, and dependency ratios rise substantially. In Japan the dependency ratio remains approximately at the same level above baseline.

Finally, we include a simulation of the projected changes in government expenditures related to aging and a simulation of the combined effects.

Effects of Aging on Consumption Expenditure

As discussed in the Appendix, a shift in the dependency ratio affects the economy through several channels. The first channel is through the effect on consumption expenditure; as the ratio of dependents to the working-age population increases, consumption increases (for given values of income and wealth).

Table 4 presents the results of a simulation of the effects of a shift in dependency ratios over the period 1996–2025,[15] operating only through the change in consumption behavior. In this simulation the labor force is held exogenous in each country, and no change is made to government expenditure. As shown in the table, the private saving rate in the United States is above its baseline level (which was assumed to be constant) throughout the simulation; it rises through 2015 (relative to the baseline, it is almost 3 percentage points higher then), and then drops back somewhat, as the dependency ratio first falls, and then rises. The rise in the saving rate is mirrored in the movement of domestic demand, which is below the baseline throughout the simulation, reaching its lowest level in 2005 before beginning to recover. The reduction in domestic demand is offset by an increase in demand for U.S. exports from abroad due both to lower saving rates abroad and to a real depreciation of the dollar. As a result, real GNP in the United States is above the baseline after 2005.

The increase in the saving rate initially leads to a modest increase in investment, but this effect is offset later on by an increase in the real interest rate resulting from higher aggregate demand. The government balance is largely unchanged, as a share of GNP, so the increase in private saving is manifested primarily in the current account, which improves by up to 3 percent of GNP over the simulation range. As a result, the net foreign asset position of the United States improves steadily, and is higher by more than 30 percent of GNP at the end of the simulation.

[15] Because the model requires that terminal conditions be imposed on expectations variables, and in order to minimize the effects of those terminal conditions, the simulation period was extended to 2040. After 2025, the changes in dependency ratios were assumed to be gradually reversed.

Table 4. *Demographic Shift: Consumption Effects*
(Deviations from baseline)

Country	2000	2005	2010	2015	2020	2025
United States			*(in percent)*			
Real GNP	−1.0	−0.2	1.1	1.9	2.2	2.1
Real domestic demand	−2.8	−3.8	−3.7	−3.0	−2.2	−1.5
Real interest rate	0.6	−0.2	−0.5	−0.0	0.9	2.0
Real effective exchange rate	−6.2	−11.6	−12.8	−11.3	−8.4	−4.9
GDP per worker	−0.9	−0.6	0.0	0.4	0.4	0.1
Capital stock per worker	−0.5	−0.7	−0.4	0.0	−0.0	−0.8
			(as a percent of GNP)			
Current account balance	0.8	2.0	2.8	3.0	2.8	2.6
General government financial balance	−0.4	0.0	0.2	0.1	−0.0	−0.1
Private saving	1.3	1.4	2.3	2.6	2.3	1.6
Gross private investment	0.1	0.3	0.4	0.2	−0.3	−0.9
Net foreign assets	1.9	7.9	16.7	25.0	31.0	34.5
Government debt	1.3	1.7	0.7	−0.3	−0.7	−0.6
Japan			*(in percent)*			
Real GNP	2.1	0.7	−0.9	−2.8	−4.6	−6.1
Real domestic demand	7.1	9.6	9.9	8.2	5.1	1.8
Real interest rate	−2.3	−0.3	1.0	2.4	3.4	3.7
Real effective exchange rate	14.2	27.5	33.8	33.1	26.1	17.1
GDP per worker	2.5	2.1	1.2	0.0	−1.2	−2.2
Capital stock per worker	1.8	2.6	2.2	0.7	−1.4	−3.7
			(as a percent of GNP)			
Current account balance	−2.1	−3.5	−4.3	−4.5	−4.4	−4.2
General government financial balance	0.5	0.4	0.3	0.0	−0.3	−0.5
Private saving	−2.9	−4.8	−5.9	−6.2	−5.8	−5.2
Gross private investment	−0.2	−1.0	−1.4	−1.7	−1.7	−1.5
Net foreign assets	−11.3	−23.9	−35.7	−45.8	−53.6	−58.5
Government debt	−1.7	−3.2	−3.3	−2.5	−0.7	1.6
Germany, Fed. Rep. of			*(in percent)*			
Real GNP	0.7	0.0	−1.0	−1.5	−1.2	−0.5
Real domestic demand	1.1	2.4	2.6	1.8	1.0	1.2
Real interest rate	−0.3	−0.2	0.0	0.6	1.5	2.4
Real effective exchange rate	0.2	1.3	1.9	1.8	0.9	0.9
GDP per worker	0.5	0.5	0.1	−0.2	−0.2	0.0
Capital stock per worker	0.2	0.5	0.6	0.4	−0.2	−1.2
			(as a percent of GNP)			
Current account balance	−0.1	−1.3	−2.3	−2.2	−1.7	−1.2
General government financial balance	0.2	0.0	−0.1	−0.2	−0.2	−0.1
Private saving	−0.3	−1.3	−2.1	−2.0	−1.8	−2.1
Gross private investment	0.0	0.0	0.1	−0.0	−0.3	−0.9
Net foreign assets	−2.3	−6.6	−13.0	−18.2	−20.8	−21.4
Government debt	−0.4	−0.8	−0.4	0.3	0.9	1.0

Continued overleaf

Table 4 (*concluded*).

Country	2000	2005	2010	2015	2020	2025
Other Industrial Countries			*(in percent)*			
Real GNP	−0.2	0.1	0.2	0.7	0.3	−0.3
Real domestic demand	−0.3	−0.4	−0.6	−0.2	−0.4	−1.1
Real interest rate	−0.1	−0.1	−0.0	0.3	1.4	2.4
Real effective exchange rate	−0.8	−1.7	−2.5	−2.8	−2.4	−2.1
GDP per worker	−0.1	−0.0	−0.2	0.3	0.0	−0.4
Capital stock per worker	−0.1	−0.0	0.0	0.2	−0.2	−1.4
			(as a percent of GNP)			
Current account balance	0.2	0.6	0.7	0.6	0.4	0.2
General government financial balance	0.1	0.0	0.0	−0.1	−0.4	−0.4
Private saving	0.1	0.5	0.7	0.6	0.4	−0.2
Gross private investment	0.0	0.0	0.0	0.0	−0.4	−0.8
Net foreign assets	1.1	3.1	5.3	6.5	6.6	5.8
Government debt	0.5	0.3	0.1	−0.6	−0.0	1.7

In Japan, the private saving rate falls steadily through 2015 as a result of the aging of the population, leading to substantial increases in domestic demand. Real output is initially higher than in the baseline as a result of the increase in demand, but the real interest rate rises above the baseline, tending to crowd out domestic demand. The real exchange rate appreciates by about 30 percent at its peak, and the current account is substantially lower, as a share of GNP, throughout the simulation. As a result, Japan's net foreign asset position deteriorates substantially, by almost 60 percent of GNP, by 2025.

In the Federal Republic of Germany saving is also lower and domestic demand higher as a result of the demographic shift. The results for the external sector are, however, quite different: the real exchange rate appreciates very little, though the current account ratio falls substantially, by about 20 percent of GNP. The extent of the demographic shift is smaller in Germany than in Japan, which accounts for some of the difference. Also, imports of manufactures are a much larger share of GNP in Germany, so that a given change in the real exchange rate can achieve a larger demand shift in Germany than in Japan.[16]

The effects of the demographic shift on all other industrial countries taken as a group are smaller in comparison. These countries include Canada, with demographic projections that resemble those for the

[16] If relative price elasticities were the same, a unit change in the real exchange rate would bring about a larger change in imports as a share of GNP in Germany than in Japan as a result. In fact, the price elasticity of imports of manufactures is also higher in Germany; see Masson, Symansky, and Meredith (1990).

United States, and European countries, with projections for aging that are closer to Germany's, but less severe. The saving rate, domestic demand, and real output for other industrial countries taken together are all roughly unchanged for most of the period, although by 2025 the real interest rate rises significantly and output declines.

In MULTIMOD, foreign and domestic assets are assumed to be perfect substitutes, so that real interest parity holds. Differences in real interest rates across countries therefore reflect expected future appreciation or depreciation of the real exchange rate, and the overall level of real interest rates reflects global saving and investment (or aggregate demand and supply). From 2015 onwards the demographic shift is toward more aging in all industrial countries, leading to global excess demand, and higher real interest rates in all countries. Before 2015, it is the composition of global demand that is shifting, leading to changes in real exchange rates, while the global real interest rate remains (approximately) unchanged.

Effects of Aging on Production

Demographic shifts also operate through a change in the labor force, which, assuming that the participation rate is constant, changes one-for-one with the decline in those aged 15–64. Aging of the population reduces the labor force and thereby reduces potential output, leading to excess demand for domestic output. As a result, real output would also be expected to fall, and the real exchange rate, to appreciate. The effect on real interest rates is ambiguous, since, on the one hand, a reduction in supply creates excess (global) demand for goods, which tends to raise the real interest rate, and, on the other hand, a fall in the labor force tends to lower the marginal product of capital and hence tends to lower the equilibrium real interest rate. In the long run, however, for a given saving rate a smaller labor force should lead to a proportionate contraction of the capital stock and output, leaving real interest rates unaffected.

Table 5 shows the results of a simulation in which the demographic shift affects only the total labor force in each country.[17] The results are consistent with the analysis given above—in both Germany and Japan real output falls steadily relative to the baseline, while the real exchange rate appreciates. In both countries the real interest rate is initially below the baseline, and then rises above it at the end of the simulation. In both

[17] That is, the direct effects on consumption discussed above are ignored. However, changes in output do induce changes in human wealth and, hence, in consumption.

Table 5. *Demographic Shift: Production Effects*
(Deviations from baseline)

Country	2000	2005	2010	2015	2020	2025
United States			*(in percent)*			
Real GNP	1.0	2.9	3.7	2.4	−0.2	−2.9
Real domestic demand	0.8	2.2	2.9	1.8	−0.2	−2.5
Real interest rate	−0.3	−0.7	−0.8	−0.3	0.3	0.9
Real effective exchange rate	−1.0	−2.6	−3.1	−2.7	−2.2	−1.3
GDP per worker	−1.0	−1.2	−0.4	0.6	1.5	1.9
Capital stock per worker	−1.6	−2.6	−1.6	0.9	3.4	4.9
			(as a percent of GNP)			
Current account balance	0.0	0.2	0.2	−0.0	−0.3	−0.5
General government financial balance	0.2	0.4	0.2	−0.2	−0.5	−0.6
Private saving	0.0	−0.9	−0.5	−0.1	0.0	−0.1
Gross private investment	0.0	0.1	0.2	0.2	0.1	0.0
Net foreign assets	−0.1	0.3	1.0	1.1	0.2	−1.4
Government debt	−0.3	−1.5	−2.3	−1.6	0.3	2.7
Japan			*(in percent)*			
Real GNP	−1.8	−3.7	−5.7	−6.8	−7.0	−6.7
Real domestic demand	−1.4	−2.6	−4.2	−5.5	−6.2	−6.3
Real interest rate	−1.1	−1.0	−0.3	0.3	0.9	1.2
Real effective exchange rate	1.5	3.9	5.9	6.0	5.1	4.1
GDP per worker	1.5	3.2	3.6	3.4	2.5	1.7
Capital stock per worker	3.1	6.4	7.9	7.5	5.7	3.3
			(as a percent of GNP)			
Current account balance	−0.1	−0.3	−0.3	0.1	0.6	1.0
General government financial balance	−0.2	−0.3	−0.4	−0.3	−0.2	−0.0
Private saving	0.7	0.7	0.7	0.7	0.6	0.4
Gross private investment	0.5	0.7	0.6	0.3	−0.2	−0.6
Net foreign assets	−0.1	−1.1	−1.8	−1.2	0.7	3.6
Government debt	0.6	1.6	2.8	3.5	3.5	3.0
Germany, Fed. Rep. of			*(in percent)*			
Real GNP	−1.0	−2.1	−2.4	−2.2	−2.9	−4.7
Real domestic demand	−1.2	−1.8	−2.2	−2.5	−3.4	−5.1
Real interest rate	−0.6	−0.7	−0.6	−0.2	0.3	1.2
Real effective exchange rate	0.1	0.8	0.8	0.2	0.6	1.9
GDP per worker	0.3	0.9	0.4	0.4	1.4	2.5
Capital stock per worker	1.0	2.5	2.2	2.1	3.7	5.5
			(as a percent of GNP)			
Current account balance	0.2	−0.0	−0.0	0.3	0.5	0.9
General government financial balance	−0.1	−0.2	−0.1	−0.1	−0.2	−0.4
Private saving	0.5	0.4	0.4	0.6	0.7	0.7
Gross private investment	0.2	0.3	0.3	0.2	−0.1	−0.6
Net foreign assets	1.1	1.7	1.9	1.9	1.8	3.6
Government debt	0.5	1.0	1.3	1.3	1.6	2.5

Table 5 (*concluded*).

Country	2000	2005	2010	2015	2020	2025
Other Industrial Countries			*(in percent)*			
Real GNP	−0.0	0.4	0.5	−0.4	−2.4	−3.7
Real domestic demand	−0.0	0.3	0.4	−0.4	−2.4	−3.7
Real interest rate	−0.5	−0.6	−0.7	−0.2	0.6	0.9
Real effective exchange rate	−0.1	−0.3	−0.6	−0.5	−0.6	−1.0
GDP per worker	−0.0	0.1	0.2	1.0	1.0	1.8
Capital stock per worker	0.1	0.3	0.7	2.3	3.2	3.9
			(as a percent of GNP)			
Current account balance	−0.0	0.1	0.0	−0.1	−0.2	−0.3
General government financial balance	0.0	0.1	0.1	−0.2	−0.5	−0.4
Private saving	0.1	0.2	0.2	0.2	0.2	−0.0
Gross private investment	0.1	0.2	0.2	0.1	−0.1	−0.1
Net foreign assets	−0.1	0.0	−0.0	−0.2	−0.6	−1.5
Government debt	0.1	−0.4	−0.9	−0.6	1.8	3.6

countries also, the capital stock per worker is higher throughout, though investment as a share of GNP is below the baseline.

In the United States until 2010, the demographic shift leads to a larger labor force (and therefore to higher output), a depreciation of the real exchange rate, and a lower real interest rate. After 2010 the dependency ratio begins to rise, and these effects are in large part reversed.

In the other industrial countries, there is no substantial effect until 2020, when real output drops off significantly and real interest rates rise. There is only a negligible effect on the current account position of these countries. In sum, for all countries the net foreign asset implications of aging are simulated to be considerably less important through their effects on production reported here than those operating through consumption.

Effects of Aging on Government Expenditures

An increase in the elderly dependency ratio would be expected to increase government expenditures on medical care, while a decline in the youth dependency ratio would lead to lower education expenditures. Furthermore, an increase in the number of retirees would increase payment of government pension benefits. Heller and others (1986) report projections for these components of government spending in individual Group of Seven countries for the years 2000, 2010, and 2025 (see Table

2 above); we interpolated these estimates to obtain annual series.[18] Education and health care are components of government expenditure on goods and services, and so they directly increase aggregate demand. Pension benefits take the form of a transfer, which we treat in MULTIMOD as if it were a negative, nondistortionary tax. We do not examine the impact of funding social security expenditures, including pensions, and taxation is assumed not to be linked to those benefits.

Table 6 reports the results of a simulation of these changes in government expenditure. In the United States, government expenditure is reduced throughout the simulation, relative to the baseline, leading to a reduction in domestic demand of only ¼ of 1 percent in 2025. The reduction in Japanese net exports is enough to lead to a slight reduction in output, despite the increase in government expenditure resulting from an increased dependency ratio in that country. In Germany real output rises slightly as a result of higher government expenditure; in other industrial countries output is lower. In sum, although government debt rises substantially in Germany and Japan, effects on output and net foreign assets are relatively modest.

Combined Effects

The combined effects of the demographic shifts are shown in Table 7 (including results for France, Italy, the United Kingdom, Canada, and the remaining smaller industrial countries). The interpretation of the results is straightforward, since they are approximately a simple sum of the results for the three partial simulations just discussed. What is of interest is the magnitudes—the simulation shows that demographic shifts can be expected to have very substantial effects on the global pattern of external balances over the next 35 years. In the United States the net foreign asset position improves by over 35 percent of GNP in 2025, compared, for instance, with an assumed net debtor position in 1995 of about 23 percent of GNP.[19] In Japan and Germany the net foreign asset positions in 2025 are lower by about 60 and 25 percent, respectively, as compared with assumed net creditor positions in 1995 of 26 and 38 percent of GNP. It is clear that the aging of the population in the

[18] We used a simple average of the increases in the Group of Seven countries for the aggregate of smaller industrial countries.

[19] An alternative comparison would be what the net foreign asset position would be in 2025 *without* the shift in dependency ratios. In our baseline projection, which extrapolates medium-term trends but which is not intended to be a forecast, the net asset share in 2025 is −39 percent for the United States, 37 percent for Japan, and 85 percent for Germany.

Table 6. *Demographic Shift: Government Expenditure Effects*
(Deviations from baseline)

Country	2000	2005	2010	2015	2020	2025
United States			*(in percent)*			
Real GNP	−0.0	0.5	0.2	0.3	0.2	0.2
Real domestic demand	−0.6	−0.0	−0.3	−0.1	−0.2	−0.2
Real interest rate	−0.3	−0.1	−0.0	0.1	0.1	0.1
Real effective exchange rate	−1.7	−1.3	−1.2	−1.0	−1.0	−1.1
GDP per worker	−0.1	0.3	0.0	0.1	0.0	0.0
Capital stock per worker	0.0	0.2	0.2	0.2	0.1	0.0
			(as a percent of GNP)			
Current account balance	0.3	0.3	0.3	0.3	0.3	0.3
General government financial balance	0.9	0.5	0.3	−0.2	−0.5	−0.6
Private saving	−0.4	−0.2	0.0	0.5	0.8	0.8
Gross private investment	0.2	0.0	0.0	−0.0	−0.0	−0.1
Net foreign assets	0.6	1.9	2.6	3.2	3.6	4.0
Government debt	−2.4	−4.7	−4.8	−3.3	−0.6	2.0
Japan			*(in percent)*			
Real GNP	0.0	−0.4	−0.3	−0.5	−0.4	−0.5
Real domestic demand	1.2	0.9	0.9	0.5	0.6	0.6
Real interest rate	−0.0	0.0	0.1	0.0	0.1	0.1
Real effective exchange rate	2.8	3.0	2.9	2.4	2.4	2.5
GDP per worker	0.2	−0.0	0.0	−0.1	−0.1	−0.1
Capital stock per worker	0.1	0.1	0.0	−0.1	−0.1	−0.2
			(as a percent of GNP)			
Current account balance	−0.5	−0.6	−0.5	−0.4	−0 5	−0.5
General government financial balance	−3.1	−3.0	−2.9	−1.8	−1.3	−1.1
Private saving	2.3	2.3	2.3	1.3	0.8	0.5
Gross private investment	−0.2	−0.1	−0.2	−0.1	−0.1	−0.1
Net foreign assets	−2.7	−4.1	−5.2	−5.5	−6.1	−6.5
Government debt	9.0	19.7	27.0	29.3	27.6	24.9
Germany, Fed. Rep. of			*(in percent)*			
Real GNP	−0.0	−0.4	−0.2	−0.3	−0.3	−0.4
Real domestic demand	0.9	0.4	0.4	0.5	0.4	0.5
Real interest rate	−0.1	−0.0	−0.0	0.1	0.1	0.1
Real effective exchange rate	0.7	0.6	0.3	0.5	0.5	0.5
GDP per worker	0.2	−0.1	0.1	0.1	0.0	0.0
Capital stock per worker	0.1	0.1	0.1	0.1	0.1	−0.0
			(as a percent of GNP)			
Current account balance	−0.6	−0.5	−0.5	−0.5	−0.6	−0.6
General government financial balance	−2.0	−1.5	−1.2	−1.2	−1.2	−1.2
Private saving	1.5	1.0	0.7	0.7	0.6	0.6
Gross private investment	0.0	0.0	0.1	0.0	0.0	0.0
Net foreign assets	−2.2	−3.5	−4.6	−5.6	−6.5	−7.3
Government debt	6.1	11.6	14.0	15.3	16.2	16.9

Continued overleaf

Table 6 (*concluded*).

Country	2000	2005	2010	2015	2020	2025
Other Industrial Countries			*(in percent)*			
Real GNP	0.0	0.3	−0.0	0.1	0.0	0.0
Real domestic demand	−0.1	0.1	−0.1	−0.0	−0.1	−0.1
Real interest rate	−0.2	−0.1	0.0	0.1	0.1	0.1
Real effective exchange rate	−0.2	−0.3	−0.2	−0.3	−0.3	−0.3
GDP per worker	−0.0	0.2	−0.0	0.1	0.0	−0.0
Capital stock per worker	0.0	0.2	0.1	0.1	0.0	−0.1
			(as a percent of GNP)			
Current account balance	0.1	0.1	0.1	0.1	0.1	0.1
General government financial balance	−0.4	−0.5	−0.6	−0.7	−0.9	−0.9
Private saving	0.5	0.6	0.6	0.8	0.9	0.9
Gross private investment	0.2	0.0	0.0	0.0	0.0	−0.1
Net foreign assets	0.3	0.6	0.8	0.9	1.0	1.0
Government debt	1.4	2.5	4.2	6.0	7.9	9.7

Table 7. *Demographic Shift: Combined Effects*
(Deviations from baseline)

Country	2000	2005	2010	2015	2020	2025
United States			*(in percent)*			
Real GNP	−0.1	3.2	4.9	4.7	2.5	−0.1
Real domestic demand	−2.7	−1.7	−1.0	−1.0	−2.2	−3.8
Real interest rate	0.1	−1.1	−1.4	−0.5	1.1	2.9
Real effective exchange rate	−9.1	−15.5	−16.6	−14.0	−9.9	−5.3
GDP per worker	−2.0	−1.4	−0.4	1.1	2.0	2.2
Capital stock per worker	−2.2	−3.1	−1.7	1.2	3.7	4.3
			(as a percent of GNP)			
Current account balance	1.1	2.5	3.1	3.0	2.8	2.7
General government financial balance	0.8	0.9	0.7	−0.3	−1.0	−1.3
Private saving	0.7	2.1	3.0	3.6	3.6	3.0
Gross private investment	0.3	0.5	0.6	0.3	−0.2	−1.0
Net foreign assets	2.7	10.4	19.9	27.9	33.1	36.2
Government debt	−1.5	−4.7	−6.5	−5.3	−1.3	3.5
Japan			*(in percent)*			
Real GNP	0.4	−3.1	−6.4	−9.5	−11.8	−13.2
Real domestic demand	6.8	7.2	5.8	2.4	−1.3	−4.7
Real interest rate	−3.3	−1.2	0.6	2.5	4.1	4.8
Real effective exchange rate	18.8	35.0	43.0	41.4	32.7	21.5
GDP per worker	4.4	5.1	4.8	3.2	1.2	−0.5
Capital stock per worker	5.1	9.1	10.2	8.3	4.3	−0.5

Table 7 (*continued*).

Country	2000	2005	2010	2015	2020	2025
			(as a percent of GNP)			
Current account balance	−2.5	−3.8	−4.4	−4.5	−4.4	−4.0
General government financial balance	−2.5	−2.6	−2.8	−2.1	−1.9	−1.6
Private saving	0.1	−1.7	−2.7	−3.8	−4.2	−4.3
Gross private investment	0.0	−0.5	−1.1	−1.5	−1.7	−1.8
Net foreign assets	−13.4	−26.7	−38.5	−48.0	−55.0	−59.0
Government debt	7.5	16.3	23.0	26.1	26.9	27.3
Germany, Fed. Rep. of			*(in percent)*			
Real GNP	−0.2	−2.3	−3.6	−4.0	−4.6	−5.8
Real domestic demand	0.8	1.0	0.8	−0.4	−2.1	−3.9
Real interest rate	−1.1	−1.0	−0.7	0.3	1.7	3.6
Real effective exchange rate	1.0	2.7	3.0	2.3	1.9	3.2
GDP per worker	1.0	1.3	0.5	0.1	1.2	2.6
Capital stock per worker	1.3	3.2	3.0	2.7	3.6	4.2
			(as a percent of GNP)			
Current account balance	−0.5	−1.8	−2.7	−2.5	−1.8	−0.9
General government financial balance	−1.9	−1.5	−1.5	−1.5	−1.6	−1.5
Private saving	1.7	0.1	−0.8	−0.7	−0.5	−0.9
Gross private investment	0.3	0.4	0.4	0.2	−0.3	−1.5
Net foreign assets	−3.3	−8.1	−15.0	−20.9	−24.0	−23.5
Government debt	6.1	11.4	14.6	16.6	18.1	19.0
France			*(in percent)*			
Real GNP	−0.4	1.1	1.5	1.0	−0.3	−1.6
Real domestic demand	−0.9	−0.1	−0.1	−0.9	−2.2	−3.7
Real interest rate	−0.3	−1.0	−1.0	0.0	1.5	3.0
Real effective exchange rate	−1.2	−4.1	−5.4	−5.5	−4.8	−3.3
GDP per worker	−0.8	−0.2	−0.3	0.7	1.6	2.1
Capital stock per worker	−0.7	−0.7	−0.1	1.9	3.4	3.2
			(as a percent of GNP)			
Current account balance	0.5	0.7	0.8	0.8	0.9	1.3
General government financial balance	−0.3	−0.2	−0.4	−0.8	−1.1	−1.2
Private saving	0.9	1.2	1.6	1.9	1.8	1.6
Gross private investment	0.0	0.4	0.5	0.2	−0.2	−0.9
Net foreign assets	2.1	4.3	6.5	8.5	9.8	11.8
Government debt	2.2	2.9	2.9	4.1	6.6	9.0
Italy			*(in percent)*			
Real GNP	0.8	−0.2	−2.0	−1.6	−4.4	−3.3
Real domestic demand	2.1	1.1	−1.4	−1.9	−6.0	−5.2
Real interest rate	−1.4	−0.1	−0.0	0.3	2.8	2.0
Real effective exchange rate	1.8	4.1	1.3	−2.3	−3.7	−7.6
GDP per worker	1.7	1.6	−0.9	0.3	−1.5	1.8
Capital stock per worker	1.8	3.0	1.3	1.8	0.5	0.7

Continued overleaf

Table 7 (*continued*).

Country	2000	2005	2010	2015	2020	2025
			(as a percent of GNP)			
Current account balance	−0.4	0.4	0.7	0.5	1.2	0.2
General government financial balance	−0.7	−1.2	−0.9	−1.7	−2.8	−2.5
Private saving	0.6	1.1	1.4	2.1	3.2	2.6
Gross private investment	0.3	−0.4	−0.1	−0.1	−0.7	−0.1
Net foreign assets	−0.6	0.1	1.9	2.7	5.6	7.4
Government debt	0.3	2.2	12.0	15.6	22.9	29.0
United Kingdom			*(in percent)*			
Real GNP	0.0	0.8	1.2	0.6	−1.4	−2.3
Real domestic demand	−0.8	−0.8	−1.1	−1.9	−4.3	−5.8
Real interest rate	−0.7	−0.9	−0.9	0.3	2.0	2.9
Real effective exchange rate	−2.0	−3.3	−4.9	−5.1	−5.9	−7.0
GDP per worker	−0.1	−0.4	−0.5	0.4	−0.1	1.0
Capital stock per worker	−0.1	−0.3	0.0	1.6	1.7	1.3
			(as a percent of GNP)			
Current account balance	0.4	1.1	1.0	0.9	0.3	−0.1
General government financial balance	0.0	−0.1	−0.3	−0.6	−1.1	−1.1
Private saving	0.7	1.4	1.8	1.8	1.4	0.7
Gross private investment	0.3	0.2	0.5	0.2	−0.0	−0.2
Net foreign assets	0.9	4.8	7.7	9.4	8.9	6.3
Government debt	0.2	0.2	1.0	2.7	6.1	9.5
Canada			*(in percent)*			
Real GNP	0.2	2.8	3.5	2.4	−0.2	−3.3
Real domestic demand	−1.1	1.2	1.7	1.0	−0.7	−2.9
Real interest rate	−0.5	−1.4	−1.5	−0.4	1.1	3.3
Real effective exchange rate	−5.5	−7.7	−7.1	−4.9	−1.8	2.4
GDP per worker	−0.3	−0.0	0.5	1.8	2.5	3.0
Capital stock per worker	−0.3	−0.5	1.1	3.7	5.5	5.8
			(as a percent of GNP)			
Current account balance	1.3	2.4	3.0	2.8	2.1	1.5
General government financial balance	1.6	1.3	0.8	−0.4	−1.3	−1.9
Private saving	0.0	1.3	2.2	2.5	1.8	0.4
Gross private investment	0.3	0.2	−0.0	−0.7	−1.6	−2.9
Net foreign assets	4.1	12.2	21.3	28.1	31.0	30.2
Government debt	−4.0	−9.2	−10.8	−8.0	−2.0	4.8
Smaller Industrial Countries			*(in percent)*			
Real GNP	−0.2	0.8	0.3	−0.7	−3.1	−5.3
Real domestic demand	−0.1	0.8	0.5	−0.3	−2.3	−4.2
Real interest rate	−0.8	−1.1	−0.7	0.3	1.9	3.3
Real effective exchange rate	−0.2	−1.0	−1.0	−1.3	−1.2	−1.1
GDP per worker	−0.2	0.6	0.4	1.1	1.4	1.7
Capital stock per worker	0.1	0.9	1.7	3.1	3.7	3.0

Table 7 (*concluded*).

Country	2000	2005	2010	2015	2020	2025
			(as a percent of GNP)			
Current account balance	−0.0	0.2	0.0	−0.3	−0.8	−1.1
General government financial balance	−0.5	−0.5	−0.8	−1.1	−1.5	−1.6
Private saving	0.7	1.0	1.1	0.8	0.3	−0.6
Gross private investment	0.3	0.3	0.3	0.0	−0.4	−1.1
Net foreign assets	1.1	1.6	1.2	−0.7	−3.4	−6.8
Government debt	2.1	3.3	5.0	7.4	10.8	14.5

industrial countries has the potential to generate large swings in foreign indebtedness over time, and that a simple extrapolation of present current account positions is likely to be well off the mark.

The projected aging of the population also has significant implications for real GNP. In the simulation, the contraction in the labor force in the industrial countries after 2015 reduces real GNP in 2025 by 13 percent in Japan, by 6 percent in Germany, and by a somewhat smaller amount in the other industrial countries outside the United States. However, it should be noted that output per worker is higher in several countries, as is the capital stock per worker. In the United States aggregate output is roughly unchanged in 2025, and it is in fact higher for most of the simulation, as a result of the increase in the working-age population in the early part of the next century.

Fiscal deficits do not evolve as dramatically as external positions in these simulations, in large part because of endogenous tax increases. The real cost to the world economy shows up in the effect on production through a smaller labor force and a lower capital stock. Government financial positions do nonetheless weaken toward the end of the simulation period, as tax revenues fall and pension expenditures increase substantially in all industrial countries. In particular, government debt rises significantly in Japan and Germany.

Given the magnitude of the effects on net creditor and debtor positions, it is of interest to see how sensitive they are to estimated parameters and projections of key exogenous variables. Two such experiments are reported in Table 8. The first reduces the coefficients on the dependency ratio (which were not very well determined statistically) by a factor of 2. The second supposes that aging of the population induces an increase in participation rates (for instance, because of delayed retirement or increased labor supply of those who must support aged relatives). In particular, participation rates are assumed to offset half of the effect on the labor force of the rise in dependency ratios.

Table 8. *Effect of Aging on Net Foreign Assets in 2025 Under Three Alternative Assumptions*

(Deviations from baseline as a percent of GNP)

Country	Standard Model[a]	Consumption Coefficient[b]	Participation Rate[c]
United States	36	23	36
Japan	−59	−34	−59
Germany, Fed. Rep. of	−24	−16	−23
France	12	4	13
Italy	7	3	7
United Kingdom	6	−2	9
Canada	30	25	25

[a] From Table 7.
[b] The consumption coefficient of *DEM*3 is assumed to be halved.
[c] The participation rate is assumed to rise by one half of the proportionate decline in those aged 15–64.

The first change makes a substantial difference for net foreign asset positions, as can be seen in Table 8. The second assumption, in contrast, has only minor effects—as might be expected from the discussion of production effects above. Taken together, these simulations suggest that the numerical results discussed above should at best be considered rough orders of magnitude, and that they are especially sensitive to assumed effects of aging on saving rates.

IV. Concluding Remarks

The paper has isolated some of the implications of the aging of the population that is projected for the next three and a half decades. Using MULTIMOD to simulate the net effect of aging through three channels—reduced saving rates, a lower labor force, and higher government expenditure—suggests that macroeconomic effects may be substantial by 2025. Moreover, though some of the effects are common to all countries—higher real interest rates and lower output in the later years of our simulation period—some of the effects differ substantially because of differences in the extent and speed of aging across countries. As a result, there are substantial long-run changes in current account and net foreign asset positions, in a direction that reverses recent tendencies among the three largest industrial economies.

A number of policy issues arise in the context of population aging; they are not, however, the subject of this paper. Governments can influence capital formation by their expenditure and tax policies; a key question is whether the capital stock will be adequate to support a higher consumption ratio and greater demands for government medical services in the future. Questions of intergenerational equity are at the heart of the debate over whether anticipated increases in government expenditure should be financed through government saving today, or through taxes on the working population in the next century (see Halter and Hemming (1987) and Aaron, Bosworth, and Burtless (1989)). Another important question relates to the prospects for capital accumulation and sustained growth in developing countries when industrial countries are saving less.

It is important to stress once again the limitations and uncertainties associated with our analysis. The prospect of substantial migration within Europe and North America makes any demographic projections 35 years into the future extremely tentative. Moreover, our model of household behavior is rudimentary, and the effects on consumption estimated over a historical period with a much younger population may not provide a good guide to the future. Other effects, which we have not considered, include an endogenous response of participation rates—for instance, because of a rise in two wage-earner households or an increase in the average retirement age—and effects of the age composition of the working population on productivity levels. We have also not analyzed the effects of a continued slowdown of population growth—which, in itself, might be expected to lower real interest rates and increase the capital stock per worker (see the Appendix). Clearly, more research into these various questions is in order.

APPENDIX

Steady-State Effects of Demographic Changes

In this Appendix we work out analytically the long-run effects of having an older population. In MULTIMOD the effects of aging operate through three channels. (1) The consumption equation has an estimated positive coefficient on the dependency ratio, which is consistent with greater consumption during one's retirement years relative to income and wealth. (2) Potential output depends on the labor force, which is reduced when a larger fraction of the population is retired. (3) An older population is associated with higher government spending (based on estimates in Heller and others (1986)). We also consider a decrease in the birthrate β, which for an unchanged mortality rate implies slower population growth, although these effects are not discussed in the text, given difficulties in simulating MULTIMOD with different population growth rates in different countries (implying the impossibility of ever reaching a steady state) and because of uncertainty concerning birthrate projections. The macroeconomic effects that one would expect to result through these linkages can be described in a simplified version of MULTIMOD, as laid out below.

If we ignore monetary factors and, as a result, can express all variables in real terms, we can represent MULTIMOD for the global economy as follows:[20]

$$C = (\rho + \lambda + \alpha\Delta)(B + H) \quad (1)$$

$$\dot{H} = (r + \beta)H - (Y - \delta K - T) \quad (2)$$

$$\dot{B} = rB + G - T \quad (3)$$

$$Y = F(K, L) \quad (4)$$

$$F_1(K, L) = r + \delta \quad (5)$$

$$Y = C + G + \delta K + \dot{K}. \quad (6)$$

Consumption C is modeled as in Blanchard (1985) and Buiter (1988), with the addition of a multiplicative term in the dependency ratio; liquidity constraints are ignored here. It is assumed that the birthrate β is exogenous; population (and all stock and flow variables in steady state) grows at rate $n = \beta - \lambda$, where λ is the mortality rate (constant, and independent of age), and ρ is the rate of time preference for any given individual. Productivity growth is assumed to be zero. As a result, consumption is proportional to wealth, with the constant of proportionality depending positively on the dependency ratio Δ (equation (1)). The only forms of wealth are government bonds B and human capital H; that is, discounted future after-tax income (including net income to capital K) (equation (2)). The government budget constraint makes bonds grow with the deficit (equation (3)), and bonds pay a real rate of interest r. Output is given by a production function that depends on capital K and the labor force L (equation (4)), and conditions for profit maximization imply that the marginal product of capital (F_1) equals the real rate of interest plus the rate of depreciation (equation (5)).[21] Finally, output produced has to equal demand on the part of households and the government (equation (6)), plus replacement investment.

In a steady state with growth at rate $n = \beta - \lambda$, $\dot{H}$, $\dot{K}$, and $\dot{B}$ have to be equal to nH, nK, and nB, respectively. To consider steady-state effects, we therefore replace equations (2) and (3) with the following equations:

$$H = (Y - \delta K - T)/(r + \lambda) \quad (7)$$

$$B = (T - G)/(r - \beta + \lambda) \quad (8)$$

$$Y = C + G + (\beta - \lambda + \delta)K. \quad (9)$$

The effects of a greater proportion of the elderly show up in three exogenous variables: Δ, G, and L—the first two increase, and the third declines.[22] A decrease in birthrates produces a fall in β and therefore a fall in real growth n. We

[20] Implications for a single open economy are discussed below.

[21] Corporate taxes are ignored; taxes are assumed to be lump-sum levies on households.

[22] For a given population P and participation rate R, Δ and L are related as follows: $L = \Delta RP$. In order to understand the mechanisms at work, we separate the labor force effects of a change in Δ from its effect on consumption.

therefore differentiate the above system of equations (1), (7), (8), (4), (5), and (9) with respect to Δ, G, L, and β (noting that $dn = d\beta$). The results are as follows:

$$dC = (\rho + \lambda)(dB + dH) + \alpha d\Delta(B + H) \tag{10}$$

$$dH = (dY - \delta dK - dT)/(r + \lambda) - [(Y - \delta K - T)/(r + \lambda)^2]dr \tag{11}$$

$$dB = (dT - dG)/(r - \beta + \lambda) - [(T - G)/(r - \beta + \lambda)^2](dr - d\beta) \tag{12}$$

$$dY = F_1 dK + F_2 dL \tag{13}$$

$$F_{11}dK + F_{12}dL = dr \tag{14}$$

$$dY = dC + dG + (\beta - \lambda + \delta)dK + Kd\beta. \tag{15}$$

Equations (10)–(15) give six equations in seven endogenous variables—dC, dH, dB, dT, dY, dr, and dK. The underdetermination results from government variables; we take the steady-state bond stock to be exogenous (as is the case in MULTIMOD for the bond/GNP ratio). Moreover, to simplify the analysis, we consider the case where the primary deficit $(G - T)$ is zero; so from equation (12) $dT = dG$ (and also $B = 0$). In this case, lower birthrates have no effect on the long-run equilibrium real interest rate, except through the steady-state rate of investment, in (15).

It is straightforward to reduce the system of equations to three equations in three endogenous variables, dC, dK, and dr:

$$\begin{bmatrix} 1 & -\theta(F_1 - \delta) & \theta H \\ 0 & F_{11} & -1 \\ -1 & F_1 - \mu & 0 \end{bmatrix} \begin{bmatrix} dC \\ dK \\ dr \end{bmatrix} = \begin{bmatrix} \alpha H & \theta F_2 & -\theta & 0 \\ 0 & -F_{12} & 0 & 0 \\ 0 & -F_2 & 1 & K \end{bmatrix} \begin{bmatrix} d\Delta \\ dL \\ dG \\ d\beta \end{bmatrix}, \tag{16}$$

or

$$Ady = Bdx,$$

where $\theta = (\rho + \lambda)/(r + \lambda)$ and $\mu = \beta - \lambda + \delta$. It can be shown that $\rho \leq r < \rho + \lambda$ (provided bonds B are positive, but less than some upper limit), so $0 < \theta < 1$.

Now the determinant of the matrix A is equal to

$$\det(A) = F_1(1 - \theta) + F_{11}\theta H - (\mu - \delta\theta). \tag{17}$$

The marginal product of capital is positive, $F_1 > 0$, and by diminishing marginal returns, $F_{11} < 0$; det (A) can therefore not be signed a priori. However, stability of the dynamic system (not analyzed here) requires that at a point of equilibrium, an increase in the real interest rate should increase saving net of investment. This can be shown to imply that det $(A) < 0$, as follows. The change in net savings dS is equal to

$$\begin{aligned} dS &= dY - dC - \mu dK \\ &= [(1 - \theta)F_1 + \delta\theta]dK + \theta H dr - \mu dK \\ &= (1 - \theta)F_1 dr/F_{11} + \theta H dr - (\mu - \delta\theta)dr/F_{11}. \end{aligned} \tag{18}$$

Multiplying by F_{11} (which is negative) shows from equation (17) that the condition that $dS/dr > 0$ is equivalent to det $(A) < 0$.

Calculating $A^{-1}B$ and simplifying gives the following comparative static results:

$$\begin{bmatrix} dC \\ dK \\ dr \end{bmatrix} = \frac{1}{\det(A)} \cdot \begin{bmatrix} \alpha H(F_1-\mu) & D_1 & -\theta H F_{11}+n\theta & \theta K(F_1-\delta-HF_{11}) \\ \alpha H & D_2 & (1-\theta) & K \\ \alpha H F_{11} & D_3 & F_{11}(1-\theta) & F_{11}K \end{bmatrix} \cdot \begin{bmatrix} d\Delta \\ dL \\ dG \\ d\beta \end{bmatrix}, \tag{19}$$

where

$$D_1 = \theta H[F_{11}F_2 - (F_1-\mu)F_{12}] - n\theta F_2$$
$$D_2 = -(1-\theta)F_2 - \theta H F_{12}$$
$$D_3 = -(1-\theta)F_{11}F_2 + F_1F_{12}(1-\theta) - F_{12}(\mu - \delta\theta).$$

Noting that $F_{12} > 0$, $F_{11} < 0$, $F_1 - \mu = r - n > 0$, and $\mu - \delta\theta > 0$, and recalling that $\det(A) < 0$, the signs of the comparative statics results are as follows:

	$d\Delta$	dL	dG	$d\beta$
dC	−	+	−	−
dK	−	+	−	−
dr	+	0[23]	+	+

Let us consider in turn the changes in the exogenous variables. An increase in private consumption due to aging ($d\Delta > 0$) paradoxically *decreases* steady-state consumption. The reason is that it raises the real interest rate and lowers the capital stock, leading to lower output. Though there is short-run stimulus to consumption and to output demand, in the long-run steady state, aggregate supply effects dominate: an economy that saves less has a lower capital stock.[24] The effect of increased government spending $dG > 0$ is similar; it drains resources away from capital formation. A decrease in the labor force due to an increase in retirees ($dL < 0$) tends to *lower* aggregate consumption, capital, and output, but has no effects on per capita variables or the real interest rate, given the somewhat artificial assumption that the aggregate consumption/wealth ratio is unaffected and if one makes the further assumption that government spending per capita is unchanged. Such a change in L just corresponds to a scale change in the econ-

[23] Assuming that G changes proportionately.
[24] Provided it is below the golden-rule capital stock.

omy. A decline in population growth ($d\beta < 0$) should increase capital intensity and consumption and decrease the real interest rate.

Some intuition about long-run effects can be obtained with the help of a simple diagram, taken from the neoclassical growth literature (Figure 1). All variables have been put in per capita terms; that is, divided by the labor force. A constant returns to scale production function (and the assumption that G grows with LF, discussed above) allows us to do this. In equilibrium, saving must equal investment. For the equilibrium to be a steady state, investment must be sufficient to maintain a constant capital/labor ratio k; that is, the capital stock must grow at the growth rate of the labor force n. Hence, saving per capita ($sf(k)$, where s is the saving rate) must equal investment per capita (nk).

Now a change in the level of the labor force would just scale up or down all macroeconomic flow and stock variables, but have no effect on such variables as capital intensity (plotted on the horizontal axis) or saving per capita (the curve $sf(k)$). The level of the real interest rate can be inferred from the value of the capital/labor ratio k; from the production function and the equilibrium condition that the marginal product of capital is equal to the real interest rate plus the depreciation rate, a higher value of k is associated with a lower real interest rate.

A permanent change in the age structure toward an older population, leaving population growth unaffected, would shift down the saving schedule because the aggregate saving rate would be lower. This would occur because the government would spend more in order to provide increased services and because the elderly

Figure 1. *Steady-State Equilibrium with Different Saving Rates and Population Growth Rates*

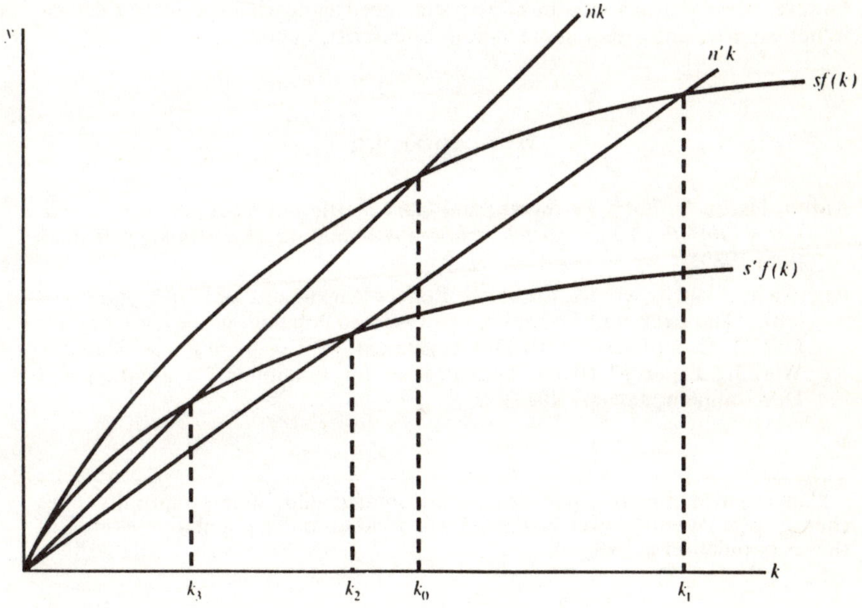

save less. Lower saving for a given population growth would shift the $sf(k)$ curve down to $s'f(k)$ and lead it to intersect with investment at a lower capital labor ratio, k_3. In other words, capital intensity would be lower, and the real interest rate higher, with an older population.

A permanent decline in the population's growth rate, keeping age structure unchanged,[25] would have the opposite effect. It would shift down the investment line to $n'k$; with slower population growth, the economy can devote a lower proportion of its output to investment and yet maintain its standard of living. As a result, with unchanged saving behavior capital intensity rises to k_1, and the real interest rate falls. The net effect of slower population growth and an older population depends on the extent of the demographic changes and the size of effects on saving: k can either rise or fall.

In the case of an open economy facing the above demographic shifts, the results would be modified in several important ways. Suppose, first, that the country is small and that it alone experiences the demographic shifts. In the long run the home country's interest rate will equal the exogenous world rate. Therefore, instead of raising interest rates and lowering the capital stock, population aging will lead to a rundown of net claims on foreigners. Another channel will involve changes in the terms of trade. Increases in consumption demand and decreases in supply (through a shrinkage of the labor force) will each lead to an appreciation of the home country currency in real terms, which will also have the effect of pushing the current account position into deficit and leading to a decline in net foreign assets. Thus, in a small open economy model, crowding out of excess demand for the home good will occur through net exports and not through declines in investment and the capital stock, as in the closed economy model.

To the extent that the economy is large, there will be a combination of effects on real interest rates and on the foreign balance. Moreover, if the demographic shifts occur in a large number of countries, then the closed economy results will be approximated at the global level. If the shifts are of different magnitudes, however, the countries with the more pronounced aging will experience a decline in net exports, and a real appreciation, as described above.

REFERENCES

Aaron, Henry J., Barry Bosworth, and Gary Burtless, *Can America Afford to Grow Old? Paying for Social Security* (Washington: The Brookings Institution, 1989).

Auerbach, Alan, Lawrence Kotlikoff, Robert Hagemann, and Guiseppe Nicoletti, "The Economic Dynamics of an Ageing Population: the Case of Four OECD Economies," OECD Department of Economics and Statistics Working Paper 62 (Paris: Organization for Economic Cooperation and Development, January 1989).

[25] In practice, the two phenomena are interrelated: unless mortality rates change, permanently lower birthrates will yield an older population as well as slower population growth.

Blanchard, Olivier, "Debt, Deficits, and Finite Horizons," *Journal of Political Economy,* Vol. 93 (April 1985), pp. 233–47.

Bös, Dieter, and Robert Weizsäcker, "Economic Consequences of an Aging Population," *European Economic Review,* Vol. 33 (March 1989), pp. 345–54.

Bovenberg, A. Lans, and Owen Evans, "National and Personal Saving in the United States: Measurement and Analysis of Recent Trends," *Staff Papers,* International Monetary Fund (Washington), Vol. 37 (September 1990), pp. 636–69.

Buiter, Willem H., "Death, Birth, Productivity Growth and Debt Neutrality," *Economic Journal,* Vol. 98 (June 1988), pp. 279–93.

Davidson, James E. H., and others, "Economic Modelling of the Aggregate Time-Series Relationship Between Consumers' Expenditure and Income in the United Kingdom," *Economic Journal,* Vol. 88 (December 1978), pp. 661–92.

Dean, Andrew, and others, "Saving Trends and Behaviour in OECD Countries," OECD Department of Economics and Statistics Working Paper 67 (Paris: Organization for Economic Cooperation and Development, June 1989).

Hagemann, Robert, and Giuseppe Nicoletti, "Ageing Populations: Economic Effects and Implications for Public Finance," OECD Department of Economics and Statistics Working Paper 61 (Paris: Organization for Economic Cooperation and Development, January 1989).

Halter, William A., and Richard Hemming, "The Impact of Demographic Changes on Social Security Financing," *Staff Papers,* International Monetary Fund (Washington), Vol. 34 (September 1987), pp. 471–502.

Heller, Peter, "Aging, Savings, and Pensions in the Group of Seven Countries: 1980–2025," *Journal of Public Policy,* Vol. 9 (April/June 1989), pp. 127–53.

———, and others, *Aging and Social Expenditure in the Major Industrial Countries, 1980–2025,* Occasional Paper 47 (Washington: International Monetary Fund, September 1986).

Hendry, David F., and Thomas von Ungern-Sternberg, "Liquidity and Inflation Effects on Consumers' Expenditure," in *Essays in the Theory and Measurement of Consumer Behaviour,* ed. by Angus Deaton (Cambridge: Cambridge University Press, 1981).

Herd, Richard, "The Impact of Increased Government Saving on the Economy," OECD Department of Economics and Statistics Working Paper 69 (Paris: Organization for Economic Cooperation and Development, June 1989).

Horne, Jocelyn, Jeroen Kremers, and Paul Masson, "Net Foreign Assets and International Adjustment in the United States, Japan, and the Federal Republic of Germany," IMF Working Paper WP/89/22 (Washington: International Monetary Fund, March 1989).

International Monetary Fund, *World Economic Outlook: A Survey by the Staff of the International Monetary Fund,* World Economic and Financial Surveys (Washington: International Monetary Fund, October 1989), pp. 28–34.

———, *World Economic Outlook: A Survey by the Staff of the International Monetary Fund,* World Economic and Financial Surveys (Washington: International Monetary Fund, May 1990), pp. 100–13.

Lee, Ronald and Shelley Lapkoff, "International Flows of Time and Goods: Consequences of Slowing Population Growth," *Journal of Political Economy,* Vol. 96 (June 1988), pp. 618–51.

Masson, Paul, Steven Symansky, and Guy Meredith, *MULTIMOD Mark II: A Revised and Extended Model,* Occasional Paper 71 (Washington: International Monetary Fund, forthcoming 1990).

Ritzen, Jozef, and Hendrick P. van Dalen, "Taxation and Public Debt under a Demographic Transition," paper presented to the 45th Congress of the International Institute of Public Finance, Buenos Aires, August 28–31, 1989 (unpublished; Rotterdam: Erasmus University).

[32]

Effects of the Changing U.S. Age Distribution on Macroeconomic Equations

By RAY C. FAIR AND KATHRYN M. DOMINGUEZ*

The effects of the changing U.S. age distribution on various macroeconomic equations are examined in this paper. The equations include consumption, housing-investment, money-demand, and labor-force-participation equations. There seems to be enough variance in the age-distribution data to allow reasonably precise estimates of the effects of the age distribution on the macro variables. (*JEL* 131)

A striking feature of postwar U.S. society has been the baby boom of the late 1940's and the 1950's and the subsequent falling off of the birth rate in the 1960's. Figure 1 shows a plot of the number of births by year for the period 1900–1986. The number of births rose dramatically from 2.5 million in 1945 to 4.2 million in 1961 and then fell back to 3.1 million in 1974. Figure 2 shows the consequences of this birth pattern for the percentage of prime-age (25–54) people in the working-age (≥ 16) population. In 1952 this percentage was 57.9, whereas by 1977 it had fallen to 49.5. Since 1980 the percentage of prime-aged workers has risen sharply as the baby boomers have begun to pass the age of 25.

In this paper, we examine the effects of the dramatic changes in the U.S. population age distribution on the behavior of several macroeconomic variables. Previous empirical studies of aggregate behavior have typically ignored age-distribution effects, relying instead on the representative-agent paradigm. While this approach is attractive in that it derives macroeconomic relationships from a well-specified individual's optimizing problem, it explicitly assumes that the population is homogeneous. Thomas M. Stoker (1986) shows that, in order for representative-agent models to describe accurately aggregate behavior, all marginal reactions of individuals to changes in aggregate variables must be identical. This condition seems particularly unlikely to hold across individuals from different age cohorts.

Here, we abandon the representative-agent approach in favor of models that explicitly allow for age-based population heterogeneity.[1] In Section I, we test the

*Fair: Cowles Foundation for Research in Economics, Yale University, New Haven, CT 06520, and National Bureau of Economic Research; Dominguez: Kennedy School of Government, Harvard University, Cambridge, MA 02138, and National Bureau of Economic Research. We are indebted to the referees for many helpful comments.

[1]Previous studies using a similar modeling approach have used both population and income data to examine the influence of distributional changes on interest rates, saving behavior, and commodity expenditures. Henry McMillan and Jerome Baesel (1987) find that real interest rates are negatively related to the ratio of savers to borrowers in the postwar United States. Their simulation results predict negative real interest rates beginning in the 1990's as baby boomers reach the saving phase of their life cycle. Charles Lieberman and Paul Wachtel (1980) find that the saving rate in the 1970's would have been substantially smaller if the demographic structure that existed in the 1960's had remained unchanged. Dale Heien (1972) includes the median age of the population over 24 in his life-cycle study and finds that the saving rate has increased with the median age of the adult population. Frank Denton and Byron Spencer (1976), however, using both Canadian and U.N. census data, find no age-distribution influence on aggregate saving and consumption.

Alan S. Blinder (1975) tests for the effect of the income distribution on saving behavior and reports no systematic relationship. Blinder concludes, however, that this result may stem, not from the lack of a relationship, but rather, from the relative stability of the U.S. income distribution since World War II. Stoker (1986) finds a significant relationship between income distribution and commodity expenditure, although he

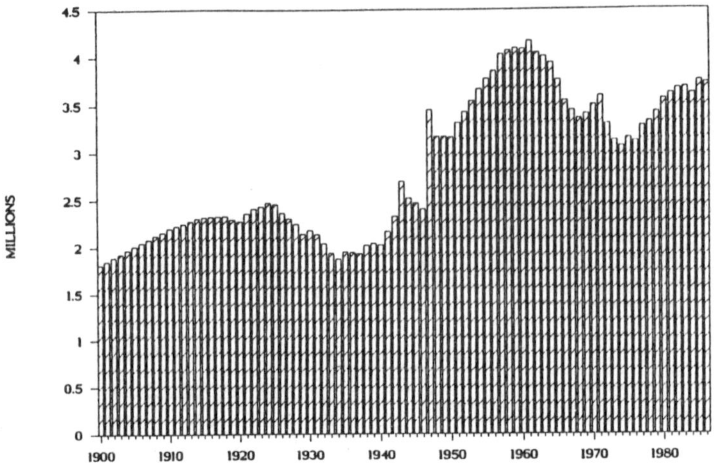

FIGURE 1. NUMBER OF BIRTHS BY YEAR, 1900–1986

Source: Current Population Reports, Series P-25, numbers 310, 519, 917, 965, and 985 (U.S. Department of Commerce, Bureau of the Census).

hypothesis that the changing age distribution is significant in explaining aggregate consumption and housing investment. The life-cycle model of Franco Modigliani and Richard Brumberg (1954) and the extension by Albert Ando and Modigliani (1963) predict that people in their prime working years consume a smaller fraction of their current income than do people younger and older. Further, if housing consumption is roughly proportional to the stock of housing, then the life-cycle model implies that the housing stock relative to current income should likewise vary with age. Prime-age people should consume less housing relative to their income than those younger or older.

The money-demand models of W. J. Baumol (1952) and James Tobin (1956) predict that there is a positive relationship between the transactions costs associated with obtaining money and the optimal amount of money held by individuals. If the opportunity cost of bank visits is higher for prime-age people, which seems likely, then prime-age people will hold more money relative to their transactions than will people younger or older. We also test this hypothesis in Section I.[2]

Richard A. Easterlin (1987) and Mark C. Berger (1985) argue that larger cohorts face a lower wage rate, on average, because of the increased competition for jobs. If this is the case, then the size of the cohort should affect the labor-force participation of individuals in the cohort. People in a large cohort will work less if the substitution effect dominates (other things equal) and will work more if the income effect dominates. We examine the relationship between co-

shows that the data are unable to distinguish statistically between a static model including distributional effects and one allowing for dynamics but excluding distributional effects.

The advantage of the age-distribution data used in the present study is that there is considerable variation in the data over the sample period. Thus, there may be a good chance of picking up the effects of the changing age distribution on coefficients in macroeconometric equations.

[2]Thomas Mayor and Lawrence Pearl (1984) estimate, using cross-section census data for the 1950–1970 sample period, that 7.3 percent of the increase in the velocity of money was due to the decrease in the population's median age.

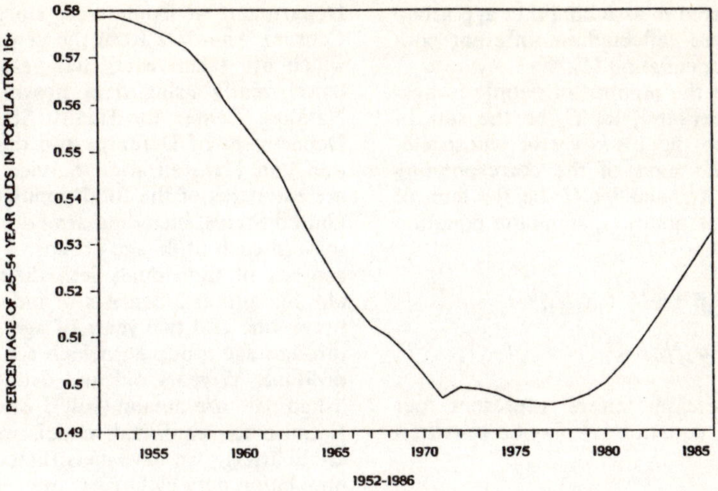

FIGURE 2. PERCENTAGE OF PRIME-AGE PEOPLE IN WORKING-AGE POPULATION

Source: Current Population Reports, Series P-25, numbers 310, 519, 917, 965, and 985 (U.S. Department of Commerce, Bureau of the Census).

hort size and labor-force participation in Section II.

I. Consumption, Housing Investment, and Money Demand

A. *The Methodology*

Divide the population into J age-groups. Let $\mathrm{D1}_{it}$ be 1 if individual i is in age-group 1 in period t and 0 otherwise; let $\mathrm{D2}_{it}$ be 1 if individual i is in age-group 2 in period t and 0 otherwise; and so on through DJ_{it}. Consider the following equation:

$$C_{it} = \mathbf{X}_{it}\boldsymbol{\beta} + \gamma + \alpha_1 D1_{it} + \cdots + \alpha_J DJ_{it} + U_{it} \qquad i = 1,\ldots,N_t \quad t = 1,\ldots,T \tag{1}$$

where C_{it} is the dependent variable (e.g., consumption or money demand of individual i in period t), $\mathbf{X}_{it}$ is a $1\times k$ vector of explanatory variables excluding the constant, $\boldsymbol{\beta}$ is a $k\times 1$ vector of coefficients, and U_{it} is the error term. The constant term in the equation is $\gamma + \alpha_j$ for an individual in age-group j in period t. N_t is the number of people in the population in period t.

Equation (1) is restrictive, because it assumes that $\boldsymbol{\beta}$ is the same across all individuals, but it is less restrictive than a typical macroeconomic equation, which also assumes that the constant term is the same across individuals. Given $\mathbf{X}_{it}$, C_{it} is allowed to vary across age-groups in equation (1). Because most macroeconomic variables are not disaggregated by age-groups, we are unable to test for age-sensitive $\boldsymbol{\beta}$'s. For example, suppose that one of the variables in $\mathbf{X}_{it}$ is Y_{it}, the income of individual i. If the coefficient of Y_{it} is the same across individuals, say β_1, then $\beta_1 Y_{it}$ enters the equation, and it can be summed in the manner discussed in the next paragraph. If the coefficient differs across age-groups, then the term entering the equation is $\beta_{11}\mathrm{D1}_{it}Y_{it} + \cdots + \beta_{1J}\mathrm{D}J_{it}Y_{it}$. The sum of a variable like $\mathrm{D1}_{it}Y_{it}$ across individuals is the total income of individuals in age-group 1, for which data are not generally available. One is thus restricted to assuming that age-group differences are reflected in different constant terms in equation (1).

Let N_{jt} be the number of people in age-group j in period t, let C_t be the sum of C_{it}, let $\mathbf{X}_t$ be the $1 \times k$ vector whose elements are the sums of the corresponding elements in $\mathbf{X}_{it}$, and let U_t be the sum of U_{it}. Given this notation, summing equation (1) yields

$$(2) \quad C_t = \mathbf{X}_t \boldsymbol{\beta} + \gamma N_t + \alpha_1 N_{1t} \cdots + \alpha_J N_{Jt} + U_t \qquad t = 1, \ldots, T.$$

Letting lowercase letters represent per capita terms, equation (2) may be rewritten as:

$$(3) \quad c_t = \mathbf{x}_t \boldsymbol{\beta} + \gamma + \alpha_1 p_{1t} \cdots + \alpha_J p_{Jt} + u_t \qquad t = 1, \ldots, T$$

where, for example, $p_{jt} = N_{jt} / N_t$.

A test of whether age distribution matters is simply a test of whether the α_j coefficients in equation (3) are significantly different from zero.[3] If the coefficients are zero, one is back to a standard macroeconomic equation. Otherwise, given $\mathbf{x}_t$, c_t varies as the age distribution varies. Since the sum of p_{jt} across j is 1 and there is a constant in the equation, a restriction on the α_j coefficients must be imposed for estimation. The age-group coefficients are restricted to sum to zero, $\Sigma_{j=1}^{J} \alpha_j = 0$; if the distributional variables do not matter, then adding them to the equation will not affect the constant term.

B. *The Data*

The age-distribution data are from the *Current Population Reports*, Series P-25 (U.S. Department of Commerce, Bureau of the Census). The data from the census surveys, which are taken every ten years, are updated yearly using data provided by the National Center for Health Statistics, the Department of Defense, and the Immigration and Naturalization Service. The data are estimates of the total population of the United States, including armed forces overseas, in each of 86 age-groups. Age-group 1 consists of individuals less than one year old, age-group 2 consists of individuals between one and two years of age, and so on through age-group 86, which consists of individuals 85 years old and over. The published data are annual (July 1 of each year). Because the empirical models we estimate are quarterly, we have constructed quarterly population data by linearly interpolating between the yearly points.[4]

We consider 55 age-groups in this study: ages $16, 17, \ldots, 69$, and ≥ 70. The "total" population, N_t, is taken to be the population at least 16 years of age. In terms of the above notation, we have created 55 p_{jt} variables ($j = 1, \ldots, 55$), where the 55 variables sum to 1 for a given t.

C. *Constraints on the α_j Coefficients*

It is obviously not sensible to estimate 55 unconstrained α_j coefficients. For the basic results in this paper we have imposed two restrictions on the age-group coefficients. The first, as mentioned above, is that they sum to zero. The second is that they lie on a second-degree polynomial. The second-degree-polynomial constraint allows enough flexibility to see whether the prime-age groups behave differently from the young and old groups while keeping the number of unconstrained coefficients small. A second-degree polynomial where the coefficients sum to zero is determined by two coefficients, and so there are two unconstrained coefficients to estimate per equation. We denote the two variables associated with

[3]Stoker (1986) characterizes this test (that all proportion coefficients are zero) as a test of microeconomic linearity or homogeneity (that all marginal reactions of individual agents are identical). He shows that individual differences or more general behavioral nonlinearities will coincide with the presence of distributional effects in macroeconomic equations.

[4]The quarterly data for the 86 age groups from 1952 through 1988 are available on diskette from the authors upon request.

two unconstrained coefficients, Z_{1t} and Z_{2t}.[5]

We have also examined the robustness of our results to the use of the quadratic restriction. We do this by including four age categories separately in each regression and examining whether the pattern of coefficient values is consistent with the quadratic constraint.

D. *Consumption and Housing Investment*

In this section, we test the hypotheses that age variables have significant explanatory power in consumption and housing-investment equations and that prime-age people consume less relative to their income than those younger or older. To guard against the danger of having the age results depend on a particular model, we estimate equations that are general enough to encompass several different specifications. We start with the equations in the Fair (1984) model and then successively add variables to these equations to make them more general.

The theory behind the specification of the consumption equations in the Fair model is that households choose consumption and labor supply to maximize a multiperiod utility function, possibly subject to a "disequilibrium" constraint regarding the amount that they can work at the current set of wage rates. The explanatory variables include the real value of wealth (A), the after-tax nominal wage (W), the price level (P), the after-tax interest rate (r), the real level of transfer payments (YTR), and a "labor-constraint" variable (Q), which is designed to pick up possible disequilibrium effects.[6] The lagged dependent variable is also included to pick up partial-adjustment and expectational effects.

Labor income is *not* a direct explanatory variable in the consumption equations. If households jointly determine consumption and labor supply and are not constrained in their labor-supply choice, labor income is endogenous. If, on the other hand, households are constrained in their labor supply, then labor supply is no longer a decision variable, and it is appropriate to consider labor income as a determinant of consumption. Q, the labor-constraint variable, is zero when there is full employment (and thus no binding labor constraint on households), and it becomes larger (in absolute value) the more the economy deviates from full employment. In low-employment periods, Q is highly correlated with hours worked, and Q and W together are highly correlated with labor income. Therefore, in low-employment periods the consumption equations reflect the "Keynesian" specification in which income is an explanatory variable. The specification more closely approximates the classical story as the economy approaches full employment.

[5]The age variables enter an equation as $\Sigma_{j=1}^{55}\alpha_j p_{jt}$, where $\Sigma_{j=1}^{55}\alpha_j = 0$. The polynomial constraint is $\alpha_j = \gamma_0 + \gamma_1 j + \gamma_2 j^2$, $j = 1,\dots,55$, where γ_0, γ_1, and γ_2 are coefficients to be determined. The zero-sum constraint on the α_j's implies that

$$\gamma_0 = -\gamma_1(1/55)\sum_{j=1}^{55} j - \gamma_2(1/55)\sum_{j=1}^{55} j^2.$$

The way in which the age variables enter the estimated equation is then

$$\gamma_1 Z_{1t} + \gamma_2 Z_{2t}$$

where

$$Z_{1t} = \sum_{j=1}^{55} j p_{jt} - (1/55)\sum_{j=1}^{55} j \sum_{j=1}^{55} p_{jt}$$

and

$$Z_{2t} = \sum_{j=1}^{55} j^2 p_{jt} - (1/55)\sum_{j=1}^{55} j^2 \sum_{j=1}^{55} p_{jt}.$$

Given the estimates of γ_1 and γ_2, the 55 α_j coefficients can be computed. This technique is simply Shirley Almon's (1965) polynomial-distributed lag technique, where the coefficients that are constrained are the coefficients of the p_{jt} variables ($j = 1,\dots,55$) rather than coefficients of the lagged values of some variable.

[6]Q is equal to $1 - J^*/J$, where J is the ratio of total hours worked to the total population aged 16 and older and where J^* is an estimate of the full-employment value of J (see Fair [1984] for data references).

We consider four components of household expenditures: service consumption, nondurable consumption, consumer durable expenditures, and housing investment. We estimate five specifications for the service and nondurable consumption equations. The first specification for each equation includes all the variables described previously, plus the age variables; the second specification drops variables whose coefficient estimates are of the "wrong" sign (see Fair, 1990);[7] the third specification adds real disposable income to the variables from the first specification; the fourth specification adds values of all the explanatory variables from the third specification lagged once (except the age variables); and the fifth specification adds values of all the explanatory variables from the third specification led once (except the asset variable, the lagged dependent variable, and the age variables).

The third, fourth, and fifth specifications are clearly more general than the Fair-model specification. Adding disposable personal income in the third specification incorporates the Keynesian specification. Adding the lagged values in the fourth specification incorporates a richer dynamic structure. For example, David F. Hendry et al. (1984) show that adding the lagged dependent variable and lagged values of all the explanatory variables is quite general in that it encompasses many different types of dynamic structures. Adding lead values in the fifth specification allows for the possibility that agents form rational expectations (see Fair, 1990).[8]

All the equations were estimated by two-stage least squares. The first-stage regressors include the main predetermined variables in the Fair model (see table 6-1 in Fair [1984] for the first-stage regressors; see appendix A in that book for the construction of all the variables). The data are quarterly and are seasonally adjusted where appropriate. The estimation period for the equations with lead values was 1954:1–1988:3. For the other equations, the estimation period ended in 1988:4. The significance of the age variables (i.e., the joint significance of Z_{1t} and Z_{2t}) was tested using a chi-square test.[9]

[7]Because of collinearity among explanatory variables and the fairly large number of variables per equation, one would not expect all the coefficients to be estimated precisely. This is an argument for leaving in variables that are not statistically significant at, say, the 5-percent level if their coefficient estimates have the expected sign. Variables with wrong signs were dropped to see if the age results were sensitive to the inclusion of these variables. It will be seen that the results are not.

Note also that the nominal wage (W) and the price (P) have been included separately rather than as W/P. There are two reasons for this. One is to see whether the data support opposite signs on the variables. The second, and more important, reason is that one does not necessarily expect W and P to enter as W/P. The P used for each equation is the own price of the good (the price deflator for services for the services equation, the price deflator for nondurables for the nondurables equation, and so on), and in principle the prices of the other goods should be included in the equation as well. There is, however, too much collinearity among the various price deflators to pick up sensible effects in the aggregate data. Therefore, only the own price was included (but included separately).

[8]When future values for, say, period $t+i$ appear as explanatory variables, Lars Hansen's (1982) method-of-moments estimator can be used. Basically, this estimator is a modification of the two-stage least-squares (2SLS) estimator to account for the moving-average property (of order $i-1$) of the error term. If the lead values are only for period $t+1$ and if equation (A2) in Fumio Hayashi and Christopher Sims (1983) is used to estimate Hansen's "**M**" matrix, which is commonly done, then Hansen's estimator and 2SLS are the same. For the work in this paper, only $t+1$ was used, and so only the 2SLS estimator was needed.

[9]The chi-square test is as follows. The 2SLS objective function is $\mathbf{u}'Z(Z'Z)^{-1}Z'\mathbf{u} = S$, where $\mathbf{u}$ is a $T \times 1$ vector of error terms and $\mathbf{Z}$ is a $T \times K$ matrix of first-stage regressors; u is a function of the coefficients and the endogenous and predetermined variables in the equation. If the equation is estimated under the assumption of first-order serial correlation of the error term, which is done here for nondurable consumption, u is a nonlinear function of the coefficients if the serial correlation coefficient is counted as a structural coefficient, which is the treatment here. Assume that there are r restrictions on the coefficients. (In the present case, there are two zero restrictions.) Let S^* be the value of S when the restrictions are not imposed, and let S^{**} be the value of S when the restrictions are imposed. Let $\hat{\sigma}^2$ be the estimate of the variance of the error term in the unrestricted case. Then $(S^{**} - S^*)/\hat{\sigma}^2$ is asymptotically distributed as chi-square with r degrees of freedom. A general proof of this is in Donald T. M. Andrews and Fair (1988). If the ordinary least-squares estimator is used, which it is in a few cases in what follows, S is simply $\mathbf{u}'\mathbf{u}$.

TABLE 1—ESTIMATES OF THE SERVICE AND NONDURABLE CONSUMPTION EQUATIONS

	Consumption of services (CS/POP)			Consumption of nondurables (CN/POP)		
Explanatory variable	(1)	(2)	(3)	(1)	(2)	(3)
Constant	0.0773 (3.10)	0.0700 (2.85)	0.0689 (2.61)	0.614 (5.55)	0.606 (5.33)	0.671 (4.40)
LDV	0.845 (22.19)	0.843 (22.10)	0.822 (18.08)	0.199 (1.70)	0.202 (1.67)	0.210 (1.75)
$(A/\text{POP})_{-1}$	0.00064 (1.38)	0.00103 (2.63)	0.00037 (0.69)	0.00335 (4.29)	0.00335 (4.29)	0.00347 (4.24)
r	−0.00279 (5.59)	−0.00253 (5.36)	−0.00262 (5.00)	0.00150 (1.24)	—	0.00175 (1.33)
YTR/POP	0.0500 (1.43)	0.0266 (0.84)	0.0358 (0.95)	0.0800 (1.72)	0.0738 (1.61)	0.116 (1.42)
W	−0.065 (0.52)	0.130 (4.74)	−0.100 (0.77)	0.669 (5.26)	0.599 (5.09)	0.777 (3.31)
P	0.126 (1.59)	—	0.150 (1.81)	−0.468 (4.78)	−0.402 (4.76)	−0.541 (3.27)
Q	0.143 (3.14)	0.117 (2.75)	0.117 (2.20)	0.321 (3.48)	0.353 (3.92)	0.384 (2.60)
YD/POP	—	—	0.020 (0.89)	—	—	−0.037 (0.55)
Z_1	−0.0788 (4.73)	−0.0680 (4.46)	−0.0779 (4.73)	−0.131 (4.78)	−0.141 (5.30)	−0.145 (3.91)
Z_2	0.00157 (4.61)	0.00139 (4.32)	0.00156 (4.60)	0.00256 (4.40)	0.00276 (4.91)	0.00285 (3.62)
$\hat{\rho}$:	—	—	—	0.639 (6.58)	0.649 (6.67)	0.635 (6.47)
SE:	0.00532	0.00534	0.00525	0.00646	0.00641	0.00656
X^2:	24.11	21.30	24.29	34.61	39.75	21.41
α_1:	0.50	0.39	0.49	0.89	0.94	0.96
α_{55}:	1.00	0.93	0.99	1.55	1.69	1.76
j^*:	25	24	25	26	25	25
α_{j^*}:	−0.41	−0.37	−0.41	−0.66	−0.71	−0.74
X^2 (lags):	—	—	27.46	—	—	11.59
X^2 (leads):	—	—	13.47	—	—	8.46

Notes: The estimation technique is two-stage least squares. Sample period = 1954:1–1988:4 (1954:1–1988:3 when leads are used). Numbers in parentheses are t statistics (in absolute value). Statistics reported at bottom of table:

$\hat{\rho}$: estimate of first-order serial correlation coefficient of the error term;

X^2: test of the hypothesis that the coefficients of Z_{1t} and Z_{2t} are zero; critical values ($d.f.$ = 2) are 5.99 at the 5-percent level and 9.21 at the 1-percent level;

j^*: value of j for which α_j is at a minimum;

X^2 (lags): X^2 value for the equation with the lagged values of all the explanatory variables added (including the lagged value of the lagged dependent variable) except for Z_{1t} and Z_{2t};

X^2 (leads): X^2 value for the equation with the values of r, YTR/POP, W, P, Q, and YD/POP led one quarter added.

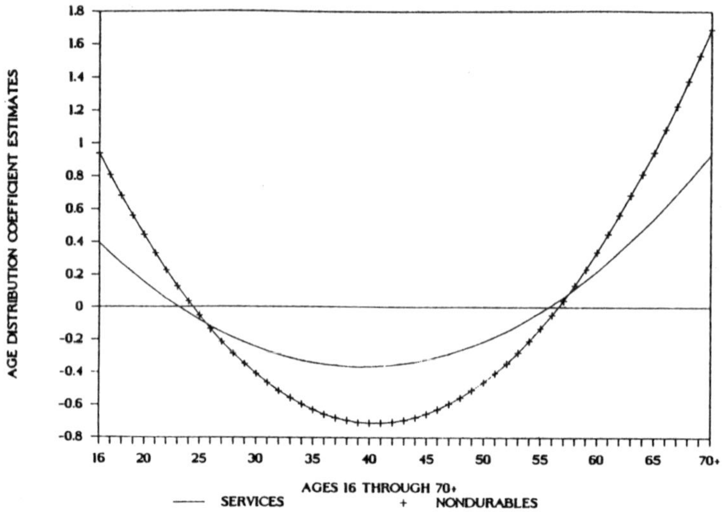

FIGURE 3. CONSUMPTION EQUATION: AGE-DISTRIBUTION COEFFICIENT ESTIMATES (SEE TABLE 1)

Table 1 presents estimation results for the service and nondurable consumption equations.[10] Detailed results are presented for the first three specifications, and X^2 values are presented for the fourth and fifth specifications. The results for all specifications strongly support the hypothesis that age variables matter. The lowest X^2 value is 8.46 (significant at the 0.01 level) in the nondurable equation with the leads added. Further, the patterns of the age-variable coefficients are consistent with the life-cycle hypothesis; prime-age people consume less relative to their income than do the young and old. Figure 3 presents the computed α_j coefficients from the second service and nondurable consumption-equation specifications for each of the 55 age-groups. For service consumption the lowest value of α_j occurs at $j = 24$ (age 40), and for nondurable consumption the lowest value occurs at $j = 25$ (age 41).

Going from equations (1) to (2) to (3) in Table 1 has very little effect on the age results. Similarly, adding the lags and leads had little effect on the age results. Since the specification with the lags added is quite general, the age results appear to be quite robust to alternative specifications of the consumption equations.

The equations for expenditures on durables and housing investment in the Fair model are similar to those for service and nondurable consumption, except that they include a lagged stock variable. So long as consumption of housing services is proportional to the stock of housing, the variables that affect consumption, including the age variables, also affect the housing stock. However, unless the actual stock adjusts instantly to the desired stock, an allowance must be made for partial adjustments. Let KH** denote the desired stock of housing if there are no costs of adjusting both the stock and the level of housing investment, where

$$\text{KH}^{**} = f(\cdots) \qquad (4)$$

[10] The population variable POP in Table 1 that is used to put the equations in per capita terms differs slightly from the population variable N that is used to construct the p_j variables. POP is constructed from monthly data from the Bureau of Labor Statistics, and N is constructed from yearly data from the *Current Population Reports*. N is used in the construction of the p_j variables so that they will sum to 1 across j.

where the arguments in f are the same as for consumption. Two types of partial adjustment are considered. The first is an adjustment to KH** assuming no costs of adjusting investment:

$$(5)\quad KH^* - KH_{-1} = \lambda(KH^{**} - KH_{-1})$$

where KH* denotes the desired stock of housing if there is no cost of adjusting the level of housing investment. The physical depreciation of the housing stock is assumed to be proportional to the size of the stock, with depreciation rate δ. Gross investment in housing (IH) is thus equal to $KH-(1-\delta)KH_{-1}$. Given KH* from (5), desired gross investment is thus

$$(6)\quad IH^* = KH^* - (1-\delta)KH_{-1}.$$

The second type of adjustment is an adjustment of gross investment to its desired value:

$$(7)\quad IH - IH_{-1} = \gamma(IH^* - IH_{-1}).$$

Combining (4)–(7) yields

$$(8)\quad IH = (1-\gamma)IH_{-1} + \gamma(\delta-\lambda)KH_{-1} + \gamma\lambda f(\cdots).$$

This treatment thus adds the lagged dependent variable and the lagged stock of housing to the housing-investment equation, both of which seem to be important explanatory variables in practice.

According to (8), the age variables affect housing investment to the extent that they are arguments in f (i.e., to the extent that they affect housing consumption). One problem with this specification is that the age variables may affect the adjustment parameters λ and γ. In particular, adjustment may be faster for the young than for the old.[11] Unfortunately, as discussed previously, the requisite data are not available to allow parameters other than the constant term to be a function of the age variables, and so it must be assumed that λ and γ do not vary by age. The housing equations may thus be less reliable than those for consumption.

The justification for including the stock of durable goods in the durable-expenditure equation specification is analogous to that described for housing. We estimated four durable-expenditure and five housing-investment equation specifications. (We only estimated four equations for durable expenditures because none of the coefficient estimates in the first equation was of the wrong sign.) Again, the last three specifications are more general than the Fair-model specifications. The values of the explanatory variables in the housing equation are lagged once because housing investment depends in large part on housing-starts decisions made at least a quarter earlier.

Table 2 presents the estimation results for durable expenditures and housing investment. Consider housing investment first. The age variables are highly significant for all the housing-investment equation specifications. Further, the pattern of the α_j coefficients, which are plotted for the second housing equation in Figure 4, is similar to that found for service and nondurable consumption.[12] The lowest value of α_j occurs

[11]Eric A. Hanushek and John M. Quigley (1979) hypothesize that households' consumption of housing in any given period will deviate significantly from their desired level due to the substantial transactions and search costs associated with the housing market. They find (based upon reinterview data gathered on low-income renter households) that young households initially consuming "too little" housing close the gap between actual and desired consumption more rapidly than do older households who are consuming "too much" housing. If there are capital-market imperfections, budget constraints might be less binding for the old than for the young, which would help explain why the young consume too little housing.

[12]Figure 4 suggests that not only do prime-age people consume less housing relative to their income than do those younger and older; but also older people consume more housing relative to their income than do younger people. Louis B. Russell (1982) points out that older people have been major contributors to housing trends because of the rising rate of household (as opposed to individual) incidence in that age-group. The decision not to disband existing households when a spouse retires or dies means that older people continue to occupy the existing housing stock, which requires younger households to buy new rather than existing houses and, thus, for there to be more housing investment.

TABLE 2—ESTIMATES OF THE DURABLE-EXPENDITURE AND HOUSING-INVESTMENT EQUATIONS

	Durable expenditures (CD/POP)		Housing investment (IH/POP)		
Explanatory variable	(1)	(2)	(1)	(2)	(3)
Constant	0.0493 (0.67)	−0.105 (0.85)	0.367 (5.27)	0.399 (8.06)	0.344 (4.65)
LDV	0.555 (6.92)	0.529 (6.51)	0.874 (31.71)	0.881 (32.47)	0.864 (29.33)
Lagged stock	−0.0266 (2.95)	−0.0214 (2.26)	−0.0424 (7.20)	−0.0427 (9.76)	−0.0440 (7.16)
$(A/\text{POP})_{-1}$	0.00270 (3.98)	0.00200 (2.49)	0.00185 (3.78)	0.00127 (3.19)	0.00166 (3.11)
R	−0.00673 (5.27)	−0.00721 (5.54)	−0.00585 (6.09)	−0.00480 (6.05)	−0.00605 (6.14)
YTR/POP	0.164 (2.69)	0.090 (1.17)	0.142 (3.57)	0.124 (4.17)	0.119 (2.55)
W	0.443 (2.81)	0.211 (0.98)	0.154 (2.62)	0.254 (7.88)	0.091 (1.02)
P	−0.165 (1.42)	−0.002 (0.01)	0.078 (2.03)	—	0.116 (2.05)
Q	0.247 (2.75)	0.108 (0.86)	−0.023 (0.50)	—	−0.081 (1.03)
YD/POP	—	0.081 (1.56)	—	—	0.028 (0.92)
Z_1	−0.0519 (3.47)	−0.0053 (0.16)	−0.157 (7.15)	−0.150 (8.03)	−0.151 (6.60)
Z_2	0.000706 (2.29)	−0.000291 (0.41)	0.00353 (6.60)	0.00340 (8.12)	0.00344 (6.31)
SE:	0.00943	0.00934	0.00701	0.00707	0.00702
X^2:	16.83	8.98	59.68	70.57	48.10
α_1:	0.67	0.45	0.60	0.53	0.53
α_{55}:	0.003	−0.72	2.77	2.72	2.75
j^*:	37	55	22	22	22
α_{j^*}:	−0.23	−0.72	−1.00	−0.98	−0.99
X^2 (lags):	—	4.86	—	—	16.42
X^2 (leads):	—	0.77	—	—	33.22

Notes: The estimation technique is two-stage least squares for the durable-expenditure equations and the fifth housing-investment equation. The estimation technique is ordinary least squares for the other housing-investment equations. Sample period = 1954:1–1988:4 (1954:1–1988:3 for durable expenditures when leads are used). Numbers in parentheses are t statistics (in absolute value). For the housing-investment equation, R, YTR/POP, W, P, Q, and YD/POP are lagged one quarter. Statistics reported at the bottom of the table:

X^2: test of the hypothesis that the coefficients of Z_{1t} and Z_{2t} are zero; critical values ($d.f.=2$) are 5.99 at the 5-percent level and 9.21 at the 1-percent level;

j^*: value of j for which α_j is at a minimum;

X^2(lags): X^2 value for the equation with the lagged values of all the explanatory variables added (including the lagged value of the lagged dependent variable and the lagged value of the lagged stock variable), except for Z_{1t} and Z_{2t};

X^2(leads): X^2 value for the equation with the values of R, YTR/POP, W, P, Q, and YD/POP led one quarter added for durable expenditures and the contemporaneous values added for housing investment.

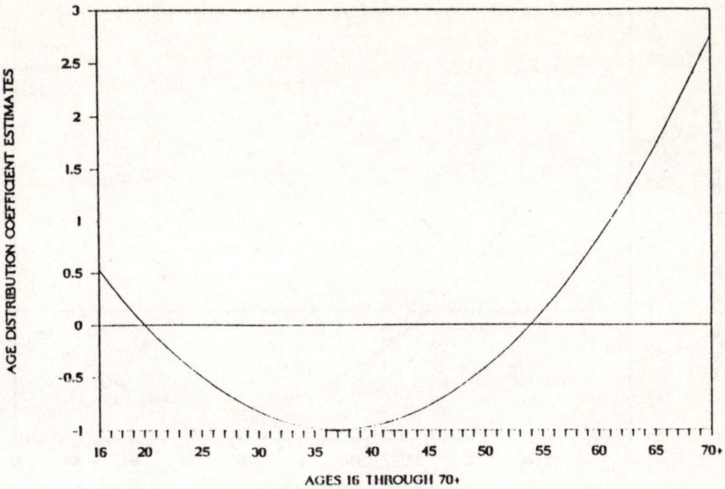

FIGURE 4. HOUSING-INVESTMENT EQUATION: AGE-DISTRIBUTION COEFFICIENT ESTIMATES (SEE TABLE 2)

for $j=22$ (age 38).[13] Again, going from (1) to (2) to (3) has little effect on the age results, as do the additions of the lags and leads.

The results for durable expenditures are mixed. The age variables are significant and have the expected U-shaped pattern for the first equation (plotted in Fig. 5), with the lowest value at $j=37$ (age 53). However, once we include disposable income and the leads and lags of the other variables, the estimates of the age-variable coefficient are no longer consistent with the life-cycle hypothesis. The age results are thus not robust for durable expenditures.

As noted above, we have examined the robustness of the age results to the use of the quadratic constraint. Instead of imposing the quadratic constraint, the age categories 16–25, 26–35, 36–65, and ≥ 65 were entered separately,[14] with the coefficients on the four variables constrained to sum to zero. This means that three unrestricted age coefficients were estimated rather than two. These results were similar to the results reported above. Consider the equation for each expenditure category with the variables that have the wrong signs dropped. For all four equations, the age variables were significant at the 1-percent level. The chi-square test statistic for the hypothesis that the three age coefficients are jointly zero is 22.13 for service consumption, 39.52 for nondurable consumption, 25.21 for durable consumption, and 64.55 for housing investment.[15] The patterns of the coefficients were also as expected—lower values

[13] N. Gregory Mankiw and David N. Weil (1989), using cross-sectional data for 1970 and 1980, find that the quantity of housing demanded is highest for people between ages 20 and 30 and that it declines after age 40 by about 1 percent per year. Recall that the results presented in this paper suggest that prime-age people consume less housing *relative to their income* than do those older and younger. Therefore, the combined results indicate that prime-age people earn significantly more than those older and younger. This implication is tested directly in the final section of the paper.

[14] The first variable is the percentage of people aged 16–25 in the total population aged ≥ 16; the second variable is the percentage of people aged 26–35 in the total population aged ≥ 16; and so on.

[15] The critical χ^2 value at the 1-percent level with three degrees of freedom is 11.34.

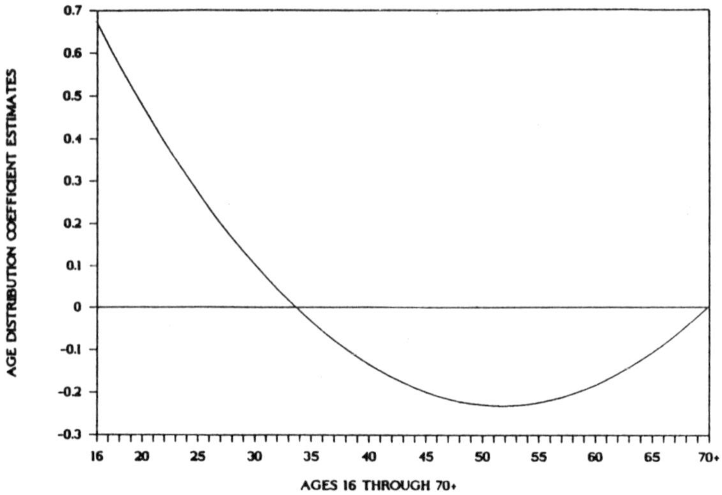

FIGURE 5. DURABLE-EXPENDITURE EQUATION: AGE-DISTRIBUTION COEFFICIENT ESTIMATES (SEE TABLE 2)

for coefficients on the second and third age categories than for the first and fourth—except for durable consumption. For durable consumption, the coefficient estimate for the second age category (26–35) was larger than that for the first (16–25), although the other two coefficient estimates were as expected. In general, the results seemed very robust to the different age aggregation.

Overall, the results in Tables 1 and 2 strongly support the hypothesis that age variables matter. Even when lags and leads are added, which are quite general specifications, the age variables retain their explanatory power in all the equations with the exception of durable expenditures. Also, the patterns of the age coefficients are consistent with the life-cycle hypothesis, with the minimum points occurring quite close to where one would expect them. The equation estimates themselves seem reasonably good, with nearly all the coefficients being significant and of the expected sign.

We now turn to money demand, for which one expects the pattern of the age coefficients to be the opposite of that found for the expenditure equations.

E. *Money Demand*

A typical demand-for-money model begins by postulating that the long-run desired level of real money balances (M_t^*/P_t) is a function of real income (Y_t) and a short-term interest rate (r_t). Assume that the equation, in per capita terms, is

$$(9)\quad M_t^*/(P_tN_t) = \alpha + \beta(Y_t/N_t) + \gamma r_t.$$

An adjustment equation is then postulated, in which the adjustment may be either in real terms [$M_t/(P_tN_t)$ adjusting to $M_t^*/(P_tN_t)$] or in nominal terms [M_t/N_t adjusting to M_t^*/N_t]. The results in Fair (1987) strongly support the latter specification, which is used here. The hypothesis is

$$(10)\quad (M_t/N_t) - (M_{t-1}/N_{t-1}) = \lambda(M_t^*/N_t) - (M_{t-1}/N_{t-1}) + \mu_t.$$

Combining (9) and (10) yields

$$(11)\quad M_t/N_t = (1-\lambda)(M_{t-1}/N_{t-1}) + \lambda\alpha P_t + [\lambda\beta(Y_tP_t)/N_t] + \lambda\gamma r_tP_t + \mu_t.$$

If it is assumed that the age variables enter equation (9) as $\gamma_1 Z_{1t} + \gamma_2 Z_{2t}$, then they enter equation (11) as $\lambda\gamma_1 Z_{1t} P_t + \lambda\gamma_2 Z_{2t} P_t$.

Table 3 presents the results of estimating equation (11) with the age variables added. An equation has also been estimated with the lagged values of the explanatory variables added (except for the age variables) to encompass a more general dynamic specification. The age variables in the money-demand regressions are significant at the 10-percent level (although not the 5-percent level) for both specifications. Figure 6 presents a plot of the α_j coefficients for the first equation. The age-variable pattern is as expected. Prime-age people hold more money, other things being equal, than do those younger and older. The largest value of α_j occurs at $j = 23$ (age 39).[16] These estimates can be interpreted as providing at least mild support of the hypothesis that people in their prime working years demand more money relative to their transactions than otherwise because the opportunity cost of their time is higher.

The other coefficient estimates in the money-demand equation seem reasonable. The implied value of λ is 0.167, and the implied value of β is 0.449. The long-run elasticity of money demand with respect to income at the point of means is 0.62.

TABLE 3—ESTIMATES OF THE MONEY-DEMAND EQUATION: DEPENDENT VARIABLE IS MH/POP

Explanatory variable	Coefficient
P	0.253
	(2.77)
MH_{-1}/POP_{-1}	0.833
	(20.06)
$(YD \cdot P)/POP$	0.0749
	(4.29)
$r \cdot P$	−0.00872
	(3.53)
$Z_1 \cdot P$	0.0938
	(2.15)
$Z_2 \cdot P$	−0.00207
	(1.80)
SE:	0.0319
X^2:	4.92
α_1:	−0.38
α_{55}:	−1.59
j^*:	23
α_{j^*}:	0.58
X^2(lags):	4.10

Notes: The estimation technique is two-stage least squares. Sample period = 1954:1–1988:4. Numbers in parentheses are t statistics (in absolute value). Statistics reported at bottom of table:

X^2: test of the hypothesis that the coefficients of Z_1 and Z_2 are zero; critical values ($d.f. = 2$) are 5.99 at the 5-percent level and 9.21 at the 1-percent level;

j^*: value of j for which α_j is at a maximum;

X^2(lags): X^2 value for the equation with MH_{-2}/POP_{-2}, $YD_{-1}P/POP_{-1}$, and $r_{-1}P$ added.

II. Labor-Force-Participation Equations

A typical labor-force-participation equation is of the form

$$(12) \quad L^s_{jt} = X_t \beta + u_t \qquad t = 1, \ldots, T \quad s = \text{m}, \text{f}.$$

where L^s_{jt} is the ratio of the number of individuals of sex s in age-group j in the labor force to the total population of people of sex s in age-group j. X_t typically includes the real wage and variables intended to pick up possible "discouraged worker effects."

Although the left-hand-side variables in equations like (12) are disaggregated by age and sex, the right-hand-side variables are typically not age–sex specific. The aggregate real wage is used in place of the more appropriate but unobserved real wage of the particular age–sex group. The implicit assumption in this treatment is that the real wage relevant to age-group j (say W_{jt}) is proportional to the aggregate wage (W_t): $W_{jt} = \lambda_j W_t$. The Easterlin hypothesis suggests that λ_j is a negative function of the percentage of people in age-group j in the total population. Berger (1985) finds that λ_j for baby-boom cohorts is low relative to the λ_j for other age cohorts.

[16] When the four age categories mentioned above were used in place of the quadratic constraint, the age variables were significant at the 5-percent level ($X^2_{[3]} > 10.96$), and the coefficient pattern was as expected.

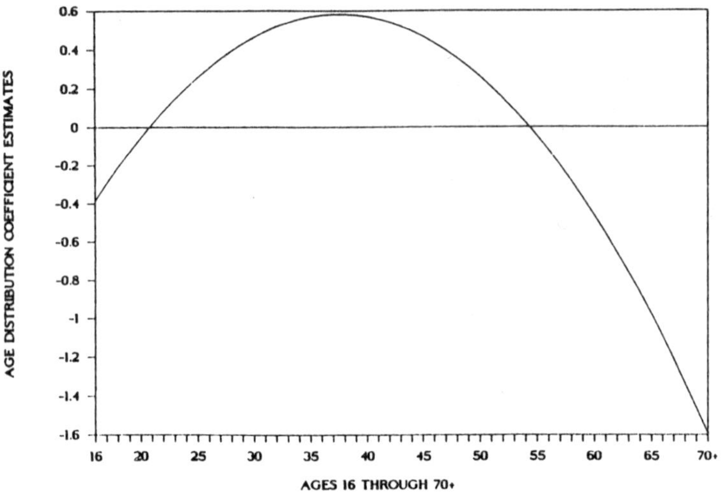

FIGURE 6. MONEY-DEMAND EQUATION: AGE-DISTRIBUTION COEFFICIENT ESTIMATES (SEE TABLE 3)

A way to test the Easterlin hypothesis is to postulate that the ratio of the real wage relevant to age-group j (W_{jt}) to the aggregate wage (W_t) is a function of the proportion of people in age-group j (p_{jt}):

$$W_{jt}/W_t = \gamma_0 + \gamma_1 p_{jt} \tag{13}$$

where γ_1 is negative. Assume that $\beta_1 W_{jt}$ is one of the terms in equation (12). Substituting (13) into (12) results in the terms $\beta_1\gamma_0 W_t$ and $\beta_1\gamma_1 p_{jt} W_t$ in the equation. Since γ_1 is negative, one expects the coefficients of W_t and $p_{jt}W_t$ to be of opposite signs. If the substitution effect dominates, β_1 is positive, and so one expects the coefficient of W_t to be positive and the coefficient of $p_{jt}W_t$ to be negative. The opposite is true if the income effect dominates.

Two aspects of the Easterlin hypothesis should be distinguished. The first is that there is not perfect substitution across age-groups in the labor market, so that more people in an age-group implies a lower average wage for that group. This aspect is represented by equation (13). The second part, termed the relative-income hypothesis, says that young peoples' consumption aspirations are shaped by their parents' living standards. In the face of unfavorable labor-market conditions, a large cohort will adjust demographic and economic behavior in order to maintain its consumption aspirations. More specifically, Easterlin suggests that the baby-boom generation delayed marriage and children and increased labor participation of young women[17] in response to lower average wages.[18] That is, Easterlin postulates

[17] Easterlin notes that, since most young men (in the family-forming ages) are already committed to the labor force, increased labor-force participation will come primarily from young women, although possibly also via moonlighting by the men.

[18] An alternative, sociological, explanation for the increased labor participation (and drop in fertility) of women, as discussed for example in George L. Perry (1977), is based not on the economic incentives brought about by the decline in the relative earnings of the baby-boom generation, but on the changing attitudes about the role of women in society brought about by the "women's movement."

William R. Johnson and Jonathan Skinner (1986) find support for the hypothesis that future divorce probabilities increase current labor supply for married women. They conclude that the rise in the frequency of divorce since 1960 may account for one-third of the unexplained increase in women's postwar labor-force participation.

TABLE 4—ESTIMATES OF THE LABOR-FORCE-PARTICIPATION EQUATIONS

Explanatory variable	Prime-age men L1/POP1	Prime-age women L2/POP1
Constant	0.356	0.0638
	(5.19)	(4.04)
LDV	0.632	0.836
	(8.94)	(19.79)
W	−0.133	0.237
	(4.99)	(4.50)
P	0.0344	−0.0210
	(3.49)	(1.64)
Q	0.0080	0.0366
	(1.07)	(3.21)
Wp_j	0.131	−0.267
	(4.20)	(4.56)
SE:	0.00186	0.00290

Notes: The estimation technique is two-stage least squares. Sample period = 1954:1–1987:1. Numbers in parentheses are t statistics (in absolute value).

that the income effect dominates for women, in which case β_1 should be negative for women, and $\beta_1\gamma_1$ should be positive.

Table 4 presents estimated labor-force-participation equations for prime-age (25–54) men and women. Participation is a function of the after-tax nominal wage (W), the price level (P),[19] the labor-constraint variable (Q), the lagged dependent variable, and the wage rate times p_{jt}. The labor-constraint variable is meant to pick up discouraged-worker effects (discouraged in the disequilibrium sense of not being able to find a job at the current set of wage rates, not discouraged in the sense that the current set of wage rates is low).

For prime-age men, the coefficient estimate for W is negative, and for P it is positive, suggesting that the income effect dominates. The sign of the coefficient on the $p_{jt}W_t$ variable is positive as expected.

For prime-age women, the coefficient estimates indicate that the substitution effect dominates. The results thus support Easterlin's hypothesis that relative wages vary inversely with cohort size but fail to support his other hypothesis that the income effect dominates for women.[20]

It is fairly clear from examining the data why the income effect dominates for men. The after-tax real wage generally grew from the beginning of the data set (1952) to about 1974, after which it flattened out. The participation rate of prime-age men fell slightly from 1952 to 1967, fell at a faster rate from 1967 to about 1976, and then flattened out after that. The estimates thus attribute the fall in the participation rate to the rise in the real wage and the flattening out of the participation rate to the flattening out of the real wage. This thus seems to be the income effect at work. The participation rate of prime-age women, on the other hand, has risen fairly steadily over the entire 1952–1987 period, and the estimates are attributing at least some of this rise to the rise in the real wage before 1974. This thus seems to be the substitution effect at work.

III. Caveats

The results in this paper are rather striking. The changing age distribution of the U.S. population has significant explanatory power in consumption, housing-investment, money-demand, and labor-force-participation equations. There seems to be enough variance in the age-distribution data to allow reasonably precise estimates of the ef-

[19]As was the case for the expenditure equations, W and P were entered separately in the equations, rather than as W/P.

[20]Michael L. Wachter (1977) regresses labor-force participation by 14 different age–sex groups on the proportion of the population aged 16–34 in the population at least 16 years of age, the unemployment rate, a time trend, and lagged labor-force participation. He finds that the coefficient estimates for the young-worker variable (aged 16–34) are significantly negative for men aged 25–64 and women aged 45–65+ over the period 1949–1976. However, because the regressions do not include the wage rate, it is not possible to interpret the results in terms of income and substitution effects. Further, it is somewhat unclear as to the expected effects of one age-group's relative size on other age-groups' labor-force participation, which makes the regressions difficult to interpret.

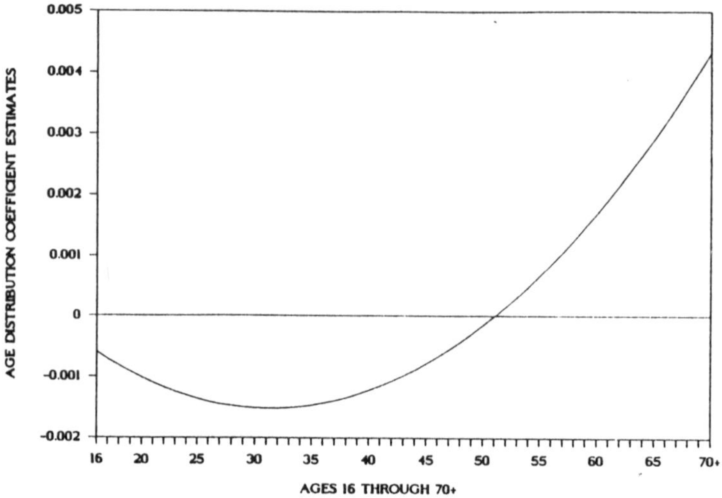

FIGURE 7. REAL-WAGE EQUATION: AGE-DISTRIBUTION COEFFICIENT ESTIMATES

Note: Other right-hand-side variables included a constant, time, and the lagged dependent variable.

fects of the age variables on the aggregate variables. The results show that prime-age people consume less relative to their income (including less housing) and demand more money relative to their income than others. The results also show that the labor-force-participation rate of both prime-age men and women is affected by the percentage of prime-age people in the total population. The relationship between cohort size and labor-force participation is positive for men and negative for women.

There are, however, some negative results that should be reported. One might expect that when the age variables are added to an equation explaining real per capita disposable income or the real wage they would be significant and have a sign pattern that implies that prime-age people earn more than those younger and perhaps also more than those older. To test this, Z_{1t} and Z_{2t} were included in a regression of real per capita disposable income on a constant, time, and lagged real per capita disposable income for the 1954:1–1988:4 period. The age variables were not significant ($X^2 = 1.51$). When the two age variables were included in a regression of the real wage on a constant, time, and the lagged real wage, they were significant ($X^2 = 10.91$), but the sign pattern, which is depicted in Figure 7, is not quite as expected. The lowest α_j coefficient occurs at $j = 16$ (age 32), whereas one would expect it to occur at $j = 1$. Also, one would not necessarily expect the curve to keep rising through the last age-group, although this may be because the quadratic constraint is too restrictive.

One might also expect that when the age variables are included in an equation explaining the aggregate personal saving rate they would be significant and have a sign pattern that implies that the saving rate is highest for prime-age people. When Z_{1t} and Z_{2t} were included in a regression of the saving rate on a constant, time, and the lagged saving rate, they were highly significant ($X^2 = 21.03$), but the sign pattern, depicted in Figure 8, is not sensible. The shape of the polynomial implies that those in the

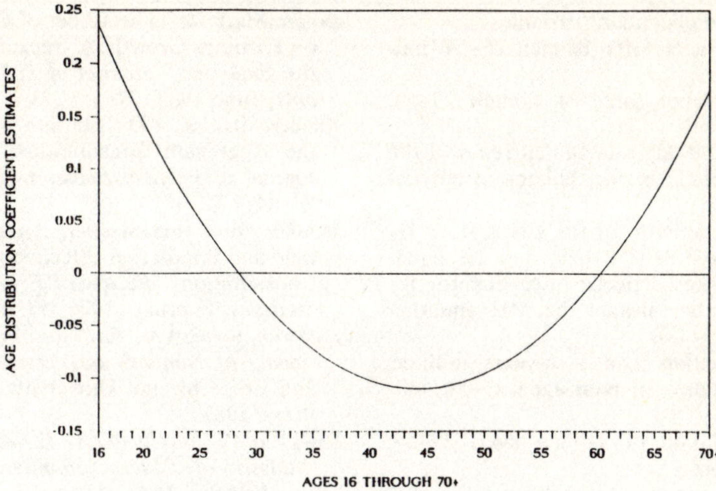

FIGURE 8. PERSONAL-SAVING EQUATION: AGE-DISTRIBUTION COEFFICIENT ESTIMATES

Note: Other right-hand-side variables included a constant, time, and the lagged dependent variable.

prime years save less than those older or younger.

Is there an explanation for these seemingly conflicting results? One possibility is the following. Figure 2 shows that the percentage of prime-age people in the population was low in the 1970's relative to the 1960's and 1980's, which is also true of the state of the economy. There is thus a positive correlation between the percentage of prime-age people in the population and the state of the economy. Since poor states of the economy generally correspond to high saving rates, we can expect there to be a negative correlation between the percentage of prime-age people in the population and the aggregate saving rate. This correlation presumably has nothing to do with long-run life-cycle considerations; it is simply a cyclical fluke in the data.

If this reasoning is valid, then the simple, nonstructural saving-rate regression run above may be spuriously attributing cycle effects to the age variables, whereas the structural equations considered in previous sections may have adequately taken cyclical factors into account with the inclusion of the other variables. Likewise, the disposable-income regression may be contaminated by cycle effects. If so, then the results reported in this section are not of much concern. Nevertheless, the basic results of this paper should be interpreted with some caution. At least part of the significant effects in the previous sections may be from fluke business-cycle correlations rather than from true life-cycle considerations. More work with the age data is clearly needed, but the present results are encouraging.

APPENDIX: VARIABLE DEFINITIONS

A: real value of total net worth of the household sector
CN: real value of the consumption of nondurables
CS: real value of the consumption of services
CD: real value of durable expenditures
IH: real value of housing investment

LDV: lagged dependent variable
L1: total labor force of men 25–54, millions
L2: total labor force of women 25–54, millions
MH: demand deposits and currency of the household sector, billions of current dollars
P: price deflator for CS, CN, CD, or IH in the CS, CN, CD, and IH equations, respectively; price deflator for domestic sales in the MH equation (1982 = 1.0)
POP: population aged ≥ 16 years, millions
POP1: population of men aged 25–54, millions
POP2: population of women aged 25–54, millions
Q: labor-constraint variable
r: after-tax short-term interest rate
R: after-tax long-term interest rate
W: after-tax nominal wage rate
Wp_j: W times the percentage of the population between 25 and 54 years old
YD: real value of disposable personal income
YTR: real value of the level of transfer payments
Z_1: first age variable
Z_2: second age variable

See Fair (1984) for data sources. All real values are in billions of 1982 dollars.

REFERENCES

Almon, Shirley, "The Distributed Lag Between Capital Appropriations and Expenditures," *Econometrica*, January 1965, *33*, 178–96.

Ando, Albert and Modigliani, Franco, "The 'Life Cycle Hypothesis' of Saving," *American Economic Review*, March 1963, *51*, 55–84.

Andrews, Donald T. M. and Fair, Ray C., "Inference in Econometric Models with Structural Change," *Review of Economic Studies*, October 1988, *60*, 615–39.

Baumol, W. J., "The Transactions Demand for Cash: An Inventory Theoretic Approach," *Quarterly Journal of Economics*, November 1952, *66*, 545–56.

Berger, Mark C., "The Effect of Cohort Size on Earnings Growth: A Reexamination of the Evidence," *Journal of Political Economy*, June 1985, *93*, 561–73.

Blinder, Alan S., "Distribution Effects and the Aggregate Consumption Function," *Journal of Political Economy*, June 1975, *83*, 447–75.

Denton, Frank and Spencer, Byron, "Household and Population Effects on Aggregate Consumption," *Review of Economics and Statistics*, February 1976, *58*, 86–95.

Easterlin, Richard A., *Birth and Fortune: The Impact of Numbers on Personal Welfare*, 2nd Ed., Chicago: University of Chicago Press, 1987.

Fair, Ray C., *Specification, Estimation, and Analysis of Macroeconometric Models*, Cambridge, MA: Harvard University Press, 1984.

______, "International Evidence on the Demand for Money," *Review of Economics and Statistics*, August 1987, *69*, 473–80.

______, "Testing the Rational Expectations Hypothesis in Macroeconomic Models," mimeo, Yale University, 1990.

Hansen, Lars, "Large Sample Properties of Generalized Method of Moments Estimators," *Econometrica*, July 1982, *50*, 1029–54.

Hanushek, Eric A. and Quigley, John M., "The Dynamics of the Housing Market: A Stock Adjustment Model of Housing Consumption," *Journal of Urban Economics*, January 1979, *6*, 90–111.

Hayashi, Fumio and Sims, Christopher "Nearly Efficient Estimation of Time Series Models with Predetermined, but Not Exogenous, Instruments," *Econometrica*, May 1983, *51*, 783–98.

Heien, Dale, "Demographic Effects and the Multiperiod Consumption Function," *Journal of Political Economy*, January/February 1972, *80*, 125–38.

Hendry, David F., Pagan, Adrian R. and Sargan, J. Denis, "Dynamic Specifications," in Z. Griliches and M. D. Intriligator, eds., *Handbook of Econometrics*, Amsterdam: North-Holland, 1984, pp. 1023–1100.

Johnson, William R. and Skinner, Jonathan, "Labor Supply and Marital Separation," *American Economic Review*, June 1986,

76, 455–69.

Lieberman, Charles and Wachtel, Paul, "Age Structure and Personal Saving Behavior," in George von Furstenberg, ed., *Social Security versus Private Saving*, Cambridge, MA: Ballinger, 1980, pp. 315–57.

Mankiw, N. Gregory and Weil, David N., "The Baby Boom, the Baby Bust, and the Housing Market," *Regional Science and Urban Economics*, May 1989, *19*, 235–58.

Mayor, Thomas and Pearl, Lawrence, "Life-Cycle Effects, Structural Change and Long-Run Movements in the Velocity of Money," *Journal of Money, Credit and Banking*, May 1984, *16*, 175–84.

McMillan, Henry and Baesel, Jerome, "Demographic Influences on Real Interest Rates," mimeo, University of California, Irvine, 1987.

Modigliani, Franco and Brumberg, Richard "Utility Analysis and the Consumption Function: An Interpretation of Cross-Section Data," in K. K. Kurihara, ed., *Post Keynesian Economics*, New Brunswick, NJ: Rutgers University Press, 1954, pp. 388–436.

Perry, George L., "Potential Output and Productivity," *Brookings Papers on Economic Activity*, 1977, (1), 11–47.

Russell, Louise B., *The Baby Boom Generation and the Economy*, Washington, DC: Brookings Institution, 1982.

Stoker, Thomas M., "Simple Tests of Distributional Effects on Macroeconomic Equations," *Journal of Political Economy*, August 1986, *94*, 763–95.

Tobin, James, "The Interest Elasticity of the Transactions Demand for Cash," *Review of Economics and Statistics*, August 1956, *38*, 241–7.

Wachter, Michael L., "Intermediate Swings in Labor-Force Participation," *Brookings Papers on Economic Activity*, 1977, (2), 545–76.

U.S. Department of Commerce, Bureau of the Census, "Estimates of the Population of the U.S. by Age, Sex and Race: 1952–1985," in *Current Population Reports*, Series P-25 (Numbers 310, 519, 917, 965, and 985) Washington, DC: U.S. Government Printing Office, various years.

Name Index

The International Library of Critical Writings in Economics

1. Multinational Corporations
   Mark Casson
2. The Economics of Innovation
   Christopher Freeman
3. Entrepreneurship
   Mark Casson
4. International Investment
   Peter J. Buckley
5. Game Theory in Economics
   Ariel Rubinstein
6. The History of Economic Thought
   Mark Blaug
7. Monetary Theory
   Thomas Mayer
8. Joint Production of Commodities
   Neri Salvadori and Ian Steedman
9. Industrial Organization
   Oliver E. Williamson
10. Growth Theory (Volumes I, II and III)
    R. Becker and E. Burmeister
11. Microeconomics: Theoretical and Applied (Volumes I, II and III)
    Robert E. Kuenne
12. The Economics of Health (Volumes I and II)
    A.J. Culyer
13. Recent Developments in Macroeconomics (Volumes I, II and III)
    Edmund S. Phelps
14. Urban and Regional Economics
    Paul C. Cheshire and Alan W. Evans
15. Modern Public Finance (Volumes I and II)
    A.B. Atkinson
16. Exchange Rate Economics (Volumes I and II)
    Ronald MacDonald and Mark P. Taylor

17. The Economic Value of Education: Studies in the Economics of Education
Mark Blaug

18. Development Economics (Volumes I, II, III and IV)
Deepak Lal

19. The New Classical Macroeconomics (Volumes I, II and III)
Kevin D. Hoover

20. The Economics of the Environment
Wallace E. Oates

21. Post Keynesian Theory of Growth and Distribution
Carlo Panico and Neri Salvadori

22. Dynamic Labor Demand and Adjustment Costs
Giorgio Galeazzi and Daniel S. Hamermesh

23. The Philosophy and Methodology of Economics (Volumes I, II and III)
Bruce J. Caldwell

24. Public Choice Theory (Volumes I, II and III)
Charles K. Rowley

25. Evolutionary Economics
Ulrich Witt

26. Economics and Psychology
Shlomo Maital and Sharone L. Maital

27. Social Choice Theory (Volumes I, II and III)
Charles K. Rowley

28. Non-Linear Dynamics in Economic Theory
Marc Jarsulic

29. Recent Developments in Experimental Economics (Volumes I and II)
John D. Hey and Graham Loomes

30. Monopoly and Competition Policy (Volumes I and II)
F.M. Scherer

31. The Economics of Technical Change
Edwin Mansfield and Elizabeth Mansfield

32. The Economics of Exhaustible Resources
Geoffrey Heal

33. The Economics of Institutions
Geoffrey M. Hodgson

34. The Economics of Transport (Volumes I and II)
Herbert Mohring

35. Implicit Contract Theory
Sherwin Rosen

36. Foundations of Analytical Marxism (Volumes I and II)
John E. Roemer

37. The Economics of Product Differentiation (Volumes I and II)
Jacques-François Thisse and George Norman

38. Economic Growth in Theory and Practice: A Kaldorian Perspective
John E. King

39. Markets and Socialism
Alec Nove and Ian D. Thatcher

40. Recent Developments in the Economics of Education
Elchanan Cohn and Geraint Johnes

41. The Theory of Inflation
Michael Parkin

42. The Economics of Location (Volumes I, II and III)
Melvin L. Greenhut and George Norman

43. Financial Intermediaries
Mervyn K. Lewis

44. The Political Economy of Privatization and Deregulation
Elizabeth E. Bailey and Janet Rothenberg Pack

45. Gender and Economics
Jane Humphries

46. Macroeconomics and Imperfect Competition
Jean-Pascal Bénassy

47. Labor Economics (Volumes I, II, III and IV)
Orley C. Ashenfelter and Kevin F. Hallock

48. The Economics of Altruism
Stefano Zamagni

49. The Economic Analysis of Rent Seeking
Robert D. Tollison and Roger D. Congleton

50. Economics and Biology
Geoffrey M. Hodgson

51. The Economics of Ageing
John Creedy

Future titles will include:

Economics and Discrimination
William A. Darity, Jr

The Economics of Information
David K. Levine and Steven A. Lippman

Fiscal and Monetary Policy
Thomas Mayer and Stephen Sheffrin

Transaction Cost Economics
Oliver Williamson and Scott Masten

Long Wave Theory
Christopher Freeman

International Trade
J. Peter Neary

Agricultural Economics
G.H. Peters

International Debt
Graham Bird and P.N. Snowdon

Small Firms and Economic Growth
Zoltan Acs

Business Cycle Theory
Finn E. Kydland

General Equilibrium Theory
Gerard Debreu

The Money Supply in the Economic Process
Marco Musella and Carlo Panico

Producer Cooperatives and Labor-Managed Systems
David L. Prychitko and Jaroslav Vanek

The Foundations of Public Finance
Peter Jackson

International Finance
Robert Z. Aliber

Welfare Economics
William J. Baumol and Janusz A. Ordover

The Theory of the Firm
Mark Casson

The Economics of Inequality and Poverty
A.B. Atkinson

The Economics of Housing
John M. Quigley

Population Economics
Julian L. Simon

The Economics of Crime
Isaac Ehrlich

The Economics of Integration
Willem Molle

The Rhetoric of Economics
Donald McCloskey

Ethics and Economics
Alan Hamlin

Migration
Oded Stark

Economic Forecasting
Paul Ormerod

The Economics of Training
Robert J. LaLonde and Orley Ashenfelter

The Economics of Defence
Keith Hartley and Nicholas Hooper

Consumer Theory
Kelvin Lancaster

Law and Economics
Judge Richard A. Posner

The Economics of Business Policy
John Kay

Microeconomic Theories of Imperfect Competition
Jacques Thisse and Jean Gabszewicz

The Economics of Increasing Returns
Geoffrey Heal

The Balance of Payments
Michael J. Artis

The Economics of the Family
Nancy Folbre

Cost-Benefit Analysis
Arnold Harberger and Glenn P. Jenkins

The New Growth Theory
Gene M. Grossman

Economic Theory and Chaos Theory
W. Davis Dechert

The Economics of Unemployment
P.N. Junankar

Mathematical Economics
Graciela Chichilnisky

Economic Growth in the Long Run
Bart van Ark

Gender in Economic and Social History
K.J. Humphries and J. Lewis

The Economics of Communication and Innovation
Donald M. Lamberton

The Economics of Uncertainty
John D. Hey